EARLY MATTERS

EARLY MATTERS

Essays on the History of Buddhist Art in Zangskar, Western Himalaya

Rob Linrothe

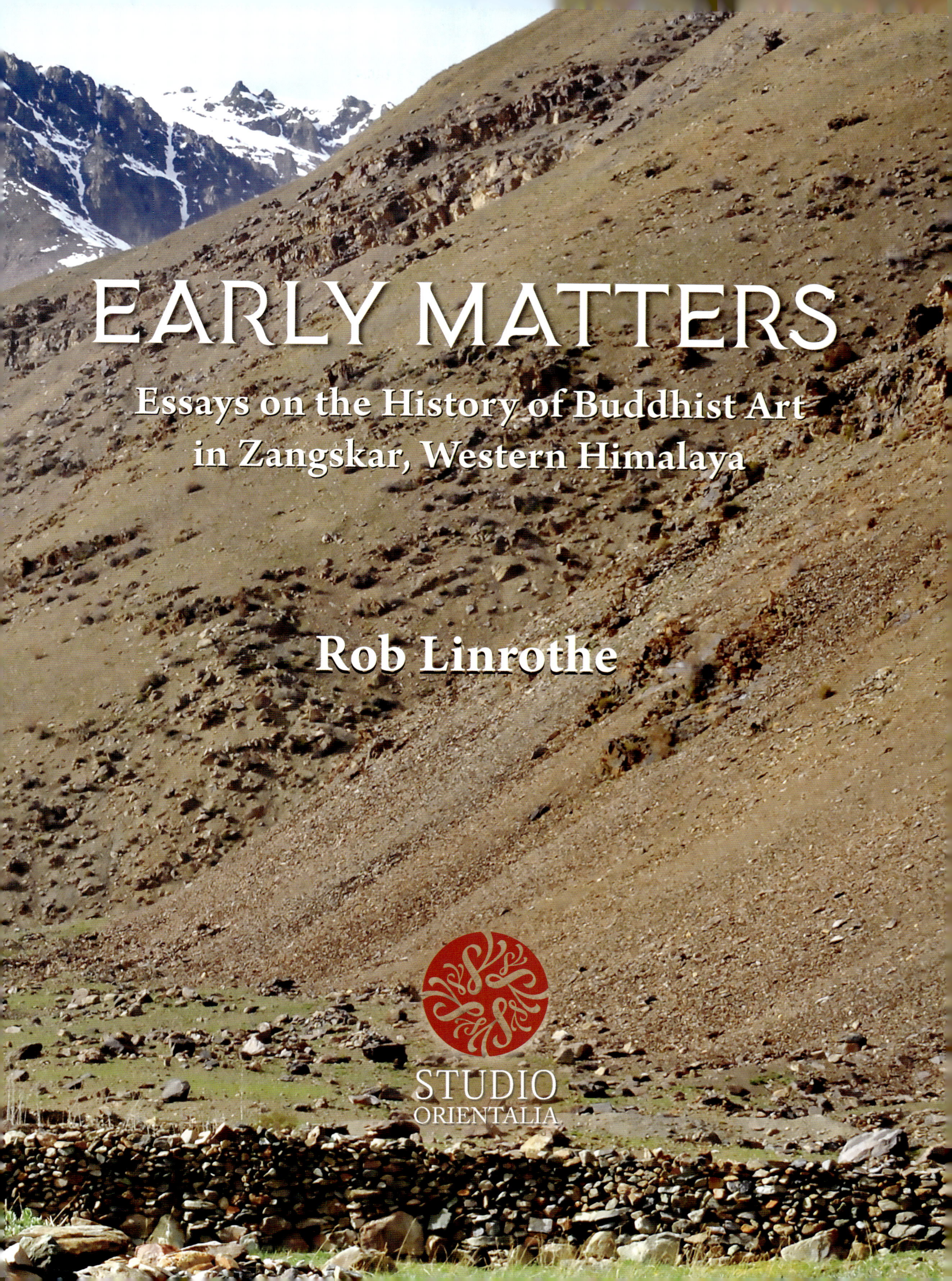

STUDIO ORIENTALIA

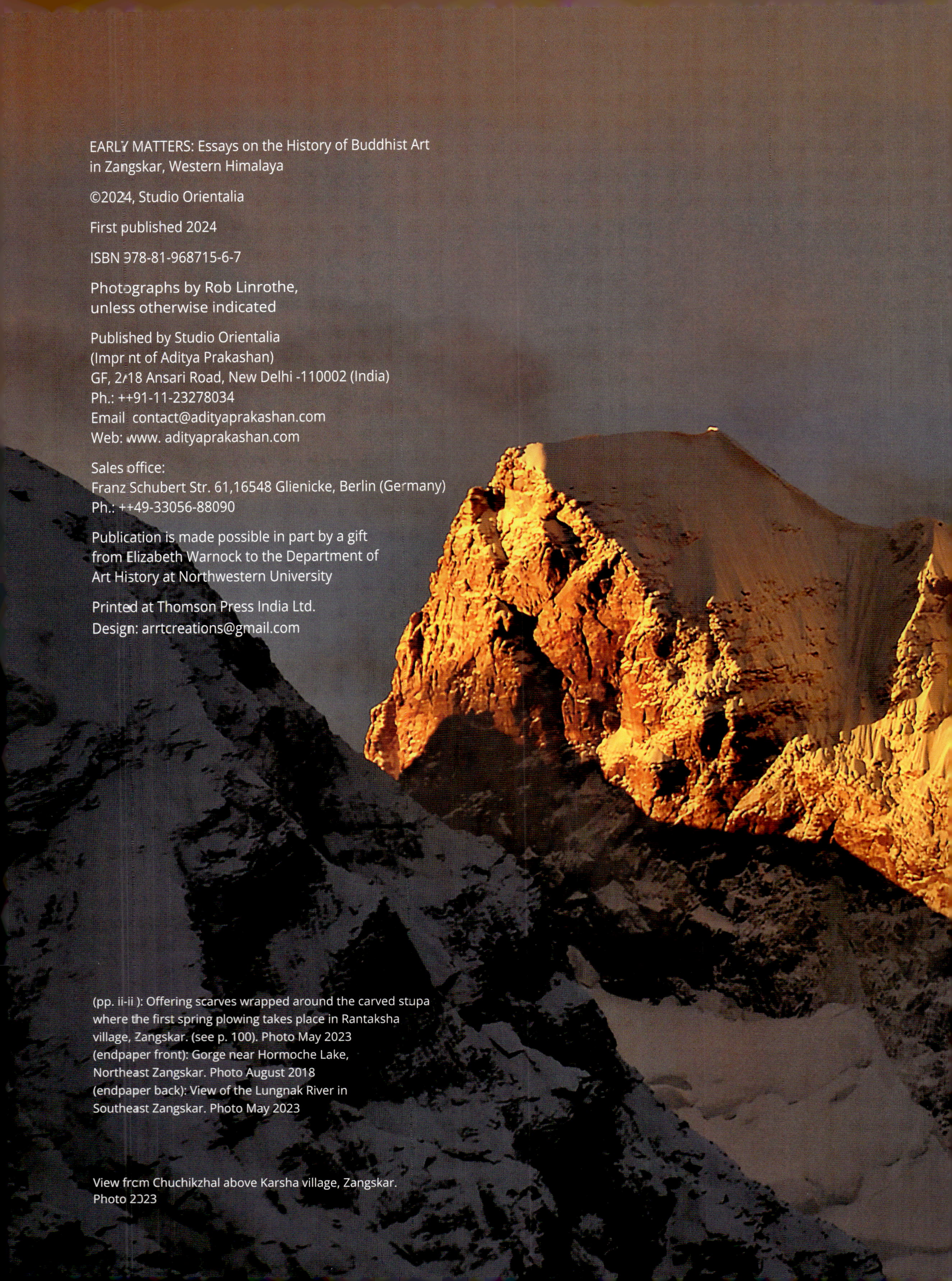

EARLY MATTERS: Essays on the History of Buddhist Art in Zangskar, Western Himalaya

First published 2024

ISBN 978-81-968715-6-7

Photographs by Rob Linrothe, unless otherwise indicated

Published by Studio Orientalia
(Imprint of Aditya Prakashan)
GF, 2/18 Ansari Road, New Delhi -110002 (India)
Ph.: ++91-11-23278034
Email contact@adityaprakashan.com
Web: www. adityaprakashan.com

Sales office:
Franz Schubert Str. 61,16548 Glienicke, Berlin (Germany)
Ph.: ++49-33056-88090

Publication is made possible in part by a gift from Elizabeth Warnock to the Department of Art History at Northwestern University

Printed at Thomson Press India Ltd.
Design: arrtcreations@gmail.com

(pp. ii-ii): Offering scarves wrapped around the carved stupa where the first spring plowing takes place in Rantaksha village, Zangskar. (see p. 100). Photo May 2023
(endpaper front): Gorge near Hormoche Lake, Northeast Zangskar. Photo August 2018
(endpaper back): View of the Lungnak River in Southeast Zangskar. Photo May 2023

View from Chuchikzhal above Karsha village, Zangskar. Photo 2023

Contents

Buddha painted in the Nyingpa gateway stupa of Padum, Zangskar (see Chapter 4). Photo May 2023.

Preface and Acknowledgements

This land truly exists, yet one could search a long time to find its name on a map. . . . 'Unexplored', mentioned the *Indian Gazetteer* at the beginning of the century, and strangely enough in 1976 one could have written nearly the same thing, for no one has studied the area.
MICHEL PEISSEL, *ZANSKAR: THE HIDDEN KINGDOM*, 11.

Is there a need for studies of the visual heritage of Zangskar? Compared to the relatively plentiful documentation of sites, objects, and cultural currents in Spiti and Ladakh since 1974 (when travel restrictions were lifted), there have been pitifully few of Zangskar. It seems that Zangskar has largely escaped the attention of the cartographers compiling the art historical map of the western Himalaya. Apparently it has been off the radar range as other monuments have drawn our attention. No historians of art or visual culture participated in the otherwise extraordinarily comprehensive (from Agriculture to the Zodiac) "Zangskar Project" of 1980 with its invaluable results published in 1994.[1] Of the 198 black and white photographs included in Khosla's 1979 *Buddhist Monasteries in the Western Himalaya*, only 22 depict sites in Zangskar, and many are picturesque rather than documentary: "Zangskar Valley seen from Karsha," "Yak as a mode of transport in Zangskar," "Padam folk dance."[2] Of the fifty eight technical drawings in this specialized study of Buddhist architecture, six are of sites in Zangskar. In Christian Luczanits' 2004 book on the early sculptural art of the western Himalaya, which one reviewer rightly called a "profound assessment" (K. Paul) and another "a major scholarly work of enormous significance" (P. Pal), Zangskar art plays no substantial role. The "Alchi Group of Monuments" of Ladakh occupies more than 75 pages of this well-illustrated work, but Zangkar, a substantial area formally incorporated as the southern region of Ladakh and with at least two dozen monasteries and nunneries, is scarcely mentioned and no illustrations of any sculptures or murals appear.[3] A full decade later, a volume of 400+ pages entitled *Art and Architecture in Ladakh*, contains more than a dozen scattered references to Zangskar among its sixteen essays,[4] and (progress!) one of the essays includes two sites in Zangskar among the ten discussed.

1 Crook and Osmaston, *Himalayan Buddhist Villages*.

2 Khosla, *Buddhist Monasteries in the Western Himalaya*, black and white plates 9, 16, and 18.

3 Luczanits, *Buddhist Sculpture in Clay*.

4 Lo Bue and Bray, eds., *Art and Architecture in Ladakh*.

The authors also illustrate the two Zangskar sites with five photographs (one in color), and two drawn plans and elevations.[5] To site just one more example of the relative invisibility of Zangskar, in the 2005 *Ladakh: Culture at the Crossroads*, edited by Monisha Ahmed and Clare Harris, not a single town or village of Zangskar appears marked on the double-page map with more than thirty such sites in Ladakh around and west of Leh. The vast space of Zangskar remains *terra incognita*, "unexplored." The index to the volume includes 6 entries for the word "Zanskar." Four refer to the Zangskar "river," one to the Zangskar "Valley" and one to the Zangskar "area." By contrast, more than fifty entries are found for Leh alone, the capitol city of Ladakh. Zangskar's art, architecture, and artists receive no attention in the eight essays or the introduction, and its extensive monasteries, stupas, and royal shrines are figuratively and literally not on the map.

Singling out these examples is not meant to be a criticism of the distinguished authors who have contributed so much to the study of western Himalayan culture. Not negligence on their part, rather, it is quite typical, and reflects Zangskar's perceived isolation and the difficulties that (used to) prevail in getting in and getting out. Compared to Ladakh, Zangskar is "[e]ven more secluded."[6] "One of the reasons why Zanskar has escaped investigation, study, or exploration," Peissel explained in 1979, "is that it is surely one of the most inaccessible and highest valleys of our planet."[7] The isolation—but not the altitude—has changed in the last few years with two new motorable routes to and through it having opened, added to the existing one. None, however, are dependably open year-round. There is still no airport there, though that is coming, the government promises, within the next decade. Nor are all its major monasteries or villages connected to the growing network of external and internal roads. That too is changing. Remoteness and inconvenience in terms of transportation is no longer a viable reason to overlook the "Hidden Kingdom," as Peissel named it forty years ago.

The introduction to Quentin Devers' recent (2022) inventory of historical sites in Zangskar gives an excellent condensed summary of the geography, topography, climate, history, and contemporary population numbers, and the reader is encouraged to refer to it.[8] Briefly, two major rivers coming from opposite directions (southeast and northwest) meet just north of Padum to form the mighty Zangskar River which flows north till it joins the Indus in Ladakh (See maps p. x). A few dozen villages are located along both banks of these conjoined rivers as well as along various tributaries. The rivers form valleys separated by high Himalayan mountain ranges. Devers summarizes its scale relative to Ladakh: "Zanskar represents about 15% of the territory and 5% of the population of Ladakh, with a density

5 Devers, Bruneau and Vernier. "An Archaeological Account," 109–114, 135–138.

6 Crook and Osmaston, introduction to *Himalayan Buddhist Villages*, xxv.

7 Peissel, *Zanskar*, 11.

8 Devers, *Historical Sites of Zanskar*, 3–23. James Crowden also gives a beautifully written description of the geography of Zangskar and its routes, based on very intimate knowledge of the place in the 1976–77; Crowden, *Frozen River*, 8–9.

of roughly 1.5 inhabitants per square kilometer," well under other regions of Ladakh.[9] In a 2012 publication, the population of Ladakh was given as above 270,000, with some 14,000 in Zangskar.[10] These number are no doubt higher now; one sees rough population estimates as high as 20,000. Ahmed and Harris and others give the total area of Ladakh as 82,000 square kilometers, including Changtang, Nubra, the Suru Valley and Zangskar, which is estimated at 7000 square kilometers.[11] The Zangskar interior is so little traversed by commentators, however, that an erudite specialist on the western Himalaya (who shall remain unidentified) can confidently but mistakenly claim that "Zanskar certainly does not have a single lake." I personally know of three cold, clear, glacier-melt lakes and confess to swimming across one of them on more than one occasion, as my trekking partners at those times can attest. Two of these lakes are in Shun/Shadé, not near any motorable roads, but they do appear on the Olizane maps.[12] Despite having walked in and out of Zangskar along each of a half-dozen known paths aligned along all the primary directions, including the frozen-river *chadar*,[13] I would not venture to claim that these three were the only lakes in Zangskar. There may be more, as yet unnoticed. Indeed, in May 2023, as this was being finalized for publication, I learned of another lake above Dzonkhul monastery! It is a minor matter, to be sure, but illustrates prevailing attitudes and unrealized unfamiliarity with its physical and cultural environment.

Is this neglect justifiable? Perhaps there is little there to capture the attention of archaeologists and art historians? In fact, given how under-documented and under-explored it remains, as small as it is, with as low a population as it supports, ironically Zangskar punches above its weight in terms of material culture. Devers lists 272 sites of pre-15th date "which is more than we imagined for a region so scarcely populated. Of these, about 130 have been published previously."[14] The abundant petroglyphs in Zangskar have attracted somewhat more attention than the Buddhist art.[15] There may not be Buddhist monuments in Zangskar as spectacular as that of Alchi or Tabo, but there is an extensive body of Buddhist sculpture, painting and architecture going back more than a thousand years that deserves to be—indeed, *needs* to be—incorporated into the discourse of western Himalayan art while there is still time. Endangering it first have been the trappings of development (imported educational systems, building materials, foodstuffs, transportation infrastructure, entertainment, etc.).[16] Now, the global climate crisis is also dramatically affecting it. Neither phenomenon have been kind to Zangskar. Both have been and continue to be increasingly destructive of the culture and way of life in Zangskar,[17] as well as its cultural inheritance from the past. The bell is already tolling on the material culture in this region, and gives urgency to the project of first

9 Devers, *Historical Sites of Zanskar*, 3.

10 Powers and Templeman, *Historical Dictionary* 387, 747.

11 Ahmed and Harris, introduction to *Ladakh*, 11; Powers and Templeman, *Historical Dictionary*, 746.

12 Charles Genoud and Philippe Chabloz, *Ladakh-Zangskar: Guides Olizane* (Genève: Editions Olizane, 2008). A full-page color illustration of the lake near Normoche appears in Linrothe, *Seeing into Stone*, vxii. The other is named Tso Tok on the Olizane map; I first noticed it looking down from the pass at Nialo Kontse and have visited the western shore on several occasions.

13 On the *chadar* journey, see Crowden, "Butter Trading Down the Zangskar Gorge," 287–292," and Crowden, *The Frozen River*.

14 Devers, *Historical Sites of Zanskar*, 1. Devers' listings, each a half page with one photograph (a minority are given one or more larger details), gps locality, a "grade" of historical and archaeological importance, state of conservation, brief description, approximate date (usually "1st millenium CE?," "approx.. 8th–13th centuries," "last few hundred years," or "difficult to assess") and extensive mapping, are excellent tools compiled in a handbook form.

15 More than 70 of Devers' listings are of pre- or non-Buddhist petroglyphs; also of note in this regard are the work of Francfort et al., "Archaic Petroglyphs of Ladakh and Zanskar;" and Martin Vernier *Exploration et Documentation des Pétroglyphes*, and Vernier,"Zamthang, epicenter of Zangskar's rock art heritage." My own book on Zangskar's pre-Buddhist petroglyphs commenced as the first chapter of the present work before attaining independent form. It can still be considered both background and introduction to the present material. See Linrothe, *Seeing into Stone*.

16 The anthropologist Helena Norberg-Hodge, who participated in the 1980 "Zangskar Project," insightfully critiques the unintended consequences of development in her *Ancient Futures*.

17 For an excellent 2015 study of how the climate crisis is affecting one village in Zangskar, see Mingle, *Fire and Ice*. Things have only gotten worse since it was published (2015), across the entire area. For a 2018 ethnographic study in the shadow of climate change in the Sham area of Ladakh (Nyemo to Khalatse village along the Indus, west of Leh) of "affect-driven" attitudes toward the non-human that cultural transformations are eroding see Gagné, *Caring for Glaciers*.

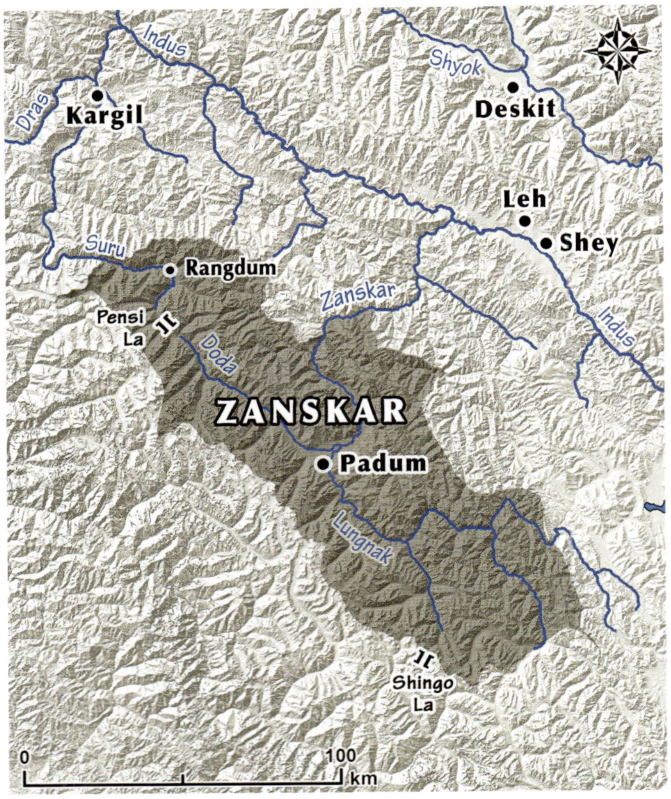

(*left*): **Map 1** Outline of the Zangskar region with rivers indicated. Created by Quentin Devers, used with permission.

(*below*): **Map 2** Map of the Zangskar and Ladakh region with Spiti, Baltistan and Kashmir indicated. Created by Mel Keiser.

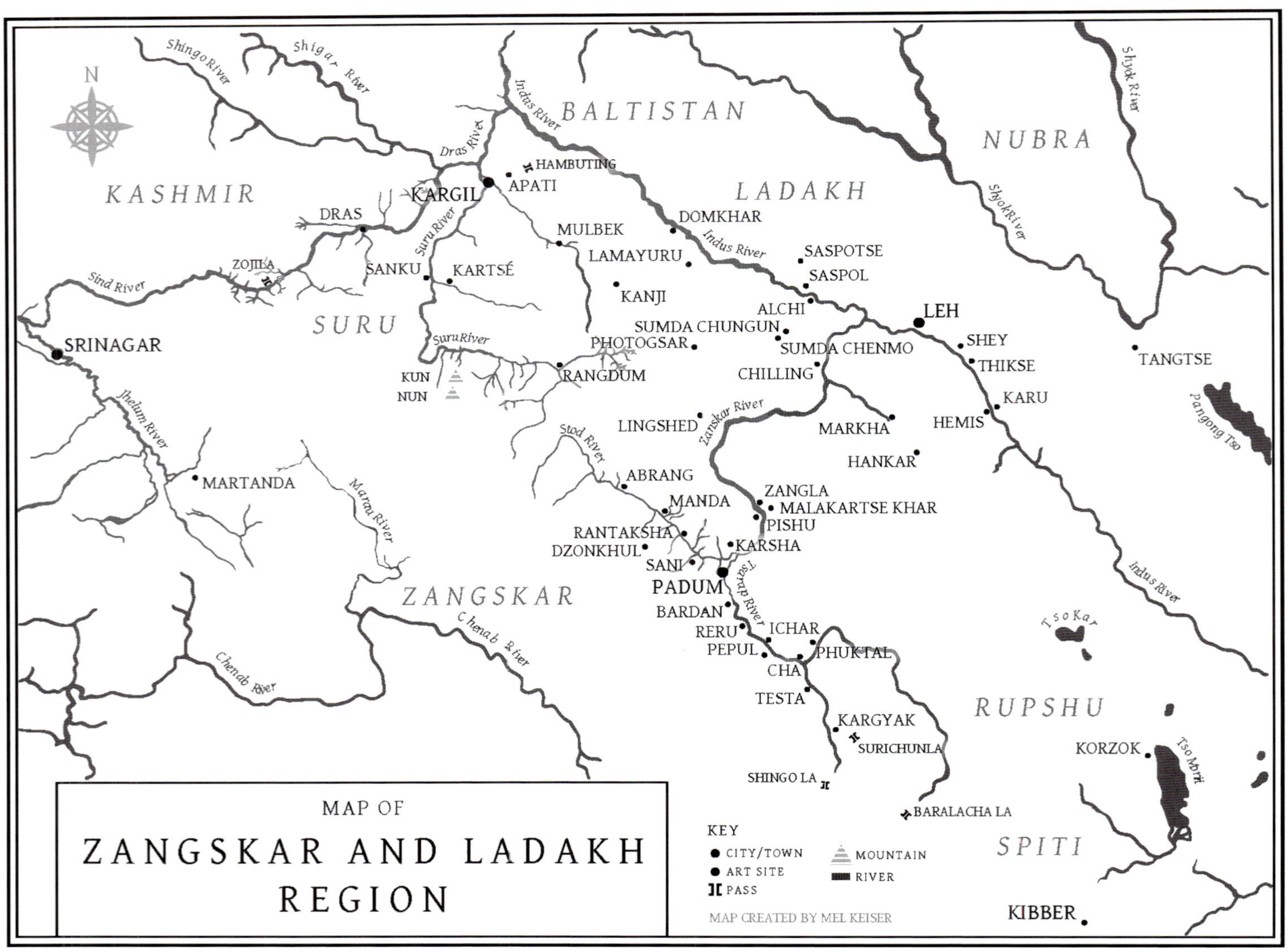

surveying what remains, as Devers has succeeded in doing in remarkable fashion, and then to analyze it in greater depth and in concert with the related art of surrounding regions, as this book aims to do for a much smaller but still sizeable concentration of objects.[18]

✣✣✣

The chapters of this book illustrate both the plenitude and the diversity of artistic remains in Zangskar. They explore aspects of its formation and evolution over time, and its formal and conceptual relationships to trends of thought and art in its neighboring regions and those even farther afield. The chapters also manifest different potential approaches to what we today take to be "art." It is worth noting that there is no simple word for what (all) we mean by "art" that we know of in pre-modern Zangskari Tibetan. Art in terms of "skill" or craftsmanship is certainly known (lag rtsal (ལག་རྩལ་, "hand capacity"), and there were plenty of words for paintings and tapestries of deities, painted, sculpted, and woodblock printed portraits and self-portraits of religious figures. With very few possible exceptions, all of the objects and images discussed and reproduced in this book were and are produced and used for religious purposes and settings, and most express Buddhist values and meanings. But it is the historical and the formal properties that are foregrounded for the most part in the chapters of the book. Thus the "etic" nature of the analyses that follow make no claim to represent the meaning of values of their makers, except in a limited technical sense related to the identifications of iconography.

The first two chapters are focused on theoretical matters, trying to escape from the embrace of received opinions about the "Tibetanness" of the culture and art of Zangskar and the western Himalaya more broadly, and out from under the shadow of the much lauded "father" of Tibetan art history, Giuseppe Tucci. The first, "Stretched to Fit," looks at the history of nomenclature for this region, and the misleading tendency to conflate Ladakh, Zangskar and other subregions of the western Himalaya as Tibet, or as "Little Tibet." The chapter is not meant to be a comprehensive examination of the history of the region's treatment by Westerners, but its controlling argument is to identify reductive patterns that deny the region a history apart from that of Tibet. The second chapter, "*Tibetan Painted Scrolls* and the Practice of Art History," diverges from my previous work (in *Collecting Paradise*) on Tucci's (and others') unscrupulous and manipulative collecting practices, based on the testimony of his own published works. The chapter in this book focuses instead on his underdeveloped art historical methodology. It is not meant to be part of a smear campaign against him, ostracize him, or to censor him from the canon of tibetologists.

18 I am particularly indebted to the publisher of Studio Orientalia, Aditya Goel, for allowing me to include so many more photographs than is typical of books produced by US and European academic publishers. The photographs are in themselves a contribution, I hope, to the documentation of this endangered resource.

Too often it seems that his textual and linguistic prowess, pioneering efforts to reconstruct Tibetan Buddhist history, fieldwork, and eloquent writing has led to an attitude of near idealization if not idolatry. Such loyalty to one's predecessors and teachers is understandable, even commendable in terms of human feeling, but should not blind us to concomitant weaknesses and inherited flaws to which we all are susceptible. Thus this chapter is intended to critically assess one influential but unexamined aspect of his contributions, and salvage those that are valuable. Indeed, over the course of the book, his other insights are frequently quoted and utilized in various places.

The next three extended essays, chapter 3 to 5, give visual evidence for unlocking Zangskar art from the prison of Shangri-la, as it were. They literally illustrate that before Zangskari artists and patrons were aware of Tibetan Buddhist sculpture and painting—perhaps even before there WAS recognizable Tibetan Buddhist sculpture and painting for them to be aware of—they were making art aligned in form and meaning with those on their southern, western and northwestern borders. In that sense, the chapters are protreptical: they each argue a particular point related to the controlling argument of the first chapter. They do not attempt open-ended exploration of what is found, but marshal what is found as visual evidence that Zangskar has a history that needs to be unmoored from Tibet or from that of Tibet. "Early Buddhist Stūpa Reliefs in Zangskar," chapter 3, considers the transition in Zangskar from pre-Buddhist to early Buddhist engravings in the form of stupas outlined on rock, stones, boulders and cliffs. The fourth chapter, "Early Buddhist Figural Art in Zangskar," focuses on early figural art, mainly but not exclusively in Zangskar, and attempts to classify several different early modes of visual language that can be traced to the cultures surrounding the western Himalaya, including Tibet and Nepal, but not exclusively so. The scope and period are wide and the attributions experimental and, in some instances, intentionally provocative, inviting consideration, correction, or refutation. In such instances, they are initial attempts to take seriously and account for works that are generally ignored or passed over. The fifth chapter, "Looking Westward," narrows the focus to two roughly contemporary sites, one in Zangskar and the other in west Tibet. Both are oriented towards the Kashmiri mode of painting as far as we can reconstruct it.

They also share damaged and incomplete condition, as well as a number of identical Esoteric Buddhist themes. Comparison of what is present and what is missing in each helps to reconstruct the otherwise incomplete iconographic program of the one in Zangskar. In turn, the two closely related sites prompt a reassessment of the dating of a host of early Buddhist sites in the western Himalaya. The chapter concludes by offering a relative chronology for tenth to late twelfth century sites in the western Himalaya and Ngari (west Tibet).

The last three chapters of the book are less didactic. They each take on works of art at a different scale than the others. Chapter 6 looks at two *sets* of sculptures, just a few kilometers apart from each other, that represent two related pantheons of Buddhist exemplars, the Mahāsiddhas, done in radically different formal vocabularies. Titled "Mahāsiddha Stone Engravings of Tungri Nunnery and Manda Village," the related pantheons are done in distinct modalities that align remarkably well with what are designated as "linear" and "painterly" in Western art history. The second to last chapter, chapter 7, "Discovery, Deconsecration, Rebuilding and Reconsecration: Revisiting the Art, Architecture, and Relics in Karsha's Chuchikzhal Complex," takes on *a single site*, that of Karsha Chuchikzhal, in Zangskar, which in the last three decades has yielded a great deal of information about Buddhism and patterns of its visual expressions from the last millennium in the western Himalaya. The final chapter focuses on *a single painting* in a monastery in Zangskar. "Reflections on a Buddhist Painting of Sarasvatī in Zangskar" unpacks the probable significance to its maker by revealing the transmission of the theme of the goddess with a *vīṇā* from early India to the later monastic institutions and leaders in Central Tibet and into the western Himalaya.

By no means a simple or comprehensive survey of art in Zangskar, the chapters nevertheless range across different times, locations, artists, types of sponsors. They feature several classes of media, and diverse approaches or methodologies in documenting, studying, and writing about objects created not merely as objects beautiful or interesting for their own sakes, but as 'supports' for transcendental in-sight. To one extent or another, regardless of dates, they are rooted in, and, I hope, prove the point that, *early matters*.

Among those in Ladakh and Zangskar to whom I am forever in debt are the Karsha Lonpo Sonam Wangchuk and many of his family members including Gelong Angchug, Konchok Dolma and "Pali" Stanzin Chosgyal, Dolma and Stambha Gyaltsen, Sonam Phuntsok and Phuntsok Angchuk. Also, Jisul Tsephel Gongmapa, Geshé Tashi Wangdus Kargyakpa and their colleagues at Lingshed and Phuktal, Lochen Tulku, Gelong Sangyas Tsering of Hemis Monastery, the patient, calm and always wise Anwar Ullah, the incomparable guide and loyal friend Lobsang Gyatso Pishupa, many horse-handlers over the decades including Pali of Hanumil, Norbu of Pidmo, Gelek of Lingshed, Topi Gyatso Pishupa, Tsering Choedak of

Choglamsar, and several others, not to forget the dozens of horses who have uncomplainingly [or just silently] carried my gear for weeks at a time. Jigmet and his parents in Leh always made me feel welcome and comfortable. Among other friends, scholars, and trekking partners, I am especially grateful to Melissa Kerin, Joel Reed, and Victoria "Tori" Andrews for their generosity and shared interests in both Zangskar and western Himalayan art and the mountain environment. Several of the images included in this book were produced jointly as part of the Andrews and Linrothe Fieldwork Summer 2022 Project.[19] Siddiq Wahid has been a font of wisdom and inspiration even before I ever traveled to Ladakh; his younger brother Gafoor—who accompanied me on my very first trek in Ladakh in 1983—models a fearless and contagious love of the region. Others I have had the privilege to meet, know, encounter or travel with in the region include Kim Gutschow, Quentin Devers, Caroline Riegel, Gerald Kozicz, Christian Luczanits, the late Roger Goepper, Jaroslav Poncar, Martin Mills, Pascale Dollfus, Monisha Ahmed, Martin Vernier, Nils Martin, Wolfgang Heusgen, Tara Sharma, Elena Pakhoutova, Nawang Jinpa, John Harrison, the late André Alexander, Laura Strand, Christina Bitter, Jeanet Snijders, Krista Martin, Nicholas Ferlatte, and Margo Mensing. Still others I have come to know elsewhere but who shared their passion for the area, consisting of the distinguished Deborah Klimburg-Salter, Christiane Kalantari, Yannick Laurent, Heinrich Pöll, the late John Clarke, Mark Aldenderfer, Chiara Bellini, Eva Allinger, Hugh Raynor, Olaf Czaja, Amy Heller, John Bray, the late Helen Abbott, Ge Wanzhang, and many others, from all of whom I learned a great deal. Also, it is a pleasure to remember a number of Chinese colleagues for their generosity: Xie Jisheng, Liao Yang, Luo Wenhua, and Zhang Changhong. A special thank you to Aditya Goel, Ritu Topa, Shanker Sharma, Catherine Becker, Sarah Jacoby, Antonio Terrone and colleagues in the Department of Art History at Northwestern, especially Ann Gunter, Holly Clayson, Christina Kiaer, Jesús Escobar, Hannah Feldman, Mel Keiser, as well as Liz Warnock for her generous funding. That enabled the peerless Mary Gladue to attempt to corral my stampeding prose, and Ritu Topa find ways to allow the images to do much of the heavy lifting. Gerald Kozicz and Eric Huntington contributed elegant and important drawings, Mel Keiser outlined hard-to-decipher linear engravings for chapter 6 as well as a map. Mr. Skarma from Zangskar, Christian Luczanits, Jaroslav Poncar, Melissa R. Kerin, Daniel Majchrowicz, and Hugh Raynor generously allowed me to use some of their photographs, as did the Bentley Historical Library of the University of Michigan. Others were equally gracious in permitting the use of drawings and maps, including Olaf Czaja, Caroline Riegel and Quentin Devers. Though I am indebted to all those named, and more, none are responsible for errors or deficiencies, or can be assumed to share opinions expressed.

19 These include Figures 4.19–21, 4.85–86, 4.111, 4 116, 5.11–12, 5.51, 5.80, 5.153, and 5.156–157.

Theoretical and Methodological Matters

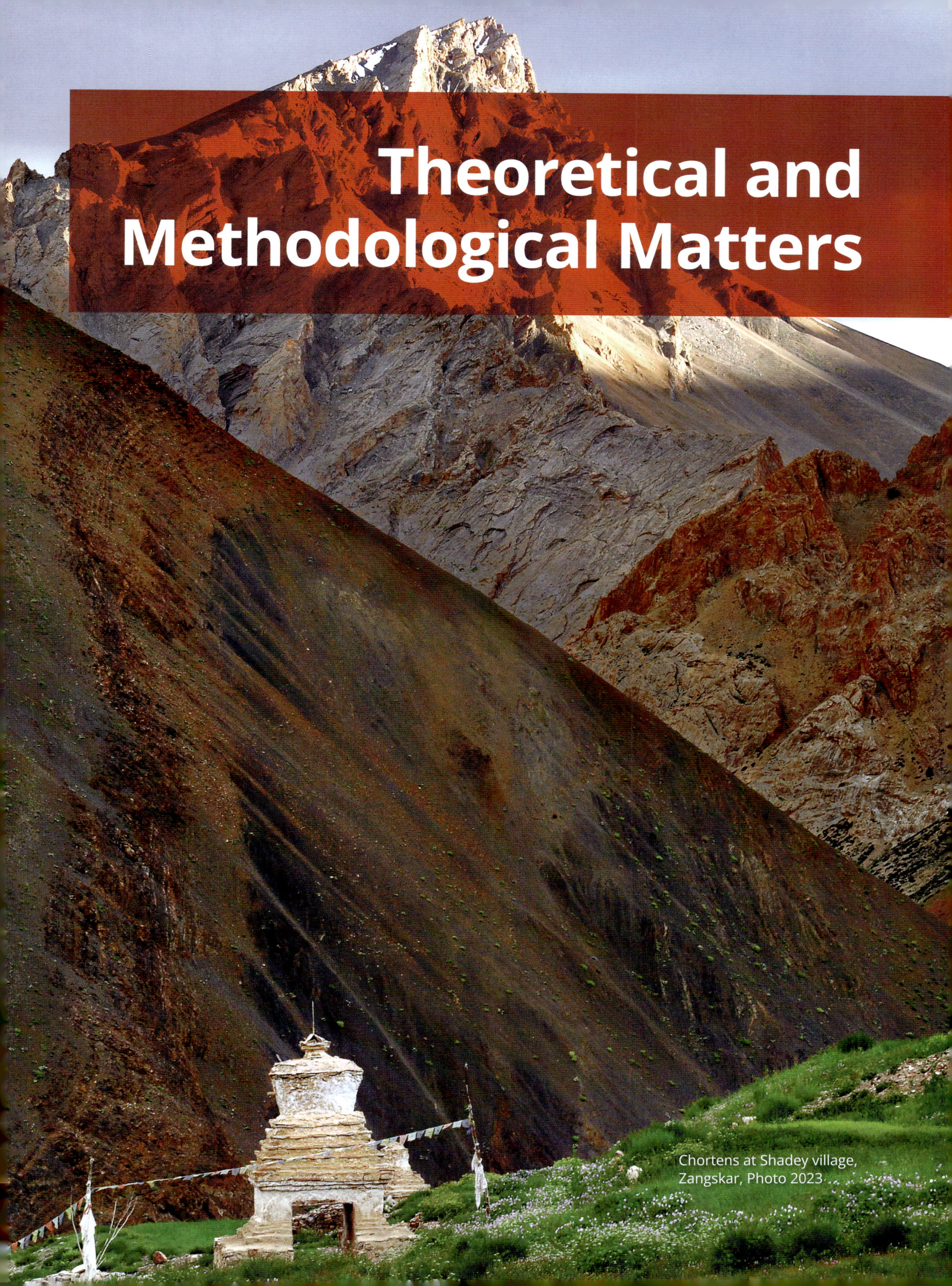

Chortens at Shadey village, Zangskar, Photo 2023

CHAPTER 1

Stretched to Fit The Western Himalaya: A Himalayan-Scaled Archive of Linguistic Tokens[1]

Ladakh is not solely a 'Little Tibet', since it includes a much richer set of material, cultural and religious [inspirations].
—DEVERS, "ARCHAEOLOGICAL LADAKH," 103

In ethnography and Tibetan studies in general, it is common practice to describe and analyze Ladakhi society, people, and culture from a general Tibet-centered frame. Monographs on *the* Ladakhi are produced which operate from a unified, unambiguous Tibetan or Buddhist frame. . . . Moreover, local actors (politicians, institutions, 'key informants,' 'ordinary people') and their interventions are also actively engaged in the production of classifications.
—VAN BEEK, "CONTESTED CLASSIFICATIONS OF PEOPLE IN LADAKH," 35 (EMPHASIS IN ORIGINAL)

[S]ince the time the foreigners called the British have ruled India, they have changed the borders of India to exclude places they have not entered, such as Kapila and Oddiyana, and include parts of Tibet, such as Ladakh and Sikkim, which they have brought under their dominion. . . . Sometimes the name of a small place remains the name of a large region, and sometimes the opposite occurs. Even among those who wish to relate real history without errors, there are very few who investigate this [question].
—GENDUN CHOPEL, *GRAINS OF GOLD*, 74

Introduction

Arguments about nomenclature are as inevitable as they are ineffectual. The "classic administrative pastime, the rectification of names"[2] occupies bureaucrats and pedantic academics. Etic names used by outsiders naturally reflect different values than emic ones. They will and must evolve as the outsiders learn more. Like language itself, names are never final or permanent. They are heuristic, but also powerful and have extensive, if sometimes subtle, effects. Contingent denotations produce unintended but misleading connotations. When we can, it makes sense to use names that are accurately indexical, and grounded in known history regardless of passing or conflicting fashions, occupations, or affiliations.

1 This essay was originally drafted in direct response to a call for participation in a panel entitled "Looking Askance at 'Himalayan Art'" sponsored by the American Council of Southern Asian Art at the 2016 College Art Association national conference. In the panel abstract, Nachiket Chanchani, the organizer and chair, wrote that one of the panel's aims was to "initiate a rethinking of the applicability of the term 'Himalayan art' to ensembles traditionally subsumed within it as well as those excluded" in the light of the "underproblematized . . . issue of whether geographically oriented terminology used to describe this subfield is useful in interpreting visual culture produced in this landscape." I attempted to grapple with the term's historiography and applicability. The recent archaeological and historical work of Quentin Devers (and to a lesser extent that of Nils Martin) have subsequently underlined the poverty of the term *West(ern) Tibet* for the Himalayan regions that are now divided between India and Pakistan, and inspired me to reframe the essay. I have benefited immensely from the wise comments of Melissa Kerin, who read an early draft and discussed the reframed version with me, and from the encouragement, interest, and help from Siddiq Wahid.

2 Strickmann, "Longest Taoist Scripture," 347.

In that context, I argue here for the preference and validity of the collective term *western Himalaya* to refer to Ladakh and its divisions—including Zangskar—as well as Spiti, Kinnaur, Lahaul (Garzha), Baltistan (and other areas), in contradistinction to the very commonly used terms *West(ern) Tibet*, *Indo-Tibet*, and *Indian Himalayas*. I prefer to reserve *west(ern) Tibet* to the province of Ngari in what is now the Tibetan Autonomous Region (TAR) of the People's Republic of China (PRC). This is already followed by some (but by no means all) writers of scholarly and popular writing. Use of *west(ern) Tibet* and *western Himalaya* is analogous to referring to Kham as *east(ern) Tibet*, and to Sikkim and Bhutan as *eastern Himalayan*. This preference for *western Himalaya* and reservations about the other terms extend to their use in identifying archaeological remains from the respective regions, as is discussed more fully in chapters 3 and 4, "Early Buddhist Stūpa Reliefs in Zangskar," and "Early Buddhist Figural Art in Zangskar: Tracing Sources Upstream." The long history of reference to Ladakh and related areas as "Greater Tibet," "Second Tibet," "Little Tibet," "West Tibet," or in fact *as* Tibet (at a time when Tibet proper was largely unknown in the West) must be recognized and contextualized. My own avoidance of the use of the term *Tibet* for this region stems from a concern with misleading, even insidious, denotations and connotations; in particular, some subtle assumptions described below that are unintentionally smuggled in with the term.[3]

As I will demonstrate in the first section of the chapter after this introduction, use of the terms *Tibet*, *Little Tibet*, and *west(ern) Tibet* in western languages to refer to Ladakh and Zangskar, Spiti, Kinnaur, Lahaul, Baltistan, etc. (hereafter LZSKLB) has an extensive history in various types of publications and commentary, starting from a period when they were as imperfectly known as their borders were undefined and modified through conquest and complicated historical events. The term *west(ern) Tibet* certainly does have its functionality even today, but is logically channeled to refer to the so-called Ngari Prefecture, including Purang (Puhrang). This area, at least since the eighth century or so, has been integrated into a system of governance and culture that is now recognized as Tibet. Of course, its earlier history calls even this into question, since west Tibet was the center of the still ill-defined state of Zhangzhung, defeated militarily by the Pugyal Tibetans of Central Tibet. Still, since the eighth century, Ngari's political, social, and cultural ties to Central Tibet have been severed only very occasionally, as by the seventeenth-century invasion

3 It has already been the practice of some specialized institutions to use "Himalaya" or "Himalayan" either instead of "Tibet" or "Tibetan," or together with it. Among them are the Western Himalaya Archive Vienna, the Himalayan Art Resources website, the Tibetan & Himalayan Library, and the Rinchen Shah Center for Western Himalayan Cultures in the Islamic University of Science and Technology, Awantipora, Jammu and Kashmir, and other organizations. I am or have been a supporter of these institutions, and have long been persuaded by their choice of terms, although in my 1999 book *Ruthless Compassion* I used both "Indo-Tibetan" and "Western Tibet," each of which I now find misleading (the first term is embedded in the subtitle itself: *Wrathful Deities in Early Indo-Tibetan Esoteric Buddhist Art*).

by a Ladakhi army. Those ties were relatively quickly restored through the intervention of a mainly Mongol army sent from Central Tibet to attack Ladakh. Overall, however, *west(ern) Tibet* fits the Gugé-Purang area quite well, much better than it applies to LZSKLB.[4]

It is when, as in examples I will specify to illustrate the point, the term *west Tibet* is loosely used to imply the inclusion of Spiti, Ladakh, Zangskar, Kinnaur, Lahaul, etc. that inaccuracy and confusion reign. To give one minor but revealing example: the title of Jane Duncan's 1905 memoir of her travels in Ladakh, *A Summer Ride through Western Tibet*, was taken literally by an (apparently) non-specialist historian, who in a 1996 publication innocently but mistakenly includes Duncan with the other accounts of Victorian travelers who actually went to Tibet. The author writes that Duncan "found in Tibet the kind of vacation experience most people associate with a deluxe hotel," and that "Duncan was, after all, fifty-six years old when she visited Tibet."[5] Similarly, in his masterful biography of William Moorcroft, who in 1812 actually did penetrate into western Tibet in disguise, Garry Alder misleadingly if not mistakenly describes the Rohtang Pass of Himachal Pradesh, near the borders of Lahaul, Zangskar and Ladakh but far from Tibet, as the place where "the empty Buddhist world of Tibet begins . . . an austere and empty moonscape of orange, brown and purple rock with not a tree, house or field visible . . . at one's feet . . . a vast amphitheatre of bare rock, snow peak and glacier."[6]

The second section of this essay attempts to demonstrate why *Tibetan*, however economical and convenient a term, is inaccurate and inappropriate as a geographic, socio-political or regional denominator for those regions or districts—especially Ladakh and Zangskar—by summarizing their history as far back as is known. To be sure, at least for the last half millenium religious practices there were tightly spliced with west Tibetan and particularly with Central Tibetan Buddhism. Since the time of the Central Tibetan imperial invasions of LZSKLB in the eighth and ninth centuries, and the later invasions of west Tibetan armies in the tenth and eleventh centuries, elites from Tibet have instantiated themselves into the regions as nobles and leaders. As a consequence of their religion and politics, the "high" language and literature since that time has been similarly Tibetan in script and grammar.

4 Tibetan language terminological practices, precision, idiosyncrasy, or regional variation is a separate issue not tackled here. *Nub byang*, literally "northwest," in Mustang refers to "the Guge-Purang region of Western Tibet or— more generally—Western Himalaya, including Ladakh" (Vinding and Sørensen 2021: 9[illegible]1) but of course implies a standpoint east of there, not a Ladakhi perspective.

5 Procida, "A Tale Begun in Other Days," 188, 19[illegible].

6 Garry Alder, *Beyond Bokhara*, 249.

Contemporary sentiments of many inhabitants of LZSKLB—especially the religious elites—often embrace an identification with Tibet. Now that Tibet itself is occupied by the PRC, exilic Tibet brings many benefits, including regular visits by His Holiness the Dalai Lama, which never previously occurred. This attitude colors their view of their history of engagement with Tibet, which assumes a benevolent aspect. The "deep historical relationship between Ladakh and Buddhist Tibet"[7] is celebrated, not interrogated. A few recent examples give a sense of this. According to Eshey Namgial, Kyidé Nyimagon ("whose origin and lineage can be traced to the great kingdom of Tibet") "became Ladakh king [*sic*] *winning the heart of Ladakhi people*, and built his first palace in Shey village near Indus, which had not only brought the impact of classical Tibetan but also brought cultural and religious reformation in Ladakh."[8] Two other contemporary western Himalayan writers observe that the "faces and physiques," the food and the clothes, the geographic and climatic conditions, all are closely akin to that of Tibet because Tibet's cultural "pressure has been extraordinarily uniform"; it even "provided Ladakh with a western Tibetan dialect."[9] In a word, "culturally, Ladakh *is* Tibetan."[10]

Yet this ideological alignment is itself historically situated and created, not a matter of "essence," "race," or "origin." Previously, such a conflation with Tibet was vigorously, and militarily, resisted on the part of western Himalayans, and one wonders if ordinary Central Tibetans didn't in fact deny that such border "barbarian tribes" had a pure "Tibetan" identity.[11] There is no more justification for calling Ladakh and neighboring regions "Little" or "western Tibet" than there would be to calling India "Little" or "eastern Britain," despite British rule over India, its intelligentsia's embrace—however ambivalent or regretted—of the English language, of bequeathed bureaucratic systems of rule, of banking, of transportation, to highlight a few.

Such issues will be considered more intensively in the second section of this essay. If the second section focuses on why I believe scholars could be more precise in distinguishing west Tibetan from western Himalayan, and what these latter regions were and are not (i.e., Tibetan in any meaningful sense), the third and final section attempts to outline what it was before and after it was occupied by central and west Tibetan armies. A model based on its distinctive Himalayan geography adjacent to an unusual number of discrete cultures to the north, west, south, and east made these western Himalayan

7 Joldan, *Ladakh's Traditional Ties with Buddhist Tibet*, 7.

8 Namgial, "Ladakhi," 40 (emphasis added).

9 Jolden and Tundup, *Cultural Relationship*, 68.

10 Ibid., 66 (emphasis added). According to the two authors, in central and eastern Ladakh "Tibetan traits were predominant, culturally as well as racially." The kingdom of Ladakh was "founded in about AD 917 by Skyid-lde Nyi-ma-mgon, a direct scion of the Tibetan king Lang Darma . . . He chooses Shey as his capital"; ibid., 67. "Ladakh and Bhutan share most of the culture of Tibet, which shows that the origins of these cultures are from Tibet and they have greater contact earlier . . . the source of inspiration [upon which] these civilizations [Ladakh and Bhutan] were founded will undoubtedly be Tibet"; ibid., 68. Methinks they doth protest too much.

11 Sara Shneiderman points to "ample evidence of indigenous Tibetan ontologies which use the term 'barbarian' to describe those at the borders, but it is less clear that Tibetans use anything like the terms 'race' or 'ethnic' to describe themselves"; Shneiderman, "Barbarians at the Border and Civilising Pojects," 20.

regions contested "borderlands," though not in the traditional sense of stable borders between two nation-states with unequal power relations, or the distant periphery to a dominant center, "where the sharpness of ethnic and other cultural limits and differentiations clashed with the groups' need to interact with other groups on the other side of the dividing lines."[12] In the present instance, merchants, missionaries, and militarists flowed into the regions from multiple directions and left their imprint in the constantly evolving lifestyle and visible culture, which then played a role in transmitting it eastward. Buddhism stands as a perfect example of this. Defined by the geography, then, the area was not a soupy melting pot of Tibetan "influence" so much as a pliant builder of social structures and cultural expressions, and one of the most fertile regions for the production of art in Asia, particularly factoring in its minuscule population. It deserves terminological clarity, at the minimum: *west Tibet* refers to the western regions of *bod yul* proper; *western Himalaya* refers to regions with different origins and histories, not consistently Tibetan except as the result of military invasions and gradual assimilation.

Let me try to articulate what I think are the stakes. This is not just about names, for language shapes thought.[13] And it can do so unconsciously. Terms, which are specific to particular contexts and thus change over time, represent concepts that "have consequences; they determine and limit what we can say, what we believe, and thus how we feel justified to act. Concepts are the building blocks not just of knowledge claims but of social practices."[14] When those regions of the western Himalaya are fixed in our minds as Tibetan, the contributions of other social groups become intruders, "outsiders," and can be discounted. With "Tibet" and "Tibetan language inscriptions" as the norm, "non-Tibetan" variants become borrowings or transcriptions of increasingly distant linguistic sources, not local ones. One witnesses erudite but fruitless searches as far afield as Arabic, or Chinese, instead of assuming forms preserved from the autochthonous languages. In art history, as is documented in chapters 3 and 4, those forms that do not conform to the evolution of Tibetan form-idioms, or are independent of them, tend to evoke slight interest.
I am certainly not the only one to warn against the reduction of Ladakh and other non-Tibetan regions to a provincial branch of Tibetan culture. Martijn van Beek perceptively formulated a similar thesis decades ago. His frame of reference was not art history but the ethnography and colonial and post-colonial classification of the population of Ladakh across race,

12 Zarman, "Identity, Movement, and Response," 4.

13 Lakoff and Johnson, *Metaphors We Live By*.

14 O'Donnell, "Revisiting David Summers' *Real Spaces*," 28.

class, caste, and religion. Martijn van Beek's meticulous survey of census records from 1891 to 1941 resulted in startlingly similar conclusions: "Ladakh tends to remain imagined as essentially homogeneously Tibetan and Buddhist."[15] Scholars are not immune from this constructed vision, which is reinforced by the Tibetan-speaking Buddhists who support this identification with Tibetan culture; we also tend "to capture and frame Ladakhi society, to make it fit our received frame: to describe it in ideal-typical terms, suspended in time and space."[16]

Why Thibet, Little Tibet, Greater Tibet, and Its Variants?

> We do not know the ancient name of Ladakh; when first mentioned by Hsüan-tsang, it is called *Mo lo so (muat lā sā)* which Francke (*JRAS*, 1908, p. 189) interpreted as *Mar sa* "the low land". Pelliot 1959–73, p. 706, proposed *Mra-sa, Mar sa, Ma-rāsa*. All such hypotheses have a weak point: they suppose that the name transcribed by Hsüan-tsang is a transcription of a Tibetan name. . . . Since the Tibetan dynasty had not yet conquered Ladakh it is useless to search for a Tibetan original at the basis of 'Moloso', 'Molop'o'.
>
> —Tucci, "On Swāt," 73

> It may be noted here, that the only name for the province of *Ladak* ever used by Mirza Haidar is *Tibet*. . . . The inconvenient circumstance, however, is that throughout the *Tarikh-i-Rashidi* the name of *Tibet* is applied not only to *Ladak*, but to the whole of the provinces under the rule of the priestly government of Lassa—that is, to the region generally known in Europe as *Tibet*. In reading the *Tarikh-i-Rashidi*, therefore, it is necessary to discriminate between *Ladak* and *Tibet* proper, on every occasion that the word occurs.
>
> —Elias, the editor, in Mīrzā Haidar, *Tarikh-i-Rashidi of Mirza Muhammad Haidar, Dughlát*, 135n2 (italics in original)

From artists to officials and missionaries, from the nineteenth to the twenty-first century, observers have been calling Ladakh and its parts and neighbors "Western Tibet," or even just "Tibet." It is not as if there were an earlier consensus term for the area. The further back we go, the more challenging it is to know to what, exactly, the terms that Chinese and other travelers employed actually referred. While it is not possible to present an exhaustive survey here, what follows is a (hopefully representative) sampling mainly of the nineteenth- and early twentieth-century usages.

15 van Beek, "Contested Classifications of People in Ladakh," 48.

16 Ibid.

For the nineteenth and early twentieth centuries they can be clustered by the writers' professions: scientists and naturalists, explorers and mountaineers, missionaries, colonial officials and military men, hunters engaged in "sport," journalists, and other travelers. A few more recent examples include academics in various disciplines but mainly historians, of language, social groups, political forms, religion, and art. The categories are certainly not fixed or inviolable; there are some differences in terms used within and across groups. The inconsistencies—one might even say the confusion—began early but seem to have staying power.

One or another version of "Bolor" (Po-lu-lo)—"Greater" or "Lesser"—seems to have been in use when the Korean Hyecho (Hui Chao; 704–787) commented on them, and even earlier, in the description of the Chinese traveler Xuanzang (604–664).[17] According to Zeisler, "*Lesser* means *Closer* to a particular reference point . . . The term *Greater* would thus apply to territories further away from the reference point."[18] Unfortunately, despite close examination by Zeisler and Denwood, we really do not know the observer's point of reference. Zeisler and Denwood encounter a number of inexplicable inconsistencies, possible copyist mistakes in directions, and the like.[19] Rarely can one conclude that the name definitely in- or excludes Gilgit, Chilas, Baltistan, Hunza, a certain Dardada, Skardo, or even Upper Ladakh or Lower Ladakh. To paraphrase Zeisler, the problems might never be resolved.[20]

Xuanzang mentions Kullu, Lahaul, and farther north, "travelling by a road dangerous and precipitous, where icy winds and flying snow (assault the traveller), we come to Mo-lo-so (called also San-po-ho)."[21] Cunningham reconstructs the former as Mar-po-yul, and the latter as Tsang-po, or "the river," referring to the Indus.[22] (As it happens, north of Lahaul is actually Zangskar.) This assumes Tibetan was spoken there in the seventh century. Giuseppe Tucci, on the other hand, as already quoted, points to the essential weakness of such arguments: they mistakenly assume that seventh-century names as transcribed into Chinese were originally Tibetan.[23] We do not know what the inhabitants called it then; the earliest mention of the term *Ladakh* is found in the Alchi Sumtsek.[24]

Starting in 1532 the Central Asian military leader Mīrzā Haidar Dughlat (1499/1500–1551) began a multi-year series of campaigns, invading and occupying Nubra, Ladakh, Zangskar, and Balti for various lengths of

17 Yang, Jan, Shotaro, and Preston, *Hye-Ch'o Diary*, 47–48; Beal 1884, bk. 3, ch. 2; Xuanzang, *Great Tang Dynasty Record of the Western Regions*, 79–80.

18 Zeisler, "East of the Moon and West of the Sun?," 372–73 (emphasis in original). See also Zeisler, Review of *Historical Dictionary of Tibet*, 239–240. An analogous situation—"greater" and "lesser" applied to Russia and Ukraine—in which "lesser" had the meaning of "close by" and "greater" of "further away," but conflating the two as if they were variants of the same, is pointed out in a recent *Politico* article by Rory Finnin, "How the west Gets Ukraine Wrong." I am indebted to Siddiq Wahid for noticing the similarity of the changing usages of such terms and the dire consequences of the confusion of size, distance, relative position and "geopolitical fortunes" between the two different historical relationships; personal communication March 2022.

19 Zeisler, "East of the Moon and West of the Sun?," 384–88; Denwood, "Tibetans in the West, Part I," and "Tibetans in the West, Part II."

20 Ibid., 386.

21 Beal 1884, bk. 4, ch. 4; Xuanzang, *Great Tang Dynasty Record of the Western Regions*, 103–4.

22 Cunningham, *Ladák*, 4. See also Howard and Howard, "Historic Ruins in the Gya Valley," 86.

23 Tucci, "On Swāt," 73.

24 Howard and Howard, "Historic Ruins in the Gya Valley," 87; and Devers, "Archaeological Ladakh," 113.

time. Later he took control of Kashmir. He also seems to have had some experience with westernmost Tibet, which he claims to have traveled through on his way to Central Tibet (if indeed "Ursang" refers to Ütsang).[25] The relevant chapter in his memoir, the *Tarikh-I-Rashidi*, fails to convince that he knew those places the way he did the locations in the western Himalaya.[26] At any rate, Mīrzā Haidar refers to all of the above-named regions as Tibet, but distinguishes *Tibet-i-Khurd* (Little Tibet) for Balti, and *Tibet-i-Kalan* or *Tibet-i-Buzur* (Great Tibet) for Ladakh.[27] He also seems to have recognized Maryul and Ladakh[28] as separate political entities, with Shey the capital of the former and Leh of the latter, and corresponding to the upper Indus Valley of what is now Ladakh, and the middle-western Indus Valley, respectively.[29] Mīrzā Haidar also mentions "Balur," which, from the description and stated location, may very well be the regions around Gilgit, and thus an echo of "Bolor."[30]

Jigar Mohammed brings two other Mughal sources in Persian, which again use *Tibet-i-Kalan*, or "Great Tibet" for Ladakh.[31] The first is by Abul Fazl, *Ain-i-Akbari* of 1595, during Akbar's reign. The second is the *Shahjahan Nama* on the reign of Shah Jahan (r. 1628–58), written by the son of the Mughal governor of Kashmir. Given the consistency with which Baltistan and Ladakh (which would have included Zangskar, Nubra, Rutok, Suru, etc.) were called Little and Great Tibet, respectively, it should not surprise that François Bernier (1620–1688), who visited Kashmir and seems to have gone out of his way to inquire about "those imperfectly known regions,"[32] "followed contemporary [Mughal/Persian] practice in referring to Ladakh as 'Great Tibet' and Baltistan as 'Little Tibet.'"[33] John Ogilby's discussion of Mughal Kashmir in the seventeenth century, clearly based on compiling references from French, Dutch, and other reports, describes Kashmir as "the farthest part of *Indostan* to the Northward from *Lahor*, and inclos'd by Mount *Caucasus*, the Mountains of the Kingdom of great and little *Tibet*."[34] He notes, closely following Bernier's comment, that the women of Kashmir are accounted particularly beautiful, and lack the unattractive features of those of Kashgar or "great *Tibet*, their neighbors."[35]

Things do not resolve into blissful clarity by the eighteenth century. The written accounts of the Jesuit missionaries Ippolito Desideri and Manoel Freyre of their travels from Kashmir to Ladakh, then on to Ngari, and then to Lhasa in 1714–15 reveal that from their perspective, there were actually three Tibets. Yet, when they traveled to Kashmir and then started

25 This is the suggestion of the editor, who further states that what is meant is Lhasa; Mīrzā Haidar, *Tarikh-I-Rashidi of Mirza Muhammad Haidar, Dughlát*, 16n3.

26 Mīrzā Haidar, *Tarikh-I-Rashidi of Mirza Muhammad Haidar, Dughlát*, chap. 108. On the unreliability of dates as well as puzzling and unidentifiable place names, very unlike most of the rest of the narrative, see especially the editor's extended note (ibid., 456–58n1).

27 See Mohammed, "Mughal Sources on Medieval Ladakh" [2nd ed.], 148, who points out that Hashmatullah Khan (b. 1860) uses the same terms in his 1939 Urdu history of Jammu, Kashmir, Ladakh, and Baltistan, on which see more below.

28 On these terms and the (changing) geographic positions they represent, see Howard and Howard, "Historic Ruins in the Gya Valley," who see a version of Maryul in Xuanzang's account. Ibid., 86.

29 This is discussed in N. Howard, "Sultan Zain-ul Abidin's Raid into Ladakh," 136–37. See also Mīrzā, *Tarikh-I- Rashidi of Mirza Muhammad Haidar, Dughlát*, 410n1.

30 Elias, the editor of Mīrzā Haidar's *Tarikh-I-Rashidi* also suggests that Balor might be Bolor, and "included Hunza, Nagar, Gilgit, Yasin, Chitral, etc." Mīrzā, *Tarikh-I-Rashidi of Mirza Muhammad Haidar, Dughlát*, 135n1. He elsewhere equates it with the Chinese version, *Po-lo-lo*, and states that "[i]n one form or another the name is found in writings dating from the seventh century down to the eighteenth. Even at the present day it may not be entirely extinct." Mīrzā, *Tarikh-I-Rashidi of Mirza Muhammad Haidar, Dughlát*, 385n.1.

31 Mohammed, "Mughal Sources on Medieval Ladakh" [2nd ed.], 154–57.

32 Bernier, *Travels in the Mogul Empire*, 425.

33 Mohammed, "Mughal Sources on Medieval Ladakh" [2nd ed.], 157.

34 Ogilby, *Asia, the First Part*, 199 (emphasis in original).

35 Ibid., 202 (emphasis in original); compare Bernier, *Travels in the Mogul Empire*, 404.

east, they labored under the assumption there were only two. The first was "Little Tibet, otherwise called Baltistan or Middle Tibet,"[36] the borders of which they only skirted. The second was "Great(er) Tibet," or Ladakh Yül, which "[is that] which in the Persian and Hindustani languages is called by everyone Bara Tubat (Bará Tibet) and Tubat-i-Kalan (Thibet Kalaân), that is Great Tibet, and in the local language Ladakh Yül."[37] It was only when they reached Leh ("which is also called Ladakh"[38]) that, according to Freyre's report, "a Kashmiri coming from Ruthok told us that there was a third Tibet larger than the other two."[39] This was the "third and Greatest Tibet." They were further informed that the "first locality under the jurisdiction of the third and Greatest Tibet"[40] was Tashigang, today still nearest to the line of control between India and the PRC in Ngari province. At the time, Tashigang and Gartok were both under the control of "a sizeable army of Tartars [i.e., Mongols] and Tibetans subject to the king of the third Tibet."[41] Desideri was aware that Tibet was only the name that "we Europeans and Persian texts simply call Tibet . . . . [But in] the language of the country itself, however, it is called Bö (Po), pronounced like the French work *peu*, or Ütsang . . . named after its two principal provinces without taking into account its entire extent and immensity."[42]

Such European accounts of travel did not seem to be remembered in the early nineteenth century. H. T. Colebrooke (1765–1837), who introduced the account of William Moorcroft (1767–1825) of his foray in disguise to Kailash and Lake Manasarovar in Ngari, west Tibet, describes Moorcroft's 1812 journey as to "that part of little *Tibet* in *Chinese Tartary*.[43] Apparently unaware of Desideri's journey, Colebrooke, a well-regarded British judge in Company-ruled India and scholar of Hindu law, also adds that Ngari was "a country never before explored."[44] Moorcroft in his account refers consistently to "Tatary" and uses it meaning what we would call Tibet.[45] He clearly recognized that Ladakh was not part of Tibet and indeed "were extremely troublesome to the inhabitants" of Ngari who resented "their depredations" and wished they would "desist from their incursions."[46] The "Chinese Tatars then invaded Laták whose inhabitants applied to the Cashmírians for assistance,"[47] after which a treaty stopped the hostilities. However, he still considers Ladakhis, like the inhabitants of "little Tibet" (i.e Ngari Tibetan), to be Tatars.[48] Moorcroft uses "U'ndés," "U'n-des," and "Urna Déśa" to refer to west Tibet and "U'ndes," and "U'niyas" to western Tibetans, alongside "Chinese Tartary," "little Tibet" and "Tatars."[49]

36 Desideri, *Mission to Tibet*, 211.

37 Ibid., 161. "Second Tibet was originally divided into various principalities: Gugé, Ruthok, Ladakh, and several others that, at present, are entirely under the sole rule of the king of Ladakh." Ibid. As we will see later, Gugé (or Goghé, as they spelled it) had ruled Ladakh much earlier, and in the seventeenth century had been ruled by Ladakh, but by Desideri's time Gugé had been restored to Central Tibetan control.

38 Ibid., 159, also 163.

39 Ibid., 614.

40 Ibid., 166, 167. The fact that Desideri sites both "Ngari Jungar" and then "Ngari Giongar" (the latter referring to Mt. Kailash) suggests that Ngari was the current term in use locally, though he was also aware of Gugé. See ibid., 681n466.

41 Ibid., 168.

42 Ibid., 211.

43 Moorcroft, "Journey to Lake Mánasaróvara," 380.

44 Ibid., 381.

45 Ibid., 421, 493. Moorcroft refers to Lhasa as "Ouchong;" ibid. 485.

46 Ibid., 434.

47 Ibid., 454. See also ibid., 437–38.

48 He refers to "the independent *Tatars* of *Ladák*; ibid., 434 (emphasis in the original); elsewhere he refers to "three *Tatar* musicians from Laták;" ibid., 449 (emphasis in the original). The article usually spells it "Laták" but is explicit that both spellings refer to the same state; ibid., 443.

49 Ibid., title, map, 466, and passim. On the map, "To Ling" (i.e. Tholing) is labeled as "The Place of Residence of the head Lama." He also uses "Bootan," apparently to refer to Buddhist areas in what is now Himachal Pradesh nearest the border of Ngari along what is now Uttarakhand. Ibid., 423, 493. It appears as "Bhutant" on the map. The term "U'n des" and its variants including Hundés apparently derive from the term locals on the Indian side called west Tibet and western Tibetans.

Alexander Csoma De Kőrös travelled through many of the same portions of the western Himalaya as Moorcroft; in fact, they crossed paths and travelled together for several months in 1822 including in Ladakh.[50] He also spent nearly two and a half years in Zangskar, studying Tibetan language first at the Zangla Palace (1823–24) and later at Phuktal Monastery (1825–26), so one might expect his perspective to be shaped by local understanding and textual knowledge. Like Moorcroft, he too recognizes that Ladakh is both independent and yet dependent:

> Ladak, formerly called *Mar-yul*, still has its own prince, but he must accommodate himself to the political views of the Chinese. *Zanskar*, *Purik* , *Ñubra*, form part of the Ladak principality.[51]

Unfortunately, De Kőrös' distribution of the Tibets in his 1832 "Geographical Notice of Tibet" introduces still more variants: Baltistan is "Little Tibet," central Tibet is "Middle Tibet," Kham in eastern Tibet is "Great Tibet," and "the north-western part towards Ladak is '*Nári*.'"[52]

I hope at this point the contingency and irregularity in the names used for these regions has been adequately illustrated for the pre- and early-modern periods, as well as the consistency in conflating, to various degrees, Ladakh and Zangskar with Tibet.[53] There is some overlapping, depending on the experience and native language of the author, and shifting application of a few relatively invariable sets of terms. In the nineteenth century, expressions for the physical and political divisions are hardly utilized in more standard, uniform, distinct, or accurate manners. Under the scientists, there is a glimmer of hope as they tend to focus on the geography, geology, and botany of those regions that cross political borders. But such optimism is often dashed. On the other hand there are some clear-sighted Britishers who distinguish Tibet (or Thibet) from Spiti and Ladakh, perhaps because of their consciousness of the limits of colonial control.

Among the most contradictory is the 1842 two-volume work by Godfrey Thomas Vigne (1801–1863) describing his yearlong travels (1838–39) in Kashmir and along the Indus, from Baltistan to Skardo to Ladakh. His map refers to the Indus Valley below "Iskardo" as "Little Tibet" and, above it, "Bultistan or Suri Butan" (Fig. 1.1).[54] Just after Dah, Hanu, and "Achina Thung" begins "Middle Tibet or Butan or Bod," which is also indicated as "Ladak" in larger letters (Fig. 1.2). (Vigne also makes a point of calling the capital "Ladak, or, more properly Leh".[55]) In the text, mention is made

50 Duka, "Life and Works," 29.

51 De Kőrös, "Geographical Notice," 124, emphasis in the original.

52 Ibid., 121.

53 Duka, whose1885 work on the life of Csoma De Kőrös has just been cited, refers to De Kőrös' travel to study in Phuktal Monastery in Zangskar as "his second visit to Tibet;" Duka, *Life and Works of Alexander Csoma De Körös*, 68.

54 Vigne, *Travels in Kashmir*, map.

55 Ibid., 1:165; he refers to it as Ladakh in 2:249, 2:340, and 2:349. On Moorcroft's 1818 map of his 1812 journey, he notes that a river "runs from hence N.W. under [sic] Ladakh the Capital of independent Tatary;" Moorcroft, "Journey to Lake Mánasaróvara."

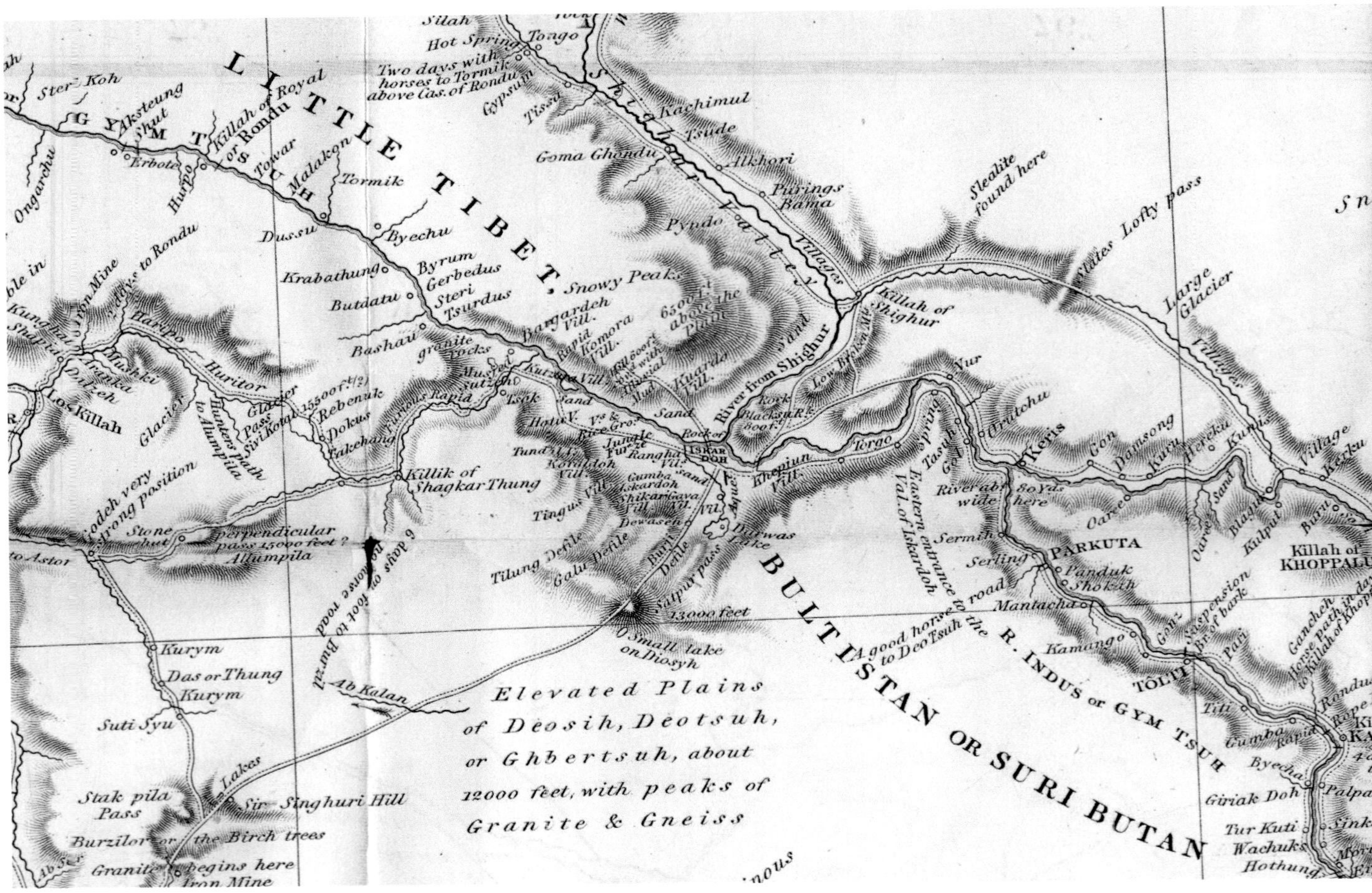

Fig. 1.1 Detail of map depicting "Little Tibet" and "Bultistan or Suri Butan." From Vigne, *Travels in Kashmir*.

Fig. 1.2 Detail of map depicting "Ladak, Middle Tibet or Butan or Bod." From Vigne, *Travels in Kashmir*.

of "the Tibets" more than once.[56] In addition to referring to Iskardo and/or "Bultistan" as "Little Tibet," and Ladakh "Middle Tibet" as on the map, he refers to "Great" and "Upper Tibet."[57] This "Great Tibet" is sometimes a reference to what we would call Tibet proper, "of which Lassa is the capital," but like Desideri, Vigne sometimes used it to denote Ladakh, as in "at Hanu, in Great Tibet."[58]

One might have high expectations for a work published in 1852 with the title *Western Himalaya and Tibet*, which appears to hit the proverbial nail on the head. It was written by the surgeon-turned-botanist Thomas Thomson (1817–1878), who was recruited into an "official" frontier study of 1847–48,[59] along with Alexander Cunningham and Henry Strachey (on whom, more anon). They each took diverging itineraries, and each produced a book recounting their findings, what one scholar labels "fine examples of heroic exploration scholarship."[60] Thomson's route was through Zangskar itself, of great pertinence in the present context. Unfortunately, it turns out that, though he never reached any farther east than Hanlé, in eastern Ladakh—decidedly NOT in Tibet—he speaks of "my journey in Tibet . . . my observations in that country . . . [and] my appointment to the Tibet Mission."[61] Ironically, after completing his journey in the western Himalaya, he joined Joseph Dalton Hooker (1817–1911), and "had the good fortune to travel in the Eastern Himalaya" with him.[62] According to Hooker's narrative of their nine-month journey together, it was mainly in northern Bengal, Assam, and what is now Meghalaya near Shillong.[63] "Eastern Himalaya" seems in this case to be an accurate geographic, not political, designation. But on the western side Thomson uses the political misnomer "Tibet" to refer to Ladakh, Zangskar, etc. As we will see, he is not alone in this inconsistency.

Thus it is rather ironic that he criticizes on convincing grounds whenever boundaries (and their names) are fixed on the basis of political divisions rather than on environmental features. His argument is worth presenting in essence, even if he himself did not extend this advice to his own naming protocols. "To the north-west and south-west [of "Western Tibet"] its boundaries are somewhat arbitrary, unless the political division of the country be had recourse to, which, depending on accidental circumstances entirely unconnected with physical geography or natural productions, is so liable to change, that its adoption would be extremely inconvenient."[64]

56 Vigne, *Travels in Kashmir*, 1:164, 1:264, 2:329.

57 Ibid., 2:248–49; 2:331.

58 Ibid., 1:367. He refers to clerics he notices "seated at the windows, and on the flat roofs," of a monastic building in Skurbuchan in Ladakh, as "Lamas and Gelums, or priests and priestesses, of *Great Tibet*;" Ibid., 2:332. Both Hanu and Skurbuchan are both villages in western Ladakh; Vigne never entered Tibet as we know it.

59 Cunningham, "Correspondence."

60 N. Howard, *Development of the Boundary*, 221n3.

61 Thomson, *Western Himalaya and Tibet*, iii. At Wanla, in Ladakh, he mentions seeing plants he was familiar with from a previous visit "but which I had not seen during *my present visit to Tibet*." Ibid., 386 (emphasis added).

62 Ibid., iv.

63 See Huxley, *Life and Letters of Sir Joseph Dalton Hooker*, 31n2, 317, 324, 328–29; and O'Brien, *In the Footsteps of Joseph Dalton Hooker*, 268–70.

64 Thomson, *Western Himalaya and Tibet*, 465.

For Thomson, this preference for abstraction is consistent: his nearly 500-page narrative is singularly devoid of any expression of interest in people, politics, culture, religion, architecture, or art, but almost monomaniacally lists the types of rocks, clay, and glaciers, and, most of all, the Latin names of plants. He gives us clues to his detachment from the social aspects and attractions of latter: "[T]he phenomena of vegetable life . . . are not affected by accidental irregularities, and therefore form an unerring guide" to the "traveller who penetrates directly to the Tibetan interior [sic]."[65] None of the many local men and porters who helped him are named, and one of the few mentions of "my servants" occurs three quarters of the way through the book. It is only then that one discovers he has been traveling by horseback. Of crossing the Shyok River in Nubra he writes:

> In the more difficult parts, two men placed themselves on each side of my horse's head, to guide him in the proper road, and two more at each stirrup to give him support in case of need. When in the centre of the current, where, from the necessity of keeping my eye on the horse's motions, I had to look at the water, I found it impossible to avoid a feeling of giddiness.[66]

These six men supporting his horse were naturally crossing the river, each on two feet, not on a horse's four.

One of Thomson's partners in the "Tibet Mission" carried out a fortnight foray into actual west Tibet in disguise in 1846. This was the thirty-something Lieutenant (later Lt. Colonel) Henry Strachey (1816–1912) of the 66th Regiment of Bengal Native Infantry. Unusually, in the report on his probe of the geography of the west Tibetan frontier published the next year, he mostly used the place names currently in use by the people of eastern Kumaon (now Uttarakhand) for Tibet, but actively sought out the Tibet equivalents.[67] Strachey began in Askot, Kumaon, near the Nepalese border. He took four yaks and two zho along with a number of "Bhotiya"[68] porters, cooks, and the like; at one point, when he complained of "being lamed by tight shoes," they carried him over the steepest part of a pass in a *dandi*, or hill litter.[69] He is explicit that *Tibet* and *Thibet* are terms used only by outsiders, mainly by Muslims from Central Asia.[70] According to one of his informants, its "true name is Húndés," related to "Hun," and refers to the "aboriginal inhabitants of the country north of the Himálaya."[71] By "true name," he seems to mean the name regularly spoken by locals from Kumaon, on the British side of the border. Strachey generally uses

65 Ibid., 469.

66 Ibid., 403.

67 H. Strachey, "Narrative of a Journey."

68 Ibid., 333.

69 Ibid., 333.

70 Ibid., 104.

71 Ibid., 103.

"Húndés" to refer to Tibet proper, rarely calling it Tibet. To refer to the government of Tibet proper, he tends to use "the Lhassan authorities" or even just "the enemy."[72] He is aware, however, of a form of the term *Ganden Phodrang* (the Gelukpa government of the Dalai Lamas) as a political designation and not "a native proper name indigenous to the land."[73] Henry Strachey is definitely interested in terminology, and is aware of "Bod" as "the general name of the country to Lhassa inclusive," opining that it includes Ladakh and Balti and perhaps even Kham.[74] He also refers to the "Indian Himálaya" and the "Nípál Himálaya," and another of his publications refers to "the British Himálayan Frontier,"[75] but he avoids "Tibetan Himalaya." For westernmost Tibet he is well informed enough to use "Todh Gnari Lungpa"—or simply "Gnari"—for that part of west Tibet up "to the Shikpi frontier" of Kinnaur.[76]

Like his slightly younger, more botanizing and geologizing brother Richard, who followed nearly the same route two years later,[77] once they neared and then crossed the border into west Tibet, they and their Bhotiya companions tried to avoid notice. Henry and his party at times traveled at night, giving locals a wide berth. He made a point of wearing "Hindustani" costume, and before starting he poured his port wine and rum into wooden flagons lest the English bottles give them away.[78] They thought they succeeded in avoiding detection.

Henry Strachey's expedition appears to have been a straightforward political-intelligence sortie, testing the frontiers, gathering information about passes, streams, forts, and settlements, including the Buddhist *gompas*, the district divisions, how the mail was organized, the trade items, and the location of gold mines.[79] He reported in detail on the military preparedness of Ngari (west Tibet):

> The Lhassan Government have no other military force in the province of Gnari than a Militia of the country people, in the extremity of disorder and undiscipline . . . at best it is represented to be a most unwarlike rabble, utterly useless against an organized enemy . . . [The militia] is assembled for two or three summer months . . . [but] the men get no pay, subsist, arm, and accouter themselves, and at the end of the exercising season are dismissed to their houses with—a fine of 3 Rupees each for their bad performance![80]

72 Ibid., 153.

73 Ibid., 330.

74 Ibid., 330.

75 H. Strachey, "Note on the Construction of the Map." He also uses cis-Himalayan to refer to the parts nearer to British territory, and trans-Himalayan to indicate those areas farther away, i.e., in West Tibet proper (Gartok, Kailash, Purang, etc.). Such terms that are only in relation to the speaker's position, like "Greater" and "Lesser" as discussed above, seem unsuitable for wider usage.

76 H. Strachey, "Note on the Construction of the Map," 331.

77 See below, and R. Strachey, "Narrative of a Journey to the Lakes."

78 H. Strachey, "Note on the Construction of the Map," 132.

79 Ibid., 344, 348, 349.

80 Ibid., 347.

Both brothers, but particularly Henry, appear to have been intent on providing support for the "forward" clique of British administrators of India advocating aggressive policies of expanding the northern border of "British Himalaya."

The third member of the boundary party, besides Strachey and Thomson, was the one most involved with Ladakh: Alexander Cunningham. In his book on the subject, he lays his position out clearly: "Ladák is the most westerly country occupied by the Tibetan race who profess the Buddhist faith."[81] Tibet proper he refers to as "the Lhasan kingdom of Great Tibet."[82] He writes of the "pure Tibetans of Ladák and Balti," and likewise "Rukchu, Zanskar, Purik, and Drás"; the inhabitants of Spiti, Kullu, Lahaul, Kishtwar, and Kashmir "are chiefly a mixed race of Indo-Tibetans"; and in Gilgit is a "mixed race of Dardo-Tibetans." Obviously, he is rooted in the nineteenth-century European race theory.[83] As with many other European observers in the western Himalaya, many plants and animals, such as hares, ibex, marmots, and mastiffs, are "Tibetan" species. The climate in Ladakh is Tibetan.

Cunningham was also very well experienced in the geography of the portion of the Himalaya accessible from British-controlled India, and shares that knowledge of the mountain chains in his *Ladák* book. He offers an analysis of the "system" of its ranges, dividing them into the Eastern Himalayan, the Trans-Himalayan, the Trans-Tibetan, the Kailash, the Mid-Himalayan, the Outer or Sub-Himalayan, and the Western Himalayan (which he also calls the Bara-Lacha). It is clear from the spectacularly inventive color illustration of these ranges (Fig. 1.3), done well before the trigonometric survey had identified Everest, that he was most impressed with the western Himalaya.

A little more than a decade later, another British military officer, Henry D'Oyley Torrens (1833–1889), a lieutenant colonel (later promoted to lieutenant-general) in the Royal Welsh Fusilliers, trekked from Simla to Lahoul, Ladakh, and on to Kashmir during three months of summer leave, along with several other officers and the deputy commissioner of Simla, Lord William Hay. They took servants and "coolies" with them. If there was a serious purpose to the trip and not just a combined sightseeing, sketchbook-filling, shooting-for-sport outing, it is well disguised in a relatively lighthearted narrative. Some passages read as comic descriptions of the journey, the humor at the expense of the British participants as much as the named or nicknamed servants. Unlike many such accounts, there

81 Cunningham, *Ladák, Physical, Statistical, and Historical*, 17.

82 Ibid., 19.

83 On race theory's deleterious impact on the development of art history, see Michaud, *Barbarian Invasions*. Sara Shneiderman also points out the continuing conflation by much more recent prominent Tibetan studies scholars of the Tibetan race and the Tibetan ethnicity, in which the "concept of 'race' seems to imply a greatness linked to 'civilisation' and literacy," with "tribes" at the borders; Shneiderman, "Barbarians at the Border and Civilising Projects," 19.

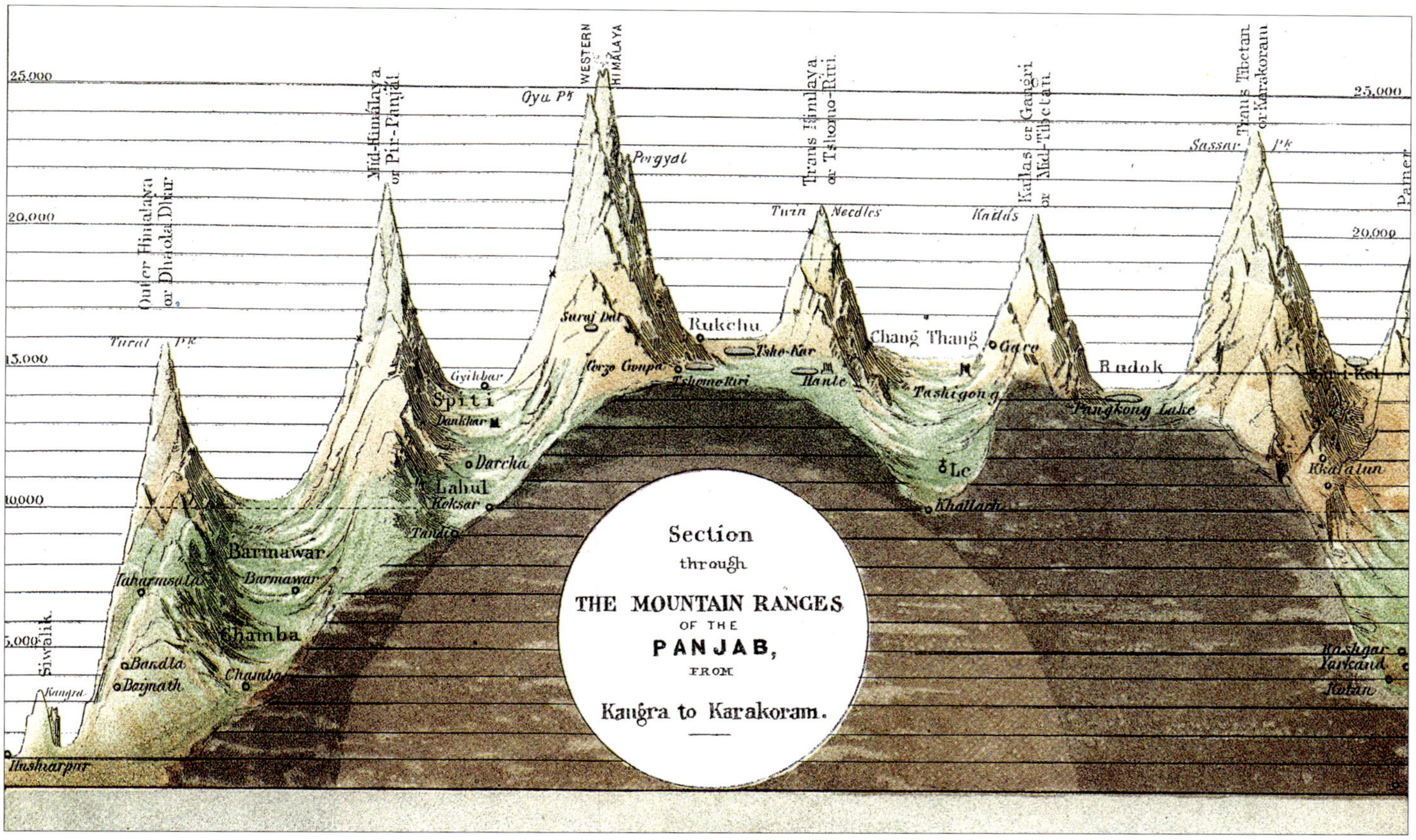

Fig. 1.3 "Section through the Mountain Ranges . . . from Kangra to Karakoram." From Cunningham, *Ladák, Physical, Statistical, and Historical*, pl. 1.

is some praise for the "hardy Ladakhis"[84] and only comparatively minor mockery of the people, places, and local practices, despite the standard topoi raised: the discordant sounds of music in monasteries, the women as hard working as they are unattractive, the sly shikharis, and the duplicitous Kashmiris. Overall, however, "they are very jolly dogs, these Botis of Ladakh."[85]

As for nomenclature, one can only sigh in confusion, starting with the title: *Travels in Ladâk, Tartary, and Kashmir*. "Tartary," it seems, is used as identical to "Thibet," which includes Ladakh. Consequently, the route they devised from Simla led "over the high table-lands of Thibetan Tartary, into the verdant vale of Kashmir."[86] Torrens and company did not cross into west Tibet but trekked from Lahaul to Ladakh to Kashmir. The best that can be said is that at least they didn't call it "Western Thibetan Tartary," though why Tartary has to be involved at all is a mystery: aside from its use in the title, it rarely appears, but when it does, "Thibetan Tartary" is equivalent to "Chinese Tartary." The latter, cited more than once, definitely denotes Tibet proper, as in "Lhassa, the metropolis of Chinese Tartary."[87] Torrens is explicit in his awareness that Ranjit Singh and the Sikhs conquered Ladakh, that Tibet does not rule it. He is aware that it was then sold to the Dogras to indemnify a Sikh debt to the British, that it was—in his time—the territory of the Maharaja of Kashmir.[88] Nonetheless, he uses "Thibetan" as qualifier for the language he hears spoken in Ladakh, for the ibex, the furze, the kyangs (wild asses), and for the nobles he encounters there, and the Ladakhi representation of deities.

84 Torrens, *Travels in Ladâk, Tartary, and Kashmir*, 8.

85 Ibid., 181.

86 Ibid., 3.

87 Ibid., 364; "Chinese Tartary" in relation to Lhasa is used twice on that page. Hooker and Thomson criticize the use of "Chinese Tartary" as "an unmeaning term, and one which should be disused in geographical and botanical works." Hooker and Thomson, *Flora Indica*, 207.

88 Torrens, *Travels in Ladâk, Tartary, and Kashmir*, 146.

Fig. 1.4 "Pass of Bara Lacha." From Torrens, *Travels in Ladâk*, opposite p. 137.

Fig. 1.5 "Upper Spiti Valley." From Egerton, *Journal of a Tour through Spiti*, pl. 18.

The Baralacha La pass (Fig. 1.4) "forms a natural boundary between India and Thibet"[89] and, since it leads from northern Lahaul to southern Ladakh, for Torrens Ladakh is Tibet. Of his entrance into the clean-swept Moravian mission at Kyelong, he exclaims, "You are no longer in Thibet—you are thousands of miles away back in dear old Deutschland!"[90] Yet in the book he writes "Ladâk" twice as many times as he does either "Thibet" or "Himalaya." In sum, Ladakh is Tibetan without being ruled by Tibet, and both are Tartar (i.e., Mongolian, which seems to mean Inner Asian), and Thibet is simultaneously Chinese. Perhaps it is the people who are Tibetan? On the other hand, near Baralacha La they encounter "Tartar shepherds, and ladies dressed in the height of Thibetan fashion, aided by a few sheep-dogs, were in charge."[91] One can only conclude that it is pointless to insist on "foolish consistency."

Another official, Philip Henry Egerton (1824–1893), Deputy Commissioner of Kangra, documented his journey "to the frontier of Chinese Tibet" in 1863 and included a number of excellent photographs that he had taken himself (Fig. 1.5).[92] He refers to the "re-establishment of the old boundary between Ladakh and Thibet," and of the kingdom of "Cashmeer on the western frontier of Thibet," the latter a reflection of Ladakh and Zangskar's incorporation into the Dogra state.[93] He does, however, use "Bhotunt" as an alternate name for Tibet, and "Chânthâng" for its western portion, and is aware of the name "Naré Khorsum" for the region up to the border of Ladakh.

Samuel Bourne (1834–1912), an accomplished technical master of early photography, documented a few expeditions into the western Himalaya in a series of four essays published in the *British Journal of Photography* between 1863 and 1869.[94] Like Egerton, Bourne also exposed prepared glass plates at relatively high altitudes, including in Spiti (Fig. 1.6). He was probably correct in his belief that at that point in time, compared with the ones made at Manirung Pass (Fig. 1.7), which he rightly understood to be at approximately 18,600 feet, no "other photographs have ever been taken at so great an elevation as this."[95] In his published reports, Bourne consistently mentions traveling in the Himalayas and to the "wild and desolate regions of Spiti as far as the borders of Thibet."[96] He refers to Ladakhis, but does not call them Tibetans or any of the places he reached Tibet. The Ladakhis who Bourne hired as bearers come in for singularly cruel treatment. As they approached the snows and high passes, the hired hands were reluctant to continue. "On seeing this I took a handy stick, and layed it smartly about

89 Ibid., 239.

90 Ibid., 121.

91 Ibid., 149.

92 Egerton, *Journal of a Tour through Spiti.*

93 Ibid., 42, 45.

94 Rayner, *Photographic Journeys in the Himalayas.*

95 Ibid., 110.

96 Ibid., 63.

Fig. 1.6 "The Manirung Pass, elevation 18,600 feet." Photograph by Samuel Bourne in 1866, negative no. 1468, approx. 29.5 x 23.5 cm, albumen print from glass collodion negative. Collection of Hugh Ashley Rayner, used with permission.

Fig. 1.7 "The Top of the Manirung Pass." Photograph by Samuel Bourne in 1866, negative no. 1469, approx. 29 x 23 cm, albumen print from glass collodion negative. Collection of Hugh Ashley Rayner, used with permission.

the shoulders of several of them till they lay whining on the ground . . . This bit of seasonable sovereignty had a good effect."[97]

With the work of Frederick Drew (1836–1891), in particular his *The Northern Barrier of India* (1877), we plunge deeper into the terminological morass: the Ladakhis belong to the "Tibetan race"; crossing the Zoji La means entering "Tibetan ground"; in Ladakh, "we are completely in Tibet"; there are "two subdivision of the Tibetan race, the Ladâkhi and Châmpâ"; the people of Lahaul and Kulu are people of both "pure and of mixed Tibetan blood."[98] The state of Tibet, starting east of Ladakh, is distinguished from the latter by being referred to as "Chinese Tibet." Drew's other observations are sharp and generally hold up, for he certainly knew Ladakh and Zangskar well and deeply, more than most at that time. A geologist, he advised the Maharaja of Jammu and Kashmir for a decade starting in the 1860s, was eventually made governor of Ladakh, and later became a master at Eton.

Others were also not chary about using the term *Tibet* extremely loosely. Such was the case with William Simpson (1823–1899), the celebrated British artist famous for his war reporting. In his posthumously published autobiography, which recounts his travels to northern India in the 1860s, he calls "Tibet" the region he visited north of Simla—including Chini, the Parang La (the pass between northern Spiti and southern Ladakh) and Tsomori Lake in east Ladakh, definitely west of Tibet proper.[99] Starting in 1894 the Indian Rev. Ahmad Shah, a medical missionary of northern India, spent "Four Years in Tibet" (i.e., Ladakh) as he titled his book published in 1906. He regularly calls it "Lower Tibet."[100] Many more examples exist, but these serve to give a sense of the instability surrounding the critical cognomen *Tibet*.

The jingoist journalist Edward Frederick Knight never saw any "reform" imposed by "our Imperial interest" on "the hill countries" that did not "bring about a great amelioration in the condition of the population," or was ever "forced upon a people against its will."[101] He attached himself to the 1891–1892 military campaign—today, we would call it embedding—in Gilgit, Chitral, Hunza, and Nagar when those venerable mountain societies north of Kashmir sought independence from the Dogras and the Britishers alike. This "little war" was fought midwinter in the context of anxieties about a Russian aggressive encroachment on colonial India, fought for the

97 Ibid., 71. This disturbing example of violent "imperial racism," along with a few others in the following pages, are of the kind which Shashi Tharoor exposed and excoriated in his *Inglorious Empire*. As he writes, "The Empire's heroes were . . . men who used barbarity to pacify the supposedly barbarous." Such violence, as here, was "proudly deployed," in the imperial enterprise. Ibid., 66; see also 89–95. The pattern deserves greater contextualization and analysis than I can offer here, especially given the status of the celebrated Samuel Bourne's "artistic brilliance" and incontestable images of the "sublime" in histories of nineteenth century photography. I cannot in good conscience utilize the data and the images and elide the disturbing attitudes, even if they do not directly contribute to my primary argument in this work. Ignoring them would be tantamount to brushing them off. Unfortunately, shocking as they are, these episodes of brutality are not the most egregious; see for example the chapter "Burn Everywhere Their Dwellings," in Amitav Ghosh, *The Nutmeg's Curse*. Nor, for that matter, were the Maharatta depredations in Orissa and Bengal in the late eighteenth century, less brutal or more benign.

98 Drew, *The Northern Barrier of India*, 88, 123, 251, 251, and 300, respectively.

99 Simpson, *Autobiography of William Simpson*, 115, 141, 146–50.

100 Shah, *Four Years in Tibet*.

101 Knight, *Where Three Empires Meet*, 29; see also ibid., 285, *passim*.

Fig. 1.8 "Rock Image Near Mulbek." From Knight, *Where Three Empires Meet*, opposite p. 144.

purpose of "locking the door on our side"[102] against them.

The subtitle to Knight's book is "Kashmir, Western Tibet, Gilgit and the Adjoining Countries." As might be expected by this point, its "Western Tibet" does not refer to west Tibet but to Ladakh, and Baltistan is referred to as "Little Tibet."[103] When Knight refers to Tibet proper, he calls it "Chinese Tibet" more than a dozen times, and "Tibet proper" at least once.[104] After arriving in Kashmir in the spring of 1891, he "visited the mystic land of Ladak with Captain Bower, the explorer of Tibet."[105] Bower ultimately sets off from Ladakh on a mission into "Chinese Tibet" and, "resolved to clear up the geographical problems of this mysterious and unknown land" and to "fill up that great blank space on the map of Asia," he eventually "traversed Chinese Tibet from end to end."[106] In Knight's narrative, "mysterious" crops up frequently to describe the views of nature: in these mountains, he confronted "the savage ruggedness beneath a mysterious region stretching out calm and solemn under the pure thin air."[107]

Knight devotes eight of his thirty-two chapters to various parts of Ladakh in the "Western Himalayan range" east of the Zoji La, when the "scenery was becoming more Tibetan as we advanced."[108] The book is well illustrated, with some of his own photographs (see Fig. 1.8).[109] The sky, the wind, and the "table-lands" were "Tibetan" once across the pass, along with the "tongue" or language of the inhabitants.[110] The people in Ladakh are of a "pure Tibetan type" (that is, race), even though the men wear "pigtails . . . in the Chinese fashion."[111] It is worth noting that never having been to Tibet did not stop Knight

102 Ibid., 290.

103 Ibid., 242.

104 Ibid., 131.

105 Ibid., viii.

106 Ibid., 183–84.

107 Ibid., 298.

108 Ibid., 112.

109 Knight refers to himself as a "book-wallah as well as a picture-wallah"; Ibid., 324.

110 Ibid., 122, 114.

111 Ibid., 126.

from describing its climate, sky, wind, and so forth. He is rather sarcastic toward Ladakhis, with their "eccentric conduct" and their abhorrence of regularity. He includes the usual mocking description of Ladakhi women dancing.[112] As for the monasteries, they were packed with the "usual grotesque objects of Tibetan worship," including "images of many groveling demons,"[113] "barbarous music," and "strange ceremonies."[114] He calls out the "mummery" of the "Mystery Play" at Hemis with its "hideous" expressions of the "malice of infernal beings," as "they danced to the wild music with strange steps and gestures, [and] howled in savage chorus."[115] He bestowed more than one chapter to the Hemis masked dance festival. Despite the lack of cultural understanding Knight displays in his write-up of his relatively brief sojourn (about four weeks) in what he called "Western Tibet" (i.e., Ladakh), it would be churlish not to acknowledge his literary skills in telling ripping yarns of "holding in check the unruly tribes."[116] The latter half of the book is devoted to the Nagar-Hunza campaign northeast of Gilgit under Colonel Algernon Durand (b. 1854),[117] which Knight calls "one of our little wars."[118]

"Today we entered Western Tibet." So begins chapter 8 of a book of 1893 by Charles A. Murray, 7th Earl of Dunmore (1841–1907). He was then lieutenant-colonel of the Queen's Own Cameron Highlanders, and what he actually meant was that in May 1892 he arrived in Ladakh, which, he asserts, is one of three provinces of "Ngarees-Kharsum."[119] He is quite clear on Ladakh's frontiers: the "Lhasa government" to the east and China to the north.[120] This was a lengthy journey, from the British Trans-Indus Empire ("from the Indus to the Khyber") and on into Chinese Kashgar, to Samarkhand, Bokhara, to the Caspian Sea, Baku and then Constantinople. In the interlude before heading into Central Asia, he visited the Ladakh region. There, he attracted the help and advice of various political officers, among them H. Ramsay, the British Joint-Commissioner in Ladakh and the author of a "practical dictionary" of "the several districts of Western Tibet, *viz.*, Ladák, Nubra, Roopshoo, and Tángtsey, which are collectively spoken of by Europeans as 'Ladák.'"[121] As a result, Murray is actually rather well informed, especially compared with many authors of such travel narratives. Chinese, Sanskrit, and Tibetan script, transliterations, and translations are included in the book. Ramsay is credited, as is the Rev. F. Weber, the head of the Moravian mission at the time. The latter explained Buddhism to the Murray, who affirms that Weber "knows more about their religion than they [Ladakhi Buddhists] do themselves."[122]

112 Ibid., 199.

113 Ibid., 226.

114 Ibid., 204.

115 Ibid., 211.

116 Ibid., 288. The tales convey events of a frequently cruel nature, rather adolescent, and at times exaggeratedly masculine and ethnocentric if not racist. What saving grace there is in his account is his sympathetic description of the fraternization (women were never seen) of the Hunza gallants once the war was over. The former enemies shared food, music, dance and pantomime together, their former enmity set aside if not forgotten. Knight compares these "hearty ruffians," to "Scotch highlander" or "Norse freebooters," standing "quite apart from all other races of Asia;" Ibid., 510.

117 See Durand, *Making of a Frontier*. He does not refer to Ladakh as Tibet, only to Baltistan as "Little Tibet," on p. 12 and listed as such on the map he provides.

118 Knight, *Where Three Empires Meet*, 453.

119 Murray, *Pamirs*, 1:80. That Ladakh is another name for Western Tibet is repeated in ibid., 1:130.

120 Ibid., 1:83.

121 Ramsay, *Western Tibet*, preface (unpaginated). He implies that he was reduced to titling his book *Western Tibet* because Cunningham's book had already appropriated "Ladák," which would have been preferable. Yet he uses them as equivalent.

122 Murray, *Pamirs*, 1:110.

Nevertheless, Murray displays an ugly arrogance (familiar from Samuel Bourne's) when one of his ponymen, who had earlier been fined for damage to two of Murray's boxes of luggage, pulled out a couple of Murray's tent pegs that night and one side of the tent's roof fell in. Murray had his "servants" catch the man, "ordered out my cutting whip . . . had the man held by two coolies," and commanded one of his other servants to give him two dozen strokes of the whip.[123] Later Murray declared he was "sending back all my [local] servants as a lazy useless thieving lot; there is not one to be trusted."[124]

Besides the crass colonial cruelty and arrogance, there are points of confusion or contradiction in the aristocratic Murray's account relevant to nomenclature. While all of Ladakh is west Tibet as far as Murray is concerned, the Zoji La pass between Kashmir and Ladakh "may be called the entrance to the Western Himalayas," while the Fotu La pass (west of Lamayuru) is the exit from that range.[125] Does that not seem to imply that Ladakh is actually part of the Central Himalayas and not west Tibet? In fact he goes further and suggests that when viewing the mountains north and east of Hemis from its upper terrace he was seeing "the southern wall of the great range of the *Eastern* Himalayas, which formidable barrier divides Western Asia from the great Chinese Empire."[126] One assumes his active duty in the military did not depend on acute or advanced geographic orientation.

By way of contrast to the repeated use of "Tibet" and "West Tibet" for cultures well west of the Tibetan border, a contemporaneous contribution to the geography of the area by the Surveyor-General of India itself used the term *North-West Himalayas* for surveys undertaken between 1850 and 1862 "reaching from Nepal on the east up to and including Kashmir on the west."[127] As with all the usages, there is a discernible method at work here. Official surveys generated from the side of colonial India, as well as scientific ones in general, have a double ideological investment in transcending political borders and names. Similarly, the report of an Italian expedition carried out in 1909 in the name of science (to study glaciers and the physiological effects of high altitude on humans) avoided the term *Tibet* altogether.[128]

Another densely scientific paper, filled with Latin names of flora and fauna and commenting constantly on the rivers, streams, fossils, and geology, was published in the *Geographical Journal* in 1900. Written by Richard Strachey

123 Ibid., 1:97–98. See comment in note 97.

124 Ibid., 1:109. In chapters 11 and 12 Murray includes passages ridiculing the smells, the sounds of music, the ritual practices at Spituk and Hemis.

125 Ibid., 1:94.

126 Ibid., 1:149 (emphasis added).

127 Gore, "Mr. Freshfield's Paper," 236.

128 De Filippi, *Karakoram and Western Himalaya 1909*.

(1817–1908), Henry's younger brother, it records in great detail a short trip from Kumaon into west Tibet, to Lake Manasarowar, made a half-century earlier, in 1848. Richard is also clear about the distinction between the Himalaya and west Tibet. He even points out "an old dry stone wall, which we were told was a traditional boundary between Tibet and *Juhar* [in Kumaon, now in Uttarakhand] . . . [though] I do not think that our Bhotiya subjects have any definite ideas as to the boundary between the British possessions and those subject to Lhasa."[129] He describes where the principal passes into west Tibet are located, and the trade that is carried out by "Bhotiyas" on the Indian side with the "Huniyas" on the "Chino-Tibetan" side. Strachey is quite meticulous is providing the names used on both sides of the border; for example, "*Manasarowar* is the Indian name of this lake, which in Tibet is called *Mapham*."[130] He is also aware of the term Gugé for west Tibet, as in "*Lama-chorten* is the first halting-ground in the open plain of *Guge* on the way into Tibet from the Himalayan valley of *Darma*."[131] It is worth noting that Richard Strachey and his companion J. E. Winterbottom, along with sixteen Bhutiyas from the Juhar valley on the Indian side of the border, were defying the "jealous policy of the Chino-Tibetan Government [which] rigorously excludes all strangers from its territory."[132] The two Europeans affected a disguise and avoided as much as possible any contact with the locals. In fact he seems to wish to tweak the Tibetans: once he returned, a Tibetan official sent an inquiry having heard of their unauthorized entry, seeking to determine where they had been. In response Richard wrote, "I desired a message to be sent in return to tell him exactly where we had been, and I added, that if it suited me to go into Hundes [i.e., the country of the Huns, as the locals on the Indian side called Tibet] again next year I should certainly do it." In fact, he did go back the next year, with his brother Henry.

Ultimately, despite the bravado once safely back in Kumaon, the report's reams of botanical, biological, geological, and social data verge on intelligence gathering. The tone of the writing is very much of the moment, not the views of someone reflecting back on a journey made fifty years earlier. One wonders if it was originally submitted to the British colonial government in 1848 and only declassified in 1900.[133] I will return to scientific methods of constructing productive models of regional nomenclature in the final section of this chapter.

As a contrast to several of the accounts so far surveyed, that of Charles

129 R. Strachey, "Narrative of a Journey," 263 (italics in original).

130 Ibid., 263 (italics inoriginal).

131 Ibid., 251 (italics inoriginal).

132 Ibid., 158.

133 This might explain the cryptic footnote by the journal's editor on the first page: "As this narrative has not before been published, the information it contains has been considered by the Council of sufficient value to be placed on permanent record"; Ibid., 150.

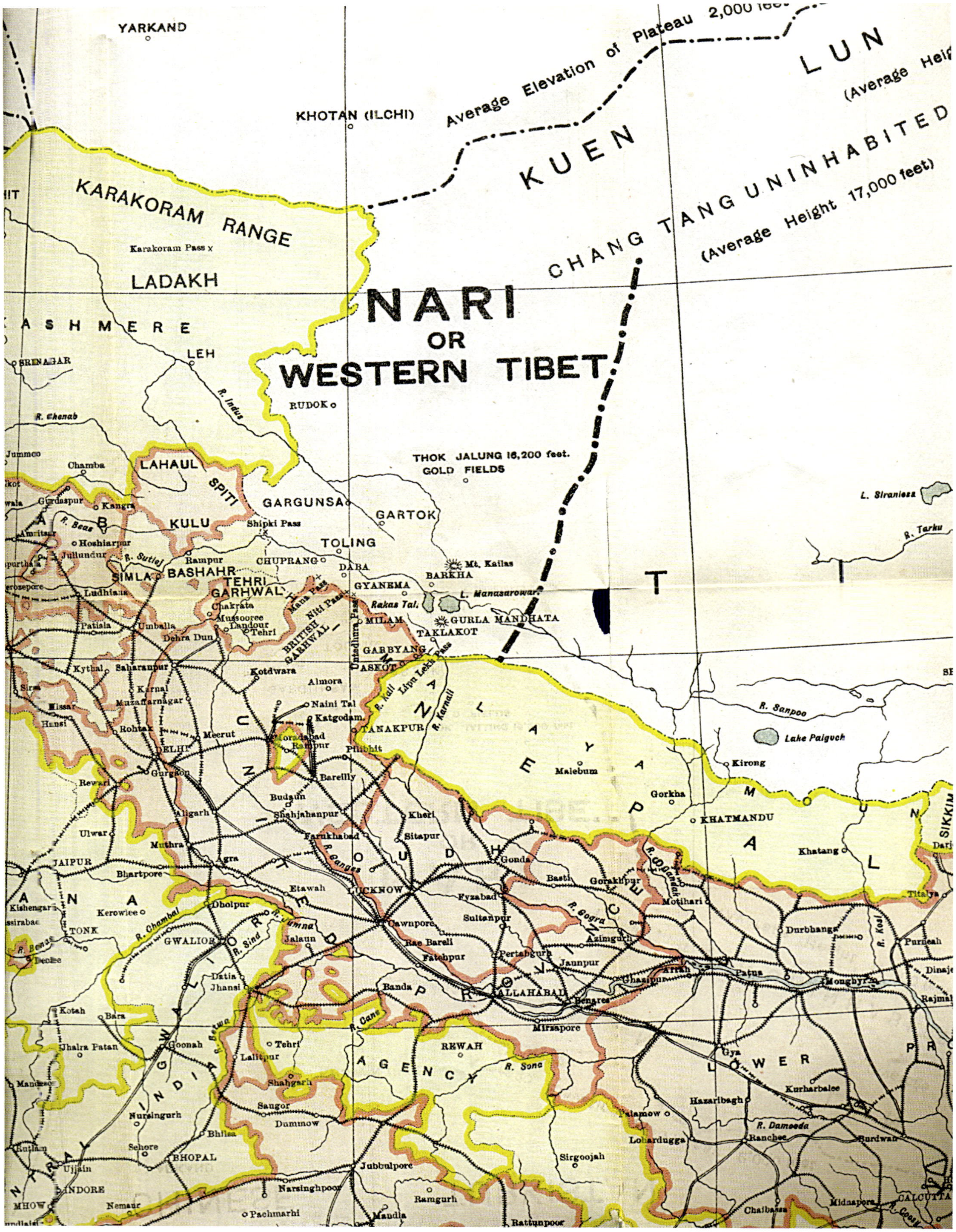

Fig. 1.9 Detail of map depicting "Nari or Western Tibet" as part of Tibet, not "Kashmere." From Sherring, *Western Tibet and the British Borderland.*

Fig. 1.10 "Kailas (21,850 feet)." From Sherring, *Western Tibet and the British Borderland*, frontispiece.

Fig. 1.11 "The Tomb of Zorawar Singh." From Sherring, *Western Tibet and the British Borderland*, p. 198.

Atmore Sherring reflects personal experience in west Tibet, and less obfuscation about the difference between it and the British- and Kashmiri-ruled areas of the western Himalaya.[134] He consistently distinguishes west Tibet from "the British Borderland." In this regard, the map he includes could not be clearer (Fig. 1.9). An official in British Indian service posted in the Almora district, a year after the 1904 Younghusband-led invasion of Tibet, he was able to make an expedition into West Tibet, including to Kailash (Fig. 1.10). Sherring was cordially received by various officials in West Tibet, but he asserts that his 1906 book "is entirely non-political . . . as is befitting a Government servant whose appointment and duties preclude him from entering upon such subjects."[135] His real interest and expertise, however, seems to be the administration of various parts of Western Tibet, the organization of Tibetan armies or militia in the region, the conduct of the officials in relation to treaties imposed after the Younghusband expedition, trade and markets, and the geography of the approaches into Western Tibet from British-controlled India. Sherring emphasizes the rights of Hindus to come to Kailash freely from British-controlled territory, as well as the "horrible cruelty" of the Tibetans toward the Dogra general Zorowar Singh after his plundering of monasteries. Sherring includes a photograph he took purporting to be "a very big Chorten erected to Zorawar Singh at Toyo [in Purang] over his bones" (Fig. 1.11).[136]

Continuing with a survey of the history of the usage of terms related to Tibet to identify western Himalayan cultures, Christian missions to the region, along with adventure-travelers, continued to call these areas "Tibet" or "Western Tibet" for half a century or so. Tibet's mystique, enhanced by its self-proclaimed and selectively enforced closure, is too well studied to require discussion here.[137] For missionaries in the field, as it were, engaged in fundraising for their synods and organizations, Tibet was well known for its veiled aloofness—and its "popish" paganism—much more so than

134 Sherring, *Western Tibet and the British Borderland.*

135 Ibid., vi–vii.

136 Ibid. vi–vii.

137 Brauen 2004; Bishop, *Myth of Shangri-La*; Bishop, *Dreams of Power*; Dodin and Räther, *Imagining Tibet.*

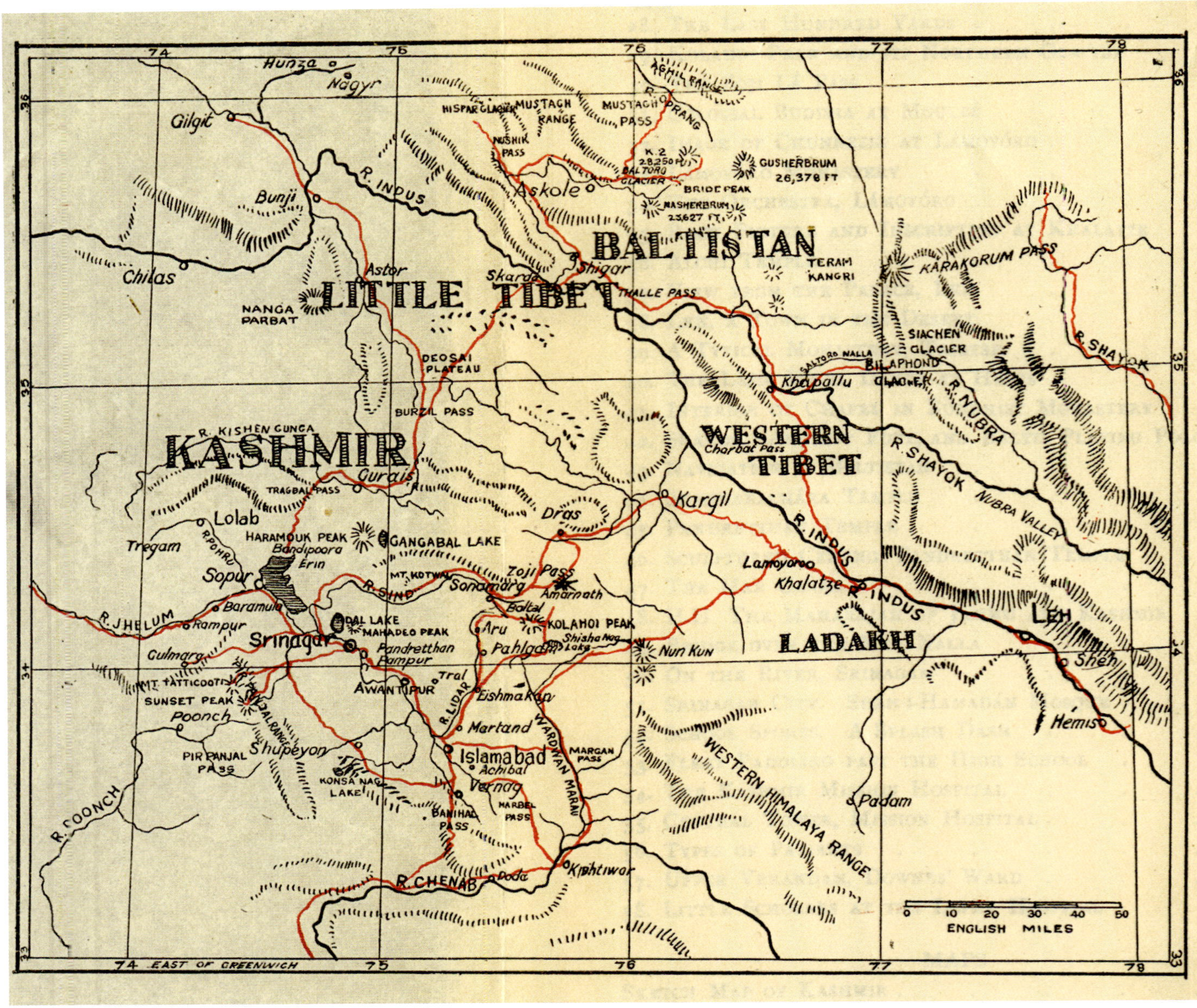

Fig. 1.12 "Sketch Map by Dr. Ernest Neve." From Neve, *Beyond the Pir Panjal.*

any other regional term such as *Ladakh* or *Lahaul*. One understands the preference for a familiar term for an exotic location over a name requiring explanation. Thus one of the founders of the study of the western Himalayan cultures, the Moravian[138] missionary August Hermann Francke, who contributed so much to uncovering the history of the entire western Himalayan region, was relentless in calling it "Tibet" in one or another compounded form. Francke's titles of essays and books include *Antiquities of Indian Tibet*, "Archaeology in Western Tibet," "The Dards at Khalatse in Western Tibet," "Historische Dokumente von Khalatse in West-Tibet (Ladakh)," *A History of Western Tibet*, and "A Language Map of West Tibet," to list just a few.

Ernest Neve, a contemporary of Francke, was much less empathetic toward the culture of the area of what he called—and referred to on his map (Fig. 1.12)—as "Western Tibet" (meaning Ladakh), to which he traveled. He also called the area "Kashmiri Tibet," a reflection no doubt of his

138 Much work, including by John Bray, has been done on the Moravians; see Bray, *Ladakhi Histories*; Heyde, "Early History of the Moravian Mission in the Western Himalayas." See also Tobdan and Dorje, *Moravian Missionaries in Western Trans-Himalaya*; and Beszterda, *Moravian Brethren and Himalayan Cultures*. The Moravians in Lahaul and Ladakh chose to translate the Bible into registers of "classical" Tibetan since the regional vernacular languages in Lahaul, where they first settled in the 19th century, "did not have written forms" (Beszterda 2013: 81; also 188). The "Moravians were surprised to discover that the [three] largest of these local languages . . . were not Tibetan dialects at all, as they had first thought;" (ibid., 186–187). Only the nobility and monks tended to be literate in Tibetan, but the choice was still in line with "the group's plans to carry out evangelization in Tibet proper" (ibid., 286), the anticipated move to Tibet never actually taking place (ibid., 167).

Fig. 1.13 "Rock Picture and Inscription at Khalatze." From Neve, *Beyond the Pir Panjal*, opposite p. 186.

heightened awareness that it was ruled by the Dogra Maharaja, whose summer capital was in Srinagar, Kashmir. Neve was, after all, an English doctor called to serve in the missionary hospital in Srinagar, part of the Kashmir Mission of the Church Missionary Society. He saw himself as on "the fighting line of Christianity," whose "battle is prolonged,"[139] in a competition for the souls of benighted heathens. This certainly colored his observations about Ladakh, summed up by his statement that "After Kargyl the population is Buddhist and you feel that you are in a strange country."[140] His attitude to Buddhism was also permeated by superior Anglican hostility and the widespread idealization of European-created Buddhism[141] as reflected in the last sentences of his chapter "A Glimpse of Kashmiri Tibet":

> But neither in them [the monasteries] nor in the villages and towns of Ladákh does one meet with the Buddhism of romance. Along with much that is quaint and weird and fascinating from an artistic standpoint, there appears to be only too much that is gross, sensual and depraved. Ignorance and pride as usual go hand in hand. There is no 'Light of Asia' here.[142]

At Francke's request Neve photographed one of the boulders at Khalatse that bore both Tibetan and Kharoṣṭhī inscriptions on them. Neve then printed the image and sent it to the Dutch epigrapher Jean Phillippe Vogel, then working with the Archaeological Survey of India. Francke later published it and wrote that Vogel read it as being Maurya-period Brāhmi for "Bharad[v]ayasa," which he suggests is the name of a northwest Indian.[143] Neve included it in his book as plate 35 (Fig. 1.13).

Another Moravian missionary, Adolph Reeve Heber, and his wife, Kathleen, used both "Lesser Tibet" and "Western Tibet" to refer to Ladakh, Zangskar, and other regions in their 1903 publication.[144] One more Moravian missionary, who also collected art and artifacts for museums in Europe, was Walter Asboe. In the 1930s and 1940s, he continued to call the local people in Keylong in Lahaul, "Tibetans,"[145] and that region and Ladakh itself as "Western Tibet."[146]

139 Neve, *Beyond the Pir Panjal*, 202.

140 Ibid., 176.

141 Almond, *British Discovery of Buddhism*.

142 Neve, *Beyond the Pir Panjal*, 183–84.

143 Francke, "Historische Dokumente von Khalatse," 592. This boulder is referred to in Salomon, Devers, and Ldawa, "Kharoṣṭhī and Brāhmī Inscriptions from Ladakh," 93. At the time they drafted their essay, they were unaware of the published photograph. I thank my Northwestern University colleague Mark McClish, who I consulted about the Brāhmī, for bringing it to their attention, and sharing Salomon's comments after seeing the photograph, that Francke's eye copy is "pretty accurate," although the "third and last character are very uncertain." He also shared their forthcoming article, which Salomon had forwarded him. Personal communication, October 2021.

144 Heber and Heber, *Himalayan Tibet & Ladakh*, 1976 (1926), 204, 226.

145 Asboe, "Sacrifices in Western Tibet," 75.

146 Ibid.; and Asboe, "Pottery in Ladakh, Western Tibet."

As a bona fide "explorer" who had walked the borders of Tibet, entering and exiting from various directions, Sven Hedin (1865–1952) had no reason to inflate his accomplishments by falsely associating them with blank spaces on the map he was actually filling in. Moreover, he had every reason to be clear about where the borders lie, since he faced many difficulties and setbacks in crossing them. Nor, as a Swede, would he have had any particular desire to curry favor with the British alone: to further his goals he needed permits from them, yes, but not at the expense of equally necessary cooperation from officials in China, Tibet, and Russia.

Hedin could not be clearer about what was on each side of the Ladakh-Tibet border: "I saw the eternal snow-fields on the Himalaya ridges . . . On the other side was Tibet."[147] In 1906 he planned to enter Tibet from British territory but was denied permission and decided to start from Leh and enter Tibet unofficially from the north. That plan succeeded but it was the permission from the Chinese authorities he had acquired as backup insurance that held up well in Tibet, despite the British refusal. Eventually, after going as far east as Shigatse and exploring Rakas-tal and Manasarowar lakes, in August 1908 "we crossed the border-line of Tibet and India"[148] near the Shipki-la, connecting Ngari to Lahaul, passed through Poo on his way to Simla (in his diary, "Camp no. 500") and back to Europe. No "West(ern) Tibet" referring to Spiti or Ladakh muddies the stream of Hedin's narrative.

As noted earlier, Mughal-era sources distinguish among Balti (*Tibet-i-Khurd,* Little Tibet) and Ladakh (*Tibet-i-Kalan or Tibet-i-Buzur*, Great Tibet). A later author with extensive firsthand knowledge of those areas in the late nineteenth and early twentieth centuries was al-Haj Maulana Hashmatullah Khan Lakhnawwi, a high official (*Wazir e-wazarat*) who had served the government of Jammu and Kashmir in Gilgit, Muzaffarabad, Kargil, Ladakh, and the Baramula region of Kashmir.[149] After his retirement in 1928, he wrote an extensive history of northern India and Tibet in Urdu, the title translated as *A History of Kishtwar, Real Tibet (Lhasa), Little Tibet (Baltistan), Purig (Kargil and Zangskar) and Gilgit (Dardistan).*[150] According to Siddiq Wahid, Hashmattulah Khan followed earlier practice for Balti and Ladakh (as *Tibbat e-khurd* and *Tibbat e-buzurg*, respectively), but now also includes Tibet proper as "Real Tibet," or *Tibbat e-asli.*

Walter Koelz, the American ornithologist who supported his expeditions by

147 Hedin, *My Life as an Explorer*, 377.

148 Ibid., 523.

149 Hashmattulah Khān, *History of Tibet and Great Tibet*, iii, in the foreword by Ambassador Salman Haidar, grandson of Hashmattullah Khān. This is a translation only of the parts of Khan's text that relate to Tibet.

150 This translation was kindly provided by Siddiq Wahid; personal communication, October 2021.

shooting birds by the hundreds, stuffing and selling their bodies to natural history museums, subtitled a portion of his published diary of a collecting expedition to Lahaul, Ladakh, and Zangskar "A Traveler in Tibet." In the body of the essay itself, while using the term *Tibetan* some twenty times, Koelz refers to Hemis as "the largest and best known in West Tibet," and Zangskar as "the Tibetan province of Zanskskar [*sic*]."[151] Giuseppe Tucci was also in Ladakh at some of the same time as Koelz, though Tucci did succeed in traveling on to west Tibet. He used "Western Tibet" (in Italian, *Tibet occidentale*) in the titles for both of his popular books: *Secrets of Tibet: Being the Chronicle of the Tucci Scientific Expedition to Western Tibet (1933)*, written with E. Ghersi, as well as the more academic, multi-volume series he called *Indo-Tibetica*. Volume 3 is *The Temples of Western Tibet and Their Artistic Symbolism*, and Part 1 consists of temples in Spiti, so he too implies Spiti is west Tibet. In one of Tucci's expedition accounts, he explicitly refers to inhabitants of Spiti he meets as "Tibetans" (1936: 45–46).[152] Marco Pallis was in the same regions at the same time—indeed he encountered Tucci in Spiti near the Tibetan frontier and described a dinner in which the latter was distracted by negotiations for "an antique ceremonial apron made from carved plates of human bone . . . being offered for sale by a mysterious person hovering in the background."[153] Pallis was an enthusiastic mountaineer and a thoughtful seeker of wisdom who seems to have been intrigued with the contrast he saw in "traditional" and "modern" ways of living. He had experience in both the eastern and western Himalaya, and was familiar with "the peoples living on the borders of Tibet"[154] such as those in Spiti, Ladakh, and Sikkim, which he called the "antechamber to Tibet."[155] Pallis recognizes that his mountaineering expeditions were "Himalayan journeys," but he writes of his excitement at "the prospect of re-entering a Tibetan country" when leaving Kargil and entering Buddhist Ladakh, and essentializes the "Tibetan race."[156] At roughly the same period—in the 1930s and early 1940s—that "cosmopolitan traveler" from Amdo Tibet, Gendun Chopel who spent twelve years in India, wrote that Ladakh was a part of Tibet but due to British imperialism, was now, in his time, within India.[157] Both are arguable propositions, but it does reflect the assumption of many Tibetans that Ladakh, with its many monks training in central Tibetan monasteries, was in some sense "Tibetan."

In more recent times, in museum publications and in the art market and its handmaidens, it is not uncommon to use "West Tibet" to cover a wide area. In an article with the subtitle of "Kashmirian Influence on the Sculpture of

151 Koelz, "Roof of the World," 291, 289.

152 Tucci and Ghersi, *Shrines of a Thousand Buddhas*, 45–46. In Losar village in Spiti, he observes, "These Tibetan people, who are dominated by Lamaism, live under the spiritual rule of the Lamas;" ibid., 51.

153 Pallis, *Peaks and Lamas*, 70–71. Pallis later complained about Tucci's collecting to the British authorities.

154 Ibid., 370.

155 Ibid., 97.

156 Ibid., 3, 200, 376.

157 Chopel, "Grains of Gold," 74. John Bray cites evidence provided by an early British Trade Agent at Gyantse in the early twentieth century that common people in Tibet misinterpreted the triennial Lochak (lo phyag) trade mission from Ladakh to Lhasa as a tribute mission signifying fealty, fostering the mistaken belief among Tibetans that Ladakh was ruled by Lhasa; Bray, "Lapchak Mission from Ladakh,"92.

West Tibet," John Siudmak mainly discusses Kashmiri art, his speciality in scholarship and the art market. The only "West Tibetan" works illustrated are labeled as from Ladakh, twelfth or thirteenth century.[158] Here again "West Tibet" is shorthand for Ladakh and surrounding regions, although the definition is assumed, not specified, and can be misleading. Nathalie Bazin of the Musée Guimet recently illustrated how "Western Tibet played a major religious and artistic role . . . and [produced] some of the most beautiful mural paintings of Tibet art history" by discussing the Sumtsek of Alchi, in Ladakh.[159] Here "Tibet" and "West Tibet" presumably indicate artistic modes that transcend political borders. But do they, really? Is Alchi Sumtsek's painting purely "Tibetan," when the proto-Śāradā script used by Kashmir artists has been detected underneath its pigments?

There is or was a certain commercial cachet, a popular appeal to using the term Tibet, at least in Europe and the US, and in my experience publishers and museums use it for marketing and authors acquiesce. Some hit all the buttons, as in an exhibition and book of photographs which, in the later English translation, was titled *Indian Tibet / Tibetan India: The Cultural Legacy of the Western Himalayas.*[160] That led to well-intended reviewers spreading such advertising-copy-like statements as "The real Tibet is in India. Not just since 1959."[161] The book, which features many interesting comparisons of early landscape and architectural photographs with ones by van Ham, recounts the history of the exploration of the western Himalaya, leans heavily on the Tibet connection (as its title suggests), and falls back on the trope of Ladakh as "Little Tibet."[162] By contrast, such statements today cause alarm among officials and publishers in India, as they seems to provide ammunition for Chinese claims of sovereignty (and regular incursions) over more and more areas along the four-thousand-kilometer border.

In one of his final books, Michel Peissel (1937–2011) utilized "Greater Tibet" so as to include Balitstan, Ladakh, Zangskar, Sikkim, Bhutan and much of Sichuan in his map of the "Tibetan language area." This despite the fact that, as John Bray points out, "there are significant variations in the dialects spoken in different villages and districts within Ladakh; and spoken Ladakhi and Lhasa Tibetan are not mutually intelligible."[163] The various dialects, categorized as Ladakhi, including Zangskari, differ "not only in their pronunciation and lexicon from Central Tibetan and among themselves, but more importantly also in their grammar."[164]

158 Siudmak, "Development of the Classical Buddha Image from Kashmir," figs. 22–24.

159 Bazin, "Fragrant Ritual Offerings," 31.

160 The German edition is van Ham, *Indiens Tibet—Tibets Indien*; a revised English translation—van Ham, *Indian Tibet / Tibetan India*—was produced in 2015, six years later.

161 https://kunstundfilm.de/2011/01/indiens-tibet-tibets-indien/.

162 Chapter title, "Ladakh: Little Tibet of High Passes," van Ham, *Indian Tibet / Tibetan India*, 189. An extensive chapter titled "Exploration and Travel," including subsections on pilgrimage, early exploration by British and other foreigners, mountaineering and trekking is found in Zurick and Pacheco 2006: 143–186.

163 Bray "Early Protestant Missionary Engagement," [2nd ed.], 3.

164 Zeisler, Review of *Historical Dictionary of Tibet*, 242.

One absorbs Peissel's idea from the title, *Tibet: The Secret Continent*, the book's purpose being to "reveal the cultural unity of this Great Tibet and the true dimension of a great nation."[165] Peissel's infectious Tibetophilia, facility with Tibetan dialects, and adventurous willingness to go to great lengths to follow up on his hunches, cannot but endear him, despite the fearless idealism underlying claims that "Tibetans still constitute a dynamic and united people—a nation that still inhabits the entire extent of that 'secret continent' set in the heart of Asia . . . , a nation awaiting an opportunity to rise again."[166]

Many Ladakhis in recent times conflate Ladakhi history with Tibet, starting from the ancient period. Besides the examples given in the introduction of this chapter, one finds it expressed in one or another capsule history based on Buddhist sources on the history of Ladakh. In ones written by devout Ladakhi Buddhists Ladakh can still be seen as "Little Tibet," a "living museum."[167] Together,

> Tibet and Ladakh formed a great island in a lake surrounded by snow mountains . . . In the year 127 B.C. there arose Nakhri Tsanpo, the first king to gain control over the whole of Tibet . . . In the year 900 A.D. the descendant of the Tibetan kings . . . came to Purang in the province of Stod Naris, it not being desirable for him to continue residing in Central Tibet. He was installed as the king of Naris-skor-sum. He had three sons whom he disposed in different parts of Naris. The eldest, Palgyigon, gained Ladakh and so in 930 he won authority over Maryul-Ladakh.[168]

Ladakhi is merged into a great island-continent with Tibet, and Ladakh's history begins with Tibet. To be sure, knowledgeable Ladakhis do register their resistance to such widespread reduction. Nawang Tsering, after pointing out that "Ladakhis assert that they have received their spiritual and cultural tradition from Tibet," goes on to point out that, "[a]s a matter of fact, however, Buddhism was introduced in the upper Indus Valley earlier than the seventh century."[169]

The contemporary insistence by many inhabitants of their intrinsic "Tibetaness," and the inherited pre-colonial and colonial legacy of chaos and conflation of appropriate terminology and identity by outsiders has led to more confusion, particularly in accounts of non-specialist outsiders. Just one example will suffice. In a relatively well-informed treatise based on first-

165 Peissel, *Tibet*, 6–7.

166 Ibid. Peissel's earlier work on Zangskar is particularly inspirational for me, and in fact photographs of Zangskar and Ladakh surely form a plurality if not a majority in the book under discussion.

167 Paljor, "Ladakh," 184. In an introduction to a book of memories of their periods of study and travel in Tibet by two Ladakhis, Francesca Merritt also points out that "Ladakh is very similar to Tibet and it is often referred to as 'Little Tibet'. Culturally it is the same as Tibet used to be." Tharchin and Namgail, *Recollections of Tibet*, iii.

168 Paldan, *Guide to the Buddhist Monasteries*, 3.

169 Tsering, *Buddhism in Ladakh*, 7.

person interviews conducted in Ladakh, we are told that the Ladakh region is "politically Indian, but culturally and morphologically Tibetan . . . Ethnically the Changpa [nomads] of Ladakh are Tibetan. They reached this area around the eighth century . . . most are indigenous Ladakhi".[170] One of the largest entities of the western Himalaya is thus caught between the pincers of "India" and "Tibet." Even for well-meaning, sympathetic researchers who have traveled to the region, those are its only options, it seems, in terms of its identity and those of its people. This binary obscures a situation that is much more complex, as one would expect specialists to explicate clearly.

Of course, aspects of culture in relatively recent times might be sufficiently cross-regional that separately referring to them as "West Tibetan" versus "western Himalayan" would in fact introduce differences that are not necessarily inherent. For example, in the realm of religious practices in the last few centuries, although we might still refer to "Tibetan Buddhism" as practiced in the western Himalayan region, it makes little sense to me to suggest that western Himalayan Buddhism is fundamentally different or distinct from (west) Tibetan or Tibetan Buddhism. Linguistically, to describe the Tibetan script and language as "western Himalayan" is similarly excessive and inaccurate. H. A. Jäschke in his 1881 Tibetan-English dictionary, groups Ladakh and Lahaul under Western Tibetan, as separate from Spiti, which is grouped with Central Tibetan, as opposed to Khams in eastern Tibet.[171] No doubt there was some empirical evidence for this classification.

As with "Lesser" and "Greater," so too "Inner" and "Outer." It is fascinating to learn that terminological slippage is relevant also for locals in Kham, in what is generally called Eastern Tibet. Buffetrille points to the following inter-Tibetan set of tensions around these terms:

> Khampas were even members of a militia which, alongside the Muslim warlord Ma Bufang (1903–1975), fought against the Tibetan Army . . . During those years, the Khampas considered that they were in "Tibet proper" when they were on the other side of the Drichu . . . which marked the frontier between "Inner Tibet" (Kham) under Qing authority and "Outer Tibet" (Bö) under the Ganden Phodrang, thus following and respecting the Simla Convention of 1914. It was only with the advent of the People's Liberation Army that "the hatred between Drawu and Dege faded" . . . since they had to fight side by

170 Garrone, *Cashmre Journey and the Nomad Shepherds*, 46–47.

171 Jäschke, *Tibetan-English Dictionary*, xvi–xxi.

> side against the same enemy. . . Khampa traders appealed to the Lhasa government for help and were "amazed" not to receive an answer.[172]

Apparently they thought they were "proper" Tibetans. The Lhassans apparently thought not.

Alternatively, it may be the case that scholars use the ambiguity of the term west *Tibet(an)* purposefully, when unsure whether a physical object is from Ngari or from west of there. And it must be acknowledged that Ngari might itself not be excluded from an inclusive definition of "western Himalaya." It is, after all, among the Himalayan chains of mountains and is west of Central Tibet. In that case, one would not be doing an active injustice to west Tibet to call it (a part of the) western Himalaya in the way that, I will argue in the next section, it is inappropriate historically to call Ladakh, Zangskar, etc. Tibet(an). Ngari is both Himalayan and Tibetan. LZSKLB are Himalayan but not part of Tibet. This is why I advocate clarity and specificity: define the way one is using such terms. In an important recent essay, for instance, the art historian Eva Allinger discussed an intriguing manuscript located at Hanlé monastery in eastern Ladakh.[173] She insightfully compares some of its illuminations to those on manuscripts and to architecture in Tabo, Pooh, Nako, and Lalung in Himachal Pradesh, at the Alchi Dukhang and Sumtsek in Ladakh, and at Khorchag in Purang (PRC). She concludes that it is from a "local workshop" whose locale is unknown. One of the manuscript's motifs (which it shares with manuscripts in Tabo and Pooh) is "a uniquely West Tibetan idiosyncrasy,"[174] and the title of the essay specifies that it is an "early West Tibetan manuscript." Are we to understand that Allinger believes it was made in Gugé-Purang and then imported to Hanlé in southeastern Ladakh? "Local" in this instance means *somewhere in Ngari*? Or are we meant to understand, as I believe was intended, that it could be from either Gugé-Purang (i.e., west Tibet) or Ladakh or Spiti (i.e., western Himalayan)? Or perhaps what is west Tibetan is the style followed by the artists, and we are meant to comprehend that this style was followed in both west Tibet and in Spiti and Ladakh?[175] The reader would benefit from having this made explicit.

Amy Heller and Giacomella Orofino seem to have gotten it exactly right with their edited volume *Discoveries in Western Tibet and the Western Himalayas* (2007). No explicit explanation was offered for this in the introduction, but since both terms are present and distinguished from

172 Buffetrille, "Increasing Visibility of the Tibetan 'Borderlands,'" 92.

173 Allinger, "An Early West Tibetan Manuscript from Hanle Monastery."

174 Allinger, "An Early West Tibetan Manuscript from Hanle Monastery," 149.

175 See chapters 3 and 4, in which I address the related issue of aesthetic modalities and their names and misnomers in greater detail.

each other in the very title, it was a promising start. Disappointingly, the contributors did not seem to recognize the distinction, or the title was made after and regardless of the volume's essays. According to Huo Wei, one of the contributors, "greater west Tibet" includes Tabo and Alchi.[176] According to another contributor, Elena de Rossi Filibeck, both Tabo and Ladakh are in west Tibet.[177] Even such meticulous scholars as Christian Jahoda, peerless in studies of social formation, in his essay included in the volume writes of western Tibet as "including Spiti," and on his map, Spiti, Kinnaur, and Gugé are all labeled "western Tibet" in the caption.[178] The reader is informed that Rigzin Tsewang Norbu (1698–1755) of Kathog monastery in eastern Tibet was sent by the 7th Dalai Lama to "western Tibet" in order to mediate a dispute between the related Ladakhi and Purig rulers and conclude a treaty among them at Hanlé, which is in eastern Ladakh, so in fact he was sent west, through west Tibet, to Ladakh.[179] To be sure, the title of Jahoda's essay itself makes it clear the focus is on sites in Spiti so it does not cause confusion, but it does then reinforce the reductive notion that Spiti is Tibetan, whatever that may mean.

Examples are numerous by superb Tibetologically-trained scholars and fieldworkers imbued with the conviction absorbed from language and professed ideologies of many contemporary Buddhist western Himalayans that, for example, "Zanskari cultural identity is deeply Tibetan."[180] In studying the folk or local religious practices in Zangskar, "underneath," if you will, the orthodox Buddhist practices (the distinction of *mi chos* or "people's religion," vs. *lha chos* or "divine and royal religion," according to Eva K. Dargyay[181]), Riaboff's aim is to demonstrate the reality and intentions behind "old Tibetan representations of the king."[182] This might actually work, but if it does, it depends on some kind of seamless and timeless continuity between Central Tibetan seventh- or eighth-century beliefs and practices and twentieth-century Zangskar. That was precisely Dargyay's view: "the Tibetan civilization as present in Zanskar is a cultural fossil insofar as many of the cultural elements of the early Tibetan dynasty (seventh to ninth century C.E.) are still alive in Zanskar while they were displaced by more recent developments in other parts of the Tibetan world."[183] These jaw-dropping Tibeto-centric assumptions stem at least in part from or perhaps the result of the acceptance of imprecise and inconsistent geographic terms (see Table 1.1). I believe both need to be challenged, and not only for Zangskar, or Ladakh, but for Tibet itself, just as it must be also for regions like Mustang.[184]

176 Huo, "Newly Discovered Early Buddhist Grottos in Western Tibet," 29.

177 de Rossi Filibeck, "Poetical Prefaces of Manuscripts from Western Tibet," 152–53.

178 Jahoda, "Socio-economic Organisations of Village Communities and Monasteries in Spiti," 220, 240. It is possible I am misinterpreting the caption to the map—"Spiti and Sutlej valleys, western Tibet"—as Spiti and Sutlej valleys OF western Tibet," when it may have been meant to be understood as Spiti and Sutlej valleys AND western Tibet.

179 Ibid., 222. On this episode, see also Schwieger, "Kathog Rigzin Tsewang Norbu's (Kah-thog-rig-'dzin Tshe- dbang-nor-bu) Diplomatic Mission."

180 Riaboff, "Gzhon nu mdung lag, Mountain God of Zanskar," 23.

181 Dargyay, "Buddhism in Adaptation," 125.

182 Riaboff, "Gzhon nu mdung lag, Mountain God of Zanskar," 34.

183 Dargyay, "Buddhism in Adaptation," 126.

184 In a recent learned essay on how Thakali clans in Mustang narrativize their ancestry we are told that "*some* of the ancestors of the present-day Tamang Thakali indeed were emigrants from Jumla or Western Tibet (incl. Ladakh)." Vinding and Sørensen, "Miscellanea Himalaica," 993 (emphasis in original).

Table 1.1 Place-names

Western Himalaya (LZSKLB)	LZSKLB & West Tibet	West Tibet / Tibet
Antechamber to Tibet		Bhotunt
Bará Tibet		Bö
Bara Tubat		
Bod		
Bolor		
British Himálaya		Chângthâng
Bultistan		Chinese Tartary
Butan		Chinese Tibet
Changthang	Gnari	Chino-Tibet
Great Tibet	Greater West Tibet	Ganden Phodrang
Greater Tibet	Guge, Gugé	Great Tibet
Indian Himalaya	Hundés, Hundes	Greatest Tibet
Kashmiri Tibet	Huniyas (=Tibetans)	Hundés, Hundes
Ladak		Huiyas (=Tibetans)
Ladakh Yül		Lhasan kingdom of Grt Tbt
Lesser Tibet		Lhassan authority, govt
Little Tibet		
Lower Tibet		
Middle Tibet		
Mo lo so (muat lā sā)		
Mar-po-yul		
Mar sa		
Maryul		
Naré Khorsum	Naré Khorsum	Nare Khorsum
Ngarees-Kharsum	Ngari	Ngari
Po-lu-lo		
San-po-ho		Po
Second Tibet		Real Tibet (Tibbat e-Asli)
Suri Butan		
Tartary		
Tibet		
Tibet-i-Buzur		Thibetan Tartary
Tibet-i-Kalan		Third Tibet
Tibet-i-Khurd		Tibet proper
Tsang-po	Todh Gnari Lungpa	U'n-des, U'ndés
West Tibet		Ursang
Western Tibet	West(ern) Tibet	Ütsang

While I am perplexed by the nearly uniform projection of an assumed identity of "Tibetan-ness" onto the western Himalayan cultures, in western language studies in particular, fundamental questions are also being raised—if not answered—by scholars of classical, early, and contemporary Tibetan language, literature, and ethnography about the Tibetan-ness of Tibet and Tibetans. The anthropologist Charles Ramble compares ethnic identity to "the Buddhist notion of the self, that is, rather like the hole in the donut that needs something around it in order even to pretend to exist at all."[185] Sara Shneiderman points to the fact that although "ethnic Tibetan" and "ethnically Tibetan" "are used frequently in Tibetan Studies, there is very little discussion of what these terms actually signify."[186] "'Tibet' and 'Tibetan' are particularly challenging terms because they have been used to mean so many different things within as many contexts over time."[187] In the process of interrogating assumptions that "have been taken for granted as belonging to or representing the 'Tibeto-sphere'" from the perspective of imperial times in Central Tibet, Joanna Bialek asks,

> What does "Tibetan" mean in the [imperial] period? Was "Tibetan culture" any culture within the territory controlled at a given time by the Tibetan army, including Feryana and Kabul? Did "Tibetan society" include all the peoples subject to any form of taxation imposed by the "Tibetan" overlords . . . . To what extent did the texts written in Tibetan script of Tibetan language mirror the "Tibetan" "state of mind"? . . . No term corresponding to the English "the Tibetan Empire" appears to have ever been in use . . . Thus, the urgent question is: what are we talking about when we are talking about "Tibetan"?[188]

The same questions need to be asked about later periods as well, the same doubts raised, as Tsering Shakya has done,[189] before applying the term to the various distinct people of LZSKLB.

It is not the task I set myself to be the word-police in Tibetan or western Himalayan studies (of whatever origin). I approach the work of early and contemporary scholars to learn. In this issue I am left somewhat confused by what these foundational terms mean. I do not exempt my past work for similar ambiguity and imprecision, but am convinced there is merit in a simple solution: west Tibet in my mind refers to those regions that were meaningfully and consistently integrated into that's state's administration, and continue to be in the present; western Himalaya refers to current

185 Ramble, "Whither, Indeed, the Tsampa Eaters," 22.

186 Shneiderman, "Barbarians at the Border and Civilising Projects," 11.

187 Ibid., 12. Shneiderman importantly points out that the victimhood narrative of exilic Tibetan, however justified, has allowed for the "less pleasant aspects of the Tibetan national past" to be unacknowledged; ibid., 15; also 28 on the lack of critique.

188 Bialek, "'Tibetan'—All Inclusive?," 7. Unfortunately, Bialek goes on to write that it is not the aim of her study to answer those questions.

189 Shakya, "Whither the Tsampa Eaters?"

or former states or self-defined cultures, their identities and boundaries generally geographically reinforced, west of Tibet, including Spiti, Ladakh, Nubra, Zangskar, Kinnaur, Lahaul, Baltistan, up to the southern Karakoram. These were invaded by Tibet, sometimes occupied by Tibet, and have participated in aspects of Tibetan culture. One can even say that Tibet has figured large on some of their horizons. But they are not Tibet, western or otherwise. Local or regional histories for LZSKLB that uncover and respect self-naming practices and governance as well as shifting status, are certainly possible for the later periods. The earlier periods are much more difficult to decipher, but it is more profitable to acknowledge gaps in our knowledge than to assume early, essential, or consistent "Tibetaness" by fiat.

Why Is It *Not* "Little Tibet"?

Naturally, there was no distinct dividing line, and no doubt Tibet had stronger or weaker connections at times with the more westerly regions of what I am calling the western Himalaya, (including Spiti, Lahaul, Ladakh [Leh Valley, Changthang, Purig, Kargil district, the Suru Valley, Zangskar], and even farther west, in Bruzha, Baltistan, and Gilgit). While some observers emphasize the Tibet connections with these areas, still there are fundamental distinctions that can be observed between west Tibet (Ngari prefecture) and the western Himalaya that go back to pre-historical and proto-historical times. These I call the "rule of ibex versus yaks." In the Changthang region of northwest Tibet, including northern Ngari province, the predominant animal motif of petroglyphs, painted or carved, is the yak. Of course ibex are also depicted, but many more yaks are featured.[190] The opposite is true overall in Ladakh and Zangskar: ibex are much more often represented on rock carvings. In this regard there is continuity into northwest India and southern Central Asia, which in fact is in line with other traits noted of different types, from architecture to ceramics to language.[191] Before the Tibetans came from the east, there were sturdier and long-standing connections between the western Himalaya and northwest. How close the Tibetans of the Changtang were to Mongolia, the Altai, and southern Siberia, I cannot say. But the proximate connections to the western Himalaya were multiple, and were not exclusive to or dominated by relations—trade, religious, etc.—with Tibetans.

The status of Ladakh before the seventh century is not known from discursive textual records. It is often assumed that it was part of the (Bön?)

190 Linrothe, *Seeing into Stone*, 36–37.

191 Devers, "Buddhism before the First Diffusion?" On architecture, see Devers, "Fortification of Ladakh," 48–50. Issues related to language are discussed below, including in the last section of this chapter. Several essays in Rather, Shah and Yatoo, *Revisiting Himalayan Borderlands* discuss the early and enduring connections between the western Himalaya and Central Asia.

Zhangzhung state, the capital and center of which were in west Tibet, though there is no conclusive proof of that. Some Bön adherents believe that the Zhangzhung kingdom stretched from Persia to China, but more conservative accounts see it as centered in west Tibet (now known as Ngari prefecture) and extending east into what is now western Nepal.

John Belleza, a learned Bön practitioner and writer, "maintains that the pillars, rock paintings, and carvings of western Tibet establish close cultural links with Iron Age cultures in Mongolia, the Altai, and southern Siberia, yet are sufficiently distinctive in style to indicate that they belong to a separate cultural enclave."[192] On the other hand, Dan Martin believes that there are "linguistic connections" between Zhangzhung and "Kinnauri and other western Tibetan languages"—even "Darma" as spoken in Uttarakhand, as well as Old Newari, although those may be later survivals, not hints at shared origins.[193]

If the western Himalayan regions were in fact part of Zhangzhung as the legendary accounts maintain, its "ghosting"—that is, its destruction in the seventh century through the treachery of the Pugyal forces by order of Songtsen Gampo, the brother-in-law of Zhangzhung's then ruler—would not have endeared the distant Pugyal kingdom of central Tibet to Zhangzhung's inhabitants. Subsequently, the Pugyal armies invaded Ladakh, Zangskar, Gilgit, and Baltistan, and stationed soldiers there. Indeed, an "astounding discovery made during the 2018 surveys" by Devers revealed a fortified courtyard at Anley (Hanlé), south of Nyoma, that Devers suggests could have been "a convenient platform for launching [imperial Tibetan] troops further west in the second phase of expansion in the 8th century."[194] It is often suggested that Ladakh was incorporated into the Pugyal empire as a result of this military invasion and occupation. For example, John Bray, one of the leading historians of the region, states that "From the late 7th or early 8th century until some time after 842 AD it [Ladakh] was part of the Tibetan empire."[195] That might technically be true at one level, but an equally valid way of putting it, one that accurately reflects what we actually think we know, is that a powerful antagonistic army was occupying it and controlling the routes in and out of the territory. After all, one accurate translation of Ngari (mnga' ris) is "the Subjugated Territory."[196] Bray certainly does not conflate the western Himalaya with Tibet—in the same essay he states categorically that "the region cannot be taken simply as a sub-set either of India or Tibet."[197] Nevertheless, stating

192 G. Jinpa, Ramble, and Dunham, *Sacred Landscape and Pilgrimage in Tibet*, 145.

193 D. Martin, "Zhangzhung Dictionary," 17–18.

194 Devers, *Historical Sites of Changthang*, 11.

195 Bray, Introduction to *Ladakhi Histories*, 1. [1st ed.]

196 G. Jinpa, Ramble, and Dunham, *Sacred Landscape and Pilgrimage in Tibet*, 152.

197 Bray, Introduction to *Ladakhi Histories*, 2. [1st ed.]

it was part of the Tibetan empire[198] is an example of the consequence of reading a military occupation as participation, leading to a false identification. This is in keeping with a pattern of assumptions "made in the Tibetan context: First that Tibetanisation was/is a positive experience of liberation rather than one of subjugation, and second, that the process of Tibetanisation is essentially complete, and therefore the concept of 'Tibetan culture' [is] a unitary juggernaut subsuming" groups on the margins.[199] From there it is one short step to "identification." If even so perceptive a historian as Bray unintentionally reinforces these assumptions, the rest of us are even more prone to see Ladakh as Tibetan. After the Pugyal troops were withdrawn (or were absorbed there) following the mid-ninth-century collapse of their empire, in the tenth century the ruling family's scion, Kyidé Nyimagon, was said to have been made king of west Tibet and came to rule Ngari Korsum, including Ladakh. Yet if the population, the culture, the language, the customs were already "Tibetan" in any meaningful sense, why would they need to forcibly occupy these areas?

In fact the early accounts of west Tibet and the western Himalaya are based on oft-repeated but later narratives about the development of Buddhism, the collapse of the Tibetan Pugyal empire due to Langdarma's anti-Buddhist measures in the mid-ninth century, the arrival of Kyidé Nyimagon into Ngari and Purang in the early tenth, his heir Lha Lama Yeshe Ö (947–1019/24), Rinchen Zangpo (958–1055), and so on. This literature is no doubt studded with shining gems of retrospective understanding but it cannot be accepted as syntheses of unbiased accounts created at the time. In fact,

> We do not have much information about the development of Buddhism in Mnga' ris before the advent of Lha bla ma, not to mention other forms of religious practices and worship. Indeed there are still a large number of unclarities about what exactly transpired upon the dissolution of Tubo that must have taken place after the assassination of its last ruler. Khri dar ma 'u dum btsan (d. ?842), alias Glang dar ma. Not unproblematically, the tradition asserts that he had two sons, 'Od srung[s] and Yum brtan, whose descendants ruled, respectively, over the vast area that later came to be known as Mnga' ris and central Tibet.[200]

Even the transmitted literature about the Pugyal Empire of Tibet and its Buddhism-promoting kings, much less the accounts of the origins

198 The *Historical Dictionary of Tibet,* which can be taken as a representative illustration of the received understanding, states that Ladakh "came under the control of the Yar klung kings [i.e. the Pugyal Tibetan Empire]" Powers and Templeman, *Historical Dictionary of Tibet*, 388. In the entry on Zangskar, we find the following: "During Tibet's imperial period (seventh–ninth centuries), the region was incorporated into the Tibetan empire. With its collapse, Zangs dkar reverted to local control" (ibid., 747). Military occupation is not necessarily incorporation, much less identification. One pertinent example derives from the other, eastern frontier of the Pugyal empire. Some Han Chinese areas now part of Gansu were captured and occupied by the Tibetan armies in the eighth and ninth centuries. The Han population, occupied and ruled by the Tibetan empire continuously for decades, for as long as eighty years, did not become Tibetan. When the Tang armies pushed the Tibetan lines of control south and west, and recaptured these areas, they were welcomed with joyful tears by thousands still maintaining Han-style traditions; see Sperling, "A Captivity in Ninth Century Tibet," 27–28, 59. Why assume it was different in Ladakh and Zangskar? Sperling suggests that the "forced assimilation that so often accompanies the artificial creation of modern nation states," was not part of "traditional" imperialism. In contemporary times, we lose sight of the fact that "imperial nations usually sought only the submission of other states, not their cultural destruction;" ibid., 59–60.

199 Shneiderman, "Barbarians at the Border and Civilising Projects," 28.

200 Kuijp, "Bird-faced Monk," 407.

of the line of kings, reproduce, in Jahoda's view, "a mythic formula with reference to a divine ancestor who came from (the gods of) heaven to earth as the lord of men," phrases that continue to be applied to the Tibetan royal lineage into the tenth century.[201] Comparison of this type of literature with the Dunhuang manuscripts provides similar checks on accepting these narratives as presenting an accurate picture of the historical situation, including the position of Buddhism between the seventh and tenth centuries in Tibetan-controlled territory. The *Old Tibetan Chronicle* (PT 1287) and the *Old Tibetan Annals* (PT 1288, IOL Tib J 750, and Or. 822/187) found at Dunhuang provide "glimpses of the texture of the Tibetan world prior to the emergence of Buddhist tropes through which the empire was later viewed. By the time the Dunhuang manuscripts were sealed into the cave [in the early 11th century], Buddhism was no doubt a potent force, but it had not yet thoroughly pervaded Tibetan culture."[202] Still, even if Buddhism was underdeveloped in Tibet (and Ngari) in the early tenth century, the fact that the lineage of west Tibetan rulers of regions of the western Himalaya can be traced back to Tibet does not "make Tibetan" those regions, as if that alone settled the matter, or overrides the much more complex histories, both before or after the installation of Kyidé Nyimagon and his sons.

In his critically important 2018 essay, the archaeologist Quentin Devers makes an excellent case for the multiple cultural connections maintained by the western Himalayan people in proto- and early historical times. Among them are the nomad states of the Changtang, as well as Bruzha or Gilgit, Baltistan, Kashmir, and even farther afield in southern Central Asia; basically, the same connections can be shown to be operative in the Neolithic period.[203] Later inscriptional evidence demonstrates such links to cultures to the south, west, north, and northeast, who wrote in Brāhmī, Kharoṣṭhī, proto-Śāradā, and even Chinese. As another archaeologist, Laurianne Bruneau, points out, "The diversity of scripts found engraved all over the regions (*kharoṣṭhī, brāhmī, śāradā,* Chinese, Sogdian, Tocharian, Tibetan, Arabic) proves that during the 1st millennium AD Ladakh already was in contact with its powerful neighbours, including [those in the subcontinent of India]."[204] Salomon, Devers, and Ldawa conclude that the Kharoṣṭhī and Brahmī inscriptions seen in Ladakh can be "convincingly interpreted as artifacts of the flourishing trade routes between India and Central Asia in the early centuries of the Common Era."[205] Further, these "Ladakh routes . . . were significant enough to be chosen for display of

201 Jahoda, "Social and the Religious in Early Post-Imperial Tibet," 178. "Historical records show that although Songtsen Gampo is credited with introducing Buddhist ideas to Tibet, he himself was never a Buddhist but rather practiced territorial deity worship"; Shneiderman, "Barbarians at the Border and Civilising Projects," 26, citing Dreyfus.

202 M. Howard, "Translator's Introduction," xxviii.

203 Linrothe, *Seeing into Stone*, 92–93.

204 Bruneau, "Influence of the Indian Cultural Area in Ladakh," 179. Warikoo mentions the "[t]housands of rock carvings, inscriptions, petroglyphs etc. spanning the Karakoram-Himalayas," and the Brāhmī and Kharosthī inscriptions at Chilas and other regions," as discussed in greater detail below in Chapters 3 and 4 in relation to their Buddhist imagery; Warikoo, "Making of a Frontier, 98.

205 Salomon, Devers, and Ldawa, "Kharoṣṭhī and Brāhmī Inscriptions from Ladakh," 106.

Kuṣāṇa power [which in turn] suggests that the routes were fairly well traveled during the heyday of the Kuṣāṇas in the later first century and the second century C.E."[206] Art-historical evidence also tentatively supports links with the peoples on the southern side of the Himalayan hills and farther south and east.[207] Devers writes that he does not provide Wylie transliterations to local place-names because "multiple ethnic groups coexisted and succeeded one another in the region [between the Pamirs and the Himalayas]. Not all toponyms are therefore of Tibetan origin. As a result, providing random artificial Wylie spelling only creates confusion about the toponymy and etymology of these places."[208]

For the protohistorical era, Devers discusses four "distinct influences": Upper Tibet; the Baltistan and Gilgit region; Northern Central Asia; and Kashmir. Upper Tibet is the most marginal, but can be seen in the stone-roofed architecture and perhaps most clearly in the Changthang region, although even there "a number of cultural, material and religious traditions can be observed. Some are tied to Central Asia (or more precisely the Tarim Basin), so to the so-called Mon populations, and some are more difficult to pinpoint."[209] The archaeologist sees the Kharoṣṭhī and Brāhmī stone inscriptions as evidence of contact with regions connected to Baltistan and Gilgit. He cites the evidence of "animal style" petroglyphs for connections to northern Central Asia, while various remains in Dras and the Suru Valley demonstrate relations with Kashmir, though other types of evidence can be cited. In addition, one might add other visual evidence for interchange with groups on the southern slopes of the western Himalaya, as well as ethnographic and linguistic evidence reinforcing some of these long-standing links to Ladakh and Zangskar's neighbors through the so-called Mon (a generic categorization for local peoples originating south of the Himalayas) and Brogpa ("Dardic," from the northwest) inhabitants.

Although typically engaged in pious exaggeration, Xuanzang reported hundreds of Buddhist monasteries and monks in Baltistan in the early seventh century. Could Ladakh and Zangskar have been unaffected by the surge of Buddhist pilgrims, missionaries, and traders between Kashmir and Central Asia from Kushan times onward? The Gilgit kingdom of the Patola Shahis flourished or was active at least between the sixth and ninth centuries in the Karakoram Himalayas, along routes directly connected to Ladakh and Zangskar. "Notwithstanding its difficult terrain—high and cold mountains, and very limited material resources—the Karakoram-

206 Ibid., 107.

207 See Chapters 3 and 4 in this volume.

208 Devers, "Archaeological Ladakh," 103. If I understand him correctly, what he is pointing to is something akin to the inevitable distortions and sometimes inexplicable inaccuracies that come with transcribing toponyms from one language and script to another, especially when the source language is unknown. Take, for example, the Tibetan place-name Tsaparang, capitol of Gugé in the 17th century when it was conquered by the Ladakhi ruler Sengge Namgyal (which incidentally is transcribed in Wylie as *rtsa hrang, tsa brang* and other variations!). Tsaparang is transliterated into Chinese as Zhaburang (札布让) in the *pinyin* system of transliterating the three Chinese characters into English. At best, the Chinese is a loose approximation of the Tibetan pronunciation. However faithfully the Chinese is transcribed into English, it is still at some distance from the Tibetan pronunciation. So it is with a Wylie English transcription of a Tibetan version that approximates (at best) a place-name from an unknown and very possibly unwritten (thus, spoken) language source in, for instance, the far western Himalaya of the seventh or eighth century. Accurately transcribing the Tibetan approximation is highly unlikely to precisely convey the actual local name of the place in question. However, it might give a false sense of confidence that it was in fact originally in language and by some measure culture.

209 Devers, *Historical Sites of Changthang,* 16.

Himalayan region acted as the transit zone for the transmission of Buddhism to Central Asia. Traders, monks, and local patrons, particularly the Patola Shahi dynasty of the 7th–8th Century AD, contributed to the establishment of Buddhist presence in the region."[210] Of some 5,000 inscriptions found in the Baltistan-Gilgit region in Brahmi, Sogdian, Chinese, and Tibetan languages, 80 percent of the inscriptions are in Brahmi.[211] Given the flourishing of Indian Buddhism in an arc to the south, west, and north of Zangskar, can it be doubted that the early remains, the pre-Tibetan remains, in Zangskar, are as early as the fourth century through the ninth, well before the Tibetan state was in contact with the western Himalaya, or, at the earliest, in the seventh century, with Buddhism itself? [These issues are taken up with examples in chapters 3 and 4, which focus on visual evidence.]

Not only does Devers's essay clarify the mistaken presumption that Maryul and Ladakh are synonymous (as was referred to earlier), but it reinforces some basic distinctions about some of the non-Tibetans who populated the regions. Devers argues that "Mon are mostly found in Upper Maryul, whereas those attributed to the Brogpa are mostly in Lower Maryul." The dividing lines are roughly the confluence of the Zangskar and Indus rivers west of Leh, and Upshi, south of Leh. "[S]ites attributed to the Mon are strictly found along the Indus valley from Upper Tibet to the Indus-Zanskar confluence, while remains attributed to the Brogpa can be located all the way from Baltistan to near Ubshi."[212] This is perhaps slightly oversimplified, and is hard to sustain when we look at the same groups—or rather at sites reasonably attributed to those groups—in Zangskar. There are villages along the left bank of the Doda (Stod) River with strong Brogpa connections, and Devers has also identified an early site, known locally as Mon Khar, which "presents the usual plan of Mon fortifications" on the south bank of the same river.[213] Nevertheless, with a few exceptions this is an important distinction that may be the general pattern.

For Ladakh, the basic division between Upper Indus and Lower Indus, or eastern and western Ladakh, continued well into the historical period. Devers argues that eastern Ladakh (Upper Indus area) was more accommodating to the neighboring west Tibetan culture, including to the imposed rule of descendants of Kyidé Nyimagon ruling from Ngari/Gugé-Purang. The region south of Upshi along the Indus Valley, closer to Spiti and Ngari, seems to have been incorporated into the Gugé-Purang state

210 Warikoo, "Karakoram Himalayas and Central Asia," 17.

211 Ibid., 17–18.

212 Devers, "Archaeological Ladakh," 105.

213 Devers, "Buddhism before the First Diffusion?," para. 37.

with little resistance, and appears as Maryul with its regional center at Shey in the eleventh century.[214] In stark contrast, Zangskar apparently suffered a violently contested invasion. Nils Martin combines the translations of the *Zangs skar chos kyi lo rgyus* by Dieter Schuh and Francke (in brackets) for this account of the Gugé-Purang invasion: "In response, the ten-thousand army of Guge was sent and all the villages of Zangskar and so forth [were destroyed by fire. Many people were slaughtered.] All that remained was carried away and the land became empty. Thereafter, people came from various places [and the land was repopulated]."[215] The passage goes on to itemize the "implantation of prominent West-Tibetan clans" and Gugé-Purang officials into Zangskar's Padum, Jangngos (i.e., Karsha) and Stongde. Such an influx of Tibetans into Zangskar is described by Dargyay, although she believes it happened several centuries earlier, at the time of the collapse of the Pugyal dynasty: "Tibetan princes settled in these western territories [and] brought along with them their attendants, aristocrats, officers, servants, and craftsmen. Apparently, the local Dard population submitted to the Tibetan intruders and since then the Tibetan element became predominant throughout these areas."[216]

The relatively uncontested rule over Maryul nevertheless ended by the thirteenth century, when its local leaders revolted against the imposed rule. Western Ladakh seems to have undergone a different experience, more akin to Zangskar's. Devers lists a series of pecked inscriptions, some surrounding Buddhist stupas, at Alchi, Balukhar, Khaltse and Kharool (north of Kargil), with the names of eleventh-century soldiers that he and Nils Martin believe were part of "the same [West Tibetan] army traveling between Maryul and Gilgit via Sham and Purig." [217] The inscriptions appear at strategic river crossings, trade and travel routes with observation posts along the way, the routes themselves protected by "forts that appear to have been built by the Ngari armies."[218] By contrast, they do not seem to have left evidence of such campaigning around Shey. It was in the central and western areas of Ladakh, especially those that culturally maintained close links to Baltistan, Gilgit, and Kashmir—a major portion of Ladakh and Zangskar—where resistance to Tibetans or west Tibetans was countered with military force and occupation. Devers comes to the reasonable conclusion that in those areas, a significant part of the population consisted of Brogpas,[219] by which in this context are meant the so-called Dards or Daradas.[220] Shared customs, history, language, and familiar forms of Buddhism were lacking. If anything, there would have been the historical

214 "Ngari appears to have controlled Shey since at least Yeshe Od's time." Devers, "Archaeological Ladakh," 115.

215 N. Martin, "Solemn Praise," 209.

216 Dargyay, "Buddhism in Adaptation," 124. This is supported by the sources Vitali examined which suggests that Zangskar "was devastated at an unspecified date during the period of the Yar.lung [Pugyal] dynasty by the advance of the Yar.lung.pas," and was then repopulated by various clans from west Tibet; Vitali, *Kingdoms of Gu.ge Pu.hrang*, 192n271.

217 Devers, "Archaeological Ladakh," 107.

218 Ibid., 108.

219 Ibid., 109.

220 Clark, "Who Were the Dards?" See also N. Howard and K. Howard, "Historic Ruins in the Gya Valley," 90–91. Call them what you like (except "Tibetans"), they seem to have been in Ladakh and Zangskar, early and late. Peissel prefers "Minaro"; Peissel, *Tibet*, 49–50, 54–56.

memory of the Pugyal Tibetan invasions of a few centuries earlier, and a disinclination to welcome the intruders.

Nils Martin brings forward evidence that shows just how fraught was the rule of the descendants of the Tibetan royal family who relocated to west Tibet, including Purang, when they tried to impose themselves on the western part of Ladakh just north of Kargil at Kharul in Purig. Although there remain some questions about the interpretation of the weathered, damaged inscription, at least in Martin's understanding it and an inscription farther west naming the same person "testify to the military nature of the rule exerted" by the Purang king 'Od lde (r. ca. 1024–1037/1060) and his deputed representative.[221] The inscription seems to have commemorated the successful handling of territorial conflicts against the Tibetan invaders' rule, and includes a number of "foreign" names—that is, foreign to Tibetans but no doubt local people with non-Tibetan names.

Gradually, some local groups accommodated the powerful rulers and became brokers and translators and adopted west Tibetan language, script, religious practices, and culture. These compradors would have steadily risen in status. Similarly, as with the 'Bro[222] and Smer clans, officials with their families sent from Ngari settled within these contested areas and as local elites were integrated into the society. However, such acclimatization did not run in only one direction. Even as they had an impact on local society, they were also changed. In fact it would not be unusual if in time claims were made to elite status, to origins and identification with aristocratic clans rooted in centuries-old histories, despite tenuous actual connections (through marriage or indirect descent) or outright fabrication.

Nevertheless, by the end of the thirteenth century, west Tibet's militarily imposed rule over the western Himalayan region collapsed, and local rulers "unrelated to Western Tibet"[223] organized fragmented, temporary states. Devers links this to frequent raids carried out by various Kashmiri and Central Asian armies, culminating with the relatively well-documented occupation of Kashgari Mīrzā Haidar in the sixteenth century.[224] At that point, even in the regions of Ladakh most proximate to Ngari, the Maryul region (south of Shey), west Tibet's power was eclipsed. Out of the ruins emerged the Namgyal dynasty, which unified the disparate subregions of what we call Ladakh.[225] By this time, however, the westernmost regions,

221 N. Martin, "Solemn Praise," 208. Among the doubts raised by Martin's extensive and ambitious explication of the inscription is the fact that two of the three syllables of the name of the person being commemorated, dPal 'dus sgra, are spelled differently in the same short inscription, not to speak of the fact that each differently spelled name is given a different title. Ibid., 217. There is in fact a tendency to supply missing Tibetan letters rather freely, or to "correct" what is there, filling in gaps with a predetermined preference and even overturning the readings of specialists such as Orofino and Takeuchi. Ibid., 202. In many cases Martin gives extensive reasons for his intervention in supplying missing letters, yet one is still left with uncertainty built upon uncertainty. Although one must be grateful that an effort was made to publish in English, there are awkward and quizzical terms (*lapicide* and *tricuspidate finial*, among others), and passages such as "Further mechanical and intentional alteration of the surface of the south face [of the boulder] constitute the core of the present contribution." Ibid., 190. The inscription praises someone "for having set 'the paragon of a resolution of eminent bravery,'" ibid., 201, and "the decline that struck the rule exterted [*sic*] by the *mnga' bdag* of Purangs 'Od lDe," ibid., 209. Just because the repatination of the inscription—which is divided into two sections and overlaps the central, more deeply scored image of a *chorten*— does not appear to the unaided eye to be markedly different to that of the *chorten*, this does not conclusively demonstrate, contra the conclusion on p. 200, that they were done at the same time by the same "lapicide(s)."

222 Nils Martin reminds us that the great-grandfather of the founder of the Sumtsek (Tshul khrims 'Od of the 'Bro clan) had migrated from Gugé-Purang, where the 'Bro clan had estates, to Nyarma in Ladakh; ibid., 209–10.

223 Devers, "Archaeological Ladakh," 116.

224 Mīrzā Haidar, *Tarikh-I-Rashidi of Mirza Muhammad Haidar, Dughlát*.

225 Devers, "Archaeological Ladakh," 112–14.

including "Little Tibet," had turned fully away from Tibet, even as a beacon of Buddhism.

> [I]t is especially striking that we have not even a single report about similar activities [as in Ladakh, Nubra and Zangskar] of Buddhist clerics in the area of Drass, the Suru-valley, Sod, Paskyum, Shakar-Cigian and the area of present-day Baltistan. Quite obviously already in the 15th and 16th century the rulers of the Drass, the western and northern parts of Purig and present Baltistan showed no special interest in Buddhism.[226]

It is a historical irony that in 1630 Sengge Namgyal (1570–1642) actually had the major role in the final destruction of the Gugé-Purang kings who claimed descent from Tibet. The *casus belli* as related by the Jesuit Francisco De Azevedo[227] has a remarkable symmetry with the idealized accounts of Songtsen Gampo's stated cause of war in the seventh century with the Zhangzhung ruler. Songtsen Gampo's sister, unhappy living in distant Khyunglung, plotted with him to take it over. A millennium later, in the Namgyal-Gugé conflict, it was Sengge Namgyal's sister who was betrothed to the king of Gugé. She was on her way to Tsaparang when the marriage was called off by the Gugé king, an unbearable insult. Sengge Namgyal invaded and took the last west Tibetan king hostage back to Leh. This took place just at the time when Central Tibet's power was expanding into an empire, and ultimately Ladakh paid a heavy price for its aggression. The takeover of the monasteries in Gugé by the Namgyal king, as well as the supposed defunding of the Gelugpa monasteries by the Ladakh ruler who was dazzled by the Drukpa teacher Taktsang Repa Ngawang Gyatso (1574–1651), was not looked upon favorably by the Fifth Dalai Lama (Ngawang Lobzang Gyatso, 1617–1682).[228] No doubt this in turn contributed to the invasion of Ladakh by armed forces under Ganden Tsewang (1644–1697), ordered by the Fifth Dalai Lama. To the extent that in the western Himalaya they remembered it clearly, this must have seemed like an eerie echo of the successive Pugyal and Gugé-Puhrang invasions. The Pugyal occupation may have been the most relevant, for the Fifth Dalai Lama was a kind of re-embodiment of Pugyal kings wielding religious and secular power and destroying the Zhangzhung state. In this case, the so-called Great Fifth's army drove the Ladakhi rulers into the arms of the Mughals in Kashmir, forcing lasting changes to Ladakh's organization. Once again, even in this late stage, western Himalayan engagement with its non-Tibetan neighbors returned to the fore.

226 Schuh and Munshi, *Travel into the History of Purig*, 61.

227 Le Calloc'h, "Francisco De Azevedo's Travels in Guge and Ladakh." This source includes a translation of De Azevedo's description of the person of Sengge Namgyal, who he avers to have met in person twice; ibid., 63.

228 See N. Jinpa, "Why Did Tibet and Ladakh Clash in the 17th Century?"; Emmer, "dGa' ldan Tshe dbang dPal bzang po"; Ahmad, "New Light on the Tibet-Ladakh-Mughal War of 1679–84."

Despite this fraught history, the majority of the Buddhists in Ladakh and Zangskar that I have encountered identify as, or at least abstractly with, Tibet or Tibetan culture; they did not consider themselves "Indian" (I have less experience in Spiti, but I would not be surprised if they held similar attitudes).[229] In the 1980s and 1990s when I first starting going to the western Himalaya, it was not uncommon for locals to say when they were leaving to go to Jammu or Delhi, "I'm travelling to India next week." They were Ladakhi or Zangkari with strong Tibetan affiliations, particularly, of course, with H.H. the Dalai Lama. That kind of self-identification should not be taken lightly or dismissed, even though I do not believe it has deep historical roots. "The need for a clear identity sometimes leads people to resurrect symbols from the very archaic past, or from someone else's past, or even from a past that never was."[230] With Tibet now having been taken over by China, it is "safe" for western Himalayans in Ladakh and Zangskar to consider themselves a branch of the Tibetans, as many outsiders seem to have believed, going back to Xuan Zang and Hui Chao, and Christian missionaries going back to the seventeenth century.[231]

At present, the association with Tibet is used as a marketing ploy by locals and outsiders to attract international and domestic Indian tourists. Such centers as Leh abound with cafes and shops with one or another variation of "Lhasa Café," "Lhasa Crafts," "Tibet Café," "Tibet City Corner," "Potala Medicos," etc. Tibet today is not in a position to attempt to re-colonize Ladakh, Zangskar, or Spiti, to rule them from afar if requested, or to invade them, which as we have seen they had a history of doing. The most profound benefit western Himalayans receive now is of course more frequent and more convenient access to the person of His Holiness and other Tulkus who in recent decades visit and give teachings there regularly. Tibetan Buddhist institutions—Geluk along with those of the other lineages—have been "relocated" from Tibet to northern and southern India and Nepal, and many western Himalayan monks and nuns find opportunities for advanced education and teaching in them.

Yet when floods of ordinary Tibetans came out of Tibet in the early 1960s, they were hardly universally welcomed in Ladakh. The Tibetan refugees still struggle in poverty, living in the equivalent of poor ghettos, with substandard transportation and schooling. I have heard local Ladakhis express resentment that the refugees are supported internationally, while they themselves are not. Nevertheless, the refugees were certainly not

229 Interestingly, others have noticed that in contemporary times, "[t]o a large extent, the people that live along the margin of the former Tibetan polity no longer show a great affinity or loyalty" to Tibet; Klieger, *Tibetan Borderlands*, 1.

230 Ramble, "Whither, Indeed, the Tsampa Eaters," 25.

231 Peissel has an excellent summary of the history of European missionaries traveling to Tibet and the western Himalaya; Peissel, *Tibet*, 143, 148–49, 152–53, 156.

treated as long-lost cousin-brothers.[232] This has to be understood in a long historical context, not merely as mean-hearted western Himalayans, which they are not. To a degree, this provides more indirect support for my central point, that referring to these subcultures of Ladakh, Spiti, Lahaul, and Zangskar as "Indo-Tibetan," or "west Tibetans," reinforces a fundamental misunderstanding. The people in these related but distinct areas are dealing with different sets of neighboring states and cultures than those of central, eastern, and northern Tibet. They may be more aligned with west(ern) Tibet (i.e., Gugé or Ngari) but they have had an even longer history of being occupied and occupying west Tibet, fighting wars against armies sent by the Central Asian *and* central Tibetan rulers.

If Not "Tibet," What Do We Call It Then?

> The Western Himalaya is a loose term which describes a region that includes the Indian districts of Ladakh, Spiti and Lahoul. There are no specific physical or political boundaries which could coincide with the term and it has been used here more as a convenience than as a precise geographical definition.
>
> —KHOSLA, *BUDDHIST MONASTERIES IN THE WESTERN HIMALAYA*, 17

> Places are singular concretions made up of plural experiences. They accumulate sediments of time, layers of meaning linked to the evolution of landscape and the multiple histories of human activities that have contributed to shaping them. They are also contested spaces subjected to internal and external forces that often work against each other and contribute to variegated place-making processes.
>
> —Gros, *Frontier Tibet*, 41

In this section of the chapter I briefly consider an alternate conception of LZSKLB, a modified "borderlands" notion in which Tibet is a continuous factor but not a unique or a determinative one. I then attempt to explicitly lay out the factors that must be considered in creating such a designation as "western Himalaya" to signify, when heuristically necessary, the collectivity of LZSKLB. Those factors, borrowed from botanists already encountered in this essay, include geography and climate, ethnicity, history, political borders, and intelligibility or "customary" denotations.

The discussion of the history of LZSKLB and their relations with Tibet that appears in the second section of this essay, is, I would be the first to

232 Jolden and Tundup make the bold claim that there was an "easy adaptation of Tibetan refugees in Ladakh," that the "Ladakhi community gave a welcome to them . . . when Tibetan[s] were in dire need of help"; Jolden and Tundup, "Cultural Relationship," 68, 69. They do finally acknowledge that "economic disparity leads occasionally to friction and conflict" due to "funding and regular grants from foreign agencies"; Jolden and Tundup, "Cultural Relationship," 70. That the refugees are economically privileged is belied by visits I have made to the refugee "camps" in the desert and by personal accounts by Tibetan refugees struggling for basic amenities.

concede, imbalanced. I emphasized the "dark side" of Tibetan incursions to compensate for two or three factors affecting studies of the area, or studies of aspects of Tibet that involve those areas. The first is a tendency to idealize Tibet, reinforced by contemporary Buddhists who associate the advanced teachings and teachers they hold in reverence with Tibet. The second and third are related: the habit of identifying language with ethnicity, and an underdetermined concept of "Tibetan-ness." Both stem from the inherited legacy of imprecision with regard to these regions that was illustrated in the first section of the essay, the bulging archive I sampled based largely on "unofficial knowledge, produced by travellers and enthusiasts."[233] Without being obliged to follow the disparate examples they document, it must be admitted that "travellers and missionaries had a chance to see and hear things which, when put in their proper context, provide us with an additional perspective" on frontier history.[234] For political reasons, colonial and otherwise, because of the romantic ideas of Tibet as a receptacle for the fantasies of Westerners, or due to the contextualized knowledge of our predecessors, we have inherited multiple uses of the terms *Tibet* and *Tibetan*. Stéphane Gros identities three of those registers:

> We often use "Tibet" in various ways as a macro-regional category to refer to three overlapping layers: the Geological expanse of the Tibetan Plateau, the "Land of snow" (*gang jong*); the ethno-cultural entity that is conventionally called "ethnographic Tibet"; and finally the political entity. All three layers encompass different places and societies, and there is generally no single term to describe them collectively.[235]

Yet there are even more ways that they are applied. Tibetan Studies—if one can use that term, which is itself contested and compromised by the very term at issue—is only beginning to deal with that inheritance.

With reference to two of the usages identified by Gros, the national and the ethnic, Sara Shneiderman advocates separation, careful definition, and contextual application:

> I have argued that "Tibetan" as an ethnic category and "Tibetan" as a national category must be analytically separated and carefully defined according to the specifics of each empirical situation. Doing this requires us to situate the concept of ethnicity without broader national frameworks, and look beyond the particular "ethnically

233 Anand, "Archive and the Poetics of 'Exotica Tibet,'" 58.

234 Sperngen, "Chone and Thewu," 210.

235 Gros, *Frontier Tibet*, 45.

> Tibetan" groups and historical moments we describe to consider the overarching web of social relations constituting ethnicity in the Tibetan context. These moves pave the way for a more thorough examination of the dynamics of power within the "Tibetanisation process", wherever and whenever it is occurring.[236]

A fourth, and perhaps most obvious usage of "Tibetan" is in reference to the spoken language and the script; it also is probably the most overlooked in terms of questioning its presumed relevance in determining identity. After all, native Tibetan speakers are generally identified as, well, Tibetan. "Aren't the Tibetan-speakers of the borderlands already Tibetan?" asks Ramble. In answer, he replies, "rather less than is often thought."[237]

Turin argues against the direct linkage of language and ethnic identity, or cultural worldview, which he regards as an "imprudent mainstreaming of linguistic classification to map ethnic or social categories," for the "linguistic classification of a spoken language is clearly not diagnostic for the cultural habits or ethnic worldviews of its speakers."[238] His focus is "on the need for precise terminology for describing and analysing Himalayan cultural diversity," and against the conflation of ethnic and linguistic categories.[239]

In the case of LZSKLB, a Tibeto-centric approach may actually hinder historical inquiry. Denwood concluded that the language (and thus the culture) of Ladakh and Baltistan, was already (or originally) Tibetan or "Tibetanised," easing a seamless incorporation into Tibet's empire: "[I]t is hard to avoid the proposition that the incorporation of Ladakh into the old Tibetan empire was either a cause or an effect of the Tibetanisation of the local population—perhaps a bit of both."[240] Both he and Zeisler sought to explain the deviations of Ladakhi and Balti Tibetan in terms of grammar, pronunciation, and vocabulary from older, archaic forms of Tibetan.[241] Zeisler concludes that they "have their origin in an earlier stage of the Tibetan language, possibly *Archaic Northeast Tibetan variety from which *Old Amdo Tibetan as well [as] Old Tibetan developed."[242] Some deviations "may be due to intensive contact with the New Indo-Aryan and Dardic languages."[243] If instead we are prepared to accept that Tibetan language was imposed on non-Tibetan-language speakers, then the process is just the reverse: non-Tibetan speakers gradually adopting the language of the elite (who were themselves cut off from the wellsprings of Central Tibetan language) and bringing with them certain patterns from their original language.

236 Shneiderman, "Barbarians at the Border and Civilising Projects," 23–24.

237 Ramble, "Whither, Indeed, the Tsampa Eaters," 24.

238 Turin, "Rethinking Tibeto-Burman," 36, 39.

239 Ibid., 46. Ramble, somewhat ambivalently, considers that "the rather clumsy term 'Tibetan-speakers' is probably the least unsatisfactory terms English has to designate the totality of ethnic Tibetans within and outside the frontiers of the modern Tibet Autonomous Region." Ramble, "Whither, Indeed, the Tsampa Eaters," 21. The *more* unsatisfactory defining characteristics are "eating *tsampa*" and "being Buddhist."

240 Denwood, "The Tibetanisation of Ladakh," 286.

241 Zeisler, "On the Position of Ladakhi and Balti" [2nd ed.]; Denwood, "Early Connections between Ladakh/Baltistan and Amdo/Kham."

242 Ibid., 59.

243 Ibid., 57.

Tucci is even more adamant about the inhabitants of Ladakh and farther western Himalayan people not originally being Tibetan speakers.

> Up to the time of the establishment of the royal dynasty, there is no reason to suppose that those people [in Ladakh] spoke Tibetan: some tribes might have already been converted to Buddhism through Dardistan or Kashmir, perhaps on account of the geographical proximity; their language and culture might also have been influenced in the Western or N.W. parts by that of [Zhang Zhung], but Dardic must have predominated.[244]

There are thus two sides to the Tibeto-centric coin: exclusion of the supposedly non-Tibetan practices that have fed into Greater Tibetan culture; and a tendency to superimpose "Tibetan" practices onto those exposed to more than one culture at the same time—nearly everyone today!—to color the rich patchwork in a monotone. Prioritizing Tibet flattens out the complexity.

As I hope to have indicated (and have tried to demonstrate in chapters 3 and 4 with visual evidence), the cultures of Ladakh, Zangskar, and Spiti were not meaningfully or dominantly Tibetan until well after the eleventh century, and even then not exclusively. This is true, I believe, linguistically, culturally, and politically, and certainly in terms of religion and heredity. A close study of pre-Buddhist culture in the region demonstrates much greater affinities with Central Asia in the northwest than with Tibet to the east, and the farther west one looks, the more pronounced they are.[245] The Tibetan empire stationed troops at strategic points in these areas starting in the eighth century, and elites claiming dynastic Tibetan descent insinuated themselves into the local power structures in the late ninth or tenth century. In subsequent centuries, however, the majority of the inhabitants were only beginning to be "Tibetan-ized" in a linguistic and cultural sense, after which a process of reorientation toward Central Tibet was initiated. This reorientation coincided with the wholesale Buddhicization of Tibet—not just among the elites—in which the western Himalaya, already long exposed to Buddhism from its other borders—played a significant part. It took place parallel to political independence from Tibet and west Tibet after the thirteenth century. To refer to early western Himalayan Buddhist paintings and sculptures as "Tibetan" in any meaningful sense confounds the ethnic or political slippage in the name with the religious aspect.[246]

244 Tucci, "On Swāt," 74.

245 The evidence for this conclusion is argued in Linrothe, *Seeing into Stone*.

246 As Snellgrove points out, "Tibet was no more Buddhist [in the eighth and ninth centuries] than England was Christian as the immediate result of the mission of 597 of Augustine . . . But in England, as much as in Tibet, several centuries of self-sacrificing proselytizing and arduous scholarly work were necessary before either country could really be said to be converted to the new faith. Thus is it probably true to claim Tibet as generally Buddhist by the 13th century, and scarcely before." Snellgrove, "Indo-Tibetan Liturgy," 37.

The point is that the constellation of LZSKLB was not merely adjacent to Tibet's western frontier. This region was a contact zone for Kashmir, Gilgit and Swat, Central Asia (Samarkand's Sogdians, Kashgar, and Yarkand), China, Nepal, and north and northwest Indian kingdoms. Even such kingdoms as the one ruled by Harsha (ca. 590–647) at its furthest extent was not too distant to be connected through trade routes. Such multidimensional contact zones were (and are) dynamically active ethnically, politically, culturally, religiously, economically, and linguistically. Elements within them were mobile in terms of exchanging goods and ideas, as well as relative power and position along the multiple concentric patterns of center and periphery.[247] The point is emphasized by Katia Buffetrille:

> "Borderlands are inhabited territories located on the margins of a power center, or between power centers, with power understood in the civilizational as well as the politico-economic sense . . . they are continually in movement." This type of definition, however, gives prominence to power relations and centrifugal forces that need to be counterbalanced with proper acknowledgement of the dynamics alluded to above and the forms of agency that also contribute to shaping change.[248]

We have inherited the modernist obsession with borders which define and divide states, and so much of the tension in the nineteenth and early twentieth century in the region was due to the British seeking to impose such boundaries as well as Tibet's attempt to selectively close them.[249] Rather, following Gros's suggestion for the frontier zone between eastern Tibet and China, it might be more accurate to think of the western Himalaya as "a kind of borderland-cum-frontier zone, which should be addressed *as a process*."[250] By that I understand it as having a Kubleresque "manifold shapes of time" which we must take into consideration. Since borderlands are "essentially local reactions to past and present stimuli . . . . their memories are long."[251] One of the patterns that we can discern must certainly be its geographical location, the time of its space. The eco-geography of the western Himalaya allowed for, perhaps even necessitated, multiple interactions in different directions for economic and military or security reasons and in some cases simultaneously or nearly so. There were periods of radical movement of the tectonic plates of culture. These are most clearly literally illustrated from that time by the engraved and carved sculpture and painting in the western Himalaya, as chapters 3 and 4 demonstrate. The forms of the objects reflect the formal idioms at work

247 See Neelis, *Early Buddhist Transmission and Trade Networks*.

248 Buffetrille, "Increasing Visibility of the Tibetan 'Borderlands,'" 87, quoting Zartman, "Identity, Movement, and Response," 2.

249 N. Howard, "Development of the Boundary."

250 Gros, *Frontier Tibet*, 53 (emphasis in original).

251 Zartman, "Borderland Policy," 249.

in those other areas simultaneously and across time along the frontiers or incorporated borders of successive states and serial empires, of greater or lesser formality. These included the Kushan, the Kashmiri dynasties, the Tibetan (repeatedly), the Mughal, the British, Sikh, Dogra, and, it must not be forgotten, their own dynasties, states, and empires, competing and rivaling each other (particularly among Ladakh, Zangskar, Lahaul, Kulu, Spiti, and Balti). Ultimately, at least in this context, it is as much about a highlands "cultural borderland" as it is about a political one. As for the latter, the regions in need of clearer naming practices are less the borderlands of other states than states themselves *as* borderlands, their identities formed by contesting being incorporated by any of their multiple neighboring, more powerful states.

This attitude and a conscious awareness of the multiple dimensions of Ladakh's engagement with its surrounding areas are embedded in some wedding songs Francke collected in the late nineteenth century. He is convinced that "there can be no doubt as to the pre-buddhist origin" of the songs.[252] Song no. IV is structured like most of them, as a challenge by the bride's family and supporters to the groom's representatives who have arrived to claim the bride, followed by the latters's response. They are asked, when you came from the eastern (*shar*) country, who was the king and what are the customs there, followed by the same questions for the countries of the south (*lho*), the west (*nub*), and the north (*byang*). The responses include the names of kings, praise for the customs, and provide some positive characteristic association with the direction. For east it is the sun, "the umbrella of the sun"; for the south it is "all kinds of grain"; for the west it is "all kinds of medicines"; and for the north it is "all kinds of dyes."[253] Francke points out that in another marriage song, which he did not include in his article, "the four points of the compass come in again [as well as] actual geographical kingdoms, for instance China and India."[254] These reflect familiarity with geographic, ecological, botanical, and cultural zones of the directions surrounding the western Himalaya, not just of Tibet—multiple grains to the south being a striking example of the association of the sub-montane regions of India with its rice, wheat, millet, amaranth, and so forth.

Social life in particular—immersed as it is in the natural realm, its stage but also its source—is "a complex interweaving of very many concurrent cycles," "interlocking cycles of experience," to use Tim Ingold's evocative

252 Francke, "Ladakhi Pre-Buddhist Marriage Ritual," 141.

253 Ibid., 140–41.

254 Ibid., 141.

phrasing.[255] In its daily and seasonal cycles, it fosters relationships even across cultures near and more distant. Marriages, pilgrimages, trade, hunting animals, tracking down semi-domesticated animals left to graze freely, and gathering medicinal plants, wood, fuel, juniper for ritual fumigation (*sangchö*), all require crossing boundaries and borders, and enable encounters, exploration, exposure, and experience. Even plagues, epidemics, crop failures, droughts, overpopulation, revolution, succession disputes, and raids stimulate trans-cultural interaction, not to speak of curiosity, a hunger for adventure, and other states of misery and desperation. Seekers of technology, craft, knowledge, wisdom, or mystic experience sought teachers in all directions, inner and outer. After finding them, many returned. Change happens.

Shifting engrained habits of naming is no easy task. To be convincing, it rightly requires compelling justification and exposure of the hidden consequences of existing practice. By far the most perceptive and explicit explanation for choices made in creating named categories and subcategories involving Tibet, India, and the Himalaya that I have encountered is that found in *Flora Indica* of 1855 by Joseph Dalton Hooker and Thomas Thomson, two scientists mentioned above. Their account demonstrates the validity of Ronald Davidson's proposal, made in a very different context and purpose, that "the discipline of biogeography be employed as a heuristic device, not as an end, but to afford a moment in which paradigms from the empirical sciences may be suggested to contribute some sense of how complexity could be envisioned"—and perhaps accounted for as well.[256] Hooker and Thomson provide the elements that they took into consideration in defining and then naming botanical regions within the Himalayas that reflected their direct experience there. These elements or factors included botany, geography and extant political boundaries, but they were intersecting and not of equal value, validity, or utility. Political boundaries—after all, this was supposed to be "A Systematic Account of the Plants of British India"—gave them the most trouble. This was "partly from the constantly shifting political and other boundaries of our [British] dominions and its subdivisions, and partly from the necessity of selecting as far as possible such provinces as are defined by physical features rather than by arbitrary lines."[257] An additional imperative that factored into choice of the names of the geographical divisions they first decided on was to "endeavor to choose such as are already familiar to persons conversant with the outlines of Indian geography."[258]

255 Ingold, "Temporality of the Landscape," 157, 160.

256 Davidson, "Himalayan Buddhist Valleys as Tantric Ecologies," 135.

257 Hooker and Thomson, *Flora Indica*, 88.

258 Ibid., 90.

The "natural divisions" based on botanical principles took priority, and were intrinsically aligned with geography along three axes: "length, breadth, and height." Each was further divided into three subsections so the scheme, which can thus also account for climate, is: longitudinally: eastern, central and western Himalaya; latitudinally: exterior (rainy), interior (intermediate), and Tibetan Himalaya (arid); altitudinally: tropical, temperate, and alpine Himalaya.[259] Only when greater detail was needed, below the subsection level, "we shall either make use of the river valleys (a very convenient mode of indicating the regions), or of the political subdivisions usually recognized."[260]

The details of the further divisions of the western Himalaya and West Tibetan categories need not detain us. In brief, they were laid out in parallel latitudinal tiers on southern and northern slopes of the Himalayan mountain chains, in the beds of the Indus and Sutlej, and on the southern slope of the Kunlun mountains as they join the Karakoram. Here too are anomalies that one would want to correct: Ladakh and Balti are called "Tibetan provinces," even though Hooker and Thomson were aware that they had already become "appanages of Kashmir";[261] they insist on calling Gugé "a Chinese Tibetan district";[262] and "Little Tibet" (i.e., Balistan) is designated as "forming the western termination of the Great Tibetan Plateau,"[263] standard for the mid-nineteenth century. However, what would be our humanities equivalents of the elements they factored into their scheme: botany, geography, political boundaries? Geography and political boundaries certainly factor in, as well perhaps as pre-, early-, and recent historical experience. In addition, multiplicity of ethnicities and neighboring cultures perhaps contributing over time. If so, I give history and geographic situation (surrounded by larger cultures) bigger roles in calling the region "the western Himalaya" over the customary inclusion of "Tibet" into a hybridized name. At the same time, I acknowledge the inconsistency in that "West Tibet" explicitly reflects present-day boundaries (however contested on the granular level) of a politically formed nation-state (PRC's prefecture of Ngari in Tibet), but western Himalaya does not include "India" in the name of the grouping, either as "Indian Tibet" or as the "Indian Himalaya." This acknowledged inconsistency is based on a reluctance to resort to the name "India," which today is a recognized Republic but for most of South Asia's history was an arbitrary designation of the subcontinent. Like Hooker and Thomson, I confess that this attempt to disambiguate the western Himalaya from

259 Ibid., 174.

260 Ibid., 175.

261 Hooker and Thomson, *Flora Indica*, 84.

262 Hooker and Thomson, *Flora Indica*, 85. Gugé is also called "Hundes" and is stated to be "wholly under Chinese influence." Hooker and Thomson, *Flora Indica*, 223.

263 Hooker, *Sketch of the Flora of British India*, 11. This short article is an introduction to the more extensive *Flora Indica* volume.

West(ern) Tibet was "a very much more difficult task than might have been supposed."[264]

Conclusion

This book focuses mainly on a region now part of Ladakh known as Zangskar. Like Ladakh and its other parts (Purig, Suru, the eastern parts, including the so-called Changthang or the main Upper Indus Valley), it interacted broadly with many neighboring entities on all sides, and so Zangskar's history is very much tied up with that of its neighbors. Each of these individual regions had distinct historical experiences. This initial essay examines some of the early histories, in order to look at the region as a whole and Zangskar's place in it, before delving into the more specific art-historical legacy of the western Himalaya and Zangskar in particular. We began with a consideration of how the region has been referred to, often as a province or a version of Tibet. Neither universally employed nor avoided, on a literal level such designations present significant contradictions of historical reality. Contemporary ideological preferences, inherited historical customs, and apparent linguistic and cultural continuities coincide in occluding the incongruities. It is certainly understandable from some standpoints how we have come to see and understand the region as "Tibetan" in a provincial modality. The second part of this chapter argues for a different perspective—mainly based on archaeological evidence—from which to examine the regions' interactions with Central Tibet and Ngari. The latter has greater cause to be considered Central Tibet's actual western province ever since the eighth century or so. Rather than seeing this entire region as "Tibetan" in any meaningful sense, these regions formed a borderland "zone of contact" with a host of other highly developed cultures divided and united by the Himalayan chains of mountains. "Mountain chains have often integrated rather than isolated peoples . . . The seasonal pastoral movements in the northern part of the subcontinent constitute a vertical communications system connecting lower and upper valleys."[265] As Yudru Tsomu describes the pattern, such zones are "where traders, migrants and indigenous people participated in fluid interaction and exchange."[266] To the categories listed we must add indigenous leaders, officials and envoys, missionaries, artists, and also the armies of military expansionist empires. In such cases, "along with the exchange of goods [the activities of such groups] provided a conduit for new ideas."[267]

264 Hooker and Thomson, *Flora Indica*, 88.

265 Stacul, "Neolithic Inner Asian Traditions," 712. David Zurick eloquently describes in personal terms the dawning realization of mountains as connecting not isolating cultures: "Early on, I thought the rugged terrain of the Himalaya would separate people and make cultural convergences there unlikely. I thought that isolated societies would prevail amid geographical circumspection. I imagined places in a state of acute separation. I have found just the opposite to be the case. The mountains are traversed by passes and caravan routes, valley trails and modern roads, and people are on the move today as much as they always have been. Mountain society is fluid and mobile, despite the mighty grain of the Himalaya;" Zurick, *Himalaya: Encounters*, 90.

266 Tsomu, "Traders as Cultural Brokers," 178.

267 Ibid.

Art-historical evidence for these new *visual* ideas is examined in separate chapters, but their findings can be brought to bear as evidence to support and confirm the conception—and the naming—of these regions as more in the nature of mountainous borderlands than as intrinsically Tibetan.

The geology and the geography of this region (marked by the chains of mountains that include the highest in the world), with its concomitant climate and environment, clearly and unmistakably constrained and directed the economic, cultural, and political organization of the cultures within it. Scientific mapping of that environment also provides a method through which to seek an understanding of the underlying broad cultural model of development. In sum, just as a number of major rivers flowing into China, South Asia, and Southeast Asia originate in the Himalaya, so too there have been rivers of goods, ideas, religions, scripts, texts, and people streaming into the western Himalaya, successively and in some cases simultaneously shaping the development of its culture. It might be stating the obvious since the Zangskar, the Indus, the Sutlej dominate these regions, but as K.D. Bajpai reminds us, "From the prehistoric period to the later times, the rivers have played their role in the cultural formation and development."[268] Thus a geographic element in the preferred name for the region "western Himalaya" takes precedence over the contrived name of a political formation ("Tibet"), whose people do not even use it themselves.

268 Bajpai, "Role of Indian Rivers," 24.

CHAPTER 2

Tibetan Painted Scrolls and the Practice of Art History

Giuseppe Tucci's contributions to the study of Tibetan religion and history were extraordinary. In this chapter I provide the results of an analysis, not of those aspects of his scholarship but of the art-historical methods, practices, judgments, and assumptions expressed in his acknowledged masterwork, *Tibetan Painted Scrolls* (*TPS*) of 1949.[1] I do not take up the numerous mistakes Tucci committed in the text, as many have been pointed out.[2] A work of such length and erudition, published in a language other than the scholar's mother tongue, is sure to have errors on different levels, certainly understandable and forgivable. Nor do I discuss his well-documented affiliation with Italian fascists, such as his patron Giovanni Gentile and Benito Mussolini,[3] the questionable methods by which he acquired his collection, the problematic ethics of concealing the precise provenance for works he acquired in Tibet and the western Himalaya in the name of science at monasteries or shrines, nor the dubiousness of the project of writing the history of a medium based solely on his personal collection.[4] Here I focus on his art history, which has not received the kind of critical scrutiny that the continuing, expanding reach of *TPS* warrants.[5]

Tucci (1894–1984) did not consider art-historical inquiry to be possible with much of Tibetan art; he alternately disparaged and idealized artists, reduced their agency, and promoted essentialized notions of "national" styles. Generally, the passages I highlight here demonstrate naïve or prejudicial incoherence and unfamiliarity with the best art-historical technical concepts, terminology, and disciplinary practices of his day. I conclude that despite his reputation as a founder of Tibetan art history,[6] aside from his salutary emphasis on historical and religious contextualization, his attention to inscriptions, and the direct experience of the visual object, his art history and many of his conclusions have been eclipsed and are unsuitable as a model for emulation.

Tucci makes no coherent theoretical statement on his practice of art history.

1 I thank Melissa Kerin, the late Helen Abbott, and Liao Yang for their perceptive comments; errors and opinions are my own. This paper was originally presented as a talk at the Fifth International Conference on Tibetan Archaeology & Arts, in Hangzhou China. It was then prepared for the proceedings, edited by Liao Yang, but they were never published. That version has been modified and illustrations added.

2 Lo Bue, review article of *Tibetan Painted Scrolls*.

3 Benavides, "Giuseppe Tucci, or Buddhology in the Age of Fascism."

4 These aspects have been considered in Linrothe, *Collecting Paradise*, 1–27, *passim*.

5 One of the few scholars to (mildly) question Tucci's art historical conclusions was the late John C. Huntington, who occasionally cast doubt on particular instancing of dating or pointed out the lack of reasons given for such dating in Huntington, "Gu-Ge Bris: A Stylistic Amalgam."

6 For example, David Jackson credits Tucci with founding the "modern" study of Tibetan art history; Jackson, *Painting Traditions of the Drigung Kagyu School*, 19.

The closest he comes is to deny that Tibetan art has a history.

> [The] vicissitudes of Tibetan art . . . cannot properly be called a history, for the history of art is written through the succession of artistic personalities, the development of their genius, and in centuries of Tibetan painting on canvas [i.e. cloth ground] we only see the *alternating of schemes which, once they have been formed, are handed down, anonymous and unchanged.*[7]

Art history for Tucci is, apparently, like that of Giorgio Vasari, an ordered series of biographies. Since Tibetan art traditions are not based on the "great man" or "genius" mode, ergo, art history is not applicable in Tibet.

Tucci explicitly repudiates the power of art history to comprehend Tibetan art. He theorizes that there are "two different standards of classification." The first is the "stylistical and the chronological, attempting to distribute the tankas [i.e. paintings on cloth] according to their school and epoch." We can take this to be fundamentally art-historical. His other standard, the one in which he is invested, is built solely on religious subject matter, basically a religious studies approach. He frankly preferred "totally ignoring the first [stylistic] standard"—the art-historical—and instead classifying the art "according to their subjects or to certain peculiar characters [*sic*; characteristics?]" in the manner of religious studies.[8] The reasons he gave for this surrender of art history is that on the one hand "this art repeats itself, copies itself, has the hieratic uniformity proper to all sacred things," and on the other "there are some types of tankas bound to their subject or to their technique to such an extent that it will never be possible to date them with certainty."[9] He listed the following types as not datable by stylistic analysis: printed *thangka* (i.e., par ma; Fig. 2.1); gold- and red-ground *thangka* (i.e., gser thang and its variants; Fig. 2.2); textile *thangka*, whether embroidered, appliquéd, or, presumably, woven (Fig. 2.3); mandala of all sorts (Figs. 2.4–5); and paintings "of the *mGon khang*" (i.e. the protector shrine in monasteries with many wrathful deities; Figs. 2.6–7).[10] Tucci has not been proven correct, as it is perfectly possible, albeit challenging, to provide stylistic and chronological parameters for this rather arbitrarily assembled list of *thangka* or murals, some defined by media, others by subject matter or location. He did not give any additional explanation for why woodcuts, gold-, silver-, or red-ground *thangka* textiles, mandala, and paintings of wrathful deities cannot be formally analyzed and dated.

7 Tucci, *Tibetan Painted Scrolls*, 285 (emphasis added).

8 Ibid., 316. To paraphrase Otto Pächt, Tucci treated Tibetan art as little "more than a post room in which intellectual and religious values are wrapped and unwrapped on their way from consignor to consignee;" Pächt, *Practice of Art History*, 84.

9 Tucci, *Tibetan Painted Scrolls*, 316.

10 Ibid., 317. The Figures included in this chapter are not those specifically mentioned by Tucci in the passages of *TPS* cited. They are included to illustrate the type of paintings or book covers that are discussed by him; they are all examples of works still in monasteries or shrines in Tibet and the western Himalaya.

(clockwise from left):

Fig. 2.1 First Panchen Lama Lobzang Chokyi Gyaltsen (in an alternative number system, the fourth). Printed *thangka* with added colors. Painting dimensions inner 68.7 x 40 cm; with mounting, 128 x 62.5 cm, ca. 19th century. In Kyi Monastery, part of a set devised in the 17th century and attributed to the Tashilhunpo artist Choying Gyatso. Photo 2004.

Fig. 2.2 White Tārā painted on red-ground *thangka*, ca. 18th century. In Spituk Monastery, Ladakh. Photo 2009.

Fig. 2.3 Yama Dharmaraja and Yami, silk applique *thangka*, ca. 18th–19th c. in Drepung Tsomchen hall, Lhasa, Tibet. Photo 2005.

Fig. 2.4 Mañjuvajra Guhyasamaja Maṇḍala, mural in Dungkar Cave 1, 12th c. Photo 2007

Fig. 2.5 11-headed Avalokiteśvara Maṇḍala, painting on cloth, ca. 18th c. in Zhalu Monastery in Tibet. Photo 2007.

(facing page):

Fig. 2.6 Four-armed Mahākāla mural, ca. late 15th c., in the Phugtal Muldung shrine, Zangskar. Photo 2012.

Fig. 2.7 Rakta Yamari with consort; painting on cloth, ca. early 16th c., in Zhalu. Photo 2007.

It may be because he had minimal exposure to or training in art history and had only a superficial, dated, or popular understanding of or interests in its methods and capabilities.[11] It is striking that the "father of Tibetan art history" abandons in principle the "stylistical and chronological" standard of classification for much of the art under consideration.

Tucci admitted that for classifications based on schools, "epoch and style can be determined." He writes that Central Asian- and Nepalese-inflected Tibetan paintings (Figs. 2.8 and 2.9–10, respectively) are "comparatively simple to distinguish," for example, but was concerned that "as different trends" become blended, "the difficulty of determining school and epoch with any accuracy increases." Tucci then pivoted in the text to religious history, with which he was much more comfortable.[12] With only two exceptions, he denied the existence of "original and independent" schools of art in Tibet.[13] In fact, he had a very unorthodox understanding of schools, styles, and manners. He posited that eastern Indian, Nepalese, and Tibetan art were merely "manners" that "may be considered as the various modulations of one and the same style,"[14] whereas Tibetan painting derived from the "Kashmiri" schools (Fig. 2.11) and the "Bengali-Nepalese" (Fig. 2.12) and were "branches of the same trunk . . . like two provinces of the same kingdom, where the same language is spoken but dialectical varieties, easy to recognize, are noticeable."[15]

Because he repudiated the art-historical approach in favor of those of religious studies, Tucci had no obligation to explain his art-historical methodology.

11 Tucci was a student at the University of Rome during the tenure of Adolfo Venturi (1856–1941), who was chair in Medieval and Modern Art at the University of Rome between 1896 and 1931; *Dictionary of Art Historians* 11/20/21. Venturi was the author of the eleven-volume *Storia dell'arte italiana* (1901–1940), as well as studies on Pisanello, Paolo Veronese, and Piero della Francesca.

12 Tucci, *Tibetan Painted Scrolls*, 323.

13 Ibid., 324. The exceptions are art on the Chinese frontier and in Gugé.

14 Ibid., 272.

15 Ibid., 275–276.

Fig. 2.8 Arhats in Central Asia mode, mural at Drathang Monastery, ca. 12th c. Tibet. Photo 2005.

Fig. 2.10 Nepalese-style architecture, ca. 14th c. mural Zhalu Serkhang Khorlam. Photo 2007.

Fig. 2.9 Siddhas on mountain receiving teachings, ca. 14th c. mural in Nepalese mode, Zhalu Yum Chenmo Khorlam. Photo 2007.

Fig. 2.11 Ratnasambhava Tathāgata, mural in "Kashmiri revival" mode, ca. 15th c., at Tsaparang Lhakhang Karpo, Ngari, Tibet. Photo 2007.

Nevertheless, he made judgments and groupings and offered dates based on visual characteristics, and so in practice employed art-historical methods. Since he denied the effectiveness of such methods, we must deduce from Tucci's statements his assumptions and ideas of how the formal visual idioms he identified developed. The religious approach to art certainly constitutes the vast majority of his statements about any of the 195 mobile

Fig. 2.12 Ratnasambhava Tathāgata, mural in "Bengali-Nepalese" mode, ca. 14th c., at Zhalu Segoma Lhakhang, Tibet. Photo 2005.

scroll paintings covered in *TPS*, nearly all of them in his personal collection. Secondarily, and relatively rarely, were such visual objects to be looked at for the aesthetic reaction they provoked in him as a viewer.[16] For Tucci, religious and historical significance was primary, his aesthetic response was secondary, and the evidence a work might provide about a history of forms or a history of vision was tertiary and appeared sporadically. There was no balance among the three. He was only faintly interested in forms or their history; occasionally he responded to objects as works of beauty, but primarily he used them as documents in the development of religious history, the discipline in which he trained. There is nothing "wrong" with Tucci's approach, and it led to huge achievements in the realm of religious history and the identifications of subject matter depicted in paintings, early and late. However, it did little to bring to light the development or evolution of Tibetan art, except indirectly, which is why it is rather surprising to see his contributions lauded as the foundation for Tibetan art history.

One of the fundamental assumptions in Tucci's practice of art history was the notion of a kind of national essence, or spirit, that pervaded the art and allowed it to be grouped into broad categories based on that national character.[17] Also expressed as "the Tibetan people's artistic sensibility," this *volksgeist*, he wrote, became clearer and more well-defined over time.[18] Within art history, this notion of a national essence struggling for expression was something of a stock belief dating to the late nineteenth century,[19] and was woven into a central tenet of Fascist ideology,

16 Eloquent passages in TPS evoke Virgil or Ovid such as: "[in this painting] the gold is deftly blended with silver [giving it] a fascinating sheen and subtlety. The figures, drawn with an exquisitely accurate touch, emerge, willow-slender, out of the diaphanous background, like a landscape just awakened, breaking loose from the nightmist, kissed by the sun's first rays." Tucci, *Tibetan Painted Scrolls*, 580.

17 Phrases such as "national spirit," Tibetan "artistic spirit" or "genius" appear in ibid., 139, 187, 269, 271, 278, 283, 285, and 323.

18 Ibid., 280.

19 See Wölfflin, *Principles*.

Fig. 2.13 Dragon, ca. 14th c. mural in "Chinese" mode; Zhalu Gonkhang. Photo 2007.

although it has since been discredited. Even after the defeat of Fascism in Europe, however, Tucci continued to use the concept of national essence as the basis for his division of *thangka*s into Tibetan, Chinese, Central Asian, Nepalese, and Indian work.

A related recurrent tendency was to remove the agency of the artist and to speak of the art styles as acting directly on each other. "Currents of art" flow into Tibet from various other nations or peoples and blend with "old motifs" without intermediaries or human agents.[20] Styles and manners compete with each other, as at Zhalu (Figs. 2.5, 2.7, 2.9–10, 2.12–14), where "the Chinese manner is to a very great extent overcome by the Indian manner."[21] Tucci fell into the historical fallacy of attributing an organic life cycle to styles, describing them as gestating and ripening after centuries but growing "barren, shriveled up, and finally languish[ing] . . . extinct, to rise no more."[22] At the same time, he projected agency onto abstract notions of styles and then anthropomorphized and personified them as in, "Here the Central Asian manner takes the upper hand."[23]

As Tucci describes it, styles act upon artists rather than the other way round:

> Central Asian reminiscences are in evidence [at Gyantse; Fig. 2.15] . . . affinities, echoes which show in the Tibetan artists a knowledge, perhaps remote, of those styles, but also an immaturity as to means of expression, or at least an inadequate absorption of ideals which, *often against their will*, seemed almost to force themselves upon them.[24]

20 Tibet "assimilated Indian, Chinese and Central Asian influences;" ibid, 171. Sakya Monastery was "a place where the two cultures [of India and Yuan China] met;" ibid., 172, apparently without intermediaries. "[N]ew violent contact" with China "stirred Tibetan painting;" ibid., 283.

21 Ibid., 177.

22 Ibid., 275.

23 Ibid., 192.

24 Ibid., 184, emphasis added.

Fig. 2.14 Vaiśravaṇa surrounded by members of this mounted army, ca. 14th c. mural in "Chinese" mode, Zhalu Gonkhang. Photo 2007.

Fig. 2.15 Vaiśravaṇa on a white lion, 15th c. mural with "Central Asian reminiscences," at Gyantse Kumbum, Tibet. Photo 2007.

Although at times the tendency to deny artistic agency may be a problem more of rhetoric or grammar, of using the more formal passive tense, than of attitude, it does reflect a widespread and pernicious tendency in early art-historical writing that disenfranchises the artist from artistic decisions.[25] In this regard, Tucci's successors would be well advised to avoid this type of elocution which we all, myself included, find it easy to fall into.

Taking these assumptions together—that there are national styles or essences, and they act independently upon each other and/or upon artists—we see that Tucci's main idea of Tibetan art was that it was (or is) a kind of mixing bowl where the essences of other nations or peoples mingle and blend. Tibetans contributed nothing other than a field of action and perhaps a catalyst for inert agents to interact. For example, in discussing the paintings in Tāranātha's Phuntsokling (Fig. 2.16), the manner of painting was described as "a well-balanced blending of Indian and Chinese manners [; it] may be called a good specimen of that art in which the different inspirations and characters of Tibetan taste met and were harmonized."[26] This was not elaborated on, but he seems to be saying that what makes it good is that the Tibetans mixed Indian and Chinese manners (elsewhere: Chinese and Newar manners[27]) to produce a Tibetan manner, without actually contributing anything Tibetan except knowing the appropriate proportions of India and China to satisfy themselves (or him).

In Tucci's analyses of certain sites, he frequently drew analogies with purported Chinese or Indian manners. One example is from an ambiguous passage immediately succeeding the section cited in the previous paragraph, this one regarding the now-destroyed Phodrang of Tāranātha:

> The atrium has magnificence and grandeur; spacious and severe, it is ornamented with large paintings . . . in the [Chinese?] traditional style, although the Chinese pattern, with which the representation of this cycle is bound up in Tibet, has become fainter and gentler; the grim expression of the four keepers of the points of space has softened. . . . The rest of the wall is covered with figures of other deities of the same cycle, all by the same hand. But it is clear that the Indian manner of these frescoes [*sic*] is very different from the one which inspired the artists of the mKha' spyod lha khang. . . . The traditions inspiring the unknown author of these powerful compositions are surely Indian too, but they suggest other schools.

25 For critiques of the term *influence*, see Baxandall, *Patterns of Intention*, 58–62; and Tartakov and Dehejia, "Sharing, Intrusion, and Influence."

26 Tucci, *Tibetan Painted Scrolls*, 198.

27 "Hence the development of Tibetan painting consists in a mutual approach and blending of the Chinese and Nepalese manners;" ibid., 280.

Fig. 2.16 View of ca. early 17th century murals on two walls on the 3rd floor Nyong-nyes Lhakhang in Tāranātha's Phuntsokling Monastery. Photo 2007.

> Analogy with the styles of Central and Southern India are self-evident. [28]

All too often Tucci made circular arguments like this one in which nothing incisive is said about the visual qualities *except* that they derive from other unspecified paintings. Such derivations are then termed so "self-evident" or "clear" that they do not need to be elucidated, demonstrated, or described in any detail. From such passages we learn little except that certain things, mostly unstated, look like certain other (unstated) things—Chinese and Indian.

The essential model was that of "influence," clearly evident in this astounding paragraph:

> Their [Indian and Chinese] influence was so great that Tibetan art, born out of that contact, continued to live on its past, modulating those influences in various manners, but without ever attempting new paths. The Tibetans for a long time wavered undecided between different artistic manners, and [just] as translators were not free to alter a single syllable of the text they were transposing into their own language, without committing sacrilege, so artists, once they had been

28 Ibid., 199.

> educated in a given style, whether Indian or Chinese, handed down its technique and bewared [i.e., were frightened] of introducing any arbitrary change.[29]

The denial of agency was not the only form of condescension Tucci expressed toward Tibetan artists. A rarely recognized subtheme in the book was the denigration of Tibetan artists for whom "an interior urge and a creative impulse are absent."[30] At best, since their "technical resources are poor,"[31] the artist "dwells on a painstakingly accurate ornamental decoration" but in vain; "the figures do not lose their hieratic fixity,[32] unmoved by the least throb of life. They are lifeless and limp projections of a world of remote ideas."[33]

Tucci seems to have admired most deeply the Indian sources and those Tibetan works that hark back to "India's best work."[34] Yet at other places in the text he described this loyalty of taste as a kind of slavery. While he praised Tibetan artists for staying faithful to Indian models, he elsewhere condemned them because the "imitation of those models . . . would inevitably have lapsed into barbarism like all arts sluggishly and effortlessly drawing from past experiences, free from shocks and effort."[35] The loyalty to Indian models that in some places in *TPS* was the greatest virtue of Tibetan artists suddenly became "the yoke of a tradition which had forced them to be nothing but imitators of outlandish currents."[36] Even the denigration of the artist is reversed and suddenly "he" was idealized since, "led through yoga to a state of ecstasy, he sees the images of the gods with the eye of the spirit, not with those of the flesh." In a state of "cosmic consciousness" the artist becomes "assimilated with the first principle of things" and "one with the spiritual planes which he wants to reproduce."[37] This literal reading of idealized prescriptive religious texts with regard to the "misconception of the thangka painter as yogi" has subsequently been thoroughly discredited as a Western misapprehension.[38]

There are other contradictions in Tucci's assessments. In an article published in 1947, he discussed the Tibetan book covers (Fig. 2.17) in his personal collection: "No. V reactes [*sic*], as it were, with its sober ornamentation and the classical simplicity of its volutes, to the baroque sumptuousness of the specimens studied above."[39] This quotation embeds art-historical language along with subjective judgments, from which one can also detect criteria marking his preferences. For instance, "classical

29 Ibid., 271.

30 Ibid., 285.

31 Ibid., 286.

32 Tucci pairs "hieratic" with questionable effect with a number of negative terms beside "fixity," such as "hieratic rigidity" "hieratic uniformity" and "hieratic grimness" , the latter two making the least sense; ibid, 207.

33 Ibid., 285.

34 Ibid., 173.

35 Ibid., 278.

36 Ibid., 280.

37 Ibid., 289–90.

38 Jackson and Jackson, *Tibetan Thangka Painting*, 12–13; Kapstein, "Weaving the World."

39 Tucci, "Tibetan Book-Covers," 67.

Fig. 2.17 Tibetan book cover, carved and gilded wood, ca. 15th c., in Kyi Monastery, Spiti. Photo 2004.

simplicity" and "sober ornamentation" were contrasted with "baroque sumptuousness." However, the normal temporal order of the "classical" coming before the "baroque" is reversed. Tucci's preference for classical simplicity is also manifested when he recognizes in a "graceful interlacing of the volutes . . . a reminiscence of Hellenistic art" and pronounces that the example that reminds him of the "classical" and the "Hellenistic" derives from "the best period of Tibetan art."[40] This "best period of Tibetan art" for Tucci was the fifteenth century and is found at Tsaparang (see Figs. 2.11, 2.18), Narthang, Zhalu (see Figs. 2.9–10, 2.12–14),[41] and Gyantse (see Fig. 2.15), collapsing the distinctions between schools of west Tibet and Tsang. That a hierarchy of value was assumed here should not be surprising, for Tucci was himself an obsessive collector describing his own possessions—as already stated, *TPS* was in the final analysis the catalog of his personal collection.

Tucci's own partialities are also evident in his frequent negative references to elaborate decoration. "That horror of a void, which [Tibetan] artists used to Indian schools of painting cannot overcome, has induced the author of this tanka to fill up every empty place with the images of an extremely vast pantheon . . . ."[42] "[In] Tibet we constantly see that dislike of void which is one of the most constant traits of ancient Indian painting . . . ."[43] This flaw Tucci found in Indian, Tibetan, and also Newar art.[44] (See Fig. 2.19, an example of a painting on cloth from Zhalu with a "vast pantheon" that the artist used "to fill up every empty place.") "Nepalese images of the best style" are those

> made before the art of Nepal became confined to those iconographic and decorative schemes which, notwithstanding its ornamental vividness, very often caused it to become cold and conventional . . . . [B]esides the most ancient specimens, in which these faults are still slight and do not smother the simple levity[45] of the style, there are many later works, due not to artists but to *craftsmen*.[46]

40 He also stated that the wreath of flowers placed on the Buddha's head "also has a Hellenistic origin;" Tucci, *Tibetan Painted Scrolls*, 306.

41 Zhalu's later paintings are generally held to be fourteenth century, not fifteenth.

42 Ibid., 601–02. The painting beings referred to, an unusual one of Hevarja and consort seated, is now in an unidentified private collection. A color scan of it appears on the Himalayan Art Resources website, item no. 19049 (https://www.himalayanart.org/items/19049), where it is dated to the fifteenth century and is stated to have originated in the Sakya lineage.

43 Tucci, *Tibetan Painted Scrolls*, 282.

44 The local style at rGyang is described as "stressing a habit of Nepalese art, [that is,] all free spaces are filled up with flowers, small trees and leaves," ibid., 185.

45 The primary meaning of "levity," which Tucci uses several times in *TPS* (ex. pp. 173, 285, 286, 299) is humorous frivolity. It appears to be employed mistakenly. Perhaps the translator from the Italian, Virginia Vacca, confused it with "vitality", or level, as in balanced?

46 Ibid., 173, emphasis added.

Fig. 2.18 White Tārā, ca. 15th c. mural in the Tsaparang Lhakhang Marpo, Ngari Tibet. Photo 2007.

Fig. 2.19 Kālacakra Mandala retinue figures, each inscribed; painting on cloth, ca. 16th c. in Zhalu Monastery in Tibet. Photo 2007.

After reiterating his preference for "classical simplicity" rather than "Baroque sumptuousness," this last remark also insinuates a hierarchical distinction between fine art and decorative art, and between artists, who are creative, and craftsmen, who execute formulaic decorative schemes. It also entrenches the idea that old is gold, and the recent is indecent. Tucci was quite explicit that the best works of Tibetan art are "precious remains of artistic currents now extinguished."[47] Painters contemporary to Tucci were excoriated as "modern daubers [who] paint horrible scrawls after their manner."[48] The half-millennium between the time of the "best" art, the fifteenth century, and when he wrote is less than best. In fact much of Tucci's writing that is understood as art historical takes up this rhetoric of decline, in which the political and the cultural were in lockstep, both downhill. He was forward-thinking in paying attention to patronage and material resources, but conservative if not reactionary in simplistically linking "[p]olitical decay" with "languour [*sic*] in art schools."[49] This idea, as the art historian Christian Luczanits has shown, became entrenched in

47 Ibid., 173.

48 Ibid., 192.

49 Ibid., 185.

the approaches of most scholars, curators, dealers, and collectors and is only recently, slowly, being overturned.[50]

Earlier, we quoted Tucci's assertion that Tibetan art history is merely a matter of "the alternating of schemes which, once they have been formed, are handed down, anonymous and unchanged."[51] Yet simultaneously, Tucci evidently subscribed to the idea of evolution, of gradual change in the arts. He posits several different evolutionary scenarios, at macro and micro levels, of Tibetan art in general and of specific motifs in particular. Some of the evolutions described contradict each other. We have seen that in one of his formulations Baroque sumptuousness preceded classical simplicity. Elsewhere, however, three-dimensionality and naturalism give way to ornamentalism. Originally, painters copied sculptural models, he wrote, but then indulge "the arabesques of his fancy."[52] Those become "a mere ornamental motif . . . whose existence thus has no excuse."[53] However, within two pages of dismissing elements of a painting as becoming "a mere ornamental motif," Tucci stated flatly that "none of the motifs appearing on the tankas has a purely ornamental value."[54]

Alongside the negativity toward *horror vacui*—which in Indian art might more accurately be considered a response to the aesthetic desideratum of *alaṃkāra*, or a beautification or elaboration appropriate to honoring sacred subject matter[55]—is Tucci's similar preference for naturalism and spaciousness.[56] Despite the condemnation of overelaboration, Tucci was also in fact drawn to fineness and detail, a repeatedly stated value,[57] and to golden luster, grandly but vaguely designated "the symbol of purity but also of truth."[58] Paintings were praised for delicacy, accuracy, and color that was "ably graded, so as to produce chiaroscuro shadows and cause the figures to bulge out with a plastic relief."[59] Suppleness of posture, as opposed to "archaic stiffness," he appreciated.[60] These binaries reveal his rather conventional tastes and preferences for "classical" naturalism as opposed to "Baroque" ornamentation or archaic rigidity.

Many elegant turns of phrase that were pleasing to the ear but upon reflection do not actually signify much descend in Tucci's text into lyrical puffery. For example, "India's best work" is characterized by "thoughtful intimacy."[61] In another example, China "looked with joy and admiration upon the slumber of nature, which moved her heart to share its life," while "India only considered spiritual values and closed her eyes to the world,

50 Luczanits, "Methodological Comments Regarding Recent Research on Tibetan Art."

51 Tucci, *Tibetan Painted Scrolls*, 285.

52 Ibid., 304.

53 Ibid.

54 Ibid., 306.

55 Gonda, "Meaning of the Word Alaṃkāra."

56 When "trees . . . show signs of leaves" and "[s]pace is not so full of floral patterns . . . [i]n a word[,] there is more breadth and freedom;" Tucci, *Tibetan Painted Scrolls*, 191.

57 Hairs "drawn one by one" are singled out; ibid., 285.

58 Ibid., 289.

59 Ibid., 273–74.

60 Ibid., 275.

61 Ibid., 173.

which is indeed the raiment of God; but raiment is not the soul; it is worn out and falls to pieces . . ." and so on and so forth.[62] Echoing prominent art historians of the late nineteenth and early twentieth centuries, Tucci expounded eloquently about Tibetan painted hands, which "foreshadow the spirit, its embodiment in a form where matter, fading out before its levity [?], becomes almost rarefied and diaphanous."[63] Tucci's pleasing but obfuscating eloquence has tended to mask the nearly invariable substitution of iconography for art history with each topic taken up, whether it is composition or consecration, technique or Tāranātha, influence or iconometry, color or *chiaroscuro*.

As for *TPS*'s contribution to Tibet's history and the history of Tibet's religion and religious iconography, the work is unparalleled. Frankly, it is difficult to reconcile Tucci's so-called art history with the depth of his understanding of tantric ritual, and the sensitivity and eloquence with which he pointed to the profundity of its underlying actions, which so many previous Western observers had condemned out of hand as idolatry, demon worship, or mummery. Nevertheless, the unquestionable contributions he made to the understanding of Tibetan religious history should not blind us to the strict limitation of his knowledge of, and therefore his work's usefulness for, art history per se. His art-historical and visual analyses are not remotely as sophisticated or ambitious as his knowledge and fluid expressiveness lead us to expect. If he is the father of Tibetan art history, those of us who consider ourselves historians of Tibetan art may be forgiven for questioning, lamenting, or repudiating our paternity.

62 Ibid., 283.

63 Ibid., 285. Tucci's description of drawn hands recalls the studies of Italian painters by the connoisseur Giovanni Morelli (1816–1891), the billowy descriptions of art historians Walter Pater (1839–1894) or Bernard Berenson (1865–1959) on Renaissance art; Morelli, *Italian Painters*.

Early Matters

CHAPTER 3

Early Buddhist Stupa Reliefs in Zangskar

[The forms of the *stūpa*, in the Indus Valley from the first to the eighth century] rather than revealing an indigenous homogenous style, mirror developments of the *stūpa* which can be associated with the broad spectrum of northern and central Indian, as well as Central Asian art.
—Ebert, "Niches, Columns, and Figures," 268

The *Tīrtha* and Earliest Buddhist Art in Zangskar

In *Seeing into Stone* I argued that the concept of the *tīrtha* provides a useful interpretative framework by which to investigate the locations, functions, and characteristics of the earliest Buddhist engraved-rock art sites in Zangskar, where South, Inner, and Central Asia intersect.[1] I focused on sites with both pre-Buddhist petroglyphs—mainly of ibex and other animals layered with cultural significance for the makers—and early Buddhist imagery.[2] This chapter shows that early Buddhist engraved-rock artists of Zangskar recognized boulders and cliffs as appropriate locations for chiseled-outline images that conveyed their deepest, most cherished beliefs. Buddhists appropriated the same sites as had inspired earlier petroglyph carvers, and marked them as Buddhist without erasing the signs of a pre-Buddhist dispensation. The hunting and animal figures are manifestly beneath, and therefore earlier than, the later stupa markings, which, where they are present as superimpositions, tend to dominate the surface, whereas the animal imagery recedes into the background but is not erased (Figs. 3.1–2). The mixed pastoral-agriculturalists who gradually settled in Zangskar and Ladakh, even after they became Buddhists, continued to recognize the same sites as their predecessors as being of *tīrtha*-like importance. Instead of continuing with the hunting iconography, however, they marked it with the imagery most meaningful to them, the stupa. An analogous situation had taken hold in the Chilas area of Gilgit. There too one finds a comparable addition of Buddhist imagery and inscriptions alongside pre-Buddhist compositions. Similarly, later "rock-carvings were not condemned after the conversion to Islam"[3] and Arabic inscriptions such as "*Yā Allah yā ʿAlī madat*" were added to Buddhist petroglyphs.[4]

1 Linrothe, *Seeing into Stone*, 134.

2 Ibid., 134–68.

3 Jettmar, "Paṭolas, Their Governors and Their Successors," 97.

4 Stein, *Innermost Asia*, 46–47.

Fig. 3.1 Boulder with petroglyphs and engraved stupas at Char *doksa* (Zamthang), Zangskar. Photo 2004.

Fig. 3.2 Stupa and ibex on boulder of Fig. 3.1. Photo 2004.

Early Buddhists used the stupa as a primary motif to mark the presence of a new belief system. Stupas are powerful indexical signs of the Buddha, his teachings (*dharma*), and his followers. They proved to be a prevalent and enduring non-figural sign. Early Buddhists in Zangskar, however, also created other kinds of iconic art, including images of the Buddha, bodhisattva, and donors. Stylistically, those are among the early Buddhist sculptures remaining in Zangskar, as will be explored in chapter 4. They are still offered *pūja*s in the form of butter lamps by villagers in the region. This chapter focuses on early outlined stupa-forms. It employs them to help trace the multiplicity of sources from which Zangskaris derived Buddhism and its signs, even as they added some characteristics that appear to be distinctive to the region.

The Early Outline and Low-relief Stupa Carvings in Zangskar

Significance of Stupa Representations

Three terms are used in Buddhist literature to refer to early structures that commemorate the Buddha and the Buddha's *dharma*, or teachings: stupa, *caitya*, and *dhātugarbha*. Even though *dhātugarbha* is frequently defined as a reliquary, no consistent, non-contradictory, or simple use-patterns are observable in all regions or periods to distinguish stupa and *caitya* (although there are recurrent attempts to impose greater clarity than actually prevails in the historical record). Clearly there were differences in the use of the terms, circling around whether relics (of different types) were intended to be inserted, whether the object referred to was intended as a funerary or merely a commemorative memorial, or emphasis on function versus structure.[5] For example, Brancaccio, who discussed this issue in some detail, is convincing that the term *caitya* referred to "dome-shaped monuments placed in major pillared halls while the word *stupa* is employed to designate the dome-shaped structures built in small secondary units or clustered together at the margins of sites,"[6] at least in the western Deccan.[7] Elsewhere there is evidence that *caityas* were understood as not necessarily containing relics (at least of the Buddha) but were animated by the presence of the Buddha, whereas stupas, as funerary monuments, did contain *śarīra* (bodily) relics of the Buddha.[8] Yijing gives evidence that by the end of the seventh century, when he studied Buddhist practice in India, the names were interchangeable: "Another name for it [*caitya*] is Stūpa, the meaning being the same as Caitya."[9] Starting in the ninth century, Tibetan practice was also to translate both terms as *chorten* (mchod rten), another piece of evidence suggesting that the usage of the two terms had rendered them indistinguishable.[10] I therefore will use stupa, *caitya*, and chorten interchangeably to refer to a structure or miniature representation (2D or 3D) which functioned as a literal reliquary (one with a relic or an implied relic) or as a symbol of the presence of the Buddha and the Dharma (the latter two understood as equivalent).[11]

Stupas were pre-Buddhist, and Jains and Bönpo[12] also used them, though usually they are most strongly associated with Buddhists. In Buddhist thought there were three types of relics associated with stupas: *paribhotta-cetiya/paribhogika-stūpa*, referring to reliquaries containing objects used by the Buddha (or other saintly Buddhists); *dhātu-ceitya/śarīra-stūpa* containing bodily relics of the Buddha or others, and *dhamma-cetiya/uddeśika-stūpa*, which can be formed by inserting the *pratītyasamutpāda* formula outlining dependent co-arising, the essence of the Buddha's teaching.[13] Since the third type, also known as *dharmakāya-caitya*, concerns the enduring legacy of the Buddha and has little or nothing to do with holding bodily or other physical relics associated with the Buddha after his passing, Tucci, following Foucher, asserts that:

> not all the caityas were built to contain relics, but . . . most of them had a symbolic value . . . . We should not, therefore, attribute only a funerary character to the numberless stupas (mchod-rten) rising in every shape and in every dimension on Tibetan plains which are said to be derived from Indian ones . . . . The construction of a stupa

5 Goswamy, "Introductory Speech"; Lokesh Chandra, introduction, viii–xvii; Pakhoutova, "Reproducing the Sacred Places," 18, 22n33.

6 Brancaccio, *Buddhist Caves at Aurangabad*, 43–51.

7 Ibid., 43.

8 Roth, "Symbolism of the Buddhist Stūpa," 195; Brancaccio, *Buddhist Caves at Aurangabad*, 49–50.

9 Yijing, *Record of the Buddhist Religion*, 121; Yijing, *Buddhist Monastic Traditions of Southern Asia*, 113.

10 De Körös, *Sanskrit–Tibetan–English Vocabulary*, 83.114 and 157.64; Lokesh Chandra, introduction, vii, xvi.

11 On the derivations proposed for *caitya*, and the ambiguity of the distinction between it and stupa, see also Strong, *Relics of the Buddha*, 19n50.

12 "Bön" is a contemporary Tibetan religious tradition that traces itself far back in time, to a pre-Buddhist origin, and to the Zhangzhung state, which may have overlapped with the western Himalaya as discussed in chapter 1. "Bönpo" refers to practitioners of Bön. The history of Bön in western Tibet, and the geographic extent of the Zhangzhung, centered at times in the regions of Ngari that became Gugé, is beyond the purview of this inquiry. It recently has been examined in Denwood, "Tibetans in the West, Part I," and Denwood, "Tibetans in the West, Part II."

13 Lokesh Chandra, introduction, x; De Marco, "Stūpa as a Funerary Monument," 229; M. Willis, "Relics of the Buddha," 138–39.

> (mchod rten) comes into the category of those several meritorious works consisting either in propagating faith or in rendering homage to its revealers, by edifying sacred images, copying and transcribing books of the doctrine, erecting religious buildings.[14]

Yijing also noticed that "priests and the laymen in India make Caityas or images with earth, or impress the Buddha's image on silk or paper, and worship with offerings wherever they go . . . . They sometimes form these Stūpas in lonely fields, and leave them to fall in ruins."[15] He also stresses that "Any one may thus employ himself in making the objects for worship,"[16] not just specialists, artists, or ordained members of the clergy. Worship of these self-made images with "offering[s] of incense and flowers is a cause of riches and joy in every life to come. Do it yourself, and teach others to do the same, then you will gain immeasurable blessings."[17]

The features mentioned so far—that stupas need not literally contain relics, that they may be made in out-of-the-way places, that anyone may make them, and that the practice of making and offering worship generates merit—are particularly relevant to the carved petroglyph representations of stupas. This helps to explain, for example, the great variety of quality in the petroglyphs; many seem to have been made by those with more enthusiasm than skill. Importantly, outlined stupas could not have contained literal, physical relics, but as recognizable shapes were nevertheless imbued with significance for the makers and viewers. We also gain insight into the motivations of the maker who becomes a *kalyāṇamitra* (spiritual friend) and *dānapati* (Tib. sbyin bdag), generating merit for him- or herself by creating reminders of the Buddha and the Dharma, and providing passersby an opportunity for mindfulness and reverence. "[T]he dynamics of the relic cult suggest that simply 'seeing' stūpas is equivalent to beholding and worshipping the Buddha or saint whose relics the stūpa contains . . . . Spiritual merit is gained by the sight . . . . For the Buddhist monks, this mechanism was a means of quite literally 'presencing' the Dharma in foreign ground."[18]

The equivalence between the *caitya*, the Buddha, and the Dharma can be explored further. At some level, the idea of reliquary is never lost as a primary association with the stupa, even as it serves a "symbolic" function. Images and structures alike simultaneously referenced commemorations of the Buddha's life, his *parinirvāṇa*, and his Dharmakāya or eternal body in

14 Tucci, "Stupa and Votive Stupa," 24–25.

15 Yijing, *Record of the Buddhist Religion*, 150; Yijing, *Buddhist Monastic Traditions of Southern Asia*, 137.

16 Yijing, *Record of the Buddhist Religion*, 150.

17 Ibid., 152; Yijing, *Buddhist Monastic Traditions of Southern Asia*, 138.

18 J. Shaw, "Stūpas, Monasteries, and Relics in the Landscape," 128.

the form of the teaching. This teaching was, as indicated above, considered to have been encapsulated in the *pratītyasamutpāda* formula. Willis explains this further:

> By the early centuries CE, the *Dharma*-body—the teachings of the Buddha and his essential qualities as a Buddha—were located in the philosophy of causal genesis or dependent origination. Termed *pratīyasamutpāda* . . . . its core tenets were summarised in a single verse . . . . 'The Buddha alone has explained the conditions that arise from causes, and the great mendicant has also proclaimed their confinement.' This verse . . . was seen as having talismanic properties and became a source of speculation in its own right. Equally important were the parallels made between the verse and the Buddha, the *Dharma* and the *Dharma*-body. Extending earlier equations between seeing, knowing and the Buddha, the *Majjhima Nikāya* (1:190–191) states: "He who sees the *pratīyasamutpāda* sees the *Dharma*, and he who sees the *Dharma* sees the *pratīyasamutpāda*."[19]

In most of the cases I will examine, the outlined *caityas* are votive stupas, in the sense that they were offering-images, not reliquaries. However, many three-dimensional stupas, in some cases no larger in height than many of the petroglyphs and in others much larger, actually contain relics of one sort or another. In both India and Tibet, such objects "are now regarded by some scholars as 'burial *ad sanctos*' stūpas, built to contain the mortuary remains of ordinary monks and the laity and positioned at removed distance from more important stūpas in deference to the hierarchical structure of the relic cult."[20] By contrast, like *tsha tsha* in the shape of stupas, the petroglyph outlined *caitya* are "*stūpas* without relics, *śarīras*; but the *dharma-paryāya* (gate of the teaching) is also *śarīra*, along with the relics of the Enlightened One . . . Teaching and making of small *stūpas* therefore have the same meaning, that of the 'gift of the [Dharma].'"[21] However, as we will see, even these outlined stupas invited the response on the part of engaged viewers to add "fetish" marks, which I believe represent actual relics. In this sense they make visible that which is implied by the stupa shape.

Sites for Early Outline and Low-Relief Stupa Carvings in Zangskar

In Devers's recent listing of heritage sites in Zangskar, he documents "45 sites sheltering 190 individual stupa stones (or fragments of them)," and he illustrates many of them.[22] Rich as his listings are, they cannot be complete,

19 M. Willis, "Relics of the Buddha," 140.

20 J. Shaw, "Stūpas, Monasteries, and Relics in the Landscape," 120. See also Schopen, "Burial '*Ad Sanctos*' and the Physical Presence of the Buddha in Early Indian Buddhism," and Schopen, "*Stūpa* and *Tīrtha*."

21 Taddei, "Inscribed Clay Tablets and Miniature Stūpas from Ġaznī," 82.

22 Devers, *Historical Sites of Zanskar*, 2.

Fig. 3.3 Stupa with staircases engraved on stone at Khangwar (Tsetang), Zangskar. Photo 1998.

though the ones I discuss are for the most part included in his survey. This chapter cannot aspire to comprehensiveness in documenting the generous amount of relevant material in Zangskar. Along with sheer numbers, there is also significant variety. Before surveying the different types of early stupa carvings in Zangskar, suggesting sources or typology, and attempting to date them, the sites where some of the principal types and examples are located will be introduced. Among the most prominent locations for the outlined engraved stupas are those that also have prehistoric petroglyphs.[23] There are, however, some new sites. The sites familiar from the study of animal-style petroglyphs include Char *doksa* or Zamthang (see Figs. 3.1–2);[24] Pipula; the bridge near Pibiting; and Khangwar (Tsetang) (Fig. 3.3), all of which have a significant number of Buddhist and pre-Buddhist carvings, particularly Char *doksa*.[25] Sites that do not have much in the way of pre-Buddhist motifs but have outlined stupa carvings include two sites in the western part of Zangskar, along the sTod ("Doda") river. One is a *maṇi*-wall on the east or Padum side of Phé (phye) village, opposite the valley with Dzonkhul Gonpa (Fig. 3.4).[26] The same site includes a number of older sculptures of Buddhist figures, some of which are considered in chapter 4. The second is Rantaksha (rang thag sha), a village downstream of Phé but also on the north side of the river. A number of early sculptures and outlined stupas are found on stone and small steles in various places right in the village, among the houses and enclosures (Fig. 3.5).[27] North of the *prayag*

23 Linrothe, *Seeing into Stone*, 134–68.

24 Devers, *Historical Sites of Zanskar*, 241, 248.

25 Linrothe, *Seeing into Stone*, 12–18, 23. In 2018, Karsha Lonpo told me that the site I had understood as "Tsetang" was actually "Khangwar." Devers, who also included these stupas and dates them "Approx. 8th–13th centuries," refers to the site as Kamal Togpo; Devers, *Historical Sites of Zanskar*, 147, 149. Here I use "Khangwar (Tsetang)."

26 Devers refers to the area between Phé and Rantaksha as "Chorten Korlo"; Devers, *Historical Sites of Zanskar*, 65, 76–79.

27 Ibid., 81–82.

Fig 3.4 *Maṇi*-wall, east of Phé village, Zangskar. Photo 2008.

Fig. 3.5 Pillar with stupa engravings, Rantaksha village, Zangskar. Photo 2003.

Fig. 3.6 Boulder with stupa engravings near Rinam village, Zangskar. Photo 2004.

Fig. 3.7 Boulder with multiple stupa engravings at Zangla, Zangskar. Photo 2003.

where the sTod and Lungnak rivers form the Zangskar river are two villages that have large boulders nearby scored with multiple Buddhist *caitya*-outlines. Rinam is on the west side, between Karsha and Pishu. Although this village or hamlet of five households is near the river, the boulder is close to the base of the mountain where the original village was settled (Fig. 3.6).[28] Across the Zangskar river, and farther downstream, is the seat of one of the kings of Zangskar, Zangla. As we will see in chapters 4, 5, and 7, there was a fort and Zangskar's earliest Buddhist paintings in the Kashmiri mode to the east of Zangla, and a disused palace above the present village as well, where Csoma de Kőrös spent a year studying Tibetan. At the northern end of the village itself is a large boulder with cultic associations and hundreds of small chortens carved (and painted) on it (Fig. 3.7).[29] I will introduce other areas with a few carvings, including the area around the hamlets to the south of Karsha village and the rock outcrops near Padum by the bank of the Longnak river.

28 Gutschow and Gutschow, "Landscape Dissolved," 118. GPS reading: N 33° 33.223'; E 076° 58.960'; alt. 11,510'. Devers, *Historical Sites of Zanskar*, 148.

29 Devers, *Historical Sites of Zanskar*, 207.

According to local belief and to the *Phug thal gyi 'Bo yig*, both Rantaksha and Rinam were among the earliest settlements in Zangskar.[30] Sonam Phuntsok, a P.W.D engineer at Padum whose family home is at Rantaksha, states that some of the stone pillars with *caitya* carvings set up in Rantaksha village have roles in local festivals, including the spring festival of first plowing.[31] Sonam Phuntsok is the son-in-law of the Karsha Lonpo. In November 2003, when the photograph of Figure 3.5 was taken, he explained that the pillar with the stupa renditions on it was painted red in order to fend off malevolent spirits from the village. While hardly proof of their antiquity, the fact that these carvings are deeply integrated into the current agricultural customs of the villagers suggests that, as with the Shambhala Gate (discussed at some length in chapter 4), they may have played important roles going back to ancient times.

The Kashmiri-type Stupa in Zangskar

The most common type of stupa-carvings in Zangskar are those that can be related to Kashmiri-style forms. Let us take a few representative examples in the Karsha area (Figs. 3.8–11) and in Rantaksha (Figs. 3.5, 3.12). All are characterized by a rectangular platform (of varied heights, in some examples with indications of lotus petals), multiple bases which diminish in size as they ascend, a relatively small, often-bulbous *aṇḍa*, a square or slanted *harmikā* (from which the *yasti*-mast rises), elaborate *chattrāvalī*-umbrellas, and *dhvaja-patāka*, that is, banners, streamers, and flags hanging down from the *uṣṇisa* or topmost finial. In addition, several of them are depicted with staircases running down from the *aṇḍa* to the top of the base.

We can compare these forms with extant examples of Kashmiri-type stupa-reliquaries, such as the seventh- to eighth-century metalwork example from Gilgit in the Peshawar Museum,[32] a stone relief with a suggested date of ca. ninth century,[33] and the pair depicted on the famous eighth-century crowned Buddha framed by a pair of stupas now in the Asia Society Museum in New York.[34] The latter is datable by inscription to the early eighth century.[35] These forms of the stupa are slightly elongated versions of the plaques recovered from Harwan (Fig. 3.13) which, according to Kak, have inscriptions of "the Buddhist creed, *Ye dharma*, etc., [i.e. the *pratītyasamutpāda* formula] in Brahmi characters of about the fourth century A.D."[36] Siudmak dates them to the fifth century, but points out that "Evidence from sculpture dating from the eighth century demonstrates that the form of the *stūpa* had not greatly changed in the

30 Francke, *Antiquities of Indian Tibet*, 2:156; Gutschow and Gutschow, "Landscape Dissolved," 118n35.

31 K. Gutschow, *Being a Buddhist Nun*, 58–59; Riaboff, "Notes sur les rituals agraires au Zanskar"; Khoo, "Preliminary Remarks."

32 Luczanits, *Gandhara, the Buddhist Heritage of Pakistan*, no. 290.

33 Pal, *Arts of Kashmir*, fig. 39.

34 Pal, *Himalayas*, no. 63; Linrothe, *Collecting Paradise*, fig. 1.28.

35 Fussman, "Chilas, Hatun et les Bronzes Bouddhiques du Cashemire," 43–47.

36 Kak, *Ancient Monuments of Kashmir*, 108. See also Shali, *Kashmir*, 132.

Fig. 3.8 Standing stones with stupa engravings, near Pikongma House, south of Karsha village, Zangskar. Photo 1998.

Fig. 3.9 Outlined stupa against stone wall near Kasar village, Karsha region, Zangskar. Photo 1992.

Fig. 3.10 Five stupas etched on a boulder near Nangwaphal hamlet, Karsha region, Zangskar. Photo 1998.

Fig. 3.11 Detail of Fig. 3.10. Photo 1998.

Fig. 3.12 Engraved stupas on stone at Rantaksha village, Zangskar. Photo 2003.

Fig. 3.13 Three clay molded plaques found at Harwan, Kashmir. From Kak, *Ancient Monuments of Kashmir*, pl. XVIII.

intervening centuries."[37] All of the Harwan stupas "have a triple basement with three flights of steps, the drum with a line of beading, and plain moldings with plain dome. A row of projecting brackets makes up the *harmikā*, above which is a succession of eleven umbrellas of diminishing size, with fluttering ribbons tied at the very top."[38]

In turn, these structural characteristics can be closely compared with a related molded-plaque from Malakhartse Khar, east of Zangla (Fig. 3.14), the paintings inside which might be as early as the late eleventh century, as is discussed in chapter 5. Closely related *tsha tsha* were recovered in a dilapidated stupa at Karsha Chuchikzhal, discussed in chapter 7, which illustrates one of them (see Fig. 7.27). The so-called Alchi group of paintings, executed by Kashmiri or Kashmiri-trained painters, also provides datable examples of stupas with very similar proportions, *aṇḍa* to base and superstructure ratios, stepped bases, staircases, and hanging streamers. Three examples—from the Small Chorten at Alchi (Fig. 3.15), from Sumda Chung (Fig. 3.16), and from the painting on the dhoti of Maitreya in one of the side towers at Mangyu (Fig. 3.17)[39]—can be dated to about the twelfth century, with the early thirteenth as the outside limit. Thus, we should be able to date the Kashmiri-style chortens from Zangskar to between the seventh and thirteenth century. It should be reinforced, however, that the Alchi-group paintings of the ca. twelfth century closely follow a model that is considerably older. In many particulars, among them the elaborate slanting *harmikā*, the three-storey base, the tall superstructure, and the small *aṇḍa*, the paintings resemble a brass model, 62.5 cm in height, now in the Potala's Lima Lhakhang, which von Schroeder dates to the seventh century.[40] He also proposes that it is itself a model of the Kaniṣka-stupa of Puruṣapura (in modern Peshawar), and comes from the "Greater Kashmir Region," which could include Gilgit.[41] The extremely small, rounded *aṇḍa*,

37 Siudmak, "Religious Architecture (500–1200)," 55–56.

38 Ibid., 55.

39 See Linrothe, "Dating the Mangyu Style."

40 von Schroeder, *Buddhist Sculptures in Tibet*, 1:100.

41 Ibid., 1:100–105.

Fig. 3.14 Molded clay plaque depicting a stupa attached to the exterior of the stupa at Malakartse Khar, Zangla, Zangskar. Photo 2018.

Fig. 3.16 Painted stupa, wall mural at Sumda Chung Lhakhang, Ladakh, ca. 12th–13th c. Photo 2008.

Fig. 3.15 Painted stupas inside small chorten at Alchi, Ladakh, ca. 12th c. Photo 2008.

Fig. 3.17 Painted stupa on Maitreya sculpture at Mangyu village Lhakhang, Ladakh. Photo 2010.

Fig. 3.18 Kashmiri-type stupa engraved on boulder at Skitmartse village in Suru valley, Purig district, Ladakh. Photo 2013.

with an exaggeratedly narrow, towering superstructure, is also found carved into a rock at Skitmartse in the Suru Valley (Fig. 3.18), literally on the eastern border of Kashmir and the western border of Zangskar.[42] It was probably done by a Kashmiri artist, as was likely also the case with the one that the intrepid British artist William Simpson (1823–1899) drew at Dras and published (Fig. 3.19).[43] Only a fragment of the stupa survives at Dras today, but among the other sculptures is an inscription in *śāradā*, the script used in Kashmir. After an extensive examination of the sculptures and other evidence, I concluded that they date to the seventh or eighth century.[44]

Compared with earlier stupas in Gandhāra and in central, eastern and southern India, the Kashmiri *aṇḍa* are quite small in relation to the base and superstructure. To illustrate the difference, consider the low-relief stupa carved on the back of a sculpture of a seated Buddha from Bodhgaya, Bihar (Magadha), which is dated by the Indian Museum to the sixth or seventh century (Fig. 3.20). The ones from Zangskar and Ladakh are much closer to the Kashmiri type. Indeed, in her study of ca. first century BCE to tenth–thirteenth-century stupas along the Karakoram highway, Jorinde Ebert contends that "most *stūpa* depictions in the petroglyphs can be

42 See also Devers, *Historical Sites of Purig*, 130; Schuh and Munshi, *Travel into the History of Purig*, 110.

43 Simpson, "Sculptured Tope on an Old Stone at Dras, Ladak."

44 Linrothe, "Origins of the Kashmiri Style in the Western Himalayas," 150–62.

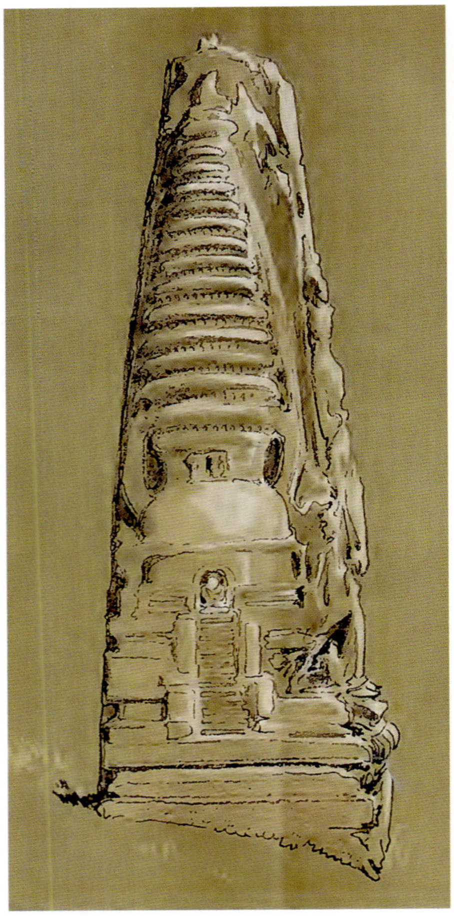

Fig. 3.19 Stupa at Dras, Kargil district, Ladakh, as drawn by William Simpson. From Simpson, "Sculptured Tope on an Old Stone at Dras, Ladak," frontispiece.

Fig. 3.20 Stupa engraved on the back of a sandstone sculpture of Buddha protected by the serpent Muchalinda, ca. 6th/7th c., from Bodhgaya, Bihar, in the Indian Museum, Kolkata, acc. no. 6290. Photo 2016.

arranged in a rough chronology according to the size of their cupola [i.e., *aṇḍa*] (including the drum) in relation to the rest of the structure," with the earliest about 62% of the total and the latest at about 15%.[45] After the ca. 13th century, however, *aṇḍa*s tend to get larger, as well as change shape from a round form to a somewhat tapered, eventually angular form seen in later Tibetan-style chorten found in Ladakh and Zangskar.[46]

The Staircase and the Set of Eight Stupas

The prevalence of the stairs on many Zangskari (and Ladakhi) representations of *caityas* requires comment. There is a tendency to interpret this feature as signifying one of the eight types of stupas associated with the life and miracles of the Buddha, in particular the miraculous descent at

45 Ebert, "Niches, Columns, and Figures," 269. See also Thewalt, "Rockcarvings and Inscriptions along the Indus."

46 Dorjee, *Stūpa and Its Technology*, 86–87, 89–90.

Sāṇkāśya from Trayastriṃsā heaven, where the Buddha went to preach to the gods and then descended accompanied by Indra and Brahma. Tucci, for example, notes that in the region comprising Ladakh, Spiti, and Lahul (presumably including Zangskar), stairs on stupa representations are "rather frequent."[47] Denwood also mentions that all of the stupa-petroglyphs at the Alchi petroglyph field near the bridge across the Indus "are modeled on the early set of eight stūpas which were associated with eight events in the life of Śākyamuni Buddha, particularly the 'many-doored stūpa of good fortune' . . . and the 'stūpa of the descent from the gods.'"[48] In certain circumstances, when it is clear that a group of eight stupas differentiated by the shape of the base and *aṇḍa* signify a set, it seems appropriate to designate those representations with staircases as Descent from Heaven types. However, many structural stupas had such staircases, in one or all four directions, as at Taxila[49] and Parihasapura.[50] The many representations of *caitya*s with staircases in Zangskar and Ladakh **(see Figs. 3.3, 3.8–10, 3.12, 3.14–19)**—including two side-by-side as in Figure 3.10—may have been intended to reflect conventions of actual architecture, rather than the set associated with the Buddha's life. For example, Figure 3.15 shows two registers of stupas, front and back, and all the rear examples have the staircases painted red to emphasize them. One boulder at the so-called Alchi petroglyph field or reservoir[51] has five stupas with only minor variations, but all with the staircase depicted. It is very unlikely in such cases that all the stupas were meant to refer to the Descent from Heaven miracle, but instead depict one of the conventional modes of stupa construction. In this, they are again following their Kashmiri and even Gandhāran models, for all three of the Harwan plaques in Figure 3.13 have such stairs, as do the Kashmiri metalwork examples cited above. Pakhoutova, following Lawson, comes to the similar conclusion for *tsha tsha* depicting stupas with staircases: "There seems to be no direct association of this type of stūpa with the Event of the Buddha's Descent from the Heaven of the Thirty-three Gods at the time [ca. tenth century]."[52]

The standard set of eight stupas substituting for the narrative figural representations of major events and miracles (as opposed to the "original" eight or rather nine stupas housing his relics and the bowl that contained them) has a complicated history, as Pakhoutova's study demonstrates.[53] The standardization of the eight sites seems to have a different chronology than that of the establishment of a set of eight recognizably different stupas associated with them.[54] Pakhoutova documents earlier sets of four

47 Tucci, "Stupa and Votive Stupa (mchod-rten and tsha-tsha)," 51.

48 Denwood, "Rock Inscriptions," 155–58.

49 Luczanits et al., *Gandhara, the Buddhist Heritage of Pakistan*, fig. 6.

50 Pal et al., *Arts of Kashmir*, fig. 40.

51 Linrothe, *Seeing into Stone*, 24–25.

52 Pakhoutova, "Reproducing the Sacred Places," 34.

53 Ibid.

54 Ibid., 47.

Fig. 3.21 Stupa engraving on *maṇi*-wall in Rantaksha village, Zangkar. Photo 2003.

stupas in the fifth century that do not correspond to the later set, and multiple stupas in the seventh century that are "part of an extensive pilgrimage network of Indian Buddhist sacred places."[55] She provides evidence for a "newly emerging emphasis" on the eight great sites in the eighth century,[56] but suggests that it was only after "around the tenth–eleventh century the Eight Great Events *and their stūpas* are popularized in the textual sources."[57] Only then do the connections with particular stupa forms (in some cases preexisting) move toward standardization. This period overlaps the one under consideration, but generally the early outlined stupa forms seen in Zangskar and Ladakh were made earlier, during the nascent period of standardization. They were made when individual stupa forms were probably already in existence in India[58] but were deployed as a part of a vocabulary of Buddhist forms independent of, at times, any of the groupings of eight stupas forming sets. Nor did they necessarily indicate the location associated with the event (i.e., Bodh Gaya for the Enlightenment stupa or Sarnath for the first sermon) but may have been used to mark any sanctified location.[59] Conversely, even by the late ninth and tenth centuries in eastern India, the stupa added to a figural depiction of the Descent from Heaven is not always of the staircase variety.[60] Thus, despite the understandable inference of earlier scholars, we must not assume that stupas with staircases or lotus petals conveyed then what they did later.

Aśokan Pillar references

The Rantaksha examples already included (see Figs. 3.5, 3.12) also have a small feature that I believe can be traced directly back to Kashmir and ultimately to Gandhāra. It is perhaps most clearly seen in another example, (Fig. 3.21). Like the one on the left of Figure 3.12 and all four of those depicted on Figure 3.5, T-shaped signs appear atop the drum on

55 Ibid., 28–29.

56 Ibid., 29–30.

57 Ibid., 24 (emphasis added).

58 Pakhoutova suggests that the stupa with stairs preexisted its association with the Descent, as did the so-called Heaped Lotus type later associated with Buddha's birth. Ibid., 49.

59 Ibid., 45.

60 Ibid., 35, 42, figs. 1.9, 1.13.

either side of the *aṇḍa*. Above the crossbar of the T are round dots; they look like small standing stick-figures. Many of the Kashmiri-type sculptures of stupas have four small, Aśokan-style pillars placed on the drum at the corners (see Fig. 3.16). Two are clearly visible in two of the Harwan plaques (see Fig. 3.13) and are also depicted in Gandhāran representation of stupas going back to at least the second century.[61] The Zangskari versions may be abstracted, possibly misunderstood references to such pillars.

The So-called Cruciform Stupa, Tibet, Nepal, and Inscriptions

Cross-shaped vs. Cruciform Base Stupa and Sino-Tibetan Rivalry

Due to the frequent misattribution of early Buddhist rock-cut stupa forms in Ladakh and Zangskar to Tibet, it is important to emphasize the Kashmiri antecedents. Tibetan forms of the stupa circulated within and across a wide Tibetan cultural zone, including in Ladakh and Zangskar, but only later, after the eleventh or twelfth century at the earliest. However, since there was a wave of contact in the western Himalaya with imperial Tibet (i.e., the Pugyal dynasty) during the late seventh through the ninth century, including soldiers who left inscriptions at Alchi and other places during the occupation of the eighth and ninth century, there is a potential to assume that the forms, and not just the inscriptions, were intrusions of Tibetan origin. Denwood argues that the names, titles, and terms employed in the inscriptions have much in common with written materials associated with Tibetan military personnel and units who were in Central Asia during the same period, particularly in the struggle with the Chinese and local rulers over Khotan.[62] Without mentioning which publication, Denwood also suggests that he is following Jettmar in that some of the forms found, including a so-called cross-shaped stupa, "seems to be an innovation of the Tibetan period, and it leads on to the distinctive Tibetan form of later centuries."[63] Jettmar's position, at least in a 1990 publication, was slightly more nuanced. Jettmar observed that in Baltistan, "elaborate *stūpa*s with a long spire and many disc-like umbrellas... [may] render monuments erected in Kashmir," while the *caityas* "shaped like a sort of stepped pyramid" with *aṇḍa* and spire reduced in size "were made before the 8th century AD, still in the time of the Bolorian state," after which "[t] he Tibetans seem to have taken over just this type as a starting point for the subsequent evolution which led to what Aurel Stein called 'cruciform type of stūpas.'"[64] The anchor images in question, cited by both Denwood and Jettmar,[65] are in Stein's 1928 publication *Innermost Asia*.[66] One is a

61 Yaldiz, *Magische Götterwelten*, 35; Luczanits et al., *Gandhara, the Buddhist Heritage of Pakistan*, 200; Bandini- König et al., "Rock Art in the Upper Indus Valley," fig. 3; Gupta, *Kushāṇa Sculptures from Sanghol*, fig. 3.6.

62 Denwood, "Rock Inscriptions," 163; Denwood, "Inscriptions at Balukhar and Char Zampa," 85. Denwood recognizes that the stupa drawings at the Alchi petroglyph field "could go back to an early Kashmir-inspired phase of Buddhism;" "Rock Inscriptions," 155.

63 Denwood, "Tibetans in the Western Himalayas and Karakoram, Seventh–Eleventh Centuries," 49.

64 Jettmar, "Exploration in Baltistan," 808.

65 Denwood, "Tibetans in the Western Himalayas and Karakoram, Seventh–Eleventh Centuries," 53n5; Jettmar, "Exploration in Baltistan," 808.

66 Stein, *Innermost Asia*, 2:1051, and 3: plan 1.

Fig. 3.22 Drawing of stupa engraving on stone found by Francke in Ladakh. From Francke, "Tibetan Inscription of the Darkōt Pass," 1051.

Fig. 3.23 Three stupa engravings with Tibetan inscription above, at Alchi petroglyph field, Ladakh. Photo 2008.

photograph Stein made of an inscribed stupa outline-carving he saw near the Darkot Pass[67] on the way to Wakhan (northwest of Baltistan and Gilgit), and an associated drawing.[68] The other is a drawing provided by Francke to Stein of a stupa Francke saw in Ladakh (Fig. 3.22).[69] It was included in *Innermost Asia* in order to suggest that the unusual cross-like shape of the exaggerated base had counterparts in Ladakh. It is an exaggeration to suggest that "this 'cross-type' occurs frequently in Ladakh."[70] To be sure, Stein quotes a letter written to him by Francke in which the latter noted he had seen cruciform bases in Ladakh.[71] But Francke's own comment on this type (which he cited in Appendix L in *Innermost Asia* accompanying the drawing [see Fig. 3.22]) belies its frequency. Referring to cross-shaped bases in Ladakh, he indicates, "This form is quite unique: at least I have not yet seen anything similar to it in this country."[72] That is my experience as well: I've seen little like it outside of Christian graveyards; certainly not on carvings of Buddhist motifs. At any rate, this image is no basis for grounding an art-historical development of a "distinctive Tibetan form," as suggested by Jettmar and Denwood.

Before moving on, in light of the attention given by scholars to the anomalous stupas—one near Gilgit, one in Ladakh—it may be worth briefly attending to the inscription on the former. Francke interpreted the Tibetan inscription next to the stupa outline as a clan- or place name, preceding a personal name, and believed the script to be of the eighth or ninth century.[73] The name itself, he notes in the same place, "does not appear to be of Tibetan origin." Denwood seems to agree: he states that it is difficult to make out but that the syllable "*li*" indicates the person was from Khotan.[74] Stein, the only one to actually see the stone in question, savvily observes that the "stupa is contemporary with, *if not older than*, the Tibetan inscription."[75]

67 Darkot Pass, at 4,575 meters (over 15,000 feet) is known to be steep. It is quite striking to find a Tibetan inscription at this historically important location. It "is recorded as the place where the Chinese were able to launch an invasion [of Tibetan controlled territory from the north] in 747 A.D. Kao Hsien-chih led ten thousand soldiers, including cavalrymen, from Kucha, via Kashgar, Tashqurgan and Pamir, to Wakhan on the Oxus. After brutal fighting with the Tibetans at Sarhad in Wakhan, seven thousand soldiers crossed the glacier-covered Darkot Pass and in the face of formidable obstacles succeeded in invading Yasin, a part of ancient 'Little P'o-lu', and defeated the Tibetans." Tsuchiya, "Tracing Ancient Routes in Northern Pakistan," 356. See also Denwood, "Tibetans in the West, Part I," 14.

68 Stein, *Innermost Asia*, 2: fig. 46, and 3: plan 1.

69 Francke, in *Innermost Asia*, 2:1051.

70 Jettmar, "Exploration in Baltistan," 808.

71 Stein, *Innermost Asia*, 1:46.

72 Francke, "Notes on Rock-Carvings from Lower Ladakh," 399, and pl. II fig. 1a, and pl. IV fig. 1. A drawing of what looks to be a rubbing of a much more elaborate stupa with an inscription on a stepped, pyramidical lower base and a vertical pillar leading to a cross-shaped support for the *aṇḍa* is illustrated in Ujfalvy, *Westlichen Himalaja*, opp. 248, and identified as from Baltistan.

73 Francke, *Innermost Asia*, 2:1050.

74 Denwood, "Tibetans in the Western Himalayas," 49.

75 Stein, *Innermost Asia*, 1:46 (emphasis added).

Fig. 3.24 Composite (?) stupa of stone in Mahābodhi grounds, Bodhgaya, Bihar. Photo 2022.

Fig. 3.25 Stupa of khondolite stone with Vajrasattva relief in niche, Ratnagiri, Odisha. Photo 2017.

Fig. 3.26 Stupa of khondolite stone with Tārā relief inside niche and seated Buddha carving in *chandraśālā*; Udayagiri, Odisha. Photo 2017.

To be sure, a much milder version of a "cruciform" base for stupas is found in several stupa-images previously published,[76] as well as one on either side of the boulder at Alchi with three stupas and a Tibetan inscription written with archaic features (Fig. 3.23). As we will see, two of the largest outlined stupas at Rinam (see Fig. 3.6) also have cross-shaped bases, as does the one near Kasar village in the Karsha region (see Fig. 3.9). In none of these cases appears features other than the cross-shaped base—actually more of a slightly indented midsection than a cross—to suggest some other radically different prototype, say from eastern India, that would then have been transmitted to Ladakh via Tibetans.

Kashmiri, Tibetan, and Subcontinental Stupa Forms

While we cannot compare Tibetan examples of the eighth or ninth century (to my knowledge), we can examine images of stupas from the major centers of Buddhism in eastern India, including Bodh Gaya as well as Ratnagiri and Udayagiri in Orissa (Figs. 3.24–3.26) datable to the ninth or tenth century and most often including a figural niche.[77] They likely would have been among the sources for stupas made by the Tibetans *in Tibet* at that time, though of course Central Asia and China might have been sources as well. What is immediately apparent in the eastern Indian

76 See Linrothe, *Seeing into Stone*, figs. 14.1, 14.4, 14.6, 14.8, 15.1.

77 For more examples of miniature stupas from eastern India, see Bénisti, *Contribution à l'Étude du Stūpa Bouddhique Indien.* Along with putting funerary remains inside the stupa, an image enshrined in a niche on the *anda*, as in Figures 3.24–26 activates it visually in accord with the well known formula that those who see the Buddha see the dharma, "the Buddha as enshrined image and as internal relics." Dobbins, *Behold the Buddha*, 180.

examples is the much larger relative size of the *aṇḍa*, which is also more bullet-shaped than round. The width of the *chhattrāvalī* (when they survive intact, which is much rarer in eastern India) at times matches that of the *aṇḍa* in the Kashmiri examples, but generally is also significantly different. The *harmikā* in the eastern Indian examples is also more emphatic and *ratha*-like, even in examples where they are depicted and remain whole, without the losses of the superstructure as in Figure 3.25. Naturally, there are no banners or streamers,[78] which are nearly ubiquitous and exaggerated in the low relief or painted Kashmiri (and Kashmiri-inspired) stupas. Finally, based on the dozens of examples gathered by Bénisti (1981), the eastern Indian stupas are no more "cruciform" or "cross-shaped" than the Kashmiri examples. In Kashmir, this base shape is commonly used in the eighth and ninth centuries to support Buddhist and Hindu figures.[79] This is thus another feature of the Kashmiri-based visual vocabulary of many of the stupa-carvings under consideration.

In general during the Pugyal dynasty, "craftsmanship was probably imported from nearby Nepal."[80] Rhie points out that "foreign artists were especially invited to Tibet from Nepal, China and Khotan,"[81] while von Schroeder notes the "ample literary references demonstrating that Nepalese, Indian, Chinese, and Central Asian craftsmen were actively involved not only in the construction of the early temple and monasteries, but especially with the artistic decoration of them."[82] One of the few central Tibetan sites to survive, the Jokhang Tsuglhakhang, has been intensively studied, with the conclusion that Newar artisans dominated the workforce.[83] Gutschow goes so far as to refer to it as "the only surviving example of Licchavi architecture."[84] Given Tibet's proximity to Nepal and the Tibetan reliance on Nepalese craftsmen in the seventh-eighth centuries, one reasonably imagines Tibetans following their lead in the shaping of stupa structures. *Caitya*s of the Licchavi period (5th–9th c.) have been extensively surveyed by Niels Guschow.[85] Many have lost their *chattrāvalī*s and have been resituated, particularly in the seventeenth century. Gutschow notes that the domes come in a rich variety, but none takes the ball-like return of the *aṇḍa* of Kashmir, Ladakh, and Zangskar (see Figs. 3.11–3.19). Some are bullet-shaped while a few exceptional cases display the wide, squat profile of Bodhnath. Another difference between the Kashmiri[86] and Nepalese forms is that in the former the *harmika* is nearly as wide as the *aṇḍa*, but the *chattrāvalī* appears to be of similar height in both. As one would expect, the Nepalese stupas resemble those of eastern India, not the Gandhāran-Kashmiri model.[87]

78 Huntington, *"Pāla-Sena" Schools of Sculpture*, figs. 39–40, 85.

79 Pal, *Arts of Kashmir*, 60, 63, 74; Pal, "A Brāhmanical Triad from Kashmir," fig. 1. Pal points out that "the *aiḍūka* of the *VDP* [Viṣṇudharmottarapurāṇa] is basically a Buddhist structure in a Brahmanical garb." Pal, "The *Aiḍūka* of the *Viṣṇudharmottarapurāṇa*," 52. The *VDP* description is of a three-layer base to support a *liṅga*. In such a structure depicted in a sculpture, the middle layer is narrower than the top or bottom one, giving rise to a somewhat cruciform shape. Pal, "A Brāhmanical Triad from Kashmir," fig. 1.

80 N. Gutschow, *Architecture of the Newars*, 1:186.

81 Rhie, "Interrelationships," 1217.

82 von Schroeder, *Buddhist Sculptures in Tibet*, 2:726.

83 Alexander, *Temples of Lhasa*, 68.

84 N. Gutschow, *Architecture of the Newars*, 1:186.

85 Ibid., 1:194–215.

86 Pal notes that in the *Viṣṇudharmottarapurāṇa*, "What little Saiva bias there is was obviously dictated by the closer resemblance of the hermispherical middle section of the *aiḍūka/stūpa* to the *liṅga* than to any comparable Vaiṣṇava shrine" (Pal, "*Aiḍūka* of the *Viṣṇudharmottarapurāṇa*," 55). Perhaps the distinctively Kashmiri rounded *aṇḍa* was meant on the part of Buddhists to resist this resemblance on the part of Hindu syncretists, for the similarity is heightened with the "bullet-shaped" *aṇḍas*.

87 Nevertheless, it must be acknowledged that at Bodhgaya, the bases, superstructures, and *aṇḍa*s seem to have been reconstituted as composites in the late nineteenth-century "renovation" of the grounds by Alexander Cunningham (1814–1893) and J. D. Beglar (1845–1907).

This dependence on Nepalese craftsmen in central Tibet undermines the notion that the stupas with early (7th–9th-c.) Tibetan inscriptions follow a type "popular" in central Tibet. In fact, they are strikingly absent there, whereas even the practice of shallow relief carvings of figures "was probably introduced into Tibet in imitation of carvings in the north-western provinces of India."[88] Petech notes that "The Tibetan troops who crossed Ladakh en route to Baltistan and Gilgit about the middle of the 8th century cannot be expected to have exerted any religious influence, since Buddhism was only just penetrating their own home country."[89] I am reluctant to make so sweeping a statement, but at least in relation to the petroglyph stupas, his reasoning is sound. Speaking of "the military expansion of the Tibetans in the 7th century A.D.," Snellgrove and Skorupski point out that they "doubtless established military posts at different points, but at that early period their culture can have made no real impact on the indigenous population. Prior to this first Tibetan invasion and for several centuries afterward the cultural inspiration came almost entirely from the west, namely from Kashmir."[90] They go on to point out that the rock carvings like the ones to be discussed here and figural ones in chapter 5 "clearly witness to the existence of Buddhist religion before it was finally taken over by the Tibetans."[91] While the exact nature of the Tibetan "takeover" is still in question, the visual evidence of the carvings of stupas, not just the Kashmiri-style sculptures, lends support to this conclusion. These are not distinctive Tibetan forms introduced from Tibet or by Tibetans.

Although none of the Kashmiri, Gilgit-related, and painted examples of Alchi-group stupas takes the exact form of a base with a narrow waist that then expands to a wider width just before the drum, a number of early examples of Gandhāran and Kashmiri-related stupas with forms are tantalizingly close. For example, the copper miniature stupa in the Peshawar Museum from the eighth or ninth century in Swat[92] has a constricted waist and then a flaring platform on which the drum and dome sit. Other, even older examples have similar wide markers of stepped series that schematically could lend themselves to such a shape.[93] Even the top of the Mangyu painted stupa (see Fig. 3.17) has an hourglass shape at the very top level above the stairs which could—if one were so inclined, as Francke was—be seen as cross-shaped. The same applies to the throne-bases depicted on banners and murals at Dunhuang during the Tibetan occupation.[94] As will be considered in greater detail and illustrated in the next chapter, some of the bodhisattva banners appear to be inspired

88 von Schroeder, *Buddhist Sculptures in Tibet*, 2:729, citing Tucci, *Transhimalaya*, 196.

89 Petech, *Kingdom of Ladakh*, 165.

90 Snellgrove and Skorupski, *Cultural Heritage of Ladakh*, 2:9.

91 Ibid.

92 Luczanits, *Gandhara, the Buddhist Heritage of Pakistan*, no. 291.

93 Ibid., 185; Ghosh, *Fashioning the Divine*, fig. 24.

94 See the throne of Vairocana with eight bodhisattva in Yulin Cave 25, ARTstor MIDA_104473, and the same theme on a banner now in the British Museum OA 1919. 1-1.050, illustrated in Heller, "Early Ninth Century Images of Vairochana," fig. 9.

by Kashmiri-style sculpture if not painting.[95] Kashmiri art was known, however indirectly, at Dunhuang, and could have been encountered there by Tibetans as well. Thus I am reluctant to agree that bases with constricted waists and flaring edges should be considered (central) Tibetan by definition, or that they necessarily are markers of Tibetan involvement. They also appear to be covalent with the stepped type, and there are as well other slight variants in stupa design, introduced below, which suggests that there was not a sole evolutionary path from stepped to cruciform, but that the basic form arrived in Zangskar and Ladakh from the west (i.e., Gandhāra, Kashmir, Gilgit).

Synchronous (and Asynchronous?) Inscriptions and Stupas

There are other possible scenarios for the creation of the inscribed outlined stupas at the Alchi petroglyph reservoir. The stupa-images could have been engraved by locals in Ladakh familiar with contemporary and earlier Kashmiri and Gilgit art, before the Tibetan soldiers came. If the inscriptions were added later, the makers tend to add them beside, above, or underneath the stupas (Fig. 3.27), not at an oblique angle to them as those who added stupas to pre-Buddhist animal motifs did. There are, however, a number of exceptions to this, where the writing does not really share the orientation with the carved stupas, or is squeezed in among them, not laid out as if planned together with the images (Figs. 3.23, 3.28) that could support the asynchrony of stupa and inscription. The patination does not show enough difference between the image and the inscription to suggest a significant lapse of time, though if they were even one or two hundred years apart, with current tools it is impossible to measure repatination so precisely.[96] Thickness or fineness of line also does not register much in the way of suggesting different hands or periods, although the stupa on the left in Figure 3.23 appears to have been added at a different time or by a different hand than the other two. Of course, there are many stupa-carvings without inscriptions.

The functions of the association of personal names early stupas in central South Asia have been plausibly identified by Gregory Schopen through extensive study of donative inscriptions and texts:

> [H]aving one's name carved in stone and permanently placed near a powerful religious "object" must have placed the person there as well, regardless of whether that person was otherwise occupied, absent, or

95 See subsection "The Central Asian Models" and Figures 4.50 and 4.51 of chapter 4.

96 Linrothe, *Seeing into Stone*, 4–6.

Fig. 3.27 Boulder with animal-hunting petroglyph on right (now out of alignment), stupa with staircase and banners in center, Tibetan inscription on the right, at Alchi petroglyph field, Ladakh. Photo 2008

Fig. 3.28 Tibetan inscription near Kashmiri-inspired stupa engraving on boulder in Alchi petroglyph field, Ladakh. Photo 2008.

> what we call dead . . . . precisely the purpose behind the early donative inscriptions at Sāñcī when seen from the point of view of the donor . . . They did not intend to leave a record . . . they wanted only, it seems to leave their presence in proximity to another, more powerful presence.[97]

Even though the purpose might have been to associate a person (not just a name) with the sacred presence as represented by the stupa, it is striking how little explicitly Buddhist terminology or sentiments are expressed in such inscriptions, at least those translated by Orofino and Denwood.[98] One might have expected references to religious gifts, merit making, or *caitya*s such as one frequently finds in inscriptions in central India,[99] or also in some Baltistan inscriptions on rocks or on metalwork.[100] The Alchi Tibetan inscriptions—which generally mention only the name and official title, and occasionally a date such as "in the snake year"—appear to resemble a kind of traveler's graffiti, a point made by Denwood when he considers that they "are essentially graffiti of the type 'So-and-so wrote this.'"[101] Such inscriptions are also frequent in Gilgit and Baltistan.[102] If we at least consider the possibility that the inscriptions were added by Tibetan soldiers after the stupas were created, the names and titles still play an important role. What the inscriptions do is provide a *terminus post quem*: most of the stupas do not postdate the eighth and early ninth centuries, the time when the Tibetan army was camped at Alchi, Khalatse, and

97 Schopen, "What's in a Name," 392.

98 Orofino, "A Note on Some Petroglyphs of the Ladakh Area"; Denwood, "Temple and Rock Inscriptions at Alchi."

99 See, e.g., Schopen, "An Old Inscription from Amarāvatī"; and Efurd, "Early Buddhist Caves of Western India," 870–91.

100 Hinüber, "Brāhmī Inscriptions on the History and Culture of the Upper Indus Valley," 67; Fussman, "Chilas, Hatun et les Bronzes Bouddhiques du Cashemire," 30–47.

101 Denwood, "Rock Inscriptions," 158.

102 Hinüber, "Brāhmī Inscriptions on the History and Culture of the Upper Indus Valley," 44–46.

campaigning in Gilgit-Baltistan. In that case, the stupas must have been done, at the earliest, by the late seventh century, when the inscriptions began to be added, for the inscriptions are fitted around the stupas, not the other way round.

If, on the other hand, we accept that the stupas were done at the same time as the inscriptions, then we would have image-makers among the Tibetan soldiers using what we must accept as Kashmiri-derived stupa forms. These might have been more familiar to them than any other type. At face value this might seem unlikely, but it is by no means implausible. Given the connections established by Denwood between the inscriptions and soldiers employed by the Pugyal dynasty—not necessarily ethnically Tibetan—in Central Asia or during or after their campaigns in Great and Little Bolor,[103] they would have been exposed to Gilgit- and Kashmiri-style stupas (seemingly synonymous) that were also exported into Central Asia. By the same token, based on what little we know of Tibetan art in the eighth and ninth centuries, the Tibetans did not already have a strong tradition of stupa-making of their own. As just indicated, they were still in the process of absorbing examples from eastern India, Nepal, and Central Asia. The Korean monk Hyecho, also known by his Chinese name, Huichao, in his account of his journey to India before 728, accurately points out that Baltistan was then under the rule of the Tibetans, and that the "Tibetans do not follow the Buddhist teachings and there are no monasteries in Tibet."[104] While he did not travel to Tibet, he apparently encountered Tibetans as he traveled from Kashmir to Anxi. Evidence such as this requires us to be cautious in reading the later predominance of Buddhism in Tibet into the seventh and eighth centuries.

Central Tibet's later history makes clear that Buddhism and its art had to be largely re-imported into Tibet starting in the tenth century. In the late seventh century, Yijing, who spent several years in India, specifically includes the Tibetans among the "Pārasas, the Naked People, the Tibetans, and the Turkish tribes [who] have no Buddhist law [i.e., *dharma*]."[105] Some have pointed out the difficulties in dating the stupas in central Tibet: "[D]ue to the lack of good archaeological evidence, the extent of *stūpa*-building during the *snga-dar* [seventh–ninth century] is a matter for speculation,"[106] while what evidence there is suggests reliance on eastern Indian, Nepalese, and other imported models. This is true not only for stupas and other architecture, but for figural sculpture as well. In order

103 Tucci, "On Swāt"; Jettmar, "Paṭolas, Their Governors and Their Successors"; Denwood, "Tibetans in the Western Himalayas and Karakoram"; Denwood, "Tibetans in the West, Part I"; Denwood, "Tibetans in the West, Part II."

104 Vohra, "Ethno-Historicity of the Dards in Ladakh-Baltistan," 540; also translated in Yang et al., *The Hye-Ch'o Diary*, 47, and Lopez, *Hyecho's Journey*, 28. See also Deeg, "Has Huichao Been Back to India?" As Lopez points out, the first monastery in Tibet, Samye, "was not constructed until the late eighth century (perhaps between 775 and 779) . . . Thus, at the time of Hyecho's writing there were no Buddhist monasteries in Tibet." *Hyecho's Journey*, 28.

105 Yijing, *Record of the Buddhist Religion as Practised in India*, 68; Yijing, *Buddhist Monastic Traditions of Southern Asia*, 66.

106 Huber, "Some 11th-Century Indian Buddhist Clay Tablets."

to analyze the style of purported central Tibetan sculptures of the eighth and ninth centuries, Rhie must rely on comparisons to works from as varied and far away as Japan, China, Korea, Persia, and Afghanistan, to Sogdia, Dunhuang, Gandhara, and Mathura, but has no local Tibetan *comparanda.*[107] So while we might legitimately attribute the inscriptions to military personnel employed by the Pugyal dynasty, we should not necessarily attribute the stupa-images to a putative central Tibetan style brought by those soldiers. Rather, the images were already in place in Ladakh before the soldiers were there, or the latter saw and absorbed the Kashmiri-style stupa forms in Central Asia, Gilgit, or Baltistan on their way to Ladakh. Alternatively, a more recent detailed study tentatively concludes that "these rock carvings near Alchi were made by the troop leaders who migrated to Ladakh after the collapse of the Tibetan Empire to establish the first Ladakh kingdom, having been inspired by the regional tradition of rock carvings."[108] In that case, they date between the second half of the ninth century and the eleventh century. This is a telling reminder of the challenges of dating these materials.

Other Early Stupa Types

Low Relief and Non-Standard Types of Stupa-Carvings

The classic Kashmiri-type stupa, which had a relatively long currency in Zangskar, is far from the only type found there. As already indicated, several variants, minor or otherwise, as well as some outliers and oddities are also found.[109] First, more variants: at three different sites in Zangskar, we find stepped bases which flare outward and upward at each level. The stupa-carving at Rinam next to one of the cruciform-base stupas has a rectangular base, and five steps with sharply flaring edges (Fig. 3.29). Three adjacent *caityas* at Khangwar (Tsetang) also have pointed steps, but only four not five of them and those three *caityas* have indications of stairways as well (see Fig. 3.3). Above Manda village, along the sTod river and above a broken, Kashmiri-style standing Maitreya bodhisattva (discussed in chapter 4) is the most exaggerated version of the flaring stepped bases (Fig. 3.30). Four platforms above a T-shaped base are sharply pointed and extend diagonally. Otherwise, the stupa forms are relatively familiar: a small rounded *aṇḍa* and a high *chhattrāvalī* which, though damaged, flares outward before tapering in, resembling the form taken at Mangyu (see Fig. 3.17).

107 Rhie, "Statue of Songzen Gampo in the Potala, Lhasa."

108 Takeuchi, "Old Tibetan Rock Inscriptions near Alchi," 55. Takeuchi transcribes and translates the inscription next to the stupa depicted in Figure 3.27 (his plate 23, text no. 30A) as "/*stong pon zhang 'bar gyis bzheng; Stong-pon* Zhang-'bar erected [this stupa];" ibid., 36. The title "stong-pon," "head of a thousand [men/districts]" is frequently found on these inscriptions. None of the other inscriptions on the Alchi stupas I include in this chapter (Figs. 3.23, 3.28, and 3.47) were illustrated and worked on to my knowledge in the relevant works by textual specialists I have cited including Takeuchi, Denwood, and Orofino.

109 The variety of stupa forms in Zangskar, and several "unusual recurring features," has also been noticed and listed in Devers, *Historical Sites of Zanskar*, 13.

Fig. 3.29 Stupa with upturned, sharp-edged foundation layers engraved on stone at Rinam village, Zangskar. Photo 2006.

Fig. 3.30 Stone engraved stupa with upturned, sharp-edged bases at Manda village, Zangskar. Photo 2010.

Fig. 3.31 One of the Eight Great stupas in a mural painting at Lhakhang Marpo in Tsaparang, Ngari, Tibet. Photo 2005.

Fig. 3.32 Detail of low-relief stupa at Shambhala Gate, Karsha village, Zangskar. Photo 2008.

It is possible that this feature was meant to designate one of the eight stupas, as it apparently does later at the Lhakhang Marpo in Tsaparang (Ngari, Tibet), where one of the eight stupas has pointed corner braces (Fig. 3.31). If, however, the stairs are not yet indicative of the Descent from Heaven miracle, but are generic, as I suggested earlier, then we could consider the stairs less relevant in this case. On the other hand, if the stairs do not indicate one of the types of the eight stupas but the corner flares do, why are two next to each other? I can only leave this question open, and consider the possibility that this was one among a number of acceptable variants in the shapes of the stupa bases. As Niels Gutschow reminds us, "A *caitya* or *stūpa* has never been thought of as ever attaining a final shape. It is rather an object that invites offerings and thus undergoes change as a result of what are considered meritorious acts."[110] What is true for a single example that transforms itself over time, seems also to be true for the type in its protean variety.

So far all of the Zangskari and Ladakhi stupas introduced have been two-dimensional, with outlines carved in stone. At Karsha and at Padum, however, are found low-relief versions of Kashmiri-style *caitya*. At the Shambhala Gate at Karsha village, to the far right in the triangular composition that is discussed in the next chapter (see Fig. 4.65), on the proper left of Mañjuśrī (see Fig. 4.67), is a low-relief sculpture of a stupa (Fig. 3.32) It has the small rounded *aṇḍa* and the tapering superstructure atop a stepped base familiar from the representations seen so far. At Padum, above

110 N. Gutschow, *Architecture of the Newars*, 1:196.

Fig. 3.33 Boulder near government office compound at Padum, Zangskar. Photo 2008.

Fig. 3.34 Stupa low-relief carvings on boulder near government office compound at Padum, Zangskar, detailed view of Fig. 3.33. Photo 2008.

Fig. 3.35 Detail of *aṇḍa* of stupa carved in low relief on boulder near government office compound at Padum, Zangskar, detail of Fig. 3.34. Photo 2008.

the outcrop with figural sculptures discussed in chapter 4 on which the standing bodhisattva is carved (see Fig. 4.56), a large boulder with three-dimensional stupas has been carved on the side facing the old palace to the south (Figs. 3.33–34). The *caitya*s are somewhat recursive, with extra examples, sans *chhattrāvalī* at the base of the largest one, and an additional one as if carved into a niche within the latter's *aṇḍa* (Fig. 3.35). There is a great deal of detail in the large central stupa: one sees the struts supporting the umbrellas (see Fig. 3.35), much as in the plaques at Harwan and Malakhartse Khar (see Figs. 3.13–14). Down the hill toward the river is one of the huge rocks on which a number of carvings are found (see Fig. 4.147), including an overlife-size standing bodhisattva, with simplified but related examples of stupas on either side of his legs and feet (Fig. 3.36). Their bases are of the mild cruciform variety.

On the side of the same huge rock facing the river, are some examples of what appear to be another variant type, again in slightly raised relief, one in which the superstructure is left off (Fig. 3.37). In that case, it may have been because the rock surface was too uneven to accommodate the umbrellas. The stupas seem to emerge on the roiled surface of a nearby boulder just to the south (Fig. 3.38).

Fig. 3.36 Outlined stupas engraved at the feet of figure at the river edge of a large boulder above Lungnak River at Padum, Zangskar. Photo 2008.

Fig. 3.37 Outlined stupas without *chhattras* carved into rock at the river edge of a large boulder above Lungnak River at Padum, Zangskar. Photo 2008.

Fig. 3.38 Multiple stupa carvings in low relief on large boulder near Lungnak River in Padum, Zangskar. Photo 2008.

Those stupas give the impression of being in relief, though actually they are outlined on the stone's uneven surface. The recursiveness of the repetition appears to constitute a variant seen in some concentration in Zangskar, one that features multiples of similarly sized units, or else larger stupas enclosing smaller ones. Both types are visible on boulders near Tahan, close to Tungri Village, on the north bank of the sTod River (Figs. 3.39–40).[111] The similarly crowded, *chhattrāvalī*-less stupas on the ancient stone at Zangla (Figs. 3.7, 3.41) also appear be part of that mode.[112]

Another candidate for an archaic, fifth to tenth-century Kashmiri type of structure is the tower-like stupa. At the Pibiting camp site, there are two examples of stupas in which the steps or layers of the base leading to the *aṇḍa* seem to replace the dome or superstructure (Fig. 3.42). They resemble the simplified stupas found at Chilas,[113] Kinro Kor,[114] and at Alchi bridge.[115] These might be clumsily executed versions of stupas which, like one shown on the Rinam rock, have a very high plinth and stepped platforms (Figs. 3.6, 3.43). What form, if any, the superstructure took is no longer possible to determine because of damage to the rock at that place. The Rinam boulder prominently features three large stupas, each quite different from the other (see Fig. 3.6). Two of them have "cruciform" bases, though in form they are quite different. The one next to the tower-like form has a simple trident or *triśūla* atop the dome (Fig. 3.44); whether that was original, added by some wandering Śaivite ascetic, or as discussed further below, is a Bön signifier, cannot be determined at present.

111 I am indebted to Quentin Devers, who pointed out this petroglyph site to me in 2018.

112 Francke appears to be writing of this rock here: "Near the village of Zangla there is a boulder by the roadside, one side of which is covered all over with pictures of pyramidal chaityas. These pictures are carved in the rock, and the lines are painted with red color"; Francke, *History of Western Tibet*, 24. Devers includes this in his listings; see Devers, *Historical Sites of Zanskar*, 207.

113 Dani, *Human Records on Karakorum Highway*, 36.

114 Khan, "Rock-Carvings at Kinro Kor," fig. 26.

115 Orofino, "Note on Some Petroglyphs of the Ladakh Area," fig. 3.

Fig. 3.39 Multiple stupa engraved on boulder near Tahan village, Zangskar. Photo 2018.

Fig. 3.40 Engraved stupas enclosed within the *aṇḍa* of a larger stupa on boulder near Tahan village, Zangskar. Photo 2018.

Fig. 3.41 Close view of the boulder at Zangla, Zangskar depicted in Fig. 3.7 with multiple stupa outlines engraved in stone. Photo 2001.

Fig. 3.42 Tower-like stupa pecked into stone outcrop at Padum near Pibiting bridge, Zangskar. Photo 2008.

Fig. 3.43 Stupa engraving on boulder at Rinam village, Zangskar. Photo 2006.

Fig. 3.44 Stupa engraving on boulder at Rinam village, Zangskar. Photo 2004.

Fig. 3.45 Stupa engraving on rock at Pipula, Zangskar. Photo 1996.

Ones at Chilas also have similar simplified finials,[116] and they are found at Alchi bridge as well. Other smaller *caitya*s on the same stone at Rinam also have minimal superstructure. If the wide variety in types was intended to suggest the standardized eight stupas, then perhaps the lotus petals on the plinth of the tower-like example (see Fig. 3.43) was intended to suggest the stupa of heaped lotuses referring to the birth of the Buddha in Lumbini garden at Kapilavastu. However, other stupas in Zangskar, including some with clearly indicated stairs, also feature lotus petals on the lower base (see Figs. 3.9, 3.12, 3.21). At any rate, we can suggest that within the acceptable spectrum of stupa depictions between the sixth and ninth centuries in Zangskar, overlapping with but not identical to the period of the Tibetan army's occupation of sites in Ladakh, Gilgit, and Baltistan, a spectrum of recognizable structures served the purpose of Buddhists to affirm the presence of a Buddhist worldview.

At Pipula, on the south bank of the Lungnak River, which I speculated was a hunting camp in pre-Buddhist times to explain the dozens of Neolithic petroglyphs there,[117] is a large, outlined stupa with a tapered *aṇḍa* betraying its relatively late date (ca. 12th c.?) (Fig. 3.45). I will come back to this image for its "fetish" additions, but at the same site is a highly unusual, though not unprecedented, outlined stupa with inscribed letters inside and below the lowest register (Fig. 3.46). Its base is recognizably cruciform, and it resembles the original Darkot carving[118] (see Fig. 3.22). An inscribed petroglyph at Alchi bridge might also be profitably compared (Fig. 3.47). Like the

116 Dani, *Human Records on Karakorum Highway*, 36; Denwood, "Tibetans in the Western Himalayas and Karakoram, Seventh-Eleventh Centuries," fig. 5.

117 Linrothe, *Seeing into Stone*, 13–15.

118 Stein, *Innermost Asia*, fig. 46; Denwood, "Tibetans in the Western Himalayas and Karakoram," fig. 4.

Fig. 3.46 Stupa engraving on rock at Pipula, Zangskar. Photo 2008.

Fig. 3.47 Stupa engraving with Tibetan inscription on boulder at Alchi petroglyph field, Ladakh. Photo 1996.

Rinam *caitya* just discussed (see Fig. 3.44), the superstructure of the Pipula *aṇḍa* (see Fig. 3.46) appears to have been added later; at any rate, it is unusual in that it is composed of two antenna-like arms enclosing a single dot. It may originally have had only the vertical extensions. It also has two lines of faint inscriptions in Tibetan, a "ma" and two "na" letters being readable. Is it possible that Tibetan merchants or militarists traveled through Zangskar between the seventh and ninth centuries, when the Tibetan army forces were also pushing through Ladakh and, via Gilgit, into the Pamirs and Central Asia? Such a proposition is enhanced by an inscription at nearby Char (or Zamthang) *doksa*, discussed next.

At Char *doksa*, where so many animal and hunting petroglyphs remain, there are also a number of Buddhist stupas, as mentioned already (see Figs. 3.1–2). Most were superimposed over the earlier motifs, but at least one example of an isolated *caitya* occurs (Fig. 3.48). On a high rectangular base, with four stepped platforms, a Kashmir-style small round *aṇḍa* supports a high triangular *chhattrāvalī* with faint lines suggesting banners hanging down. Overall it is a type that is simplified but standard throughout a wide region of the western trans-Himalaya. Also at Char *doksa* is a three-word inscription, "li ma bod."[119] Denwood argues that "this follows the pattern of the personal name of a person from Khotan as recorded in Tibetan texts of the early period. *Li* denotes the ethnic or geographical original 'Khotanese', the remaining

119 Denwood and Howard, "Inscriptions at Balukhar and Char Zampa," 85.

Fig. 3.48 Stupa engraving on rock at Char *doksa* (Zamthang), Zangskar. Photo 1998.

syllables (normally two) being the personal name."[120] Again we are confronted by possible Tibetan-script inscribers with Central Asian associations, traveling via Gilgit and Baltistan, where there were important Buddhist traditions, as documented by the Gilgit manuscripts and a fascinating travel itinerary from the mid-tenth century between Central Asia and Kashmir via Gilgit that mentions the many stone *saṅghārāma*s (Buddhist temples, monasteries) in Gilgit.[121] We are reminded that Zangskar continued to participate in the cultural exchanges along both north-south and east-west axes. In this case the cultural center was most likely in Kashmir but with participants in valleys to its north and west (Gilgit, Hunza, Baltistan, Swat), some of whom traveled along river routes to Ladakh, Zangskar, and Central Asia. Increasingly, into this web of contacts were woven Tibetans who voyaged through or settled in these regions between the seventh and ninth century. They seem to begin to supplant the previously dominant cultural mode in the valleys north of Kashmir, the mode that for lack of a better term we can call, loosely, Dardic.

Bön Chortens?

Some of the variants in Zangskar and Ladakh may actually be Bön chortens, not Buddhist stupas. Among the best candidates are those with finials that terminate in tridents or horns. This would include two of the images fom Zangskar just mentioned, the ones at Rinam (see Fig. 3.44) and Pipula (see Fig. 3.46).

120 Ibid.

121 Bailey, "Itinerary in Khotanese Saka."

Fig. 3.49 Bön stupa (?) engraved on stone at Alchi petroglyph field, Ladakh. Photo 2008.

Similar examples can be found at the Alchi bridge, where instead of the tall stack of umbrellas, there is a simplified superstructure of a *yaṣṭi* terminating in a *triśulā* (Fig. 3.49). Several horn-topped stupas are among the ones drawn by Karl Eugen von Ujfalvy in Baltistan in 1880.[122] More have been found in Gilgit and at Gakuch, northwest of Gilgit. Klaus Sagaster has transcribed and where possible translated the Tibetan inscriptions added to them, "charakteristisch fur die fruhe tibetische Orthographie (8.–10. Jh.)."[123] Some of these early inscriptions refer to official titles, again presumed to be those of Pugyal officers or officials occupying this territory. Sagaster has suggested that in a few cases inscriptions accompanying trident-topped chortens are Bön mantras.[124] This type of finial has also been identified with Bön chorten: "All Bon chorten can be immediately distinguished from the Buddhist *stūpa* by a representation of a set of horned eagle horns that are placed on the top, sometimes resembling an upright trident."[125] In Bön images the *khyung* or eagle-like Garuda plays a significant role, and a petroglyph at Alchi with an eagle or falcon with wings outspread at the top of a conventional mast (Fig. 3.50) certainly lends support to the idea that at least some of these stupas were made, or later claimed, by Bönpos. I suggest the possibility of a later appropriation because in at least two cases (see Figs. 3.44, 3.46), the Bön-type finials appear to have been added subsequent to the rest. They might, however, have later merely been emphasized or scored more deeply rather than newly added, since except in the case of the bird finial, there was no other finial above the *aṇḍa*. This type of finial seems to be a

122 Ujfalvy, *Aus dem Westlichen Himalaja*, fig. xviii.

123 Jettmar, Sagaster, and Dagyab, "Ein Tibetisches Heiligtum in Punyal," 130.

124 Ibid., 129–30.

125 Watt, "Introduction to Bon Art," 34. Gendun Chopel refers briefly and somewhat cryptically to Buddhist stupas being "related in many ways to the Bön custom of placing a white sphere between two yak horns at the top of a tiered castle;" Chopel, *Grains of Gold*, 75. Such a configuration resembles the finial of Figure 3.46.

Fig. 3.50 Bön stupa (?) with eagle-shaped finial engraved on stone at Alchi petroglyph field, Ladakh. Photo 2008.

Fig. 3.51 Bön stupa (?) engraved on large boulder at Trangtse, Ladakh. Photo 2008.

relatively consistent characteristic of those we might need to consider Bön, particularly in light of the claims by Bön practitioners and others that the Zhangzhung state included much of the western Himalaya, as discussed in chapter 1.

One hundred and twenty drawings of Bön stupas published in 1998 are all examples that relate closely to contemporary Tibetan stupas, rather than the archaic ones found in petroglyphs far from central Tibet.[126] However, a sizable majority features a pair of horns at the top enclosing a flaming pearl. The author, Namdak Tsukphu (rnam dag gtsug phud), makes clear that they function in a similar manner to the Buddhist ones:

> Whosoever builds a stupa . . . earns a great amount of merit, a positive potential for destroying negativities. The merit earned by virtue of building stupas is extra-ordinarily powerful and can purify even the deadly sins. Therefore, building stupas is an essential part in the religious life of the Bonpos.[127]

At Trangtse in eastern Ladakh, a highly eccentric structure is outlined in stone in the same area as other pre-Buddhist and Buddhist forms along with Sogdian inscriptions (Fig. 3.51). The base and drum are as peculiar as the finial. Once again, the *chhattrāvalī* above the *aṇḍa* consists solely of a *yaṣṭi* terminating in a *triśulā*. Most unusual is the crossbar beneath it with two more such tridents, resembling a weathervane. These images are remarkable in every sense, although a precise understanding of the circumstances of Bön adherents leaving petroglyphs of chortens in Zangskar, Ladakh, and far western Gilgit still eludes us. Should they be

126 Namdak Tsukphu, *mChod rten gyi dpe ris blo gsar mgul rgyan bzhugs.*

127 Ibid., x.

accounted for by assuming Bön soldiers were among the Pugyal army units stationed in Ladakh and Gilgit during the imperial-period occupation? Were the members of the former Zhangzhung military units recruited after the defeat of that western Tibetan kingdom in the seventh century and then sent into Central Asia and the regions north of Kashmir? Or do these Bön artifacts (if that is what they are) predate the Pugyal dynasty's destruction of the state, as discussed in chapter 1?

Regardless, these intriguing hints of a palpable Bön presence raise important questions about their relationship to—or even identity with—settled or transient populations in Zangskar and other areas of Ladakh. Eventually, after further study, these unusual forms might help provide firmer dates for the more standard Buddhist stupas alongside them.

"Fetishes" or Indexical Relics?

In Zangskar, at Pipula, Khangwar (Tsetang), and Rantaksha there are examples of stupa-carvings with one or three dots added within the *aṇḍa* or above the *chhattrāvalī*. In the Pipula "Bön chorten" discussed above (see Fig. 3.46), the horns of the two-horned eagle embrace a single dot. This is known in Bön belief as the *thig le*, which approximates the Sanskrit term *bindu*. Snellgrove glosses it as "dot, seed, vital fluid (viz. semen virile), drop (of semen), essence,"[128] and the ca. fourteenth-century text he translates, known by its abbreviated title of the *gZi brjid*, describes it as follows:

> This precious thing, the Thought of Enlightenment
> the state of primeval Buddhahood,
> the essence of knowledge in its natural state,
> the absolute purity of the unconditioned . . .
> Divided into its separate distinctions,
> it spreads out into 84,000 parts,
> but in its compressed form it becomes a single dot.[129]

It is tempting to read the finial at the very top of the main low-relief stupa on the boulder at Padum (see Figs. 3.33, 3.34, 3.52) as an eagle topped by such a *thig le*. However, it could also be interpreted as a crescent moon and a solar symbol.

That Bön and Buddhist texts share many ideas and terms is well known. One expects that the Buddhist use of such imagery is not radically different from that of the Bön—and vice versa. Buddhists in western

128 Snellgrove, *Nine Ways of Bon*, 298.

129 Ibid., 227–29.

Fig. 3.52 Finial of main stupa in low relief on boulder near government office compound at Padum, Zangskar. Photo 2008.

Himalaya also place a single dot above the *chhattrāvalī* in some cases, as at Rantaksha (see Fig. 3.21). One also finds an example on the right-hand stupa in the photograph of Khangwar (Tsetang), at the top of the stack of umbrellas, directly below the uppermost finial (Fig. 3.53). More frequent is the placement of a single *bindu* within the *aṇḍa* which appears on stupa-carvings at Chilas.[130] More common still in Zangskar is that the single *bindu* within the *aṇḍa* take the shape of a *triratna*, the three dots standing for the three jewels of the Buddha, the Dharma, and the Saṅgha. That is found on both the *caitya*s documented at Khangwar (Tsetang) (see Fig. 3.53) even though they have been scored so deeply into the stone they almost look like a single divot. At Pipula, however, the triple-dot motif just below the *harmikā* is clearly visible on a stupa which in 1996 was standing upright but now has been knocked over (Figs. 3.45, 3.54).

Ebert, following Dani, calls the round dots usually placed within the *aṇḍa* as the "cupola fetish." She feels it "seems to indicate a special religious connotation whose meaning is difficult to grasp."[131] I propose, however, that it is meant to indicate the presence (symbolic or metaphorical) of relics which animate the stupa. As already discussed, such relics are implied by all stupas because of their association with the Buddha. The *triratna* symbolism is particularly apropos in this regard, since it references the Buddha and the Dharma, interchangeable as the most esteemed of relics.

130 Ebert, "Niches, Columns, and Figures," pls. 4, 7b, 8.

131 Ibid., 271.

Fig. 3.53 Stupa with staircases engraved on stone outcrop at Tsetang (sKhangwar), Zangskar. Photo 1998.

Fig. 3.54 Outlined stupa engraving on stone at Pipula, Zangskar, same carving as in Fig. 3.45. Photo 2008.

Fig. 3.55 Remains of walls of shrine-retreat locally known as Chang Gonpa directly in front of rock-painting site above Karsha village, Zangskar; view facing northwest. Photo 2018.

The Early Stupa Rock Paintings in Zangskar

In 1998 Karsha Lonpo's second son, Lama Angchug, guided me above Karsha Chuchikzhal, about an hour and a half up the mountain at its rear (west, slightly south).[132] A boyhood friend of his grazed the village sheep there and recalled seeing rock paintings. I have since been a few more times, most recently in 2018 when Victoria Andrews and I disturbed a brown bear with a cub who had taken up residence in that lonely spot. After roaring most frighteningly at us as we labored up the mountainside, she fortunately ran up and away from us, her agile cub following close behind. In front of the steep cliff are the ruins of walls with courses of stone foundations below mud bricks (Fig. 3.55). The building in front of the shallow cave is perched on a promontory with a view of the *prayag* (meeting) of the two tributaries of the Zangskar River. Quentin Devers, whose expertise on buildings and fortifications in the western Himalaya is unmatched, describes it as a "temple ruin and meditation cave."[133] Julia Shaw has observed a pattern of "monastic rock-shelters" at Sanchi and surrounding sites. "These consist of prehistoric rock-shelters showing signs of adaptation for monastic use . . . [with] Buddhist paintings/inscriptions on their walls, or nearby stūpas."[134] That fits the case here quite well. The rock shelter is in the form of a shallow cave, open to the east (Fig. 3.56). From the back of the rock comes a meager dribble of precious water, probably seasonal but enough at times to sustain a few inhabitants. Ibex also take shelter there, probably in the winter when they come down to avoid the deep snow and the wind. The ground in front of the cliff wall was covered with pellets of dung that my local companions identified as

132 Discussed in Linrothe, "A Summer in the Field," 60–61 and figs. 5–6. Kim Gutschow also accompanied us. Quentin Devers includes them as nos. 96 and 97 in his survey of historical sites in Zangskar; Devers, *Historical Sites of Zanskar*, 126, 132, 133. He dates the structure and the paintings between the eighth and the thirteenth century.

133 Devers, *Historical Sites of Zanskar*, 126.

134 Shaw, "Stūpas, Monasteries, and Relics in the Landscape," 124.

Fig. 3.56 Rock shelter with paintings of stupas, above Karsha village, Zangskar. Photo 1998.

that of ibex. Locally, this place is called the Cha (bya) or Chang (byang) Gonpa, the northern shrine.[135]

On one relatively smooth and continuous register of what is otherwise uneven rock are paintings of stupas (Fig. 3.57). They are monochromatic in a thick, ochre red, probably a local mineral pigment. Sections of the mountains above nearby Pishu Village are still harvested by villagers from a wide region for their red pigment properties, often used to paint the *lhato* [lha tho] or spirit-shrines of certain fearful mountain deities. The painting appears to be executed onto a prepared white (lime plaster?) ground, though in many places that has washed away. The largest painted *caitya*s are more than sixteen inches tall and number about forty in all.[136] To the right of the stupas are some large Tibetan letters, in reserve against the bluish stone, spelling out "Oṃ mani padme hum."

It is likely that there were eight stupas in a row at one time, although the ones on the left side are damaged by the exposed, friable rock. A few stray *caitya*s are outlined somewhat randomly on other surfaces of the cliff side, but this is the largest concentration of paintings. It is important to observe that each of the four nearly complete images is distinctly different from the others. If these were intended to depict the eight great stupas, as at first seems likely, then it is possible to suggest that the first on the right is the Heaped Lotuses stupa associated with the birth of the Buddha, and the

135 Another variant is Chyadral (bya bral, "ascetic") Gonpa; personal communication, Karsha Lonpo and Lama Angchug, 3 August 1998. Devers understands it to be "Chha Gonpa." Devers, *Historical Sites of Zanskar*, 128. The Lonpo told me that the eleventh-century teacher Zangskar Lotsava is believed to have meditated or lived in the Chang Gompa cave; personal communication, 8 July 2018.

136 Devers, *Historical Sites of Zanskar*, 126.

Fig. 3.57 Paintings of stupas at rock shelter above Karsha village, Zangskar. Photo 2018.

second from the right is the Descent from Heaven stupa since it alone has the prominent staircase. The third from the right might represent either the Parinirvāṇa or the Enlightenment. The others are not distinguished by individualized features, and thus might reflect the ambiguity during the early stages of the standardization of the eight great stupas. As Pakhoutova has argued, the "various types of bases were not formalized as a set and, it appears, became clearly differentiated as the eight types of various stūpas only around the end of the twelfth-or-thirteenth century."[137] Until that date, identifying the individual stupas in the set of eight is fraught with difficulties.

The first and third from the right have the so-called cruciform or "cross-shaped" base. They all have distinctly rounded, bulbous *aṇḍa*s, in some cases quite small. The *chhattrāvalī* are wide and tall, and the second one has long banners hanging down at the sides. In other words, these all correspond quite well to the types of three-dimensional reliquaries, painted versions, and outlined on stone, found in Zangskar, Ladakh, Baltistan, Gilgit, and Kashmir. The major differences between those examined so far are twofold. First, of course, is the medium of painting. I know of very few paintings on stone of this age in either Ladakh or Zangskar.[138] The only other ones I have seen are also monochrome in red, mostly enhancing outlined images of Buddhas and bodhisattvas on the rock outcrop near the

137 Pakhoutova, "Reproducing the Sacred Places," 56.

138 Devers has located a meditation cave (a shallow rock shelter) in Tibuk in far southwestern Zangskar with a related painted-outline stupa. Devers, *Historical Sites of Zanskar*, 37, 50.

Fig. 3.58 Painting of a Kashmiri-style stupa with "cruciform base" painted on boulder north of Padum near Lungnak River's west bank, Zangskar. Photo 2012.

Lungnak river at Padum but also including a painting of a similarly cruciform-base stupa (Fig. 3.58). Otherwise, the paintings in the rock shelter are singular in my experience of Zangskar.

The other crucial difference between this set of paintings and the many individual or clusters of scratched or carved stone stupa-outlines has to do with the presumed makers of their respective types. Most of the other stone carvings can be assumed to have been made, with few exceptions, by either travelers or monk- or lay-dwellers passing along trade or grazing routes at fords or springs. They do not help establish or signify a monastic retreat so much as instantiate into the landscape a reminder of the Buddha teachings which, as Yijing states (quoted above), was appropriate for monastics and laity to execute.[139] By contrast, the remoteness of the site of these paintings above Karsha, relatively far from those routes or larger locales of lay habitation, strongly suggests that they were made by Buddhist specialists. In fact, they must have been made by members of a tiny community of Buddhist recluses, if not solitary hermits or yogins. The fact that they were renunciants with the ability to read or recite Buddhist narratives of the life of the Buddha accounts for their more advanced knowledge of different stupa types with associations to events in the Buddha's life and his miracles. The intended audience, not just the makers, was also significantly distinct. These are not the large, eye-catching carvings at Padum or Shambhala sGo, meant for lay-villagers—among others—nor the outlined stupas presumably

139 The exception might be the rocks at Padum with a pair or more of caves underneath them. Francke presumes that they are "the last remnants of an ancient monastery," evidence for which he cites the niches for beams to support a façade on the rock above. Francke, *History of Western Tibet*, 23. This remains questionable. The current Padum king, Phuntsok Dawa, told me in 2008 while showing me the caves that he thought an early Lotsava (translator of Sanskrit Buddhist texts into Tibetan) lived there, but also that people with contagious diseases were forced to live there in the past. He said that in one of the caves a lot of bones that are believed to be human had been found. Personal communication, 24 July 2008. On the other hand, nearby is the only other early site with rock paintings, the ones referred to above.

Fig. 3.59 Ruins of a monastery (at center) on the hillside south of Chang Gonpa, southwest of Karsha village, Zangskar. Photo 2003.

Fig. 3.60 Detail of ruined monastic structures south of Chang Gonpa, Zangskar. Photo 2003.

intended for travelers at fords or camps. They are relatively small, executed with an erudite finesse, placed well off the beaten track, and intended for the incumbents of the retreat.

Just to the south and down below it, still on the hillside above Karsha village and visible from the promontory at Chang Gonpa, is a much more extensive monastic ruin called Gonmoche (dgon mo che) **(Figs. 3.59–60)**.[140] There are partially collapsed walls of shrines, three-dimensional stupas, and *vihāra*-enclosures, presumably living quarters for monks. The structures might have been built around the same time or later than the Cha(ng) Gonpa, and perhaps the monks at Gonmoche went into meditation retreat at the upper site. On the evidence of the style of the rock paintings, they may be as early as the sixth or seventh century, and have little or nothing to do with Tibet or Tibetan art. Once again, the orientation is not so much toward Tibet as toward the Buddhism of the Kashmir-Gilgit area, which we know was thriving from the Kusāṇa period onward, at least until the twelfth century.

There are very few rock paintings (as opposed to rock carvings) known in Baltistan, Gilgit, and Swat as well. At Kafir-kot in Swat, some appear on a "shallow semi-circular cavity about 1.50 m in depth by the same height . . . . The images are painted with a red pigment."[141] A number of figures, including archers holding bows, are mixed with stupas, some of which have

140 Devers was apparently informed that its name is the "Gonbo Che Lhakhang." *Historical Sites of Zanskar*, 125.

141 N. Khan et al., "Recent Discovery of Cave Paintings in Swat," 335–36.

Fig. 3.61 Drawing of paintings on rock at Chaghdo, Baltistan, Pakistan. After Khan, "Chaghdo Rock Paintings, Baltistan, Northern Areas," fig. 1.

Fig. 3.62 Two stupas painted at rock shelter above Karsha village, Zangskar. Photo 2018.

garlands or banners hanging from them. The red pigment was analyzed and determined to "very probably" be ochreous hematite (Fe_2O_3).[142] A date of "between the 1st and 4th century A.D." is proposed for these images, and the clear stylistic linkage with images from the Upper Indus are pointed out.[143]

A more sophisticated painted composition, complete with fourteen male and female sponsor figures kneeling, has been discovered in Baltistan at the site of Chaghdo.[144] It is much closer to Ladakh and Zangskar than Swat (Fig. 3.61). It is along the Indus river, east of Skardu.[145] As Tucci pointed out:

> one of the still unknown centres [of Buddhism] was certainly Skardo, where there are huge rock reliefs; the extension of suzerainty of Tibet upon Baltistan may have facilitated the diffusion of Buddhist art, and given impulse to local artistic schools . . . many bronzes may have been carried into Ladak, Baltistan, Gilgit by travelling monks.[146]

In the Chaghdo painting, the three stupas beneath which the lay-figures stand and kneel (see Fig. 3.61) resemble those of the Karsha rock paintings (Fig. 3.62) to a remarkable degree, and also include a Descent-type stupa—at any rate, one with a staircase on the base—between two stupas with rounded *aṇḍas* supported by bases with indented waists. If anything, the Karsha rock paintings are more archaic, as they lack the ornamental band encircling the width of the *aṇḍas* of the two outer stupas at Chaghdo, a feature seen in some later *caitya* at the Alchi Dukhang and Sumtsek[147] and also visible in Figures 3.17 and 3.18. The Chaghdo males with turban-like headdresses and the women with capes—again resembling some early donors at Alchi who emulate Sogdian, Persian, Turkic, or Ghaznavite court culture[148]—will be discussed in chapter 4. Two red pigments, a dark and an ocher color, have been observed in use at the Chaghdo site.

142 Ibid., 345. As Mary Gladue informed me, ochreous hematite is the same as ferric oxide.

143 N. Khan et al., "Recent Discovery of Cave Paintings in Swat," 350.

144 M. Khan, "Chaghdo Rock Paintings." Unfortunately, no photograph, only the drawing, by an unidentified hand, was included in the article.

145 See map in Hauptmann, "Pre-Islamic Heritage in the Northern Areas of Pakistan," 22.

146 Tucci, "On Swāt," 103.

147 Goepper, *Alchi*, pl. 29; Goepper and Poncar, *Alchi*, 85, 143.

148 See the discussion of this version of "cultural cross-dressing" in Flood, *Objects of Translation*, 65–75.

The composition is once again on a rock shelter rather than on the interior of a cave. Khan dates the scene very roughly to between the eighth and the turn of the fifteenth century,[149] but Hauptmann considers that it represents the "'Golden Era of Buddhism' [in Gilgit and Baltistan] between the eighth and tenth centuries."[150] Hauptmann, however, identifies these stupas as "of Tibetan style" which is patently implausible, as there was no "Tibetan style" of stupas in the eighth century, and the specific structure has already been shown to closely resemble those associated with Kashmir, not Tibet. Given the resemblance of the Karsha rock paintings to those early ones of Swat on the one hand, and to ca. eighth- or ninth-century Chaghdo paintings on the other, this helps to reinforce the dating of the Karsha paintings to the sixth or seventh century, though possibly as early as the fifth or as late as the tenth.

The many stupa representations, painted on, pecked into, and engraved onto stone, in Zangskar, Ladakh, Baltistan, and Gilgit suggest a stupa-focused cult of sorts—as there was in early Buddhism in subcontinental India—during the second half of the first millennium CE. Presumably, that would include the period when the famous Gilgit manuscripts were enclosed within painted wooden covers and buried in a stupa, although some of the manuscripts go back earlier. Tsuchiya Haruko located the findspot of the Gilgit manuscripts at Naupur (just upriver from Gilgit) and notes that they were found on a ridge with four stupas, one of which, it is argued, was carefully prepared to house the chest in which the Gilgit manuscripts were found.[151] Tsuchiya suggests that the stupa in question was constructed in such a way as to resonate with chapter 10 of the *Saddharma-puṇḍarīka* (Lotus) *Sūtra*, a copy of which was included among the manuscripts discovered, datable to the sixth century. Within that text, "the stupa is emphasized as a chaitya hall for worship of sutra, and sacred manuscripts were to be housed within the stupa to be worshipped."[152] Certainly it suggests a very active Buddhist community there, along the Gilgit River, upstream of the *prayag* with the Hunza river, which in turn flows into the Indus, its current running south and then east where the many images between Chilas and Shatial that are documented by Jettmar, Dani, Hauptmann, and others were produced. Tibetans were much more likely to have been *exposed* to the specific forms of the stupas in this area than to have brought them with them when they started mobilizing into southern Central Asia in the eighth and ninth centuries.

149 M. Khan, "Chaghdo Rock Paintings," 103.

150 Hauptmann, "Pre-Islamic Heritage in the Northern Areas of Pakistan," 35.

151 On a review of the art-historical and archaeological data related to the finding of the Gilgit manuscripts and their painted covers, see Linrothe et al., *Collecting Paradise*, 39–54.

152 Tsuchiya, "Preliminary Report [I]," 34.

Dating, Historical Considerations, and Introduction to Early Buddhist Sculpture in Zangskar

The dating of early Buddhist art of Zangskar is fortunately not as open-ended or challenging as the region's pre-Buddhist petroglyphs.[153] Yet it is still not as straightforward as one would wish. It has been necessary to deal with this topic in each section of the present chapter in the course of examining stupa engravings. It will also be necessary in the next chapter (chapter 4) in considering early figural sculptures. In certain cases, iconography and formal qualities can assist in the assigning of dates. For example, once the *kha che lugs*, or the Kashmiri-inspired mode, appears in Zangskar and Ladakh (the subject of chapter 5), we can usually date the images to the ca. tenth century and after. One of the complications is that the poor quality of some local productions makes them hard to place. Related is the lack of recognizable formal characteristics, disguised in some cases by the mixing of features from different formal idioms, and compounded by the still sparse knowledge of the early-period relations maintained by inhabitants of Zangskar (and Ladakh) with their neighbors. Furthermore, the early Buddhist art of neighboring regions such as Baltistan and Gilgit also reflect idiomatic formal mixtures, with elements of Gandharan, Kashmiri, and even post-Gupta visual qualities. Goetz testifies to "a provincial Gupta tradition still alive in Kashmīr" in the eighth century.[154] The dates proposed here then are admittedly provisional, less than secure.

Given the complicated interwoven history, there does not appear to be a single evolutionary path to follow. By contrast to well-marked links to western, northern, and southern neighboring cultures, there is little evidence of Tibetans in these areas of western Himalaya until the late seventh or early eighth century. Even then, visible traces of Buddhism do not reflect Tibetan characteristics. Only beginning in the eighth century, was Ladakh to a greater or lesser extent and for a longer or shorter period, incorporated into the empire of the Pugyal dynasty,[155] or at any rate was occupied by its army—beginning sometime between the mid-seventh century and 721, but mainly the second half of the eighth century until around 842, when the dynasty collapsed.[156] According to Tibet's own legendary histories, Buddhism was introduced into the Pugyal court in the seventh century. Despite the best efforts of Indian monks and wizards, a majority of the Tibetan people did not become Buddhist until the tenth and eleventh centuries.

153 Linrothe, *Seeing into Stone*, 81–93.

154 Goetz, "Beginnings of Medieval Art in Kashmir," 53.

155 Bray, introduction to Bray, *Ladakhi Histories*, 4–5.

156 Orofino, "Note on Some Petroglyphs of the Ladakh Area," 176–77.

Fig. 3.63 "Kanika Chorten" at Sani Gonpa, Zangskar. Photo 2004.

That is when the stimulus of the western Himalaya on central Tibet (and not the other way around) was at its height, during the so-called Chyidar (phyi dar) period, or later dissemination (of Buddhism).

Yet the absence of evidence of interactions with Tibetan culture did not mean a dearth of opportunities for the inhabitants of Zangskar and Ladakh to have contacts with Buddhist missionaries, practitioners, or Buddhist visual traditions. Lower Ladakh—including Khalatse and downstream of it along the Indus where Kharoṣṭhī inscriptions have been found (among them one mentioning Vema Kadphises)—may actually have formed a part of the Kuṣāṇa empire for a period of time after the first or second century CE.[157] While there is no contemporary evidence proving the seventh-century legends that four Aśokan stupas were built in Kashmir, by the Kuṣāṇa period, Buddhism was flourishing there.[158] In Zangskar, "Sani is traditionally associated with the time of the Kuṣāṇa King Kaniska I" of the ca. early second century CE.[159] While Luczanits remains agnostic on whether Buddhism reached Ladakh during the Kushana period, he feels the "chörten at Sani, as it stands today, certainly does not support this claim."[160] I am also very hesitant to uncritically accept local traditions as historical actualities. However, there is no question that the dome of the Sani stupa (Fig. 3.63) preserves an unusually rounded shape that is more consistent with Kushana reliquaries and stupas[161] than it is with those of either later Kashmiri or Tibet. Even the sixth–seventh-century stupa from Bodhgaya (see Fig. 3.20) is a closer match.

157 Petech, *Kingdom of Ladakh*, 6–7; Bray, introduction to Bray, *Ladakhi Histories*, 6.

158 Lamotte, *History of Indian Buddhism*, 255–56, 299.

159 Luczanits, "Early Buddhist Heritage of Ladakh Reconsidered," 66.

160 Ibid.; also Snellgrove, "Buddhism in North India and the Western Himalayas," 66.

161 Luczanits, *Gandhara, the Buddhist Heritage of Pakistan*, 122; Yaldiz et al., *Magische Götterwelten*, 52.

Quentin Devers has recently found tentative evidence for early Buddhism of the pre-tenth-century period at Tarungtse village near Sani and ingeniously argues the following:

> Whether Kanishka actually built this [Sani] stupa is of little concern, the main element [of my argument] being that the stupa would have predated the Western Tibetan annexation [of Zangskar in the ca. 10th c.] and would have [originally] been from a different tradition of Buddhism. For Ladakhis [and Zangskaris], Kanishka was probably to be understood as eponymous for whatever happened before Zanskar came under Tibetan rule.[162]

Kashmir may be said to have exerted its strongest imperial and Buddhist influence in all directions during the reign of Lalitaditya (ca. 725–760), at the same time that the Tibetans were expanding, temporarily, into Ladakh, Baltistan, and Gilgit. Precisely then, however, an even stronger rival to the Kashmiri kingdom, that of Kānyakubja under the Yaśovarman (ca. 725–754), was expanding the control of Himalayan border regions all the way to Kangra and the southeastern frontiers of Kashmir, as argued by Michael Meister.[163] There were and are a number of routes into Zangskar from Kangra into Chamba and from there over the Omasi La into Padum, or from Chamba into Lahul and over the Shingo or Zangskar passes into Zangskar. From the perspective of Zangskar then, Kangra, Chamba, Kulu, and Lahul were actually much closer than Gilgit, so it should not surprise us if there were connections between the art of Zangskar and Ladakh not only with Kashmir, Gilgit, and Baltistan to the west and north, but also to sites to the south, along the borderlands of the Himalayas.

Unfortunately, the textual or inscriptional evidence for interactions with representatives of Gupta and post-Gupta Buddhism, apart from Kuṣāṇa and Kashmiri Buddhism, is very tenuous. That makes the visual evidence—which is much more extensive—all the more important. It is on this basis, along with parallel evidence including the textual in neighboring areas, that we can indulge in educated speculation. In the not-too-distant region of Hunza to the northwest, for example, Brahmi inscriptions of the fifth century have been documented. In them, local rulers claim affiliation with the Guptas or else deputed Gupta officials celebrate victories and establish religious monuments.[164] They suggest that trade and missionary routes between Indian and Central Asia were kept open at this period, with branches continuing to incorporate Ladakh and Zangskar.

162 Devers, "Buddhism before the First Diffusion?," 23.

163 Meister, "Mountain Temples and Temple-Mountains."

164 Verma, "Chandra Śrī Deva Kikramāditya of the Sacred Rock of Hunza," 109–31.

As the ca. ninth-century inscriptions left by Sogdians in Ladakh document, these inveterate traders carried out long-distance trade through the western Himalaya, probably by following the upper Indus along networks connecting India, China, and Sogdiana.[165] Thus, there is every reason to expect that there were contacts with Kushan and even Gupta Buddhists, as well with merchants and travelers to and from Central Asian sites such as Bamiyan and Khotan or even Kizil and Dunhuang between the third and the sixth centuries. Subsequent to that, Buddhists on the periphery of Pāla, Sena, and successor states to the south and east of Zangskar may have also played a mediating role. Such contacts might have stimulated, converted, or inspired a number of Buddhists within Zangskar and Ladakh, and help to explain the look of images that visually and iconographically are neither particularly Tibetan, Nepalese, nor Kashmiri. When we see anomalous images that are difficult to square with well-attested Kashmiri (much less Tibetan) art, we need to be open to the possibility that they reflect exposure to imagery and artists coming from northern India, either directly from the south via Lahul, or through the Indus, Dras, and Suru valleys.

The most important point is to acknowledge a diversity of sources and orientations. Contemporary Zangskaris, Ladakhis, and their historians are generally wedded to either a Tibetan or an Islamic emphasis, often depending on expertise in the relevant textual sources. This is true despite the lessons of nineteenth- and twentieth-century local experience not of isolation but of well-established, even routine connections with adjacent cultures. Among pertinent examples, Muslim traders were entrusted with the obligatory triennial tribute (imposed after the seventeenth-century war with Tibet) to the Lhasa government by Ladakhi authorities (the *lo phyag* missions). Along with bringing gifts to the Dalai Lama from western Himalayan monasteries, they were accompanied by novices and young clerics eager for advanced Buddhist teachings in central Tibet.[166] Economic, political and cultural networks with Central Asia remained strong until 1950.[167] Zangskari migrant labor went regularly to Kulu-Manali for work, even those from the high-status families.[168] Hindu Mahārājas at times employed British viziers to oversee Dogra interests in Leh.[169] Nineteenth- and twentieth-century Ladakh was hardly more *uniformly* "Tibetan" in culture than it had been in the seventh century. The reductive notion found even in works that emphasize the importance of Kashmir or Central Asia, embedded in statements like "culturally it [Ladakh] has always been dominated by Tibetan civilization"[170] or "After the establishment of

165 Neelis, *Early Buddhist Transmission and Trade Networks*, 270–71.

166 Radhu, *Tibetan Caravans*, 7.

167 Fewkes and A. Khan, "Social Networks and Transnational Trade"; Warikoo, "Political Linkages between Ladakh and Eastern Turkestan"; Sheikh, *Reflections on Ladakh*, 101–12.

168 Rizvi, "Trade and Migrant Labour."

169 Examples are Frederick Drew and William Johnson. Sheikh, "Economic Condition in Ladakh," 344.

170 Pal, "Kashmir and the Tibetan Connection," 59.

Tibetan Buddhism in the area, i.e. 8th Century A.D. onwards"[171] need to be resisted. As was argued in chapter 1, such notions have deep roots. Despite his vantage point and perspective gained from extended time in Leh—or perhaps because of it—Moorcroft, writing in the early nineteenth century, declares that the "earlier history of Ladakh is that of Tibet in general."[172] Long-standing as it may be, it is still a subtle assumption that tends to be reinforced, then and now, by a contemporary allegiance to Buddhism and Tibet as fundamental to Ladakhi and Zangskari culture, as discussed in chapter 1. It seeps almost unconsciously into the discourse, even, for example, into the analysis of two Buddhist organizations in the Indian Himalayas founded in the twentieth century, the origins of which are in Ladakh and Zangskar.[173] In an otherwise insightful ethnography of their founders, Thierry Dodin, referring to the populations of those regions, writes:

> The southern slopes of the Himalayas have been populated predominantly by ethnic groups *linguistically and culturally related to the Tibetans since the prehistoric.* Although historically the greatest part of the region remained outside the centralized Tibetan state, which emerged in the 7th century, its inhabitants were subject to the *strong influence of Tibetan Buddhism at an early point in time.*[174]

No doubt that is true to a considerable extent, and increased over time. However, rather than a unilinear model of cultural development springing *from* Tibet, a diversity of sources for Buddhism, including several prior to the gradual (and never absolute) Tibetanization of culture must be entertained. That is exactly what is demonstrated by the early stupa forms examined in this chapter. It is also manifested by the roughly contemporary figural sculpture considered in chapter 4. A variety of ethnic origins, including the so-called Dards associated with the regions northwest of Zangskar and Ladakh, and the "Mons" associated with the Indian regions to the south, must be accommodated, as well as Tibetans. So too, as discussed in *Seeing into Stone*,[175] Zangskar's early economy was analogously multiple, even within typical households that entwined agriculture with herding and pastoralism, along with trade and hunting. The sources of Buddhism and its forms follow such multiple directions. As Bray rightly points out, Ladakh did not solely look "east to Tibet, but also north to Eastern Turkestan (Xinjiang), south to the plains of India and west to the regions that are now the Northern Areas of Pakistan."[176] Yet against the backdrop of contemporary politics, in which Muslims and Buddhists see

171 Fonia, "Ladakh Corridor to Central Asia," 39n1.

172 Wilson, *Travels in the Himalayan Provinces*, 336.

173 The two organizations are the All India Frontier Buddhist Mahasabha and the Himalayan Buddhist Cultural Association.

174 Dodin, "Transregional Buddhist Organizations in Indian Himalayas," 189 (emphasis added).

175 Linrothe, *Seeing into Stone*, 92–93.

176 Bray, introduction to Bray, *Ladakhi Histories*, 3.

themselves as rivals for resources, too often the other ethnic, cultural, and linguistic roots and dimensions are minimized, forgotten, or exoticized, as with the "colorful" Drokpa (Dards) of Da-Hanu.

This, then, is the subject of chapter 4, which applies the insights and arguments of chapter 1 and the findings of this chapter to the diversity of artistic sources and connections we find in the early Buddhist period, following from its geographical connections to the various cultural formations surrounding it. Building and expanding on the sources analyzed in this chapter for stupas, it focuses instead on early figural Buddhist sculpture.

Fig. 3.64 "Kanika Chorten" at Sani Gonpa, Zangskar, detail of the dome. Photo 2022.

Coda

A fitting addendum to chapter 3 is the introduction through description of an elaborate engraved stupa on a flat boulder with a chocolate-colored patina in Ramala village, Zangskar (Figs. 3.65–70). The composition reaches significant proportions and reflects even greater ambition. It is one of the most involved rock-cut stupas in Zangskar if not the western Himalaya as a whole.[177] The ornate central stupa is more than a meter and a half in height[178] with flying *deva*s above it and complemented with elements of a landscape setting, flora, and fauna. Several of the features discussed in chapter 3 and singled out as distinctive traits of Zangskar treatments of stupas appear on this intricate example. Note-worthy characteristics include the staircase bifurcating the four-level foundation, the flared and pointed profile of graduated levels of the stupa foundation, and a profusion of relic-like scored dots. Given the tapered shape of the *aṇḍa*, which narrows towards the bottom, I would place it late in the series of stupas in the region, possibly the thirteenth century.

This final example demonstrates the continuities of the formal vocabularies of stupa engravings and also highlights an important example of ingenuity and creativity. It is a clear signal that chapter 3's treatment of the stupa as an important Buddhist and cultural signifier was necessarily heuristic and incomplete. That is, the chapter does not attempt a general exploration of the creativity of early artists working in the western Himalaya, but focuses on emphasizing the multiple roots of its early art, not simply Tibetan in inspiration or identity. Following the chapter by recognizing this at least acknowledges alternative explorations.

The stupa itself is detailed and intricate in structure, starting with a large lotus-petaled base, half-obscured now by the ground (Figs. 3.65–66). The tapered ladder with eight steps is built up with multiple relatively fine short lines, uniting the lower foundation to the bottom of the *aṇḍa*. On the *harmika* or balustrade at the summit of the *aṇḍa* stand four splayed-legged caryatids resting on the three-level cornice or plinth with X-shaped patterns on the widest molding. The four load-bearing caryatids support the prominent spire or *yaṣṭi* of twelve levels (see Fig. 3.70). It is unique in being formed of thirteen thin horizontal beams (*chhattra*-disks seen on edge?) which shorten in width as they rise, with large dots scored into the stone, ninety in all (Fig. 3.68). Ribbons or banners both wide and narrow flutter illusionistically along the sides of the *chhattrāvalī*. *Vajra*-handled bells hang straight down from the canopy, which supports a finial of a crescent moon cradling a *cakra*-wheel. A flower garland hangs from the edge of the fringed canopy, draped over the widest section of the *aṇḍa*.

Most if not all of these features draw on the developed vocabulary of features of the standard South Asian Buddhist stupa as found in the rock carvings considered in chapter 3. What is unparalleled are the features that ornament the stupa, that literally grow out of and around

177 Devers, *Historical Sites of Zanskar*, 60. Devers generously alerted me to this carving and its location, northeast of Remala village, at the base of the mountains behind the village. Quentin Devers's encomium that it is "the most outstanding stupa carving I have seen in the whole of Ladakh and Zangskar" is all the more telling given the archaeologist's extensive travels throughout the regions of this territory.

178 H. of the stone: 196 cm; h. of stupa, 164 cm.

Fig. 3.65 Stupa engraved on rock behind Remala village, Zangskar. Photo 2022.

it, or inhabit the space that it projects and dominates. A pair of lotus flowers curve along the lower outer edges of the base, as if to perfume the air around the foundation of the stupa (see Fig. 3.66). Above them, a leafy, flowering tree elegantly leans out of each side of the *aṇḍa*. They might call to mind the overgrowth on abandoned structures, but these probably are meant to evoke the sacred trees associated with the enlightenment of each of the past, present, and future Buddhas, starting with the Bodhi tree (*fiscus religiosa*) under which Śākyamuni sat.[179]

Fig. 3.66 Details of stupa featured in Fig. 3.65. Photos 2022.

Fig. 3.67 Details of stupa featured in Fig. 3.65. Photos 2022.

179 Some of the leaves look a little like those of Bodhi-trees, but others do not—it is hard to know how well and how early people in Zangskar knew of such regional botanical details from a distant and different ecological zone.

Fig. 3.68 Details of stupa featured in Fig. 3.65. Photos 2022.

Fig. 3.69 Details of stupa featured in Fig. 3.65. Photos 2022.

Fig. 3.70 Details of stupa featured in Fig. 3.65.

Other living creatures also animate the space surrounding the stupa, their attention riveted to it. A long-tailed monkey seems to swing toward it on one of the willow-like branches that hangs low, directly above the large lotus flower on the right (see Fig. 3.66). Above the tree, also on the right, a miniature antlered stag stands upright, facing the stupa, with one foreleg lifted behind an alert doe lying down at about the midway point of the superstructure (Fig. 3.69). Above them, two male *deva*s emerge from the sky to honor the stupa as a reliquary of the Dharmic enlightened body, speech and mind (Fig. 3.67). Looking like bodhisattvas, each *deva* has one knee bent, the other leg raised behind him in the standard convention for the flight of the gods. They are each contained within a cusped cloud, the upper one with double outlines. A large bird in flight swoops toward the stupa beneath the lower cloud-vehicle. Unfortunately, the upper left side of the stone is broken; most likely it featured more *deva*s in clouds scudding across the sky to revere the stupa, symmetrically opposite the ones on the right. More birds and other animals and plants were probably also indicated on the missing portion.

The reason that I follow chapter 3 with this extraordinary example of stupa carving is to emphasize that the stupas discussed in this chapter have the potential to be more than (a) ciphers for Buddhist dharma; (b) surviving indications of formal characteristics to be traced back to their cultural sources; or (c) clues for dating. Those are the ways that chapter 3 mainly treats the stupas of Zangskar. This ambitious composition serves to remind us that Zangskari artists were at times inspired to make images that go beyond mere necessity for stupa recognition. The artist (or artists) who created this one were pushing against conventional limits of basic iconography. They were on the cusp of setting the stupa in a landscape setting, unprecedented in early Zangskar visual art, and also worthy of our attention.

CHAPTER 4

Early Buddhist Figural Art in Zangskar: Tracing Sources Upstream[1]

Buddhism may have penetrated Tibet from its margins, and following a long-term sequential process.
—Scherrer-Schaub, "Perusal of Early Tibetan Inscriptions," 125

I think that Ladakh has surely known Buddhism much before [the time] this religion was introduced in Tibet proper . . . (VIII century). The rough sculptures in stone, representing Buddhist divinities, and not infrequent in Ladakh, in Baltistan, in Lahul, seem to me totally before the foundation of the Ladakhi dynasties.
—Tucci, "Stupa and Votive Stupa," 52

But what is Tibetan art? Is it art made by Tibetans or the art made for Tibetans? Can an imported object be considered as Tibetan art as well, and if yes under which circumstances?
—Luczanits, "Methodological Comments," 128

The Issue and Previous Studies

In the introductory chapter of this volume I argue for unlatching our conception of the history of western Himalaya from that of Tibet, following from freeing the nomenclature in use in some Western scholarship from its misleading identification of the area as a "lesser Tibet" or, indeed, as Tibetan by definition. This chapter focuses the argument on an examination of the early Buddhist visual arts of the region, particularly Zangskar, to demonstrate its multiple origins independent of Tibet. As with the larger historical identity of the western Himalaya, Zangskar's distinctiveness flows from its unique geographical and topographic features, which determined at least to an extent its social, economic, political, cultural, religious, and artistic history. To be sure, the later history of Zangskar cannot adequately be assessed without incorporating its connections—and conflicts—with Tibet. However, for the earliest period of the historical evolutionary development of something recognizable as Zangskar, from, say, the sixth through the eleventh century, the regions we now refer to as Tibet formed only one—and probably not the most important—contiguous source providing inspiration, knowledge, techniques, and artistic models. The rivers and passes that penetrated or

1 This chapter was initially a part of what is now chapter 1, drafted as a talk in a 2016 College Art Association conference panel. After comments and suggestions by Melissa Kerin, I separated the art-historical arguments from the terminological ones, and focus on the former here.

crossed the mountains and connected Zangskar to surrounding cultures provided routes to and from not only the east, where Tibet lies, but especially to the south, west, and north. Archaeological and material evidence supports a scenario that is neither singular nor static but one of multiple interconnections, of cross-fertilization of pluralities of ideas and forms. The targets of esteem in the form of compelling, awe-inspiring Buddhist art objects (in a matrix of Buddhist thought and practice) were absorbed from outside and then indigenously developed, so that the objects simultaneously resonated as both here and there, as local but transcendent,[2] linked to the admired canonical legacies from afar. These admired sources of artistic and religious inspiration were, most proximately, Lahaul, Kulu, Kashmir, Gilgit, Baltistan, and Bactria; more distantly, Magadha (eastern India); and, beyond the Karakoram, the Pamirs, and the Kunlun mountains skirting the Tarim Basin in southern Central Asia. Blended, mingled, hybrid forms predominated, but traces of the appropriated sources can still be tracked.

The sheer variety of art-making in the geographically defined area of Zangskar and Ladakh before the fourteenth century tends to be underemphasized or overlooked.[3] Works that do not register along an imposed "universal" aesthetic standard tend to be neglected, despite their power, local response, and impact on other scales. The importance of recognizing the multiplicity of modes of art-making within this period and region—the working-out of various artistic problems—was insightfully pointed out in 2015 by Deborah Klimburg-Salter in the process of attempting to recognize and name two contemporary modes at Tabo in the late eleventh century. She acknowledged that museum exhibitions and their catalogs tend to reify only one mode of art-making, since they feature and "proudly display elegant examples" of those objects "only recently acquired on the art market," resulting in "a descriptive terminology which *de facto* obscures the existence of a different and earlier artistic school" (or better, I believe, of different schools, not just one giving way to a second). Since the other modes of art-making are not featured in museums and art-market catalogs, she continues, "there is no motivation to explore this visual tradition. The picture is different when the art historical discussions evolve in the context of a study of the *in situ* monastic arts."[4] Taking a cue from this insight, nearly all of the examples I use here are still *in situ*, not in museum collections, and the study is based on extensive periods of fieldwork in Zangskar, Ladakh, and neighboring regions.

2 Larry Silver makes a similar point, that "[l]ocal canons can also be compositive fabrications, at once mingling disparate pictorial traditions while still serving as a consciously constructed identity . . . a centripetal melding . . . of surrounding contemporary visuality." Silver, "Introduction: Canons in World Perspective," 9.

3 By contrast, Ahmed and Harris rightly observe that "Ladakh is by no means a mono-culture but rather a place whose uniqueness may be characterized by its diversity," and "For centuries Ladakh has been a place for the transmission of goods and ideas from many different locations." Ahmed and Harris, introduction to *Ladakh*, 15.

4 Klimburg-Salter, "Tibetan Himalayan Style," 462–63. Although not mentioned by Klimburg-Salter, the exhibition and catalog I recently organized could aptly illustrate her point that they feature only those collected objects (generally of small scale) that represent a single mode, not a representative range. At the same time, the focus on the Kashmiri mode of western Himalayan and its "renaissance" in the fifteenth and sixteenth centuries was intentional; see Linrothe, *Collecting Paradise*.

Fig. 4.1 Petroglyph of ibex on boulder (foreground) at Zamthang (Char doksha) on the left bank on Lungnak River, Zangskar. Photo 1996.

Fig. 4.2 Petroglyph of *bharal* (*nabo*), wild caprid, at Zamthang (Char doksha), Zangskar. Photo 2013.

A few rare examples, expedient comparanda, are in museums outside Zangskar or Ladakh. On the other hand, not all of the examples discussed are monastic in any meaningful sense. Although a number of them have been preserved in or near contemporary Buddhist monasteries, others are in village shrines, not monasteries. By "monastic arts," the Buddhist nature of the art discussed is implied. In contrast, the earliest visual remains in Zangskar and surrounding areas are non- or rather pre-Buddhist, taking the form mainly of animal-themed petroglyphs that abound in the western Himalaya (Figs. 4.1–2).[5] With the introduction of Buddhism in the first centuries of the Common Era, a flood of connections, not always traceable, comes into play. Nevertheless, one must acknowledge that other systems of belief—such as animism, shamanism, and Bön—were potentially active in the area, as was mentioned in chapter 3.

When dealing with objects of religious value and functionality, even the term *art* can be problematic. In the present context, however, it is accepted with just a grimace and used without demur. Even while

5 On such petroglyphs, see Linrothe, *Seeing into Stone*.

endeavoring to distinguish modes of making on the basis of morphological differences, I have attempted to avoid, where possible, the even more problematic and ill-defined term (and concept) *style*.[6] *Style* is linked to, and aspires to be expressive of, broader cultural tendencies. We still know all too little about the early Zangskari society, so here I often substitute "form-idiom" (borrowed from Stella Kramrisch[7]) or "mode" of making. This helps to limit the claims to visual characteristics instead of larger social patterns. This does not solve the problems with *style*, embedded as it is within the Euro-American discipline of art history, and without exact correlates in pre-modern Asian languages. The hope is that perhaps the very awkwardness of less familiar substitutes serves as a reminder of our predicament: saddled with misunderstandings based on nearly monolithic derivation of culture from Tibet, and with an inadequate understanding of the early historical western Himalaya before Tibetans invaded.

Deborah Klimburg-Salter has wrestled with issues of formal development in Tibet and the Himalaya for decades, almost always using Tabo in Spiti as a fulcrum. Identifying and defining the evolution of idioms of form are central concerns in her pivotal work.[8] Her early and ongoing analyses of the Tabo complex—especially the 1997 landmark study *Tabo: A Lamp for the Kingdom*—helped put the western Himalaya on the art-historical map. After at first identifying four different phases of painting at Tabo and considering them in relation to other monuments in west Tibet and the western Himalaya,[9] she later merged them and proposed a two-phased sequence for the late tenth and eleventh centuries,[10] a "regional style"[11] and a "true Kashmiri style"[12] for what was considered the "western Tibetan artistic school" with Tabo as its central classroom, as it were.[13] More recently the nomenclature she employs for these two modes is "Tibetan Himalayan" and "Indo-Tibetan" styles. Although emerging from her critical studies of Tabo, she applies these phases of art-making beyond Spiti, although Zangskar rarely appears in the extensive spectrum of her published work.

Christian Luczanits, who studied with Klimburg-Salter, has also explicitly addressed issues of western Himalayan formal modalities in his seminal book on sculpture, *Buddhist Sculpture in Clay* (2004) and a 2005 essay, "The Early Buddhist Heritage of Ladakh Reconsidered" (2005). His brief but important article, "Styles in Western Himalayan Art" (2009), reconsiders his earlier classifications and extends them "to cover the

6 For critiques of the concepts and usage of "style," see Kubler, *Shape of Time*, and Kubler, "Shape of Time: Reconsidered"; Bagley, "Styles, Period, and the Life Cycle of the Goblin"; McCorkel, "Sense and Sensibility." To be sure, "It is difficult to defend our traditional system of stylistic concepts but it is also difficult wholly to dispense with them." Bialostocki, review of *The Shape of Time*, 136.

7 Kramrisch, "Pala and Sena Sculpture," 111, 114.

8 Klimburg-Salter, "Is There an Inner Asian International Style 12th to 14th Centuries?"; Klimburg-Salter, "Some Thoughts on Style in Tibetan Art."

9 Klimburg-Salter, "Tucci Archives Preliminary Study, [illegible]."

10 Klimburg-Salter, "Tucci Himalayan Archives Report, 2"; Klimburg-Salter, "Style in Western Tibetan Painting."

11 Klimburg-Salter, "Tucci Himalayan Archives Report, 2," 27.

12 Ibid., 37.

13 Klimburg-Salter, "Style in Western Tibetan Painting," 320. Although framed as a study of style in western Tibetan painting as a whole, of the twenty illustrations, eleven are from Tabo and two are from Nako, both sites in Spiti.

full range of the distinctive Western Himalayan art school up to the seventeenth or eighteenth century," well beyond the period covered here and with scant reference to Zangskar.[14] Melissa Kerin also made groundbreaking contributions to the study of fifteenth- to seventeenth-century painting in the western Himalaya with the chapter on "Gyapagpa Temple's Painting Style and Its Antecedents" in her book *Art and Devotion at a Buddhist Temple in the Indian Himalaya* (2015) and in her essay "From Emulation to Interpretation: Trends in the Late-Medieval Ngari Painting Tradition of the Guge Kingdom and Beyond" in the exhibition catalog *Collecting Paradise* (2014). Kerin's work extends beyond the timeframe dealt with in this chapter, however. Marylin Rhie, Heather Stoddard, Eva Allinger, and Christiane Papa-Kalantari (née Kalantari)[15] have also made detailed studies of questions of style that are critical to the issues taken up in this and other chapters and are cited accordingly. Erberto Lo Bue's distinguished body of work has been inspirational and, to cite just one, his essay "Sculptural Styles according to Pema Karpo" (1997), on the later Tibetan understanding of earlier visual modalities, is foundational.[16]

Examining the early Buddhist images, of Zangskar as a whole but in relation to its neighbors in the western Himalaya, we can identify, with varying degrees of certainty, more than the two alternatives that Klimburg-Salter identified and dated from their occurrence at Tabo, what she termed the "Tibetan Himalayan style" (8th c. to before 1042) and the "Indo-Tibetan style" (established by the mid-11th c.).[17] In this case, at least six different distinguishable types or modes reflect sources that can be traced between about the fourth and fourteenth centuries, with a seventh being a hybrid. These are of course purely etic designations and descriptions. They are marshaled here for a single purpose. That is to illustrate the spectrum of visual sources available to Zangskari image-makers in this period. Since most of these classifications are non-Tibetan, they help counteract the sustained impression that Zangskar—and the western Himalaya more broadly—stands upon a Tibetan foundation, visually or otherwise. I do not claim that early viewers or even artists were necessarily aware of or concerned with identifying or distinguishing their sources, and never in the same terms or categories presented here. In roughly chronological order, but with some overlap or simultaneity, these can be heuristically categorized as follows:

14 Luczanits, "Early Buddhist Heritage of Ladakh Reconsidered," 134.

15 Kalantari, "Art of Khorchag and Khartse in the Fabric of Western Himalayan Buddhist Art."

16 Many others, of course, have worked on issues of style. Amy Heller's 2001 article distinguishes an "Indian Style" (meaning from eastern India) from a "Kashmiri style," juxtaposing a painting *made in Tibet* in an eastern Indian modality with a metalwork sculpture *made in Kashmir*, both in private collections. The dating of the painting in pristine condition to the eleventh century is rather unfortunate; Heller has, of course, made many contributions to the study of Tibetan and west Tibetan art, as is acknowledged elsewhere in this volume. Jane Casey and Steven Kossak (*Painted Images of Enlightenment* [(2010]) have also done studies that relate to formal issues in works from Tibet but not Zangskar or Ladakh. As chapter 2 discusses, Tucci, not a trained art historian, addresses mainly the thematic and religious aspects of Tibetan art in the western Himalaya; issues of style he occasionally raises are more confounding than illuminating.

17 Klimburg-Salter, "Tibetan Himalayan Style," 455.

1. Kuṣāṇa (ca. 1st–4th c. CE) Buddhist images of Gandhāra and regions to Zangskar's west and northwest (sculpture)
2. Post-Gupta, pre- or early Pāla (ca. 5th–10th c.) images (mainly Buddhist) entering indirectly from Kashmir and directly from the south
3. Trans-Himalayan (Gilgit-Baltistan-Kashmir) and Southern Central Asian mode (ca. 8th–10th c.)
4. Kashmiri-inspired (Khaché) (7th–12th c.)
5. Eastern Indian via central Tibet (Gyalu, Shari) (ca. 12th c. onward)
6. Newari- or Nepalese-derived (Balri) (ca. late 12th c. onward)
7. Local mixtures or interpretative mélanges of the above modes (ca. 4th c. onward), including those from Chamba and Lahaul, etc.

In this chapter I lay out the chronologically overlapping modes and provide primary examples from Zangskar when possible, as well as some potential comparisons. Chapter 3 concentrated on representations of stupas. This chapter instead focuses on figural sculpture, though in some cases the two chapters coincide in presenting some of the same sites or monuments. In the process, I provide a limited but representative inventory of early figural sculpture preserved in Zangskar.

The Earliest Buddhist Sculptures in Zangskar

Localized Mode Inspired by Kuṣāṇa (ca. 1st–4th c. CE) Buddhist Images of Gandhāra and Regions to Zangskar's West and Northwest (Rock Carving)

A few suggestions of archaic sculptures seem to reflect Kuṣāṇa treatment of the Buddha theme. There are certainly reports of Kuṣāṇa—even Mauryan—inscriptions in Ladakh (as mentioned in chapter 1) so such knowledge is not completely implausible. Some examples of such sculptures have been noticed at a monastery on the right (east) bank of the Zangskar river.

Tongde (sTong de; alt. Thongde) Gompa overlooks the Zangskar river, between Padum and Zangla.[18] It is now a Geluk monastery, though popular belief claims it was founded by Marpa while looking for Narōpa. As Crook and Shakya noticed, slightly below the monastery along the old walking path leading from the village to the monastery is "a line of some fifteen handsome chortens" (Fig. 4.3). Gathered near these monuments are

18 Devers, *Historical Sites of Zanskar*, 186–99.

Fig. 4.3 Stupas near Tongde Monastery, Zangskar. Photo 2018.

Fig. 4.4 Archaic-looking sculpture at Tongde Monastery, Zangskar. Photo 2002.

Fig. 4.5 Kuṣāṇa coin of Kaniska I. From Foucher, *Beginnings of Buddhist Art*, pl. 14.

some "magnificent stone panels of great antiquity featuring early Buddhist ikons [*sic*]."[19] These and others nearby "doubtless predate the monastery and testify to the antiquity of the site."[20]

Of these stone images, probably the earliest is a slender standing figure with a robe ending above the ankles, splayed feet, left hand in *abhāya mudra* and the other arm reaching down below the knee, and simple curves of the outlined head- and body-nimbus (Fig. 4.4). The top of the head is somewhat ambiguous; possibly it is an *uṣnīṣa*, a chignon, or even a stack of heads as borne by the eleven-headed Avalokiteśvara. The ears are similarly only roughly delineated; again, they might be the exaggeratedly extended ears of the Buddha, or possibly earring-bearing lobes of a bodhisattva. Overall several of these features surprisingly resemble the image on the famous gold coin of the Kuṣāṇa king Kaniṣka I. Labeled the "*Boddo*" (or "Buddha" inBactrian script), the images makes the *abhāya mudra* with the proper right hand instead (Fig. 4.5).[21] Compare the head and body nimbus formulation, the splayed feet, and the termination of the robe above the ankles.

According to Tanabe, five such Buddha coins, in both gold and bronze, and in two denominations of gold, survive.[22] A copper drachm issued by Kaniṣka I features a "Sakamano Boudo" whose proper left hand is in front of his chest,

19 Crook and Shakya, "Monastic Communities in Zangskar," 565.

20 Ibid., 568.

21 After Foucher, *Beginnings of Buddhist Art*, pl. 14.

22 Tanabe, *Silk Road Coins*, 92 and figs. 125–127. See also Cribb, "Origin of the Buddha Image."

like that of the Tongde image, and he also has a large, somewhat indistinct chignon.[23] The one reproduced most often, however, even in surveys, is the gold one in the British Museum.[24] Of course, many large images of the standing Buddha were produced in the Kuṣāṇa period and regions, but the tiny scale of the image on the coin, which allows for little detail, correlates to the weathered stone, which is approximately two and a half feet tall (76.2 cm). Thus by making this suggestion, I am not implying the Tongde image is literally dated to the Kaniṣka I reign, which according to Cribb's recent calculations began in 127 CE, or has a direct relationship to the coin.[25] However, the forms of the sculpture tenuously intimate that a similar template might have been in the mind of the early artist, local or visiting but working in the western Himalaya.

A date of as early as the ca. second to fourth century is possible, since contact between Kuṣāṇa representatives and Ladakh is demonstrated by the stone inscription in Kharoṣṭī, which actually depicted Kaniṣka I's predecessor, Vima Kadphises, in a manner slightly less detailed than in the coins depicting Kuṣāṇa rulers,[26] and calls him "Maharaja." It was found at Khalatse in Ladakh, first noticed by Francke and then studied by, among others, Sten Konow.[27] The inscription includes a date (still problematic) and the name of the Kuṣāṇa ruler. Kharoṣṭī, written right to left, is "derived from Aramaic, the official script of the Persian state chancelleries," and "was used for official documents mainly in the middle-Indian language Gāndhārī at the court of the Greco-Indian and Indo-Scythian kings (third–fourth century AD)."[28] A few other Kharoṣṭī inscriptions are reported at Khalatse, but even the one that Francke found and Tucci photographed (apparently in 1928)[29] is now missing and believed to have been destroyed.[30] Whether the inscription and idealized "portrait" of the ruler justified the conclusion made by Petech that this "inscription proves that in the 1st or 2nd century A.D. Lower Ladakh was included in the Kushana empire,"[31] which I doubt, it nevertheless lends support to Crook's conclusion that the "earliest monuments in Zangskar itself date from the Kushan period."[32] I believe Crook would have been better off using this kind of image as evidence than the local belief that the Sani "Kanika Chorten" (see Fig. 3.63) was built by Kaniṣka, as discussed briefly at the end of the chapter 3.

A second image at Tongde, perhaps even further from Kuṣāṇa prototypes, is also a possible candidate for consideration as a local version of a Kuṣāṇa image. It is a slender standing figure, two-armed, with a thickly outlined

23 Luczanits, *Gandhara, the Buddhist Heritage of Pakistan*, cat. no. 99.

24 Zwalf, *Buddhism*, no. 121; Dehejia, *Indian Art*, fig. 47.

25 Cribb, "Coins and the Chronology of Gandhara," 67.

26 Ahmad, *Kushans in Kashmir*, pls. following p. 72.

27 Konow, *Kharoshṭhī Inscriptions*, 79–81.

28 Hauptmann, "Pre-Islamic Heritage in the Northern Areas of Pakistan," 29.

29 See Orofino, "Note on Some Petroglyphs of the Ladakh Area," 181 and fig. 33.

30 Tucci points out that this important inscription found near the bridge at Khalatse was already missing by 1930: "In 1930 and 1931 I had intensified my researches near Khalatze in order to find the inscription again, but I could not trace it. Almost surely it has been broken during works for the construction of the bridge of Khalatze." Tucci, "Stupa and Votive Stupa," 52n2.

31 Petech, *Kingdom of Ladakh*, 7. Petech's conclusion probably was based at least in part on Tucci's assertion that "the Kharosthi inscription of Vema Kadphises [shows] that the culture and hegemony of India had already penetrated these countries since the time of first Kushans. The very fact that the inscription was found together with others in Brahmī, near the bridge over the Indus, lets us suppose that since the first centuries of our era an active commerce united, as today Kashmir with the upper valley of the Indus." Tucci, "Stupa and Votive Stupa," 52–53.

32 Crook, "History of Zangskar," 438.

Fig. 4.6 View of stupa with rock carving in front near at Tongde Monastery, Zangskar. Photo 1998.

Fig. 4.7 Standing bodhisattva at Tongde Gonpa, Zangskar. Photo 1998.

head nimbus (Figs. 4.6–7). The stone around the figure is damaged, so it cannot be determined whether, like the Buddha(?) in Figure 4.4, it also had a body nimbus. The headdress marks it as definitely a bodhisattva, but which one is impossible to say. The hands are both twisted awkwardly but appear to be making the gesture of gift-giving with the proper left. Something appears at the upper right shoulder, which would be unusual in a Kuṣāna-period bodhisattva, but what is more reminiscent of that period's costume is the elaborate headdress. As in several examples of Gandhāran bodhisattvas, the figure wears a projecting diadem with ribbons that curl out and up along with fantails;[33] an example of such sculptures is in the Central Archaeological Museum, Lahore,[34] of the second–third century.

A few other simplified, slender standing figures are found at various places in Zangskar, and might be related to this group. Among them is a small (approximately 35.5 cm in height)

33 Faccenna and Filigenzi, *Repertory of Terms for Cataloguing Gandharan Sculptures*, pl. 107.3.

34 https://dsal.uchicago.edu/cgi-bin/huntington/show_detail.py?ObjectID=11113.

Fig. 4.8 Headless standing figure sculpture at Pibiting, near Padum, Zangskar, h. approx. 36 cm. Photo 2000.

stone sculpture, unfortunately headless, at Pibiting, just north of Padum (Fig. 4.8).[35] Like the Tongde standing Buddha, he has splayed feet and a straight right arm extending into a large open-palmed hand. Such images are all too often ignored or set aside as "ancient" but not seriously examined. They appear at other sites in the western Himalaya besides Zangskar and deserve to be carefully scrutinized.

Localized Sculptural Modes (Coarser and More Refined) Inspired by Post-Gupta, Pre- or Early Pāla (ca. 5th–10th c.) Imagery (Mainly Buddhist) Entering Indirectly from the South (Rock Carving)

The second mode to which I would call attention is one manifesting attributes attributable to a Post-Gupta model of heavy set, fleshy, and somewhat rounded figures. Naturally, they are modified by the process of the transfer of forms from a cultural and geographic distance into local situations with artists apparently largely unfamiliar with sculpting in relief and in the round. Earlier image makers in the area, the makers of petroglyphs (see Figs. 4.1–2) and stupa designs (as discussed and illustrated in chapter 3), created them by lines engraved or pecked into flat stone. There appear to me to be two different types or qualities within this new modality: one is coarser or less refined; the other is rather more sophisticated, in which the Post-Gupta references to sculptures found in northern India are more clearly visible. It is tempting to suggest that the coarser type is earlier, and features mass and bulk over more tempered roundness, although at this time such a sequence can neither be confirmed nor shown to be false. On the other

35 Devers, *Historical Sites of Zanskar*, 173.

Fig. 4.9 Group of archaic stone sculptures of Buddhist figures, Sani Village, Zangskar. Photo 2017.

hand, they may have been produced simultaneously.

A Coarser Subtype

The primary examples of the coarser type are those near the site of the Sani Kanika stupa (see Fig. 3.63). Until recently, a group of older sculptures of various sizes were arranged in a rough circle to the west of the monastery, and even though they are still nearby, they have been moved close to a newly built stupa (Figs. 4.9–10).[36] In the early twentieth century, possibly in 1933 while on one of his collecting expeditions, Walter Koelz or his partner Rup Chand photographed them at Sani (Fig. 4.11).[37] An even earlier photograph, taken in 1907 by Eric Upton on a "shooting tour in Kashmir territory" and published by Francke, definitely depicts the larger sculpture (the Maitreya bodhisattva discussed below), and possibly a second surviving sculpture of a standing deity.[38]

Fig. 4.10 Seated Vajrapāṇi among archaic stone sculptures of Buddhist figures, Sani Village, Zangskar. Photo 2017.

36 Ibid., 157.

37 Photograph taken by Walter Koelz or Rup Chand, 1933(?); courtesy of the Bentley Historical Library; labeled on the back, "Buddha Seni Gompa one of the sanctuaries of Budhism [*sic*]."

38 Francke, "Remarks on a Photograph," 332 and opposite unnumbered illustration.

Fig. 4.11 Sculptures near Sani Monastery, Zangskar. Photographed by Walter Koelz or Rup Chand, probably during 1933 expedition. Used with permission of the Bentley Historical Library, University of Michigan; Walter Koelz Papers (0158 Aa2), Box 7 Photos A11.

Fig. 4.12 "Old Stone Figures, Dèkoo near Padum, Zaskar," lithograph by H. M. Smith, April 1864. From Godwin-Austen, "On the System Employed," pl. IV.

Fig. 4.13 "Stone Figures, Dèkoo, near Padum, Zaskar," lithograph by H. M. Smith, April 1864. From Godwin-Austen, "On the System Employed," pl. V.

Remarkably, a group of eight of those sculptures, most of which still survive, appear in two published drawings by then Captain (later Lt. Col.) Henry Haversham Godwin-Austen (1834–1923) of the Survey of India (Figs. 4.12–13).[39] The Maitreya just mentioned is featured in both of the cited drawings, and is still the main image in the circle of sculptures; right next to him is the Vajrapāṇi (see Fig. 4.10), also in both drawings.

The principal image dominating the Koelz and Upton photographs as well as the Godwin-Austen sketches and the grouping today is a standing Maitreya image with a small stupa carved on the central plaque on his crown (Figs. 4.14–15),[40] though that iconographic detail does not appear in the drawings. The sheer mass and force of the standing image and the lack of details make it difficult to assess. There is no question, however, about the sanctity of this image. The dark stains on the crown, face, and torso, the result of anointing with butter, as well as the necklace of offering scarves (*katag*), attest to that. As a foreigner and non-Buddhist, I was not allowed to touch it or even brush the snow off it before photographing it. When I started to do so in the winter of 2003–4, my late friend Tashi Dorje (youngest son of Karsha Lonpo)

39 Godwin-Austen, "On the System Employed in Outlining Figures," pls. IV–V.

40 See also Snellgrove and Skorupski, *Cultural Heritage of Ladakh*, 2: fig. 8.

Fig. 4.14 Standing Maitreya bodhisattva sculpture, near Sani Monastery, Zangskar. Photo 2003.

Fig. 4.15 Close view of head of standing Maitreya bodhisattva sculpture near Sani Monastery, Zangskar. Photo 2003.

leapt forward to do the honors himself. It is now close to 183 centimeters in height, though a note on Godwin-Austen's drawing, when more of the head nimbus survived, states that in his day it was 228.6 centimeters in height. Francke attributes this example to "the most ancient sculptures," from when Zangskar was "in the hands of an Indian (perhaps Buddhist) tribe," and dates it to around 1000 AD.[41] Snellgrove and Skorupski agree that the image "would certainly appear to predate the Tibetan occupation."[42]

The abbreviated forms closely resemble sculptures found directly south of Zangskar, in Lahaul such as those at Keylong (Figs. 4.16–18). These in turn appear to be abstracted versions of more classical Post-Gupta forms that appear remarkably close to Zangskar, geographically, in the Kulu Valley and with which it has continuously been in contact.[43] One can follow the abstraction process at three sites in the Kulu Valley, from the Gupta-inspired *chandraśālā* at the Bajaura Mahādeva Temple of the ca. eighth century (Fig. 4.19), to the similar but more stylized forms at the Gauri Shankar Mandir in Jagatsukha village which the ASI dates to the eighth–ninth century (Fig. 4.20), to the Gauri Shankar Mandir at Dassar village

41 Francke, "Remarks on a Photograph," 332.

42 Snellgrove and Skorupski, *Cultural Heritage of Ladakh*, 2:10.

43 Heinrich Pöll has identified a number of motifs and architectural features within Ladakhi art that he identifies as deriving from Gupta and Post-Gupta art via the mediation of artists in the Himachal region. See Pöll, "Trees-of-Life, Aquatic Creatures, and Other Enigmatic Motifs."

Fig. 4.16 Standing crowned Buddha or bodhisattva, stone carving at Keylong, Lahaul, Himachal Pradesh. Photo 1996.

Fig. 4.17 Close view of Fig. 4.16. Photo 1996.

Fig. 4.18 Standing crowned Buddha or bodhisattva, stone carving at Keylong, Lahaul, Himachal Pradesh. Photo 1996.

Fig. 4.19 Śiva in *chandraśālā* on Mahādeva Temple of the ca. 8th c., Bajaura Village, Kulu Valley, Himachal Pradesh. Photo 2022.

Fig. 4.22 Standing Maitreya bodhisattva, government compound, Padum, Zangskar. Photo 2018.

Fig. 4.20 Śiva in *chandraśālā* on Gauri Shankar Mandir of the ca. 9th c., in Jagatsukha Village, Kulu Valley, Himachal Pradesh. Photo 2022.

Fig. 4.21 Śiva in *chandraśālā* on Gauri Shankar Mandir at Dassar Village, Kulu Valley, Himachal Pradesh. Photo 2022.

with the much simplified abstraction (Fig. 4.21). The Keylong sculptures obviously relate to the latter, as do the Zangskar epigones (see Fig. 4.15). Even some of the early metalwork *mohras* (masks attached to deity sculptures) provide insight into antecedents for the puffy almond-shaped eyes and cheeks, the thick lips, and simplified three-peaked crowns.[44] Other examples in this mode are plentiful in Zangskar, near Padum, one of the early royal centers of the region (Figs. 4.22),[45] at Reru village (Figs. 4.23–24),[46] and at Tongde.[47] Above the site with the Kuṣāṇa-like sculpture (see Fig. 4.4), a massive boulder carved on both sides is half buried on the northern slope of the hill on which Tongde monastery is perched (Fig. 4.25, 4.26). A bulky seated and crowned Buddha (?) faces south toward the monastery, while a standing Avalokiteśvara, with a lotus at his shoulder, faces north. The aboveground part of the stone is 170 cm in height and 130 cm at its widest. It appears as if natural white inclusions in the stone have been imaginatively utilized to suggest the parallel ridges of the bodhisattva's garment. If the object cradled in the arms of the seated crowned figure is an *amrit* vase, it is possible the figure was meant to be Amitāyus, the Buddha governing Avalokiteśvara's *padmakula*. The eyebrows and eyes are distinctly raised in relief against the rather flat surface of the face. The swollen eyelids and lips, the triangular nose, the bulky simplified forms and the crown with triangular tines resemble the Keylong standing figure in Lahaul (see Fig. 4.17). The Tongde sculpture, like the Sani Maitreya, receives exceptional reverence, as can be ascertained by the accumulation of "special" auspicious stones, mostly white in color.

The abbreviated, abstracted version of this mode assumed by the Keylong, Sani, Reru, and Tongde images elicits the pejorative adjective "folkish." Interestingly, something similar seems to have been recognized as an option that spread north along with a finer mode of Post-Gupta sculpture from eastern India, from Nalanda in Bihar, and from twenty-four Parganas district in West Bengal.[48] Bose noticed more than forty small, slabs identified during the Nalanda excavations (Figs. 4.27–28).[49] Lacking the "plasticity" of the contemporary Pāla-Sena sculptures, the eyes and lips bulge and they stand relatively stiffly, yet it is clear the compositions emulate the highly articulated contemporaneous sculptures. What is useful in the present context is the example, that "two or more schools or idioms could have flourished along with the acknowledged Pāla-Sena School of Art during the early mediaeval period in Eastern India."[50] The Nalanda so-called "folkish" images (see Figs. 4.27, 4.28)—which in fact might be

44 An example is the ca. seventh-century mask in the Kronos collection; Pal, *Himalayas: An Aesthetic Adventure*, no. 53.

45 Devers, *Historical Sites of Zanskar*, 169.

46 Ibid., 228.

47 Ibid., 187–88. The latter illustrates a sculpture inside a house in a village, the same one that a clear black-and- white photograph published earlier shows in a field: Crook, "History of Zangskar," pl. 79.

48 In 1989 I acquired two black-and-white photographs from the Asutosh Museum in Calcutta in the same format, depicting Vishnu (14.5 x 8.5 cm; neg. no. SC.329, ref. sc. 406.5067) and Mahiṣāsuramārdinī (14.5 x 7.5 cm; neg. no. sc 316; acc. no. T-3666). The museum dated them to the eighth century. A few others from Nalanda are published in Misra, *Nālandā*: F.135 (2:85); F.136 (2:186); F.140 (2:188); F.227 (3:156); and F.238 (3:162). Misra dates them much later, to the thirteenth through the fifteenth century, but does not explain why.

49 Bose describes them as "crudely carved," "unsophisticated," and "simply decorated," regrettably negative even if understandable given their difference from the finely rendered form of deities with much greater mimesis; Bose, "Note on Some Interesting Icons from Nalanda," 85. In 1989 I photographed three such stone plaques on display at the Nalanda Museum; unfortunately, I wrote down (and preserved) the accession number and height of only one of them, the Mahiṣāsuramārdinī of Fig. 4.27 (acc. no. 1125, h. 20.3 cm). The other one (Fig. 4.28), of similar size and format apparently depicts the standing female form of Lalitā.

50 Bose, "Note on Some Interesting Icons from Nalanda," 86.

Fig. 4.23 Boulder with carved Buddhist figures in barley field at Reru Village, Zangskar. Photo 2013.

Fig. 4.24 Close view of Buddhist figures on boulder depicted in Fig. 4.23. Photo 2013.

Fig. 4.25 Seated crowned Buddha (?) carved on stone near Tongde Monastery, Zangskar, h. 170 cm. Photo 2005.

Fig. 4.26 View from the side of relief carving of Fig. 4.25. Photo 2018.

Fig. 4.27 Stone sculpture of Mahiṣāsuramārdinī in Nalanda Museum, acc. no. 1125, h. 20.3 cm. Photo 1989.

Fig. 4.28 Stone sculpture of Lalitā in Nalanda Museum. Photo 1989.

Fig. 4.29 Stone sculpture of standing crowned Buddha (?) in pavilion on northwestern outskirts of Leh, north of the Tisseru Stupa. Photo 2022.

Fig. 4.30 Wooden sculpture of standing Maitreya in Sumda Chenmo Village, Ladakh. Photographed before 2006.

Fig. 4.31 Stone sculpture set up on a *maṇi* wall in Changspa neighborhood, Leh, Ladakh. Photo 2022.

said to have modernist analogies—however, are all very small in size. Still, the degree of relief and the relation of figure to the stone slab is somewhat comparable to the larger stone sculptures in Zangskar. There are, however, several other instances of the coarser subtype in the Leh area (Fig. 4.29), a wooden sculpture in Sumda Chenmo, Ladakh (Fig. 4.30),[51] next to some houses in Changspa on the outskirts of Leh (Fig. 4.31), and elsewhere including a group of more than a dozen archaic sculptures at the shrine known as Dorje Chenmo in Shey.[52]

A More Refined Subtype

Post-Gupta characteristics come through clearly and strongly in a more refined example found in Changspa village near Leh in Ladakh, northeast of Zangskar. Changspa village has now been absorbed into Leh town. A few extraordinary sculptures are found around a Many-Doors (sgo mang) Stupa. One is a tall stone (more than 6 feet tall, 182.88 cm) with Śākyamuni Buddha carved on one surface (Figs. 4.32–33),[53] Avalokiteśvara on the other, and two stupas (in a generally Kashmiri mode) on the sides. Recently, they were moved into a low concrete pavilion, but for years they were open to the elements; here I use earlier photographs. The Gupta-like interiority of the Buddha's expression, the subtle modeling of his fleshy face, and the line marking the undergarment are hallmarks of Post-Gupta sculpture. These are even more evident on the other side of the same sculpture, depicting a four-armed Avalokiteśvara with Hayagrīva (Figs. 4.34–35). More elements of Post-Gupta treatment are visible there, including rounded treatment of the body, broad (rather than oval) faces with a tall head of hair, and a pointed nimbus.

For contrast, consider a four-armed Śiva from Kashmir: the label in the Sri Pratap Singh Museum in Srinagar identifies it as dating to the eighth century and from the site of Pāndrethan (Fig. 4.36). The muscular chest, tapered ribcage, pouched belly, long *vanamālā*—these are all features that can be seen in many other sculptures and paintings in Zangskar and Ladakh in the Kashmiri and the Khachélu (kha che lugs, Tibetan versions of the Kashmiri mode), but they are not ones exhibited by the Changspa Avalokiteśvara. The hard, muscular handling of the body at Pāndrethan is quite different from the Changspa bodhisattva. Instead, there is much greater affinity between the Changspa Avalokiteśvara and the extraordinary standing figure from the Nagara-style temple at Lākhamaṇḍal, near Yamnotri in what is now Uttarakhand, near the Himachal Pradesh border,

51 Namgyal Institute, *Legacy of a Mountain People*, 2:476.

52 Ibid., 2:345.

53 It has been identified as Maitreya Buddha for reasons that are not clear to me, although it is possible; Snellgrove and Skorupski, *Cultural Heritage of Ladakh*, 1: fig. 109. Filigenzi reproduces a photograph taken in 1909/1910 illustrating the bodhisattva which she identifies as "Maitreya?"; Filigenzi, *Il Bodhisattva Maitreya nell'arte rupestre dello Swat*, 51. The bodhisattva is definitely not Maitreya.

Fig. 4.32 Standing Buddha, carved on a boulder at Changspa neighborhood, Leh, Ladakh. Photo ca. 1992.

Fig. 4.33 Close view of head of standing Buddha in Fig. 4.32. Photo ca. 1992.

Fig. 4.34 Standing Avalokiteśvara and Hayagrīva; back of the standing Buddha stone at Changspa neighborhood, Leh, Ladakh. Photo 2008.

Fig. 4.35 Close view of Hayagrīva on standing Avalokiteśvara carving in Changspa

Fig. 4.36 Stone Śiva from Pāndrethan, Kashmir, 8th c., in the Sri Pratap Singh Museum, Srinagar. Photo 2011.

Fig. 4.37 Stone standing *dvārapāla* at Lākhamaṇḍal, Uttarakhand, late 7th or early 8th c. Photo 2006.

south of the western Himalaya but contiguous with its borders (Fig. 4.37). Notice the relaxed stance, with the hips at an angle, the attention to ribbons and scarf-ends, the bands at the wrists, the size and shape of the necklace, as well as the swelling eyes, admittedly damaged. All of these are comparable with the Changspa Avalokiteśvara—though of course it is in much lower relief and comparatively rather stiff—who wears a similar pair of shorts beneath his dhoti (see Fig. 4.34).[54] According to Maxwell with respect to the Lākhamandal sculpture, "The treatment of anatomy and dress suggests that these sculptures are post-Gupta works of the late 7th or 8th century."[55] Perhaps a date range of seventh–ninth century is acceptable for the Changspa sculptures as well.

54 However, the Changspa sculpture is sometimes roughly, and unjustifiably, grouped with the Kashmiri-derived sculptures of Dras and Mulbekh as "concrete evidence of Kashmiri influence." Ahmed and Harris, introduction to *Ladakh*, 11 and fig. 3, depicting Avalokiteśvara again misidentified as "Chamba" (i.e., Maitreya).

55 Maxwell, "Lākhamaṇḍal and Trilokināth," 15.

Three ca. eighth- to tenth-century bodhisattvas from eastern India (Figs. 4.38–40) align much better with the Changspa bodhisattva sculpture than does the Pāndrethan image, especially in terms of ornaments, scarves, belts, and the soft, even plump, body type. They also have the advantage, for our purposes, of showing wrathful attendants as well. The latter are all chubby and relaxed. In the Changspa sculpture (see Fig. 4.35), Hayagrīva leans insouciantly on his upturned club, as does the Hayagrīva from Telhara (Bihar) in the Rietberg (Fig. 4.41). The point of these comparisons is not to suggest any specific linkage to Bengal or Bihar, or for that matter Lākhamaṇḍal (see Fig. 4.37). Rather it is on the one hand to provide visual evidence of particular images in Ladakh and Zangskar that predate anything we can recognize as a developed Tibetan style. On the other, in general orientation, these sculptures are more closely aligned to the contemporary art of the Indian regions to the south of the Himalayas than they are to most of the sculptures of the Kashmiri and Baltistan-Gilgit regions to the west. This is a relatively rare and short-lived movement, and, like the possibility of Kuṣāṇa-style images in Zangskar, constitutes a largely unrecognized phenomenon in the study of early western Himalayan art.

Take for example the sculptures on the large boulder just before Shey (shel, she ye) palace and temple when heading south along the main road from Leh (Figs. 4.42–43). They are quite well known.[56] As mentioned in chapter 1, Shey was the capital of Maryul and territories to the south along the upper Indus, and Leh was the capital of Ladakh or the middle-western Indus Valley. Like the Shambhala sGo (gate) sculptures above Karsha, discussed below (Figs. 4.58, 4.63–67), the important set of carvings on a boulder in Shey is arranged along a triangular flat rock-face with a significant fissure running diagonally along its length, clearly visible in Figure 4.43.

The Shey carvings depict the five directional Tathāgatas, a theme that will be discussed at greater length later in the chapter. Briefly, the central Buddha, Mahāvairocana (Fig. 4.44), is crowned; the other four are in monk robes. All five are standing, and each has his proper *vāhana* or symbolic vehicle on the base of the lotus throne below his feet. At the sides and at the lowest register are sponsor figures holding incense braziers and other offerings. The forms of the Buddhas are more sophisticated in the smoothness of integrating body parts and the subtlety of the low relief than any of the early Zangskar sculptures seen so far. The Shey and

56 Snellgrove and Skorupski, *Cultural Heritage of Ladakh*, 1:11; Snellgrove, "Buddhism in North India and the Western Himalayas," 76; Denwood, "Tibetans in the Western Himalayas and Karakoram," figs. 7–10; G. Bhattacharya, "Buddha Śākyamuni and *Pañca-Tathāgatas*," 355, fig. 1.

(left to right):

Fig. 4.38 Standing Mañjuśri with Yamāntaka, stone, from Nalanda (Bihar, India), ca. 8th c., h. 116 cm. New Delhi National Museum, acc. no. 59.528. Photo 2008.

Fig. 4.39 Standing Mañjuśrī with Yamāntaka (on left), stone sculpture from Guneri (Bihar), ca. 9th–10th c., h. 127 cm. Bodh Gaya site museum. Photo 2016.

(left to right):

Fig. 4.40 Standing Avalokiteśvara with Hayagrīva, stone, ca. 9th c. Bihar. Rietberg Museum, Zurich. Photo 2012.

Fig. 4.41 Close view of Hayagrīva on Avalokiteśvara sculpture in Fig. 4.40. Photo 2012.

Fig. 4.42 Carvings of the Five Transcendent Lords (Tathāgata) on boulder near Shey, Ladakh. Photo 2009.

Fig. 4.43 Five standing Transcendent Lords (Tathāgata) on boulder near Shey, Ladakh. Photo 2008.

Fig. 4.45 Close view of elephant *vāhana* under Akṣobhya Buddha on boulder near Shey, Ladakh. Photo 2008.

Fig. 4.44 Close view of standing Mahavairocana Buddha on boulder near Shey, Ladakh. Photo 2009.

Changspa sculptures (Figs. 4.32–35, 4.42–45) exemplify the finer non-Kashmiri mode of sculpture in Ladakh, in which elements of the Post-Gupta bulky but rounded treatment of the body, broad (rather than oval) faces with high-piled hair, pointed head nimbus, prominent jewelry (on the Mahāvairocana and Avalokiteśvara) and other advanced iconographic characteristics are infused into the forms.

One look at the elephant beneath the standing Akṣobhya, his *vāhana* (Fig. 4.45), is enough to convey the fact that the model for such an image comes from places where elephants were familiar to artists: definitely not Tibet; in Kashmir they were certainly known but not native. In Gilgit, the presence of elephants on rock carvings "may be explained by visitors from the south [i.e., India]."[57] Although elephants were integrated into Kashmiri military divisions—and the well-known Rockefeller seated crowned Buddha with two Kashmiri stupas was dedicated by a princess Deva Śriyā and Saṅjara Sena, Mahāgajapati ("chief of the elephant corps"[58])—the animals were recruited from other parts of India.[59] The convincing anatomy of the Shey elephant, the way it turns its head and bends its front right leg, suggests close familiarity with elephant bodies and behavior. That the elephant is looking backward is one of the characteristics that the Indian fifth-century Buddhaghoṣa points out about this distinctive animal in explanation of a *Mahāparinirvāna* verse that describes the Buddha as "with an elephant look": "Buddhas were accustomed to looking backwards, to turn the whole body round as an elephant does because the bones in their neck were firmly fixed."[60]

57 Hauptmann, "Pre-Islamic Heritage in the Northern Areas of Pakistan," 30.

58 Deambi, *Corpus of* Śāradā *Inscriptions of Kashmir*, 140.

59 Bamzai, *Culture and Political History of Kashmir*, 1:218–19; Linrothe, *Collecting Paradise*, 70.

60 Kramrisch, "Emblems of the Universal Being," 136.

Fig. 4.46 Seated Buddha in earth-touching posture, Pāla (eastern India), ca. 10th c., h. 43 cm. New Delhi National Museum, acc. no. 70.2. Photo 2008.

Fig. 4.47 "Rock-Cut Standing Figure at Kargah, near Gilgit." Creative Commons image, http://en.wikipedia.org/wiki/File:Buddha_at_Kargah_Gilgit.jpg#filehistory.

This is not the only strikingly Indian (or elephantine) characteristic of these sculptures. Notice the broad shoulders gracefully flowing into the upper arms (see Fig. 4.44). This corresponds to one of the eighty lesser *lakṣaṇa*, that the Buddha's "shoulders were like those of the royal elephant,"[61] and the comparison is made between the arm emerging from the shoulder and the elephant's trunk flowing from its head. In particular, Akṣobhya's left shoulder and arm (see Fig. 4.43, second standing figure from the left), with the hand cupped at the waist and the end of the robe placed near to where an elephant's floppy ear would be, makes the resemblance to an elephant's head and curling trunk almost literal or intentional. One finds a number of shared characteristics in Buddha images of the ninth and tenth centuries from eastern India, such as the seated Buddha in the National Museum in Delhi (Fig. 4.46) with a comparably shaped base and lotus petals. Other examples can be cited as well, including late seventh-century seated stone full-relief Buddhas from Patna district.[62]

A Gilgit Post-Gupta Example

There is at least one exceptional image in the Gilgit region—indeed, within sight of the location where the Gilgit manuscripts were found[63] near Naupur village—in a related style. Known as the Kargah (alt. Kar Gah) Buddha, it is some three meters in height carved onto the perpendicular surface of a large rock (Fig. 4.47).[64] Tsuchiya dates it, with reservations, to the seventh century.[65] According to Dar, the sculpture "can be dated easily in the late 7th or early 8th century" and he cites A. H. Francke, *Antiquities of Indian Tibet* (1914) as his authority,[66] though the basis is its purported

61 Hardy, *Manual of Buddhism*, 369.

62 Asher, *Art of Eastern India*, pl. 78–80.

63 Tsuchiya, "Preliminary Report on Field Research [I]," 33.

64 Dar, "Rock-Cut Standing Figure at Kargah, near Gilgit." A clear, color photograph is available at http://en.wikipedia.org/wiki/File:Buddha_at_Kargah_Gilgit.jpg#filehistory (consulted February 2012), a Creative Commons image that one is free to "copy and redistribute . . . in any medium or format" as long as credit is given: CC BY-SA 3.0; File: Buddha at Kargah Gilgit.jpg; Created: 17 November 2006. A clear color photograph taken by Klimburg-Salter is reproduced in her "Tibetan Himalayan Style," fig. 15.9.

65 Tsuchiya, "Preliminary Report on Field Research [II]," 23.

66 Dar, "Rock-Cut Standing Figure at Kargah, near Gilgit," 195, 199.

"haunting resemblance" to the Mulbekh Maitreya of Ladakh,[67] which is not nearly so early. While the Kashmiri "trefoil arch and pentagonal frame of the shrine/shelter of this figure" is accurately observed,[68] the figure itself, like that of another lesser sculpture (at Bubur in Gilgit), is soft and round in contour, which Tsuchiya notes has greater resemblance to earlier Indian prototypes including those at Ajanta and Kanheri.[69] In fact its resemblance to Mulbekh is confined to the shape of the now-missing (in both cases) shrine above it, and does not extend to the style of the carving. I agree with Dar that the Kargah sculpture "has definitely not been derived from Gandhara and Swat,"[70] but the attribution to "Tibetan influence in the wake of Tibetan occupation of the area during the 8th and 9th centuries A.C."[71] is not sustainable given what we now know of the state of Buddhist art (or the lack thereof) among Tibetans at that time. Dar quotes a source unavailable to me—a work by Nancy Hatch Dupree, who rightly points to "affinities to art styles developed further east and south, but not in the tradition of Gandhara."[72] It has greater form-feeling affinity with the large- and round-headed, puffy-eyed, soft-contoured images of Shey and Changspa than the muscular naturalism of Kashmir.

Even though the sculptures discussed so far at Changspa and Shey in Ladakh are of the best quality, they are not the only ones that could be considered as belonging to this category. Other related Post-Gupta examples in Zanskar and Ladakh have the same puffy or rounded, soft features. A slender bodhisattva on the side of a four-sided stone sculpture just to the north of the main mosque and Islamic bakery area of Leh, Ladakh (below the palace), is also a candidate (Fig. 4.48), despite the *vanamālā* extending to its shins, which is more typical of Kashmir sculpture.[73] A decade ago, a stone Maitreya buried up to its knees was identified and moved from the courtyard of an abandoned house below the palace in Leh to a nearby location (Fig. 4.49). It was then given a new face by a Western professional conservator, but my photograph shows it in its earlier position and before the new face was attached. The authors of the essay about it, André Alexander and Sam van Schaik—specialists in architectural conservation and textual analysis, respectively—conclude that the inscription found on the sculpture was added later, much like the examples suggested in chapter 3, fitting around preexisting stupa low-relief outlines.[74] They term it a graffito and, based on the inscription's paleography and comparison with other loosely dated sculptures, place it in the tenth or eleventh century but "no later than the early eleventh

67 Linrothe, "Origins of the Kashmiri Style in the Western Himalayas," figs. 5.13–5.18; Linrothe, "Kashmiri 'Loving-Kindness' in Ladakh," forthcoming; Devers, *Historical Sites of Purig*, 75.

68 Dar, "Rock-Cut Standing Figure at Kargah, near Gilgit," 199.

69 Tsuchiya, "Preliminary Report on Field Research [II]," 20.

70 Dar, "Rock-Cut Standing Figure at Kargah, near Gilgit," 193.

71 Ibid., 196.

72 Ibid., 193.

73 In 2015, a pavilion was erected over the sculpture and a plaque placed at the sculpture's feet asserting that it and four sculptures moved in 1885 to a shrine near Sankar Monastery marked the source of a spring.

74 Alexander and van Schaik, "Stone Maitreya of Leh."

Fig. 4.48 Standing Buddha on one face of the four-sided stone sculpture on the west side below the Lhachen Palkar palace in Leh, Ladakh. Photo 2010.

Fig. 4.49 Damaged stone sculpture of Maitreya bodhisattva on the south side below the Lhachen Palkar palace in Leh, Ladakh. Photo 2008.

century."[75] They link it to a cult of Maitreya sponsored in central Tibet during the period of the Tibetan empire and later in western Tibet, but concede that the attributes derive "more directly from Gilgit and other regions to the west."[76] I agree that formally it does not sit well with what we know of Tibetan or west Tibetan art of the period, but except for the resemblance in general terms to the Kargah sculpture (which they mention in a footnote), I see the mode to which it belongs as deriving ultimately from northern India in the Post-Gupta phase. There may be similarity to a few images in Gilgit, but that is because the same mode penetrated that area as well, though not as thoroughly as it did Ladakh and Zangskar.

Dates Of Shey And Other Examples

The resemblances between the Shey carvings and some of those from Zangskar, however remote or indirect, warrant a brief digression into the dates of the Shey carvings, and thus of the others in the same stylistic mode. I maintain that the Zangksar petroglyphs and rock carvings discussed

75 Ibid., 433.

76 Ibid., 438.

to this point should be considered earlier than the tenth or eleventh century when the impact of direct Kashmiri involvement in Buddhist art in Zangskar, Ladakh, Spiti, and Ngari becomes visible. Before that, connections with Kuṣāṇa, Gupta, and Post-Gupta Buddhists from northern India had a significant impact in the first millennium CE in Kashmir, Central Asia, Ladakh, and Zangskar, as well as the regions to the immediate south of the Himalayas. The routes for that impact were both along the Indus River coming in from the south and west, and directly from the south and southeast (from what is now Himachal Pradesh) in Zangskar. At this stage, central Tibetans were themselves grappling with the introduction of Buddhism and Buddhist art from Nepal and eastern India, from China and Khotan, and from Dunhuang. My argument here is that the Shey and Changspa sculptures represent the finest extant examples in the western Himalaya of this northern Indian artistic and religious strain, however filtered or transmitted via intermediaries, before the Kashmir or Khachélu began to dominate, and the west Tibetan invasions of the tenth and eleventh centuries modeled their own engagement with Kashmiri Buddhist art. Tibetan-language inscriptions exist on and around the Shey sculptures (mainly six lines squeezed above the standing Buddha on the viewer's right, Amoghasiddha), but aside from a few words and the phrase "making obeisance to the three jewels,"[77] they are worn and unreadable in terms of a coherent message. Denwood points to a number of early characteristics of costume in the composition and notes that the "palaeographic archaisms" in the inscriptions are prior to the twelfth or early thirteenth century. He concludes the sculptures and inscriptions could date anywhere between the eighth and eleventh centuries, "or conceivably even later."[78] Luczanits perspicaciously cautions against the tendency to suggest early dates for "the numerous rock carvings found in the region and neighbouring areas" without secure evidence, but acknowledges they "await a detailed study."[79] Snellgrove opines that the five-Tathāgata carving of Shey "certainly belongs to the earlier period before the Tibetanization of this area, thus prior to the tenth century A.D.[80] Bhattacharya, without giving reasons, dates the Shey carvings to the eleventh century.[81]

To me, the style elements of the Shey sculpture hint at a dating to the eighth or ninth century. The iconography allows this, since the five-family system was already developed in such texts as the *Sarvatathāgata Tattva Saṃgraha*, which had been translated into Chinese in the eighth century. It can also be observed that there are some "archaic" or early Tantric aspects

77 Denwood, "Tibetans in the Western Himalayas and Karakoram," 51.

78 Ibid., 51–52.

79 Luczanits, "Early Buddhist Heritage of Ladakh Reconsidered," 69; see also 67.

80 Snellgrove, "Buddhism in North India and the Western Himalayas," 76.

81 Bhattacharya, "Buddha Śākyamuni and *Pañca-Tathāgatas*," 350.

in the combination of a central crowned or bejeweled Buddha (the central Mahāvairocana) with uncrowned Buddhas (Akṣobhya and Ratnasambhava on Mahāvairocana's proper right, and Amitāyus and Amoghasiddhi on his left). This will be taken up again in relation to the Padum version of the theme.

Localized Trans-Himalayan (Gilgit-Baltistan-Kashmir) Southern Central Asian Mode (ca. 6th–9th c.) from the Regions to Zangskar's Northwest (Rock Carvings)

The Central Asian Models

A third mode appearing around the same time in the western Himalaya shows greater resemblance to some artistic activities carried on between Kashmir and Central Asia, including what is now Xinjiang Province and western Gansu Province in the People's Republic of China. In its shadows one glimpses early Kashmiri art (ca. 7th–9th c.). A group of ten painted banners depicting standing bodhisattvas was found bound together at Dunhuang by Aurel Stein. They are now divided between the British Museum[82] (Fig. 4.50) and the National Museum, New Delhi (Fig. 4.51).[83] Although attributed by some to Tibetan or Nepalese "influence" and projected to have been painted in Khotan and then brought to Dunhuang where they were removed in the early twentieth century, the British Museum Vajrapāṇi's connections to Kashmir are the most clearly visible. As Roderick Whitfield noted of the Vajrapāṇi, the eyes "are almond-shaped, bright white with black pupils. This feature above all gives the figure its Indianizing appearance, and one might make the comparison with bronze figures with the eyes inlaid in silver." He then compares it with the eyes of an eighth-century metalwork Buddha in Phyang monastery of Ladakh, and dates the group to the early ninth century.[84] The work in question is a Kashmiri metalwork (most likely brass, not bronze), and the comparison is apt. Kashmiri eyes are invariably almond-shaped and usually inlaid with silver, like the ones on the Devsar halo in the Sri Pratap Singh Museum of Srinagar in Kashmir (Figs. 4.52–53), usually dated to the tenth century but placed by some in the eighth or ninth century.[85] Another similarity is the form of the crown, with three triangular crests. The New Delhi bodhisattva, probably Padmapāṇi, a bit more clumsily painted, shares the crown form. It also has a striped patterned dhoti, unequal in length over the legs, both features frequently found in Kashiri metalwork. Almost no paintings survive from Kashmir from this period, although the related treatment of

82 Three examples of these painted banners of bodhisattvas found at Dunhuang and retrieved from there by Stein, in the manner reflecting impulses originating in various regions of the subcontinent, including and especially Kashmir, are now in the British Museum and are available online: https://www.britishmuseum.org/collection/object/A_1919- 0101-0-103 (here Figure 4.50); https://www.britishmuseum.org/collection/object/A_1919-0101-0-102; and https://www.britishmuseum.org/collection/object/A_1919-0101-0-101. Three other paintings belonging to the same set now in New Delhi (but not Figure 4.51) are illustrated and briefly discussed in Lokesh Chandra and Nirmala Sharma, *Buddhist Paintings of Tun-huang*," 221–23, where they are dated to the early ninth century.

83 The set of ten are treated in Bhattacharya-Haesner, "Indo-Tibetan Influences in Banners from Dunhuang." Well published, see the catalog entry by Chhaya Bhattacharya in Klimburg-Salter, *Silk Route and the Diamond Path*, 132, pl. 58; Klimburg-Salter, "Tibetan Himalayan Style," fig. 15.7; Lojda et al., "Tibetan Himalayan Style," fig. 4.2; and Whitfield, *Art of Central Asia*, 2: figs. 46–48.

84 Whitfield, *Art of Central Asia*, 1:334, citing the reproduction in Singh, *Himalayan Art*, 53.

85 Srinivasan and Sander, "Viśvarūpa Vyūya Avatāra," 156–60.

Fig. 4.51 Standing Padmapāṇi bodhisattva, painted banner, Tang dynasty, New Delhi National Museum, acc. no. Ch.lvi.001. Photo 2022.

Fig. 4.50 Standing Vajrapāṇi bodhisattva, painted banner, Tang dynasty, British Museum, acc. no. Ch.lvi.002. Used with permission (after payment).

Fig. 4.52 Seated figure in the Devsar metalwork aureole, Kashmir, 9th–10th c. Sri Pratap Singh Museum, Srinagar, Kashmir. Photo 2013.

Fig. 4.53 Nāgā figure in the Devsar metalwork aureole, Kashmir, ca. 9th–10th c. Sri Pratap Singh Museum, Srinagar, Kashmir. Photo 2013.

Fig. 4.54 Detail of Buddha on painted wooden manuscript cover, Gilgit, ca. 8th–9th c. Sri Pratap Singh Museum, Srinagar, Kashmir. Photo 2013

recognizes that with regard to the painting idiom, "the ten banners [to which Figures 4.50 and 4.51 belong] are different from those found in Chinese and Central Asian art. This is especially the case with the Vajrapāṇi figure [Fig. 4.50]."[88]

the eyes of the Buddha on one of the excavated Gilgit painted book covers of the ca. late eighth or ninth century (Fig. 4.54) offers an example of the kind of work that Vajrapāṇi's artist may have seen. In Gilgit, the rulers seem to have employed Kashmiri artists for high-end sculpture and painting.

Whitfield (and many others) suggests that "this group of [three] paintings may be related to the art of Khotan," pointing to the differences in the weave of the silk ground, the treatment of the selvege and edging, and the lack of cartouche for inscriptions.[86] Khotan, on the southern edge of the Tarim Basin almost directly northeast of Leh, is that much closer to Ladakh. An early eighth-century Kashmiri metalwork Buddha, closely resembling the one in Phyang that Whitfield mentioned but with a Śāradā inscription and larger, was excavated at Damagou, just east of Khotan, so we know such objects were circulating in southern Central Asia.[87] Bhattacharya-Haesner rightly

The Dunhuang Vajrapāṇi (see Fig. 4.50) appears to be a southern Central Asian treatment of Kashmiri art, one that has a number of variants in Gilgit, Baltistan, Ladakh, and Zangskar. Klimburg-Salter and her collaborators describe the Dunhuang paintings as painted in "a simple, linear and mostly two-dimensional figural style with straight, tubular legs and long arms."[89] They also point out that a related mode of depicting figural forms is apparent carved into rocks: stiff, frontal, and flat.[90] The Trans-Himalayan and southern Central Asian emulations have similar and specific traits that seem clearly to be derived from Kashmiri art, and probably were meant to be recognized as such. Carved into boulders in Trans-Himalayan regions (Gilgit, Baltistan, Skardu, etc.), however, they are much less sophisticated than the Kashmiri models.

The Dunhuang painted examples were done by artists no doubt affected by Chinese tastes and so have much more in the way of

86 Whitfield, *Art of Central Asia*, 1:334.

87 Leidy, "Kashmir and China." The transmission of Kashmiri art to Central and East Asia, all the way to Japan during the seventh through ninth century, and its transformation along the way is discussed in Rhie, "A T'ang Period Stele Inscription," 22–24, 28; Rhie, "Interrelationships between the Buddhist Art of China and the Art of India and Central Asia"; and Linrothe, *Collecting Paradise*, 51.

88 Bhattacharya-Haesner, "Indo-Tibetan Influences in Banners from Dunhuang," 487.

89 Lojda et al., "Tibetan Himalayan Style," 126.

90 Ibid., 127.

scarves draped over various limbs. Klimburg-Salter and others identify such works as Tibetan art by or for Tibetans, possibly emulating central Tibetan art with some features deriving from Chinese art but produced "under Tibetan patronage for the Tibetan community"[91] at Dunhuang. They become prototypes for a so-called Tibetan Himalayan style. Michelle Wang also proposes that certain Esoteric Buddhist themes and "Nepalo-Tibetan" modes of painting at Dunhuang were brought to Dunhuang from Tibet, rather than brought to Tibet.[92] I believe it is more likely that this mode organically grew around or out of Kashmir in the sites and peoples who were in contact with it, and that the farther away they were, the more distant were the similarities. Dynastic Tibetans are more likely to have encountered it at the Mogao Caves of Dunhuang and in Khotan than they were to have generated the style and left it there.

"Tibetan Himalayan style" is used by Klimburg-Salter to refer to a form-idiom with a wide occurrence but focused on the region of the western Himalaya, including Tabo and Tholing, before a contemporary mode that yet replaces it, an even more directly Kashmiri-derived manner variously termed "Indo-Tibetan style," "(western) Indo-Tibetan style," and "the Kashmiri influenced Indo-Tibetan style." The fact that key examples in these learned studies are from the tenth–eleventh century in Tabo in the western Himalaya seems to imply that the western Himalaya is part of Tibet which, as discussed at length in the opening chapter, is as difficult to defend as "Tibet" is to define. Neither India nor Tibet (as in central Tibet) is involved by these authors as the primary location for the occurrence of the "Indo-Tibetan style." Yet as Bhattacharya-Haesner rightly points out about this set of paintings, which have been attributed to Khotan (and to the "Tibetan Himalayan" or "Indo-Tibetan style"), in fact "pre-dates those of Tabo in Spiti valley . . . However, the early sculptures and bronzes from Kashmir and Swat valley, from the 6th century onwards, seem to be the source of the Khotanese school of art. This style travelled to Dunhuang, probably via Kucha on the Northern Silk Road."[93] The issue of nomenclature for artistic modes, styles, or form-idioms is taken up again in the conclusion to this chapter.

The Trans-Himalayan Models

At the Chilas-Jayachand site along the Indus river after the Gilgit river has emptied into it are a number of standing and seated Buddhas and bodhisattvas which are in a localized version of a formal idiom that,

91 Ibid., 125.

92 On this, see M. Wang, *Maṇḍalas in the Making*; for a critique of this idea, see Linrothe, "'Structure and Subject Matter' at Dunhuang."

93 Bhattacharya-Haesner, "Indo-Tibetan Influences in Banners from Dunhuang," 488.

Fig. 4.55 Standing Maitreya from the Chilas-Jayachand site (Gilgit, Pakistan). Drawing by Gerald Kozicz, after Dani, *Human records on Karakorum Highway*, 43.

like the Khotan set of paintings, seems to have emanated from Kashmir. Again like the paintings attributed to Kashmir, although inspired by Kashmiri art, local artists and patrons (in Khotan, Gilgit or Balti) also participated in it.[94] One example at the Chilas-Jayachand site is the standing Maitreya (Fig. 4.55) that Jettmar dates to the sixth century,[95] whereas Fussmann suggests it should be dated to about 600.[96] Etched into rock, the bodies are somewhat lumpy and ill-defined compared with the later tripartite structure of the torsos in Kashmiri art (discussed below), but the crowns, dhotis ending above the ankles, and thrones with evenly upward- and downward-pointed lotus petals without interior markings are all associated with Kashmir. The crowns have three triangular crests and long, wide ribbons hanging down. The dhoti has horizontal design registers on each leg. The feet are splayed and there is a head- and body-nimbus that intersects at the level of the upper arms. It is slightly naïve, even childlike.

The Zangskari Versions

We have already described examples of works in Zangskar that most closely follow models in the Trans-Himalaya. In chapter 3, we discussed the shallow cave or rock shelter above Karsha Village that is the site of archaic paintings of stupas (see Figs. 3.56–58, 3.62). The closest comparison for them is with the ca. eighth- to ninth-century rock paintings at Chaghdo in Baltistan (see Fig. 3.61) near Gilgit, between Kashmir and southern Central Asia. Another such Zangskari example is a rock art site on the west bank of the Kargyak river before the *prayag* where it joins the Stod (Doda) river flowing from Pensi La to form the Zangskar river proper, a few minutes' walk northeast of Padum in central Zangskar. Sometime before the ninth century, to judge from the carvings, two naturally occurring rocky outcrops were recognized as suitable locations for sculpture and consecration. Those seats for the deities, at a river crossing and along a path, would be seen by a large number of people. The earliest and most archaic-looking images are standing Buddha-like bodhisattvas such as the one depicted near a low, shallow cave or rock shelter (Fig. 4.56).[97] It is carved in flat, low relief emphasizing the head- and body-nimbus on an outcrop of rock on the riverbank overlooking the river. The head is depicted as if bearing an *uṣṇīṣa*, and the skirt could be that of a Buddha's robe, but the band at a wrist and elbow suggests it is a bodhisattva, as does the gesture of holding up a lotus like Padmapāṇi.[98] The roundness of the face and the curving outlines look much more like Post-Gupta brethren than Kashmiri.
The same is true for an outlined Buddha with one shoulder covered

94 Thewalt, "Rockcarvings and Inscriptions along the Indus"; Jettmar and Thewalt, *Between Gandhāra and the Silk Roads*, pl. 16; Hinüber, "Brāhmī Inscriptions on the History and Culture of the Upper Indus Valley," pls. 157–159; Dani, *Human Records on Karakorum Highway*, 40–41, 43; Hauptmann, "Pre-Islamic Heritage in the Northern Areas of Pakistan," fig. 22.

95 Jettmar and Thewalt, *Between Gandhāra and the Silk Roads*, 34.

96 Fussman, "Chilas, Hatun et les Bronzes Bouddhiques du Cashemire," 23.

97 Devers, *Historical Sites of Zanskar*, 170, 178; Francke, "Kleine archäologische Erträge," photo by J. B. Riddell captioned "Flache Reliefﬁguren auf dem Felsen über der Klosterzelle," opp. p. 661.

98 Francke, who also illustrated this figure in a set of five standing next to each other, describes them as "standing Buddhas." He also notes that they are above a shallow cave, which he identifies as formerly a monastery. Francke, *History of Western Tibet*, 22–23, pl. opp. 21.

Fig. 4.56 Standing Buddha figure carved on cliff above cave site northeast outskirts of Padum, Zangskar. Photo 2008.

Fig. 4.57 Standing Buddha figure carved in outlines on a rock near the government compound in Padum, Zangskar. Photo 2008.

(Fig. 4.57) on the plateau above the riverbank, near what is now the government precincts of Padum. He has large shoulders with rather narrow hips. The lower part of the robe is marked with the similar wave-like lines (to indicate garment folds or textile patterns) as on the bodhisattva. The tall, slightly oblate nimbus is pointed and given a double outer border, as one finds in sculpture from eastern India in the eighth century.[99] Quite archaic in form are the stupas nearer the bodhisattva (see Fig. 3.37). As with *caitya*s of the ca. second or third centuries from Kushan regions, the *aṇḍa* is very rounded, and the superstructure is minimized.[100] Later, we will take notice of a number of other, perhaps slightly later, low-relief sculptures nearby.

Most of the features in the Chilas rock carving (see Fig. 4.55) can also be seen in, for example, the standing bodhisattvas of the Karsha Shambhala sGo site (discussed more comprehensively below), especially the Vajrapāṇi to the left of the vertical fissure (Fig. 4.58). Although the Gilgit sculpture is only outlined against the cliff, the Karsha image has slight relief. As already discussed, the nearby stupas, particularly the one on the proper left of Mañjuśrī (see Fig. 3.32), have small rounded *aṇḍa*s, flattened at the top

99 Asher, *Art of Eastern India*, 77, 100, pls. 143, 253.

100 Compare Gupta, *Kushāṇa Sculptures from Sanghol*, no. 25A; Nagaraja Rao, "Stupa at Sanghol," fig. 3.6.

Fig. 4.58 Standing Vajrapāṇi bodhisattva carved on Shambhala Gate, Karsha Village, Zangskar. Photo 2002.

Fig. 4.59 Standing Mañjuśrī bodhisattva carved on a stone pillar in Rantaksha Village, Zangskar. Photo 2003.

and bottom, with a bulging set of umbrellas, and topped by a single wide finial. In some ways it resembles a squatter version of the ca. seventh- to eighth-century metal miniature stupa in the Peshawar Museum.[101]

A Mañjuśrī grasping a book carved on a stone pillar at Rantaksha (see Fig. 4.59), purely linear, might also be profitably considered as deriving from artists more acquainted with the depiction of bodhisattvas originating in Kashmiri art via the near-northwestern regions (at least from the point view of Zangskar of Baltistan and Gilgit). While probably later than the Chilas or Karsha sculpture, it has a protruding right hip similar to the latter. In Rantaksha it is used as one of the points from which observations of the position of the sun at sunset in relation to the mountain tops were used for calendrical calculations with agricultural implications.[102] The Maitreya carved in slight relief on one side of a pillar, also in the government compound in Padum, and which was mentioned in relation to coarse

101 Luczanits, *Gandhara, the Buddhist Heritage of Pakistan*, no. 290.

102 Personal communication, Sonam Phuntsok, 4 November 2003.

Fig. 4.60 Standing bodhisattva with splayed feet carved on a boulder at Stok Village in Ladakh. Photo 2004.

Fig. 4.61 Detail of Fig. 4.62 showing bodhisattva head and crown; carved in relief on boulder in government compound, Padum, Zangskar. Photo 2010.

Fig. 4.62 Standing Maitreya bodhisattva (?) in relief on boulder, Padum, Zangskar. Photo 2010.

versions of Post-Gupta sculptures (see Fig. 4.22), could possibly belong here instead (note the wavy lines on his dhoti which also appear on the dhoti of the very low-relief stone bodhisattva with splayed feet at Stok in Ladakh [Fig. 4.60]). With the cruder images it can be difficult to determine their affiliations, though certainly, either way, it is a pre-Tibetan image of the ca. sixth–ninth century. He has a stepped-base stupa in the central triangular crest of his crown, and a vase on a lotus near his ear. Remarkably, a similar but unidentified bodhisattva (Figs. 4.61–62)—probably Maitreya if the stepped structure on his crown is interpreted as a stupa—is on one of the sides of the nearby pillar-like rock.[103] A much more sophisticated outlined Mahāvairocana Buddha is on one of the other faces (Fig. 4.106), to be discussed below in the section on the eastern Indian or Magadha mode. The fact that the same pillar has a seated crowned Buddha in a relatively fluent outlined mode of the eastern Indian form-idiom and a stiffly standing relief bodhisattva in a localized version of the Gilgit-Baltistan mode is intriguing. Admittedly, the two modes may overlap in terms of date range, but it is hard to know which was done first (probably the bodhisattva). Their presence on the same tall piece of rock indicates that locally they were not seen as inharmonious together.

Karsha's Shambhala Gate

Northwest of the Padum boulders overlooking the Lingti river, across the Doda river just before the *prayag* with the Lingti, lies the village and monastery of Karsha. Next to a stream flowing out of the higher mountains behind the village is a series of low-relief sculptures found on the cliffside. They are considered the oldest and most sacred in the village, predating the

103 Devers, *Historical Sites of Zanskar*, 168, 177.

Fig. 4.63 Shrine enclosing Maitreya carved on cliffside below Karsha Monastery, Karsha Village, Zangskar. Photo 2003.

Fig. 4.64 Triangular niche in cliffside known as Shambhala sGo ("Gate") in Karsha Village, Zangskar. Photo 2004.

Fig. 4.65 Three bodhisattvas carved into the triangular niche of Shambhala Gate in Karsha Village, Zangskar. Photo 2012.

monastery above the village. The themes are straightforward: Mahāyāna bodhisattvas and stupas. The largest is a rough outline carving of an over-lifesize Maitreya bodhisattva, now enclosed by a shrine constructed within the last fifty years (Fig. 4.63).[104] The original form of the large Maitreya inside it is no longer visible after erosion, re-cutting, the blackening by butter lamps, and the ritually renewing application of clay and lime plaster, but it remains the site of regular community prayers.

Above it and not enclosed, on the side of the cliff facing east, one can more clearly see a composition framed by a naturally occurring flat triangular niche (Fig. 4.64). There are three bodhisattvas along with lay sponsors and stupas (Fig. 4.65). The three bodhisattvas are Avalokiteśvara (holding the lotus) in the center of the triad (Fig. 4.67), Vajrapāṇi (holding the *vajra*) on his proper right (see Fig. 4.58), and Mañjuśrī (holding the *utpala* [blue] lotus) on his left (Fig. 4.66). The bodies of the bodhisattvas are somewhat lumpy, stiff, and ill-defined compared with the musculature of later Kashmiri figures or the soft modeling in the Gupta-inspired mode of,

104 Ibid., 137–38.

Fig. 4.66 Standing Mañjuśrī bodhisattva to the right of center of Shambhala Gate composition, Karsha Village, Zangskar. Photo 2012.

Fig. 4.67 Standing Avalokiteśvara bodhisattva at center of Shambhala Gate composition, Karsha Village, Zangskar. Photo 2012

for example, Sarnath sculpture. There is a notable absence of the *vanamālā* as found in Kashmiri sculptures, but the crowns, dhotis ending above the ankles, and thrones with evenly upward- and downward-pointing lotus petals are vaguely associated with Kashmir and found in the Gilgit region as at the Chilas-Jayachand site now in Pakistan (see Fig. 4.55). Along with three triangular crests, the crowns have long, wide ribbons hanging down. The dhoti has horizontal design registers ("stripes"). The feet are splayed and there is a combined head and body nimbus that intersect at the level of the upper arms. The Vajrapāṇi figure can be closely compared with the painting found at Dunhuang, now in the British Museum (see Fig. 4.50) and itself a product (as I argued above) of Kashmiri art as transmitted through the Gilgit-Baltistan region and carried into southern Central Asia. The stupa from the site (see Fig. 3.32) discussed in chapter 3 also roughly follows a Kashmiri form-idiom. Given the dates of what they most closely resemble, they should probably be assigned to the seventh- to ninth-century range. A short disquisition, examining not its form-idiom but its thematic associations of the local name for it, "The Gate to Shambhala," is inserted here, at about the halfway point of the chapter.

INTERMEZZO: A Visual Exegesis

As significant as the artistic sources and date of the Shambhala Gate sculptures is the contemporary understanding of the site and its name. It is by this that its uniqueness and its relevance to Buddhist versions of the *tīrtha* concept are constituted.[1] According to the local scholar, *amchi* (traditional Tibetan medical doctor), and historian Karsha Lonpo Sonam Wangchuk, this configuration at Karsha is believed locally to have predated the settlement of Karsha village and, by its auspicious presence, helped to convince the original inhabitants to settle there. He holds these carvings as the metaphorical heart of Karsha village, its holiest place. Furthermore, the niche on the cliff with its carvings is accepted as one of the Thresholds, or Gates, of Shambhala (Shambhala sGo), and that is the name by which it is locally known.[2]

Shambhala is a hidden Pure Land (*beyul; sbas yul*) described in the *Kalachakra Tantra*, a kind of Shangri-la with its own religious kings. Its location has been the subject of an ongoing debate among learned Tibetans.[3] Some texts place Shambhala in the mapable, traversable world we know, locating it somewhere above Central Asia.[4] Other authors, among them the Third Panchen Lama, Lobsang Paldan Yeshe (1738–1780), declare it open only to purified vision and not to the dusty steps of travelers. The great Dolpopa Sherab Gyaltsen (Dol po pa shes rab rgyal mtshan; 1292–1361) claimed to have gone to Shambhala during meditation, thanks to the Kalkin kings who rule there.[5] There was general agreement that it was located in the north. "The river Sītā, which marks the border to the hidden kingdom, serves as a line of demarcation between the outer world and Śambhala."[6] This suggests that there was a border along which were four gateways, like a mandala. Other Beyul have four gates, and the Beyul Khenbalung, in Bhutan or Nepal, east of Everest, is said to have a "hidden door."[7] It has been argued that such Pure Lands are especially resorted to during times of political and social upheaval, at which times they are taken very literally, as in the case of "Khams sprul rin po che, who presently lives in Dharamsala as an advisor to the Dalai Lama, [who in 1959] prayed for months before cliffs that failed to part."[8]

At Karsha, one of the most prominent features of the triangular niche onto which bodhisattvas, stupas, and donors were carved at an early date, are the two vertical cracks or seams (Figs. 4.64–65). One of them divides Avalokiteśvara from Vajrapāṇi, and the other is to the latter's right. These might not have been seen as "flaws" in the rock but might actually have enhanced both the sacrality of landscape formation and its identification with a gate. Rozwadowski has pointed out that:

> Numerous Asian shamanic mythologies express the belief that rock crevices such as these, along with holes in the earth and simple caves, were the gates to the world of spirits, through which the shaman travelled. . . . If a rock or a mountain was identified as the home of a spirit or of the deities, then the crevice logically might have been thought as being the doorway into them.[9]

1 The *tirtha* as a spiritual "ford" in Brahmanical Hindu and Buddhist thought is defined and discussed as it appears in early rock art in Zangskar (though not at Karsha's Shambhala Gate) in Linrothe, *Seeing into Stone*, 135–43.

2 Personal communication, December 2003.

3 Newman, "Itineraries to Sambhala"; Khamtrul, "History and Geography of Shambhala."

4 Newman locates the traversable Shambhala as the region north of the Tian Shan; Newman, "Itineraries to Sambhala," 487. Interestingly, the itinerary given crosses Ngari Mangyul, which is very close to Karsha in Zangskar; ibid., 488.

5 Stearns, *Buddha from Dolpo*, 46–47, 189n87.

6 Kollmar-Paulenz, "Utopian Thought in Tibetan Buddhism," 86.

7 Diemberger, "Beyul Khenbalung," 292.

8 Sardar-Afkhami, "Buddha's Secret Gardens," 3.

9 Rozwadowski, *Symbols through Time*, 74.

Although the locations or number of gates to Shambhala are not identified in the standard treatments, locating one on the fissured cliff of Karsha is a way of understanding the site as a potential doorway to a perfected state, and an auspicious location for religious practice and settlement. This is similar, perhaps, to the sentiment expressed in the name Har-kī-paurī, or Śivā's door, at Hardwar, where the Gangā flows out of the Himalayas, bridging mountains and plains, and the site once every twelve years of the great gathering of Hindu ascetics, the Kumbha Melā.[10] In a "dream journey" to Shambhala, Garje Khamtrul Rinpoche saw a "huge rock shaped like a door. . . [which a king of Shambhala will open] with his spear, and out of it will come many treasures, weapons and soldiers. . . [It] was just a rock, but its nature was like the crystal that comes from very old mountains."[11]

Yet, in the case of the Shambhala Go, one can hardly think of anything less overtly gate-like, less fordable, than solid rock, though perhaps that was part of the point. This leads to some reflections on one of the special paradoxes of mountains or rocks as *tīrtha*. Rock *tīrtha*s seem to partake of a contradiction that is at the heart of the notion of a *tīrtha* itself. Such a place resolves and maintains contradictions of proximity and distance, physicality and spirituality, the mundane and the transcendent. Pilgrimage collapses the physical distance, though simultaneously reifies the difference between the beginning and the end of a pilgrimage. Direct contact with the deity, expressed in the form of bliss, a boon, or merit, similarly maintains the differences between deity and devotee, even as it connects them. As Eck describes, "Like a bridge, it both separates and joins the near shore of dualities and the far shore in which those distinctions do not exist."[12]

Rock as a material participates in this simultaneous resolution and maintenance of contradictions. It lends itself to the contradiction at the heart of a rock *tīrtha*: physical solidity and transcendent permeability. Just as it is due to the nature of water that a river appears timeless and constant yet is ungraspable and unfixed, eternal and yet ephemeral, in a constant flow that changes from moment to moment, so too a mountain gateway, or crossing place, presents a paradox of the ineffable stemming from the physical nature of rocks.[13] Physical properties of grandeur—scale in inconceivable dimensions—along with obdurate hardness, and infinite variety with uniquely suggestive formations, all lend themselves to the reason-defying proposition that such a material is spiritually permeable, the basis for a "crossing beyond birth and death, crossing from darkness to light, crossing from ignorance to knowledge."[14]

The mountain's interior is inaccessible, constantly hidden from view. The mountains, the visible and tactile phenomena, are seemingly all exterior. Yet a rock or cave *tīrtha* nevertheless offers the promise of an interior passage for deities "inside" it by which they cross "downward" into the accessible space, and for those on the "outside," a gateway "upward" and inward to the unbounded infinite, its very materiality proof of the miraculous. Perhaps it is for these reasons that so many cultures and regions, including Zangskar in the western Himalaya, have considered the rock to be animated, to be "living rock," and for so many rock *tīrtha*s to be scattered throughout the western Himalayan region of Zangskar. It also explains the decision, perhaps, to settle at such an auspicious location, under the very eyes and protection of self-manifesting images of enlightened and compassionate beings.

10 Alley, *On the Banks of the Gangā*, 107–8.

11 Bernbaum, *Way to Shambhala*, 172.

12 Eck, "India's *Tīrthas*," 332.

13 See the discussion on the role of rivers in the human "spiritual perception of the world;" Devy, *Nomad Called Thief*, 157–58.

14 Eck, "India's *Tīrthas*," 341.

Localized Khaché, or Kashmiri-Derived Mode (ca. 8th–12th c.) (Rock Carving and Painting)

Definitions

This mode is identified through a more holistic if belated (in the Kublerian sense) incorporation of aspects derived from Kashmiri figural art of the ca. seventh through twelfth century, similar to the way that many stupas in the western Himalaya began to take on the forms earlier utilized in Kashmir, increasingly so into the twelfth and into the thirteenth century (see Figs. 3.14–17). So too in terms of figural art (though surely starting earlier and especially affecting the previously discussed Trans-Himalayan / southern Central Asian mode), the fourth mode has left artifacts mainly in the tenth through the early thirteenth century. During that period, the links between the western Himalaya and the successor states of the Karkoṭa dynasty in Kashmir left traces in the western Himalaya as well as in the west Tibetan visual and textual record.[105] The well-studied 1042 renovations at Tabo and the later Alchi group of monuments in Ladakh are in that mode, although the debate as to the extent to which they are by Kashmiri artists or by Kashmiri artists along with local artists trained by the Kashmiris continues. That is the mode known in Tibetan as Khaché, the Tibetan term for Kashmir, and is used here to refer to western Himalayan works that can be judged to be provincial, at times coarsened versions of art produced in Kashmir itself. In such sculpture and painting, the features of Kashmiri art are for the most part unmixed with those of other areas, and can be sharply discerned.[106] However, the differences remain in need of clarification as even knowledgeable specialists such as Clare Harris and Monisha Ahmed have confused the Changspa sculptures (see Figs. 4.32–35) as reflecting the Kashmiri style.[107] This Khaché mode overlaps with Klimburg-Salter's so-called Indo-Tibetan style.[108] It is certainly the most thoroughly documented of the various modes, and objects made in the western Himalaya sometimes reflect their inspiration most clearly, perhaps because of the proximity and availability of the models and artisan teachers. Nearly every major monastic shrine in Ladakh, Zangskar, and Spiti has impressive examples of Kashmiri metalwork, and some shrines, such as Nangwaphal (snang ba pal) in Zangskar, are built around an exquisite eighth- or ninth-century Kashmiri metal sculpture with silver inlay (Figs. 4.68–69). At Hanlé, in eastern Ladakh, a spectacular Kashmiri standing eleven-headed Avalokiteśvara (Fig. 4.70) has both *śāradā* and Tibetan inscriptions. The latter names the eleventh-century Gugé royal lama, Nāgarāja who

105 One thinks of the outstanding examples of the west Tibetan Rinchen Zangpo (958–1055) in Kashmir in the late tenth and early eleventh centuries, and the influential Kashmiri scholar Śākyaśrībhadra (d. 1225) in Tibet between 1204 and 1214. See Tucci, *Rin-chen-bzan-po and the Renaissance of Buddhism in Tibet*; Kuijp, "On the Lives of Śākyaśrībhadra"; and Kuijp, "Bird-faced Monk and the Beginnings of the New Tantric Tradition."

106 This mode of art-making has been explored at greater length in Linrothe, "Origins of the Kashmiri Style in the Western Himalayas," and Linrothe et al., *Collecting Paradise*.

107 "It is not surprising therefore [in the light of enduring connections between Kashmir and Ladakh] that the concrete evidence of Kashmiri influence is visible today in the deep relief rock engravings with Buddhist deities found at Dras, Mulbekh, and Leh (figure 3 [the Changspa sculpture]) which may date from the 8th century when the warrior king Lalitaditya-Muktapida exerted his power throughout the Kashmir valley and beyond." Ahmed and Harris, introduction, 11. The Dras and Mulbekh sculptures are rightfully Kashmiri, so much so that it is likely that they were carved by Kashmiri artists—the Dras sculptures most surely—so even here "Kashmiri influence" sounds misplaced. On these sculptures, see Klimburg-Salter, "Tibetan Himalayan Style" and Linrothe, "Origins of the Kashmiri Style in the Western Himalayas."

108 Klimburg-Salter, "Tibetan Himalayan Style"; Lojda et al., "Tibetan Himalayan Style."

Fig. 4.68 Sugatiśaṃdārśana Lokeśvara, brass with silver and copper inlay, from Kashmir, ca. 9th c. Nangwaphal shrine, near Karsha, Zangskar. Photo 2018.

Fig. 4.69 Close view of the face of Sugatiśaṃdārśana Lokeśvara of Fig. 4.68. Photo 2018.

had an extensive collection of Kashmiri metalwork to which he added his own rededication.[109] The characteristics of the Kashmiri models and local epigones in the western Himalaya and in west Tibet is taken up again in chapter 5 while discussing the murals in Malakartse Khar in Zangskar and Chyiwang ("Phyang") Cave 79 not far from Tholing in west Tibet. Therefore only an abbreviated summary is necessary here. A few lesser-known satellite examples, besides the most well-known ones just mentioned, are briefly covered.

In Zangskar Villages

One of the broken stones depicting Maitreya Bodhisattva at the original site of Manda village in Zangskar above the present-day village, and an intact closely related Avalokiteśvara[110] at the nearby village of Remala, both show cleanly incised lines depicting features associated with Kashmiri art. These characteristics include the almond-shaped eyes, the small *aṇḍa* of the stupas, flowers above the ears, notched hairline, and the like (Figs. 4.71–74). Another tendency visible in Kashmir sculpture is for the male chest to be clearly divided into three parts, as can be seen on the detail from Devsar halo already illustrated (see Fig. 4.52): a well-developed upper chest, tapered ribcage, and a slightly pouched or protruding belly with a marked navel, sometimes diamond-shaped. A sculpture in partial higher relief at Hongshet (skong tchet) village in Zangskar near Karsha shows the eleven-headed Avalokiteśvara with the long *vanamālā* characteristic of Kashmiri figures (Fig. 4.76).[111] And at Karsha Chuchikzhal, a fragment of a slightly raised relief sculpture

Fig. 4.70 Eleven-headed Avalokitesvara, Kashmiri metalwork, ca. 9th–10th c. Hanlé Monastery, Ladakh. Photo Mr Skarma or Skarma Photo, Leh.

109 von Schroeder, *Buddhist Sculptures in Tibet*, 1:84–86, 126–29. Hanlé is included (as "Anley") in Devers, *Historical Sites of Changthang*, 135–38.

110 I am indebted to Quentin Devers for originally showing me a photograph of the Remala sculpture.

111 See Linrothe, "Summer in the Field," figs. 8 and 8a; Devers, *Historical Sites of Zangskar, Kargil, Ladakh*, 117, 125.

Fig. 4.71 Standing Maitreya and Mañjuśri bodhisattvas, stone, h. 87 and 55 cm, above Manda village, Zangskar. Photo 2010.

Fig. 4.72 Close view of the head of Maitreya bodhisattva depicted in Fig. 4.71. Photo 2010.

Fig. 4.73 Standing Padmapāṇi bodhisattva, stone, h. 74 cm, in Remala Village, Zangskar. Photo 2022.

Fig. 4.74 Close view of the head of Padmapāṇi bodhisattva depicted in Fig. 4.73. Photo 2022.

Fig. 4.75 Standing eleven-headed Avalokiteśvara on lion throne, h. 181 cm. at Hongshet Village, Zangskar. Photo 2018.

Fig. 4.76 Close view of the standing eleven-headed Avalokiteśvara at Hongshet village depicted in Fig. 4.75. Photo 2012.

Fig. 4.77 Low-relief sculpture fragment of crowned figure propped on a deteriorated stupa at Karsha Chuchikzhal, Zangskar. Photo 2006.

Fig. 4.78 Close view of the face of the crowned figure in Fig. 4.77. Photo 2006.

Fig. 4.79 Carved wooden beams inside the gateway stupa marking the passageway from the upper murals at Zangla, Zangskar. Photo 2003.

survives (Figs. 4.77–78).[112] The small face has almond shaped eyes and a three-medallion crown, evidence of a Kashmiri orientation.

Early paintings in the Khaché mode are rarer in Zangskar. One exception is an entrance stupa at Zangla (see Fig. 5.10) with archaic carved wooden beams between the inner corridor and the upper murals (Fig. 4.79), and notable paintings inside that dome that can be connected to Kashmir painting (Figs. 4.80–82).[113] Note the extended eye in profile, the small pupil floating in the white sclera, and the rounded faces.[114] That these were made for, if not by, local inhabitants is indicated by the type of dress and ornamentation of the female sponsors (see Fig. 4.82), a type

112 Devers, *Historical Sites of Zanskar*, 129.

113 Ibid., 205, 211.

114 On the extended eye, see Goswamy, *Conversations*, 39–42.

Fig. 4.81 Head and upper torso of mural of Ratnasambhava Transcendent Lord (Tathāgata) on the "south" wall inside the gateway stupa in Zangla, Zangskar. Photo 2018.

Fig. 4.80 Close view of the Mahāvairocana on the ceiling of the Zangla gateway stupa. Photo 2013.

Fig. 4.82 Two seated female sponsor figures and a standing youth below the Ratnasambhava Tathāgata of Fig. 4.81. Photo 2012.

Fig 4.83 *Chandraśālā* fragment from Lākhamandal, Uttarakhand. Photo 2006.

Fig. 4.84 Standing couple, stone carving on Masrur temple in Kangra (Himachal Pradesh, India). Photo by Melissa Kerin, 2004

that is now considered western Himalayan.[115] The most elaborate examples of Kashmiri art in the western Himalaya are the early ones in the mid-eleventh century at the Dukhang of Tabo and later (ca. late 12th–early 13th c.) at the Sumtsek in Alchi, as discussed in chapter 5.[116] Even they, however, demonstrate through the textiles worn by male royal sponsor figures "the cultural forms and practices current in Central Islamic lands" rather than an orientation eastward toward Tibet.[117] These affiliations will be discussed at greater length in chapter 5.

Other Variants

There is another possible source of derivation for such an image, however. By the seventh and eighth centuries, at one of the early peaks of Kashmiri political and cultural power, the Kashmiri style had been welcomed into its northern areas of Gilgit, Swat, Baltistan and Hunza, spilling over into Ladakh and Zangskar. It also was felt to the southeast of Kashmir. As is the case of Lākhamandal in Uttarakhand, with its northern architectural-style *chandraśālā* (Fig. 4.83), the site of Masrur in Kangra, demonstrates links with Nagara architectural traditions of northern India (as opposed to Kashmir), as Meister establishes.[118] He argues that it was built in or just after the reign of Yaśovarman (ca. 725–754), overlapping that of the Kashmiri Lalitāditya (ca. 724–760). The architecture may very well be imported from that more familiar to the Kābyakubja state, in the Post-Gupta mode seen already at the Bajaura Mahādeva Temple in Kulu (see Fig. 4.19), but the images of standing figures there are strikingly Kashmiri in character (Fig. 4.84). Once again, we can point to the developed tripartite male torso and the long *vanamālā*, the egg-shaped head, although to be sure the angles are softened partly due to the chalky stone. Such a carving has more in common with the Śiva from Pāndrethan (see Fig. 4.36) than it does to the figure from the geographically closer Lākhamaṇḍal (see Fig. 4.37), which in turn has more in common with Post-Gupta sculptural forms. This Kashmiri affiliation

115 Besides stone sculpture and painting, early western Himalayan metalworking was also dependent on Kashmiri models and craftsmen, there being, to my knowledge, no artistic metalworking tradition prior to the emulations of Kashmir metal-casting in the tenth and eleventh centuries. Although the craftsmen learned quickly, the early-period works appear to demonstrate an unfamiliarity with the techniques.

116 Klimburg-Salter, *Tabo*; Goepper and Poncar, *Alchi*.

117 Flood, "A Turk in the Dukhang?," 234.

118 Meister, "Mountain Temples and Temple-Mountains."

Fig. 4.85 Gadāpuruṣā at the side of Viṣṇu, stone sculpture in a niche at Mahādeva Temple of the ca. 8th c. Bajaura Village, Kulu Valley, Himachal Pradesh. Photo 2022.

Fig. 4.86 Close view of the Kashmiri-style weskit worn by Mahiṣāsura-mārdinī, stone sculpture in a niche at Mahādeva Temple of the ca. 8th c. Bajaura Village, Kulu Valley, Himachal Pradesh. Photo 2022.

Fig. 4.89 Standing dark stone figure with Kashmiri-style vanamālā in the circumambulation corridor inside the main shrine at Triloknath, Lahaul, Himachal Pradesh. Photo 2016.

Fig. 4.87 *Śikhara* (tower) over the main shrine at Triloknath, Lahaul, Himachal Pradesh. Photo 2016.

Fig. 4.88 *Chandraśālā* with the faces of Śiva on the *śikhara* over the main shrine at Triloknath, Lahaul, Himachal Pradesh. Photo 2018.

of sculptures in otherwise Gupta-inspired architectural settings is quite apparent for the goddess figures at Bajaura. The *devīs* wear Kashmiri three-pronged crowns and even the distinctive Kashmiri weskit (Figs. 4.85–86). This is the tight bodice that often ends above the navel in V-shaped points. At Triloknath, north of the Rohtang pass and southwest of Keylong, a pattern similar to that of Masrur and Kulu can be detected. The exterior architecture is in a northern Indian mode (Figs. 4.87–88), but the sculpture is inflected by Kashmir:[119] an old stone sculpture, that I noticed in the back of the structure's circumambulation corridor, unfortunately headless, with its long *vanamālā* and tripartite chest, is derived from Kashmiri figural types (Fig. 4.89).

The Early Impact of Central Tibetan Buddhist Art in Zangskar

Adapted Eastern-Indian ("Magadha") Mode via Central Tibetan Art (ca. 11th–13th c.) (Painting and Sculpture)

The fifth mode draws on the early central Tibetan sequence of painting, itself modified from the Buddhist painting of eastern India and Nepal and known as the Gyalu (rgyal lugs) or "Indian Style."[120] The eastern Indian mode of painting practiced in Tibetan and western Himalayan Buddhist contexts is also known as "Shari" (shar ris).[121] According to some commentators, the eastern Indian mode, or the "Pala style," became prominent in central Tibet in the eleventh century "and remained dominant into the late 13th century."[122] Although a modified version of it came to dominate many areas of the western Himalaya in the later thirteenth and fourteenth centuries (and would appear also in sculpture), it manifests in a relatively early form at an entrance stupa preserved from the ca. twelfth century above Karsha monastery in Zangskar, locally referred to as the "Kadampa Chorten" (see chapter 7; Fig. 7.8).[123]

Fruitful comparisons are afforded by examining the unrestored, damaged murals inside the Kadampa Chorten (Fig. 4.90)[124] in the light of an early thirteenth-century painting from central Tibet in the Metropolitan Museum[125] or a painting in a similar mode in the Bharat Kala Bhavan in Benaras Hindu University (BHU), Varanasi (Fig. 4.91).[126] Both those examples were part of five Tathāgata sets, and in fact the Kadampa Chorten also features one of the Tathāgatas at the center of each of the four interior walls with the fifth, in this case Akṣobhya, painted on the lantern ceiling.[127]

119 After drafting this observation, I found that Gerald Kozicz had arrived at the same conclusion for the Chamba site of Swaim, "which saw the fusion of *nagara* architecture of northwestern India and the sculptural art of Kashmir." Kozicz, "Collapsed, Fragmented, and Reassembled," 100.

120 Stoddard, "'Indian Style' *rGyal lugs* on an Early Tibetan Book Cover."

121 Jackson, *Nepalese Legacy in Tibetan Painting*, 53.

122 Kossak, "Pala Painting Style and Its Tibetan Variant," 39. Kossak models the same preference for eastern India over Tibetan art noted in the analysis of Tucci's *Tibetan Painted Scrolls* in chapter 2: Indian figures "have subtly articulated postures and lively features," while the Tibetan paintings based on them are characterized as "static, frontal . . . flaccid . . . less animated . . . bland and lacking in volume." Ibid., 43–44.

123 Linrothe and Kerin, "Deconsecration and Discovery;" Devers, *Historical Sites of Zanskar*, 132, 142–43.

124 The wall murals are 2.2 meters off the ground and the height of the murals is 140 cm.

125 The Buddha Amoghasiddhi with attendants, Metropolitan Museum (1991.74), https://www.metmuseum.org/art/collection/search/37966. Others are found online at https://www.himalayanart.org/search/set.cfm?setID=4369.

126 While the stains and losses of the BHU painting are initially jarring, they actually give confidence that what we see is not the product of recent inpainting or cosmetic "improvements" of its surface.

127 On the five Tathāgata sets, see Luczanits, "On the Iconography of Tibetan Scroll Paintings (*Thang ka*) Dedicated to the Five Tathāgatas." See also https://www.himalayanart.org/search/set.cfm?setID=4369.

Fig. 4.90 Central section of the mural of Ratnasambhava Transcendent Lord (Tathāgata) on the "south" wall inside the Kadampa gateway stupa above Chuchikzhal, Karsha, Zangskar. Photo 2006.

Fig. 4.92 Close view of the head and upper torso of the Ratnasambhava Tathāgata depicted in Fig. 4.90. Photo 2001.

Fig. 4.93 Close view of the head and crown of the Mahāvairocana Tathāgata depicted in Fig. 4.91. Photo 2006.

Fig. 4.91 *Thangka* of Mahāvairocana Transcendent Lord (Tathāgata), pigments on cloth, central Tibet, ca. late 12th–early 13th c. Now in the Bharat Kala Bhavan in Benaras Hindu University (BHU), Varanasi. Photo 2006.

Fig. 4.94 Close view of the torso of the Ratnasambhava Tathāgata depicted in Fig 4.90. Photo 2018.

Fig. 4.95 Close view of the torso and hands of the Mahāvairocana Tathāgata depicted in Fig. 4.91. Photo 2006.

The BHU Vairocana makes clear the affiliation with eastern-Indian–derived forms: the shape and distribution of the tines of the multilevel crown (compare Figs. 4.92–93), the jewel-inlaid disk-like earrings, the ribbons at the ears, and the sequence of necklaces. The bow-shaped eyes and eyebrows, so different from the Kashmir almond-shaped eyes, are a telling marker of eastern-Indian affiliation. Subtle shading and color modeling is also visible, as are the scrolling patterns and the specific shape the top of the dhoti adopts around the abdomen, emphasizing its musculature (Figs. 4.94–95). The jeweled triangular fleurons emerging from the backrest at the level of the Buddha's shoulders are a distinctive trait of the mode, and can be seen on the Akṣobhya at the center of the mandala on the lantern ceiling (Fig. 4.96) and on the BHU painting (Fig. 4.97). The fleurons are also visible in a low-relief Buddha sculpture at Hongshet village in Zangskar, immediately next to the eleven-headed Avalokiteśvara in the Khaché mode mentioned above (Fig. 4.98). Nearby is a wrathful deity—Vajrapāṇi—also in the Gyalu mode (Fig. 4.99), with the bulging eyes in a higher relief, but the rest in an outline mode that succeeds in conveying an

Fig. 4.97 Close view of the jeweled earring and fleuron at the right shoulder of the Mahāvairocana Tathāgata depicted in Fig. 4.91. Photo 2006.

Fig. 4.96 Akṣobhya Transcendent Lord (Tathāgata) mural on the ceiling of the Kadampa gateway stupa above Chuchikzhal, Karsha, Zangskar. Photo 2001.

Fig. 4.98 Seated Buddha with outlines engraved on stone, h. approx. 60 cm, at Hongshet Village, Zangskar. Photo 2018.

Fig. 4.99 Wrathful Vajrapāṇi outlined engraving on stone, h. approx. 100 cm, at Hongshet Village, Zangskar. Photo 1998.

Fig. 4.100 Seated Mañjuśrī bodhisattva, underdrawing outlines on mural inside the Kadampa gateway stupa above Chuchikzhal, Karsha, Zangskar. Photo 2001.

exuberant dynamism. Among the fragmentary materials deposited into one of the Karsha Chuchikzhal stupas that were discovered and documented during the stupas' demolishment in 2013 (discussed in Chapter 7) is a torn page from an illuminated manuscript (Fig. 7.30). It depicts Amoghasiddhi Tathāgata in a central Tibetan mode of imagery. The ritual helmet, the bow-shaped eyes, the shape of the torso and other features including the fleurons all correspond to the other cited examples. Whether or not this highly mobile object was created in central Tibet and brought to Karsha, or was made in Zangskar, it illustrates one likely mode of the transmission of such painterly conventions. Aspects of this mode including the fleurons, survive into the late thirteenth or early fourteenth century in Ladakh where they appear, for example, in the Senge Gang murals at Lamayuru (Fig. 7A.4).

The Gyalu type of painting looks strikingly different from the well-published Kashmiri-inflected paintings of the Alchi group in Ladakh. Among other things, the torsos of the Gyalu figural bodies are lithe, slender, and often given to a kind of swaying movement involving a tilt of the head. This feature is illustrated by the underdrawing of a four-armed Mañjuśrī bodhisattva on one of the walls of the Kadampa Chorten that has lost most of its added pigment (Fig. 4.100), and is also visible in some of the earliest murals to survive at Zhalu (Shalu; Zhwa lu) monastery in Tsang Province of mid-western Tibet (Fig. 4.101). The latter image shows a *vajra*-bodhisattva in ritual helmet similar to those worn by the Tathāgatas in the Kadampa Chorten and BHU cloth paintings (see Figs. 4.92–93). The Zhalu mural, datable to the eleventh century, is in the Yumchenmo Lhakhang at Zhalu and is "in a characteristic Indian Pala style of [high] artistic

Fig. 4.101 *Vajra*-bodhisattva (*samādhi* deity), ca. 11th-c. mural in the Yumchenmo Lhakhang at Zhalu Monastery, Tibet. Photo 2007.

Fig. 4.102 Mahāvairocana Transcendent Lord (Tathāgata), metalwork, h. 24.7 cm, Nalanda. New Delhi National Museum, acc. no. 467.48. Photo 2022.

Fig. 4.103 Amitayūs on the "west" wall mural inside the Kadampa gateway stupa above Chuchikzhal, Karsha, Zangskar. Photo 2010.

mastery."[128] That such ritual helmets can be traced back to eastern India, not to speak of the body type, is demonstrated by the gilded metalwork Vairocana excavated at Nalanda, now in the National Museum in Delhi (Fig. 4.102).[129] Note too in the Zhalu mural the ornamented framing borders at the sides of the *vajra*-bodhisattva, painted as if inlaid with colorful gemstones. This too is a characteristic of Gyalu and can be seen in the mural of the Tathāgata Amitāyus (Fig. 4.103), among other places in the Kadampa Chorten.

128 Henss, *Cultural Monuments of Tibet*, 2:612. Henss also illustrates two clear photographs in ibid., 2: figs. 878 and 879.

129 Acc. no. 47.48; h. 24.7 cm. Singh and Singh, *Ecstasy of Classical Art*, no. 2.

Fig. 4.104 Seated Mahāvairocana Buddha, outlines carved onto stone now near government compound, Padum, Zangskar. Photo 2008.

Fig. 4.105 Outlines of Mahāvairocana Buddha and lion throne, close view of Fig. 4.104. Photo 2022.

Fig. 4.106 Close view of Mahāvairocana Buddha in Fig. 4.104. Photo 2008.

Fig. 4.107 Close view of lion supporting Buddha throne of Fig. 4.104. Photo 2022.

Also belonging to this group is on one face of a three-sided stone in the government-building area of Padum in Zangskar. While the other faces belong to other modes (see Figs. 4.61–62), the largest of the three is an outline carving of a Mahāvairocana seated on a lion throne (Figs. 4.104–107).[130]

When I visited in 2011 it was situated immediately in front of the entrance to the "Community Information Center" of Zangskar, the government-sponsored internet service office in Padum. At that time, the office was rarely open; in 2019 it had closed altogether. In most stone versions of the eastern India Gyalu mode in Zangskar, they are outlined rather than relief sculpture, including the ones from Hongshet (Figs. 4.98–99). They feature softened, taut S-curved outlines, as in the bodies and tails of the backward-looking lions on the base (Fig. 4.107). The torso of the deities are slender rather than hardened or built-up as in the Khaché mode, and lotus petals on the throne emphasize those pointing up over those pointing down. They also tend to have a

130 According to Stanzin Chosgyal ("Pali"), a son-in-law of Karsha Lonpo, his father—a retired government servant—was instrumental in relocating and re-erecting the stone during his years in office.

Fig. 4.108 Vajrasattva, painted clay sculpture on the main wall of the Serkhang, Lalung, Spiti, Himachal Pradesh. Photo 2006.

Fig. 4.109 Vajrasattva in architectural shrine, painted clay sculpture on the main wall of the Serkhang, Lalung, Spiti, Himachal Pradesh. Photo 2006.

Fig. 4.110 Crowned *vajra*-bodhisattva (samādhi deity), painted clay sculpture on main wall of the Serkhang, Lalung, Spiti, Himachal Pradesh. Photo 2006.

nimbus that is slightly wider at the top than near the shoulders, often with a slight point at the top.

Another site in the western Himalaya that retains recognizable traces of its original Gyalu orientation, despite repeated repainting and restoration campaigns, is the Serkhang of Lalung (Figs. 4.108–110). Luczanits, who has described and analyzed it extensively,[131] dates it to the second half of the twelfth century;[132] Kurt Tropper, who studied the founding inscription, dates it to between 1025 and 1250.[133] Tropper argues the inscription was probably done by a powerful member of the elite Guge-Purang rulers; it mentions more than once subduing hostile enemies, working or fighting on the borderlands. Therefore the sponsor was actively engaged in the occupation of Spiti and melding it into the west Tibetan kingdom. As Luczanits describes the sculptures, "they are slender with thin, elongated limbs and slim shovel-shaped face . . . they have beautiful, slightly angular, facial features: large eyes with a curving eyelid, a groove marking the eyebrows . . . a prominent, straight nose with slightly flared nostrils, and a pronounced crescent-shaped mouth."[134] These are not the only markers of the Gyalu form-idiom. Marialaura Di Mattia has pointed out that the sculptural shrines serving as niches for the sculptures (see Fig. 4.109) have been adapted from the architecture of Bihar and Bengal in the Pāla-Sena period.[135] Although Luczanits points out some features he considers Kashmiri-derived, I see the Lalung sculptures are fundamentally eastern Indian in inspiration.[136]

131 Luczanits, *Buddhist Sculpture in Clay*, 93–106.

132 Ibid., 106.

133 Tropper, *Founding Inscription in the gSer khaṅ of Lalung*, 13. In her report on Lalung, Klimburg-Salter dates it to the end of the twelfth century ("Tucci Himalayan Archives Report, 2," 46).

134 Luczanits, *Buddhist Sculpture in Clay*, 102.

135 Di Mattia, "Divine Palaces of the Buddha,"

136 Some distinctive iconographic features at Lalung are discussed in chapter 5.

Localized Newari-Tibetan Mode (ca. late 10th–14th c.) (Painting)

It is an understatement that Newar painters and metalworkers of Nepal were highly appreciated in Tibet. By the twelfth century or so, some of the finest monuments in Central and mid-western Tibet, such as Zhalu, were painted by Tibetan and Newar artists in a style that became associated with Nepal known as Balri (*bal ris*). Newar artists were also working at such sites as Tholing in the thirteenth century.[137] One of the foundations for the development of Balri art was the art of eastern India (Magadha in particular) during the Pāla-Sena period (8th–13th c.).[138] On this basis were added discrete characteristics, one of which is a color scheme that privileges red against a dark-blue background. Garuḍas and *makara*s are favored in compositions, often integrated into elaborate throne-backs, along with pillars in vases supporting lotus capitals, earrings lying parallel to the picture plane, and so forth.[139] It is probably only a slight exaggeration to state that by the late fourteenth century the Newar-Tibetan type of painting "was adopted in Tibet universally."[140] It certainly figures into later painting in the fourteenth and fifteenth centuries in the western Himalaya as well. Here we will use murals from two sites, one in Spiti and one in Zangskar, with relatively early dates, probably not earlier than the late thirteenth or fourteenth century. Many of the traits just mentioned are visible there, although a few comparisons with central Tibetan Balri paintings are also provided.

A clear example of this sixth mode in the western Himalaya is found in northern Spiti, near Kibber, only a few days' walk from Zangskar (closer than Shey, for example), in a village named Tashigang (Fig. 4.111). It has an entrance stupa (Fig. 4.112) with paintings on the inside of the dome in a modified version of a Newari or Nepalese mode of painting (Figs. 4.113–117).[141] Another example is in Padum, one of the capitals of Zangskar. Near the old town and royal settlement is a gateway or *kankani* chorten (stupa), as they are called locally (Fig. 4.118), this one referred to as the Nyingpa (old) *kankani* chorten. Inside are mural paintings on the four walls supporting the lantern ceiling, at the center of which is a square painting on cloth that is curling away from the beams to which it was bonded with some type of adhesive (Figs. 119–122).[142] A crowned Akṣobhya Buddha is at the center below a Garuḍa perched on his head nimbus (Fig. 4.119), a pair of bodhisattvas at his sides (Figs. 4.120–121), and two *makara*s with scrolling floriate tails on the outer finials of his throne-back (Fig. 4.122). Difficult to date and mixed with elements current in both Khaché and Pāla

137 Vitali, *Records of Tho-ling*, 124, 125. See also Vitali, *Kingdoms of Gu.ge Pu.hrang*.

138 That in the early thirteenth century, "strong Indo-Nepalese artistic affinities" in Tibet were "ultimately deriving from Pāla art in India," is recognized in Gyalpo and Kalantari, "Buddhist Monuments of Khartse Valley," 17.

139 Jackson, *Nepalese Legacy in Tibetan Painting*.

140 Ibid., xi.

141 The entrance stupa was modified and one of the entrances blocked up to create an enclosed shrine in the lower area with later murals. Kozicz, who has studied the architecture in detail, suggests a date of the thirteenth or fourteenth century. Kozicz, "One *Stūpa* and Three *Lha thos*," 237.

142 Devers, *Historical Sites of Zanskar*, 167, 176.

(clockwise from top left):

Fig. 4.111 Tashigang Village (foreground), with striped entrance stupa on right. Spiti, Himachal Pradesh. Photo 2022.

Fig. 4.112 Tashigang entrance stupa exterior, Spiti, Himachal Pradesh. Photo 2006.

Fig. 4.113 Seated Amitāyus Transcendent Lord (Tathāgata) in mural on "south" wall of Tashigang entrance stupa, Spiti, Himachal Pradesh. Photo 2006.

Fig. 4.115 Seated Amitāyus Tathāgata on the "east" wall of Tashigang entrance stupa, Spiti, Himachal Pradesh. Photo 2006.

Fig. 4.114 Close view of Amitāyus Tathāgata holding vase of *amṛta* (long-life nectar) with Garuḍa above his head, detail of Fig. 4.113. Photo 2006.

Fig. 4.116 Standing white (Padmapāṇi?) bodhisattva on "west" wall of Tashigang entrance stupa, Spiti, Himachal Pradesh. Photo 2022.

Fig. 4.118 Exterior of Nyingpa *kankani* chorten (gateway stupa) north of Padum, Zangskar, view from the north. Photo 2012.

Fig. 4.117 Amitāyus Buddha at center of Amitāyus mandala on ceiling of the Tashigang entrance stupa, Spiti, Himachal Pradesh. Photo 2006.

Fig. 4.119 Detailed view of the Akṣobhya Transcendent Lord (Tathāgata) painted on cloth on the ceiling of the Nyingpa gateway stupa, Padum, Zangskar. Photo 2018.

painting, at both Tashigang and the Padum gateway chorten, there are a number of distinct features deriving from Newar paintings of the twelfth to fourteenth century.[143] Besides the traits already listed, they include the shape of the necklaces on the chest with multiple loops (see Fig. 4.115), the mode of depicting emphatic strands of hair on the shoulders (see Figs. 4.114–115, 4.119, 4.121) that sometimes are punctuated with hooks to suggest curls, the peculiar mincing quality of the side bodhisattvas with their long arms and swaying hips (see Figs. 4.116, 4.120), as well as the profusion of scarves and the overall flatness. There is also a kind of simplicity to the figures and the faces, a childlike innocence, a guilelessness

143 Thirteenth-century examples of Newar or Newar-Tibetan paintings on cloth include ones in the Philadelphia Museum of Art (1994-148-609; HAR item no. 87054), the Los Angeles County Museum of Art (M.81.90.5; HAR item no. 85732), and the Museum of Fine Arts Boston (BMFA.67.818; https://collections.mfa.org/objects/22396/buddha-of-the-eternal-life-amitayus-and-eight-bodhisattvas?ctx=b829e8ef- baea-40dd-aa30-08b0502d409d&idx=0). See also Jackson, *Nepalese Legacy in Tibetan Painting*, 99–103.

Fig. 4.120 Standing white (Padmapāṇi?) bodhisattva on the proper right of Akṣobhya Tathāgata painted on cloth on the ceiling of the Nyingpa gateway stupa, Padum, Zangskar. Photo 2018.

Fig. 4.121 Close view of the standing bodhisattva on the proper left of Akṣobhya Tathāgata painted on cloth on the ceiling of the Nyingpa gateway stupa, Padum, Zangskar. Photo 2018.

Fig. 4.122 Floral scrolling, *makara*-finial and colored jewels on throneback of Akṣobhya Buddha painted on cloth on the ceiling of the Nyingpa gateway stupa, Padum, Zangskar. Photo 2018.

Fig. 4.124 Close view of the face and hands (holding lotus stems) of White Mañjuśrī bodhisattva mural in Newar mode, Nenying Monastery, Tibet. Photo 2007.

Fig. 4.125 Standing white bodhisattva mural with *pastiglia* in Gyantse Fort, Tibet. Photo 2007.

Fig. 4.123 Head and head nimbus of Akṣobhya Transcendent Lord (Tathāgata), mural in Segoma Lhakhang, Zhalu Monastery, Tibet. Photo 2007.

or sweetness to the expressions, especially in the less sophisticated versions in the western Himalaya.

The early fourteenth-century murals of the Segoma at Zhalu (Fig. 4.123) can be considered one of the great monuments of Balri painting in Tibet. One can see there many of the elements characteristics of early Newari painting in central Tibet, which no doubt reached Spiti and Zangskar via Tibet, and/or directly from Nepal. These features include the motif of the Garuḍa above the head-nimbus and *makara*s on the backrest, the distinct bow-shaped eyes (similar to eastern-Indian imagery but quite different from the Kashmir almond-shaped eyes), the arched eyebrows well below the high forehead, the notch in the hairline at the center of the heart-shaped forehead. The comparison is somewhat unfair to the western Himalaya, as Zhalu "is associated with the direct patronage received from the Mongol Yuan emperors of China, which made possible a massive renovation," and represents a peak of "artistic efflorescence and creativity."[144] The somewhat more modest Nenying (gnas snying)

144 Richardson, "When Walls Could Talk," 244.

Monastery ca. thirteenth or fourteenth-century murals in Tsang, also visibly Newar in inspiration, have some similarities in terms of the configuration of the necklaces and treatment of hair (compare Figures 4.115 and 4.124). Nearby Nenying, the fort at Gyantse has fine Newar-mode paintings, unfortunately in a parlous state, but one of the surviving bodhisattva paintings (Fig. 4.125) maintains something of the awkward pose, where hips and shoulders seem to bend in opposite directions, also seen in the Tashigang bodhisattva (see Fig. 4.116).

Local Mixtures and Interpretations in Zangskar

The category of early painting and sculpture in Zangskar designated as type number 4 in the list on page 146, which decidedly derived from Kashmiri art in a more direct way, not just via Baltistan, Gilgit, Skardu, and southern Central Asia—is significant enough to merit a chapter dedicated to a fuller exploration. Chapter 5: "Looking Westward: Painting in the Kashmiri Idiom" does that along with examination of early paintings that are similarly derived. So, too, the art that is inspired by central Tibetan art starting in the twelfth century (mode 5) is also expanded upon in chapter 7, "Discovery, Deconsecration, Rebuilding and Reconsecration: Revisiting the Art, Architecture, and Relics in Karsha's Chuchikzhal Complex." While not dealt with outside of this chapter, the Newar-derived category has been explored in detail by others.[145] Category number 7 in the list on page 146 is something of a miscellany, containing exceptions or hybrids when a single dominant strain is difficult to discern. Sculptures have been classed thus either because local components or ineptitude overwhelms whatever appropriated aesthetic mode lay behind the artist's intentions, or multiple sources or admixtures of elements make classification challenging. As Kubler argues, "Several formal sequences may coexist within one object . . . . A complex form . . . will contain traits belonging to different sequences."[146]

Padum 5 Tathāgatas

The most urgent of such sculptures in Zangskar to locate on a stylistic map is also iconographically one of the most intricate. The overall theme is straightforward to identify. In terms of the latter, on the same boulder near the Lungnak river on which the stone stupas discussed in chapter 3 were carved (see Figs. 3.36–37) we find reliefs of five seated Tathāgata (Figs. 4.126–129).[147] As the view from an oblique angle to the boulder (Fig. 4.129) reveals, the sculptures are in higher relief than, for example,

145 Jackson includes a section titled "Transitional Styles in Far-Western Tibet" that begins by considering paintings at the Lhakhang Soma in Alchi, paintings in the Koelz collection from Spiti, from Wanla in Ladakh, as well as in west Tibet, conflating the two regions. Jackson, *Nepalese Legacy in Tibetan Painting*, 120–29.

146 Kubler, "Shape of Time," 114.

147 Devers, *Historical Sites of Zanskar*, 172, 178, 180; Francke, "Kleine archäologische Erträge," 656, and photo by J. B. Riddell captioned "Photographie der grossen Buddhas." opp. p. 660.

Fig. 4.126 Site known as Gyalwa Rig nga (rgyal ba rigs lnga; Five Transcendent Lords) near Lungnak river north of Padum, Zangskar. Total width of the composition, 6.25 m. Photo 1998, before "restoration."

Fig. 4.127 Same site as in Fig. 4.126, after cement steps have been added. Photo 2022, after "restoration."

Fig. 4.128 Five Transcendent Lords (Tathāgata) sculpture on boulder near Lungnak river north of Padum, Zangskar. Photo 1998, before "restoration."

Fig. 4.129 Five Tathāgata sculpture depicted in Figure 4.128, depicted from oblique angle to show the depth of the carving. Photo 2022, after "restoration."

Fig. 4.130 Five Tathāgata site of Figure 4.126 receiving reverence by a nun. Photo 2015.

the bodhisattvas of the Shambhala Gate (see Figs. 4.58, 4.65–67), those of Remala and Manda (see Figs. 4.71–74) or Hongshet (see Figs. 4.75–76, 4.98–99). The site is referred to as the *rgyal ba rigs lnga*, which references the five families of Tathāgata who appear complete with their respective *vāhana* (vehicles) and making the associated mudra. Phuntsok Dawa, the late Padum king, informed me that the boulder was formerly on royal land that had been divided and the portion on which the boulder is located is now owned by his nephew.[148] It is considered particularly numinous and powerful, and it is not unusual to see local lay and monastic visitors carrying out rituals and making offerings in front of it (Fig. 4.130). Unfortunately, by 2008 a pious Ladakhi stationed in Padum with the Indo-Tibetan Border Police Force sponsored a "repair" of the sculptures, with cement. The details of the mudras, for instance, are no longer reliable (Akṣobhya's hand is now wrongly oriented, for example), so with indicated exceptions (including Figure 4.130), I will when possible employ older photographs here.

The grassy slope near the river has apparently increased in height over the centuries, and what at one time was probably well below the boulder has slowly risen to obscure part of the carving on the lower left (see Fig. 4.126). That blocked off some of the standing figures shown *en face* in a register directly below the thrones, with small *caitya*s between each figure. Very recently, the left side has been cleared away to make a path, exposing somewhat less weathered relief sculptures. This is somewhat visible by comparing the right side of overall photos Figures 4.126 and 4.127, the latter being the more recent, where the slope has been removed. One can see the effect of being protected from weathering from the much lighter

148 Personal communication, 24 July 2008. In May 2023, I met an alert and gracious Phuntsok Dawa in Padum; only a few days later, I heard that he had passed away in his sleep.

Fig. 4.131 Five Transcendent Lords (Tathāgata) metal sculpture, Kashmir or early western Himalaya, ca. 8th–9th c. Now in Sankar Monastery, Leh, Ladakh. Photo 2016.

color of the stone where it was covered (see Fig. 4.136). The five Buddhas are still clear, with a slightly larger Mahāvairocana at the center on a lion throne. On his left are Akṣobhya with elephants and Ratnasambhava with horses; on his right are Amitāyus with peacocks and Amoghasiddhi with Garuḍas. The four Buddhas around Mahāvairocana are in the unbejeweled, uncrowned state—Mahāvairocana alone is crowned. This mixed mode, crowned and uncrowned together, is a feature of early depictions of the five Tathāgatas. The texts that discuss these five families, such as the *Sarvatathāgata Tattva Saṃgraha*, must be as early as the seventh century, since by the eighth they had been translated into Chinese.

The five Tathāgata set, with Mahāvairocana at the center crowned and bejeweled and the other four in uncrowned form wearing monastic robes, in that sense resembles the Shey group (see Figs. 4.42–43), except that the Shey Buddhas were all standing and the Padum ones are all seated. An immediate connection of the Padum group can be made with Kashmiri or Khaché sculpture, as a similarly arranged set of the directional seated Buddhas in metal is preserved at the Sankar monastery in Leh (Fig. 4.131). It is most likely a product of a western Himalayan artist closely following Kashmiri precedents, such as the ca. ninth-century Kashmiri brass sculpture now in Lhasa.[149] On the other hand, the undifferentiated torsos and the simplified, somewhat puffy faces do not help much in assigning a Kashmiri origin. Nor do the very small, rounded *uṣṇīṣa*s reinforce a Kashmiri affiliation.

According to the Vajradhātu *mahāmaṇḍala*, each of the four Tathāgata barring Mahāvairocana alone has four *vajra*-bodhisattvas (or *samādhi* deities) in his train, sixteen altogether. Also part of the mandala are four inner and four outer offering deities, and four gatekeepers. In addition, there are four consorts or family mothers (*kulamātṛ*), one from each of the four Tathāgata offered to Mahāvairocana. They thus represent the four families of the

149 The brass sculpture from Kashmir has the same iconography (the five Tathāgata Buddhas, the central one a crowned Vairocana, and the other four in monk robes) now in the Lima Lhakhang in the Potala Collection, Lhasa, illustrated in von Schroeder, *Buddhist Sculptures in Tibet*, 1:138, pl. 33.

vajra, the gem, the lotus, and karma (this last represented by a double *vajra* or by a sword), governed by Akṣobhya, Ratnasambhava, Amitāyus, and Amoghasiddhi Tathāgata, respectively. Although not in the format of a fully symmetrical mandala, the Padum composition is an "unpacked," implicit, or "horizontal" mandala. That is, unlike the five Tathāgatas at Shey, all thirty-seven deities of the Vajradhātu *mahāmaṇḍala* are represented on the boulder, not just the five central Tathāgatas.

On the Padum boulder, between and slightly above the five high-relief seated Buddhas, are eight low-relief standing figures bearing objects, unfortunately now nearly indecipherable. Six are at the level of the head nimbus and two directly above Vairocana (Fig. 4.132). One, above Amoghasiddhi, definitely holds a bowl (Fig. 4.133), one a garland, and one has hands symmetrically arranged resting on the hips or waist. From this it is possible to identify them as the inner and outer offering deities, in this case in male form, which is not unprecedented though they are usually female. The clearest one appears to the upper right of Amoghasiddhi (Fig. 4.133), a post-repair photograph in which the cement added to the Buddha's face is painfully apparent. Below the five Tathāgata thrones is a row of standing figures who wear crowns and earrings and stand on a shared horizontal lotus base, with miniature stupas between each of them at head height (Fig. 4.134). Another post-restoration photograph displays the first four on the far right of this long line of standing figures (Fig. 4.135). The first two on the right appear bare-chested and perhaps are wearing dhotis. Both hands are supporting something in front of the chest. The left two wear long robes that end above their ankles, their feet splayed, and the proper left arms hanging at their sides, with an extended sleeve. The right two are protective gate guardians: the one on the far right holds a bell and is Vajraghaṇṭa or Vajrāveśa; the one on his right is probably Vajrasphoṭa holding a chain. The left pair in the photograph dressed in robes with their left arms hanging at their sides are *vajra*-bodhisattvas (*samādhi* deities), and six more follow them to the right, so that altogether there are eight identically dressed figures in a row to the right of center. There then follow four standing figures in a row who are dressed in belted robes like the *vajra*-bodhisattvas but have their left arms akimbo, their hands at their hip. They hold four different objects in their right hands; from left to right, they are vajra, gem, padma and crossed vajra. They represent the four consorts (or *kulamātṛ*) offered to Vairocana, one from each of the other four families. After them the *vajra*-bodhisattvas with the long sleeve

Fig. 4.132 Close view of the head and nimbus of Mahāvairocana Tathāgata on the Padum Gyalwa Rig nga boulder, with accompanying standing offering deities. Photo 2022, after "restoration."

Fig. 4.133 Close view of the head and nimbus of Amoghasiddhi Tathāgata with standing offering deity holding a bowl, detail of the Padum Gyalwa Rig nga boulder. Photo 2008, after "restoration."

Fig. 4.134 Standing *vajra*-bodhisattvas (*samādhi* deities and consorts below thrones of seated Amitāyus *(right)* and Mahāvairocana *(left)* Tathāgata, on the Padum Gyalwa Rig nga boulder, Photo 1998, before "restoration."

Fig. 4.135 Two standing gate-guardians *(right)* and two *vajra*-bodhisattvas (*samādhi* deities, right), on the Padum Gyalwa Rig nga boulder. Photo 2008, after "restoration."

Fig. 4.136 Two standing gate-guardians *(left)* and several *vajra*-bodhisattvas (*samādhi* deities, right), under Ratnasambhava Tathāgata on the Padum Gyalwa Rig nga boulder, after the left side slope was clear, exposing the less weathered carving. Photo 2022, after "restoration."

Fig. 4.137 Close view of the left side of the carvings depicted in Fig. 4.136. Photo 2022, before "restoration."

Fig. 4.138 Detailed view of the hands and feet of Ratnasambhava Tathāgata on the Padum Gyalwa Rig nga boulder. Photo 1998, before "restoration."

Fig. 4.139 Head and crown of Mahāvairocana Tathāgata on the Padum Gyalwa Rig nga boulder. Photo 1998, before "restoration."

Fig. 4.140 Head and face of Amitayūs Tathāgata on the Padum Gyalwa Rig nga boulder. Photo 1998, before "restoration."

hanging at their left sides pick up again. With the recent exposure of the previously covered hillside, it is possible to confirm that there are another eight standing Vajra-bodhisattvas and a second pair of gate guardians to the left of center (Figs. 4.136–137), to match the grouping on the right, one holding a noose, so identifiable as Vajrapāśa, the other probably Vajrāṅkuśa as there appears the hook of the *aṅkuśa*.[150]

In terms of the formal qualities of the sculptures, the underdeveloped sense of the human body and the relatively low level of naturalism (toes are nearly as long as fingers; Fig. 4.138) seem much more aligned with those depicted in the Trans-Himalayan and Southern Central Asian regions than the more sensuous appeal of male and female figures in Magadha or the more taut muscular stylization of hardened Kashmiri torsos. For example, the proportions of the hands are stretched, feet are twisted to give maximum recognizability, and there is a formulaic quality to the faces (Figs. 4.139–140) which closely resemble one another, somewhat like in our mode 2. This makes an analysis of form-idiom quite difficult. Nevertheless, there are small features which point in various directions, including even northeastern India to the southeast of Zangskar. Note, for instance, the particulars of the way each Tathāgata is contained

150 At first it appears that there was space for a seventeenth *vajra*-bodhisattva next to the others on the shared lotus pedestal. However, the boulder where it would have gone is deeply indented, not allowing for the carving of a standing figure. The artists added an extra head-height stupa just at that point.

Fig. 4.141 Seated Ratnasambhava Tathāgata in a pointed tripartite niche on the Padum Gyalwa Rig nga boulder. Photo 1998, before "restoration."

Fig. 4.142 Seated Amoghasiddhi Tathāgata in a pointed tripartite niche on the Padum Gyalwa Rig nga boulder. Photo 1998, before "restoration."

within a trilobed niche, with a slight point above the top of the head (Figs. 4.141–142). This is not so much a head- and body-nimbus as a contained frame. It is true that many Kashmiri figures have a pointed finial, but they are usually thickened versions of the head halo, in the case of metalwork, or, as at Payar,[151] Avantipur, or Martanda (Fig. 4.143), a tight niche with the three rounded lobes at the top within an architectural frame. The pointed head niches and the thrones at Padum might also recall certain examples from Cave 14 at Dunhuang or Cave 25 at Yulin,[152] but at least some of the original impulses were coming out of eastern India (i.e., Magadha and Gauḍa-Bengal) to begin with, and may very well have been swept through the western Himalaya on their way into Central Asia. Certainly a closer parallel with the way the trilobed head and body frames intersect on the Padum sculpture can be observed on the ca. late seventh- or eighth-century stone reliefs of Temple 2 at Nalanda (Fig. 4.144),[153] not at Kashmir (where the symmetrical side lobes are more rounded) or Dunhuang. At Padum, this is a much more delicate pointed tip to an independent head area which expands to the sides around the shoulders. The ritual helmet worn by Mahāvairocana (see Fig. 4.139) hints at the shape of the one worn by the Nalanda Mahāvairocana (see Fig. 4.102). One is even tempted to put eastern Indian sculptures side-by-side with the Padum Mahāvairocana (Figs. 4.145–146).

151 Kak, *Ancient Monuments of Kashmir*, pl. 51.

152 For example, see the ca. ninth-century "Khadgapāṇi" mural of Mogao Cave 14 (https://dsal.uchicago.edu/cgi- bin/huntington/show_detail.py?ObjectID=30015837) and the so-called "*maṇḍala* with Mahāvairocana Tathāgata" on the east wall of Yulin Cave 25; Ching, *Visualizing Dunhuang*, 8:69–71.

153 On Nalanda Temple 2 and a date of the late seventh century, see Deva, "Stone Temple at Nālandā," and Deva, "Stone Temple (No. 2) at Nālandā."

Fig. 4.144 Yaksha(?) in a niche, holding a bell(?); Nalanda Temple 2, Bihar, ca. 7th c. Photo 1989.

Fig. 4.143 Standing multi-armed god in a rounded tripartite niche, Martanda Sun Temple, Kashmir, east face, 8th c. Photo 2011.

Fig. 4.145 Mahāvairocana Transcendent Lord (Tathāgata), stone sculpture, ca. 10th c. Udayagiri archaeological site, Odisha. Photo 1990.

Fig. 4.146 Mahāvairocana Transcendent Lord (Tathāgata), on the Padum Gyalwa Rig nga boulder, h. 227.5 cm. Photo 1998, before "restoration."

Fig. 4.147 Standing Maitreya bodhisattva, on the far right of the Padum Gyalwa Rig nga boulder, Zangskar, h. approx. 4 m 72 cm. Photo 2008, after "restoration."

Fig. 4.148 Close view of the face, crown and nimbus of the standing Maitreya bodhisattva depicted in Fig. 4.147. Photo 2022, after "restoration."

into play by an artist whose reach exceeded his(?) grasp. Heavy outlines reinforce the flat relief of the gangly figure. Although two curving lines indicating the lower extension of the dhoti or robe are found at the knees, the top of the dhoti is not inscribed at the waist. Faint lines beginning above the left shoulder extending to the abdomen suggest a scarf-end of the crowned and bodhisattva-defined Maitreya. (His crown has a stupa etched on it, identitying him as Maitreya.) He stands surrounded by rather clumsy Kashmiri rounded-*aṇḍa* stupas discussed in the previous chapter, on a base with upward pointed petals (see Fig. 3.36). The petals resemble those under the three Tathāgatas on the right side, closest to the Maitreya. They also have similarly extended fingers, but the rounded relief of the Buddhas is fundamentally different from the flat outlining or scored facial features of the Maitreya.

Padum And Shey Maitreyas

A similar challenge is posed by the towering, Giacometti-like standing Maitreya bodhisattva on the river side of the large boulder on which the five Tathāgata are carved at Padum (Figs. 4.147–148).[154]
It seems to have been inspired by the form-idiom current in Gilgit-Baltistan (-Kashmir), but brought

To an extent, the situation at Shey is comparable to that just described at Padum: a large Maitreya is found not far from the five Tathāgata.[155] At Shey, until recently obscured behind a tree (Fig. 4.149), is a huge Maitreya figure, much flatter than the higher-relief five Tathāgata. Before, it was almost invisible from the road because of the young tree: the sight-line to the sculpture in

154 Devers, *Historical Sites of Zanskar*, 179.

155 Namgyal Institute, *Legacy of a Mountain People*, 2:346.

Fig. 4.149 Standing Maitreya bodhisattva carved on cliff near Shey, Ladakh. Photo 2011.

Fig. 4.150 "Sculpture at Sheh." Photograph by H. B. Marx. From Francke, *History of Western Tibet*, opp. p. 62.

the photograph by the missionary H. B. Marx is unobstructed (Fig. 4.150; the negative or the print seems to have been enhanced to bring out more clearly the lines of the sculptures depicted),[156] as is the photography of the same sculpture published by Denwood and credited to Neil Howard,[157] and again as of 2022 (Fig. 4.151). The Shey Maitreya also has a three-crested crown with a stupa in the central plaque, distorted fingers, and crudely projecting eyes and lips (Fig. 4.152). While the five Tathāgatas are, as already discussed, in a finer Post-Gupta Indian manner, the standing Maitreya at Shey appears to be more in the Gilgit-Baltistan(-Kashmir) modality. At any rate it resembles the standing bodhisattvas with hulking shoulders in the famous Satpara rock carving near Skardu in Baltistan (Fig. 4.153). Denwood gives a history of the latter's discovery and publication,[158] mentioning the reproduction of a photograph by Jane Duncan in 1905.[159] He suggests that the Tibetan inscriptions underneath were created by shallow scratching of the rock surface, whereas the sculpture was made by actually sculpting or "paring away substantial areas of the surface to leave the figures standing out slightly," with slight modeling.[160] I take this distinction between the production of the inscription and the image, coupled with the latter's style, to indicate that while Tibetans might have produced the image—in the sense of engaging a sculptor—the Tibetan writer was not the same as the (local Balti?) sculptor. Different carving methods are involved. Based on the inscriptions, Denwood dates the Satpara sculpture to the eighth to tenth century, Hauptmann to the ninth.[161] On the other hand, Sifur Rahman Dar has "no doubt that the Sadpor

156 Francke, *History of Western Tibet*, opp. p. 62.

157 Denwood, "Tibetans in the Western Himalayas and Karakoram," fig. 11.

158 One early publication not mentioned is Biasutti and Dainelli, *I Tipi Umani*, pl. 14.

159 Duncan, *Summer Ride through Western Tibet*, frontispiece.

160 Denwood, "Tibetans in the Western Himalayas and Karakoram," 50.

161 Hauptmann, "Pre-Islamic Heritage in the Northern Areas of Pakistan," 36.

Fig. 4.151 Standing Maitreya bodhisattva carved on cliff near Shey, Ladakh. Photo 2022.

Fig. 4.152 Close view of large standing Maitreya bodhisattva near Shey, with stupa in crown visible. Photo 2022.

Fig. 4.153 Standing bodhisattvas and seated Buddhas at Satpara, Baltistan (Pakistan). Photo 2017 by Daniel Majchrowicz.

[i.e., Satpara] sculptures were made earlier than the writing of the inscriptions below them. As the writing cannot be dated beyond 1000 A.C., the carved figures can be dated any time between the 8th and 10th centuries A.C."[162] He judges that the "features of the Buddha and Boddhisattavas [*sic*] are typically Tibetan,"[163] although no Tibetan comparanda are offered.

Close examination of photographs of the Satpara sculpture, however, reveals a number of very intriguing features that point in another direction. They include the rounded, rather than angular poses, the slightly pointed head nimbi, and the softly molded fleshiness of limbs and torsos. Rather than the nearly empty set of eighth- to ninth-century imperial Tibetan sculpture, these features may be deduced to reflect some awareness of Post-Gupta sculptural styles of northern or eastern India. This is not a radical or surprising suggestion, given the long-distance trade and missionary interconnections between regions of what is now India, and the reverence all Buddhists had for the "ikons" produced at Bodh Gaya in northeast India. In such a climate, styles can appear surprisingly complex and recursive, in which, as in Buddhism itself, there is both translation, performance, transmission, and adaptation.

At both Padum and Shey there are documented instances of combined modes at the same site, of subtly modeled sculpture appearing alongside gigantic but flatly outlined profiles. As with the kind of accumulation of petroglyphs of different dates and subjects at Char *doksa* (Zamthang), the Alchi bridge, and elsewhere, it may be that local artists with different backgrounds and levels of skill worked together or, more likely, serially over long periods on sculptures at these sites. Inscriptions—contemporary or, in many cases, added later—complicate the situation. Denwood dates all of the Shey sculptures to the "eighth-?tenth centuries CE,"[164] the same range as the Satpara scultpure. The exact sequence will probably always remain indecipherable, and the category into which I have placed individual sculptures can be argued about. Overall, however, Francke's conclusion is borne out that in Zangskar in particular, but also in Ladakh, there are "imposing remains of ancient Buddhist art [which] must have had some connection with the pre-Lamaist [i.e., pre-Tibetan] Buddhism."[165] This remains true even for those that were technically produced or claimed, in some cases, by writers of Tibetan inscriptions. It was in this period, in the latter part of the broad early period in which Buddhism appeared

162 Dar, "Rock-Cut Standing Figure at Kargah, near Gilgit," 196.

163 Ibid..

164 Denwood, "Tibetans in the Western Himalayas and Karakoram," captions to figs. 7 and 11.

165 Francke, *History of Western Tibet*, 20. Similar convictions about the presence of pre-Tibetan Buddhism are expressed by Tucci for Ladakh (Tucci, "Stupa and Votive Stupa," 52–53), as quoted in one of the epigraphs for this chapter.

Fig. 4.154 Detail of kneeling sponsor figure on Shambhala Gate, Karsha, Zangskar. Photo 2003.

in Zangskar and Ladakh (ca. 2nd–9th c.), that diasporic Tibetans were casting about for appropriate modalities of art to express their growing attraction to the religion they were discovering in most of the lands through which they sojourned, temporarily commandeered, or in which they eventually settled.

Sponsor Figure Comparison

Now that a number of major and minor sites have been brought into the discussion, it seems appropriate to briefly address a central issue that cuts across several of them: the depiction of sponsors or donors. While one would expect sponsors of elaborate monuments of the eleventh century and later to be west Tibetan elites working to impose or integrate themselves into local western Himalayan communities, earlier sponsors would not necessarily signal a Tibetan-derived ethnicity through clothing. Let me first point out the similarity of a Shambhala sGo sponsor figure (Fig. 4.154) to those depicted in Chagdho in Baltistan near Gilgit of the eighth–ninth century (see Fig. 3.61). I have already argued for the connection between the Chang Gompa rock paintings of stupas (see Figs. 3.56–58, 3.62) to the Chagdho rock carvings, and the Shambhala sGo bodhisattva forms (see Figs. 4.58, 4.65–67) to rock carvings at Chilas (see Fig. 4.55). There are close counterparts in the sponsor depictions in Figures 4.154 and 3.61 in the style of robe, the kneeling posture, the relative size and position compared with the venerated objects (stupas and Buddha figures). At Skitmartse in the Suru Valley, adjacent to Zangskar,

Fig. 4.155 Detail of standing sponsor couple carved below Sugatiśaṃdārśana Lokeśvara at Skitmartse, Suru Valley, western Ladakh. Photo 2018.

Fig. 4.156 *Vajra*-bodhisattvas (*samādhi* deities) dressed robes and long sleeves on the Padum Gyalwa Rig nga boulder, resembling local sponsor figures. Photo 1998, before "restoration."

and between Zangskar and eastern Kashmir, a sizable Kashmiri-style low-relief carving of Sugatiśaṃdārśana Lokeśvara has been preserved;[166] on the same boulder is the stupa discussed and illustrated in chapter 3 (see Fig. 3.18). At the level of the bodhisattva's lower leg are two sponsor figures, presumably one of the two local sponsor couples depicted (Fig. 4.155), the other one not being as clear. The male in front wears a robe cinched at the waist and ending above his ankles. The fingers of the bodhisattva's lowered right hand nearly touch the top of the male sponsor's head. While the relief itself may have been done by a Kashmiri artist, the sponsor is depicted in local dress, as is typical in Kashmiri art. (As discussed in chapter 5, such a practice is confirmed in a textual source, the *Citrasūtra*). Although the Padum five directional Tathāgata composition does not have sponsor figures, the Vajra-bodhisattvas with the long cinched robes and empty sleeves (Fig. 4.156) are dressed almost like the sponsor figures at Shey and elsewhere. Similarly dressed sponsors were carved beneath the Maitreya at Mulbekh (Fig. 4.157).

One of the kneeling sponsor figures on the Shey stone (Fig. 4.158) resembles the Karsha sponsor (Fig. 4.154), although he has wide sleeves, lapels, and a somewhat different style of headdress. The long robe that tightly wraps around the bent knees is similar, and on other sponsors it is clear the costume also includes a belt. (The sponsor-like figure making *añjali mudrā* on the Buddha side of the Changspa stone also appears to be kneeling with the robe wrapping around his knees and with labels on the front of his robe [see Fig. 4.34]; otherwise, it is hard to discern or conclude

166 Linrothe, "Art Historical Evidence for a Cult of the Triloknāth Lokeśvara in Zangskar," fig. 11; Devers, *Historical Sites of Purig*, 130.

Fig. 4.157 Sponsor figures carved below the standing Maitreya cliff sculpture at Mulbekh, Ladakh. Photo 2012.

Fig. 4.158 Kneeling sponsor figure below cliff carving of the Five Transcendent Lords near Shey, Ladakh. Photo 2008.

Fig. 4.159 Kneeling sponsor figures below cliff carving of the Five Transcendent Lords near Shey, Ladakh. Photo 2010.

Fig. 4.160 Kneeling sponsor figures with wavy-legged tripod offering stands, below cliff carving of the Five Transcendent Lords near Shey, Ladakh. Photo 2010.

Fig. 4.161 Kneeling sponsor figures, a male and two females on pedestal of Viṣṇu sculpture, ca. 11th–12th c., stone, h. 69 cm, from Giriak, Nalanda district, Bihar. Patna Museum, Bihar, acc. no. 1594. Photo 2017.

Fig. 4.162 Seated male sponsor figure holding up flower with standing youth behind, below the Ratnasambhava Tathāgata mural on the "south" wall inside the gateway stupa in Zangla, Zangskar. Photo 2012.

much about it.) At Shey, two groups of three kneeling sponsors appear—the ones at the edges smaller than the other as if to suggest children—one set on either side below the central standing crowned Mahāvairocana (Figs. 4.159–160). Directly beneath him are wavy-legged tripod stands to hold the offerings. They are exactly like the tripods depicted on eastern Indian sculptures, and reinforce the notion of the Shey carvings being the result of the artist's (or the workshop's) exposure to and emulation of the Post-Gupta mode.

In sum, there is little question of the Chaghdo sponsor being "Tibetan" or Tibetanized. These are local elites and they share a great deal, culturally speaking, with other elites in the western Himalaya, notably those depicted in the contiguous areas of Suru and Ladakh and Zangskar in this period. The details of the sponsors and their resemblance to rock carvings in the Trans-Himalayan regions help confirm a date of ca. eighth–ninth century for Shey and Padum, with a marginally earlier date possible for Karsha's Shambhala sGo.

The clothes of the sponsor figures depicted in the entrance chorten at Zangla (see Fig. 4.82), particularly the women, are in a different mode. The women appear to have adopted the hair scarf found in later Kashmiri painting and sculpture, though in fact such accessories are also frequently worn by elite female sponsors depicted in eastern Indian sculpture (Fig. 4.161, right and center), a detail from the same sculpture depicted in Figure 8.12. The male sponsors at Zangla, however, resemble those following Central Asian (Sogdian) fashion, with a belt around a robe open at the neck, narrow sleeves, holding up offerings (Fig. 4.162), and recalling the twelfth-century sponsor paintings in the Alchi Dukhang.[167] Again, these sponsor figures document artists in the western Himalaya looking north and west, rather than east toward Tibet. In the next chapter we will compare painted sponsors of the Malakartse Khar stupa murals with sponsors depicted in shrines in west Tibet, where in that somewhat later period under consideration (the 11th c. and after) the connections with west Tibet were stronger.

Conclusion

That multiple modes of Buddhist art were prized and produced during the first millennium of the common era in Zangskar and Ladakh is not

167 Flood 2009, *Objects of Translation*; Flood, "A Turk in the Dukhang?"; Papa-Kalantari, "Art of the Court," 2007.

substantially different in principle from the situation in central, northern, and eastern Tibet. The attribution to Tibetans of the images in Ladakh next to which they scratched their names is flawed for this very reason: there was no dominant mode of art that "the Tibetans" were following at this time and could have been exporting to the western territories they came to dominate. Nor were the majority of inhabitants of the various valleys of the western Himalaya—Zangskar, Ladakh, Lahaul, Spiti, etc.—"Tibetans," particularly in this early period.

Many of those who have studied the art of this period in central and eastern Tibet also emphasize a variety of sources. According to Marylin Rhie, the best information about a "Tibetan style" of the seventh–ninth century are paintings from Dunhuang that can be associated with Tibet through inscriptions. Some of such paintings are in "the Chinese style," whereas others are "clearly related to Pala India art."[168] Heather Stoddard seems to conclude that the artist dPal dbyangs working at Dunhuang "was equally familiar with two styles, the one Chinese or Central Asian-Chinese and the other Tibeto-Nepalese," since there is no substantive difference between two parts of the same painting on which the artist's inscription survives in Tibetan.[169] Amy Heller also emphasizes a mixture of Indian, Chinese, and especially Nepalese "esthetic influence" on the art of the Pugyal Dynasty.[170] The paradigmatic example is Samye, which according to its famous legend was built by Tibetan and Nepalese builders, with "Tibetan," Chinese, and Indian storeys, and with Khotan possibly lurking somewhere in the background.

The case of Kham (*khams*), on the other (eastern) extreme edge of the Tibetan cultural zone during the eighth to tenth century, is similar to what we find in Zangskar and Ladakh in the lack of a single "Tibet style" predominating. Instead, there is a range of stylistic affiliations, including with China, the nearest and most dominant state. There are also examples of art which Heller has identified as manifesting "Nepalese aesthetic characteristics," others in which garments "characteristic of late Tang garments" appear.[171] Heller, however, emphasizes the continuity and interaction between eastern and central Tibet, although given the eclecticism in both regions at that time, that could be interpreted to suggest that they were similar in not having developed a single dominant formal mode.

168 Rhie, "Tibetan Painting," 46.

169 Stoddard, *Early Sino-Tibetan Art*, 12.

170 Heller, *Tibetan Art*, 33–37, 49–52.

171 Heller, "Buddhist Images and Rock Inscriptions from Eastern Tibet," 387, 394. See also Heller, "Early Ninth Century Images of Vairochana from Eastern Tibet."

The northern Tibetan plateau offers a counterpoint and confirmation of the artistic experience of the western Himalaya as I have portrayed it. In a familiar pattern, between the sixth and ninth century the imperial Tibetans conquered the Turkic Tuyuhun who "had to submit to Tubo [i.e., Tibetan] influences."[172] Unlike the peoples in the western Himalaya, the Tuyuhun never regained an independent identity after the Pugyal empire collapsed, but "gradually fused with the Tubo, resulting from the enforcement of Tibetanizing policies."[173] What they seemed to have contributed to the Tibetans was an exposure and interest in precious objects from all the cultures that surrounded them. The archaeological evidence reveals a mixture of northern animal-style metalwork, Tibetan, Sogdian, Persian, Sui- and Tang-Dynasty Chinese painting and textiles, the Chinese silks themselves responding to Persian motifs. The site of Dulan (now in western Qinghai Province) was a "door open to eastern and western exotica" due to extensive trade with "Sogdiana in the west, Dunhuang and Turfan in the north, Xi'an as the center of Central China in the east."[174]

In all cases, Kham, central Tibet, the northern Tibetan plateau, west Tibet, and the western Himalaya (here, Zangskar and Ladakh), the sources are proximate to the geographic location. For Kham and central Tibet, it is the art of Nepal, eastern India, and China that predominate; in the western Himalaya it is mainly Kashmir and Gilgit-Baltistan reinforced along the trade routes coming all the way from southern Central Asia, with some impact of Post-Gupta art seeping up via the hillstates to the south of Zangskar. Later, Tibetan-endorsed Pāla (i.e., Gyalu or Shari) and Newar (Balri) modes were transmitted from central and west Tibet where they were championed. Thus, the lessons from a close analysis of early art in Zangskar help to underscore the heterogeneity of the artistic sources and historical experience of people many now consider culturally Tibetan. These lessons demonstrate the importance of regional histories, reminding us that those histories must not be overshadowed by conclusions drawn strictly from the perspective of central Tibet.

Deborah Klimburg-Salter has examined many of the same examples of art in the western Himalaya that have been explored in this chapter. She and her collaborators collapse what I have argued are several different discernible stages or modes into two larger groups, the so-called "Tibetan Himalayan Style" and the "Indo-Tibetan Style," sometimes also called the "(western) Indo-Tibetan Style." There are certainly a number of shared

172 Tong, *Silk Roads of the Northern Tibetan Plateau*, 150.

173 Ibid., 163.

174 Ibid., 162.

judgments and readings among our examples, and Klimburg-Salter does acknowledge at one point that "one can identify different modes of a single style."[175] Although there is overlap in the examples used, her focus and touchstone remains Tabo in Spiti. Tabo provides the undeniable advantage of having some secure dates—mainly the renovation of 1042, conveniently serving as the precise dividing line between their two modalities. She and her two coauthors work from and within a different framing assumption, in that like many others, they see the art in the western Himalaya as fundamentally "Tibetan" and in accord with, if not derived from, a putative "Tibetan" art-historical development, right from the seventh century if not earlier.

As they see it, the Purang-Gugé kings of west Tibet were "the new political rulers [of much of the western Himalaya starting in the tenth century who] descended from the Yarlung dynasty."[176] Whatever tensions or resistance to these outsider-rulers there may have been in the tenth century were generated not by the non-Tibetan communities on which the Yarlung-descendants imposed themselves by force. Rather, they see these as power struggles with "some of the local *Tibetan* communities."[177] Both rulers and ruled are equally Tibetan in this view. As is the common assumption of many scholars, they accept at face value "ancient Tibetan texts [that] tell us that this region became part of the Tibetan empire from at least the middle of the 7th century,"[178] and that inclusion turned their people into Tibetans. Even the Kargah sculpture near Naupur in Gilgit (see Fig. 4.47), we are told, needs to be reconsidered "in light of the Tibetan occupation of the region in the 8th century,"[179] suggesting that Tibetan military presence succeeded in spreading a Tibetan aesthetic into every region they invaded. As I analyze it, the use of terminology that emphasizes both Tibet and India stems from a basic framing assumption of a unified "Tibetan" identity that the western Himalayans, who at present are incorporated into India (and Pakistan), acquired once occupied or ruled by Tibetans. From the presumption of a unified "Tibetan" identity proceeds the conclusion that once ruled or occupied by Tibetans, western Himalayan agents become Tibetan, and thus their art—whether made before or after they have become Tibetan—is also Tibetan. To be sure, this is an oversimplified reduction of their much more sophisticated argument. Nevertheless, there is a subtle circularity at work there, and terms such as those inflected by contemporary categories (to wit, "Tibet" and "India") bear unintended ideological baggage.

175 Klimburg-Salter, "Tibetan Himalayan Style," 429.

176 Ibid., 457.

177 Ibid., 457 (emphasis added).

178 Ibid., 455. See also Klimburg-Salter, "Imagining the World of Ye Shes 'od," 272.

179 Klimburg-Salter, "Tibetan Himalayan Style," 449.

In Klimburg-Salter's 2015 "The Tibetan Himalayan Style: The Art of the Western Domains" and Lojda, Klimburg-Salter, and Strinu's 2016 "The Tibetan Himalayan Style: Considering the Central Asian Connection," the term "Tibetan Himalayan style" is used to refer to a form-idiom with a wide occurrence in the western Himalaya, especially in Spiti. They include within the same category examples I have distributed to modes 2 through 5. According to the authors of those essays, by 1042 the so-called Tibetan Himalayan style had disappeared at Tabo. It was replaced by a Kashmiri-derived style variously termed "Indo-Tibetan style," "(western) Indo-Tibetan style," and "the Kashmiri influenced Indo-Tibetan style," largely equivalent to my category 4, the Khaché mode. Since their arguments and key examples in their learned and wide-ranging studies almost always emerge from and return to the tenth- to eleventh-century murals and sculptures in Tabo in the western Himalaya, their argument and nomenclature states that the western Himalaya is a part of Tibet and therefore Tibetan. Neither India nor Tibet (as in central Tibet) is involved by the authors as the primary location for the occurrence of these styles, except to the extent that Kashmir is now part of India. As discussed in chapter 1 of this volume, even though starting in the tenth century some of the elites in the western Himalaya may have used the Tibetan written language, I find it anachronistic and distorting to call the people and culture throughout the western Himalaya (in LZSKLB) starting in the seventh century simply "Tibetan." Equally problematic in the term *Indo-Tibetan* is the misleading metonymic reference to Kashmir as understandably "Indo" or Indian. Kashmir in the late tenth and eleventh centuries may have been "Indic" in a vague sense, but it was not "India," and once again the term *Tibet* is inappropriately applied to people or a culture in the western Himalaya before they had become "Tibetanized" to a significant degree. Concerns about the suitability of the terms—though not the insight that at Tabo, the earlier local mode was replaced by a mode that was derived from Kashmir with the participation of Kashmiris over a fifty-year period—proceed from the ambiguity or imprecision of the terms.[180] As for the "Tibetan Himalayan style," is there a mode of Tibetan art that is *not* Himalayan? In what sense is the "Tibetan Himalayan style" at Dunhuang "Himalayan"? If the Kashmiri-inflected art is "Indo-Tibetan," then what term should be used for the so-called Gyalu or Shari art that occurred in central Tibet under the inspiration of the art of eastern India (i.e., Magadhan, Pāla-period art), the type that has been recognized above as being the inspiration for mode 5? "Indo-Tibetan art" might actually fit

180 Luczanits articulates concerns with using "Indo-Tibetan" to refer to the renovation-period murals at Tabo ("On an Unusual Painting Style in Ladakh," 152), but at that early stage in the study of this material preferred "West Tibetan" to "Indo-Tibetan." He suggested "Kashmiri style" for the paintings in the Alchi Sumtsek, and "Early Ladakhi style" for the paintings at Shangrong in Alchi, at Wanla, Lamayuru, Phyang and Saspol as they are "certainly the products of a native Ladakhi painting school" (ibid., 153).

better for the Magadha-derived art, since at least the Pālas ruled for a time over a considerable region of what is now recognized as India, whereas the Kashmiri Karkoṭas and their successors were, except for a few forays into northern India, confined to what we might now call greater Kashmir. But calling it "Indo-" anything is still problematic. In sum, "Tibetan Himalayan" and "Indo-Tibetan" in these instances are not only just as imprecise as "Himalayan," they are also much more misleading.

In the series of three essays that we have just been discussing (the first two stated to be a two-part article published some seven years apart), Klimburg-Salter and her co-authors eloquently correlate their art-historical argument with their understanding of the development of Tibetan Buddhism and political power between the seventh and the eleventh century.[181] The initial essay covered the late tenth and early eleventh century at Tabo. It used "Foundation Phase (ca. 996)" and "Renovation Phase (ca. 1042)" to refer to the same two modes of art later referred to as "Tibetan Himalayan" and "Indo-Tibetan." The second of the two-part series covers the eighth through the eleventh century and illustrates art from other sites in the western Himalaya more broadly. In fact, however, the later one is also largely focused on Tabo of the late tenth century and the 1042 renovations. The third contribution "expands the discussion [of the Tibetan Himalayan Style] primarily to Central Asia but also to Central Tibet in order to understand the distinctive socio-political contexts in which this style appears—and disappears."[182] It too uses Tabo as its keystone. The correlative argument between political and artistic developments is compelling, although it runs the risk of suggesting that governmental and military events predominantly drive the development of artistic progressions, since it would hardly be the case that art would determine the political structure and military campaigns. (A host of factors fuel artistic developments that need not be coextensive with political or social periodization.) It also might imply that the "Tibetan Himalayan Style," though occurring in the western Himalaya (beside Tabo in Spiti, they illustrate and discuss sculptures and paintings in Ladakh—Dras, Mulbekh, and Shey—Gilgit, Skardu, and Dunhuang) was dictated and imposed from the outside but by, among, and for Tibetans.

My attempt to differentiate several modes of art on the basis of visual characteristics is not integrated into a single political or ethnic narrative the way Klimburg-Salter and her co-authors are able to link them to

181 Klimburg-Salter, "Imagining the World of Ye Shes 'od"; and Klimburg-Salter, "Tibetan Himalayan Style."

182 Lojda et al., "Tibetan Himalayan Style," 122. Klimburg-Salter's earlier essays on similar themes ("Style in Western Tibetan Painting" and "Imagining the World of Ye Shes 'od") also admirably situate formal studies within social, religious, and political contexts.

Tibetan expansion and identity. The modes I propose overlap in time and in some cases share features but do not have sharply etched temporal boundaries or limits. They are not rigidly defined or separated, but are graded and shaded in a messy, somewhat chaotic, and contradictory manner. Although they are also related to external factors, they are much less driven by a single extension of Tibetan power and culture than by the complex geographic realities of the western Himalaya. They were created by scrappy local people grappling with what they learned from their more powerful, more organized, wealthier neighbors ensconced in more fertile territory. The assumption is that in the earliest periods the patrons were local and engaged either enterprising local artists aware of and inspired by art from outside, or hired equally intrepid artists from the outside. This was a voluntary, not an imposed process. Though the categories may need refinement—so too their nomenclature—and perhaps a few specific examples shifted from one to another basket of tendencies, they avoid ascription to a transregional and ultimately fictive monoculture, the idea of which so many of us have succumbed in the late twentieth and early twenty-first century. I argue that it is more topology and geology that played the formative role in producing a pluralistic, polysemic dictionary of alternative artistic trends, not a linear or inevitable positivistic teleology or movement to a predetermined goal. If Kubler is to be believed, all of the modes reflect "artistic problems" that the artists themselves were trying to solve in and through the solutions they came up with, borrowed, appropriated, modified, and the like.[183] Once the solutions are identified, Kubler would have us try to forensically discern the particular issues and problems that the new developments, new solutions, were meant to resolve. That is a hermeneutical desideratum left to the future. At the same time, there is no question that the successive phases or modes put into a consecutive (if overlapping) sequence testify to a growing representational power, versatility, and conviction among groups of artists, but there was no ultimate goal toward which they (hoped they) were moving.

To summarize my argument, what all these modes share is a relationship between the western Himalaya and one or more of the cultures that are contiguous with the borders of or nestled within the Himalayan mountain chains, including the Indus and Gangetic plains, Himachal Pradesh, the Kashmir Valley, Gilgit, and eventually Nepal, and west and central Tibet. Much of the time, those regions had more developed, varied, and wealthier economies, themselves linked into networks with even more technically

183 Kubler, *Shape of Time*; Kubler, "Shape of Time: Revisited."

capable or politically centralized ways of living than those of the sparsely populated but pastorally and agriculturally narrowly productive western Himalaya. Many local people in Ladakh and Zangskar, along with some scholars from outside, now prefer to consider all of these forms of art as a variant of early "Tibetan [Buddhist] art." Present local affinities and preferences notwithstanding, I believe the critical scrutiny to which I have subjected this understanding is justified and deserved.

Systematic and random forays of missionaries, merchants, and military forces from these contiguous regions into and across the western Himalaya, along with Himalayans themselves who traded and married across mountain ranges and valleys, forged cultural ties that manifested themselves in art-making. The result is the visible insertion into the western Himalaya of particular belated characteristics—that is, occurring late in the original, non-western Himalayan Kublerian sequence. Although initiated or developed in the neighboring regions they were inevitably modified or localized before adoption or in the process of emulation. I am aware of the dangerous implication of finding the sources for early western Himalayan modes of art-making outside of the western Himalaya, as if denying any agency to the artists of the western Himalaya. This risks slipping into the position of those like Tucci about Tibetan art who have suggested or implied that the only thing distinctively original up to the fifteenth century is the misinterpretation of outside modes, and the primary contribution of the local artists in the fifteenth century was to combine them. However, in the early period, considerably different cultural, technological, and economic levels differentiate the societies of the western Himalaya (often even at their highest registers) from those surrounding them. It is undeniable that it took several centuries—the very ones being examined here—for local artists to become as facile as the artists creating the imported work. The pattern in fact is parallel to that going on in central Tibet (though it may have begun earlier in the western Himalaya): Tibet through the dynastic and immediate post-dynastic period was "a grateful and absorbent receptacle of artistic and intellectual influences," characterized as "Newari-Nepalese, then a Khotanese, or a Sinicized Central Asian, followed finally by prolonged and massive Indian and Chinese influx."[184]

Whatever the problems with the term *art of the western Himalaya*—notably its vagueness and overly capacious inclusiveness[185]—consider

184 Sørensen, review of Ernst Steinkellner, *Sudhana's Miraculous Journey*, 69.

185 In his summary and review of Heather Stoddard's 1985 *Le mendiant de l'Amdo*, Per Kvaerne archly criticizes "those official bodies in the West (especially museums) who speak of 'Himalayan' art and 'Himalayan' culture when they mean (and when everyone, including foreign ministries as well as the Chinese, whom the same ministries imagine they thereby avoid offending, *know* they mean) 'Tibet'"; Kvaerne, "Beggar from Amdo," 68–69. In this case, I explicitly do not use "Himalayan" to mean "Tibet" because Ladakh and Zangskar were "Himalayan" before (and after) they became (to the extent that they have) culturally Tibetan.

the alternatives: terms derived from or misleadingly directed toward contemporary modern nationalities, ethnicities or nation-states such as Indian, Newari, Tibetan, Nepalese, and the like, minimizing agency of artists in Zangskar and Ladakh. In fact the imprecision of the preferred terms matches the mixture of distinguishable modalities preserved in the region which in their variety resist a singular origin or inspiration. In support of the geographic umbrella term of *western Himalayan art* in several modalities, this chapter focused on seven different modes of art produced within the western Himalaya between roughly the seventh and thirteenth centuries.[186] They are either coeval or overlapping. This period in particular was one of profound cultural shifts and development within and around the western Himalaya. What makes the term *art of western Himalaya* acceptable or appropriate for this period, despite the drawbacks, is the intersection with a host of geographically contingent but culturally distinct cultures. Such junctions, defined by the topography of the mountain chains, occur in greater magnitude and intensity than in most other regions. There is thus something suitably "Himalayan" about this pattern of interaction.

186 Eight different modes can be identified if one includes the notoriously difficult-to-date non- or pre-Buddhist petroglyphs, such as Figures 4.1–2. While not continuing to be made with the same urgency or frequency as before, in a sense being replaced by the stupa carvings discussed in chapter 3, they were still prominent in the landscape during the early Buddhist period.

CHAPTER 5

Looking Westward: Painting in the Kashmiri Idiom, 10th–12th-Century Zangksar and West Tibet

Introduction

In Zangskar, only one known site preserves extensive paintings in the Kashmiri mode of the tenth century to the twelfth: the painted murals on the interior of a stupa associated with the ruins of a fort known locally as Malakartse Khar.[1] It is an abandoned site, an hour's walk east of Zangla, one of two royal capitals of the Zangskar kingdom. Whether it was indeed created by Kashmiri artists for Zangskar patrons (as I believe), by non-Kashmiri artists from outside Zangskar who had imbibed the Kashmiri style and made it their own, or by Zangskari artists working in a painterly *Kha che lugs* (Kashmiri-derived form-idiom) is at present impossible to know with certainty. Part of the problem is because so little Kashmiri painting, as opposed to sculpture, survives in Kashmir for comparison.[2] Some murals outside of Kashmir can be tentatively attributed to Kashmiri artists, such as those at the Alchi Sumtsek,[3] and at Mangyu, where I have argued the paintings on the *dhoti* of the standing Maitreya are too deeply immersed in the minutiae of Kashmiri culture to be created by epigones.[4] For the most part, the eleventh-century murals at the Tabo Dukhang, but not the sculptures, are considered as possibly having been produced by Kashmiri artists.[5] There is also a tendency to see even these paintings as done by artists from "the area where the Sutlej reaches the Indian plains," that is, in current Himachal Pradesh.[6] In west Tibet, a few of the murals at Tholing, those of the stupa near the Gyatsa Lhakhang, and some manuscript illuminations found at Tholing are accepted as late tenth or early eleventh century and likely to be by Kashmiri artists,[7] but not the rest of the murals at Tholing, Dungkar, or Chyiwang (phyi dbang).[8] But none of these is an unchallenged attribution, and rightly so, since the issues are complex and there is no definitive evidence to settle the questions. Rather than avoiding them, however, a temptation to which some may have

1 A second site with a painting in the Kashmiri idiom but more probably by local, not Kashmiri, artists is in a gateway stupa at Zangla; see chapter 4, Figs. 4.80–82, 4.162.

2 For a discussion of the Gilgit manuscripts as evidence of Kashmiri painting, see Linrothe, *Collecting Paradise*, 39–54.

3 Goepper, "More Evidence for Dating the Sumtsek in Alchi"; Goepper and Luczanits, *Alchi*, 2:488, 543, 718.

4 Linrothe, "Skirting the Bodhisattva."

5 Luczanits, *Buddhist Sculpture in Clay*, 54.

6 Luczanits, "Styles in Western Himalayan Art," 136.

7 Luczanits, "From Kashmir to Western Tibet," 113–14, figs. 2.7, 2.19–23, 2.38; Namgyal, *Tuolin Si (Ntho-ling Monastery)*, 126–32.

8 Spelled "phyi dbang" in Tibetan, it is pronounced "chee" (as in "cheese") and "wang" (rhymes with "wrong"), though in Western literature it often appears as "Piyang" or "Phyi-wang."

(wisely?) succumbed, this chapter examines the Malakartse Khar stupa remains in greater detail than has been provided to date. It offers critiques of existing classifications and hypotheses about its origins and Esoteric Buddhist program, provided with their evidentiary basis. These too will hopefully be subject to critical scrutiny.

In the first part of this essay, I introduce the murals of the Malakartse Khar stupa, examining in detail the site, its context, the iconographic program and issues of painting forms or style. The site is heavily damaged, and in order to understand both the iconography and style, I then turn to what I consider the earliest extant paintings at the cave site of Chyiwang, in Cave 79, a cave across the border in west Tibet which has been termed the Cave of the Offering Goddesses.[9] Even though, like the Malakartse Khar stupa, it has also lost its sculptures and some of its painting, it has a more extensive iconographic layout than the one at Malakartse Khar. Some partial overlaps in Cave 79 help fill in missing features in the Zangskar program, the primary focus of the chapter. The Chyiwang murals can also be conveniently set into a stylistic and thematic evolution moving from the late tenth–early eleventh-century Tholing murals, to Tabo in Spiti, to a cave temple near Khartse in western Tibet, to three caves at Dungkar and other caves at Chyiwang near Tholing which have received little notice. Within that developmental spectrum, the Malakartse Khar murals find an early perch. In the process, Zangskar's location between Kashmir and the wealthy centers of the Gugé and Purang kingdoms is considered. In the course of the study of these two sites (Malakartse Khar and Chyiwang), a surprising continuity or currency is demonstrated for the western Himalaya of forms of Esoteric Buddhism found originally mostly in eastern and northern Indian contexts, and from there transmitted by pilgrims and travellers with its texts, teachings and art to China and Japan.

Of necessity, this study demands considerable attention to unfamiliar iconography. Not only were the sponsors, designers, and artists drawing on abstruse Esoteric Buddhist themes, they were working in a period of transition. Today, the themes and formats of later Esoteric Buddhism or Vajrayāna that dominated Tibet after the fourteenth century tend to be somewhat more familiar to historians of Himalayan art. Unfortunately, they do not help much in grappling with the earlier phases of Esoteric Buddhist art. Consequently, careful attention to nuances of iconographic signifiers is necessary, made all the more challenging by the incompleteness of sets

9 Neumann, "Cave of the Offering Goddesses."

of deities through damage. Although we may not have access to the same texts and teachings that were familiar to the creators, close looking and close reading go a long way in "equipping our organs of reception with a knowledge of the customs and practices that are unique" to this context.[10] Although Pächt rightly critiques the "current obsession with iconology,"[11] and argues that art historians "should be all the more determined to search for the meaning that lies not behind but within the image,"[12] he acknowledges the need for iconography "to reactivate whatever was spontaneously known at the relevant historical moment."[13]

The development of the textual corpus describing—however cryptically—early mature Esoteric Buddhism, what I have elsewhere called "Phase Two,"[14] had certainly begun by the eighth and ninth centuries. By the tenth and early eleventh centuries it was fully intact, at least in eastern and perhaps south India and Kashmir; its next phase was shading into substance in the form of images. The transmission of "Phase Three" Esoteric Buddhist teachings to the western Himalaya from Kashmir, however, seems to have been delayed, deferred, or resisted.[15] At any rate, compared with what was earlier transmitted and found in eastern India, Tang China, and Heian Japan, the western Himalayan experience of Esoteric Buddhism was, in Kubler's terms, relatively "late" in its sequence of progression.[16] From the point of view of the Zangskaris, however, it was still part of a radical movement in the tectonic plates of culture. As the well-preserved Tabo and Alchi group[17] of monuments demonstrate, it was Phase Two that was fully embraced through the end of the twelfth century. The Malakartse Khar stupa murals represent an earlier position in this western Himalayan trajectory of Esoteric Buddhism, transitional in the sense that they combine the *trikula*, or three-family system, and the full-throated *pañcakula* (rigs lnga) that would come to epitomize early mature Esoteric Buddhism in its so-called Mahāyoga phase. The documentation of these developmental traces alone make the mural paintings historically significant but the extraordinary figuration, rich textile patterns, complex compositions, and unique location provide a surfeit of pleasure and wonder. Together, these fully reward the effort to reconstruct, even if ultimately only partially, the original integrated program of paintings and sculptures.

10 Pächt, *Practice of Art History*, 82.

11 Ibid., 100.

12 Ibid., 85.

13 Ibid., 81.

14 Linrothe, *Ruthless Compassion*.

15 This issue and how it fits into what is believed about the early rulers and patrons of Buddhism in the late tenth and eleventh centuries will be taken up later in the chapter.

16 Kubler, *Shape of Time*.

17 The Alchi group includes Alchi Dukhang, the Sumtsek, the Mangyu complex, Sumda Chung, Saspotse, and Skyu; Luczanits, *Buddhist Sculpture in Clay*, 125–54.

Malakartse Khar

The Castle

On the north (right) bank of the Zumlung tributary to the Zangskar river, east of Zangla, one of the two old royal seats (along with Padum) in Zangskar, is an abandoned fort, palace or citadel, in ruins high on a promontory overlooking the stream (Figs. 5.1–5).[18] The walls are made of mud-mortared stone with a random texture and a slight batter (Fig. 5.4). Its location is certainly more suited for defense than for convenience, and this is confirmed by the loopholes visible in the wall fabric. They are of both triangular and rectangular shape. The origin or etymology of the local name, Malakartse Khar (ma la dkar rtse mkhar), is not known, though literally it seems to mean the Castle of the Excellent White Peak, "khar" (mkhar) being used to indicate a castle or fort. No other stories or information about it could be obtained, even from knowledgeable local people with an interest in history. Some had heard of it, but they had never visited the site.[19] Neither when it was built nor when it was abandoned has been determined with certainty based on texts or inscriptions. Its proximity to the old palace at Zangla naturally suggests a connection with the royal family. However, it is far enough away from Zangla to be useless for a rapid retreat from an imminent threat. It would require considerable advance notice to move from the much more exposed Zangla overlooking the broad Zangskar river valley to Malakartse Khar. Nor could it accommodate the village population, only an elite group with a praetorian guard-type force. On the other hand, unlike the fort at Hankar, which can be associated with the Ladakhi Namgyal sovereigns of Leh, Malakartse Khar is not far enough away from Zangla to make a substantive seasonal change of scenery or microclimate attractive to royals. Nor are the ruins extensive enough to suggest, as at Zangla and Karsha, that this was the original site of a "defensible settlement occupying the rocky outcrops of the ridge."[20]

Quentin Devers argues succinctly that "this site is completely isolated, located about an hour upstream of Zangla, in a very narrow gorge, far from any food resources."[21] His suggestion explaining its placement and function is as ingenious as it is largely convincing: "Establishing a post in Malakartse was the only chance for Zangla to get a grip on the Jumlam route and its trade, which otherwise completely avoided the village."[22] He notes the importance of the Jumlam route for the trade in butter and barley. This critical trade route, generally only open in late summer and fall, links

18 For a description of the earliest known documentation of the site, see Linrothe, "A Winter in the Field." Since then, although it has been mentioned occasionally and is included in Quentin Devers's survey of Zangskar archaeological sites (*Historical Sites of Zanskar*, 207), it has not been considered or analyzed in depth.

19 Karsha Lonpo Sonam Wangchuk and Zurba Tashi, personal communication, 2004.

20 N. Howard, "Fortified Places of Zanskar," 90. Unfortunately, Howard did not notice or investigate the Malakartse Khar during his travels in Zangskar, although that is hardly surprising. I walked below it on the Jumlam trek in September 2002 and never noticed it. If not for Gelong Angchug, one of Karsha Lonpo's sons, I would never have known of it. I described the site and my debt to him in Linrothe, "A Winter in the Field," 40–45.

21 Devers, "Charting Ancient Routes," 324.

22 Ibid.

Fig. 5.1 Malakartse Khar ruins on top of rocky promontory at center; view from the south; stupa at lower left. Photo 2018.

Fig. 5.2 Malakartse Khar ruins on top of rocky cliff at center view from the west. Photo 2012.

Fig. 5.3 Close view of the ruined structure at Malakartse Khar; view from the north. Photo 2022.

Fig. 5.4 Detail of a ruined wall at Malakartse Khar; view from the east. Photo 2018.

Fig. 5.5 Looking down on the Malakartse Khar promontory; view from the north. Photo 2004.

Fig. 5.6 Old Palace at Zangla before restoration. Photo 2003.

Fig. 5.7 Old Palace at Zangla before restoration. Photo pre-2004, digitized slide.

Zangskar with the Markha Valley and thus other trade routes connecting Lahaul, Kashmir, the southern Tarim Basin, and Ladakh. At the same time, as a military outpost, it could defend against invasions or rebellions and serve as a highly defensible retreat.

For the evaluation of the age of Malakartse Khar it is of some relevance to consider briefly, for the sake of comparison, the old palace at Zangla of four storeys, surrounded by houses,[23] now restored. It too was built on top of a promontory—locally referred to as depicting Garuda (khyung) (Figs. 5.6–8). The "royal path" leading up to it is marked by stupas (Fig. 5.9)—also visible in Figure 5.8. According to local belief, the whole village used to be up on the hill near the palace. Eventually, the village moved down to be closer to water and to the fields. The old palace was still in use during the stay there of Alexander Csoma de Körös (1784–1842) between June 1823 and October 1824.[24] In recent times, the local wife of the Zangla king (rarely in residence) and other family members have a generous, but by no means palatial, home. Gutschow implies the new house was built after the Dogra invasions of the late 1830s and the 1846 treaty by which the territory became formally part of the kingdom of the Mahārāja of Jammu and Kashmir.[25]

In Figure 5.10, a view looking down from close to the Zangla palace, many of the stupas of the "royal path" are visible beyond the gateway stupa, along with the village in the middle ground and the relatively new nunnery in the distance; to the left is the Zangskar river. In 2003, the late Tashi Dorje, the youngest son of Karsha Lonpo who is related by marriage to both the Zangla and Padum royal families, explained to me why there are so many stupas along that path. There was a powerful king, the story went, who was very devout, a *dharmarāja* or *cakravartin*. When he sat in judgment of those who had committed crimes, as expiation, he sentenced them to build such stupas. To be sure, this is an explanation given for other stupas and *maṇi* walls in both Ladakh and Zangskar.

23 N. Howard, "Fortified Palaces of Zanskar," 89.

24 Duka, *Life and Works*, 33–34; K. Gutschow, "An Economy of Merit," 95.

25 K. Gutschow, "An Economy of Merit," 86.

Fig. 5.8 View of the site of the Old Palace at Zangla (far right) and path leading up to it. Photo 2006.

Fig. 5.9 View of a group of stupas below the Old Palace at Zangla. Photo pre-2004, digitized slide.

Fig. 5.10 View of the *kankani* stupa below the Old Palace at Zangla, before restoration. Photo pre-2004, digitized slide.

Only some of the walls of the old Zangla palace still stand (see Figs. 5.6-7), though in recent years the entire exterior and interior underwent thorough conservation by Irimiás Balázs on behalf of the Hungarian organization Csoma Szobája Alapítvány (Csoma's Room Foundation). Here I use mainly pre-conservation photographs. The white-washed building next to the massive wall parallel to the picture plane in Figure 5.6 is not as old as the wall itself.[26] Howard describes it as follows:

> Its lower parts are also built of random-texture, mud-mortared stone and incorporate a good deal of light timber reinforcement—which has done its job well since the building still stands despite the many cracks, particularly in the south-west face. Mud brick has been used for the upper parts and also in places where the stone-work has been repaired or replaced with brick; and there is a large stone buttress on the north-west front.[27]

It too has rectangular loopholes. Howard concludes that "a substantial remodelling of the palace [took place] in the second half of the sixteenth century" while "the stone work is earlier."[28] The stone work he attributes on the basis of comparison to his sample in Ladakh[29] to the fifteenth century.

26 Devers, *Historical Sites of Zanskar*, 204.

27 N. Howard, "Fortified Places of Zanskar," 89.

28 Ibid.

29 Ibid.

Fig. 5.11 Detail of the face of the sculpture depicted in Figure 5.12. Photo 2022.

Fig. 5.12 Painted clay sculpture of Avalokiteśvara in the Old Palace at Zangla; ht. 129 cm., ca. 15th–16th c. Photo 2022.

When the royal family moved from this palace, they left behind a number of clay sculptures, the largest of which was, presumably, too fragile to move. Some of these sculptures support Howard's date of a founding in the fifteenth or sixteenth century. One is a very fine Avalokiteśvara bodhisattva, with Amitāyus in the headdress, and an antelope across his left shoulder and chest (Figs. 5.11–12). It is 1.29 meters in height, and 79 centimeters from knee to knee. The mode is Khaché (here used as the name for Himalayan work in the Kashmiri mode) but from the revival or renaissance version datable to the fifteenth and sixteenth centuries.[30] The almond-shaped eyes, triangular crests of the crown, reverse-widow's peak, and two flowers above the ears are familiar elements in both the original Kashmiri sculptural precedent and the later western Himalayan Khaché mode of the Zangla sculpture.[31]

Returning to the Malakartse Khar, and comparing it to the old Zangla palace, timber lacing is much less obvious at Malakartse Khar but there does seem to be the remains of a buttress (see Fig. 5.3). If mud bricks were used above the stone walls as in Zangla, they do not survive in place. There is no evidence that the Malakartse Khar is later than the Zangla palace; if anything, its less systematic building method suggests an earlier

30 Kerin, "Re-tracing Lines of Devotion"; Kerin, "From Emulation to Interpretation"; and Kerin, *Art and Devotion*.

31 The developments of art in Zangskar after the thirteenth century are largely beyond the scope of this work, but see Linrothe, *Collecting Paradise*, and Linrothe, "Origins of the Kashmiri Style in the Western Himalayas." For elsewhere in west Tibet and the western Himalayas, see Kerin, *Art and Devotion at a Buddhist Temple in the Indian Himalaya*.

Fig. 5.13 View of the ruins of the citadel and palace above Karsha Chuchikzhal. Photo pre-2004, digitized slide.

Fig. 5.14 Corner of a building among the ruins above Karsha Chuchikzhal. Photo 2013.

Fig. 5.15 View from above of the some of the ruined structure above Karsha Chuchikzhal, with Karsha Monastery in the background. Photo 2003.

construction, one which perhaps overlapped in time with the latter and was later abandoned.

Other early citadel-type settlements on promontories exist in Zangskar. The ruins above Karsha (Figs. 5.13–15), across the Zangskar river from Zangla and a little to the south, are locally called Changgos Khar, the "castle of the northern realm" (byang ngos gi mkhar).[32] This refers to the understood division of Zangskar into different realms, Zangla and Karsha being part of the northern realm, separate from Padum. The structures at Karsha, which the Karsha Lonpo believes were already in ruins by the end of the sixteenth century,[33] are accepted by Howard as "having been in existence in some form in the eleventh century."[34] The Malakartse Khar, which like Karsha's old castle, has a minimal use of timber lacing and is built of random-textured mud-mortared stone, has additional evidence nearby which similarly dates it to that period. Gutschow provides a description of such "early royal settlements (Karsha, Padum, later Stongde and Zangla) [which] tended to be fortress towns built on a cliff."[35] Despite the generalized description having been made on the basis of comparison to the other sites and without firsthand knowledge of Malakartse Khar (MkK), her account fits it quite well and perhaps helps to reconstruct the use, in principle, of this and other Khars.

> Such fortress settlements usually had a central fort and watchtower (*spi'u*) surrounded by small houses built precariously on a steep slope so that access was nearly impossible. The houses were surrounded by an outer wall with only a limited number of access gates. A covered walkway provided access to the streambed far below in times of siege. Traces of these covered walkways and watchtowers can be found at Karsha and Zangla. A network of such watchtowers along the length of the northern (Stod) and central (gZhung) valleys comprised Zangskar's earliest defense system. At the first signs of enemy attack, the watch at the top of the valley would light a huge bonfire, which could be seen by the next watch, who then lit his own fire, and so on down the valley until the king's palace in central Zangskar was informed. In the meantime, each fortress settlement would prepare for a siege, stockpiling food and water, pulling livestock within the town walls, and closing down all means of access.[36]

32 K. Gutschow, "An Economy of Merit," 79.

33 Ibid., 82n48.

34 N. Howard, "Fortified Places of Zanskar," 91; Devers, *Historical Sites of Zanskar*, 128.

35 K. Gutschow, "An Economy of Merit," 79.

36 Ibid., 70.

Fig. 5.16 View from the south of the Malakartse Khar stupa, from below. Photo 2004.

Fig. 5.17 Malakartse Khar stupa, view from above of the east facing doorway. Photo 2004.

Fig. 5.18 View from the south of the Malakartse Khar stupa, with the ruined relic shrine directly above. Photo 2018.

The MkK Stupa: Introduction

Within sight of the Malakartse Khar, not on the fort's promontory but still well above the river, is found a stupa elevated onto a constructed rectangular base or plinth (Figs. 5.16–18).[37] A view from the south, directly across the river, demonstrates how close the stupa is to the fort, though the ruins are higher and to the east—the stupa is visible to the lower right in Figure 5.1. Directly above the stupa are two much smaller additional constructions placed adjacent to each other (Figs. 5.19–20). They are invisible at the level of stupa platform because of the steepness of the cliffside, and were noticed for the first time in 2018 when Victoria Andrews brought the larger one to my attention as we were looking at the stupa from across the stream. The larger one, perhaps originally a stupa but now missing its superstructure, is hollow and had molded lotus petal designs impressed into mud plaster. They remain on only one side (see Fig. 5.20). The smaller one is much deteriorated and has a number of rocks piled on the top, disguising its original shape. When shown

37 GPS reading: N 33° 38.846'; E 077° 01.320'; alt. 11,936'.

Fig. 5.19 Looking down on the Malakartse Khar stupa (on the left), with the two ruined relic structures visible at upper right; view from the north. Photo 2022.

Fig. 5.20 The larger of the two ruined relic structure above the Malakartse Khar stupa with molded lotus pedestal relief outlines visible. Photo 2022.

photographs of them, the Karsha Lonpo Sonam Wangchuk suggested they might have functioned as a *tsha khang* to inter relics of an esteemed teacher, or possibly the kinds of relics of worn out scripture fragments, paintings or sculptures. He himself had created such a structure to accommodate the fragments and *tsha tsha* removed from the Kadampa Chorten below the old Karsha castle (see chapter 7). Although both small structures appear to be relic depositories, no relics of any sort were visible when Ms Andrews and I, along with Gelong Angchug, who had first shown me the site in 2003, climbed up there again in August 2022.

Since the Malakartse Khar stupa is built onto a steep slope, the side facing the river to the south required elevation in order to build a level platform for the base and superstructure. This support took the form of a wedge-shaped foundation, as seen on the left in Figure 5.17. It was constructed with random-textured stones, much like that of the fort. The base and superstructure are also made of stones, but with a heavy covering of mud plaster, at least until recently. The shape of the stupa is similar to the type which Kath Howard refers to as the "Lotsava mChod-rten type"[38] and which her informants assure her is "of great age and in a style no longer built."[39]

On the north side, a large opening developed on the two upper levels of the superstructure. This was closed off by Balázs during the years he was working at the Zangla palace, between 2004 when I first published the site and 2012 when I returned (Fig. 5.23).[40] He had also reinforced the platform (Fig. 5.18). Just below the pilaster marking the join of the base to the superstructure, clay molded plaques of two types have been applied to the plaster. While they no longer survive all the way around the structure, two clusters of them remain on the east and west sides. The ones of the

38 K. Howard, "Archaeological Notes on mChod-rten Types," 62.

39 Ibid., 62n5.

40 I returned in 2010 and was within a day's walk above it (to the east) when the violent rains that caused so much damage in Leh and destroyed many bridges throughout Ladakh made walking along the Zumlung Chu impossible. We (my friend and guide Lobsang Gyatso Pishupa, the horse-handler Choglamsar Tsering Choedak, and five horses) waited several days at Zangla Sumdo, hoping the level of the river would fall, but as we were running out of food after a forty-day trek we were forced to retreat, so close to Malakartse Khar and Zangla, the planned end of our trek. We started to return to the Lungnak Valley via Shadey and Phugtal, but after only a day Lobsang Gyatso found an emergency path over the snowy Siachen La (leading to Tsazar village) that normally horses are unable to cross. In August 2018 I returned with Lobsang Gyatso, Pali Hanumurpa, and Tori Andrews, and once again in 2022.

Fig. 5.21 Row of molded stupa reliefs on the west side of the Malakartse Khar stupa. Photo 2012.

Fig. 5.23 Malakartse Khar Stupa, with the hole on the northern side of the upper story repaired with stones. Photo 2022.

Fig. 5.22 Close view of one of the molded relief stupas in Figure 5.21, of the Kashmiri, Kaniska stupa type. Photo 2012.

Fig. 5.24 Close view of one of the molded relief stupas on the east wall of Malakartse Khar stupa, of the Kashmiri Kaniska type with the tip of a vajra visible below the base. Photo 2012.

west wall (Figs. 5.21–22) are of the quintessentially Kashmiri type, often referred to as modeled on the Kaniṣka stupa (see the discussion in chapter 3 and Figures 3.13–19). Below the beams splayed at an oblique angle above the small rounded *aṇḍa* marked with a band at the widest part, there is an additional element to the *harmika*, possibly a striding lion as if it had stepped off an Aśokan capital. On the east wall, the molded plaques are slightly different (Fig. 5.24). Most distinctive about the east-wall type is the protrusion of the tip of a vajra below the base of the stupa. All the ones noticed, of both types, are of the descent (lha 'bab) type.[41] It appears that the artists who created and decorated the exterior of the Malakartse Khar (MkK) stupa used at least two different clay molds for the plaques representing stupas, one of which reproduced an early and enduring form (see Fig. 5.22), and one with a somewhat later, more "tantric" form (see Fig. 5.24). Otherwise, we could assume that the original stupa's plaques, all of the earlier Kashmiri type as now found on the west wall, were partially replaced at a later date. Nevertheless, the forms depicted on east wall are still in a Kashmiri or Khaché mode, not a later Tibetan or Nepalese or locally-inflected form. They are not incompatible with the late eleventh- or twelfth-century date that will be proposed for the decorated interior.

On the east side of the stupa, there is a low doorway, supported at the top by wooden beams (Fig. 5.25). Both base and superstructure are hollow and the former can be entered. Inside is a small chamber,

41 See the discussion in chapter 3 of this type of early stupa and the caution against assuming it refers to one of the later standard eight types of stupas.

(left and right):

Fig. 5.25 Doorway entrance on the east side of the Malakartse Khar stupa. Photo 2004.

Fig. 5.26 View of the Malakartse Khar stupa ceiling with the repaired hole visible. Photo 2018.

Fig. 5.27 View of one of the wooden panels at the corners of the Malakartse Khar stupa ceiling, painted with textile pattern. Photo 2012.

around three and a half square meters. The walls are taller than they are wide, though the original height has not yet been determined since the current floor is unevenly raised well above its original level by the rubble of the fallen ceiling and other debris. At the corners where the top of the walls met the lantern ceiling, there are relatively intact remains of triangular horizontal panels decorated with textile patterns (Figs. 5.26–27). They indicate that the walls supported a lantern-style ceiling within the superstructure, common to early architecture in Ladakh and Ngari, west Tibet, including Cave 1 at Dungkar (dung dkar).[42] Unfortunately, probably due to the weight of the accumulation of snow on the roof and

42 Klimburg-Salter, "Dung dkar/Phyi dbang, West Tibet."

the destructive effects of its melting on the mud mortar, the interior roof has collapsed. Time widened the hole in the superstructure and opened up several smaller gaps in the superstructure on the other sides. They have exposed the interior to the elements, including an increasing amount of rain over the last three decades on account of recent climate change.[43]
It cannot be determined whether the entire lantern ceiling was painted—though that is likely—or with what theme. Unlike the many gateway stupas in Zangskar featuring five Tathāgatas and either Akṣobhya or Vairocana painted on the ceiling, where what remains on the supporting walls indicates what is missing above, here, as we will see, the themes of the walls do not provide straightforward clues to the destroyed portion.

The MkK Stupa: Interior Overview

All four support walls were once painted with murals, and, with the exception of the entrance wall (Fig. 5.28), clay sculptures were inserted into and suspended at or near the center of the walls (Figs. 5.29–31; Charts 5.1–5.4). The ceiling, as discussed, was neither flat nor slightly rounded but opens upward as if it to support a lantern ceiling, such as is found in the Karsha Kadampa Chorten (see chapter 7). Now it has only the four horizontal corner supports partially remaining (see Fig. 5.26). These consisted of wooden boards, and the lower surfaces were painted with lotus motifs and textile designs, but only the ones on the northeast and northwest corners show the full motif (see Fig. 5.27). Of the ceiling itself, the mud-mortared stone and a few wooden braces are all that remain in place. The focus here, then, can only be on what remains of the four walls. We can, however, examine the configuration of the sculptures' placement and their relationships, formally and thematically, to the surviving painted motifs. The main (west) wall, opposite the entrance (see Fig. 5.30), was centered on a clay sculpture in the middle of the wall. The placement of the holes at the center and below the painted circular nimbus suggests the sockets for struts to support a seated figure. In this, as will be discussed and illustrated below, it resembles the early Vajradhātu mandalas at the ruined sites of Dungkar and east of Basgo and Nyarma,[44] and those sites at Tabo, Lalung, the Alchi group, and other west Tibetan sites like Tholing of the eleventh to early thirteenth centuries preserving sculpture mounted against a shrine wall[45] (see Figs. 5.47, 5.159–5.161).

Circa eleventh-century temples at Khartse in west Tibet even retain fragments of the figural sculptures still attached to the rain-washed and

43 For the impact of the climate crisis in Zangskar, particularly its affect on Kumik village not far from Zangla, see Mingle, *Fire and Ice*.

44 Neuwirth and Auer, *Ancient Monastic Complexes of Tholing, Nyarma and Tabo*, 115–65, 313–25.

45 Luczanits, *Buddhist Sculpture in Clay*.

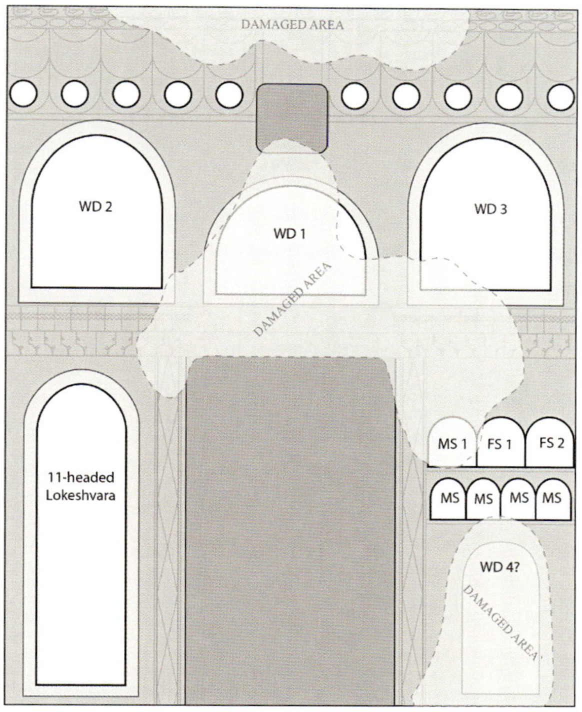

Chart 5.1 Entrance (East) Wall of Malakhartse Khar Stupa. WD = Wrathful Deity; MS = Male Sponsor; FS = Female Sponsor. Chart by Eric Huntington and Rob Linrothe.

Fig 5.28 Interior view of the east (entrance) wall of the Malakartse Khar stupa. Photo 2018.

Fig 5.29 Interior view of the south (left) wall of the Malakartse Khar stupa. Diameter of central circle 94 cm. Photo 2018.

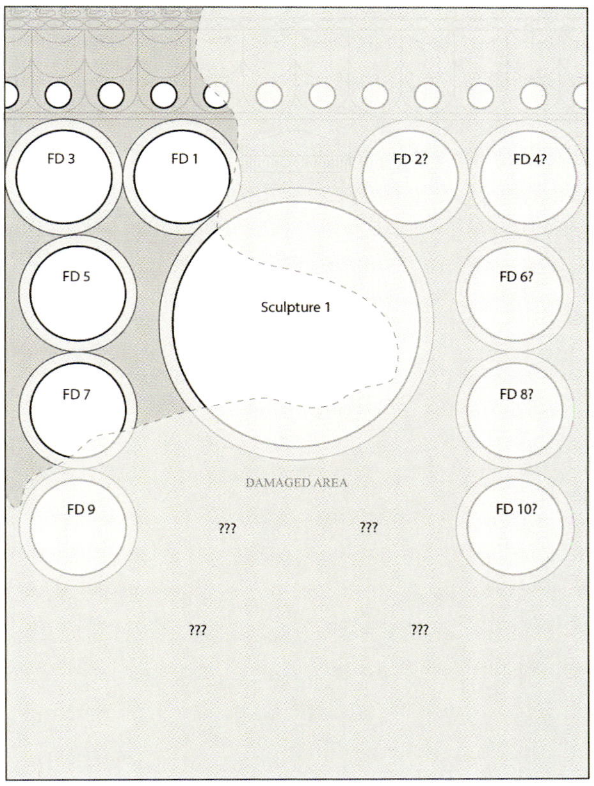

Chart 5.2 Left (South) Wall of Malakhartse Khar Stupa. FD = Female Deity. Chart by Eric Huntington and Rob Linrothe.

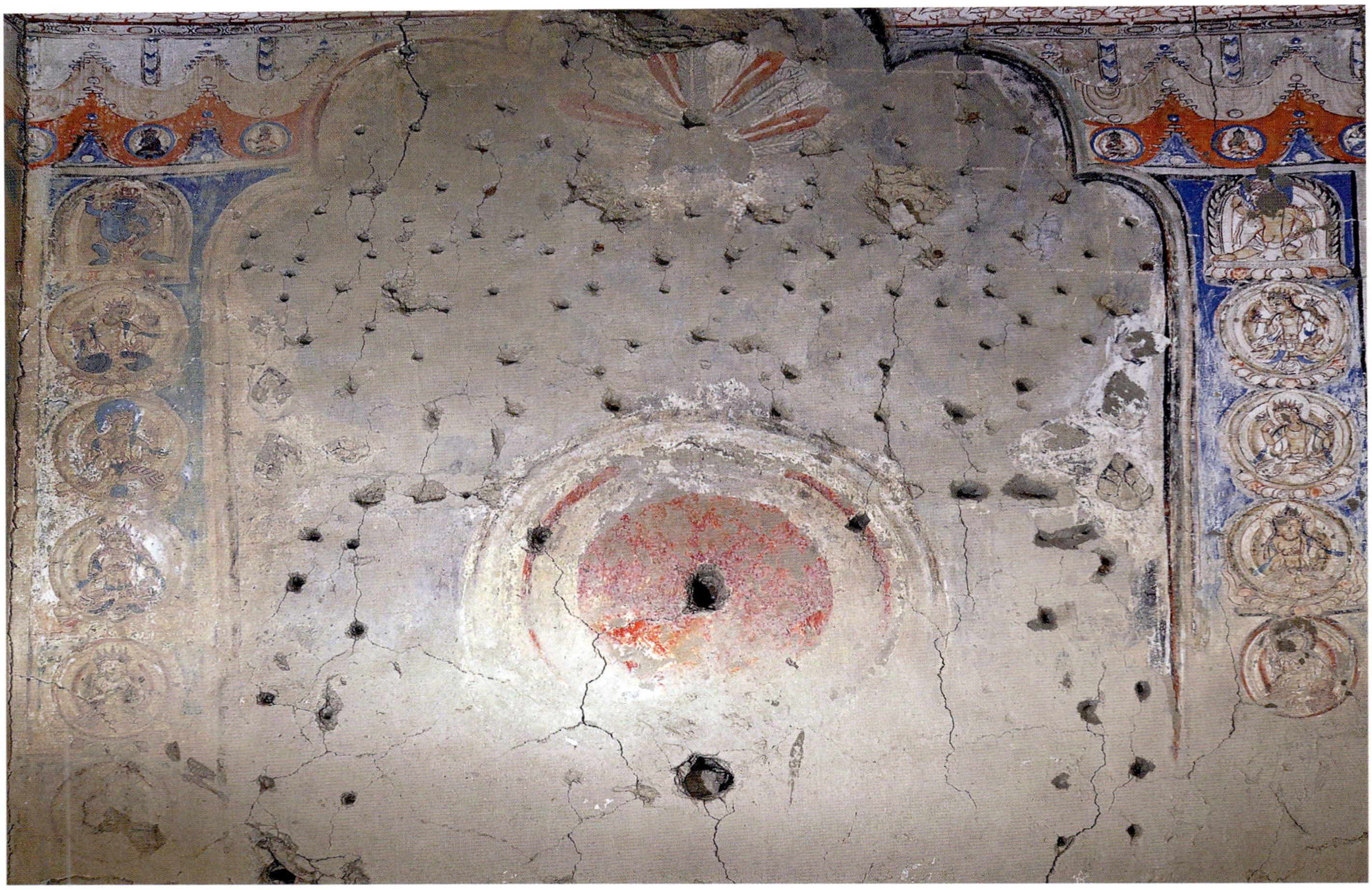

Fig 5.30 Interior view of the west (main) wall of the Malakartse Khar stupa. Diameter of central circle 64 cm. Photo 2018.

Fig 5.31 Interior view of the north (right) wall of the Malakartse Khar stupa. Diameter of inner circle 98 cm. Photo 2018.

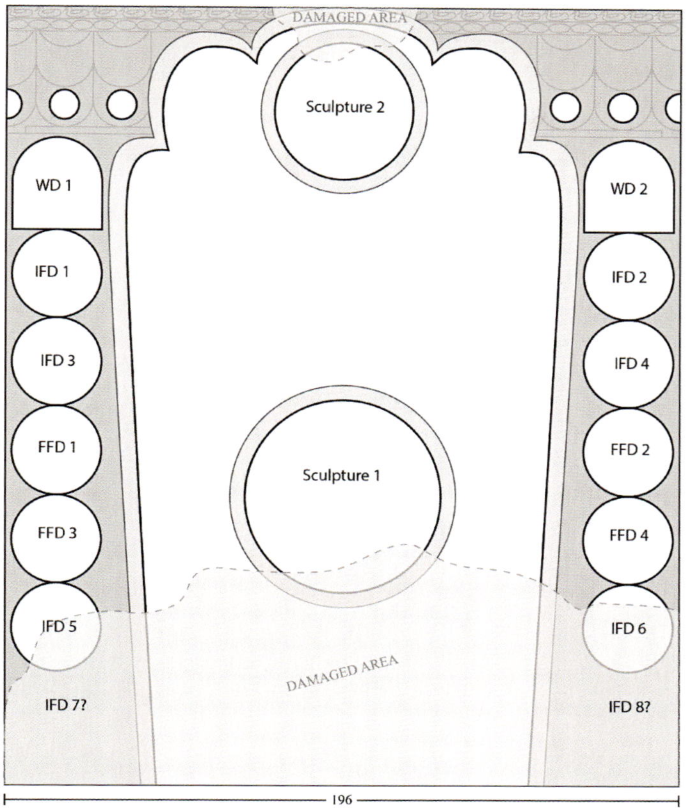

Chart 5.3 Main (West) Wall of Malakhartse Khar Stupa. WD = Wrathful Deity; IFD = Inward Facing Deity; FFD = Forward Facing Deity. Chart by Eric Huntington and Rob Linrothe.

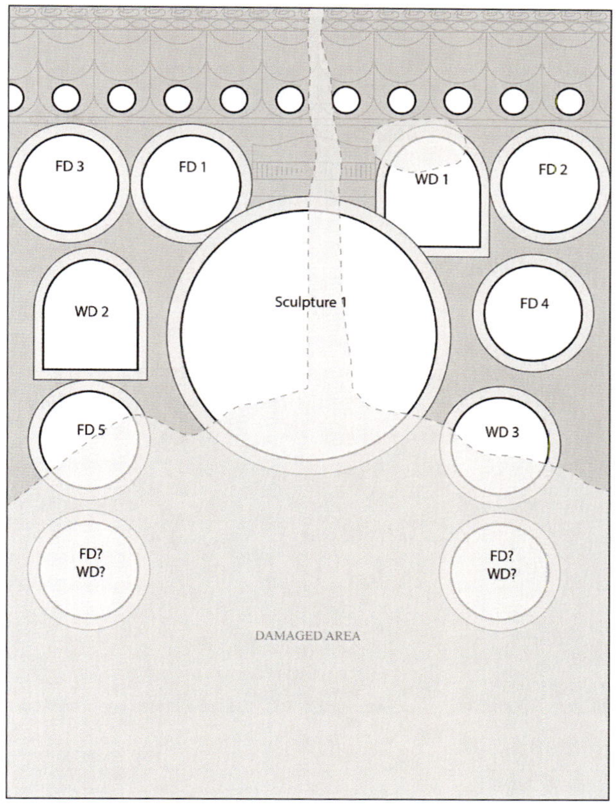

Chart 5.4 Right (North) Wall of Malakhartse Khar Stupa. FD = Female Deity; WD = Wrathful Deity. Chart by Eric Huntington and Rob Linrothe.

sun-bleached walls.[46] Based on the proportions and shape of the socket pattern, it seems safe to assume that the (missing) central figure of the main wall at Malakartse Khar (see Fig. 5.30; Chart 5.3) was a seated figure. Above him or her, an additional small figure was placed at the apex of the five-cusped painted enclosure, within the tree-like painted nimbus. A small socket-hold is visible at the center of the nimbus. Surrounding these two (absent) figures, still within the painted five-cusped enclosure, a network of holes distributed within a painted white lattice (faintly visible on the upper right in Figure 5.30) probably resembled the sculptural frames, thrones and secondary figures found in the Alchi Dukhang (Fig. 5.32),[47] Mangyu,[48] and numerous other early sites, including Lalung in Spiti (Fig. 5.33). At the Alchi Dukhang, a clay sculpture of Ratnasaṃbhava Tathāgata is attached to the painted wall (with flower buds surrounding him [see Fig. 5.32] as can also be seen on the main wall at the Malakartse Khar stupa).[49] He is seated within a five-cusped arch—sculptural, instead of painted—supported by columns. The shape is quite distinctive, and resembles not only the outlined upper framing on the central figure on the main wall, but also the frame of the Kashmiri Avantisvāmin sculpted panel depicting Kāmadeva (Fig. 5.34). To either side of the painted enclosure for the sculptural program on the main wall is a vertical column of deities, one on top of another. We will examine them shortly.

The south and north walls are similarly centered (roughly) on a painted

46 Sichuan Daxue 2009, color plates 11, 12.

47 Luczanits, *Buddhist Sculpture in Clay*, fig. 138.

48 Ibid., fig. 170.

49 With this comparison, I am *not* suggesting that the missing sculpture on the main wall of MkK stupa was Ratnasaṃbhava, only pointing out a similarly framed sculptural throne-back and setting for the figure.

(left and right):

Fig. 5.32 Clay sculpture of Ratnasaṃbhava Tathāgata in Alchi Dukhang. Photograph courtesy of Christian Luczanits.

Fig. 5.33 Vajrasattva in elaborate shrine at Lalung Serkhang, Spiti, Himachal Pradesh, India, ca. late 12th c. Photo 2006.

Fig. 5.34 Stone sculpture of Kāmadeva at Avantisvāmin, Kashmir, ca. 9th century. Photo 2004.

round nimbus. On the north wall (see Fig. 5.31) two large sockets at the center and the bottom of the nimbus and four struts in a line below it again suggest a seated figure, but beneath a painted canopy. It is without the elaborate sculptural framing found only on the main wall. Instead, the attendant deities were painted as murals. Something similar was the case for the south wall (see Fig. 5.29), though it is much more damaged. At any rate there are no other sockets for mounting other deities aside from the central one. In the late fall of 2003, when I first accompanied the Karsha Lonpo's second of three sons, Gelong Angchug, to the MkK stupa, he mentioned that a few years previously, when he had gone there for the first time, a few fragments of broken clay sculpture were still visible, though that was not the case during my initial visits of 2003 and 2004.

Figs. 5.35 & 5.36 Fragments of painted murals found among rubble on the floor of the Malakartse Khar stupa. Photo 2012.

I returned in 2012, 2018 and 2022. In 2012 I searched amidst the surface rubble of dirt and stones from the collapsed ceiling and superstructure. I documented some splinters of the wood struts, fragments of wall paintings (Figs. 5.35–36), and a few small portions of clay sculptures. The latter were too small to offer clues to the identity of the three main sculptures. To do that, we must infer who they were based on the remaining murals on all four walls and by comparison with a few rare sites in other areas. Before embarking on that endeavor in the second half of the chapter, however, the four walls must be examined in greater detail.

The overall condition of the murals is quite varied. Parts are still clear and colorful, mainly near the top of the west, north and entrance walls, but some areas of the murals have been completely or nearly obliterated by exposure to water so as to fade or discolor significantly. Others have suffered more serious intentional damage by human iconoclasts or vandals. From what remains, however, it is clear that the main upper ground against which many figures are depicted was a rich bright blue, presumably either an indigo or azurite pigment which has retained its intensity. Similar blue colors have been used as the ground for early paintings at Alchi, Tabo, Tholing, Chyiwang, and Dungkar. Using microscopic, microchemical and infrared spectroscopy, Dasser identified both azurite and indigo pigments on the walls of the Alchi Sumtsek.[50] These pigments seem to have been the preferred or the conventional background color for Kashmiri and Khaché murals, though not always so bright a blue. This azure background was relatively stable and resistant to water damage and fading. It was mainly confined to the upper third of the entrance wall, and the upper half of the other three walls. The lower portions had a different background color that, by contrast, has for all intents and purposes vanished.

While the width of each wall is straightforward enough to measure, the height from the floor to the beginning of the roof varies depending on the rubble from the ceiling that has accumulated on the interior floor. The east

50 Dasser, "Appendix," 274.

(entrance) and west (main) walls were 185 and 195 cm in width, while the two side walls were each 190 cm. The height of the entrance wall was approximately 230 cm, the south wall a little over 220, and the main and north walls 255 cm. The interior is thus approximately 3.6 square meters in area, and the interior space is approximately 8.5 cubic meters.

The MkK Stupa: East (Entrance) Wall

The entrance, or east, wall (see Fig. 5.28, Chart 5.1) has sustained considerable damage, not only due to holes in the superstructure but also from a small passage excavated into the top middle of the wall subsequent to the completion of the murals. Speculatively, it is possible that this hole was made in order to insert sacred objects such as *tsha tsha* or fragments of text and paintings. This would probably only have been done if the door had by that time been blocked, but it has subsequently been cleared. Still, in 2003 the lower part of the door retained a pile of stones that originally may have fully obstructed the doorway (see Fig. 5.25). I have not noticed the *tsha tsha* that typically fill niches or openings in other architectural stupas in Zangskar and Ladakh.[51] Perhaps they were buried under the rubble of the ceiling, but they were either cleared out and removed to Zangla, or did not accumulate significantly before the site was abandoned.

The very top of the entrance wall has three painted registers that run all the way around the inside of the entire chamber, interrupted only by the top of the central sculptural enclosure on the main wall (Fig. 5.37–38). The register on the top, bordered in red, depicts a row of *haṃsa* or geese, a motif frequently found at the top of early Buddhist structures in the western Himalaya, one with a symbolic tenure rooted in South Asian antiquity. "The Haṃsa bird, commonly identified as the bar-headed goose (Anser indicus), has a long and complex history in Indian literature as a mantra or as a metaphor, symbol, or allegory for the liberated soul."[52] Considered "the noble bird *par excellence*"[53] for its migratory life between winters in India and summers at Lake Manasarovar in west Tibet, for the fact that it feeds on the fibre of the lotus plant, and because, according to poets, it "is capable of separating the milk out of a mixture with water."[54] These features made it a favorite in Indian and especially Buddhist art as a kind of auspicious correlate for ascetics in general, and the Buddha in particular.[55] Indian ascetics are sometimes compared to the *haṃsa* "because they are wanderers, like the great birds that migrate from the jungles of the south to the lakes of the Himalayas, at home in the lofty sky as well as

51 Linrothe and Kerin, "Discovery through Deconsecration"; Linrothe, "Site Unseen"; Linrothe, "Thirty Years On," figs. 7, 8. See chapter 7, below.

52 Vasudeva, "Transport of the Haṃsas," 242.

53 Vogel, *Goose in Indian Literature and Art*, 2.

54 Ibid., 6.

55 Fisher, "Enigma of Harwan," 43; Zimmer, *Philosophies of India*, 262.

(clockwise from top left):

Fig. 5.37 Detail of the painted *haṃsa*, jeweled border, cloth banners with chevron patter, and swags of cloth on the upper part of the valance, Malakartse Khar stupa. Photo 2018.

Fig. 5.38 Section of the valance painted on upper wall inside Malakartse Khar stupa. Photo 2004.

Fig. 5.39 Detail of the *haṃsa* on the *vajrāsana* outside the Mahabodhi temple, Bodhgayā, Bihar India. Photo 2022.

on the water-surfaces of the earthly plane,"[56] "just as saints are at home in the formless sphere devoid of attributes as well as in the garb of the human individual, seemingly moving among us in the phenomenal sphere of bondage."[57] Vogel shows that the *haṃsa* motif appears on Aśokan pillars, in the Kaniṣka casket, on the *vajrāsana* slab at Bodh Gaya (Fig. 5.39), and on the Harwan clay tiles in Kashmir. In most such cases, at least one wing is raised, as here. At the two corners of the entrance wall, the surviving register shows that the *haṃsa* move in different directions, away from the center. The ones on the viewer's right move to their right and vice versa.

56 Zimmer, *Philosophies of India*, 262.

57 Ibid. 461n233. Bosch, who extends Vogel's posthumous 1962 work on the *haṃsa* cited above, writes that "the most important function the haṃsa has . . . is that of supporting things and persons, in other words, behaving as a pratiṣṭhā [i.e. support or foundation, similar to consecration];" Bosch, "Pratiṣṭhā Symbols," 536.

Fig. 5.40 Vajrasattva depicted in the *Gobu Shinkan*, after *Taishō Zūzo* 4 item no. 2974, p. 77.

Fig. 5.41 Close view of two Buddhas painted on the lower part of the valance inside the Malakartse Khar stupa. Photo 2022.

They continue these directions and would have met at the center of the main (west) wall to face each other, but the cusped sculptural enclosure interrupts the upper registers including that of the *haṃsa*.

Below the *haṃsa* is a narrow band of lozenge-shaped medallions, alternating in dark and light outlining (see Figs. 5.37–38). Just below it is a much wider register depicting three overlapping draped valances, in white, light yellow or tan, and ocher over a blue background. Each layer has a different device hanging at the center of the swag: for the upper white layer it is a narrow hanging ribbon with a chevron pattern pointing down. The tip is rounded. The light yellow layer has a round pearl hanging from a chain, and centered against the lowest swag is a roundel with a seated Buddha.[58] The Buddhas do not all make the same *mudra* or wear the same colored robe, but they all radiate the tightly undulating lines indicating light or energy (Figs. 5.40–41) as is found in the Japanese scroll known as the *Gobu-shinkan* with Kashmiri antecedents featuring Vajradhātu *mahāmaṇḍala* images and Sanskrit mantras.[59] This is one of several pieces of evidence for the transmission of Kashmiri idiomatic motifs across Asia to Japan.[60]

Both the valence and the representations of light rays convey meaning. The set of cloths and hangings providing the setting for a continuous row of Buddhas recall the opening scene of the *Sarvatathāgata Tattva Saṃgraha* (STTS) which takes places in the Jewel Hall of the palace of the king of Akaniṣṭha Heaven,

> a place frequented by All the Tathāgatas. [This palace] was variously adorned, with bells large and small and silken banners swaying in the gentle breeze, and it was bedecked with chaplets of pearls, strings of precious stones, half and full moons, and the like.[61]

58 A somewhat analogous arrangement, with the geese, geometric ornamental band, layered swags of cloth, chevron banners, and bells hanging from chains, but sans Buddhas, is found in the west tower of the Alchi Dukhang, visible in a photograph by Christian Luczanits, "AlchiDK CL98 91,03." I am very grateful to him for sharing the relevant portion of his photo archive.

59 Lokesh Chandra, *Ninth Century Scroll of the Vajradhātu Maṇḍala*, 78. See also Tanaka, *Illustrated History of the Mandala*, 145–147. The *Gobu-shinkan*, the "Meditation of [Each Image of] the Five Families," is believed to be a copy of a text brought to China from India by Śubhākarasiṃha (637–735), several copies of which survive in Japan. It has a number of Kashmiri visual conventions, suggesting the surviving copies were based on at least one made in Kashmir or by a Kashmiri-trained artist.

60 Linrothe, *Collecting Paradise*, 51–53.

61 Giebel, *Two Esoteric Sutras*, 19.

As for the light rays, they are by no means confined to Buddhas but are a frequently used visual convention to indicate one of the main visible characteristics of sacred objects in Esoteric Buddhism. Words that express this are sometimes strung together into mantras, as in the *Susiddhikara Sūtra*, an early pre-STTS ritual performance text featuring the *trikula* (three family) scheme which juxtaposes *jvāla* (to emit light), *jālaya* (cause to emit light), *dīpya* (shine), *dīpaya* (cause to shine), *tejas* (luminosity or sheen), *tejaya* (cause to be emit luminosity) with *siddhi* (success), *vardhaya* (cause to increase) and *saṃnidhim* (cause auspiciousness to be present).[62] Clearly, the emitting of light was an important concept in Tantric Buddhism—indeed, "Tantras were dominated by the concept of light"[63]—and it should be remembered that Vajradīpā is one of the eight offering goddesses, she who offers light to deity.
In the STTS, light rays move across the world systems, generating deities:

> Then, from this *vajra* [in the hand of Vairocana] there appeared [light rays in] the form of *vajra*s and of various colors and aspects, which pervaded and illuminated all world-systems. From the tips of these *vajra*[-like] light rays there appeared the figures of Tathāgatas equal [in number] to the dust-motes of all world-systems: They pervaded the Dharma-realm, went to the extremities of all empty space, pervaded the oceanlike clouds of all world-systems.[64]

Something like this was aimed at by the paintings at the upper levels, to evoke a consecrated space populated by Buddhas and the assemblies they generate.

The main area of the entrance wall is divided into two sections, upper and lower, the lower accommodating the doorway in the center. Dividing the space are three wrathful gate-guardians or protectors (see Figs. 5.28, 5.42–46; on Chart 5.1, marked WD 1–3), though the central one is damaged to the point of near absence. All three have a semi-rectangular nimbus that is rounded at the top—the same nimbus-shape reserved for wrathful deities in the sculptural Vajradhātu mandalas at the archaic, now dilapidated site near Basgo, probably of early eleventh century date (Fig. 5.47, lower right). The smaller central wrathful figure above the door is bookended by the two larger ones, WD2 and WD3 on Chart 5.1 (see Figs. 5.42–43). A close on-site examination of what remains of the east (entrance) wall WD 1 indicated that it is a light-colored wrathful *krodha-vighnāntaka* ("wrathful obstacle destroyer") with skulls in his crown and holding up a sword or staff. Given the smaller space allotted him,

62 Ibid., 262; Tanaka, *Illustrated History of the Maṇḍala*, 47–50.

63 Lokesh Chandra, "Preface: Synoptic View of the Book," xli.

64 Giebel, *Two Esoteric Sutras*, 26–27.

Fig. 5.42 Wrathful deity painted on the left side of the entrance wall at Malakartse Khar stupa. Photo 2004.

Fig. 5.43 Wrathful deity (Vajrahūṃkara?) painted on the right side of the entrance wall at Malakartse Khar stupa. Ht. 50.5 cm. Photo 2012.

Fig. 5.44 Close view of right hand of wrathful deity depicted in Figure 5.42, with snake bracelet on wrist, holding vajra. Photo 2004.

Fig. 5.45 Detail of upper torso of wrathful deity depicted in Figure 5.43 showing Kashmiri mode of depicting wrathful deity hair, and reverse widow's peak. Photo 2004.

Fig. 5.46 Close view of the arms and hands of the wrathful deity depicted in Figure 5.43, showing *mudrā* associated with Vajrahūṃkara, holding vajra and bell. Photo 2004.

he may have been depicted as seated, unlike the other two who face inward toward him and are standing in the *ālīḍha* and *pratyālīḍha* posture.

Between the heavily damaged central wrathful protector and the two on the ends are a few floating lotus buds against the blue ground, as if the sky was raining flowers. Similar closed buds appear on the two side walls, some attached to curling stems, but not against the main wall. The light-colored *krodha-vighnāntaka* on the left (see Fig. 5.42) stands with the right leg bent in *pratyālīḍha* (as used here; sources vary on which is which), and holds a *vajra* and a skull bowl in the right and left hands, respectively (see Fig. 5.44). His hair is knotted in a loose chignon on top of his head above a skull-bearing crown, with a flame-shaped wing of hair on the proper right side of his face turned towards the center of the wall, a distinctive convention originating in Kashmir.[65] Snakes adorn his wrists, and he wears an animal skin wrapped around the upper part of his *dhotī* decorated with stripes of different colors and patterns.

The *krodha-vighnāntaka* on the right (see Fig. 5.43) also faces towards the center (see Fig. 5.28). He can be identified by the blue skin color and the particular *mudrā* with the wrists crossed, the palms facing out and the little fingers intertwined while holding a *vajra* and bell in the right and left hands, respectively, as Vajrahūṃkara (see Figs. 5.45–46). (The iconography of the groupings will be discussed below, once a preliminary introduction to the subject matter has been laid out.) He has snakes on his ankles, as earrings, and as the *upavīta*. His long hair is arranged in a manner similar to that of the other wrathful standing figure on the wall, though in this case, both pointed wings of hair are visible, one on either side of his head (see Fig. 5.45).

Between the upper and lower sections of the wall, at the level of the top of the door, two registers of rusticated, cubic-form rocks are drawn in red and

65 Discussed and illustrated in Linrothe, *Collecting Paradise*, 89–91.

(clockwise from top left):

Fig. 5.47 Ruined shrine in Basgo, Ladakh, with remains of nimbi for Vajradhatu *mahāmaṇḍala* set of sculptures. Photo 2008.

Fig. 5.48 Drawing of ca. 8th c. Kashmiri Buddha etched onto a brass aureole in an undisclosed private collection published in Pal, *Arts of Kashmir*, fig. 96. Drawing by Eric Huntington.

Fig. 5.49 Close view of the stylized cubicized rocks painted below the wrathful deities on the entrance wall of the Malakartse Khar stupa. Photo 2004.

black pigments (Fig. 5.49).[66] These repeated hooked and reversed L´s, and inverted U´s, etc. have the same derivation and conventionalized function as the motifs on the seats of metal Buddhas from Kashmir, and on a line-etching of the Mount Meru, hourglass-shaped throne on the backplate of a Kashmiri aureole (Fig. 5.48).[67] The entryway opening is outlined with red and white borders, the widest outside border with vertically oriented diamond lozenges. To the left of the doorway when facing it from inside, below the cubic rock forms is a painting of a standing eleven-headed Avalokiteśvara (Fig. 5.50; Chart 5.1, lower left). Unfortunately, besides the environmental damage, the eleven heads of the bodhisattva have been singled out for intentional defacement. Little or nothing can be discerned about this figure other than his identity demonstrated by the lotus blooming at his left shoulder, and the fact that his eleven heads are arranged in the Kashmiri mode of this deity (Fig. 5.51), the one associated with Lakśminkāra, and not in the one with more wrathful heads associated with Songtsen Gampo (srong btsan sgam po).[68]

66 For further discussion of these forms, see Linrothe, "Landscape Elements in Early Tibetan Painting."

67 There is a remarkable similarity to "the curious stumpy terrain . . . derived from the terraced landscape of Late Antique and Early Christian art, which is built up by endless repetitions of the same clump of rock: identical building blocks, as it were." Pächt, *Practice of Art History*, 35.

68 On the different forms and their associations, see Kerin and Linrothe, "Recollecting Kashmir."

Fig. 5.50 Lower left side of Malakartse Khar entrance wall showing very damaged standing 11-headed Avalokiteśvara (Chuchikzhal). Ht. 75 cm. Photo 2004.

Fig. 5.51 Close view of the intentionally damaged 11 heads of the Avalokiteśvara of Figure 5.50. Photo 2022.

Fig. 5.53 Detail of the top knot on the central head of a disfigured three-headed wrathful deity depicted in Figure 5.52. Photo 2018.

Fig. 5.52 View of the area to the immediate right of the doorway on the entrance wall of the Malakartse Khar stupa depicting sponsors above and disfigured wrathful deity below. Photo 2004.

Fig. 5.54 Entrance wall of Cave 1 at Dungkar, West Tibet, depicting mandala and standing Avalokiteśvara, ca. 12th c. Photo 2007.

Opposite this form of Avalokiteśvara, on the other side of the door, on the lowest part of the right side of the door, beneath two registers of sponsors, is a smaller figure painted within a cusped arch against a blue rectangular surround (Fig. 5.52; Chart 5.1, lower right). Other than some kind of architectural frame enclosing him, even less can be identified. Still, enough remains to determine that he (?) had three heads, and a loose fan-shaped tuft of reddish hair emerges from the top of his central head (Fig. 5.53).[69] The space on the wall left for him is not as large as on the other side of the door dedicated to the eleven-headed Avalokiteśvara, because the sponsor figures are also fit into that space right of the doorway. Interestingly, the layout of the entrance wall of Cave One at Dungkar in Ngari, west Tibet, which on the other three walls is completely taken up with five mandalas (see Fig. 2.4), offers a number of similarities to the composition on the inside of the entrance wall at the MkK stupa. At Dungkar, the areas on either side of and above the doorway on the entrance wall are likewise dedicated to bodhisattvas (including the eleven-headed as one of two forms of Avalokiteśvara appearing there) along with wrathful protectors (a five-deity wrathful-wheel mandala and local protectors directly above the door) and sponsors (Fig. 5.54).

69 It is possible that it is the three-headed wrathful Ṭakkirāja.

Fig. 5.55 Two female sponsor figures (center and right) to the right of the doorway on the entrance wall of the Malakartse Khar stupa. Ht. of taller female 17 cm. Photo 2022.

At the Malakartse Khar stupa, there were seven local donors originally depicted; six are extant, all in the clothes associated with western Himalayan and west Tibetan sponsors (see Fig. 5.52, upper; Chart 5.1, MS and FS). Two women are depicted above (Fig. 5.55; Chart 5.1, FS 1 and FS 2). The third sponsor closest to the door, on their right, has been scratched out with only the left knee and a booted foot remaining, indubitably male (Chart 5.1, MS 1). Both extant female sponsors wear multiple strands of necklaces, have wide lapels, and face slightly towards the door in a three-quarter's view. The larger one has long hair and turquoise stones at her forehead. She wears an ample white cloak with a brown hem or lining, over a wheatish or dun-colored inner robe. A regal, queenly air is exuded. One hand is at her chest, the other is held up so we can see the inside of her long sleeve, but the hand itself is missing because of damage. In terms of the clothing and the turquoise at her forehead, she resembles the figures depicted in the Sudhana narratives in the Dukhang at Tabo (Fig. 5.56). One can also compare the sponsors from Saspotse, part of the Alchi group of related sites in Ladakh (Fig. 5.57). By comparison, the main female sponsor at the Malakartse Khar stupa is more individualized,

Fig. 5.56 Scene from the Sudhana narrative murals at Tabo Tsuglhakhang. Photo by Jaroslav Poncar.

Fig. 5.58 Detail of a depiction of Prajñāpāramitā from an unprovenanced manuscript illumination page offered for sale in 2003, probably from west Tibet (Tholing?). See Pal, *Arts of Kashmir*, fig. 115a. Photograph 2003.

Fig. 5.57 Two female sponsor figures depicted at Saspotse shrine, ca. 12th century. Photo 2010.

Fig. 5.59 Four male sponsor figures to the right of the doorway on the entrance wall of the Malakartse Khar stupa. Ht. of left two figures 15 cm. Photo 2004.

less stereotyped, the face fuller with the oft-noted Kashmiri chin. Beside her, a more contained, perhaps more youthful figure sits with her hands invisible, but a long stemmed lotus-bud emerging from her cloak. Both female sponsors are depicted with slight shading on the faces. The queenly figure has a protruding or extended farther eye in the grain- or almond-shape associated with Kashmir, similar to that in the Tholing-type manuscript painted in the Kashmiri mode (Fig. 5.58) that was at one time offered to the Rubin Museum for sale by a dealer, claimed to have been extracted from a closed-off stupa.

To the left of the queen was an equally large figure of a male larger than the four males directly below. One empty sleeve rests in front of the queen, and one boot is still visible (see Figs. 5.55, left, and 5.59, above left; Chart 5.1, MS 1). Otherwise he has been almost entirely eliminated from the composition due to damage. Below the three upper figures is a row of four males, slightly smaller than the three above them (see Fig. 5.59; Chart 5.1, MS). Three wear white robes with open lapels, belted at the waist. Their faces have been intentionally damaged. The first on the left wears a reddish-brown robe with white and blue lapels in the early western Himalayan or Tibetan mode of dress. The head gear worn by three of the figures is distinct in each case, with pointed extensions. All four had shoes or boots,

Fig. 5.60 Painting of sponsor figures in the Tsuglhakhang Ambulatory of Tabo, ca. 1042. Photo by Jaroslav Poncar.

Fig. 5.61 Male sponsor figures with faces intentionally disfigured depicted at Chyiwang Cave 79, Ngari, west Tibet. Photo 2007.

Fig. 5.62 Male sponsor figures with faces intentionally disfigured depicted at Chyiwang Cave 79, Ngari, west Tibet. Photo 2007.

Fig. 5.63 Sponsor couple (male and female) surrounded by other sponsors at Dungkar Cave 2, west Tibet, ca. late 12th century. Photo 2007.

Fig. 5.64 Drawing of an etched image of a couple on a ca. 9th c. metal bowl purportedly found in Gilgit, probably Kashmiri in origin, ca. 9th century, in an undisclosed private collection published in Pal, *Arts of Kashmir*, fig. 194. Drawing by Eric Huntington.

and appear in respectful gestures. The second from the left has a goatee and curling mustachios. The first two have cropped hair, while the two on the right have long hair, presumably indicating relative youth.

Once again, relatively close cognates for headgear, facial hair, robes, postures and the combination of older and younger male figures are found among the sponsor figures at Tabo, in this case in the Ambulatory (Fig. 5.60). They in turn closely resemble those depicted in the three-niche cave at Chyiwang (Figs. 5.61–62), as we will see, merely the first of a number of significant parallels. One of these Chyiwang sponsors (see Fig. 5.62, middle figure) wears a hat with pointed flaps. Near Chyiwang in west Tibet, Dungkar Cave 2 with the mandala ceiling has a number of donors depicted, including a sponsor couple (Fig. 5.63). She has the same cascade of chokers and necklaces as the MkK stupa queenly figure, a wide-sleeved cloak over a robe, long hair and her left hand held in front of her chest. Her male companion has a tightly belted robe, a wide-brimmed hat, and bobbed hair. These figures show that in terms of their dress, jewelry, and manner of self-representation, the Zangskar sponsors depicted in the Malakartse Khar stupa wished to appear as participants in a larger pan-western Himalayan and west Tibetan aristocratic court culture. Perhaps they were members of the west Tibetan elites who had installed themselves in Zangskar in the train of the Gugé-Purang invasion (see chapter 1). It should be remembered that the stupa was closely affiliated with the strongly defensible Malakartse Khar fort, itself suggesting a somewhat besieged and militant context, possibly enforcing trade levies.

That these clothes and accoutrements are local, not Kashmiri, is quite clear. The "etching" at the bottom of a shallow Kashmiri metal bowl depicts a couple who correspond to the Kashmiri aristocratic ideal (Fig. 5.64).

They are much more "Indic" than the Malakartse Khar sponsors in that he wears a *dhoti*, is bare-chested, and she wears a tight-fitting bodice. They are barefoot where the western Himalayan donors are booted. The fact that the elite *sponsors* are depicted wearing local clothing does not necessarily imply that the *artists* were local. In fact, the rest of the depictions at MkK stupa show deities dressed in attire appropriate to Buddhist images in Kashmir. The *Citrasūtra*—probably written and certainly known in Kashmir—specifically points out that it was expected that (Kashmiri) artists should adjust so as to depict figures wearing "dress appropriate to that particular country" in which they are temporarily working.[70] While the heavy modeling is typical of that found in the other sponsor figures of Tabo and Chyiwang (see Figs. 5.56, 5.60–62), what these others rarely display, however, is a clear extension of the eye beyond the outline of the face in three-quarters view. This is found in the relatively intact larger female Malakartse Khar stupa sponsor (see Fig. 5.55, center) and in some depictions of deities discussed below. It is discussed in the *Citrasūtra* as well. The text mentions that there are times when "only half of the nose is visible . . . one side of one cheek [is full, while] . . . one [entire] side [of the face is] foreshortened (*ardhakṛtakṣayam*)".[71] In other words, *how* it was painted was Kashmiri; *what* was painted was in accord with local elites' self-presentation.

The MkK Stupa: West (Main) Wall

Two clay sculptures were once affixed along the central axis of the main wall, the lower one larger than the upper one based on the sizes of the painted nimbi. Along with the surrounding thrones and attendant figures, all are missing and presumably destroyed (see Fig. 5.30; Chart 5.3). Later, we will hazard some conjectures about who they depicted, but in order to arrive at that point it is necessary to glean what we can of the surrounding deities arranged vertically on the edges of the composition (Figs. 5.65–66).

At the top of both columnar stacks of deities are two wrathful deities (*krodha-vighnāntaka*) (Figs. 5.67–68; Chart 5.3: WD 1 and WD 2). Each is enclosed in a round-topped nimbus edged with flames, turns to face the center, and is supported by a single row of downward-turned lotus petals. These minor details of shape of nimbus, orientation, and seat or platform serve to distinguish several related classes of deities vertically arranged in the two columns. The *krodha-vighnāntaka* on the viewer's left is blue, holds a sword in his raised right hand and the stem of a lotus held in the

70 Mukherji, *The* Citrasūtra *of the* Visṇudharmottara Purāṇa, 163.

71 Ibid., 83.

Fig. 5.65 Column of deities on the right side of the main (west) wall of the Malakartse Khar stupa. Ht. 22 cm. Photo 2018.

Fig. 5.66 Column of deities on the left side of the main (west) wall of the Malakartse Khar stupa. Ht. 22 cm. Photo 2018.

(left and right):

Fig. 5.67 Detail of blue wrathful deity at the top of the left column of the main (west) wall of the Malakartse Khar stupa. Ht. 22 cm. Photo 2018.

Fig. 5.68 Detail of Hayagrīva wrathful deity at the top of the right column of the main (west) wall of the Malakartse Khar stupa. Ht. 22 cm. Photo 2018.

fingers of his left hand carried at his hip (see Fig. 5.67). The lotus appears to have a gem on it, which is wrapped by a black noose or *pāśa*. The sword and the *pāśa*, along with the color blue, are the attributes of Acalanātha, one of the eight (or ten) directional guardians found in various mandalas, particularly of the Yoga Tantra variety. He is associated with the Vajra family and is directly across from the blue wrathful Vajrahūṃkara (see Fig. 5.43) on the entrance wall. In this depiction he is *lambodara* (big-bellied), has snake ornaments, his right leg bent and left leg straight, and his hair arranged like the other wrathful figures on the entrance wall: two flame-like tufts bracketing a fan-like central chignon, with a v-shaped slit above the middle of his forehead, resembling wrathful figures from Kashmir.[72] He looks inward toward the central composition, and toward his counterpart on the other side. One oddity is that his *upavīta* starts to curve under and around his left breast, leaving a gap. This is the convention encountered on the other walls with the female deities who have large breasts, but here the size is not sufficient to explain the gap. Perhaps it is an error or lapse of concentration on the part of the artist; alternatively, it could be a female form of the wrathful deity, which seems unlikely; or it is just meant to emphasize the fleshiness of the sumo-wrestler-like chest.

The wrathful deity on the right (Fig. 5.68; Chart 5.2, WD 2) is in much better condition in terms of pigments left on the surface of the wall, but it has suffered more intentional damage. He stands in the opposite pose, also looking inward, with a similar arrangement of the hair except for the addition of the band of skulls and the horse's head at the top. This indicates that it is Hayagrīva, representing the *padma* family, adjacent to the right wall which turns out to have other *padma* family associations. For that matter, he is across from the 11-headed Avalokiteśvara on the entrance wall (see Figs. 5.50–51) intimating a division between the left and right walls, of the vajra (signalled by Acalanātha and Vajrahūṃkara) and lotus (signalled by Hayagrīva and Avalokiteśvara) families respectively. What Hayagrīva holds in the upper right hand is not clear; in many Indian sculptures Hayagrīva carries a club (*daṇḍa*) or sword.[73] In an early Ladakhi sculpture (ca. 9th–10th c.) in the Changspa neighborhood of Leh, Hayagrīva leans on a club (Fig. 5.69), whereas at Mangyu he brandishes a sword.[74]

On the lotus flower at Hayagrīva's shoulder on the main wall at the MkK stupa, a chain arcs around the top (see Fig. 5.68). Since Acala has a *pāśa*, this suggests that the two of them might represent the "Attracting Deities,"

72 Linrothe, *Collecting Paradise*, fig. 1.62.
73 Linrothe, *Ruthless Compassion*, 95–128.
74 Linrothe, "Murals of Mangyu," fig. 20.

Fig. 5.69 Hayagrīva with horse's head on Avalokiteśvara stone sculpture in open-air pavilion in Changspa, near Leh, Ladakh, 9th–10th c. Photo 2008.

Vajrapāśa and Vajrasphoṭa, who serve to draw in and secure as well as restrain and bind, the deities with whom the practitioner or *ācārya* (master, teacher) bonds in the Yoga Tantra ritual; they are described thus in the STTS.[75] If so, one would expect the other two "Attracting Deities," Vajrāṅkuśa and Vajraghaṇṭa, to be represented as part of the deployment of the basic Vajradhātu *mahāmaṇḍala*, and perhaps they appeared at the lower end of the column of deities in the areas where the pigments are now washed away or covered by the rubble on the floor. In that case, they would have been at both the top and the bottom, framing the column of deities. On the other hand, possibly the two extant wrathful figures on the main wall instead represented a three-family scheme, of the Vajra family at the proper right of the central (missing) deity, and the *padma* family on the left. That would imply that the central deity and the one above belonged to the Buddha family. Note that the painted nimbus for the upper sculpture at the top of the main wall is delineated with fern-like radiating branches as if indicating the tree under which the Buddha sat while attaining enlightenment (see Fig. 5.30, top). We will return to these possibilities. In other early Esoteric Buddhist contexts one would expect Vairocana to represent the Buddha family, but as we will see, he is already represented among non-wrathful figures on the vertical stacks on the margins of the main wall, which we examine next.

Below the wrathful deities (Acala and Hayagrīva apparently also acting as Vajrapāśa and Vajraphoṭa; see Figs. 5.67–68) there are both clear and faint traces of at least five male figures on each side (see Figs. 5.65–66). Each is about 22 cm in height. The first two from the top

75 Todaro, "Annotated Translation of the *Tattvasaṃgraha* (Part 1)," 301, 306, 317.

Fig. 5.70 Third and fourth deities from the top of the left column on the main (west) wall of the Malakartse Khar stupa. Photo 2004.

Fig. 5.71 Third and fourth deities from the top of the right column on the main (west) wall of the Malakartse Khar stupa. Photo 2004.

Fig. 5.72 Fifth and sixth deities from the top of the left column on the main (west) wall of the Malakartse Khar stupa. Photo 2004.

Fig. 5.73 Fifth and sixth deities from the top of the right column on the main (west) wall of the Malakartse Khar stupa. Photo 2004.

on both the left and right (below the wrathful figures) face inward toward the center (Chart 5.3, IF 1–IF4). The next two on both sides, by contrast, face forward (Chart 5.3, FF 1–FF 4). Below them there are possibly two more on each side, facing inward (Chart 5.3, IF 5–IF8?). As examples, Figures 5.70 and 5.71 illustrate the second and third male figures (not counting the wrathful ones at the top) of the left and right column, including one facing inward and one facing forward. Though the nimbi are the same for both inward- and forward-looking deities, the latter maintain a hieratically more significant orientation. Of the two lower pairs of males looking inward, only the one on the left is fully visible but in a faded form (Fig. 5.72, lower), the other one having been almost completely obliterated (Fig. 5.73, lower). Presumably there was at least one more pair of inward looking peaceful deities further below on each side beneath the accumulated rubble now constituting the floor. At the very bottom, the counterparts to the two topmost wrathful figures (see Figs. 5.67–68), also facing inward, may be supposed on the basis of symmetry and manifest knowledge on the part of the painters of the standard sets of deities of the Vajradhatu *mahāmaṇḍala*-like program to which the visible ones clearly belong.

Assuming this, then the side panels would each have eight deities (sixteen in total), starting with a pair of *krodha-vighnāntaka* at the top and bottom (four in total). Also appearing would have been two sets of four deities turning inward (eight in total) and between them, at the same level as the main sculpture on the wall, a set of four deities looking straight ahead. In that case, the two side panels would constitute the full set of four wrathful "Attracting Deities," two sets of four offering deities (those facing inward) constituting the eight inner and the outer offering deities as found in the STTS, and, as is demonstrated below, a set of four of the five Tathāgata Buddhas. Since several figures are missing, this scenario remains speculative, based on an expectation of both visual symmetry, conceptual completeness, and the space available on the prepared wall covered by the rubble from the collapsed ceiling and sculptures.

On the other hand, it is also possible that the set of wrathful figures was completed by a pair of small sculptures attached to the wall, along with four or more bodhisattva-like figures, yielding sixteen in all, the usual number prescribed for the *vajra*-bodhisattvas (or *samādhi* deities as they are also called) associated with the four Tathāgatas (excluding the central Vairocana) in the Vajradhātu *mahāmaṇḍala*, as found in such texts as the STTS and the *Sarvadurgati Pariśodhana Tantras*. These also appear in sculptural form in the Dukhang at Tabo and at Sumda Chung, and in a combination of sculpture and painting at the Alchi Dukhang and the Nako Translator's temple.[76] The question of whether the inward-facing deities on the two side panels of the main wall are eight of the sixteen *vajra*-Bodhisattvas or constitute the full set of eight offering deities hinges on the identification of the handheld and lotus-borne attributes (*āyudha*). These will be examined shortly, with rather surprising results. First, brief comparisons with other early sites in the western Himalaya are in order.

The Alchi Dukhang, to which attention has already been drawn in relation to the shape of the cusped arch supported by pillars (see Fig. 5.32), has a number of other parallels here. Four sculptural Tathāgatas, paired on the short side walls of the apse, were each framed with a vertical painted column including the *vajra*-bodhisattvas (Fig. 5.74). The sculptures have been repaired and other later figures added, but the combination of paintings and sculptures might help indicate the original state at the Malakartse Khar stupa.

76 Luczanits, *Buddhist Sculpture in Clay*.

Fig. 5.74 Akṣobhya Tathāgata (at center, repaired) at Alchi Dukhang, surrounded by *vajra*-bodhisattvas in columns to left and right, ca. 12th c. Photo by Christian Luczanits.

Fig. 5.75 *Vajra*-bodhisattva painted in the Alchi Dukhang, ca. 12th c. Photo by Christian Luczanits.

A shared iconographic language of poses and gestures if not iconographic type is evident by comparing one of the Alchi Dukhang *vajra*-bodhisattvas (Fig. 5.75) with one of the Malakartse Khar stupa's seated Tathāgata (see Fig. 5.71, lower). Both have their left hands in *vajramuṣṭi* (*vajra*-fist) at the hip, and hold a flower or gem at the chest with the right. From the style point of view, note also the way the scarves are arranged at the crown and over the arms, the interest in textile patterning, the earrings, the slit at center of the forehead at the hairline, and the Kashmiri-style shape of the eyes and torso. Certainly, these were not the same artists, nor was it completed at the same time. One notes that the Alchi bodhisattva is rather more elongated in proportions, and the Malakartse Khar stupa bodhisattva is more compact, suggesting a somewhat earlier origin. A more detailed proposal for a relative chronology will be suggested near the end of the chapter but while discussing the Alchi Dukhang imagery, we should point out that Luczanits's analysis concludes, "there is no doubt that the Alchi Dukhang is the oldest of the three Alchi temples containing clay sculptures."[77] Luczanits concurs with Goepper in placing the Sumtsek in the very late twelfth or early thirteenth century, and the Dukhang in the third quarter of the twelfth century.[78]

Returning to the two stacks of deities framing the sculptural area of the main wall, it would be remiss not to point out that the first set of four bodhisattvas turning inward (the first two on each side below the wrathful-protectors at the top of the columns; Chart 5.3, IF1–IF 4) have some peculiarities. All four make the *vajramuṣṭi mudrā* with the left hand and grasp the stem of a lotus that appears at their proper left shoulder. In addition, each holds an attribute (*āyudha*) in the raised right hand. These latter attributes include (starting on the viewer's right column) a gem-like

77 Ibid., 137.

78 Ibid.; Luczanits, "Beneficial to See," 214–33; Luczanits, *Alchi*, 19–27.

flower with pointed leaves (Fig. 5.76) and a white lotus with rounded petals (see Fig. 5.71, upper); and on the left column a jewel (Fig. 5.77) and a sword (see Fig. 5.70, upper). The lotus, gem and sword can be identified with the *padma*, *ratna*, and *karma* families of Amitāyus, Ratnasambhava, and Amoghasiddhi, respectively. They are thus held by the primary Vajra-bodhisattvas of each of these families, as described in the STTS.

What is unexpected is that in addition to the objects held in the right hands, the stem of a lotus is held in their left hands at the hip, and the objects supported by the white lotuses at their shoulders relate more to the offering deities than to the sixteen *vajra*-bodhisattvas. For example, the first (upper) one on the right has a lick of flame emerging from the lotus (see Fig. 5.76), the symbol of Vajradīpā, while the first on the left (see Fig. 5.77) has a bowl in which incense appears to be burning, the characteristic attribute of Vajradhūpā. Vajradhūpā and Vajradīpā are the first and the third of the four "outer" offering deities generated by the four Tathāgatas "for the sake of returning the honour of the offering of the Bhagavata Vairocana" for generating the four "inner" offering deities, according to the STTS.[79] The second on the right (see Fig. 5.71, upper) has a tiny curved harp with five strings, a musical instrument according with the attribute carried by Vajragītā, the third "inner" offering deity, whose offering is song or music. The second on the left (see Fig. 5.70, upper) has blue and white jewels strung into a garland, precisely the attribute of Vajramālā, second of the four "inner" offering deities.

The eight inner and outer offering deities are also part of the essential Vajradhātu *mahāmaṇḍala* as well as related mandalas from correlated texts. We will find them as such on the north wall, but there, and as is customary for images of the offering deities, they take the form of goddesses, not male bodhisattvas. However, in some instances, the offering deities were understood to be male.[80] For example, in the fifth mandala introduced in the first section of the *Sarvatathāgata Tattva Saṃgraha*, the so-called Naya mandala with four deities surrounding Vajrasattva, these four attending deities are understood to personify "[o]ffering the joys of song, dance, drink, food, amusement, etc. to the Buddhas" and are frequently depicted as male forms of the "inner" offering deities. They are depicted as such in the so-called "Maṇḍala of Vajrasattva" in the Musée Guimet, ca. tenth century, on silk from Dunhuang (Fig. 5.78), as well as the Genzu drawings.[81] In the STTS, there are certainly a number of other instances

79 Todaro, "Annotated Translation of the *Tattvasaṃgraha* (Part 1)," 243.

80 As discussed in Linrothe, "Mirror Image: Deity and Donor as Vajrasattva"; Linrothe, "'Structure and Subject Matter' at Dunhuang."

81 Lokesh Chandra, *Ninth Century Scroll of the Vajradhātu Maṇḍala*, 331–34.

Fig. 5.77 Second deity from the top of the left column on the main (west) wall of the Malakartse Khar stupa. Photo 2004.

Fig. 5.76 Second deity from the top of the right column on the main (west) wall of the Malakartse Khar stupa. Photo 2004.

Fig. 5.78 Drawing of a painting from Dunhuang, Gansu, China, now in the Musée Guimet, Paris, on silk, ca. 10th c. depicting Vajrasattva surrounded by the Inner Offering deities in male form. Drawing by Gerald Kozicz.

Fig. 5.79 Horse *vāhana* under Ratnasambhava Tathāgata, the fourth deity from the top of the left column on the main (west) wall of the Malakartse Khar stupa. Photo 2018.

Fig. 5.80 Lion *vāhana* under Vairocana Tathāgata, the fifth deity from the top of the left column on the main (west) wall of the Malakartse Khar stupa. Photo 2022.

of gender substitution, but most often it is the substitution of the male *vajra*-bodhisattvas for female ones, as is the case for the Vajraguhya mandala and the Vajrakārya Karma mandala, the former also depicted in the Alchi Sumtsek.[82] Most unusual here is that the first set of four inward-looking deities seems to do double duty both as part of the set of *vajra*-bodhisattvas, and to stand in for four of the eight "inner" and "outer" offering deities.

The second two pairs of deities, the fourth and fifth from the top of the column who face directly forward (Chart 5.3, FF 1–FF 4), are perfectly aligned horizontally with the large central nimbus of the destroyed central sculpture. Although they appear similar to the bodhisattva figures just discussed in dress, jewelry, round nimbus, and the *vajramuṣṭi mudrā* of the proper left hand held at the hip, there are at least four significant differences: posture, orientation, *vāhana*, and the lack of a lotus at the left shoulder. (Compare the examples of one of each group in Figures 5.70–71.) As with the facing-forward orientation, the posture of these middle pairs is more formal than the "adept's pose" (*sattvaparyaṅkāsana*) of the upper bodhisattvas. Instead of having one bent leg on top of the other, they sit in full *vajrāparyank-āsana* posture, with both soles of the feet visible, and ankles crossed.

The forward-facing ones also have visible *vāhana*s (animal vehicles). On the left, a pair of horses is visible (Figs. 5.70, lower, 5.79), and on the right, peacocks (see Fig. 5.71, lower). These features conclusively identify them as Ratnasambhava and Amitāyus, two of the five directional Tathāgata Buddhas. The males directly below them on both sides also look forward and have (barely visible) *vāhana*s, in their cases lions on the left

82 Todaro, "An Annotated Translation of the *Tattvasaṃgraha* (Part 1)"; Goepper and Poncar, *Alchi*, 200–209.

(see Figs. 5.72, upper and 5.80) and garudas on the right (see Figs. 5.73, upper),[83] identifying them as Vairocana and Amoghasiddhi, respectively.

These four Jinas lack the hand-held lotus with the offerings of the eight inward-looking deities, but the *āyudha*s they hold are quite clear: the upper one on the right holds a flower bud (see Fig. 5.71, lower; Chart 5.3, FF 2), the lower one on the right holds a sword (see Fig. 5.73, upper; Chart 5.3, FF 4), the top on the left holds a gem (see Fig. 5.70, lower; Chart 5.3, FF 1), and the lower one on the left holds a wheel (see Fig. 5.72, upper; Chart 5.3, FF 3). These correspond to the *padma*, *karma*, *ratna*, and *Buddha* family, respectively.

The facts that the four of them have *vāhana* (animal mounts) below their lotus seats, their attributes and formal poses and orientation, along with their position strictly aligned with where the central sculpture was placed on the main wall allow us to float with confidence the probability that they were meant to be recognized as neither *vajra*-bodhisattvas nor inner or outer offering deities, but as four of the five directional Tathāgatas. The fifth is conjecturally the missing sculpture in the middle of the wall. The four painted ones have the *samaya*-icon of the family they represent, as well as their associated *vāhana*. They correspond to their associated directions, in clockwise order starting with Vairocana in the east, Ratnasambhava above him in the south (both on the left side) and then Amitayus above and Amoghasiddhi underneath him in the west and north (on the right side). On the other hand, it must be acknowledged that they do not make the standard *mudrā*s of the Tathāgatas. If they are not the Tathāgatas, they still represent four of the five families (*pañcakula*). It is also conceivable that these four were also somehow invested with a double identity—like Acala and Hayagrīva as *also* Vajrapāśa and Vajrasphoṭa, and others as offering deities *and vajra*-bodhisattva. In that case, they could be counted as simultaneously four of the five Tathāgtatas with their respective *vāhana and* among the sixteen *vajra*-bodhisattvas. For example, the one with the wheel could possibly be the *vajra*-bodhisattva Vajrahetu who is described in Ānandagarbha's commentary on the STTS.[84]

Alternatively, their second identity could be through referencing the four consorts who are often represented by their family *samaya*, the very attribute that is held in the proper left hands of the four. That is, Locanā carries a wheel[85] like the one in Figure 5.72, upper; Ratnavajrī holds a

83 These were only visible to me with very close inspection, bright lights and magnification on site itself. Only the eyes of the left-side lion are faintly visible in Figure 5.72, more clearly in Figure 5.80, though the right side Garuda is relatively visible when Figure 5.73 is enlarged.

84 Luczanits, *Buddhist Sculpture in Clay*, 299, no. 16 West.

85 Tucci, *Temples of Western Tibet*, 33.

jewel as in Figure 5.70, lower. Paṇḍaravāsinī holds a lotus like the one in Figure 5.71; and Karmavajri is of the *karma* family whose symbol is either a double vajra or a sword, as in Figure 5.73, upper).[86] The standard *vajra*-bodhisattvas do not appear with *vāhana*. This doubling of identities, however, would be unprecedented in my experience though that is true also for the other figures around them.

To recap the proposed identification of the composition of the main wall so far, of the two columns on the side of the missing sculptures at the center of the main wall, we have encountered three sets of different deity-types. First, wrathful gate-guardians (two extant of a likely set of four). Second, peaceful bodhisattva-like deities looking inward (six extant of a possible set of eight) who simultaneously represent (eight of sixteen) *vajra*-bodhisattvas and (eight of eight) inner- and outer-offering deities. The third set is composed of Tathāgatas facing forward (four of five). Although there is no trace of the two projected wrathful deities or two bodhisattvas at the bottom of the wall, there is space on the wall to account for them. Moreover, symmetry and completion of the sets in accord with the Vajradhatu *mahāmaṇḍala* demands them. It is possible, however, that the two missing wrathful figures and either six or more likely four of the bodhisattva figures instead appeared as sculptures surrounding the central figure.

The fact that the *krodha-vighnāntaka*, the eight inward-facing bodhisattva figures, and the four Jinas may all have double roles in this scheme requires further comment. Presumably, having a dual identity was a way of economically compacting a large number of deities into a small space. This probably was made possible because of the context of an "unpacked," "horizontal," or "implicit" mandala. That is, instead of showing all the deities of a particular mandala within the fully symmetrical circular zones of the mandalas (above, below, or to the sides of the main concentric deities), as is conventional for representing three-dimensional mandalas, the deities are removed from the circles and arranged in columns. Certainly, only initiated practitioners would have noticed at a glance that there were missing deities, and then would be able to recognize those playing more than one role. If my reading of this is correct, such an "economy" is unprecedented to my knowledge and would represent a fascinating act of creative interpretation on the part of the artists or designers. On the other hand, the intertwining of painting and sculpture so as to constitute a single programmatic unit, such as a Vajradhatu

86 I have here mixed two different system of names for these consorts; their complex relationship and identity is addressed in Luczanits, *Buddhist Sculpture in Clay*, 318n554.

mahāmaṇḍala, is commonly found at other early sites in the western Himalaya and west Tibet, including Tabo and the Alchi group of sites.

However, in order to account for a full thirty-seven–deity Vajradhātu *mahāmaṇḍala* on the main wall, we would still have to account for eight more *vajra*-bodhisattvas. Given the number of holes accommodating struts surrounding the two larger sculptures, four or more small deities could certainly be accommodated. Nevertheless, it is also possible that, as with the dual-purpose deities, there was more abbreviation by which the mandala was evoked rather than depicted. A much simpler composition is certainly possible. Unless the floor inside the stupa is excavated and reveals identifiable sculpture fragments so that the subject matter of the sculptures can be more securely reconstructed and identified, the precise program of the main wall will remain indefinite, with this possible but still hypothetical reconstruction only tentative.

A more challenging absence to understand is that of one of the five Tathāgata, Akṣobhya. It is well known that he often, perhaps even increasingly replaces Mahāvairocana at the center of mandalas, such as at the Karsha Kadampa stupa (see chapter 7), at the Padum and Nyoma painted stupas, etc. Since Mahāvairocana with lion *vahana* and Buddha-family wheel appears among the four Tathāgata surrounding the main sculpture, it seems likely that Akṣobhya would be the theme of the central sculpture on the main wall to complete the set of five Jinas. However, there are good reasons to associate the south and north walls with the *vajra* and *padma* families, respectively. Thus Akṣobhya's *vajrakula* would already be represented, and the Buddha family, which appears in a number of western Himalayan composition at the center of the three-family triad—notably Lalung—needs to be accounted for. Fortunately, there are other candidates who would not duplicate Vairocana's presence on the left side of the main wall, and still allow an intact three-family program. It is a useful reminder of the subtlety of the thematic program that each wall is not an island in and of itself. Instead, they are designed together. This principle needs to be taken into account in the reconstruction of this unfortunately damaged structure.

The MkK Stupa: South Wall

There is comparatively much less to detain us on the south wall, since so little survives (see Fig. 5.29; Chart 5.2). As with the main and north walls, the sculpture originally suspended at the center of the wall does not survive. Unlike the main wall, however, there were no supplementary or framing sculptures encircling it. By contrast, the related murals are more integrated into the overall composition and are not sequestered into a pair of vertical columns. The integration was enhanced by vines or long stems curling among the surviving figures. The graceful creepers end in buds or flower heads resembling the flotating ones on the entrance wall already referred to, as well as connected ones observable and more complete on the north wall. On both walls they may have originally emerged from vases at the bottom center, unfortunately no longer visible on either wall but attested elsewhere, even in sculpture such as at the Lalung Serkhang in Spiti which they otherwise closely resemble despite the different medium.[87] As Luczanits points out, "The lotus scroll framing . . . is probably a feature deriving from Kashmiri art."[88]

Loosely but still symmetrically arranged around the outermost painted border of the nimbus at the center of the south wall were at least twelve painted female deities, each seated on a lotus with downturned petals and surrounded by a painted circular nimbus. The diameter of each circle is between 33 and 35 cm. The arrangement of these attendant deities is considerably more informal than that on the main wall: the figures are not enclosed in strict columns. In this they mirror, at least to a degree, the composition on the opposite, north wall. As can be seen in Chart 5.2, two deities were on either side of the parasol above the central sculpture, and at least three more running down each side below the four at the top. Traces of the nimbi of at least two more deities are just inside (i.e., toward the center of) the visible ones (fourth from the top) near the bottom of the wall, but no details remain of them. Of the deities on the viewer's right, almost nothing can be determined other than that they had been there. Smaller painted roundels are interspersed between and among the female deities on both sides. One of them is well enough preserved to be recognized as containing an elephant painted in profile **(Fig. 5.81)**, indicating the roundel set must have represented the *saptaratna* (Tib. rgyal srid sna bdun), the seven jewels of the Cakravartin. In this, they are the counterparts of the *aṣṭamaṅgala* (eight auspicious emblems; Tib. bkra shis rtags brgyad), a few of which remain identifiable on the north wall.

On the viewer's left, five of the female deities are in better, if not good, condition compared to their counterparts on the right **(Chart 5.2, FD 1, 3, 5 and 7)**. Of the five deities at least somewhat recognizable on the

87 Ibid., figs. 110, 112.

88 Ibid., 259.

Fig 5.81 Painted roundel on the south (left) wall of the Malakartse Khar stupa, depicting the elephant in the set of seven jewels (*saptaratna*) of the Cakravartin (wheel-turning universal monarch). Photo 2018.

Fig. 5.82 Offering goddess painted at the top left of the south (left) wall of the Malakartse Khar stupa. Photo 2004.

Fig. 5.83 Offering goddess painted on the left side center of the south (left) wall of the Malakartse Khar stupa. Photo 2004.

Fig. 5.84 Offering goddess painted on the left side, third from the top left of the south (left) wall of the Malakartse Khar stupa. Photo 2004.

Fig. 5.85 Close view of the upper torso of the offering goddess depicted in Figure 5.82. Photo 2004.

left side, four of which are illustrated enlarged (5.82–84, 5.87), all are definitely female deities, suggesting that the ones on the right side were also female. They all have extremely tiny "wasp waists", multiple bracelets, an eye protruding beyond the further cheek, and elaborate flower-strewn headdresses. Except at the top, the faces have been intentionally ruined, but where not damaged, a thin, vertical rectangle for the *urna* or "third eye" is arranged (Fig. 5.85). In the four cases where the breasts are visible, the *upavita* falls from the left shoulder onto the left breast, over it and between the two breasts, the same convention noted above on Acala (see Fig. 5.67). This seems to be one characteristic "tic" of the style.

Fig. 5.86 Close view of the blue gem held in the right hand of the offering goddess depicted in Figure 5.83 Photo 2012.

Fig. 5.87 Upper torso of the offering goddess painted on the left side, fourth from the top left of the south (left) wall of the Malakartse Khar stupa. Photo 2018.

Others are the interest in various striped or checked textile patterns,[89] the lively swaying poses, sharp "v" at the center of the forehead, pouch of loose flesh at the belly, and multiple earrings at the lobes but also on the upper ear (see Fig. 5.85). Tightly wriggling lines alternating with straight lines indicate the emanation of light radiating from the innermost nimbus (see Figure 5.82, visible near the blue lotus at her right shoulder).

Iconographically, the top four goddesses make the *vajramuṣṭi mudra* with the left hand, from which a long stem emerges, with the blue *utpala* lotus flower blooming at the shoulder. They also all hold an object in front of their chest or to the outside. What the goddess at the top left-center holds in her right is unclear, but another (see Fig. 5.82; Chart 5.2, FD 3) holds a mass of flower petals, perhaps lotuses. The goddess directly under her holds a blue gem (see Figs. 5.83, 5.86; Chart 5.2, FD 5). The next goddess (see Fig. 5.84; Chart 5.2, FD 7) has met with environmental conditions which have reacted with the pigments, creating a kind of sepia tone which is actually quite lovely, however unintentional. The heavy modeling of the limbs and torso are enhanced by the accident. The object she held in her right hand, if there was one, is no longer legible. Fortunately, the goddess beneath her (Fig. 5.87; Chart 5.2, FD 9), despite the mutilation of the face, still retains her *āyudha*, which appears to be an arrow. It is not clear (because of damage) whether she had a lotus blooming at her left shoulder.

As already mentioned, in the fundamental Vajradhātu *mahāmaṇḍala*

89 See Appendix 5.1 for a photographic gallery of details of the textile patterns from the MkK stupa.

expounded in the first section of the STTS, the 16 Vajra- (or Mahā-) bodhisattvas usually appear in male form. However, some of the other mandalas revealed in the first and subsequent sections of the STTS substitute female deities.[90] They are usually depicted with similar attributes. Weinberger shows that in all the mandalas of the STTS, with the single exception of the first mandala of the second section (dealing with Trailokyavijaya's subjugation of Maheśvara),

> all maṇḍalas of the four main types consist of the same thirty-seven deities as those that comprise the Vajradhātu Great Maṇḍala. These thirty-seven deities appear in different forms, and under variant names . . . but there is no doubt that they are the same deities, arranged in the same configuration, as we find in the Vajradhātu Great Maṇḍala.[91]

In this way, Vajrarāga, who holds an arrow in the right hand and makes the *vajramuṣṭi mudra* in the Vajradhātu mandalas, appears with an arrow in female form as Ratirāgā in the Vajraguhya mandala and as Ānurāgaṇī in the Karma mandala.[92] We can thus tentatively identify this goddess as the female form of Vajrarāga (Vajrarāgā) in one of the iterations of the Vajradhātu *mahāmaṇḍala*. She is accompanied by the female form of either Vajraratna or Vajratejas who both hold objects that look like gems (see Fig. 5.83).[93] If the objects held in the right hand of Figure 5.82 are indeed lotus petals, she can be identified as the female form of Vajradharma, either Vajrāmbujā or Mahājñāna-gītā of the Vajraguhya and Karma mandalas, respectively.[94]

There are faint traces of at least two more painted deities on the wall, next to the lowest deities on either side. That would result in a total of twelve (female?) deities arranged around the central deity. As on the main wall, it is possible that there was enough room to include an additional four below the central sculpture, constituting sixteen, the number in the Vajra-bodhisattva set. The extant paintings on the adjacent entrance wall certainly extended well below the lowest goddess on the south wall. However, outside of an explicit mandala, it was not usually the practice to include deities fully below the main deities, as opposed to the sides. Either each wall made up an independent, coherent composition or else the three walls with sculptures combined to create a single formation. A combination may also need to be considered. Before concluding what we can about the overall iconography of the Malakartse Khar, there is one more wall to consider.

90 Snellgrove, introduction to *Sarva-Tathāgata-Tattva-Saṅgraha*, 29.

91 Weinberger, "Significance of Yoga Tantra," 76.

92 Lokesh Chandra, *Ninth Century Scroll of the Vajradhātu Maṇḍala*, 68–69, 144–45, 276–77.

93 Ratnottamā is the female form of Vajraratna in the Vajraguhya mandala; Mahādhipatī is the female form of Vajraratna in the Karma mandala, both with the gem. Ratnalokā is the female form of Vajratejas in the Vajraguhya mandala; Mahodyotā in the Karma mandala, both with the radiating gem-like orb (ibid., 148–51, 280–83).

94 Ibid., 156–57, 288–89.

The MkK Stupa: North Wall

The paintings on the entrance wall focused on wrathful deities, bodhisattva and patrons; the main wall on *vajra*-bodhisattvas doubling as the inner and outer offering deities, Tathāgatas and *krodha-vighnāntaka* deities. The south wall presented female forms of the *vajra*-bodhisattvas. The north wall (see Fig. 5.31, Chart 5.4) has a combination of at least three of the four "Attracting Deities" (WD 1–3 in Chart 5.4) and the five of the eight offering goddesses. It is not unlikely that the missing wrathful figure and the three missing offering goddesses were originally painted in the now damaged area. As with the other walls, the area closer to the top is in generally better condition, while those at the bottom have deteriorated severely. Interestingly, the wrathful deities are interspersed somewhat asymmetrically among the offering goddesses, while the latter's "inner" group are interspersed with the "outer."

Also worth noting from the outset are the variances of size of the different components of the set of gate guardians. One of the three extant *krodha-vighnāntaka* is considerably larger than the other two, the one closest to the west (main) wall. That serves to cue us to the fact that the main sculptures of both the north and the south walls were not placed in the exact center of the facing walls. In both cases, it was placed slightly closer to the entrance wall, decreasing the width of the murals on that side. Since the south wall is most damaged on the entrance wall side, this offset is hardly noticeable, but the difference is clearer on the north wall. Apparently, the artists slightly expanded one of the gate guardians on the wider side, and compressed the wrathful deity on the tighter side.

Among the three visible "Attracting Deities," one of them (Fig. 5.88; Chart 5.4, WD 1) can be identified because of the chain he holds as Vajrasphoṭa (alt. Vajrsriṅkala). He stands flatfooted, his feet splayed, large bellied, and had reddish hair though his entire head has been obliterated. The *vajra*-tipped chain with which he binds and restrains all bonds of union is clearly visible.[95] He stands at the top, just to the right of the parasol over the central sculptural deity. Another of the "Attracting Deities" stands below, in the second register on the left side (Fig. 5.89; Chart 5.4, WD 2), while the third one is shifted back to the right, into the third register (Fig. 5.90; Chart 5.4, WD 3). The second one (see Fig. 5.89) is Vajrapāśa, since he holds a noose in his right hand. He helps secure those deities who have been attracted[96] during the ritual, and stands with his right knee bent and left straight,

95 Todaro, "Annotated Translation of the *Tattvasaṃgraha* (Part 1)," 254–55, 301, 306, 317.

96 Ibid., 301, 306, 317.

Fig. 5.88 The wrathful deity Vajrasphoṭa (alt. Vajraśṛṅkala) with intentionally damaged face, second figure from the right in the top row on the north (right) wall of the Malakartse Khar stupa. Photo 2004.

Fig. 5.89 The wrathful deity Vajrapāśa holding a noose, to the left of the central nimbus on the north (right) wall of the Malakartse Khar stupa. Photo 2004.

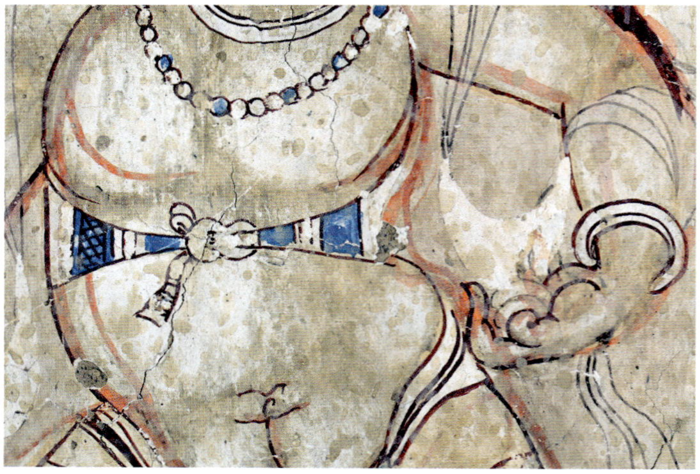

Fig. 5.91 Close view of the torso of wrathful deity Vajrapāśa depicted in Figure 5.89. Photo 2018.

Fig. 5.90 The wrathful deity Vajraghaṇṭa (alt. Vajrāveśa) holding a bell, to the lower right on the north (right) wall of the Malakartse Khar stupa. Photo 2018.

looking back over his left shoulder toward the central deity. Snakes adorn his ankles. His hair is in the standard raised and tufted mode, with one eye extended beyond the outline of his face. A wonderful detail, besides the striped *dhoti*, is the scarf which has been tied around his midriff (Fig. 5.91). The distinctive wrathful nimbus, with relatively straight sides and curved top, edged by triangular flames, encloses him. The painting of the third wrathful deity, Vajraghaṇṭa (alt. Vajrāveśa; see Fig. 5.90), has lost almost all of its color and much of his face. The *vajra*-handled bell (*ghaṇṭa*) held in the raised right hand identifies him as the last of the four "Attracting Deities." Once the deities are "hooked" by Vajrāṅkuśa (not visible here), and the self-identification has been secured by Vajrapāśa and Vajrasphoṭa, then the sound of Vajraghaṇṭa's bell "enters" (*āvesa*) "the minds and bodies causing joy."[97] He is in a pose that suggests dancing and is in fact directly below the offering goddess Vajragītī, who holds a musical instrument and is associated with the offering of music. Although his nimbus has the same flame-tipped border, it is much more circular than that of all the other *krodha* enclosures, somewhere between the circles of the bodhisattvas and offering goddesses and the straight-sided, curved-top of the other wrathful deities. At any rate, three of the four "Attracting Deities" associated with the mandalas revealed in the STTS remain on this wall. The fourth was presumably originally painted somewhere beneath the central sculpture: there are traces of paint and priming well below the sculpture's nimbus particularly on the left. A view of the corner between the north and entrance walls (Fig. 5.92) shows that Vajraghaṇṭa is about level with the stack of eleven heads framed by the red outline on the north side of the entrance wall. The whole standing figure of Avalokiteśvara (Chuchikzhal) extends below this. Vajraghaṇṭa's lotus throne is about level with the bottom of the head nimbus of the missing sculpture on the north wall. Therefore, there is plenty of room for at least one more "Attracting Deity," but whose position is not known—probably on the left. The fourth missing wrathful deity would have been Vajrāṅkuśa. There is also space for at least one more offering goddess if not three in all, to bring the total of offering deities up to the prescribed number of eight—four "inner" and four "outer." On Chart 5.4, hypothetical nimbi have been added to both sides, and labeled "FD? WD?" to indicate that either female or wrathful deities appeared there. As already indicated, the five offering goddesses currently visible represent a mixture of the two categories, so I believe these are supportable conjectures.

97 Ibid., 256.

Fig. 5.93 *Dharmacakra* (dharma wheel), one of the *aṣṭamaṅgala*, the eight auspicious emblems, painted on the north wall of the Malakartse Khar stupa. Photo 2018.

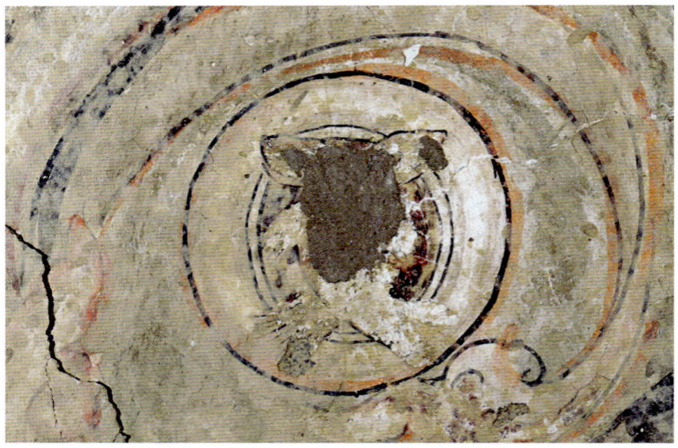

Fig. 5.94 *Suvarṇamatsya* (pair of golden fish), one of the *aṣṭamaṅgala*, the eight auspicious emblems, painted on the north wall of the Malakartse Khar stupa. Photo 2018.

Fig. 5.92 Corner shared by the left side of the entrance wall and the right side of the north wall of the Malakartse Khar stupa. Photo 2012.

Only two of the *aṣṭamaṅgala* contained within small circles are visible on the north wall. They are just beyond the outermost ring of the central sculpture's nimbus. If that nimbus were the face of a clock, then they are placed at approximately four and eight o'clock. The one on the left (Fig. 5.93) is the wheel (*cakra*), and the one on the right (Fig. 5.94) is the pair of golden fish (*suvarṇamatsya*). Two other members of the group might be recognized, despite not being enclosed in the prescribed circles. The parasol (*chattra*) at top center belongs to the set (though it also appears on the south wall so is not exclusive to the *aṣṭamaṅgala*), and free-floating lotus flowers (*padma*) are also visible against the cobalt blue background on the upper half of the wall.

The offering goddess to the left of the central parasol, the counter-part to Vajrasphoṭa on the other side, is Vajramālā (Fig. 5.95; Chart 5.4,

Fig. 5.95 Vajramālā, "inner" offering goddess with garland of gems, on the north wall of the Malakartse Khar stupa. Photo 2012.

FD 1). Instead of placing the garland of blue and white gems on top of a lotus at her shoulder, as did the male bodhisattva on the west (main) wall (see Fig. 5.70, upper) where it appears as a secondary identity, here the offering goddess is in the more usual female form, holding the ends of the garland in both hands. Her ritual function as a member of the "inner" offering goddesses, is to offer splendor and decoration to the deities who have been attracted for the rite of deity yoga.[98] Her form is nearly identical to the female *vajra*-bodhisattva transformations on the opposite (south) wall. Indeed they seem to be constructed with an identical mental model and painting formulas if not a stencil. She has extra rings in the top of her visible ear, and a black line at her eyelashes over the brown lineament, deepening her heavy-lidded eyes. The further eye is also accentuated, the profile quite angular between the forehead and the eye. The protruding chin is also emphasized.

Right behind her is another member of the offering goddess group, but of the "outer" section (Fig. 5.96; Chart 5.4, FD 3). She offers a bowl of flowers, and so can be identified with Vajrapuṣpā, who serves to adorn and decorate the atmosphere. Only subtle differences distinguish her from Vajramālā. They both have a slight greenish tinge, the same thick ankles and the signature fleshy abdomens and puckered navels. On the far right on the top register of the wall is Vajradīpā (alt. Vajrālokā), also one of the "outer" offering goddesses (Fig. 5.97; Chart 5.4, FD 2). She holds her left hand in *vajramuṣṭi mudrā* at her hip, and in her right,

98 Ibid., 300, 306–7.

Fig. 5.96 Vajrapuspā, "outer" offering goddess with bowl of flowers, on the north wall of the Malakartse Khar stupa. Photo 2012.

Fig. 5.97 Vajradīpā, "inner" offering goddess with flame in bowl, on the north wall of the Malakartse Khar stupa. Photo 2012.

a lobed or fluted bowl containing a flame. Like the other three offering goddesses at the top, her face is in excellent condition. Thus the triangular, gem-lined plaque at the center of her tiara is quite clear. She too has extra rings in her upper ears and the convention of her *upavita* looping up and over her breasts to emphasize their prominence. Unlike the others, her nipples are marked with a single circle, without the ring of dots indicating the areola (Fig. 5.98). She also has a lighter, yellowish skin tone, with highlights in white visible on her belly and cheeks. The painter has gone to some effort to detail the patterns on her skirt.

Directly below Vajradīpā, is another one of the "inner" offering goddesses, Vajragītī (Fig. 5.99; Chart 5.4, FD 4). Her face, like that of all but the top three offering goddesses, is spoiled by vandalism. Her skirt has a design of patterned squares unlike any other the others, but what is most distinctive about her is the musical instrument she holds. Unlike the tiny harp on a lotus borne by the bodhisattva on the main wall in reference to the male Vajragīti (see Fig. 5.71, upper), here she holds a bent-necked upright

Fig. 5.98 Close view of Vajradīpā depicted in Figure 5.97.

Fig. 5.99 Vajragītī, "inner" offering goddess with two-string bowed instrument, on the north wall of the Malakartse Khar stupa. Photo 2012.

Fig. 5.100 Vajralāsyā, "inner" offering goddess with both hands at her hips, on the north wall of the Malakartse Khar stupa. Photo 2012.

fretless two-string fiddle, with the bow held horizontally in her right hand. It resembles the *ghijak*, still played among Kazakh musicians in northern Afghanistan and elsewhere.[99] The fifth offering goddess on the north wall is directly below Vajrapāśa on the right side of the wall (Fig. 5.100; Chart 5.4, FD 5). Damage is severe. Not only is her face missing, but water has washed away most of the pigments, and she is very faded, few details remaining. Fortunately, her posture is enough to identify her as Vajralāsyā, the first of the "inner" offering goddesses. Her arms are bent at the elbows, pushed away from her sides, while her hands are at her hips. Her head is shown facing forward (unlike the others) but is tilted to one side. This is the identifying posture of Vajralāsyā, which can be seen in the drawing of the Dunhuang Vajrasattva painting in the Guimet illustrated earlier (see Fig. 5.78, lower right). In the STTS and its commentaries, she is associated with giving of joy and pleasure, sometimes with a sexual overtone.[100] In ritual manuals devoted to describing the identification with and internalization of her, one is instructed that "[l]owering the head a little to the left while forming two fists resting on the hips expresses respect and the practice of worship."[101]

There are, then, three "inner" offering goddesses depicted on the north wall: Vajralāsyā, Vajramālā, and Vajragītī, the first three. One would expect the fourth, Vajranṛtyā, to have been depicted lower down on the wall, along with the two other "outer" goddesses, Vajradhūpā and Vajragandhā, since the middle two, Vajrapuṣpā and Vajradīpā are present. It is worth noting, too, that three of the four offerings identified on the west (main) wall, the offering of the garland, lamp, and music, are also shown on the north wall, with the lamp and the music in identical positions relative to each other and the wall: the representative of the offering of the lamp directly above that of music on the top right of the wall (below the wrathful deity in the case of the west wall). The offering of the garland is in both cases to the left of center, but the north wall has the offering of flowers instead of incense. Altogether it signifies that six of the eight offering deities are represented at least once on one of the walls, and three of them twice, one each in male and female form. How does this help make sense of the overall iconography of the Malakartse Khar stupa? That question, along with an attempt to suggest a date for the site based on comparison with other sites in western Tibet, will occupy the rest of this chapter.

There is, first, a consequential observation of the north wall to make, the

99 *Garland Encyclopedia of World Museum Volume 5: South Asia*, 830–31. See also the Vajragīti (in male form) in the drawing of Vajrasattva surrounded by offering deities in Figure 5.78.

100 Todaro, "Annotated Translation of the *Tattvasaṃgraha* (Part 1)," 300, 306–7, 317; Linrothe, "Mirror Image"; Linrothe, *Reenchantment*, 153–55.

101 Todaro, "Annotated Translation of the *Tattvasaṃgraha* (Part 1)," 314.

Fig 5.101 White *utpala*-type lotus flower painted on the nimbus at the center of the north wall of the Malakartse Khar stupa. Photo 2012.

implications of which will be not be evident until we first examine the related site of murals in west Tibet in Chyiwang Cave 79. On the painted murals that were immediately behind the sculptures on the main (west) and south walls, I have not been able to discover any meaningful traces of paint, other than concentric bands of color and the remains of flame- or light-emitting motifs. However, on the north wall, on the right of the middle concentric beige and orange inner rings is painted a splayed *padma*-lotus on a long stem, with buds at different levels (Fig. 5.101). In shape, it most clearly resembles the *utpala*, the blue, or night lotus, which is found on the south wall, painted a brilliant blue, in the hands of female deities (see Figs. 5.82–83, 5.85), rather than the round-petaled lotus found, for instance on the main (west) wall. The one on the north wall's central sculpture's nimbus (see Fig. 5.101), however, despite whatever discoloration or fading may have occurred, was not painted blue. Instead, it was painted white. Thus, we have a significant clue as to which deity was represented by the sculpture. We need merely to find a deity, the principal attribute of which is the *padma*. Obviously, Lokeśvara comes to mind, but various forms of Tārā can also hold the white lotus, as can others. Greater conviction and precision will come from comparison with a contemporary shrine in a neighboring region in a related style and with a comparable program.

Comparisons between Malakartse Khar's Stupa and Chyiwang Cave 79

The Site of Chyiwang Cave 79

The site of Chyiwang (phyi dbang) in Ngari, west Tibet, in the same region as Dungkar (dung dkar), north of Tholing, is much more important than its treatment to date in English would lead one to suppose (Fig. 5.102). Dungkar has three main caves, all of an early (ca. 12th c.) date, and a significant later (ca. 15th c.) temple complex above with some ruined structures and a few wall paintings surviving. Other earlier ruined structures in the valley mesa are also of interest, including ones documented by Mark Aldenderfer.[102] The caves in the cliffs of Chyiwang, on the other hand, are much more extensive—more than 800 have been counted by the Chinese archaeological team in three different areas though most are small habitation or storage sites—and the decorated ones have a broad range of dates. The cave site and the ruins on the nearby mesa together suggest the continued importance of Chyiwang between the eleventh and the sixteenth or seventeenth century. This is also confirmed by the finds of a huge library near the caves, which

102 Aldenderfer, "On Text, Materiality."

Fig 5.102 View of the cliffs at the cave site of Chyiwang ("Piyang"), Ngari, west Tibet. Photo 2007.

was subsequently ransacked for illuminated folios, though these events are shrouded in secrecy, no doubt to obscure actions of dubious legality motivated by pecuniary advantage or other ambitions. As Klimburg-Salter and Thomas Pritzker point out, Tucci focused on Dungkar rather than Chyiwang, and Pritzker follows this precedent, arguing from an aesthetic rather than a historical position that neither of the early caves at Chyiwang "match the quality seen at Dungkar."[103] Thus he illustrates nineteen wall paintings from Dungkar and one from Chyiwang, while Klimburg-Salter seems not to have actually visited the Chyiwang caves because of bad weather as reported in her 2001 article. Nor does Luczanits discuss the Chyiwang caves in his thorough treatment of early western Himalayan art,[104] though it does appear in subsequent published analyses. (We visited the site together in 2007.) Van Ham published seven photographs of the murals and provides captions and a brief description;[105] Beck's chapter, "Phyang and Dungkar," has thirteen photographs—three from Chyiwang, none from Cave 79.[106] Neumann, however, discusses one of the Chyiwang caves—the one we will focus on here, Cave 79.[107]

Tibetan- and Chinese-language sources have done somewhat better by Chyiwang in including it within discussions of west Tibetan culture, although it is still put in the shadow of the two main caves at Dungkar. An excellent study of the Dungkar Cave 2 with the mandala ceiling has been produced,[108] but I am not aware of anything comparable done on any of the caves of Chyiwang. The initial archaeological report in 1997 discusses

103 Pritzker, "Preliminary Report on Early Cave Paintings of Western Tibet," 225; Klimburg-Salter, "Dung dkar/Phyi dbang, West Tibet."

104 Luczanits, *Buddhist Sculpture in Clay*.

105 van Ham, *Guge—Ages of Gold*, 163–69.

106 Beck, *Tibet–Guge*, 42–51.

107 Helmut Neumann, "The Cave of the Offering Goddesses."

108 Phun-tshogs-rnam-rgyal, *Zhongguo Xizang*.

both sites but includes fewer illustrations from Chyiwang.[109] Sichuan University issued an extensive formal archaeological report on the remains at both Dungkar and Chyiwang,[110] though again, the four caves at Dungkar are allotted twice as many pages as five painted caves at Chyiwang. In a useful compilation of photographs of west Tibetan art, among the many illustrations of Dungkar are interspersed a few from two caves of Chyiwang.[111] Huo Wei includes a discussion of the same two Chyiwang caves in his attempt to group the development of west Tibetan art into three broad stages: tenth–thirteenth century, the "Rinchen Zangpo period" with Kashmiri and Central Asian affiliations; ca. eleventh–fourteenth century, in which the eastern Indian and Nepalese modes predominate; and the fifteenth–seventeenth century with indigenous Tibetan movements including the Gugé revival style.[112] More recently, a large-format book of photographs of shrines of the Dungkar and Chyiwang and other sites in Ngari sites has been published, including Chyiwang Cave 79.[113] The authors include it in the tenth–twelfth-century category.[114]

Besides the survey of the caves, stupas, ruined structures, and petroglyphs in the region, a considerable amount of archaeological excavation has been conducted,[115] including work on pre-Buddhist excavation sites.[116] Aldenderfer, working with Sichuan University and University of California Santa Barbara archaeologists, also reports on a spectrum of calibrated Carbon-14 dates of materials from buildings and stupas in the Chyiwang area, on the mesa across from the cave site.[117] Six dates were arrived at: 997 for painting in a built room; 1192–1208 for a brick on a constructed lotus platform; 1288 for stucco wall coating on a constructed room; 1403 for a mud brick in a constructed stupa; 1427 for a stucco wall coating in a constructed stupa; and 1439 for a mud brick on the interior of a constructed stupa. (These may have been recalculated along with a calibrated C14 radiocarbon date from MkK stupa, as discussed below.) While none of these dates was derived from one of the nearby decorated cave shrines, they do attest to the fact that between the late tenth century and at least the fifteenth century, the site near the painted caves, which appears to have been a Buddhist monastery, was constructed, reconstructed, and expanded. These dates are useful counterparts for the cave sites as well, which have a similar range. Given the dearth of illustrated discussion of its caves, a brief introduction to the site as a whole precedes a more focused examination of the cave most relatable to the Malakartse Khar stupa.

109 Xizang Zizhiqu Wenwu Ju and Sichuan Lianhe Daxue Kaogu Ye, "Xizang Ali Dongga, Piyang Shiku Kaogu Diaocha Jianbao." See also Huo and Li, *Nishi Chibetto Sekkutsu Iseki*.

110 Sichuan Daxue, *Piyang, Dongga yi zhi kao gu bao gao*.

111 Huo and Li, *Xizang Xibu Fojiao Yishu*, figs. 52, 75, 88, 117–18.

112 Huo, "Xizang xibu Shiku bihua zhong ji zhong yishu fengge de fenxi."

113 Zhang and Huo, *Bod kyi mdzes rtsal kun btus*, plate pages 12–23.

114 Ibid., 37.

115 Sichuan Daxue, *Piyang, Dongga yi zhi kao gu bao gao*, chap. 8 and 9.

116 Aldenderfer and Moyes, "Excavations at Dindun"; Aldenderfer and Moyes, "In the Valley of the Eagle."

117 Aldenderfer, "Piyang," 143–44; Aldenderfer, "On Text, Materiality," 353.

Fig. 5.103 Interior of Cave 90, Chyiwang, wall murals of Buddhas and deep pile of debis and *tsha tsha*. Photo 2007.

Fig. 5.104 Illuminated folio on the altar of the "library" cave at Chyiwang in 2005. Photo 2005.

At least two early caves at Chyiwang contain murals in the Kashmiri idiom—caves 79 and 90, according to the Chinese numbering system. Cave 90 now has only the 1,000-Buddha theme covering all its walls, but at one time also had sculptures.[118] As of 2005 and 2007 when I visited the site three different times, there were thousands of *tsha tsha* in a huge heap in the cave (Fig. 5.103). Cave 79 is the cave Neumann dubbed the "Cave of the Offering Goddesses" due to the prominence of those figures in the cave.[119] Neumann apparently was unaware of the Chinese archeological report published a year earlier than his treatment of the cave,[120] since he claimed that the cave is "to be described for the first time in this paper."[121] Cave 79 appears to be from the same time as Cave 90 even though it has a much more elaborate decorative scheme, which we will examine in some detail. In 2005 and 2007, loose pages from manuscripts were piled in disarray in a freestanding temple built against the cliff near some of the painted caves. That the Chyiwang "library," the original sources for which are unknown to me, once contained manuscripts that derive from the period of Kashmiri-idiom predominance in many regions of west Tibet, is demonstrated by a damaged illuminated folio that was on the altar in the old shrine now housing the remains of the library (Fig. 5.104). Although certainly not of the finest quality, it shows the modeling and visual vocabulary of Kashmir-derived painting.

One of the most fascinating caves at Chyiwang is Cave 351. It would appear to belong late in the period of the Mongol Yuan dynasty (1271–1368) period, when many Chinese motifs were brought to Tibet, as evidenced by the dragon-and-cloud motif painted on the ceiling, along with Chinese auspicious motifs (Fig. 5.105). This is closely comparable to the dragon on

118 Zhang and Huo, *Bod kyi mdzes rtsal kun btus*, pl. p. 24 upper.

119 Neumann, "Cave of the Offering Goddesses."

120 Xizang Zizhiqu Wenwu Ju and Sichuan Lianhe Daxue Kaogu Ye, "Xizang Ali Dongga, Piyang Shiku Kaogu Diaocha Jianbao."

121 Neumann, "Cave of the Offering Goddesses," 53.

Fig. 5.105 Dragon and textile design painted on ceiling of Chyiwang Cave 351, ca. 14th century. Photo 2007.

Fig. 5.106 Three religious kings (Pugyal Gyalpo) in Chyiwang Cave 351, ca. 14th century. Photo 2007.

Fig. 5.107 Damaged mural in Chyiwang Cave 34 depicting the Mahāsiddha Saraha, ca. late 15th c. Photo 2007.

Fig 5.108 Gonkhang with painted Sakya lineage in Chyiwang Cave 32, ca. 16th century. Photo 2007

Fig 5.109 Detail of two deities from the ceiling *maṇḍala* at Dungkar Cave 2, late 12th or early 13th c. Photo 2007.

the repainted Gonkhang at Zhalu which Vitali convincingly assigns to the early fourteenth century (Fig. 2.13).[122] Dense scroll work associated with the fourteenth and fifteenth century Beri (bal bris; Nepalese style) is visible in the murals, as well as the type of cusped, gold-trimmed decorative arches found behind the three religious kings surrounded by eight great siddhas (Fig. 5.106). The cave's program demonstrates a definite Sakya (sa skya) affiliation, reinforcing the form-idiom connections with Mongol-ruled China. Zhang Changhong and Huo Wei, however, include it among their fifteenth to seventeenth-century category.[123]

One of the nearly ruined caves, with some evidence of fire singeing the walls, features the eight great siddhas on either side of Vajradhara. In the illustration (Fig. 5.107), the yogic adept Saraha tests the trueness of the arrow he has fabricated. This cave, number 34 in the Chinese survey,[124] also Sakya, appears to be part of the period of the revival of the Gugé kingdom from the late fifteenth or sixteenth century. Among the latest caves at the site dating to the sixteenth or seventeenth century features a standardized Sakya lineage (Fig. 5.108). This is Cave 32,[125] which was apparently a Gonkhang, as the huge nimbus at the center of the main wall seemed to have been the backdrop for a Panjaranātha Mahākāla. There is much more to be discovered about this multiple cave site, which largely mirrors the cluster of dates derived by Aldenderfer from scientific testing of structures on the nearby mesa. There may very well also be correspondence between the dates of the construction of the various Chyiwang cave shrines and the monuments of the Khartse valley as surveyed by Tsering Gyalpo and his Austrian collaborators.[126]

Chyiwang Cave 79 has previously been regarded as "contemporaneous with the Dungkar caves," "of the same lucid style,"[127] "so closely related to the Dungkar caves that it appears possible that they were painted by the same artists."[128] Later, the same author acknowledges that the "earliest of the caves might be the 'Cave of the Offering Goddesses' at Piyang," but reinforces

122 Vitali, *Early Temples of Central Tibet*, 109–10.

123 Zhang and Huo, *Bod kyi mdzes rtsal kun btus*, text pp. 37–38.

124 Sichuan Daxue, *Piyang, Dongga yi zhi kao gu bao gao*, 85–87.

125 Ibid., 81–85; Zhang and Huo, *Bod kyi mdzes rtsal kun btus*, pl. pp. 238–52.

126 Gyalpo et al., "Buddhist Monuments of Khartse Valley."

127 Neumann, "Cave of the Offering Goddesses," 53.

128 Ibid., 58.

the notion of "the singular style practiced by the painters of the Dungkar and Piyang caves."[129] I would submit that the cave is definitely earlier than either of the main Dungkar caves, and that this is evident both by the themes depicted (as was realized by Neumann in the later treatment[130]) and also by the painting qua painting. There are certainly areas of overlap, and both participate in the same general Kashmir-derived style but at distinctly different phases. The verve, tautness and angular agility of the figures in Cave 79 have been subdued to the point of almost featurelessness as seen in a detail from the mandala of Dungkar Cave 2 (Fig. 5.109) compared with comparably themed bodhisattvas and goddesses at Chyiwang Cave 79 as we will examine in detail. The *gandharvas* flying around the mandala in Dungkar Cave 1 (see Fig. 2.4) are not nearly as linearly abstract flickers of movement as the sixth-century Dunhuang examples to which Neumann compares them,[131] but are much more painterly, coloristic, and amorphous than Chyiwang's earlier paintings. The "precisely drawn lines" he sees in both Chyiwang and Dungkar are more aptly applied to Chyiwang alone. The Dungkar caves each have their own virtues. I believe the Chyiwang Cave 79 should be considered transitional between early painting at Tholing and Tabo and the caves of Dungkar. Through mapping a relative chronology of the relationships of the Malakartse Khar stupa murals and the paintings in Chyiwang Cave 79, and distinguishing the two Dungkar caves' murals we can contribute to the expanding chronology formulated by Luczanits and others. By this means, not only can we place Chyiwang Cave 79, but—more importantly for this context—locate the Zangskari Malakartse Khar stupa paintings through their iconographic and formal relationship to Kashmiri-derived painting of the western Himalaya and west Tibet, including Ladakh, Spiti, Kinnaur, and Ngari. First, a close reading of Chyiwang Cave 79, updating prior efforts, is in order.

Chyiwang Cave 79's Plan

Chyiwang Cave 79 is approximately 3.52 meters in width and 4.2 meters deep,[132] nearly 15 square meters in area. The original doorway is 110 centimeters wide, but the original access from the front has been swept away by a landslide of some sort. A small doorway has been carved right through the murals into the wall on the left side (when facing the main wall). The plan (Fig. 5.110) shows that originally three indented niches were clustered at the far end of the cave. In fact, one of the main similarities with the Malakartse Khar stupa is that the murals painted on the three walls were arranged around large sculptures, none of which survives.

129 Ibid., 79.

130 Ibid,.

131 Ibid., figs. 7–8.

132 Xizang Zizhiqu Wenwu Ju and Sichuan Lianhe Daxue Kaogu Ye, "Xizang Ali Dongga, Piyang Shiku Kaogu Diaocha Jianbao," 10.

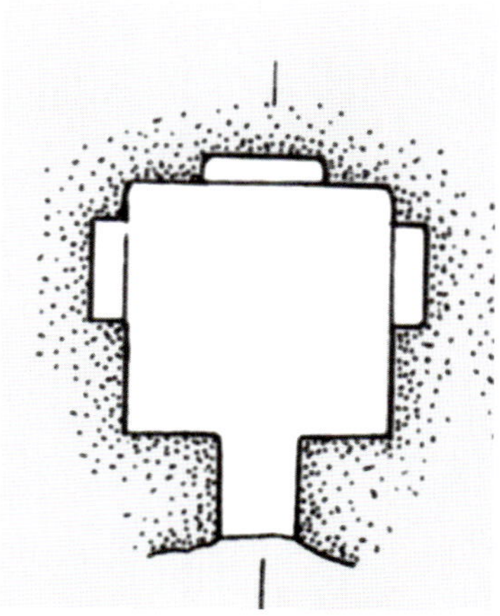

Fig 5.110 Plan of Chyiwang Cave 79, after Xizang Zizhiqu Wenwu Ju, "Xizang Ali Dongga," 15.

Fig 5.111 Detail of the valance in Chyiwang Cave 79. Photo 2007.

Remains of a circular nimbus in the lower part of each niche are extant, along with a large socket-hole where the principal strut of the sculpture affixed it to the wall. It is possible there were smaller sculptures above the main one, but the interiors of the three niches are too dilapidated to tell any more about them than at the Zangskar stupa. The niche on the main (west) wall is wider (159 cm) than the ones on the side walls (132 cm on the south wall and 134 cm on the north wall). All three niches are about 32 centimeters deep. As at Malakartse Khar, the inside of the original entrance wall did not accommodate sculptures. A related series of valances—sans *haṃsa*, but including *kirtimukha* holding up swags of cloth in their mouths (Fig. 5.111)—went all the way around the upper walls. A short corridor led from the outer entrance into the cave. It had a large wrathful figure on each side, but these have been severely degraded by exposure and the deterioration of the ceiling. As already mentioned, with that entrance no longer viable, a hole was later cut into the left side wall to allow entry.

Chyiwang Cave 79 Original Entrance (East) Wall

On the left side of the entrance wall when facing it are nine Buddhas in different mudras and colored robes (Fig. 5.112). Two more are visible over the original entryway. Below the Buddhas on the left is a five-deity *krodha cakra* (disk of wrath) mandala. It has a wheel-like internal structure, surrounded by a band of *vajras*, 96 centimeters in diameter (Fig. 5.113). It is highly unusual as far as mandalas go, but not without precedent. At nearby Dungkar Cave One, also on the entrance wall, we find a similar four-deity wheel-like mandala, surrounded by a band of *vajras* (Fig. 5.114). And, in the so-called Dukhang or eastern temple of Mangyu in Ladakh, a related *krodha* mandala of thirteen deities can also be found (Figs. 5.115–116). It is a fully developed palace-type mandala with gateways, what Luczanits refers to as the "standard Tibetan depiction."[133] The central circle at Mangyu has a similar wheel-like structure.

133 Luczanits, "On the Earliest Mandalas in a Buddhist Context," 8.

Fig 5.112 View of the left side of the entrance wall and doorway inside Chyiwang Cave 79. Photo 2007.

Fig. 5.113 *Krodha cakra maṇḍala* (wrathful wheel mandala) painted on entrance wall inside Chyiwang Cave 79. Photo 2007.

Fig. 5.114 *Krodha cakra maṇḍala* on entrance wall of Dungkar Cave 1. Photo 2005.

Fig. 5.115 *Krodha cakra maṇḍala* inside Mangyu village Dukhang, Ladakh. Photo 2008.

Fig. 5.116 Central section of the mandala depicted in Figure 5.115. Photo 2008.

Fig 5.117 Wrathful deity at the center of mandala depicted in Figure 114. Photo 2005.

In all three cases—Chyiwang, Dungkar, and Mangyu—however, the central deity is different. At Chyiwang, it appears to be a seated form of Vajrapāṇi, greenish, with his left hand at his hip. At Dungkar, he is standing, also greenish, suggesting it is a Karma, or action mandala (Fig. 5.117) At Dungkar and Mangyu the other deities are arranged as if in the cardinal directions, whereas at Chyiwang the four wrathful figures are placed at the intermediate directions.

The same deities appear to be placed in different directions as well: the dark gray deity is in the northeast corner at Chyiwang and the west at Dungkar; the blue one with a club (in both cases) in the northeast corner at Chyiwang, and the south at Dungkar. In other words, they are rotated two positions. Mangyu is different again: at the center is a six-armed form of Trailokyavijaya, placed in a triangularly shaped *homa* altar for wrathful "destroying" or subjugating (*ābhicārika*) rituals.[134] The *Hizō-ki*, an eighth- or early ninth-century text, describes such a ritual on a black triangular *homa* altar featuring Trailokyavijaya and entourage.[135] Surrounding him are

134 Skorupski, *Sarvadurgatipariśodhana Tantra*, 71–72; Skorupski, "Tibetan Homa Rites," 410–12.

135 Goepper, "Four Kinds of Rites at the Altar," 200–203. See also Giebel, *Two Esoteric Sutras*, 186.

Fig. 5.118 View of the right side of the entrance wall and doorway inside Chyiwang Cave 79. Photo 2007.

different variants related to the *vajra*, *padma*, and *karma* families.[136]

To the right of the original doorway, below another set of Buddhas (also probably at least nine), there are two registers of six wrathful figures (Fig. 5.118). A large pile of debris and *tsha tsha* covers up another register, the left side of which is just barely visible (Fig. 5.119). This was a set of nine *krodha-vighnāntaka*, with a blue two-armed Vajrahūṃkara at the center. He is larger than the other ones, implying this is an implicit Vajrahūṃkara or Traikokyavijaya mandala, the former being a two-armed form of the latter. In a way, this could be considered what Luczanits refers to as a "*maṇḍala* assembly,"[137] since there are no indications of circles, squares, or gates as is expected in the "standard Tibetan depiction." However, since the deities appear to be arranged in a geometric manner reflecting their actual positions in relation to the main deity, it is somewhere between a mandala assembly and the standard form. Only a few of the attributes can be seen. Starting at the top left and moving clockwise, there is a blue *krodha-vighnāntaka* (*k-v*) with a small *viśvavajra*; a greenish *k-v*, attribute not visible, but wearing a tiger-skin dhoti (Fig. 5.177); greenish *k-v* with an arrow; light colored *k-v* with

four blue wrathful deities each with a skullcup and a flaying knife; three are blue and the fourth is dark grey, in the south. These seem to relate most closely to the *Trilokacakra Mahāmaṇḍala* ('jig rten gsum gyi 'khor lo), the Great Maṇḍala of the Wheel of the Threefold World associated with Trailokyavijaya, from the second, *vajra*, section of the STTS. It too has several

136 Snellgrove, introduction to *Sarva-Tathāgata-Tattva-Saṅgraha*, 10; Weinberger, "Significance of Yoga Tantra," 81.

137 Luczanits, "On the Earliest Mandalas in a Buddhist Context."

Fig 5.119 Nine wrathful deities (some covered by debris), including Vajrahūṃkara at center on right side of entrance wall of Chyiwang Cave 79. Photo 2007.

a single-pointed *vajra*; blue Vajrahūṃkara with hands crossed at wrists, palms inward; and light colored *k-v* with a club or sword. The implied mandala may be related to that of the eight Bhairavas as described in the *Sarvadurgatipariśodhana*,[138] though the details of the attributes vary. At any rate we can conclude that the makers of Cave 79 at Chyiwang structured the entrance in such a way as to emphasize the presence of gateway-guarding wrathful deities there, something we also found inside the Malakartse Khar stupa. The latter also included Vajrahūṃkara in a similar position (see Fig. 5.43). As we will find to be the case generally, the Chyiwang cave is more "advanced" in the sense of having transitional, if not fully explicit mandalas, as well as the implicit ones, the only type found at Malakartse Khar. Formally, the wrathful deities are quite close at both sites in terms of the conventions of hair, ribbons, poses, midriff scarfs and the like. However, the *krodha* deities on the entrance wall are in poorer condition than on some of the other walls, so specific comparisons can wait. Also to be noted is the transfer of the sponsor figures off the entrance wall, where they appear at MkK stupa, and at other caves in Dungkar and Chyiwang.

Chyiwang Cave 79 Main (West) Wall Opposite Entrance

Turning to the main wall at Chyiwang (Fig. 5.120), which, also like that of the MkK stupa, lies in the west direction, a painted border visible on the right side of the main wall indicates the original lower limit of the murals. This reveals that the sixteen deities currently depicted, eight on each side, though damaged, reflect the entire original composition. From the ceiling to the bottom of the wall painting is 262 centimeters. Because the condition is affected more by intentional damage and the deterioration of the ceiling than by the collapse of the roof, the condition of the paint at the top and bottom is roughly equal. This is in contrast to Malakartse Khar, where, because of the position of the hole in the lantern roof and its smaller size, the upper paintings are in readable condition and the lower ones are either buried by ceiling rubble or have completely washed away.

138 Skorupski, *Sarvadurgatipariśodhana Tantra*, 59–63, corrected from "nine Bhairava *maṇḍala*" in van der Kuijp 1992, 123n17.

Fig. 5.120 Main wall opposite entrance with central inset niche at Chyiwang Cave 79. Photo 2007.

The pantheon of deities surrounding the missing main sculpture is roughly the same at both sites. There are four wrathful "Attracting Deities" within the same straight-sided, curved-top nimbus-shape, two on each side, both on the outside column, but not in the same registers. (On the left, the second and fourth register; on the right, first and third.) A representative example in the best condition (and therefore repeatedly published) is Vajrasphoṭa with the chain (Fig. 5.121; compare Fig. 5.88). As with the other *krodha-vighnāntaka* figures, his hair is in a slightly nuanced, finer version of the hairstyle found on that type at MkK stupa: the horn-like tufts of hair are thinner but equally evident. The eight inner and outer offering goddesses, four per side, are intermixed as at Malakartse Khar, though distinguishable on this wall since the outer offering goddesses wear tight weskits and appear on the outer columns, and the inner offering goddesses are naked to the waist and are closer to the central niche. Recall that the offering deities on the main wall at MkK stupa are male (on the north wall, female), which can be taken as a sign of relative earliness, when there was still some ambiguity as to their sex.[139] The Chyiwang Cave 79 sets correspond to their later standardization. In Figure 5.122, left, Vajragītī plays a bowed instrument, related but not identical to the one depicted at Malakartse Khar (see Fig. 5.99). Neumann illustrated Vajradhūpā,[140] and Vajramālā holding the garland is in the top row, second from the left in Figure 5.120. The outer offering deity next to Vajragītī (Fig. 5.122, right)

139 One finds this ambiguity in cave paintings at Dunhuang dating to the ninth and tenth centuries; see Linrothe, "'Structure and Subject Matter' at Dunhuang."

140 Neumann, "Cave of the Offering Goddesses," figs. 5–6.

Fig. 5.121 Vajrasphoṭa with chain, top right on the main wall at Chyiwang Cave 79. Photo 2007.

Fig. 5.123 Mañjuśrī holding book and sword on the main wall (second row on the left next to the central inset niche) at Chyiwang Cave 79. Photo 2007.

Fig. 5.122 Vajragītī with musical instrument (left) and Vajradīpā/ Vajrālokā or Vajradhūpā below Vajrasphoṭa (Fig. 5.121) on the main wall at Chyiwang Cave 79. Photo 2007.

apparently is Vajradīpā/Vajrālokā or Vajradhūpā, since a plume of flame or smoke rises above the damaged bowl held in her right hand, smoke generated by either a flame or by incense, respectively. All of the goddesses are enclosed within round nimbi. The four remaining deities, two per side on the inner columns, are male *vajra*-bodhisattvas or another group of bodhisattvas, also with rounded nimbi. The one in Figure 5.123 holds the sword and book of Mañjuśrī, who rarely, if occasionally appears blue, as in the *Aṣṭabodhisattvamaṇḍala Sutra*.[141] A bodhisattva on the right side, underneath Vajragītī, holds a small wheel (see Fig. 5.147). If he is a *vajra*-bodhisattva, then he is probably Vajrahetu, who, as mentioned above, is described in Ānandagarbha's commentary on the STTS.[142]

On the narrow, indented side walls of the inset niche are *makara*s at the top, separated by a band of diamond lozenges from a tall upright outward-facing *vyala* or leogryph (Figs. 5.124–125). These are associated with regal themes, and derive directly from eastern India where they are most often found on the throne backs of images of Buddha or a Tathāgata or Brahmanical Hindu deities (see Fig. 8.14).[143] As indicated below, in my opinion it is likely that the original main sculpture on this wall was the Jina Vairocana or Mahāvairocana.

Chyiwang Cave 79 South (Left) Wall

In 2005 and 2007 the south wall, on the left when facing the main wall (Fig. 5.126), had a large pile of *tsha tsha* in the lower part of its niche, spilling out to both sides and obscuring some of the deities painted to either side. It features a single framed column of deities bordering each side of the niche. All are slightly larger than the Buddhas and other deities on the left side of the wall. The ones on the left border look toward their left at the center niche, the ones on the right toward their right. One of the deities on the lower right border is completely obscured, and one at the lower left border only partially so. It is clear from the visible ones that they represented the eight inner- and outer-offering goddesses (four in each vertical column) and four "Attracting Deities," for twelve in all. Among the best preserved outer-offering goddesses is Vajrapuṣpā, at the top of the left column (Fig. 5.127). The lotus at her left shoulder bears a floriate-themed, elaborately decorated bowl of flowers, and complex textile patterns in subtle shades of color grace her skirt and scarf. In spite of the bowl of flowers, Neumann identifies her as Vajradhūpā who offers incense.[144] A different one on the same wall holds a censer, so she should be the outer-offering

141 Yoritomi, "Iconographic Study of the Eight Bodhisattvas in Tibet," 327.

142 Luczanits, *Buddhist Sculpture in Clay*, 299, no. 16 West.

143 For examples, see Linrothe, *Reenchantment*, 68, 95, 133.

144 Neumann, "Cave of the Offering Goddesses," fig. 10.

Fig. 5.124 *Vyala* (leogryph) depicted on the narrow side wall on the left of the inset niche on the main wall of Chyiwang Cave 79. Photo 2007.

Fig. 5.125 *Vyala* (leogryph) depicted on the narrow side wall on the right of the inset niche on the main wall of Chyiwang Cave 79. Photo 2007.

Fig. 5.126 Overview of the south (left) side wall of Chyiwang Cave 79 including piles of debris and *tsha tsha* as well as small doorway cut into the wall to allow access once the original entrance was no longer accessible from the cliff face. Photo 2007.

Fig. 5.127 Vajrapuṣpā, "outer" offering goddess, to the left top of the south (left) wall niche at Chyiwang Cave 79. Photo 2005.

goddess of incense. The one whose bowl holds multicolored flowers is more likely to be Vajrapuṣpā, the goddess offering flowers, noticed as well by Luczanits[145] and, apparently, by Neumann himself in a later treatment.[146] The bowl, along with others depicted in the cave, closely resembles the shape, color scheme, and decorative vocabulary of Samanid ceramics, evidence of the Persianate and Sogdian court culture in Kashmir and, by extension, among western Himalayan elites.

On this wall, the inner and outer offering goddesses are not distinguishable by costume, only by attribute. As indicated, on the left it is Vajrapuṣpā at the top (outer), followed by Vajramālā (inner), the wrathful Vajrapāṣa ("Attracting Deity"), Vajradhūpā (outer), Vajralāsyā (inner), and an unidentified *krodha-vighnāntaka* with damage to the face and covered by *tsha tsha* and debris. On the right, at the top is "Attracting Deity" Vajrasphota—the best preserved of his set (Fig. 5.128, upper, Fig. 5.181), followed by Vajradīpā/Vajrālokā (outer) (see Fig. 5.128, lower), Vajragītī (inner), Vajraghaṇṭa ("Attracting Deity"), Vajragandhā (outer), and, presumably (she is covered by *tsha tsha*), Vajranṛtyā (inner). Like the main wall, the inner and outer goddesses are consciously staggered or alternated, two from each category distributed to each side. The same is true of the *krodha-vighnāntaka* deities, demonstrating very careful planning of the composition and distribution of the deities, resulting in a slight asymmetry, alternating categories, and not repeating the same order on both sides.

This same concern to intermix the deities and yet not repeat the order on both sides is also visible in the Malakartse Khar stupa

145 Luczanits, "Styles in Western Himalayan Art," 137n24.

146 Neumann, "Wall Paintings of Western Tibet," 79.

Fig. 5.128 Vajrasphoṭa (above) with chain and Vajradīpā, with lamp, below, to the right top of the niche on the south (left) wall of Chyiwang Cave 79. Photo 2005.

North (right) wall (see Fig. 5.31). In fact, we can probably reconstruct the identities of the Malakartse Khar stupa right wall's missing or damaged figures based on the resemblance of the order of the left wall at Chyiwang Cave 779. For example, Vajrapuṣpa (outer) and Vajramālā (inner) are next to each other at Malakartse Khar, instead of one being on top of the other, with Vajrapāṣa below. Vajrasphota is similarly opposite Vajramālā at both sites, followed by Vajrālokā (outer) and Vajragītī (inner) at both sites.

With the large deity at the center of the left wall niche (now missing), the eight goddesses and four "Attracting Deities" form an implicit mandala, or mandala assembly, of thirteen deities. Or, if four more were included above the main deity, also in sculptural form, a mandala of seventeen deities. Mandalas of thirteen and seventeen deities are attested in an eighth-century commentary to the STTS.[147] Toganoo suggested that,

> the seventeen-deity *maṇḍala* centred on Vairocana or Vajrasattva (who embody the attributes of the Vajra, Gem, Lotus and Action Families) consists of, in addition to the central deity, Four Attendant Bodhisattvas (representing the Four Families), Eight Offering Goddesses and Four Gatekeepers, while the thirteen-deity *maṇḍala* is centred on any other deity symbolizing an attribute of only one of the Four Families and therefore lacks the Four Attendant Bodhisattvas.[148]

147 Giebel, *Chin-kang-ting ching yü-ch'ieh shi-pa-hui chih-kuei*, 139.

148 Ibid., 140.

The seventeen-deity mandala centered on Vajrasattva is one of the most important of those described in the *Prajñapāramitānayasūtra*, which Kimiaki Tanaka has recently shown was so critical in the development toward the Vajradhātu *mahāmaṇḍala* as found in the STTS.[149] It is possible, then, that the main niche on the west wall of Cave 79 housed a seventeen-deity mandala, of which Yoga Tantra provides several different examples including the identical deities that remain—both the STTS and the *Mahā-samaya-tattva-yoga* have seventeen-deity mandalas.[150] In that case, having Vairocana on the main wall, as Neumann suggests,[151] is the most reasonable in my opinion, although other possibilities exist. We will return to the question of the identity of the mandala on the left wall after further consideration of the other images on that wall and on the right wall.

As is visible in the plan **(see Fig. 5.110)**, the niche is not centered in the middle of the left wall, but shifted somewhat closer to the main wall, leaving more room toward the entrance wall side. The exact opposite is true at MkK stupa of the sculptures not quite centered on the north and south walls, but are shifted slightly *away* from the main wall. At Chyiwang, the space on the left wall **(see Fig. 5.126)** closer to the original entrance wall and farther from the sculptural niche, is divided into two sections. First is a smaller upper area with six Buddhas, and below them is a marked-off area, slightly larger though the bottom area was obscured by *tsha tsha*. In it was painted another nine-deity mandala-like composition **(Fig. 5.129)**. It is mandala-like in the same way that the wrathful mandala **(see Fig. 5.119)** is: the deities are arranged geometrically around a larger central one, including directly above and below the central one, but there are no gateways or other indications of the mandala palace. It is not as much like the "standard *maṇḍala* depiction" as the *krodha cakra* mandala on the entrance wall **(see Fig. 5.113)**, but it is more so than the deity assemblies found on and around the main and left wall niches. Much of four of the deities and all of two more are obscured by the pile of *tsha tsha* or by damage. Fortunately, enough remains of five of the nine deities to ascertain that all eight of the deities surrounding the central deity were female. They appear to be the offering goddesses once again; Vajradīpā/Vajrālokā holds another representation of a brown-and-white glazed bowl containing a candelabra-like lamp (**Figs. 5.130 and 5.178**; compare **Fig. 5.98**). It is not possible to ascertain whether the central deity was male or female. The only *āyudha* visible is a blue *utpala* at the left shoulder, and although we found that being held by several female goddesses on the left wall at MkK stupa,

149 Tanaka, *Illustrated History of the Mandala*, 93–100.

150 Ibid., 139–40, 149–50, 186, 188–90; Weinberger, "Significance of Yoga Tantra," 68n184, 287–88.

151 Neumann, "Cave of the Offering Goddesses," 55.

Fig. 5.129 Nine-deity mandala-like assembly, some including central deity covered by debris, on the lower left side of the south (left) wall of Chyiwang Cave 79. Photo 2007.

Fig. 5.130 Vajradīpā/Vajrālokā with lamp in the upper right corner of the nine-deity mandala-like grouping depicted in Figure 5.129. Photo 2007.

it is also one of the attributes of Mañjuśrī. At any rate, the concentration of female deities on the "left" wall echoes the female emphasis found on the equivalent wall at Malakartse Khar stupa (see Fig. 5.29), the central sculptural deity of which, surrounded by offering goddesses, has also not been identified. Regardless, it is apparent that least some of the same or similar organizing principles were at work in the two shrines.

Chyiwang Cave 79 North (Right) Wall

The right wall in its divisions matches the left (Fig. 5.131). In both cases, hardly anything of the painting remains on the back wall of the niche interior. In this case, *tsha tsha* and loose manuscript pages are placed on the lower inset. As seen on the plan (see Fig. 5.110), the niche is also shifted toward the main wall and two vertical registers frame the niche. However, in the columns of deities here are only four deities (instead of sixteen or twelve), two each on either side immediately framing the niche (Fig. 5.132). The four deities, two to a side, are in the middle, with roundels at top and bottom, each enclosing two of the *aṣṭamaṇgala*, the eight auspicious symbols—another instance of thematic overlap with MkK stupa. Neumann has published the one in the best condition, with the parasol and the victory banner (Fig. 5.180);[152] Figure 5.133 depicts the lotus and vase (damaged). The faint ocher underpainting is visible against the cream ground, suggesting that they were only basic instructions for what should go where, or that the painters somewhat spontaneously executed designs, still no doubt according to time-honored formulas. The lines are well-modulated and adeptly drawn.

The upper pair of deities are in wrathful-deity shaped nimbus-form—

152 Ibid., fig. 13.

Fig. 5.131 Overview of the north (right) wall with niche at Chyiwang Cave 79. Photo 2007.

Fig. 5.132 Close view of niche and damaged columns of painted deities framing the sides on the north (right) wall at Chyiwang Cave 79. Photo 2007.

Fig. 5.133 Lotus (*padma*) and treasure vase (*dhanakhumba*), two of the *aṣṭamaṅgala* painted in a roundel on the top right of the niche on the north (right) wall at Chyiwang Cave 79. Photo 2007.

Fig. 5.134 Hayagrīva with horse's head painted to the left of the niche on the north (right) wall at Chyiwang Cave 79. Photo 2007.

Fig. 5. 135 Four-armed peaceful Avalokiteśvara, seated with right leg down, open lotus at left shoulder, below Hayagrīva, on left side of the niche on the north (right) wall at Chyiwang Cave 79. Photo 2007.

vertical sides and rounded top—and the lower pair in circular ones. The left upper *krodha-vighnāntaka* is a four- (or more) armed Hayagrīva, identified by the horse's head (Figs. 5.134, 5.179). He is pinkish in color. The very damaged wrathful figure across from him, on the right, is greyish, apparently seated, eight- (or more) armed, holding a bow, a sword, a *vajra*, and other implements. Neumann identifies it as the black Ekajaṭī.[153] Certainly, the bow, the sword, and the *vajra* match her attributes in later times, and one can confirm that it is a female deity, for the *śāṭī* garment wraps around the knee and seems to go down to the ankle; *dhoti*s of males in this mode end at or above the knee, as with the Mañjuśrī image (see Fig. 5.123). The two peaceful deities of the columns definitely include a male on the left (Fig. 5.135) and a second female on the right. This female is Bhṛikuṭī, rather close to the description in the *Sādhanamālā* except for the hands in which one of the attributes are placed: she "carries the staff with three horns [i.e. three branches, the *tridaṇḍa*] and the Kamaṇḍalu [vase] in the two left hands. The two right show the mudrā of bowing in one and the rosary in the second."[154] Bhṛikuṭī and Hayagriva are closely tied to Avalokiteśvara, and the male four-armed figure below Hayagrīva (Fig. 5.135) holds a large pink lotus in his lower left hand, one of the principal attributes of Avalokiteśvara. He also holds a *vajra* and a noose in his right hands, and a long staff, perhaps an *aṅkuśa*-goad in the left or possibly a *tridaṇḍa*.

153 Ibid., 56.

154 Bhattacharyya, *Indian Buddhist Iconography*, 129.

At least two forms of Avalokiteśvara carry the noose and *aṅkuśa*,[155] though not in this precise alignment. Neumann argues that it is Amoghapāśa, and that they surrounded a sculptural image of a white two-armed Avalokiteśvara (Padmapāṇi).[156] At any rate given the lotus at his shoulder, it is indeed very likely that this painted deity is a form of Avalokiteśvara and that the sculpture in the niche belonged to the *padma* family, being either Amitāyus, Tārā, or, as Neumann suggests, Avalokiteśvara himself.

Given the other similarities, it is thus worth considering whether or not the Malakartse Khar stupa had a similar *padma* family emphasis on its right (north) wall (see Fig. 5.31). The identifications of the side walls have to also be considered as contributing to a larger coordinated program, namely an implicit triadic composition or to an implicit mandala or mandala assembly. Although there are five-deity mandalas, or sections of mandalas (the *krodha* mandala on the entrance wall of Chyiwang 79 is an example), the four deities surrounding the north wall niche at Chyiwang Cave 79 belong to different categories. Hayagrīva is an *āyudha-purusha*, or personification of the voice of Avalokiteśvara, Ekajaṭī is a female protector, Bhṛikutī, a consort or attendant, and Avalokiteśvara or Amoghapāśa an alternate form of the main deity, if it was Padmapāṇi. Almost invariably, the deity at the center of a mandala is surrounded by four or eight of the same class of deities, not one or two each of three or four different categories. This is another sign of the relative earliness of the iconography at work at Chyiwang Cave 79 (and at MkK stupa for that matter), since it retains, alongside the experiments with full and implicit mandalas in the *pañcakula* mode, an older, pre-STTS type of arrangement based not on the five-family system of geometrically surrounding the central deity, but rather compositions that are based on a triadic system, symmetrically extendable in the side directions. Thus in this case, the central deity had two female deities on its left side, one wrathful and one peaceful, and two male deities on the right side, one wrathful and one peaceful. Except in cultic Mahāyāna, these older compositions were generally superseded by the full five-family forms in Tantric contexts. The Chyiwang Cave 79 retains traces of the transition toward the later forms, for the five-family mode is also resorted to, as in the *krodha cakra,* or *trilokacakra* mandala. At Cave One at Dungkar, by contrast, the triadic form is relegated to the entrance wall, where, for example, the eleven-headed Avalokiteśvara is accompanied by Tārā and Bṛikutī, arranged symmetrically to either side (Fig. 5.136). The main walls of that cave are rigorously, rapturously given over to the fully

155 ibid., 137, 138.

156 Neumann, "Cave of the Offering Goddesses," 56.

Fig. 5.136 Eleven-headed Avalokiteśvara accompanied by Tārā and Bhṛkutī on entrance wall of Dungkar Cave 1. Photo 2005.

symmetrical five-family mandala, in floor to ceiling iterations, as is the Dukhang at Alchi, and two such mandala appear even on the entrance wall of Dungkar Cave 1 (see Fig. 5.54).

Nevertheless, Chyiwang Cave 79's right wall niche appears very likely to have been devoted to Avalokiteśvara and thus the *padma* or *dharma* family or division as understood in the STTS and other related Yoga Tantra texts such as the *Susiddhikara*. The former text describes many mandalas within its four sections relatable to the Buddha or *Tathāgata*, *vajra*, *dharma* (or *padma*), and *ratna* (jewel with *karma* [action]) families. Weinberger's explanation of this division is worth quoting at length:

> Divisions in the *Compendium of Principles* [i.e., the *Sarvatathāgata Tattva Saṃgraha*] primarily come in sets of four. Each of the four sections of the tantra is associated with a central Buddha figure, a Buddha family, and an aspect of enlightened expression. The first section is associated with Vairocana (the central figure in Yoga Tantra as a whole), the Tathāgata family (Tib: *de bzhin gshegs pa'i rigs*; Skt: *tathāgata-kula*), and enlightened body; the second, with Akṣobhya, the vajra family (Tib: *rdo rje'i rigs*; Skt: *vajra-kula*), and enlightened mind; the third, with Amitāyus (aka Lokeśvararāja and, in later traditions, Amitābha), the doctrine family (or lotus family; *chos kyi* or *padma'i rigs*, *dharma-* or *padma-kula*),

> and enlightened speech; and the fourth, with Ratnasambhava, the jewel family (*rin po che'i rigs, ratna-kula*), and enlightened action.[157]

This can help settle the affiliation of the right wall with the *padma* family at the MkK stupa, as confirmed by the presence of a lotus painted on the nimbus there (Fig. 5.101), an all-important identifier of Avalokiteśvara. This in turn helps validate the suggestion that, if one can judge by the set of similarities in the overall structure, the right (north) wall sculpture at Chiwang Cave 79 was indeed a form of Lokeśvara, and not Amitāyus Tathāgata. Presuming there was more symmetry across walls, that hints that the sculptures on the two left (south) walls were also bodhisattvas-types, not Tathāgatas. However, it is still possible that both were female deities, such as Tārā and Prajñaparamita on the north and south walls, respectively. Ekajaṭī and Bhṛikutī often accompany Tārā, and sometimes Hayagrīva does as well. It is only the presence of a form of Avalokiteśvara that casts doubt on the identification of the main missing sculpture on the north wall as Tārā. She frequently accompanies him, but I am unaware of examples where he attends her.

Before moving on from the niche on the right (north) wall of Chyiwang Cave 79, one minor aspect needs to be noted. Although little or nothing remains of the sculpture and painting in the niche, along the very narrow inset walls are distantly-related versions of the cubic rock forms noted above separating the wrathful protectors from the lower motifs on the entrance wall of the Malakartse Khar stupa (see Fig. 5.49). These are equally, but somewhat differently, conventionalized and abstracted (Figs. 5.137–138). That they are meant to convey a wild mountainous terrain as the setting for Avalokiteśvara in sculptural medium, is demonstrated by the damaged image of a white elephant near the center of Figure 5.137, just below the long curling tail of a tiger hanging down on the upper right. In Figure 5.138, a cave has been depicted as if excavated into the mountains, and part of a bony, seated ascetic inside it is visible. The bodies of writhing shakes climbing over the sharp hill-units can be seen to the left of the ascetic, underscoring the remoteness of the setting. Similar conventionalized abstractions of mountain forms are also found in some of the other caves in west Tibet, as well as sculptures in eastern India such as a monumental one from Udaygiri in Orissa, two others from eastern Bengal and Kurkihar in Bihar, and one at Borobudur in Java.[158] An even more stylized version of the rocky setting is found in a special

157 Weinberger, "Significance of Yoga Tantra," 42.

158 Linrothe, *Ruthless Compassion*, 109–90; S. Huntington, "Compassion in a Mountain Abode," figs. 1, 9, and 10. This is usually identified as Avalokiteśvara at Mt. Potalaka.

Fig 5.137 Abstracted elements of a mountain landscape on narrow side walls of the inset niche on the north (right) wall at Chyiwang Cave 79. Photo 2007.

Fig. 5.138 Ascetic in a cave set in a mountain landscape on narrow side walls of the inset niche on the north (right) wall at Chyiwang Cave 79. Photo 2007.

shrine at Zhalu (in Tsang province of midwestern Tibet) devoted to the four-armed form of Avalokiteśvara known as Ṣaḍakṣarīlokeśvara accompanied by Maṇidhara and Ṣaḍakṣarī Mahāvidyā.[159]

Directly below the now-empty niche of the right (north) wall is a narrow panel stretching between the two vertical columns of deities and *aṣṭamaṇgala*. On the left are two seated deities, one female and seeming to emerge from the center of a lotus (only her torso is visible, her legs "inside" the lotus; perhaps Pṛthvī?), and a male figure with leopard skin boots seated on a white horse (Fig. 5.139). These appear to be local protectors, and are larger than the sponsors on the protectors's left, arranged in two horizontal rows of sponsors and facing the protectors (Fig. 5.140). If we take into consideration here the almost obliterated unidentified three-headed wrathful deity below and larger than the registers of sponsors depicted at MkK stupa (Figs. 5.52–53) this might suggest that he (or she) too is a local protector. Another possibility would be a fourth member of four gate-guardians, but all of the other three are one-headed at MkK stupa, so a local protector, along the lines of the Zangskari mountain, clan, or village gods[160] that presumably go back into antiquity, seems just as likely.

Most of the sponsors depicted below the niche on the north wall inside Chyiwang Cave 79 are male—certainly the first five in the lower register

159 Illustrated in Linrothe, "Landscape Elements in Early Tibetan Painting," 167.

160 Riaboff, "Gzhon nu mdung lag, Mountain God of Zanskar."

Fig. 5.139 Local protectors (?) below the inset niche on the north (right) wall at Chyiwang Cave 79. Photo 2007.

Fig 5.140 Damaged rows of sponsor figure below the inset niche on the north (right) wall at Chyiwang Cave 79. Photo 2007.

from the left, seated with flat, brimmed and pointed-flap hats, wearing wide-lapeled robes belted at the waist (see Figs. 5.61–62, 5.140), much like those at Malakartse Khar. There appear to have been around twenty or so, and the ones below, including females, have red cartouches for their names but none of them have extant inscriptions. The heads of each figure in the lower register have been intentionally defaced.

On the right side of the Chyiwang Cave 79 right wall, adjacent to the entrance wall, the divisions of the murals found on the left wall are mirrored (Fig. 5.141). At the top are six more Buddhas that flow into

Fig. 5.141 Corner shared by the right side of the north (right) wall and the left side of the entrance wall of Chyiwang Cave 79. Photo 2007.

Fig. 5.142 Nine-deity mandala-like assembly, including Mahāvairocana as larger central deity surrounded by eight bodhisattvas, on the lower right side of the north (right) wall of Chyiwang Cave 79. Photo 2007.

the Buddhas on the upper part of the entrance wall. On the larger lower section is another mandala-like geometric arrangement of nine deities, in this case all male and all facing forward (Fig. 5.142). At the center is Mahāvairocana making the *dhyāna mudra*, and surrounding him is the set of eight bodhisattvas.[161] This is an archaic element, a reminder of the cult of Mahāvairocana and the eight bodhisattvas, prominent in Tibetan contents during the Pugyal (Tibetan imperial) period.[162] Most of the bodhisattvas have their left hands at the hip like the *vajra*-bodhisattvas. A few are easy enough to identify through their attributes. In the upper right corner, for instance, is Mañjuśrī with a book on an *utpala*-lotus (Fig. 5.143). The fact that he has his hair tied into tufts emerging from his crown is a sign of the closeness of the artists to Indian visual traditions. A second bodhisattva belonging to the set is blue, and holds the fragments of a banner on a staff; he sits on Mahāvirocana's left. This is likely to be Sarvanivaraṇa-Viṣkambhin, also a member of the set of eight bodhisattvas who according to the *Aṣṭamaṇḍalaka-sūtra* carries the flag.[163] Admittedly he is rarely blue, at least in the versions of the eight bodhisattvas assembled by Yoritomi.[164] Then again, the deity directly on top of Mahāvairocana holds the *vajra* in

161 Neumann identified this figure as "possibly Amitabha . . . surrounded by deities in the eight directions" ("Cave of the Offering Goddesses," 57), confusion arising due to the *dhyāna mudrā* shared by both Mahāvairocana and Amitāyus. Neumann does not discuss the five-deity wrathful *maṇḍala* on the entrance wall, suggesting the nine-deity *maṇḍala* is made up of twelve deities (ibid.). It may be that when I visited the cave in 2005 and 2007, well after Neumann published it, more was exposed, since he mentions the lower *aṣṭamaṇgala* being "only partly visible above the debris accumulated on the floor" (ibid., 56). Perhaps the debris covered up the sponsor figures, similarly not mentioned.

162 Heller, "Early Ninth Century Images of Vairochana from Eastern Tibet"; Heller, "*P.T. 7A, P.T. 108, P.T. 240* and *Beijing Bstan'Gyur 3489*"; Kapstein, *Tibetan Assimilation of Buddhism*, 51–65; Richardson, "Cult of Vairocana in Early Tibet;" M. Wang, *Maṇḍalas in the Making.*

163 Granoff, "Portable Buddhist Shrine," 90; Mitra, "Brief Survey," 64–65.

164 Yoritomi, "Iconographic Study of the Eight Bodhisattvas in Tibet."

Fig. 5.143 Mañjuśrī bodhisattva with book on blue *utpala*-flower, upper right corner of the nine-deity assembly on the lower right side of the north (right) wall of Chyiwang Cave 79. Photo 2007.

front of his heart and so would appear to be Vajrapāṇi, but he is *not* blue as one expects. Both these deities, but in precisely opposite positions, are described along with the others[165] surrounding Vairocana as corresponding to, and deifications of, the initial sections of the *Prajñapāramitānayasūtra*.[166] This format was used with a shifting set of bodhisattvas—Tanaka identifies another from the fourth tantra of the *Vajraśekharasūtra* in which Maitreya replaces Sarvamārapramardin.[167] Maitreya is possibly to be identified in the Chyiwang Cave 79 set as the bodhisattva in the lower left holding a flower that is probably meant to represent the *nāgapuspa*, his attribute. This arrangement, including Sarvanivaraṇa-Viṣkambhin's position in relation to Mahāvairocana closely resembles the wooden shrine in the Nelson Gallery which, although attributed to Central Asia with imported Kashmiri characteristics,[168] could equally well be from Kashmir or Gilgit with imported Central Asian characteristics.[169] The resemblance once again points up the connections the painters at Chyiwang and Malakartse Khar had to art from Kashmir.

Formal and Thematic Comparisons between Chyiwang Cave 79 and the Malakartse Khar Stupa

The resemblances between the iconographic themes, their distribution, the formats, and the visual forms of the paintings at Chyiwang Cave 79 and the stupa at Malakartse Khar are worth summarizing. Both sites feature three-fold programs with paintings in registers surrounding, and interacting with, sculptures.[170] The *aṣṭamaṇgala* and other auspicious devices are interspersed among the figures on the side walls, even more

165 Avalokiteśvara, Ākāśagarbha, Vajramuṣṭi, Sacitttotpādadharmacakrapravartin, Gaganagañja, and Sarvamārapramardin.

166 Tanaka, *Illustrated History of the Maṇḍala*, 91–93.

167 Ibid., 92.

168 Granoff, "Portable Buddhist Shrine," 85.

169 Linrothe, *Collecting Paradise*, 31–35.

170 In both cases, whatever was painted on the ceiling has disappeared and cannot be taken into account.

prominently at Chyiwang. Many, even *most*, of the same deities appear prominently and repeatedly, notably the offering goddesses, the *krodha-vighnāntaka* "Attracting Deities," and the *vajra*-bodhisattvas. These also appear in Yoga Tantra texts and the pantheon they describe. The entrance wall in both cases is largely, though not exclusively, devoted to wrathful deities, and is often (as at Dungkar and MkK stupa) where the sponsor figures are represented, though not at Chyiwang Cave 79. The left wall has an emphasis at both sites on female deities. At both sites there are nearly the same mandala assemblies (a category of implicit mandalas), ordered in only slightly different ways. On the other hand, the Chyiwang composition is somewhat more advanced in the sense that it includes a relatively explicit mandala on the back wall, and two more "proto-*maṇḍala*" on the entrance-wall halves of both side walls. This is in addition to the "implicit" mandala or mandala assemblies that are the main theme on two of the three niches. It is clear from the repetition of more than one depiction of the same deity at both sites that the three niches must be considered three separate but coordinated compositions, and not a single composition distributed over three walls as appears elsewhere, as at the old site near Basgo (see Fig. 5.47), a similar structure at Nyarma,[171] at Nyag and in the Khartse Valley.[172] Multiple Buddhas with varying gestures and robe colors are found on the upper areas of three of the walls at Chyiwang; they appear more widely spaced and smaller around all four walls at Malakartse Khar. There, they are part of the valance design bridging the wall and the ceiling. Also expressed at both sites is an interest in exotic material culture, including elaborate textiles, ceramics, and musical instruments. This seems to reflect an awareness of luxury objects imported into and incorporated by the court culture of Kashmir.

Before turning to formal tendencies, it must be emphasized that the interior area of Chyiwang Cave 79 is nearly four times larger than that of the Malakartse Khar stupa. This significant difference in scale certainly affects both the number of figures and motifs allowed, the scale of the themes, as well as space surrounding them. The small size may also help explain the decision on the part of the makers of the MkK stupa to have many of the painted deities represent two thematic identities simultaneously, to efficiently and economically utilize the modest space. In terms of the form-idiom and the painterly conventions employed, although the basic vocabulary and visual language of the two sites have many similarities, the differences also stand out. The way the circular nimbi rest like moon

171 Neuwirth and Auer, *Ancient Monastic Complexes of Tholing, Nyarma and Tabo*, 115–65, 313–25.

172 Sichuan Daxue, ""Xizang Ali Xiangquan he Liuyu Kazi," pls. 11, 12, 21–23; Gyalpo and Kalantari, "Buddhist Monuments of Khartse Valley."

disks on the lotuses is clearly shared. So is the convention on the female deities of the fall of a necklace interrupted by the curve of the breast, as if coiling around it, though it is less overt. Also shared are the compulsion for a blue background, for relatively dense or detailed textile patterns,[173] the tightly wound springy lines to indicate light-rays in the nimbi, pointed crests inserted at the center of the crowns, circular flowers or flower-like medallions in the hair, flowing scarves, extra earrings in the upper ear in some cases (Figs. 5.144–145), and the extended further eye. Most of these are standard in the Kashmiri idiom, fully represented in metal and ivory sculpture. But *how* the eye extends is quite different between these two sites. At the Malakartse Khar stupa, a typical offering goddess (Fig. 5.146) in three-quarter view has a more active profile, with part of the upper eye and eyelid extending beyond the forehead and cheek, not merely the lower line and the eyelashes (as in Figure 5.145). The outlines are much thicker, wetter and more fluid in the case of the Malakartse Khar stupa murals. The *V* at the forehead is more dramatic, the eyes wider and more hooded, and the eyebrows more slanted with a greater variety of thickness. The goddesses at Chyiwang have tight curls along their forehead hairlines (Fig. 5.145), which is not the case at the site in Zangskar (see Fig. 5.146).

Overall, the bodies of the deities in the MkK stupa, despite being largely painted in outlines with some modeling, are more volumetric than the Chyiwang bodies, which are painted in color with fainter outlining. Compare the shape of the torsos of a Vajrasattva-like bodhisattva on the main wall at Chyiwang, perhaps Vajrahetu, (Fig. 5.147) with one of the *vajra*-bodhisattvas *cum* offering gods at Malakartse Khar (Fig. 5.148). Both have torsos that sway between active shoulders and hips. The movement at Chyiwang is unified, a continuous sweep from shoulders to waist, and the outline is a smooth arc. Despite being smaller in size, the Malakartse Khar torso is more complex. The head moves to its right, the upper chest twists slightly to the left (note the nipples shifted farther to his left), the rib cage begins to shift back to the right, and the abdomen and hips push further in that direction. Each section of the torso has its own volume and potential for contained energy and is treated accordingly, contributing to overall movement but with parts maintaining independence. At Chyiwang, the torso is a much simpler more unified form. It depends on the belt circling the waist to convey the illusion of three-dimensionality, while the chest itself is flat and, like the earrings, the tufts of hair, and the crown, aligned with the viewing plane. This is a fundamental difference,

173 See Appendix 5.1 and 5.2 following this chapter for details of the painted textile patterns depicted in the murals at MkK stupa and Chyiwang Cave 79 respectively.

(above left and right):

Fig. 5.144 Detail of the head and upper torso of Vajradīpā (Fig. 5.97) on the north wall of the Malakartse Khar stupa. Photo 2004.

Fig. 5.145 Close view of the head, hair, crown, face and upper torso of Vajramālā on the top left side (second from the left) on the main wall (Fig. 120) of Chyiwang Cave 79. Photo 2007.

Fig. 5.146 Close view of the head, hair, crown and face of an offering goddess painted at the top left of the south (left) wall of the Malakartse Khar stupa (Fig. 5.82). Photo 2012.

Fig. 5.147 *Vajra*-bodhisattva Vajrahetu, holding wheel emblem with left hand in *vajramuṣṭi* at the hip, on the mainwall, right of the central niche, at Chyiwang Cave 79. Photo 2005.

Fig. 5.148 *Vajra*-bodhisattva *cum* offering deity on the right of the main (west) wall of the Malakartse Khar stupa (see Fig. 5.78). Photo 2012.

easy to overlook because of the expanded palette and greater detailing. If we compare the two bodhisattvas to one on the Gilgit manuscript covers (Fig. 5.149), the structure of the Malakartse Khar painting is more closely aligned to its exaggerated treatment of the body. Further comparison with examples from Dungkar Cave 2 shows that the latter, far from being nearly identical to Chyiwang Cave 79, move further in the direction of simplifying bodily volume, flattening out the structure and minimizing the twist of the torso, for both male and female figures (see Fig. 5.109). Similar contrasts can be made between the offering goddesses at MkK stupa and Chyiwang Cave 79; for example, Figures 5.98 and 5.127. The direction of development, from the seventh–ninth-century Gilgit manuscript covers[174] to the ca. late twelfth-century (or later) Dungkar Cave 2 is from graphically representing a complex bodily structure and organic movements in three dimensions, toward more painterly but flatter, more frontal, less articulated bodies. The Chyiwang paintings clearly fit between those two extremes, but closer to the latter than the MkK stupa murals.

174 Linrothe, *Collecting Paradise*, 39–54.

Fig 5.150 Seated Buddha, rock carving above Linshed Monastery, Zangskar, ca. 7th or 8th c. Photo pre-2004, digitized slide.

Fig 5.149 Bodhisattva painted on the inside of a wooden book cover found in the Gilgit District, ca. 7th century, now in the Sri Pratap Singh Museum Srinagar. Photo 2013.

Other differences include an increasing tendency of compressing the rounded head nimbus into an oblate shape, narrower at the bottom, rounder at the top. Although this type is visible at Malakartse Khar, the round nimbus is at least as prevalent, whereas at Chyiwang, it is mainly of the oblate shape. If we use the twelfth and early thirteenth century paintings of Alchi Dukhang and Sumtsek as benchmarks, then the round head-haloes are definitely earlier, and the oblate shape later, though certainly in circulation in the eleventh century. The round type is more visible in painting than in sculpture, though it is apparent there as well (see Fig. 5.48). It appears in the early manuscript painting associated with Tholing (see Fig. 5.58), as well as with the still earlier Gilgit manuscripts (see Fig. 5.149), not to mention rock carvings such as, for example, Figure 5.150, though like the Malakartse Khar paintings, both types are visible among the former.

Based on the iconographic and stylistic evidence, the forms of the paintings in Chyiwang Cave 79 are earlier than those of Dungkar, and the Malakartse Khar stupa paintings are most closely related on the same grounds to Chyiwang, but slightly earlier. Having proposed a relative chronology for the Malakartse Khar paintings in relation to Chyiwang Cave 79 and the Dungkar caves, a further step is to expand that relative chronology, and then to posit dates at least for MkK stupa and Chyiwang Cave 79 within that relative chronology, after first positing a programmatic reconstruction for the Malakartse Khar stupa.

Comparing the Overall Programs at Chyiwang Cave 79 and the Malakartse Khar Stupa

Aside from the thematic and formal similarities and difference across the two sites, it is important also to consider the overall iconographic or programmatic correspondences, if any, between the two sites. Clearly, there is a similar pantheon of deities deployed repeatedly—especially the offering deities and the gate guardians—along comparable walls. Padma family deities are clustered on the right wall at Chyiwang, and on the same wall at the MkK stupa. These includes the presence of a lotus painted on the nimbus there **(see Fig. 5.101)**, an essential identifier of Avalokiteśvara. This in turn helps validate the suggestion that, if one can judge by the set of similarities in the overall structure, the right (north) wall sculpture at Chiwang Cave 79 was indeed a form of Lokeśvara Bodhisattva, and not Amitāyus Tathāgata. Presuming there was more symmetry across walls, that hints that the sculptures on the two left (south) walls were also bodhisattvas, not Tathāgatas, which would imbalance the thematic symmetry, and duplicate what was surely on the main wall. However, it is still possible that both sides walls featured female deities, such as Tārā (also a member of the *padma* family) and Prajñāpāramitā on the north and south walls, respectively.

If, as seems most probable, the main wall at Chyiwang was devoted to the Buddha family progenitor, Vairocana, and the right wall to the *padma-kula*, then it is not unlikely that the left wall was devoted to the *vajra-kula*. The three walls would thus present a three-family system. In Buddhist visual convention, which the western Himalayans and Tibetans inherited, hierarchical precedence begins at the center then moves to the right from the perspective of the central deity, followed by the left; this would place the three families in the proper order. At Malakartse Khar, similar logic was probably at work. With a bodhisattva (a form of Avalokiteśvara) presiding over the north wall, it would be unlikely that the deity on the left would be a Tathāgata (such as Akṣobhya the head of the *vajra* family) because of the symmetrical tendencies seen here and at many other sites. The other likely representative of the *vajra-kula* is Vajrasattva, who was the principal deity depicted in the *ekamudrā* mandala in the STTS, and can appear in the thirteen-deity form,[175] or for that matter at the center of seventeen- and thirty-seven-deity mandalas. Still, we must also account for the emphasis on female deities found on the left wall, at both sites. In fact, this is not obstacle to suggesting the central sculpture may have been Vajrasattva: he is particularly associated with an all-female retinue in the *Prajñāpāramitanayasūtra* (the *Rishukyo* in Japanese Shingon).[176] Even in the STTS, the *ekamudrā* ritual in which the practitioner is enjoined to become Vajrasattva, there is the suggestive instruction that "there is no other evil like absence of passion. Therefore, you should not practice indifference to sexual love."[177] It is possible that an all-female mandala was in place there, along the lines of the Vajraguhya mandala found on the second storey at the Alchi Sumtsek,[178] though that is a full 37-deity mandala based on the Vajradhātu *mahāmaṇḍala* model. The Vajrakārya Karma mandala, the action mandala of the *vajra* family, also features female forms of the *puja* bodhisattvas, based on the fourth section of the STTS.[179] Naturally there are many possibilities, but we can use as a working hypothesis the basic structure of the Tathāgata family represented on the main wall, the Vajra family with a large contingent of female deities represented on the left wall, the Lotus family on the right wall, and the *krodha* deities, also often associated with the Vajra family, dominating the entrance wall. Vajrasattva is certainly also a candidate for the central sculptural image on the south wall opposite a form of Avalokiteśvara on the main wall in the MkK stupa since his status transitions in this period's Esoteric Buddhism from a *vajra*-Bodhisattva to a form of the Ādi-Buddha (and thus is both).[180] Moreover, in both eastern Indian and East Asian images and teaching traditions, he is often distinctively depicted surrounded by female deities.[181] A form of Avalokiteśvara and that of Vajrasattva appear paired on opposite walls in the small brick Temple 4 at Ratnagiri in Orissa in the ca. 10th century, as part of a triadic, three-family program with Vairocana making the *dhyāna mudrā* in the center (Fig. 5.151).[182] At the Lalung Serkhang, in nearby Spiti, a nearly identical three-family composition as the one I am endorsing for the three main sculptures of the Malakartse Khar stupa is found not on the main and two side walls (as at Ratnagiri), but on the back wall itself. In the center is Śākyamuni Buddha (or Akṣobhya in monk form?) making *bhūmisparśa mudrā*, representing the Buddha family. Above him and on his proper right is a nearly equally large Padmapāṇi Avalokiteśvara in an elaborate architectural throne representing the *padma-kula*, and on the Buddha's proper left is Vajrasattva (see Fig. 5.33), clearly paired with Padmapāṇi, and in a similar pillared

175 Giebel, *Chin-kang-ting ching yü-ch'ieh shi-pa-hui chih-kuei*, 139.

176 Weinberger, "Significance of Yoga Tantra," 111–117; Astley, "An Example of Vajrasattva;" Linrothe "Mirror Image"; Linrothe, *Reenchantment*, 153–55.

177 Todaro, "Annotated Translation of the *Tattvasaṃgraha* (Part 1)," 367.

178 Goepper and Poncar, *Alchi*, 200–209; Giebel, *Chin-kang-ting ching yü-ch'ieh shi-pa-hui chih-kuei*, 132; Todaro, "Annotated Translation of the *Tattvasaṃgraha* (Part 1)," 330–34.

179 Ibid., 352–56.

180 Linrothe, "Mirror Image." He appears as the equivalent of Vairocana at Dunhuang; Linrothe, "'Structure and Subject Matter' at Dunhuang." Tanaka notes that Vajrasattva "is not only the first bodhisattva but also the primordial bodhisattva among all the bodhisattvas in the Vajradhātu-maṃḍala;" *Illustrated History of the Mandala*, 98.

181 Linrothe, *Reenchantment*, 153–155; Linrothe "Mirror Image."

182 Mitra, *Ratnagiri*, 287–292, pls. 236–240; Tanaka, *Illustrated History of the Mandala*, 57–58.

Fig. 5.151 Vairocana (center, ht. 162 cm), Vajrasattva (left, 165 cm), and Vajradharma (Avalokiteśvara, right, 166 cm) in Temple 4 at the archaeological site of Ratnagiri Monastery, Odisha. Photo 2017.

palace, indicative of the *vajra-kula*.[183] The fact that Padmapāṇi and Vajrasattva at Lalung Serkhang are on opposite sides than what I am proposing for both the MkK stupa sculptures and the Chyiwang Cave 79 is not necessarily problematic. There may have been other reasons to place Vajrasattva close to the right wall dominated by Prajñāpāramitā, or Padmapāṇi near what Luczanits identifies as the Dharmadhātu Vāgīśvara Mañjuśrī at the center of the left wall. The fact that they form a pair joined to or triangulated with the Buddha is the key point. It should be recalled that the three-family program, a relatively early phenomenon, was mixed with the more dominant *pañcakula* system related to the STTS and Vajradhatu *mahāmaṇḍala* mode. As Luczanits points out in relation to Lalung, the *trikula* configuration "is extremely frequent in both late Indian and early Tibetan Buddhist art, but was a conservative iconographic group at the time the Lalung Serkhang was erected."[184] By contrast, as we will see momentarily, "both side wall [implicit] mandalas are unique" and "innovative."[185]

It is the identification of the large sculpture on the main wall at MkK (Fig. 5.30) that remains puzzling. That it represents the Buddha family is highly likely. That could include, for example, its progenitors such as Śākyamuni Buddha at Lalung and one or more form of Vairocana as at

183 Luczanits, *Buddhist Sculpture in Clay*, 93–106. Di Mattia follows Tucci in misidentifying the Avalokiteśvara as Mañjuśrī Vāgiśvara, and in the process rejects Luczanits's identification, and that of others, as Padmapāṇi; Di Mattia, "Divine Palaces of the Buddha," 62–63. Like many seated Padmapāṇi images, his right leg is down, a lotus appears at his left shoulder, and a deer skin is over his shoulder. Di Mattia offers no explanation for how or why Mañjuśrī, Vajrasattva, and the Buddha, the three principal themes of the main wall at Lalung, fit together, nor does Tucci in his treatment of the Lalung Serkhang; Tucci, *Temples of Western Tibet*, 116–121.

184 Luczanits, *Buddhist Sculpture in Clay*, 204. Elsewhere he confirms that that "In the earliest monuments three-family configurations are quite common." Ibid., 221.

185 Ibid., 122.

Ratnagiri (see Fig. 5.151), Alchi Dukhang, Sumda Chung, and presumably Chyiwang Cave 79. Why not attribute Vairocana to the MkK stupa as well? What makes that questionable is the fact that Vairocana, complete with his lion *vahana* and Buddha-family wheel (see Fig. 5.72, above) is already present in painted form along with three of the other Tathāgata on the columnar borders of the main wall. The fifth member of the set of five Jinas, Akṣobhya, might seem to be the natural candidate for the main wall, but as indicated already, he is the progenitor of the *vajra*-family, already plausibly represented by Vajrasattva on the south wall. Thus we might need to rule out both Vairocana and Akṣobhya. Śakyamuni would seem oddly cast when he is surrounded in this Esoteric Buddhist context by four Tathāgata and a host of related Vajradhātu-*mahāmaṇḍala* deities, instead of his usual two monk disciples. Who then can represent the Buddha family in this context, which calls for *two* sculptures, the large one at the center, and a smaller one above it?

I favor a surprisingly widespread but until recently unidentified form of the Ādibuddha whose mandala surmounts the main (Buddha) wall on the third level at Alchi Sumtsek, flanked by a crowned Śākyamuni mandala on his right and a Prajñāpāramitā mandala on his right. He also appears more than once at Mangyu in Ladakh, one of the Alchi group of monuments (Fig. 5.152), and at Lalung. In the latter, he dominates the left wall as its central image (Fig. 5.153),[186] facing Prajñāpāramitā on the opposite wall.

Previously misidentified, by me, and most everyone else, as the bodhisattva Mañjuśrī, in the overwhelmingly convincing case made by Anthony Tribe, the "eight-armed Mañjuśrī found in early Western Himalayan Art [sic] [can] be identified not as the *bodhisattva* Mañjuśrī but as the Ādibuddha."[187] This promotion from bodhisattva status to transcendent Buddha is not as unusual as it sounds—Vajrasattva himself is sometimes considered the Ādibuddha, at other times a *vajra*-bodhisattva, and at still other instances, the idealized practitioner-as-*ācārya*,[188] depending on context but without changing form. In the eight-armed form, Mañjuśrī is not only the (or an) Ādibuddha, he appears within the heart of Mahāvairocana and all the other Tathāgata. In forms appearing in the western Himalaya (see Fig. 5.152), four of the arms hold swords, the other four hold the *Prajñāpāramitā* text. At the Serkhang in Lalung (see Fig. 5.153), the attributes in his hands have all been lost, like almost all the other sculptures there. However, he "is flanked on each side by two columns of four further clay sculptures that

186 These important and astounding identifications were made by Anthony Tribe, in "Mañjuśrī as Ādibuddha." Tribe based these discoveries on his study and translation of ca. late eighth to mid ninth century commentaries to the *Nāmasaṃgīti* by a trio of authors known to each other, the main one being Vilāsavajra who was apparently from Swat (which helps explain its currency among the Kashmiri artists and Buddhists who served western Himalayan patrons) but also spent some ten years in Nālandā; Tribe, *Tantric Buddhist Practice in India*, 25–28.

187 Tribe, "Mañjuśrī as Ādibuddha," 539.

188 Linrothe, "Mirror Image."

Fig. 5.152 8-armed, 5-headed Mañjuśrī Ādibuddha, mural painting, in Western Tower at Mangyu, Ladakh, ca. late 12th c. Photo 2006.

Fig. 5.153 8-armed Mañjuśrī Ādibuddha on left wall, Lalung Serkhang, Spiti, Himachal Pradesh, India, ca. late 12th c. Photo 2022.

form a surrounding *maṇḍala* of sixteen figures. The inner two columns are comprised of four goddesses and the four directional *tathāgatas*."[189] Note how closely that mirrors the identity of the deities painted on columns to the side on the main wall at the Malakartse Khar stupa (see Figs. 5.65–66). Only the wrathful deities have been shifted to the entrance wall at the Serkhang, where Hayagrīva and Vajrapāṇi appear in sculptural form. Tribe also notes that in the Sumtsek Mañjuśrī Ādibuddha mandala, Mañjuśrī Ādibuddha is surrounded by the female "mothers" of the family (*kula-mātṛ*), "identifiable by the family symbols they hold," plus the four directional Tathāgatas, identifiable in part through their *vahana*, at least four of the offering deities, and likely also by the *vajra*-bodhisattvas (*samādhi* deities).[190] This too, coincides very well with the identification proposed of the doubled identities of the Tathāgata with the consorts (or mothers), and the *vajra*-bodhisattvas with the offering goddesses.

Also intriguing about the Lalung Serkhang Mañjuśrī Ādibuddha is that above him is a second, smaller but related deity. Again, this echoes the second, smaller socket and painted nimbus above the larger one at the MkK stupa (see Fig. 5.30). The text that describes the form of Mañjuśrī Ādibuddha posits it as within the heart of Mahāvairocana and of all the

189 Tribe, "Mañjuśrī as Ādibuddha," 545.

190 Ibid., 559–560. The substitution on the main wall of the MkK stupa of Mahavairocana with lion *vahana* and the wheel *samaya* (symbol), for Akṣobhya with elephant and the vajra, is a variant that so far remains vexing without good explanations or precedence.

Fig. 5.154 Mahāvairocana with Mañjuśrī Ādibuddha in his heart, mural painting in Kumbum Chapel 3Wa, Gyantse west-central Tibet, first half of the 15th c. Photo 2007.

Fig 5.155 Close view of Mañjuśrī Ādibuddha and Mañjuśrī-jñanasattva in heart of Mahāvairocana depicted in Figure 5.154. Photo 2007.

other Tathāgata and Vajrasattva Ādibuddha. Like a story within a story leading to a story, there is a third image within the heart of the Ādibuddha: on a wheel in their hearts are mantras associated with the *Nāmasaṃgiti*, and at its very center is a six-faced "gnosis-being Mañjuśrī" known as Mañjuśrī-jñānasattva. This series of recursive images are shown as such in the fifteenth century paintings at the Gyantse Kumbum in west-central Tibet—a tiny Mañjuśrī-jñānasattva at the center of the upper chest of Mañjuśrī-jñānasattva at the center of the upper chest of Mahāvairocana (Figs. 5.154–155).[191] Among the Lalung Serkhang sculptures, however, that would have been impossible to depict clearly. Instead, above the large Mañjuśrī Ādibuddha (see Fig. 5.153) is a smaller depiction of the Mañjuśrī-jñānasattva (Fig. 5.156). He holds two lotuses in hand which, according to Vilāsavajra's text, each supported a volume of the *Prajñāpāramitā* (like all such attributes in Serkhang, now missing).[192]

Interestingly, Tribe points out that textually, Mahavairocana has four faces, Mañjuśrī Ādibuddha is to have five faces and Mañjuśrī-jñānasattva six.[193]

191 Ricca and Lo Bue, *Great Stupa of Gyantse*, pls. 5–9.

192 Ibid., 547.

193 Ibid.

Fig. 5.156 Mañjuśrī-jñanasattva above Mañjuśrī Ādibuddha on left wall, Lalung Serkhang, Spiti, Himachal Pradesh, India, ca. late 12th c. Photo 2022.

Fig. 5.157 Close view of the faces of Mañjuśrī Ādibuddha depicted in Figure 5.153, showing unpainted fourth facing at the back. Photo 2022.

In the painted version of Mañjuśrī Ādibuddha at Mangyu (see Fig. 5.152), five faces are visible, but on the Serkhhang sculpture only three faces are apparent (see Fig. 5.153), and four on the Mañjuśrī-jñānasattva (see Fig. 5.156). As for the latter, Tribe rightly observes that the fourth head is floating peculiarly above the other three and that it is possible that "there were originally two further heads in between the bottom three and single top head," thus matching Vilāsavajra's description.[194] As for the two missing heads of Mañjuśrī Ādibuddha at Lalung, looking closely behind the three heads, I was recently able to document a fourth ungilded head behind the main three (Fig. 5.157). The textually prescribed fifth might have been on the other side, not available to me because of space restrictions within the shrine.

At any rate, I suggest that the main wall at the Malakartse Khar stupa featured a large sculpture of Mañjuśrī Ādibuddha and above it, as at the Lalung Serkhang, a smaller one of Mañjuśrī-jñānasattva. As the heart

194 Ibid., 553.

of the heart of Mahavairocana, the Adibuddha Mañjuśrī and Mañjuśrī-jñānasattva form the quintessential representatives of the Buddha family. They are surrounded by members of the Vajradhatu *mahāmaṇḍala* necessarily doubled in an implicit mandala configuration. On their proper right, on the south wall, was probably Vajrasattva not as Ādibuddha but as the archetype of the *vajrakula*, and on their left, Avalokiteśvara epitomizing the *padmakula* on the north wall. Opposite them, on the entrance wall, were three gate guardians. The one closest to the south wall is blue and holds a vajra and bell, both associated with Trailokyavijaya and *vajrakula* (see Fig. 5.43). Were we able to identify the other two more precisely, the one in the middle too might belong to the *buddhakula*, and the one closest to the north wall (see Fig. 5.42) might affiliate with the *padmakula*, as does Hayagrīva on the main wall immediately adjacent to the north wall (see Fig. 5.68). These identifications, though contingent, are grounded in the interlocking Esoteric Buddhist doctrines translated into spatial principles, as well as sites with comparable if not precisely identical themes. At the least, the proposed reconstruction of the overarching program at MkK stupa are compounded from what remains intact locally and in neighboring sites, and, hopefully, do not do serious violence to what was possible at that time, the ca. late eleventh or early twelfth century.

A Relative Chronology for 10th–13th-Century Buddhist Sites in Kashmiri or Kashmiri-derived Form-idiom in Ngari, Spiti, Ladakh, and Zangskar

> Self-evidently, it is only by exploring the structures of artistic phenomena, and hence the mainsprings of historical change, that we can see individual achievements for what they are, in all their uniqueness and at the historical point of origin. Whatever perils attendant on evolutionary thinking, I know of no other method—static structural analyses not excluded—whereby we can even come close to grasping the individuality of a work of art. As [Hans] Tietze long ago pointed out, what makes art history possible is that 'the work of art is totally defined by its making'; that it can and must be assigned with certainty to one particular time and place.
>
> Otto Pächt, *The Practice Of Art History*, 127[195]

I take it that Pächt is pointing to a dialectic between the individual work of art—or in this case, a site—and the longer trajectory of historical

195 In his *Practice of Art History*, 142n92, Pächt cites Hans Tietze, *Die Methode der Kunstgeschichte* (Leipzig, 1913), 174.

development in which it can be plotted. The site takes its place in a longer evolution, and both shares with what comes before and after, but what it is that distinguishes it from others in its lineage is more clearly profiled by slotting it into place. To that end and for such purposes, I have attempted to assemble in tabular form related sites in west Tibet and the western Himalaya into a stream of sites within a limited time span, before and after the Malakartese Khar stupa and Chyiwang Cave 79.

Table 5.1 constitutes a relative chronology derived from, and supplementing, many of the most intensive studies to date in this area, those of Klimburg-Salter et al. (*Tabo*), Neumann ("Wall Paintings of Western Tibet"), Pritzker ("Wall Paintings of Nyag Lhakhang Kharpo"), and Luczanits (*Buddhist Sculpture in Clay*; "Early Buddhist Heritage of Ladakh Reconsidered"; "Styles in Western Himalayan Art"), as well as those of Zhang Changhong and Huo Wei, and Sichuan University (*Bod kyi mdzes rtsal kun btus*; *Piyang, Dongga yi zhi kao gu bao gao*; "Xizang Ali Xiangquan he Liuyu Kazi hegu Fojiao Weicun de Kaogu Diaocha yu Yanjiu"; Huo Wei, "Xizang xibu Shiku bihua zhong ji zhong yishu fengge de fenxi"), and others. Luczanits's *Buddhist Sculpture in Clay* (2004) is largely devoted to sculpture rather than painting but is comprehensive, including many additional sites, particularly those mainly featuring early sculptures. The table here leaves aside several relatively minor shrines (to which category, of course, Zangskar's Malakartse Khar ultimately belongs), especially those of which I have no firsthand experience. **Table 5.1** calibrates the main Buddhist theme depicted in each shrine. That is, it indicates whether the program focuses on the three-family system, the Vajradhātu *mahāmaṇḍala*, the Dharmadhātu Vāgīśvara Mañjuśrī mandala or some combination. It also tabulates the type of mandala form, distinguishing the standard Tibetan Buddhist mandala depiction from implicit mandalas; those that combine sculptures with paintings (the majority) or are exclusively sculptural; and geometric mandalas, transitional between implicit and standard (as discussed above). There can certainly be valid debate about the exact position of most of these sites, though hopefully not by more than a relative position or two earlier or later.

Before analyzing the long-term trends that emerge from this kind of organization, first I will briefly summarize those sites which have not figured in the discussion above and indicate where further information might be or has been derived. Tholing Gyatsa Lhakhang is also known

Table 5.1: Relative Chronology of Western Tibetan Sites with Kashmiri or *Khaché* Styles of Painting Sculpture

SITE	PROGRAM	*MAṆḌALA* TYPE	REGION
Tholing Gyatsa (brgya rtsa) Lhakhang	Vajradhātu	Implicit	Ngari
Tholing Stupa NW of Gyatsa Lhakhang	Trikula (VAT?) + Vajradhātu	X? Implicit?	Ngari
Tabo Entry Hall (sgo khang)	Worldly protectors, donors	X	Spiti
Tabo Cella	Trikula	X	Spiti
Nyarma enclosure wall ruins	Vajradhātu?	Implicit	Ladakh
Nyag Lhakhang Karpo	Shakyamuni assembly	X	Ngari
Tabo Dukhang	Vajradhātu + DVM	Implicit	Spiti
Malakhartse Khar	Trikula + Vajradhātu + MA?	Implicit	Zangskar
Chyiwang Cave 79	Trikula + Vajradhātu	Implicit + Geometric	Ngari
Lalung chapel (sculptures only)	*4-fold Vairocana Sculpture*	*Implicit*	*Spiti*
Dungkar valley temple ruin	Vajradhātu	Implicit	Ngari
Basgo ruins	Vajradhātu	Implicit	Ladakh
Nako Translator's Temple	Vajradhātu + DVM	Implicit + Standard	Kinnaur
Nako Upper Temple	Pp + Vajradhātu	Implicit + Standard	Kinnaur
Dungkar Cave 1	Vajradhātu + DVM + GS	Standard	Ngari
Nyag Lhakhang Karpo	DVSM	Implicit	Ngari
Lalung Serkhang	Trikula + Vajradhātu +MA	Implicit	Spiti
Alchi Dukhang	Vajradhātu + DVM	Implicit + Standard	Ladakh
Mangyu	Vajradhātu + DVM + MA	Implicit + Standard	Ladakh
Sumda Chung	Vajradhātu + DVM	Implicit + Standard	Ladakh
Saspotse	Vajradhātu + DVM	Standard	Ladakh
Skyu	DVM (?)	Standard	Markha
Dungkar Cave 2	DVM	Standard	Ngari
Alchi Sumtsek	BSM + Vajradhātu + DVM + MA	Standard	Ladakh

Those in italics are placed very tentatively
BSM = Body-Speech-Mind, referring to the three ground floor bodhisattvas at the Sumtsek which are not arranged on the basis of the *trikula*.
DVM = Dharmadhātu Vāgīśvara Mañjuśrī *maṇḍala*
GS = Guhyasamāja *maṇḍala*
MA = Mañjurśrī Adi-Buddha
Pp = Prajñāpāramitā
Vajradhātu = Vajradhātu *maṇḍala*
VAT = *Vairocanābhisaṃbodhi Tantra*

maṇḍala type key:
Geometric = the deities arranged geometrically around the central deity (as in a standard *maṇḍala* depiction) but not within a four-gated palace
Implicit = the deities arranged around the central deity but neither fully geometrically nor within a four-gated palace; a type of *maṇḍala* assembly
Standard = "standard *maṇḍala* depiction" (adapted from Luczanits 2008).
X = not present; no painted *maṇḍala*

in Tibetan as the Nampar Nangzad Lhakhang (rnam par snang mdzad lha khang), or the Vairocana Lhakhang.[196] Its structure is a kind of three-dimensional mandala, and indeed it appears to have housed a Vajradhātu mandala, but one that was a hybrid assembly. In the center are remains of a base for Vairocana and the symbols of the four Pāramitās, but most of the rest of the deities seem to have lined the walls on which are remains of the outlines of nimbi. Moreover, Vitali reports that it was restored in the thirteenth and again in the fifteenth century, so other than a few surviving mural fragments, it is likely that the sculptures are largely if not completely restored.[197] Nevertheless, a late tenth-century date is assigned to its mural fragments,[198] which could not have been painted until the structure itself was constructed.

The stupa to the northwest of the Tholing Gyatsa (brgya rtsa) was excavated and subsequently reburied or moved.[199] As Luczanits points out, the paintings and sculptures are of "superb quality" and, in some cases, in equally vibrant condition, the colors fresh and bright. Heller calls the

196 Vitali, *Records of Tho-ling*, 92–93, passim; Phun-tshogs-rnam-rgyal and Zhang, *Tuo lin Si*, 82–92; Namgyal 2001: 126–32.

197 Vitali, *Records of Tho-ling*, 14–15.

198 Luczanits, *Buddhist Sculpture in Clay*, 72.

199 Ibid., 30–32; Phun-tshogs-rnam-rgyal and Zhang, *Tuo lin Si*, 126–32; Trinle Tharchin, *Qiangu Juehui*, 53, 97–98.

Fig 5.158 Drawing of Vajralāsyā offering goddess on painted stupa at Tholing Monastery, Ngari, west Tibet, now reburied, after Namgyal, *Tuolin* Si, 131b. Drawing by Eric Huntington.

paintings "highly sophisticated" with "a brilliant palette of bright colours, thickly applied to create an opaque yet lustrous effect."[200] The format is triadic, with a standing Buddha sculpture on the main wall, a form of Avalokiteśvara on his right and the peaceful blue Vajrapāṇī (not Vajrasattva as it is often stated[201]) on his left. These are the standard representatives of *buddha*, *padma*, and *vajra* families; Heller connects the iconographic program to the *Vairocanābhisaṃbodhi Tantra* and notes that Rinchen Zangpo (958–1055) translated a ritual offering linked to the Tantra.[202] On the back (west) wall there were no sculptures but at least two wrathful deities, one blue and holding a vajra in the raised upper left and making the admonitory *tarjani mudrā* with the left (probably Vajrapāṇi), and the other a red wrathful deity, probably Hayagrīva.[203] These two are in *alīḍha* and *pratyālīḍha* postures, one-headed and with curly reddish hair. Though the top of the hair is damaged, the hair arrangement is somewhat archaic, with so-called Gupta curls which are present in eighth to tenth-century eastern Indian sculpture.[204] The sculptures are surrounded by vertical columns of retinue figures painted on either side, four per column, and eight per deity. Bodhisattvas alternate with handsomely ornamented offering goddesses such as Vajralāsyā facing the Buddha (Fig. 5.158). Heller tentatively concludes that "each family is represented by a sculpture and by mural paintings of four goddesses and four Bodhisattvas, the latter selected among the eight Bodhisattvas and the 16 *vajrasattva/mahābodhisattva*."[205] This is thus both triadic and with some of the deities of the Vajradhātu mandala in an implicit mandala arrangement around central sculptures, much like (in the forms and the identities of the deities) both Chyiwang Cave 79 and Malakartse Khar stupa. Luczanits notes the heavy shading and considers the Tholing stupa and the nearby Gyatsa Lhakhang "foremost" among the west Tibetan sites representative of the Kashmiri style.[206] Heller also considers that these paintings are likely to have been the work of Kashmiri artists.[207] Luczanits feels they were probably constructed in

200 Heller, "Preliminary Remarks," 47, 64.

201 A number of excellent scholars conflate and Vajrapāṇi and Vajrasattva, even in contexts such as the eight bodhisattvas. I am not comfortable with such an equation. To be sure, they have some shared chareacteristics, but separate histories.Vajrapāṇi can be traced back to Kushan times while Vajrasattva is a creature of tantric teachings. They both hold the vajra, invariably, and Vajrapāṇi *may* hold a bell, which is invariable for Vajrasattva who is nearly always in a peaceful form while Vajrapāṇi assumes a wrathful form as often as a peaceful one. Only Vajrapāṇi serves as a gate guardian, and only Vajrasattva is promoted to Ādibuddha status. That they both belong to the *vajrakula* is axiomatic, but that is a distinction shared with many other deities. Vajrasattva is properly white in color. To equate Vajrapāṇi with Vajrasattva is no more viable than not distinguishing Vajrasattva from Vajradhara—both holding vajra and bell—or for that matter, Vajrapāṇī and Vajradhara—both are blue and hold the vajra.

202 Ibid., 58–64.

203 Phun-tshogs-rnam-rgyal and Zhang, *Tuo lin Si*, 130–31.

204 Linrothe, *Ruthless Compassion*, fig. 101.

205 Heller, "Preliminary Remarks," 64.

206 Luczanits, "Styles in Western Himalayan Art," 134.

207 Heller, "Preliminary Remarks," 44, 67.

the first half of the eleventh century,[208] a date with which Heller concurs. She has identified many of the sponsors as belonging to the *'hrugs wer* family to which Rinchen Zangpo belonged, and while his name does not show up among the site inscriptions to which she had access, Heller proposes that "this *mchod rten* may have been created to honour the memory of Ye she 'od on the occasion of the *dgongs rdzogs rjes dran*, the religious rites conducted on the death anniversary, celebrated a year after his death, *c.* 1025."[209] The basis for this conjecture is mainly a general concurrence of dates and the thematic involvement of Vairocana. She cites the *Sarvadurgatipariśodhana* and especially the *Vairocanābhisaṃbodhi Sūtra*, which is a largely *trikula* text of early Esoteric Buddhism.

Tabo has been well studied[210] and already mentioned repeatedly. Its founding is generally accepted as dating to 996 by the consecrated lama-king, Lha Lhama Yeshe O (ye shes 'od), and its renovations by the great nephew of Yeshe O, Changchub O (byang chub 'od) completed in 1042. The two dates create essential benchmarks for the history of art in the region. The entry hall dates to the founding and its murals appear in a relatively naïve local style derived ultimately from the Kashmiri mode and other sources. The Cella is triadic in arrangement, and the three sculptures there are rather more sophisticated than the paintings. The Assembly Hall is the result of the 1042 renovations. It forms an implicit Vajradhātu *mahāmaṇḍala*. Both iconographically and stylistically, the program of art reflects the direct impact of Kashmiri scholars and artists involved with the local scholars and artists of the eleventh century. This is visible in the strong Kashmiri-style characteristics, with delicate shading and tripartite torsos.

The Nyag Lhakhang Kharpo is dated by Pritzker on the basis of similarity with Tabo to the second quarter of the eleventh century.[211] However, there are two very different formal modes at the site. One does indeed seem in tune with the earlier, pre-renovation paintings of Tabo Assembly Hall and Cella. The Buddha Śākyamuni with an assembly of monks on the north wall at Nyag Lhakhang Kharpo may very well be early eleventh century.[212] However, the visual feel of the elaborate Dharmadhātu Vāgīśvara Mañjuśrī mandala assembly on the south wall is quite different.[213] Although as Pritzker points out, they have much in common with the Tabo murals, at the same time the figures have almost baroquely high foreheads. The offering goddesses' hairlines end in an exaggerated, nearly pointed oval, while the male *vajra*-bodhisattvas have very high flat foreheads and facial

208 Luczanits, "From Kashmir to Western Tibet," 112–14.

209 Heller, "Preliminary Remarks," 69.

210 Klimburg-Salter, *Tabo*; Luczanits, *Buddhist Sculpture in Clay*, 33–56.

211 Pritzker, "Wall Paintings of Nyag Lhakhang Kharpo," 112. For images, see also Zhang and Huo, *Bod kyi mdzes rtsal kun btus*, pls. 1–11, and Sichuan Daxue Zongguo Zangxue Yanjiu Suo, "Xizang Ali Xiangquan he Liuyu Kazi hegu Fojiao Weicun de Kaogu Diaocha yu Yanjiu," pls. 2–10. Unfortunately, I learned of and gained access to the recent publication edited by Christian Jahoda and Christiane Kalantari, *Early West Tibetan Buddhist Monuments: Architecture, Art, History and Texts* (Vienna: Austrian Academy of Sciences, 2021) only during the process of final publication preparation. Although too late to have incorporated their insights into this study, several essays look to be very pertinent especially to this chapter as well as to 3 and 4.

212 Ham, *Guge—Ages of Gold*, 153.

213 Ibid., 156–58.

features pushed down into the lower third of the face.[214] This is not found among the Tabo Vajradhātu paintings, but more closely resembles the shape of the faces in the Vajraguhya mandala on the second storey of the Alchi Sumtsek.[215] Some of those goddesses also have similarly striped scarves,[216] not found on the Tabo goddesses. One of Luczanits's criteria for dating is the greater or lesser prominence of the Dharmadhātu Vāgīśvara Mañjuśrī mandala. He argues that it has a relatively minor presence in the Tabo Dukhang which features the Vajradhātu *mahāmaṇḍala* and only comes to prominence in the late eleventh and twelfth centuries.[217] That is also visible as a trend at west Tibetan sites, rare at the beginning of the relative chronology, invariable at the end. In that case, the Nyag Lhakhang Kharpo's main composition on the south wall may be rather later than the Tabo renovation paintings. Indeed, examining the left side of the Śākyamuni assembly with the other type of composition painted in a completely different palette and background color, one notices that the latter appears to have been added to and fitted around the preexisting assembly composition.

The sculptures at the Lalung Serkhang (lha lung gser khang) have been treated in some detail.[218] The four-fold Vairocana chapel is difficult to date since the sculptures, though early, have been restored and there are no original mural paintings to go by. The Lalung Serkang is unusual in both form-idiom and in its program, which is basically triadic. The murals, including those depicting the sponsors have been repainted, apparently retracing the original themes to the extent possible.[219] Although now brightly colored, the quality of the pigments used was extremely low, and whatever subtlety they might once have had is gone.[220] The sculptures are intriguing, for the forms suggests in places a sensibility more eastern Indian (Bihar or Bengal) than Kashmiri. Luczanits places them quite late; though locally believed to be late tenth or early eleventh, they are probably late twelfth century in date.

The Dungkar Valley's temple ruins on the mesa in front of the Chyiwang caves (Fig. 5.159) and those of Basgo (see Fig. 5.47) may be introduced as examples of early Vajradhātu sculptural mandalas. Seated deities were attached to their walls. Another site in Ladakh with intriguing remains along the same lines is that of Nyarma (Fig. 5.160). Not much survives in the extant buildings but inner enclosure walls have "the remains of former clay sculptures in the form of fragmentary aureoles. These fragments

214 Ibid., 158.

215 Goepper and Poncar, *Alchi*, 203–7.

216 Ibid., 205, 220.

217 Luczanits, *Buddhist Sculpture in Clay*, 72.

218 Ibid., 89–106; Di Mattia, "Divine Palaces of the Buddha."

219 Neuwirth, "Temple of Lalung," 283.

220 See reproductions in Ham and Stirn, *Forgotten Gods of Tibet*, 133–38; Beck, *Tibet–Guge*, 156–61.

Fig. 5.159 Ruined shrine on the mesa of Dungkar Valley, Ngari, west Tibet, with the remains of nimbi for sculptural deity depictions. Photo 2007.

Fig. 5.160 Ruined shrine at Nyarma, Ladakh, with remains of nimbi behind standing sculptural deity depictions. Photo 2006.

Fig. 5.161 Ruined shrine above Tholing Monastery, Ngari, west Tibet, with the remains of nimbi for standing sculptural deity depictions. Photo 2005.

are no doubt of considerable antiquity."[221] In fact, they closely resemble the fragments of similarly standing (but probably later) sculptures above Tholing (Fig. 5.161).[222] At both sites, the nimbus around the head is distinguished from the body aureole which goes behind the head nimbus. This is all the more intriguing since, as all commentators never fail to point out, Nyarma and Tholing are two of the three somewhat more convincing attributions to their founding by Rinchen Zangpo in his biographies.[223] Regardless, the fact that the Nyarma monastery is mentioned in relation to the early training of the founder of the Dukhang at Alchi, Kaldan Sherap (skal ldan shes rab), also testifies to its earliness.

The Translator's Temple at Nako in Kinnaur, "the oldest monument in the village,"[224] is attributed by Luczanits to the "first decades of the 12th century at the earliest,"[225] in part because of the south wall with its Dharmadhātu Vāgīśvara Mañjuśrī mandala.[226] Nako's Upper Temple "may be roughly attributed to the middle of the 12th century at the earliest."[227] These two Nako shrines are significant for containing "fully developed mandalas with gates and a fire-circle"[228] and even considered the earliest mandalas preserved as wall paintings.[229]

The Dungkar caves have been attributed to the end of the twelfth century by Klimburg-Salter and compared with similarly dated caves at Yulin.[230] Pritzker also dates them to the twelfth century.[231] Neumann attributes them to the end of the eleventh century,[232] but that might be because, as discussed above, he equates the early caves at "Piyang" (i.e. Chyiwang) with the Dungkar caves, even suggesting that the same artists or workshop produced them[233] and so assigns them all such an early date. Luczanits recognizes that Dungkar Cave One is earlier than the mandala ceiling cave: "Cave One was probably constructed first as it also contains the narrative of the Life of the Buddha."[234] He assigns a later date to Dungkar in general, and provides iconographic reasons: "a late date for Dungkar is also suggested by the iconography of the temples, not only because of the prominence given to Mañjuśrī, but also from the representation of two Guhyasamājamaṇḍala on the main wall of Cave 1, the first and probably the only representation of this theme in early West Tibetan art."[235]

As for Dungkar Cave 2, Luczanits observes that the painters and the sculptors came from different traditions, and that a "date any earlier than the middle of the 12th century appears to be impossible."[236] He thus sees it

221 Luczanits, *Buddhist Sculpture in Clay*, 30. See also Neuwirth and Auer, *Ancient Monastic Complexes*, 115–165.

222 Phun-tshogs-rnam-rgyal and Zhang Jianlin *Tuo Lin Si*, 82, 85; Beck, *Tibet–Guge*, 8, upper left.

223 Snellgrove and Skorupski 1977: 4, 15, 19; Tucci 1932 [1988]: 62–65.

224 Luczanits, "Nako Monuments in Context," 22.

225 Luczanits, *Buddhist Sculpture in Clay*, 84.

226 For detailed photographs of the murals, see Ham, *Guge—Ages of Gold*, 88–133. For Nako in general, see Krist, *Nako*.

227 Ham, *Guge—Ages of Gold*, 88.

228 Ibid., 81.

229 Luczanits, "On the Earliest Mandalas in a Buddhist Context"; Ham, *Guge—Ages of Gold*, 134–46. In the 2016 examination of the early temples at Nako, Luczanits is less specific about their dating, stating that "the earliest phase of the Noko monuments can safely be placed between the two benchmark monuments of early Buddhist art in the Western Himalayas, the Tabo Main Temple (1042) and the three-storeyed Temple at Alchi (early thirteenth century), also known as the Alchi Sumtsek (*gSum brtsegs*)"; Luczanits, "Nako Monuments in Context," 22. For Nako, see also Kerin, *Art and Devotion*; Krist and Bayerová, *Heritage Conservation and Research in India*; and Krist, *Nako*.

230 Klimburg-Salter, "Dung dkar/Phyi dbang, West Tibet," 344.

231 Pritzker, "Preliminary Report"; Pritzker, "Wall Paintings of Nyag Lhakhang Kharpo," 105.

232 Neumann, "Wall Paintings of Western Tibet," 75–76.

233 Neumann, "Cave of the Offering Goddesses," 56–57.

234 Luczanits, *Buddhist Sculpture in Clay*, 313n335; see also Kalantari and Allinger, "Spiritual Quest of the Buddha in the Dungkar Cave Temple."

235 Luczanits, *Buddhist Sculpture in Clay*, 118.

236 Ibid.

as contemporaneous with most of the Alchi group shrines. The Alchi group (including Alchi Dukhang, the Sumtsek, the Mangyu complex, Sumda Chung, Saspotse, and Skyu) has been repeatedly mentioned in the course of this and the previous chapter. The Sumtsek, with its date of the early thirteenth century based on the inclusion within its lineage of Drigungpa Jigten Gonpo ('bri gung pa 'jig rten mgon po[237]), marks a heuristic end point for Table 5.1. Luczanits places Mangyu at ca. 1175, between the Dukhang and the Sumtsek, and the same makes sense for Sumda Chung, Saspotse, and Skyu.[238]

Based on these assessments of trends in west Tibetan and western Himalayan art and iconography of early Esoteric Buddhism, then, **Table 5.1** attempts to assemble a relative chronology with the two sites of MkK stupa and Chyiwang 79 included. This ordering leaves aside the various dates that have been tentatively assigned to the sites, but respects as much as possible the relative ordering of the sites, as outlined above. The table then tabulates the main iconographic program and the type of mandala if any. From this we can extract a few trends which tend to support those identified by Luczanits's criteria. They are not even, regular or exact, but, as one would expect in historical phenomena, rather widely spaced, overlapping tendencies that fade or become more distinct over time. First, the *trikula* system of organizing an iconographic program appears very early, but is eventually discarded. Even on the first floor of the Sumtsek, where there are three bodhisattvas, proffering a perfect opportunity to use the three-family system as compositional principle, we find a different triune, that of body, speech, and mind, used instead. The overall trend mirrors the development of Tantric Buddhism in India in general.

A second tendency is for the increasing prominence of the Dharmadhātu Vāgīśvara Mañjuśrī mandala (DVMm) and, as Tribe has documented,[239] of Mañjuśrī in all forms. At first, as at the Tabo Dukhang, the DVMm takes a subordinate role to the Vajradhātu *mahāmaṇḍala*, but over time becomes not only paired with the latter, but even, as at Dungkar Cave 2, replaces the Vajradhātu in a sense. The Vajradhātu is remarkably stable and important in this period, though it should be remembered that on the one hand there are many variations of the mandala explained in the STTS, and on the other that Vairocana often switches positions with Akṣobhya. This change is prefigured in the later sections of the STTS itself, but both of them will soon be nearly replaced *in toto* at the center of shrines and *maṇḍalas* by

237 See discussion in Linrothe, "Dating the Mangyu Style"; Luczanits, "Early Buddhist Heritage of Ladakh Reconsidered," 73; Luczanits, *Alchi*.

238 Luczanits, *Buddhist Sculpture in Clay*, 164; Luczanits, "Styles in Western Himalayan Art," 135–36.

239 Tribe, *Tantric Buddhist Practice in India*; Tribe, "Mañjuśrī as Ādibuddha."

Fig. 5.162 Conservation of "Alchi Group" type mandala murals at Sumda Chung, Ladakh. Photo 2008.

more contemporary developments of Indian Esoteric Buddhism, especially by Cakrasaṃvara and Hevajra but also Guhyasamāja and Vajrabhairava.

Third, regarding the type of mandala present, in the earliest phases, if there was one at all, it was implicit. In later shrines, the "standard *maṇḍala* depiction" was inevitable, though implicit mandalas were found side-by-side. In fact, as the Tabo Serkhang and Tsaparang Lhakhang Kharpo (to cite just two prominent examples), the implicit mandala (i.e., "*maṇḍala* assembly") was never completely abandoned. Yet in the early phases represented in Table 5.1, they did not supplement the standard depiction but were almost the *only* representation of the mandala available or considered suitable. This obviously changed over the course of the period covered, in the early twelfth century to judge by the conventional dating of Nako. There was no turning back, and the Alchi group has spectacular, large-sized examples on side walls (Fig. 5.162), even while retaining the implicit arrangement of sculptures in the niche on the main wall (see Figs. 5.32, 5.74).

Within this developmental trajectory, Chyiwang Cave 79 stands out as distinctly transitional. Besides the implicit mandalas featuring offering goddesses and wrathful gate guardians, it features three *maṇḍalic* groupings, of Vairocana with eight bodhisattvas, female figures, and five *krodha-vighnāntaka*s (see Figs. 5.113, 5.129, 5.142). These are not yet "standard depictions," since they do not represent gates or indications of a palace (*kuṭāgāra*) at the center,

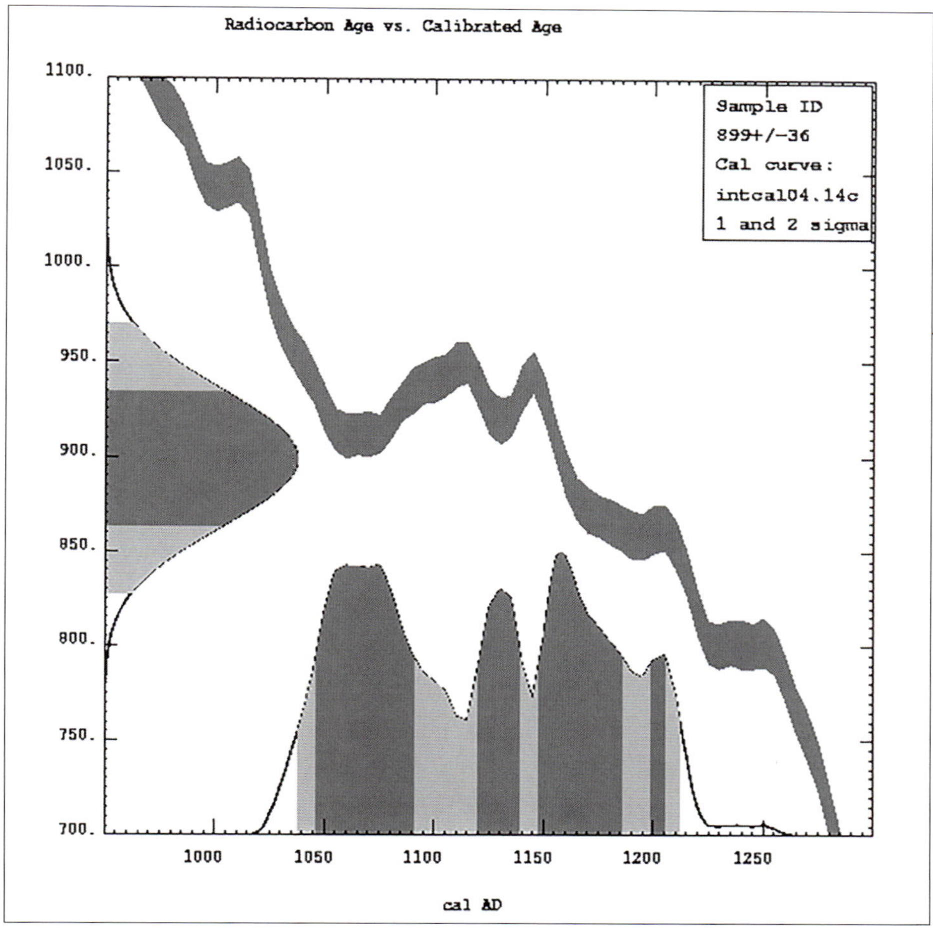

Fig. 5.163 Results from Carbon 14 test in 2007 of organic material used to prepare walls for murals, found attached to mural fragments on the floor at Malakartse Khar stupa.

but they are arranged geometrically closer to the configuration attained in the standard depiction than is found in the implicit mandala. This lends confidence to Chyiwang 79's position in the table, before the introduction of the standard mandala. In turn, because of the many similarities discovered and already discussed between the layout of Chyiwang Cave 79 and the Malakartse Khar stupa, the latter is therefore located in the table just before Chyiwang, reflecting its less-developed regime of mandalas.

Both the Malakartse Khar stupa and Chyiwang Cave 79 have been placed around 1100 by Luczanits.[240] As Table 5.1 reflects, that would be after the early monuments at Tholing and Tabo and before those of Dungkar and Alchi. It is also well within the results of Carbon-14 tests of samples taken off the floor at the Malakartse Khar stupa, kindly arranged by Prof. Mark Aldenderfer, now Dean of the Social Sciences, Humanities, and Arts at the University of California, Merced, but then of the University of Arizona, where the testing was done (Fig. 5.163). The tests used organic material, straw, or grass, part of the preparation for the murals on the north wall. At the time of the tests, the results established a date that calibrates to CE 1038–1213 at the 95% confidence interval, and was interpreted by Aldenderfer, "as being mid/late 11th c. to early 12th AD."[241] More recently, the interpretation of the data was updated, to 1040–1219 CE with a median age estimate of 1146 CE.[242] Given the constantly shifting understanding—not just in the humanities—I do not consider this as any more definitive than the judgments based on other criteria (formal analysis, iconographic development, etc.). The fact that the date ranges derived from completely different methodologies (visual, iconographic, C14 radiocarbon analysis) roughly coincide is itself heartening.

240 Luczanits, "Styles in Western Himalayan Art," 137; Luczanits, "Beneficial to See," 134.

241 Mark Aldenderfer, personal communication October 2, 2007.

242 Aldenderfer wrote, "there are two possible probabilities of the true date: 1040–1106 CE at 0.37/100 and 1114–1219 CE at 0.63/100. This situation makes interpretation difficult. So the calculated median date of 1146 CE captures this uncertainty" (personal communication September 24, 2020). For the revised "true date," he cited Reimer et al., "The IntCal20 Northern Hemisphere Radiocarbon Age Calibration Curve."

Conclusion: Toward an Iconology of Form-idiom

It is also possible to test the relative order of the sites in Table 5.1 on the basis of formal characteristics and to create groupings based on their presumed fidelity to Kashmiri models. On its own, however, this does not lead to a straightforward development, since, for example, there is a resurgence of Kashmiri characteristics in the Alchi group, particularly in the Sumtsek, which surely must have been produced with the involvement of twelfth- to early thirteenth-century Kashmiri painters.[243] By contrast, the slightly earlier or contemporaneous Dungkar Cave 2 has painted figures with a completely different scheme of rendering anatomy, one which minimizes shading but exalts colorful, even painterly, patterning. I would consider this the domestication or localization of the Kashmiri mode; it is worth recalling that Dungkar is that much more distant from Kashmir than Zangskar. Given the variants of the Kashmiri mode and its *kha che lugs* iterations, it might also be wise to acknowledge that the variety of levels of specialized patronage (which could affect the quality of the artists and pigments involved) interacted with the background, the training, and the abilities of the available artists involved. This calculus results in a condition of complexity beyond our abilities to definitively unravel at this point, if ever. Since each analyst of style tends to see different things, and see the same things differently, perhaps the preponderant reliance on iconographic benchmarks can help compensate for this surrender to relativism.

In general, I agree with Luczanits that the textual record of Rinchen Zangpo having returned to Gugé with Kashmiri artists has become a convenient but overused trope.[244] However, I do not believe that all the art of this period was produced by indigenous local artists. Nor is it merely a matter of assigning the high-quality art to Kashmiri artists and the lower quality to western Himalayan or west Tibetan artists. We know from the *Citrasūtra* that contemporaneous commentators (no later than the ca. seventh century) had already observed that there was a range of (Kashmiri) artists producing painting, including the *daiśika* (the local or provincial), the *nāgara* (the urban professional), and the mixed.[245] We should expect that the voracious demand for "authentic" Buddhism in west Tibet and the western Himalaya in the late tenth through the early thirteenth century tallied with the demand for "authentic" Buddhist art. This imperative on the part of Himalayan Buddhists intersected with economic and religious factors in Kashmir, inducing artists to travel to these neighboring regions.

243 I believe this is true of some other murals in the Alchi group, as argued in Linrothe, "Skirting the Bodhisattva."

244 Luczanits, "Styles in Western Himalayan Art," 134.

245 Mukherji, *The* Citrasūtra *of the* Viṣṇudharmottara Purāṇa, 159–64.

Zangskar, of course, is along the most direct routes to Spiti, to Ngari, from and back to Kashmir. It should not surprise us then, if a provincial, *daiśika* artist, or pair or group, were commissioned at Malakartse Khar (itself literally along a trade route that led to—or from—Kashmir via the Suru Valley) to create the sculptures and the paintings in the stupa connected to the fort at some point in the late eleventh or early twelfth century.

That, at any rate, is part of my speculative conclusion and imagined scenario about how the Malakartse Khar stupa paintings were created, based on the formal, iconographic, and comparative perspectives laid out above. Such an origin was by a relatively conservative or perhaps versatile workshop, traveling in order to take advantage of new sponsorship in Zangskar of elite Buddhists who plausibly had themselves migrated into Zangskar from west Tibet in the train of its invading army as discussed in chapter 1. The art on offer, though showing awareness of material culture such as textiles and other exotica prized in Kashmir, might not have been at the cutting edge of artistic and religious trends in more metropolitan Kashmir. Instead, it fit—or was adapted to fit—the context of the Gugé-Purang rulers' antipathy toward certain types of what is often characterized crudely as more explicitly sexualized Tantric Buddhist teachings,[246] as reflected also in the tradition of Atīśa's finding Rinchen Zangpo's Buddhism somewhat lacking, recounted in various versions of their respective biographies. In other words, as I envision it, a somewhat provincial traveling group of artists from Kashmir found a welcoming match in a group of wealthy and devout but somewhat sheltered sponsors. The result was a monument created in a transitional moment in the evolution of Esoteric Buddhism that foregrounded the older, more conservative, *trikula* scheme, utilized in a less than flamboyant manner the nascent *pañcakula* themes, and eschewed completely the latest trends related to Cakrasamvara and Hevajra (Phase Three). This adequately suited the tenor of that moment, which was fleeting and would shortly be superseded.

Yet in a wider perspective than that of west Tibet and the western Himalaya alone, the pattern exhibited by these shrines of the *trikula* scheme surviving the introduction of the *pañcakula* is not unique. As early as the ninth century in Tang China, a Chinese monk named Haiyuan, who was aware of and discussed the teachings of Amoghavajra (705–774) on both the STTS and the *Vairocanābhisaṃbodhi Sūtra*, also praises the *Susiddhikara Sūtra* teachings of the three categories, *buddha*, *padma*, and *vajra* as of

246 Karmay, "Ordinance of lHa Bla-ma Ye-shes-'od"; Karmay, "Recently Discovered *rNam thar* of Lha bla ma Ye shes 'od"; Karmay, "Decree of lHa Bla ma Ye shes 'od"; Dalton, *Taming of the Demons*, 97–109. Dalton refers to "a new conservatism" taking hold after the tenth century with "the return of monastic centers of authority" (ibid., 46). Yeshe O "was probably not wholly against the tantras" (ibid., 105) mainly against the most blatantly transgressive, which is admittedly the case with the later Phase 3 tantras.

equal importance with those in the other two Esoteric Buddhist texts.[247] The Japanese monk Enchin (814–891) received from a teacher in direct line with the Indian master Amoghavajra (705–774) the rituals and the teachings of all three texts, and Hunter understands him as writing that "the *susiddhi* rite was considered to be the most important of these rites."[248]

> The *Susiddhikara Sūtra* was important in the Tang Chinese esoteric school because it detailed the precepts of the esoteric school and provided precise directives for the threefold rites of the families of the *buddha, padma* and *vajra* that were respectively categorized as supreme, middling and inferior, as well as for the construction of *maṇḍala* and the performace of consecration rites.[249]

It was translated into Tibetan (as *legs par grub pa*) early enough to be included in the Dankar (ldan-kar) catalog of the eight century.[250] It names Hayagrīva as the representative wrathful protector for the *padma* family,[251] and has interesting directional instructions for the alignment of the three families with the (proto-) mandala: "Place the deities of the Buddha Family right along the east side of the inner enclosure, place the deities of the Lotus Family right along the north side, place the deities of the Vajra Family right along the south side."[252] The Malakartse Khar stupa most likely places the *buddha* family in the west, not the east, as does the Chyiwang Cave 79, but in both cases, that may be because of site limitations, the alignment of the cliffs, and the consequent placement of the entrance in the east and the main wall in the west. However, the *padma* and the *vajra* locations at both sites are in accord with the *Susuddhikara Sūtra* prescriptions. At any rate, this helps expand the context in which to place these two Esoteric Buddhist sites and understand their synchronization of three- and five-family schemes.

We are still left without a specific rationale for the placement of the Malakartse Khar stupa so close to, but not within, the fort. Given the fundamental association of stupas with funerary commemorations, it would seem most obvious that it was erected to house relics of either a ruler or of an *ācārya*. Since the early west Tibetan rulers were revered as *lha lamas*—that is, ordained royal figures with both religious and political charisma—and that too, with a history of investments in the acquisition of Kashmiri Buddhist art, it is not impossible that it was built to commemorate that type of authority figure, a relative, or their representative in Zangskar.

247 Hunter, "Faquan's Transmission of the *Susiddhi* Category of the Esoteric Buddhist Teachings."

248 Ibid., 59.

249 Ibid., 89.

250 Lalou, "Les Textes Bouddhiques au temps du roi Khri-Sroṅ-lde-bcan," no. 320.

251 Giebel, *Two Esoteric Sutras*, 131.

252 Ibid., 303.

In conclusion, the close examination of the remaining murals and the layout of the Malakartse Khar stupa interior, coordinated with the comparison of the slightly later, more "advanced" (doctrinally speaking) Chyiwang Cave 79 program, along with a broader overview of western Himalayan and west Tibetan sites yield the following hypotheses. The three walls with central sculptures are coordinated by an overarching theme that united the three main sculptures (now destroyed), one on each wall except the entry wall. That theme reflected a relatively early triadic, three-family organization of the Esoteric Buddhist pantheon, but in a late, transitional phase. The largest sculpture on the main wall of the stupa depicted the eight-armed Mañjuśri as the Ādi-Buddha. Above him at the top of the wall was probably Mañjuśrī-jñānasattva but possibly Śākyamuni Buddha in the *bhūmisparśa mudrā*, against a tree-like nimbus that imaginatively referred to the *bodhi* tree at Bodhgaya. Together the two represented the *buddha* family. On the left wall, surrounded by painted female offering deities, was Vajrasattva representing the *vajra* family. Opposite him on the right wall, was Avalokiteśvara, seated with one leg down, his sculptural lotus echoed by a version painted at his left shoulder on the nimbus on the wall behind him. He and his crew represent the *padma* family.

The proposed date is derived from the analysis of the form-idioms and themes in the context of the trajectory of development in western Himalayan and west Tibetan Esoteric Buddhist art. The paintings fall into the late eleventh or very early twelfth century, in the early range of the Carbon-14 test results. The patrons were based in Zangskar—probably in Zangla—and had wealth, status, and authority derived from an elevated level of rulership. They may have been indigenous Zangskaris who emulated more influential rulers from west Tibet. Alternatively, they may have been descendants within a generation or two of those deputed by the west Tibetan rulers as royal representatives in conquered territory. Originally occupying Zangskar through military force, these deputies gradually integrated into the elite stratum of independent Zangskar society even while maintaining a fading ideological loyalty to Ngari culture claiming descent and legitimacy from the centuries-earlier central Tibetan empire.

As for the artists, I see them as creative but somewhat provincial travelling artists from neighboring Kashmir. In the era proposed, competition for commissions within Kashmir must have been fierce, and dominated by the sophisticated court-trained artists like those who later painted in the

Alchi Sumtsek in the early thirteenth century. By that time, sponsorship of Buddhist and Brahmanical Hindu monuments within Kashmir was starting to erode for socio-economic reasons, sending even the best artists into adjoining regions for work. Earlier, in the eleventh and twelfth century, demand for Kashmiri trained artists in places like Ladakh and Zangskar, in Spiti and in Ngari, would have been able to draw competent but not the most prized artist groups eastward, in search of commissions. This conjecture—that the Malakartse Khar stupa works were accomplished by second- or third-tier artists, well-trained and practiced but not court-trained—helps explain the look of the surviving murals. They reflect knowledge of Indic metropolitan and Persianate courtly material culture (textiles, ceramics, musical instruments, etc.), competent knowledge of well-honed Phase Two Esoteric Buddhist themes, which were combined with patternized conventions applied somewhat indiscriminately and repeatedly, as almost internalized if not literal stencils.

Such conclusions and speculative reconstructions are, however, of no help in answering other questions. One outstanding one is what was depicted above the ceiling level—a lantern ceiling? Perhaps, but with or without figural decoration? If with, was the missing Akṣobhya the main theme there? Another, perhaps less important query is when, and by whom, were the paintings (and the sculptures?) intentionally damaged or destroyed? These latter questions can probably never by answered, but at least the general outlines of the likely date, artists, sponsors, and nominal subject matter can be established for this distinctive if desolate site.

APPENDIX 5.1: Gallery of textile details from the MkK Stupa murals

Fig. 5.164 Textile pattern on right knee of offering goddess painted at the top left of the south (left) wall of the Malakartse Khar stupa (Fig. 5.82). Photo 2012.

Fig. 5.165 Textile pattern on left knee of offering goddess painted on the left side center of the south (left) wall of the Malakartse Khar stupa (Fig. 5.83). Photo 2012.

Fig. 5.166 Textile pattern on left knee of Vajragītī (Fig. 5.99) on the north wall of the Malakartse Khar stupa. Photo 2012

Fig. 5.167 Textile pattern on the *śāṭī* of offering goddess painted on south (left) wall of the Malakartse Khar stupa (Fig. 5.84). Photo 2012.

Fig. 5.168 Textile pattern on the dhoti of a wrathful deity on the entrance wall at Malakartse Khar stupa (Fig. 5.42). Photo 2012.

Fig. 5.169 Tiger-skin stripes and textile patterns on the dhoti of a wrathful deity (Vajrahūṃkara?) on the entrance wall at Malakartse Khar stupa (Fig. 5.43). Photo 2012.

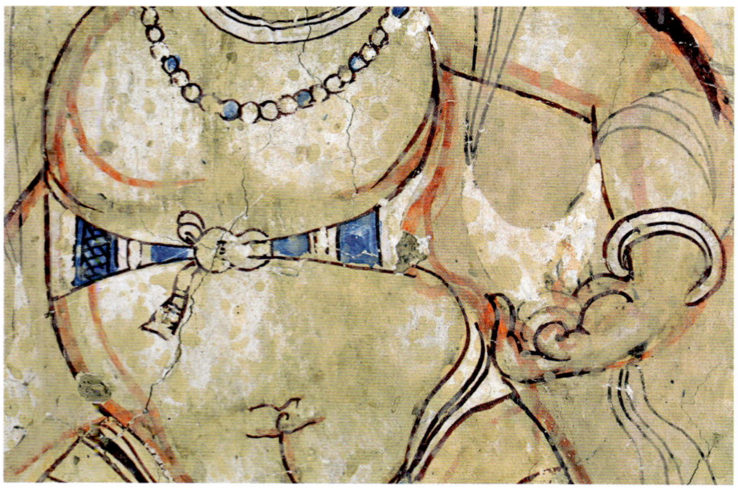

Fig. 5.170 Textile pattern on the chest band of wrathful deity Vajrapāśa (Fig. 5.89) on the north (right) wall of the Malakartse Khar stupa. Photo 2018.

APPENDIX 5.2: Gallery of textile details from the Chyiwang Cave 79 murals

Fig. 5.171 Textile pattern on the robe of a Buddha on the south (left) side wall of Chyiwang Cave 79. Photo 2007.

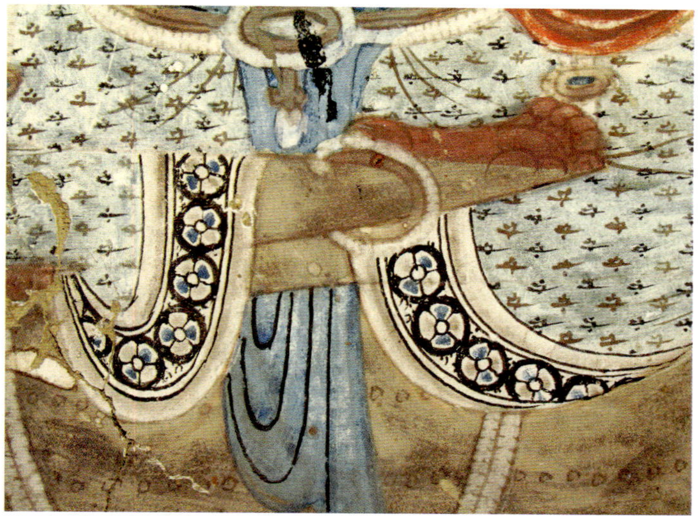

Fig. 5.172 Textile pattern on the *śāṭī* of Vajrapuṣpā (Fig. 5.127), offering goddess painted on south (left) wall of Chyiwang Cave 79. Photo 2007.

Fig. 5.173 Textile pattern on the scarf of Vajrapuṣpā (Fig. 5.127), offering goddess painted on south (left) wall of Chyiwang Cave 79. Photo 2007.

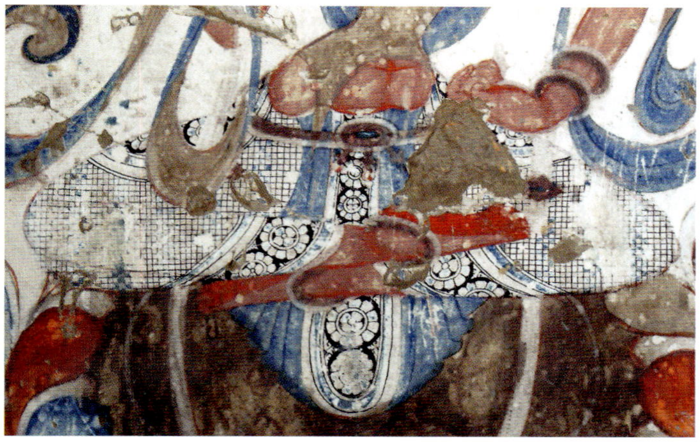

Fig. 5.174 Textile pattern on the *śāṭī* of Vajradīpā/Vajrālokā or Vajradhūpā (Fig. 5.122, right) on the main wall at Chyiwang Cave 79. Photo 2005.

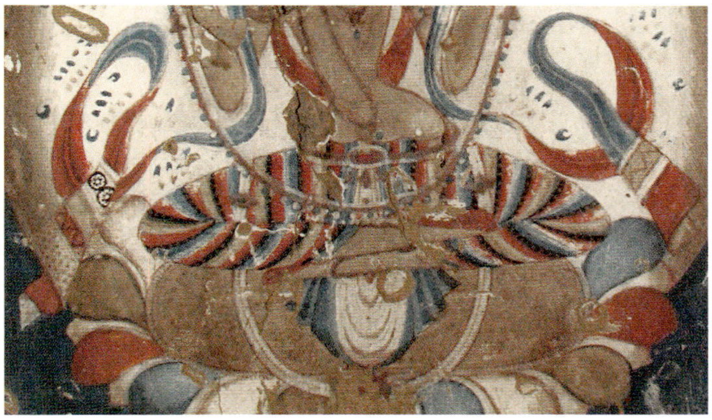

Fig. 5.175 Textile patterns on the right knee and floating scarf of Vajramālā on the south (left) wall of Chyiwang Cave 79. Photo 2005.

APPENDIX 5.3
Gallery of details from the Chyiwang Cave 79 murals (All photos 2007.)

Fig. 5.176 Detail of Vajrasphoṭa (see Fig. 5.121).

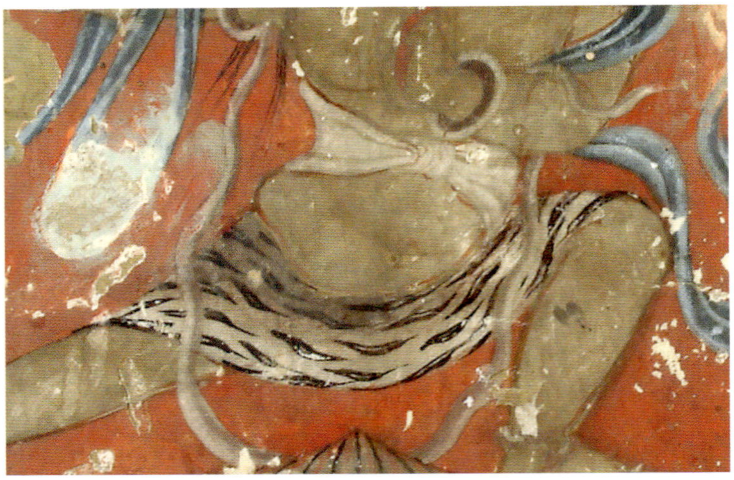

Fig. 5.177 Detail of top center wrathful deity in Figure 5.119. Compare Figure 5.169.

Fig. 5.178 Candelabra-like lamp held by Vajradīpā/ Vajrālokā (see Fig. 5.130).

Fig. 5.179 Horse head of Hayagrīva (see Fig. 5.134).

Fig. 5.180 Parasol (*chattra*) and victory banner (*ketu*) of *aṣṭamaṅgala* (see Fig. 5.132).

Fig. 5.181 Close view of Vajrasphoṭa holding chain (see Fig. 5.128).

More Recent Early Matters

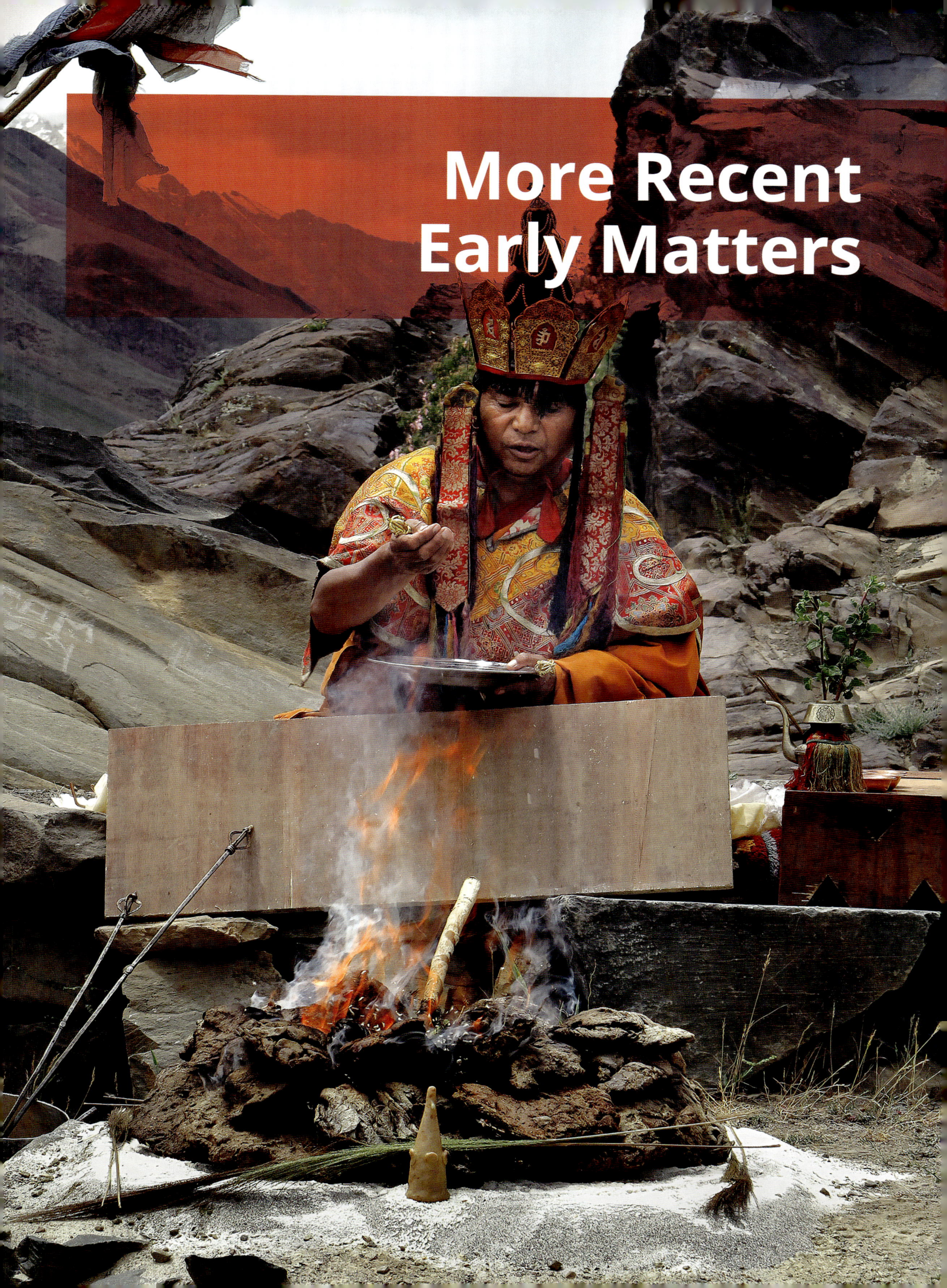

CHAPTER 6

Mahāsiddha Stone Engravings of Tungri Nunnery and Manda Village: Linear and Painterly[1]

More than fifty engraved outline stone sculptures of Mahāsiddhas—out of a set of eighty-four—have been documented in the Zangskar district of Ladakh, in the western Himalaya. They were noticed stacked on a few *maṇi*-walls behind the village of Tungri, below a nunnery on the hill above. Through comparison with other sets of Mahāsiddhas in both Zangskar and Ladakh proper, they probably can be associated with Drukpa artistic activities in Zangskar of the seventeenth or eighteenth century.

Tungri village in Zangskar today boasts a highly regarded and active Gelug nunnery, Tungri Phuntsog Ling, or Chomo Gompa (Fig. 6.1).[2] Some fifteen nuns inhabit a temple above the village, in buildings that locally are believed to have been founded as a monastery by Takstang Repa Ngawang Gyatso (stag tshang ras pa ngag bdang rgya mtsho, 1574–1651). Takstang Repa was a great traveler; originally from central Tibet, he is most renowned in the western Himalaya as the founder of Hemis, Chemre, and Hanlé Monasteries, important Drukpa institutions in Ladakh, and as the personal religious adviser to King Sengge Namgyal (ca. 1570–1642) of Ladakh. He is reputed to have visited Zangskar on his way back from a pilgrimage to Uddayana in the early part of the seventeenth century.[3]

Today, there is little in the nunnery to suggest a Drukpa heritage. The nuns themselves are affiliated with the Gelug lineage, and even though it is one of the two oldest nunneries in Zangskar, as Kim Gutschow points out, both "appear to have been monastic complexes only later occupied by nuns."[4] In 2012, while trekking to Ralakhung village, I camped for the night near Tungri and visited the nunnery. On my way up, I noticed a group of carved stones leaning on and around a *maṇi*-wall next to an old "Kaṇkani" or gateway stupa below the nunnery, just above the upper level of houses in the village (Fig. 6.2). Among the stones were old stupas engraved

1 This chapter began as a talk for The Sixth International Conference on Tibetan Archaeology and Arts in 2015 in Hangzhou China. As with the earlier chapter on Tucci, it was then expanded for the proceedings, which were never published. It was further revised and updated for this context. I benefited from the comments of several participants at the conference, including Deborah Klimburg-Salter and Helmut Neumann, as well as from the late Helen Abbott of the Rubin Museum, and Melissa Kerin who read a pre-conference draft. I also thank Caroline Riegel, Mel Keiser, and Scott Krafft for assistance with and permissions for images; the nuns of Tungri and Gelong Angchug for their assistance in Zangskar; and the Karsha Lonpo and Gelong Angchug for help in deciphering the inscriptions.

2 For more on the nunnery, see the webpages documenting the support activities there of the French hydrologist Caroline Riegel: https://baikal-bangkok.org/media/cms_page_media/103/Thigspa-Ecole-Anglais- 0615.pdf, and https://baikal-bangkok.org/en/organization/donation/. Also Riegel, *Semeuses de Joie*, her book of stunning photographs of the nuns, the nunnery and village of Tungri.

3 Schwieger, "Stag-tshang Ras-pa's Exceptional Life as a Pilgrim"; Jinpa, "Why Did Tibet and Ladakh Clash in the 17th Century?"; Jinpa and Shide, "In Praise of the Incarnation Line of 'Kyabgon Staktsang Rinpoche.'"

4 K. Gutschow, *Being a Buddhist Nun*, 100.

Fig. 6.2 Gateway stupa between Tungri village and Tungri Nunnery, Zangksar. Photo 2012.

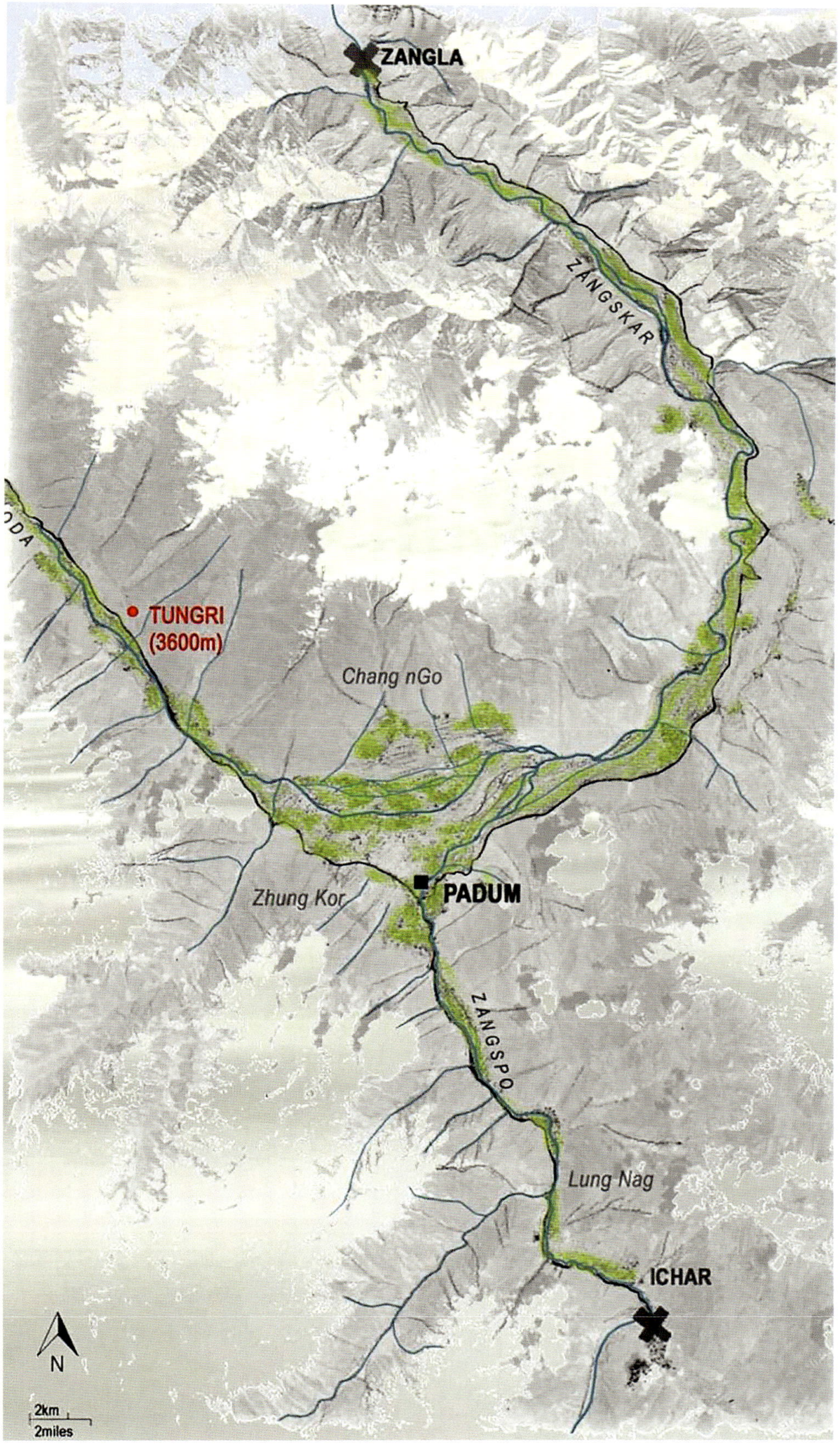

Fig. 6.1 Map by Amandine Lepers indicating Tungri village in Zangksar. From "Thigspa: A Drop of Water for Zangskar," https://baikal-bangkok.org/media/cms_page_media/103/Thigspa-Ecole-Anglais-0615.pdf. Used with the permission of Caroline Riegel.

Fig. 6.3 *Maṇi*-wall with carved stones of various ages at the gateway stupa illustrated in Fig. 6.2. At center is the Mahāsiddha carving depicting Dokaripa (A49, right) and Medhini (A50). Photo 2015.

on flat stones, contemporary prayers chiseled in stone, and pictorial representations of Mahāsiddhas. Some were stacked upon each other, spattered with whitewash, and many in damaged condition (Fig. 6.3). After informing the nuns through their benefactor, Caroline Riegel, of my opinion of the importance of the objects, and that they once had formed a set, Caroline seems to have taken it upon herself to relocate most of them to a *maṇi*-wall adjacent to the nunnery for protection (Fig. 6.4). There I was able to examine them at greater length in the summer of 2015 when I stayed overnight at the nunnery, coinciding with their observation of the Nyungné (snyung gnas) fast and a performance of a *homa* fire ritual to repulse locusts from the local barley fields (Fig. 6.5). I have had the opportunity to study them a few times since, to confirm their continuing presence at the nunnery.

Fig. 6.4 View of the *maṇi*-wall next to the Tungri Nunnery, Zangksar, with many of the Mahāsiddha engraved sculptures after they were brought up from the gateway stupa near the village. Photo 2019.

Fig. 6.5 Gelug monk performing *homa* ritual on 20 July 2015 above Tungri Nunnery, Zangksar. Photo 2015.

The stones are engraved in outline form with the likenesses and the names of the Mahāsiddhas known from the Abhayadattaśrī list of eighty-four Mahāsiddhas.[5] In 2012 only twenty-five figures of siddhas were noticed, of which eighteen could be identified through their iconography or the names that are roughly (and in some cases illegibly) inscribed beneath them. In the summer of 2015 more were found after most of the Mahāsiddhas had been moved and a thorough investigation involving retrieving carved stones from underneath others stacked on top of them was conducted. At present, a few of the larger carved stones remain below the nunnery in the location where I first noticed them. More than forty Mahāsiddhas have been identified at the two locations, mostly on the basis of readable inscriptions.[6] Several of the stones are broken and some have lost or damaged inscriptions. On the other hand, in a few cases the figures are missing but the inscriptions survive. All of the identified siddhas are found in the Abhayadattaśrī list, and while several of them also appear in some of the other well-known lists, notably that of the group of eighty-five known as the "Vajrāsana set," several of the identifiable Tungri Mahāsiddhas are exclusive to the Abhayadattaśrī list.[7] Those include three female Mahāsiddhās (Maṇibhadrā, Mekhalā, and Kanakhalā), Gorakṣa, Kaṅkāripa, Catrapa, Dhobhīpa (Figs. 6.6–6A), Bhandepa, Medhini, Jogipa, Campaka, Bhikṣanapa, Pacaripa, and Sakara. Therefore the identification of the Tungri group as representing the same set of Mahāsiddhas as the received Abhayadattaśrī set can be accepted.

Several sets of painted or sculpted Mahāsiddhas survive in Zangskar, among them mural paintings from the Tonba Lhakhang of Phuktal Monastery of the late fifteenth or early sixteenth century, later murals at Rangdum Monastery, those depicted in a manuscript from Kumik village of the mid-seventeenth century, a painting of the eighteenth century in Ralakhung village (see Figs. 6.20–21), and a partial set of perhaps eighteenth-century outlined engravings on stone near Manda village (Fig. 6.7), only about twelve kilometers northwest of Tungri.[8] (Manda is shown on Map 2 on p. x) Of those, three sets can be securely identified as to which of the two most common sets of Mahāsiddhas they represent, the Abhayadattaśri or the Vajrāsana.[9] The Kumik, Manda, and Ralakhung sets represent the Vajrāsana Mahāsiddha set and share a certain resemblance to each other, as is discussed elsewhere.[10] None of these sets, however, demonstrates any particular resemblance to the ones at Tungri village in the forms or the configuration of the individual characters.

5 Dowman, *Masters of Mahāmudrā*; Linrothe, *Holy Madness*, 195, passim.

6 Forty-one are identified, eleven are unidentified, and three small fragments might be either part of broken ones or the remains of others.

7 On the two lists, see Linrothe, *Holy Madness*, 422–23.

8 Except for the Rangdum murals, examples from these sites are illustrated and discussed in Linrothe 2016.

9 See note 7 above.

10 Linrothe, "Siddhas and Sociality," 188–99.

Fig. 6.6A Stone engraved carving illustrated in Fig. 6.6 with outlines added by Mel Keiser for clarification.

Fig. 6.6 Dhobīpa Mahāsiddha (A28) washing clothes; stone engraved carving at Tungri Nunnery, Zangksar. Photo 2015.

Fig. 6.7 Gelong Angchug, son of the Karsha Lonpo (right), and a young monk of Karsha monastery, Dorje of Phé village, searching through the maṇi-wall at Manda village, Zangksar, for Mahāsiddha engraved carvings. Photo 2015.

Fig. 6.8 Hemis monastery courtyard with Mahāsiddha stone engraved carvings, Ladakh. Photo 2008.

Fig. 6.9 The Yoginī Mahāsiddha Lakṣmīṅkarā (A82) in a cremation ground; stone engraving at Hemis monastery courtyard, Ladakh. Photo 2022.

The Tungri sculptures are, however, quite similar iconographically and expressively to the set of inscribed Abhayadattaśrī Mahāsiddhas preserved in the courtyard of Hemis Monastery (Figs. 6.8–9).[11] Figure 6.9, of one of the four female Mahāsiddhās, Lakṣmīṅkarā, depicts one of the rare unpainted stone engravings at Hemis, which makes its similarity to the Tungri Mahāsiddhas that much more apparent. The similarities include the extensive use of patterns and setting, the inclusion of attendants, subsidiary figures, and identifiable props and attributes. They also share the consistent (though not invariable) placement of the carved names in a special panel or cartouche below or to the side of the composition in which the Tibetan letters are in slight relief. In a few examples where an identifiable siddha is depicted in both the Tungri and Hemis sets, similarities are not so close as to presume the same carver at work. Nevertheless, the correspondence of the Tungri and Hemis engraved sculptures compared with the substantial differences with the other sets supports the possibility of a shared origin within the initial energetic building campaign in support of the Drukpa lineage by either Sengge Namgyal or his son Demchok Namgyal, who ruled in both Zangskar and Spiti beginning in 1647.

A singular aspect of the Tungri Mahāsiddhas is that the figural portrait is accompanied not only by a name but also by a number often to the left of the inscription. See, for example, Figures 6.10–10A, depicting Deṅgipa, where the number thirty-two in Tibetan script is quite clear. The number rarely precisely corresponds to that found in the Tibetan text of the *Grub thob brgyad bcu rtsa bzhi'i lo rgyus*, the *Legends of the Eighty-four Mahāsiddhas* as treated by both Keith Dowman

11 On the Hemis set, see Genoud, *Buddhist Wall-Painting of Ladakh*, 44–48, 77–86. Since Genoud's publication, several more stones with Mahāsiddhas (including Figure 6.9), supplementing the 77 he documented, were found in monastery storage rooms and added to the courtyard display. Several other sets or groups of Mahāsiddhas exist in Ladakh, including painted on the Alchi Sumtsek Mañjuśrī sculpture, in the Alchi Shangrong Shrine, the Lamayuru Sengegang Shrine, the Wanla Sumtsek, Phyang Guru Lhakhang, Saspol caves, Basgo Chambha Lhakhang, and in Stagna Monastery. The relatively small area of Greater Ladakh—including Zangskar—is notably rich in surviving sets of Mahāsiddha murals and cloth paintings extracted from the region or from neighboring Spiti and the TAR portion of Ngari now in Western collections such as the Rubin Museum and the Tucci collections; see Linrothe, *Collecting Paradise*, fig. 3.28; and Klimburg-Salter, *Discovering Tibet*, no. 22.

Fig. 6.10 Deṅgipa Mahāsiddha (A31) pounding rice with a pestle; stone engraved carving at Tungri Nunnery, Zangksar. Photo 2015.

Fig. 6.10A Stone engraved carving illustrated in Fig. 6.10 with outlines added by Mel Keiser for clarification.

and James B. Robinson.[12] Virūpa is a rare example in which both text and sculpture have him at number three. However, where the numbers do not precisely correspond, they are never more than a few numbers off. For example, Maṇibhadrā appears at number sixty-five (A65)[13] in the Abhayadattaśrī text but at sixty-eight in the sculpture; Medhini is A50 but number fifty-two in the Tungri set. Mīnapa (Matsyendranāth) is number seven at Tungri, but in the text is A8; Tilopa is A22 but the number twenty-three appears in Tibetan on the sculpture. This indicates to me that the sculptor had access to a text or list that was related to but a variant of the standard Abhayadattaśrī text that has come down to us. Assuming that such divergences were not mistakes by the sculptor, the consistent presence of the number as well as the name of the Mahāsiddha is suggestive of an insistence on preserving the order of the Mahāsiddha engraved sculptures, and also may have been reflected in the original arrangement, about which we speculate below.

Could the fact that the Tungri Mahāsiddhas representations are not just named but numbered—and that they reproduce the Sanskrit phonetic of the names rather than the Tibetan language translation—have dating implications? Are the numbers indications of earliness in terms of date, or unfamiliarity with the group? It is possible, and one might speculate that if a (lost) text with the same numbering and phonetic transliteration systems were to appear, and could be dated, it might give a benchmark dating. I see the consistent use of the Sanskrit name as one among several other symptoms—the use of the numbers, the detailed narrative elements—as reflections of a studious, even academic interest in the Mahāsiddha themes on the part of the creator. In other words,

12 Dowman, *Masters of Mahāmudrā*; Abhayadatta, *Buddha's Lions*.

13 In what follows, a number preceded by the letter *A* refers to the Abhayadattśrī list, and one preceded by a *V* refers to the Vajrāsana list.

it might rather tell us something about the character of the creator(s), about their antiquarian or specialized interests, rather than about the time of creation. Sanskrit studies were, and are, neither universal nor unheard of into the nineteenth century and beyond, particularly for Tibetan Buddhist scholars in Ladakh and Zangskar.[14]

Another point of interest is that for the most part, the names are uniformly Tibetan transliterations of the Sanskrit names, not translations. That is not always the case for sets of Mahāsiddhas in Ladakh and Zangskar—the nearby Manda village set of Mahāsiddha sculptures often features the Tibetan translations of the names, such as Serlingpa instead of Suvarṇadvīpa, and Lüdrup instead of Nāgārjuna. At Tungri, the combination of the presence of numbers indicating an order and the consistent transcription of Sanskrit names, which must have meant little to ordinary Tibetans unversed in Sanskrit, might reflect "scholarly" specialists' interests on the part of the maker or main sponsor of the Tungri sculptures.

Other aspects worth noting are the great variety of stone colors (gray, brown, reddish, yellowish, etc.), the relative densities of the composition of the rocks, their varied textures, hardness, size, and shapes. The stones were not standardized in size, color, texture or shape, which apparently were dictated by the flat stones found, selected, and utilized.[15] This probably indicates that there was not necessarily a single quarry or source for the stones. If there had been a highly organized or systematic aspect to the project, under royal or monastic leadership for example, one might expect greater uniformity. The gathering of such disparate stones suggests a more random effort by a few individuals, but this is only inference. At the same time, the design and the engraving does appear to be relatively uniform. Where the size and shape of the stone allowed, more than one scene related to a single Mahāsiddha is included, or, in several cases, two Mahāsiddhas are depicted on a single stone. The latter is the case with Dhokaripa (A49) and Medini (A50), barely visible at the center of Figure 6.4. In terms of the carved images, there are at least two different scales. Some of the more well-known Mahāsiddhas, like Virūpa, who come early in the Abhayadattaśrī order, tend to be larger than the rest in terms of absolute size (Figs. 6.11–11A).[16] The same is true for Tilopa (A22; Fig. 6.12).

At present, near the nunnery, they are randomly arranged, in no particular order, some stacked on top of each other. This was also the case when they

14 This aspect is discussed further in chapter 8, "Reflections on a Buddhist Painting of Saravatī in Zangskar."

15 I measured more than twenty of the stones, although almost all were damaged so the range of dimensions is misleading. The maximum height (given first) and width of those measured is: 56 x 35 cm, 33 x 23 cm, 18 x 34 cm, 20 x 34 cm, 17 x 56 cm, 18 x 25 cm, 30 x 43 cm, 44 x 35 cm, 56 x 26 cm, 19 x 46 cm, 45 x 32 cm, 34 x 27 cm, 39 x 28 cm, 26 x 27 cm, 22 x 52 cm, 31 x 32 cm, 34 x 37 cm, 36 x 41 cm, 28 x 58 cm, 30 x 66 cm, 40 x 60 cm, 25 x 56 cm.

16 The outer dimensions of the Virūpa stone are 56 x 35 cm.

Fig. 6.11 Virūpa Mahāsiddha (A3) pointing at the sun; stone engraved carving at Tungri Nunnery, Zangksar. Photo 2015.

Fig. 6.11A Stone engraved carving illustrated in Fig. 6.11 with outlines added by Mel Keiser for clarification.

were originally noticed down closer to the village. What was the original or intended arrangement, if any? Was it a linear, *pradakṣiṇa* order following the numbering of the text or list? Or, as in sets of *thangka* paintings, could they have been in an alternating mode around a central Vajradhara? Stones with two themes on a single surface, side by side, suggest a clockwise order, as if surrounding a stupa or three-dimensional mandala (Figs. 6.13–14).[17] For example, one numbered fifty-one, identified as Dhokaripa (A49), is to the right of Medini (A50), marked number fifty-two. On the other hand, there is at least one instance of a counterclockwise order, where the higher numbered Mahāsiddha is on the right and a lower number on the left. Mīnapa (A8; Fig. 6.15) is numbered seven on the sculpture, and appears to the left of Kaṅkāripa (A7), clearly numbered eight on the same sculpture. This may be, however, one of the only examples where the order moves left (no. 7) to right (no. 8), and might be an anomaly, since they are reversed in

17 See Czaja, "Commemorative Stupas at Densathil"; Czaja and Proser, *Golden Visions of Densatil*, 43.

Fig. 6.12 Tilopa Mahāsiddha (A22) pounding sesame; stone engraved carving at Tungri Nunnery, Zangksar. Photo 2015.

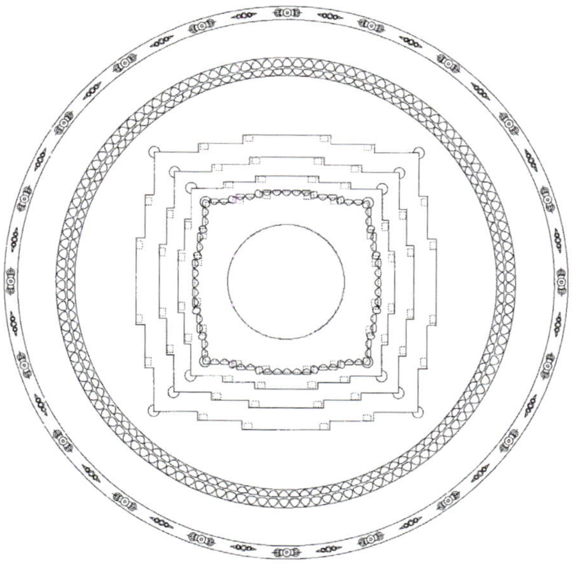

Fig. 6.13 Diagram of a *bkra shis sgo mang* stupa from above. Drawing by Olaf Czaja (not to scale). From Czaja, "Commemorative Stupas at Densathil," 268. Used with permission.

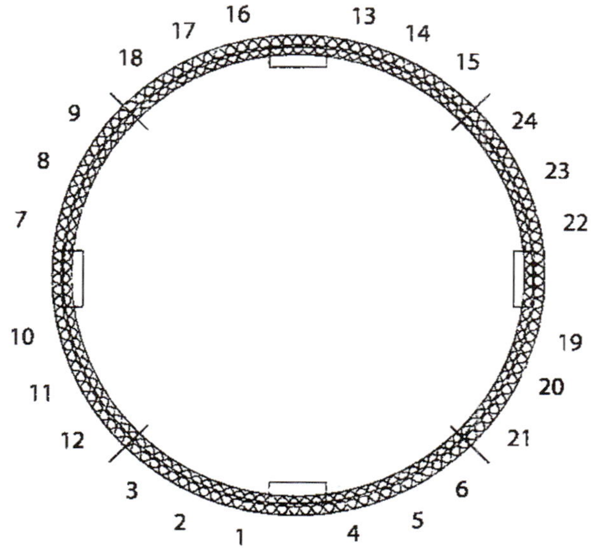

Fig. 6.14 Plan of the Sixth Tier (not to scale) of a Densatil commemorative stupa. Drawing by Olaf Czaja. From Czaja, "Commemorative Stupas at Densathil," 239. Used with permission.

Fig. 6.15 Mīnapa (Matsyendranāth) (A8); stone engraved carving at Tungri Nunnery, Zangskar. Photographed in 2012.

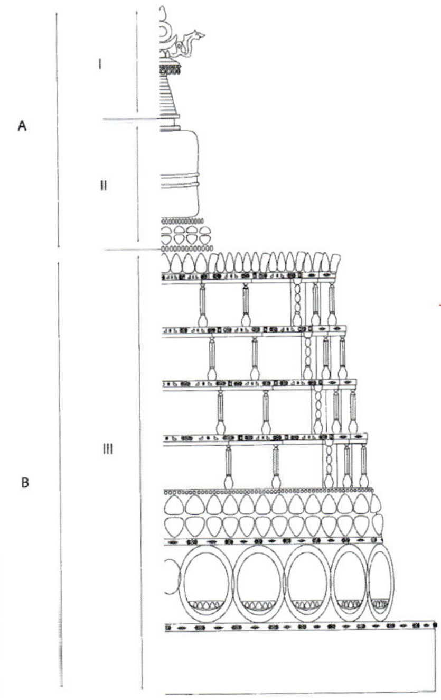

Fig. 6.16 Front elevation of a *bkra shis sgo mang* stupa. Drawing by Olaf Czaja (not to scale). From Czaja, "Commemorative Stupas at Densathil," 209.

terms of Abhayadattaśrī's order. On the other hand, there are instances of counterclockwise order elsewhere, as in Figure 6.14. Such subsections could accommodate those like the example of Mīnapa and Kaṅkāripa mentioned above, if sequences are spread out, left to right, on either side of a central image. Clockwise (*pradakṣiṇa* order) or counterclockwise, however, adjacent figures are numbered consecutively, a fact that supports the suggestion that they were arranged in the order of the numbers engraved on the stone. The scale of the larger, numerically lower siddhas (i.e., earlier in the extent version of the text and generally more well-known) is also suggestive. Were they originally stacked into tiers, like the arrangement of a mandala-like stupa platform at Densatil (Fig. 6.16)? If so, how were the two different scales accommodated into the intended arrangement? Were the larger ones set higher up and farther away from the viewer?

The Mahāsiddha sculptures at Hemis Monastery are all in a single scale and, at least as we have them now, they are on separate panel-like stones, not joined together. Currently, they are arranged in two parallel registers on the walls of the arcade surrounding the courtyard opposite the entrance to the main shrines (see Fig. 6.8). However, early photographs, such as those in Figures 6.17–6.19, demonstrate that the Hemis carved and painted stone plaques have been moved and rearranged over the years, though they have been in a similar (albeit not identical) arrangement since at least 1865.[18] Possibly the earliest photographs of Hemis were published that year, and behind the masked dancers one can clearly see the painted carvings (see Fig. 6.17). Darrah's photograph (see Fig. 6.18) was published a little over three decades later, and Vishu Nath's photograph (see Fig. 6.19) a quarter of a century after that. Detailed examination shows that individual examples are not in same location as at present.

Besides the manner of display, many other questions remain about the Tungri set. The intentions of the maker are as unknowable as his or her identity. Because of the uniform form-idiom (i.e., "style") they were not the product of a group of various villagers working together. In only a few cases might one question whether they had been contributed by a different hand. Even if one presumes that a single designer created the drawings that various hands scored into the stones, one would expect a greater variation in quality and clarity than actually one finds here. The quality of the majority is significantly greater than an average non-artist would be able to draw and execute. In my opinion, the creator(s) must have been

18 Compare the contemporary arrangement with that depicted in photographs by Alexander Brodie Melville (including Fig. 6.17) in Godwin-Austen, "Description of a Mystic Play."

Fig. 6.17 Captain Melville depicting masked dancers at Hemis, with Mahāsiddha panels in the background. From Godwin-Austen, "Description of a Mystic Play." Northwestern University Library Special Collections.

Fig. 6.18 "Gallery in Himis Monastery." From Darrah, *Sport in the Highlands of Kashmir*, p. 393. Photograph by Darrah.

Fig. 6.19 "Lama Actors in the Religious Plays." Photograph by Vishu Nath. From Tyndale Biscoe, *Kashmir in Sunlight & Shade*, opposite p. 224.

Fig. 6.20 Mahāsiddha thangka at Ralakhung hamlet. Photo 2012.

The purpose of the project, however, remains opaque. We cannot even be sure whether the most important aspect for the maker was the *process of carving* or the *subsequent display*. The creation itself may have met such ends as the fulfillment of a vow, of penance, the expression of devotion to the Mahāsiddhas, as a means of study, or inspiration. On the other hand, if the images in stone were the ultimate end, then the display was more important than the process of making them, and the intended encounter by a later party might have been designed to generate merit, to serve as a mnemonic device, to give visual pleasure, or as support for the teaching of inspiring narratives. Naturally, more than one of these possibilities may have been in play simultaneously.

The fact that Hemis and Tungri favor Abhayadattaśrī's list suggests the possibility of some kind of connection with the Drukpa lineage of the purported founder of both monasteries, Takstang Repa. A painting associated with eighteenth-century Drukpa Kagyu Zhedpa Dorje's circle at Ralakhung village is, by contrast, a depiction of the Vajrāsana list (Figs. 6.20–21), including Serlingpa (Tib. gser gling pa; Skt. Suvarṇadvīpa; V38) and Nīlapa (V48), Metogpa (V85), among others.[19]

one or two persons who worked together in a shared fluent mode of engraved two-dimensional drawing and carving. Although at first they may appear disarmingly nonprofessional, that impression needs to be resisted, and at any rate evaporates the more one studies them. They are more sophisticated than they look.

19 Linrothe, "Siddhas and Sociality," figs. 31, 34.

Fig. 6. 21 Detail of Fig. 6.20, including Jālandhara, Suvarṇadvīpa (inscribed Serlingpa), and a royal figure inscribed Nilapa. Photo 2012.

Fig. 6.22 Suvarṇadvīpa (inscribed Serlingpa) Mahāsiddha (V38) in a gesture of teaching; stone engraved carving at Manda village, Zangksar. Photo 2015.

So too the Manda group, also featuring Suvarṇadvīpa (Fig. 6.22), relates to the Vajrāsana list, not Abhayadattaśrī's.

In terms of form-idiom, one of the notable characteristics of the Tungri set is the intricate interweaving of human figures with features of landscapes and settings. Compositionally, these go beyond what is absolutely necessary for the basic identification of the Mahāsiddha's narrative, or what most other sets provide. The main actor tends to be accompanied by attendants or other characters in the narrative. That is the case for Tilopa (A22), who is shown operating the sesame-pounder with his foot while two attendants look on. He holds onto the branches of a tree with a gnarled trunk, a motif encountered frequently in the Tungri set (see Fig. 6.12; see also Figs. 6.6–6A, 6.10–10A). In the stone numbered eighty depicting Nāgabodhi (A76), both the converted thief and his teacher, Nāgārjuna, are depicted within elaborate roofed enclosures, complete with gate and doors and surrounded by foliage and clouds (Figs. 6.23–23A). In a few cases, such as that of Maṇibhadrā (A65), more than one episode in the Mahāsiddhā's story is included (Figs. 6.24–24A).[20] We are presented with a scene in her parents' home, another with her seated at a waterfall gazing at the water pot and, after the pot breaks, flying off in a cloud. The Hemis version, by contrast, selects a single representative view—flying above the water after having been enlightened by the shattering of the water vessel she had brought to the riverside (Fig. 6.25). Still, among the Hemis engraved panels there is

20 On her story and representations of her, see Linrothe, *Holy Madness*, 32–33, 278–280, 282.

Fig. 6.23 Nāgabodhi Mahāsiddha (A76) meditating surrounded by jewels provided by his teacher Nāgārjuna; stone engraved carving at Tungri Nunnery, Zangksar. Photo 2015.

Fig. 6.23A. Stone engraved carving illustrated in Fig. 6.23 with outlines added by Mel Keiser for clarification.

Fig. 6.24 Maṇibhadrā Mahāsiddhā (A65) at her parents' house (left), at the river to gather water (lower right), and flying in the sky (upper right); stone engraved carving at Tungri Nunnery, Zangksar. Photo 2015.

Fig. 6.24A Stone engraved carving illustrated in Fig. 6.15 with outlines added by Mel Keiser for clarification.

Fig. 6.25 Maṇibhadrā Mahāsiddhā (A65) flying in the sky above a river; stone engraved carving at Hemis monastery courtyard, Ladakh. Photo 2008.

Fig. 6.26 Tilopa Mahāsiddha (A22) pounding sesame; stone engraved carving at Hemis monastery courtyard, Ladakh. Photo 2008.

almost always a similar successful attempt at a landscape setting, including sky, hills, and water (Figs. 6.25–26). As we will see, the Manda set forgoes even this. Many of the Tungri Mahāsiddhas are surrounded by varieties of dense foliage, integrating figure and setting, such as in Figures 6.10–10A, where at least three different types of foliage are carefully inscribed.[21] The Hemis ones share this to an extent (compare the foliage above Deṅgipa in Figures 6.10–10A with that above Tilopa in Figure 6.26), though the later (re-?)painting on the Hemis stones may obscure some of the carved details.

The Manda Mahāsiddhas are by comparison restrained and spare, and with patterned, abstract backgrounds or empty ones rather than representational settings (Figs. 6.22, 6.27–28). Not only do the Manda siddhas not have numbers, but their names are chiseled simply, sometimes cursorily, on areas of the stone left plain and only occasionally surrounded with a simple box, not inscribed in low relief within a cartouche as at Tungri. This is the case for Indrabhūti (V15; see Fig. 6.28 top) and Suvarṅadvīpa (inscribed

21 To a certain extent, the closest comparisons with the Tungri integration of figure and setting found so far are with the partial set of clay sculptures from Nepal in the Los Angeles County Museum of Art, the Art Institute of Chicago, and the Metropolitan Museum of Art, variously attributed to the fourteenth or the seventeenth century; see Linrothe, *Holy Madness*, nos. 42–44. I recently noticed two more in the Bharat Kala Bhavan; see the Huntington Archive, scan nos. 4277 and 4282; my thanks to Susan Huntington for sending me photographs of the museum's holdings.

Serlingpa; V38; see Fig. 6.22). By comparison, in terms of inscription style and narrative settings, the Hemis set, at the seat of the Drukpas in Ladakh, resembles the Tungri ones considerably more than the Manda set. The Tungri panels, however, exceed the Hemis sculptures in terms of density of foliage and detail. There are frequently two or more smaller attendants or witnesses, or larger teachers, accompanying the main Mahāsiddha on Tungri's stones, sitting or standing under rich foliage above a gnarled Chinese-painting-style tree trunk (see Figs. 6.3 right, 6.6, 6.10, 6.12). It bears repeating that another distinctive feature of the Tungri Mahāsiddha carvings is the inclusion of inscribed numbers on each of them, which is very rare.

The Manda sculptures have their own sophisticated charm, particularly in the simplified, rounded lines and outlines, and the often rousing, kicking poses. Each siddha is invariably without attendant or teacher, and has only minimal background. Sometimes two Mahāsiddhas are paired on the same rock, one above the other (see Figs. 6.27, 6.28), rarely side by side. The Tungri sculptures are just the opposite: most are side by side, inside a web of settings that engulf the main figures accompanied by teachers, attendants, and bit players in their complex narratives. At Manda, even the inscriptions are simpler than the Tungri set, with just the Tibetan name and without the honorific "gu ru" preceding and "la na mo" (homage to . . .) succeeding the name as it is on the Tungri inscriptions. In this latter aspect, the Manda treatment of the names resembles the Hemis inscriptions, which are also missing the honorifics but, unlike the Hemis and Tungri inscriptions, the Manda writing is not in a blocked-out cartouche. If one were to calibrate density of detail with relative earliness, and clarity and continuity of line with lateness, one would say that the Tungri sculptures are earlier than the Manda set, with the Hemis sculptures bridging the two.

However, they might in fact represent two different modes of vision, or rather systems of representation, and it is possible that they were roughly coeval. Although it is usual to insist on a dominant "period eye" and "period style," in fact more than one mode of representation can operate at any one time, as a quick reflection of our own time will demonstrate. Regardless of the dating one assigns to the two sets of Mahāsiddha engraved stones, less than fifteen kilometers apart, they fit neatly into the two modes identified by Alois Riegl and Heinrich Wölfflin, termed *haptic* (tactile) and *optic*, and *linear* and *painterly*, respectively.[22]

22 "Painterly" is one sense of the German term *malerisch*, and is used not only for painting but for representational systems that complicate or suppress contour lines as opposed to linear modes that feature them.

Fig. 6.27 Two unidentified Mahāsiddhas, inscriptions broken off; stone engraved carving at Manda village, Zangskar. Photo 2015.

Fig. 6.28 Two Mahāsiddhas, including inscribed Indrabhūti Mahāsiddha (V15; *top*); stone engraved carving at Manda village. Photo 2015

The linear and haptic or tactile qualities of the Manda Mahāsiddhas can be clearly observed. The fluent, curving lines can be a source of aesthetic pleasure in their own right, aside from successfully carrying the burden of representation. The lines are generally of even width and facture, clear and often continuous. Outlines of the figures are firmly drawn, and one can, in fact, think of them as drawings in stone, disguising the technical means of chiseling lines into the hard rock. Certainly, they would transfer well from a preparatory drawing on paper to one on stone that artists must have outlined before starting to carve. Each Mahāsiddha is established as a solitary icon, complete in himself—and in the case of the Vajrāsana set, they are indeed exclusively male.

By contrast, the painterly, optical qualities of the Tungri Mahāsiddha cannot be over-emphasized. Figures and settings have been plaited together with the background into a dense overall texture that does not always allow either agents or settings to be extricated. The artist sought not to isolate but to join the near and far, objects and beings, image and ground. The lines are skittish and wobbly, though by no means uncertain. When lines are long, they cross shorter ones, as if interrupting them, and often there are series of short, angled lines that are suggestive of shading (such as on the fur of the animal on which Virūpa sits; see Figs. 6.11–11A). Some lines are given greater weight and emphasis than others, through deeper carving. The artist was less interested in having us admire his or her linear draftsmanship in an abstract way and more in conveying narratives, not icons. One might also suggest that the artist more often challenges the viewer to puzzle out the story by including attendants, helpers, and witnesses, as well as the teachers who played crucial roles in the narrative of each Mahāsiddha. The Tungri engraved stones also tend to incorporate more than one time and place into the same compositional space. They tell more complicated stories, and so require more of the viewer to be able to recognize. At times it is hard, in fact, to tell which is the Mahāsiddha and which the teacher.

The approach to forms and to the act of viewing, then, is fundamentally different in the two sets. The Manda icons emphasize conceptual and physical clarifying isolation along with boundedness—there is no confusion about who is playing which role. One time, one space, one name, one siddha. The Tungri stones are much more painterly in approach, connecting things in the foreground and background. The differences of the two approaches I would argue are significantly more clearly appreciated through the process of comparison. However useful they are for understanding the inner mechanisms of the artworks, such categorization as linear and painterly does not help much in performing the basic tasks of documentation and temporal classification and so are vulnerable to the charge of "so what?" on the part of those whose primary focus is knowing when and where something was made. And who does not want to know that? Wölfflin himself suggests that it is critical, foundational, and he sought to "establish standards by which historical transformations . . . might be defined with greater precision."[23]

While the sequence of linear to painterly documented in sixteenth- and seventeenth-century Europe does not relentlessly repeat itself in a cycle, even there it is possible to consider that both modes might have been options deployed as reactions to the excesses of the other, whether as an external change of taste or an internal transformation of perceptions. There is no reason to necessarily place the linear before the painterly if one considers episodes of a "neo-classical" revival, in what Wölfflin terms "the problem of new beginnings."[24] In this case, I would suggest that in fact the Tungri painterly set is older than Manda's linear one, but I would not go so far as to suggest that the linear set was made *in response to* the desiccation of the nerve allowing pleasure in the painterly, just so as to revive the pleasure in linear clarity.[25] In short, defining the forms in Wölfflinian terms does not automatically help in the process of relative dating by determining which came first. Nevertheless, there is something to be said for penetrating the surface of the forms, of seeing behind the curtain, as it were, to see the visual values being projected onto the stone by artists. If one were to attempt to summarize the effect of the forms on the themes, one could say that the linear mode of Manda more successfully limns each Mahāsiddha as an independent icon, whereas Tungri's more painterly mode succeeds in evoking complex situational narratives. "This is not a qualitative difference."[26] Thus neither is "better" than the other; they are "two different languages . . . each has strengths in a certain area."[27]

The differences, in relation to the Tungri and Manda Mahāsiddhas, are starkly binary. The former emphasizes narrative, the latter iconicity. One creates intricacy through engagement and interaction with the social, the other clarifies by isolating from the material world. Reading and understanding the Tungri Mahāsiddha images requires an extractive process, a focus on the dispersal of external meaning into a narrative

23 Wölfflin, *Principles of Art History*, 79.

24 Wölfflin, *Principles of Art History*, 312.

25 Wölfflin's student Ludwig Bachoffer takes a more literal view of the cyclical nature of these modes when he suggests that the development "from the stable and permanent to the transient and mobile . . . is in absolute agreement with the laws of optical development"; that when "the same phenomenon repeats itself in the history of Chinese and Japanese art, it becomes evident that we are in the presence of a law of development to which, in normal circumstances, every visual perception is subject"; that in India, "the phenomenon of the change of style is repeating itself several times"; and that the "inner law of such a development can no longer be denied to-day." Bachhofer, *Early Indian Sculpture*, 54, 118, 119.

26 Wölfflin, *Principles of Art History*, 96.

27 Wölfflin, *Principles of Art History*, 93.

of "coming into being." The Manda carved stones, by contrast, entail a reductive process revealing an achieved concentrated exalted state of being on the part of the siddha. In a phrase, expressive embeddedness versus abstract centrality. The differences may also be linked to the way the names are conveyed. Both use Tibetan script but there is once again an indirection on the Tungri transliteration of Sanskrit names compared with the immediacy of translation of a key characteristic embedded in the Tibetan version of the name, at least for the presumably Tibetan-script-reading intended audience. This is not to say that the Tungri engravings are convoluted. Their narratives in a sense are recounted in time and space, and the viewer is reminded of cultural transmission from (mainly) eastern India. In the Manda icons, the essence of the narratives must be fully known already; only the name provides a mnemonic trigger, and they transcend cultural and environmental specificity. It is extraordinary that two such different modes of image-making were applied to the same themes just a dozen or so kilometers apart in Zangskar.

In conclusion, the Tungri Mahāsiddhas appear to be related to the Hemis sculptures in technique, thematics, and format. They may be earlier or later than the Hemis and Manda sets, but reflect an enduring interest on the part of the Drukpa in Zangskar in the Mahāsiddhas as teachers of Esoteric Buddhist visualization practices. The "Chinese" landscape elements such as representations of the gnarled trees may reflect contact with art or artists of central or eastern Tibet. They might possibly be related to the time of Tungri's founding in the seventeenth century, but perhaps instead reflect active schools of either art or meditation under the Drukpa artist-abbots of nearby Dzonkhul Monastery, Ngawang Tsering[28] and Zhedpa Dorje, in the eighteenth century. Further study is required. In the appendices that follow (6.1–2) I have listed the identifiable Mahāsiddhas, with their numbers and inscriptions, along with what data can be derived from the fragmentary depictions, with siddhas without inscriptions, or undecipherable inscriptions.

28 On Ngawang Tsering, father of and predecessor to Zhedpa Dorje as Dzonkhul Monastery abbot, see Maurer, "Isn't Life Miserable?"; Tsering, *Buddhism in Ladakh*.

APPENDIX 6.1: Tungri Mahāsiddhas

44 are identified

11 others are unidentified

3 small fragments may be part of broken ones or the remains of others

Total: at least 55

Five pairs on the same stones, all consecutive

The earlier numbers (up through the 20s) are most complete,
but there are numbers in all "decades" through and including the 80s.

Identifiable by inscription or attribute
Listed in order of the number on sculpture
The Abhayadattśrī number listed as A# where known

#3
Yogi pointing to the sun, seated against architectonic throne
Virūpa (A3)

#4?
Standing *yabyum* couple
Tombhapa? = Ḍombipa? (A4)

#7
Damaged yogi (top of face and head is missing) seated on large catfish
Mi na pa = Mīnapa, Matsyendranāth (A8)
(on same stone as #8)

#8
Fragment of animal skin seat cover and inscription
Ki ka ri pa = Kaṅkāripa (A7)
(on same stone as #7)

No #
Yogi in *padmāsana*, frontal, snake *upavīta*; surrounded by buffalo
Go rak sha = Gorakṣa (A9)

#11
Layman with vīṇā
Vīṇāpa (A11)

No #
Bearded old monk with bolster, pandita's hat
"Sha nti pa"=Śāntipa (A12)

#13?
Yogi in hut next to old man weaving on a loom
Tan ti pa = Tantipa (A13)

#15?
Siddha flying in the air with sword, stūpa below (i.e. charnel ground)
"ka ga pa" = Khaḍgapa (A15)
Khaḍgapa, with sword in his hand, has a narrative that mentions a *stūpa* which appears in both the Tungri siddha and the thangka in the Tibetan House Museum (HM cat. no. 29, 2nd from the top on the viewer's right).

#16
Monk seated with snakes on head halo
"na ga . . ." = Nāgārjuna (A16)

#17
Monk with book
Kartri (= Karṇaripa or Āryadeva; A18)
(on same stone as next one)

#18 (to the right of previous one)
Yogi under umbrellas
Kāṇha (A17)

#1X?
Wild yogi
"Na ro pa" = Nāropa (A20)

#21
Robed meditator in cave
Kampala = Kambala (A30)

#23
Yogi on grain pounder, with elaborate setting (gnarled tree with leaves), an assistant and the female slave owner
Tilopa (A22)

#24
Seated monk with text in left hand, frontal view
Ca tra pa = Catrapa (A23)

#25
Two yogis seated near a stūpa (charnel ground)
Bha dra pa = Bhadrapa (A24)

#26
Head broken off of seated figure, above water or fire
Khu X X = ?

#27
Yogi washing clothes in basin, with others
Dhombipa = Dhobīpa (A28)

#28
Wealthy lay figure seated before yogi
"ka la pi"? = Kālapa, The Handsome Madman with his yogi-teacher (A27)?

#31
Monk meditating inside a cave
Ka mbha pa = Kambala (Lawapa) (A30)

#32
Kneeling yogi surrounded by bowls and ritual utensils in elaborate landscape with gnarled tree
Di hka pa (?) = Deṅgipa (A31)

#33
Seated layman, flying monk and standing layman
Jha ndhe pa = Bhandepa (A32)

#46
Peasant with axe seated in landscape
Kon ti pa = Koṭālipa (A44)

#51 (61?)
Yogi standing in front of two-storey temple
Dho ka ri pa = Dhokaripa (A49)
(on same stone as next one)

#52 (62?)
Peasant plowing with bullock
Me dhi na = Medhini (A50)
(on same stone as previous one)

#56
Mendicant-yogi standing in front of Śavaripa
Jo gi la = Jogipa (A53), disciple of Śavaripa; perhaps also the latter?
Left side of sculpture where his inscription might be is missing but it would be out of order as he is A5.

#57
Male lying on his back, another standing looking over him
Naguna = Nirguṇa (A57)

#59
Yabyum couple flying in the air with king looking on, standing Avalokiteśvara above
Ghan ta pa = Ghaṇṭāpa (A52)

#60
Seated yogi in front of Heruka
Damaged inscription X X X na la = possibly Kantalipa (A69) who receives Hevajra initiation

No #
Two seated figures, difficult to decipher
Cam pa ka = Campaka (A60)
(On same stone as next one)

No #
Two seated figures, difficult to decipher
Bhi ksha na = Bhikṣanapa (A61)
(On same stone as previous one)

#61(?)
Seated yogi, standing monk
"Pa tsa ri pa" = Pacaripa (A59)

#68
Seated woman next to waterfall
Maṇibhadrā (A65)

No #
Seated or kneeling yogi beside female siddha
Me kha la = Mekhalā (A66)

#70
Seated yogi next to Heruka like-female siddha
Inscription damaged = Kanakhalā (A67)

#77
Seated yogi next to haloed siddha with arrow (i.e. Saraha, A6)
Sarvabhakṣa (A75), student of Saraha

#78?
Seated monk w. image of Ava. bsa and lay servant
Sakara (A74)

#80
Two buildings, a monk and a yogi in window
Na ga bo X = Nāgabodhi (A76)

#81
Flying figure, broken off, above two small temples
Da ri ka pa = Dārikapa (A77)
(on same stone as next one)

#82
Layman and yogi seated below *thangka*
Pu ta li pa = Putalipa (A78)
(on same stone as previous one)

#83
Standing well-dressed layman, right hand extended and holding a lotus
Pan x x = Paṅkaja? (A51)

#84?
Wealthy layman speaking to a monk, beneath gnarled tree, peacock fan held by attendant
Ko ka li = Kokalipa (A80)

#85
Monk in a hut speaking with monk, lay (woman?) observing
A nan go = Anaṅga (A81)

#87?
Seated figure surrounded by ocean, temple rising from it
Sa mu dra = Samudra (A83)

APPENDIX 6.2: Manda Mahāsiddhās

22 identifiable by inscription or attribute
12 have unidentified or undeciphered inscription
20 are without inscription or characteristic attribute; unidentified
Total: 54

Identifiable by inscription or attribute

V1	Nāgārjuna (as yogi) (glu grub)
V2	(or V61) Āryadeva
V3	Lūipa
V4	Padmavajra
V5	Saraha (no inscription)
V7	Ḍombi Heruka
V12	Kukkuripa (no inscription)
V15	Indrabhūti (aon dra bho ti)
V21	(or V34) Śāntipa
V22	Atiśa (Mar me dzad), but a yogi, not a monk)
V23	Tilopa
V27	Śavaripa (fragment, dancing with bow) (no inscription)
V28	Dārikhapa (fragments; only "dha ri" is visible)
V35	Tantipa (Thagapa) (no inscription)
V37	Kamala
V38	Serlingpa (Suvarṇadvīpa)
V51	Mīnapa (no inscription)
V55	Ananta
V56	Sengepa
V59	Candrakīrti (zla bag grags pa)
V77	Simhapa
V83	Kālalamge (ka la la)

CHAPTER 7

Discovery, Deconsecration, Rebuilding and Reconsecration: Revisiting the Art, Architecture, and Relics in Karsha's Chuchikzhal Complex[1]

> [T]he issue of preservation of the original has now become urgent, as knowledge of traditional building methods, materials, forms, colors, architectural structure, and so on, is gradually disappearing. Fewer and fewer people possess sufficient expertise to make appropriate repairs, and even fewer still have the necessary skills to bring such edifices and works of art into existence.
>
> —E. Gruber, *From the Heart of Tibet*, 258

On my second hike through Zangskar in the western Himalaya (see map p. x), in 1992, I first met the devout, learned, and powerful patriarch, the venerable Karsha Lonpo. Sonam Wangchuk is the man's personal name, but his title is Karsha Lonpo, a hereditary position that means the headman or "prime official of Karsha village" (Fig. 7.1). Along with the title, he inherited a religious complex on a hillside, and his efforts to sustain it form the heart of this chapter's narrative. On top of the ridge on the hill are the ruins of a fortified settlement (Figs. 7.2–3), probably Karsha village's early habitation site, as discussed in chapter 5. From the tenth to the fifteenth century or so, the now-ruined structures constituted a citadel overlooking the barley fields well below. The village later moved to the bottom of the hill, while Karsha Monastery, presently perched on the hill's twin across the stream that bisects the village, and above the Shambhala Gate carvings discussed in chapters 3 and 4 (Figs. 3.32, 4.58, 4.63–67), has fine murals surviving from the fifteenth century. Between the lower village and the ruined citadel is a two-storey shrine built around an overlife-size statue of the eleven-headed Lokeśvara Bodhisattva known as Chuchikzhal (Fig. 7.4). The shrine is believed by locals, and the Karsha Lonpo himself, to have been built in the eleventh century, although since the sculpture has been repeatedly repaired and repainted, there is very little by which to assess that conviction's validity. The mural paintings on the walls surrounding the sculpture (Figs. 7.5–6) are probably fourteenth century.[2] The location of an annual *nyungné* (nyung gnas) fasting ritual,[3] the Chuchikzhal shrine is considered religiously significant by the entire

1 Originally prepared for an invited seminar at SOAS, a shortened version with fewer illustrations of this paper was published in *Orientations* (Linrothe 2020). I am grateful to Frances Macdonald for editorial suggestions, and the Yifawn Lee, editor and publisher, for permission to republish in an enhanced version, which includes substantially more documentation of paintings and sculptures found in the course of the dismantling and repair of the stupas discussed.

2 Linrothe, "Strengthening the Roots," 70.

3 K. Gutschow, "The *smyung gnas* Fast in Zangskar."

Fig. 7.1 The Ven. Karsha Lonpo Sonam Wangchuk, Chuchikzhal, Karsha, Zangskar. Photo 2004.

Fig. 7.2 A section of the stone-built ruined settlement above the Chuchikzhal shrine Chuchikzhal, Karsha, Zangskar. Photo 2012.

Fig. 7.3 View from below of the ruined settlement above the Chuchikzhal shrine, Chuchikzhal, Karsha, Zangskar. Photo 2004.

Fig. 7.4 (Left): Standing eleven-headed Avalokiteśvara (Chuchikzhal), the principal sculpture in the Chuchikzhal shrine. Photo 2009. (Right): Avalokiteśvara's heads (detail). Photo 1996. (Both): Chuchikzhal, Karsha, Zangskar.

Fig. 7.5 Part of the damaged Vajrabhairava Mandala mural on the north wall of the Chuchikzhal shrine, Chuchikzhal, Karsha, Zangskar. Photo 1996.

Fig. 7.6 Detail of lineage figures above Cakrasaṃvara Mandala on the north wall of the Chuchikzhal shrine, Chuchikzhal, Karsha, Zangskar. Photo 1996.

Fig. 7.7 View of the Chuchikzhal Shrine, with nunnery below the Kadampa Chorten, Chuchikzhal, Karsha, Zangskar. Photo 2008.

community of nuns (who have built a nunnery beside it), the Karsha Monastery monks, villagers living nearby, and even Buddhists from farther afield, who visit on pilgrimages to sacred places in Zangskar. The whole hill area of the village is now referred to metonymically as Chuchikzhal (Fig. 7.7).

Halfway between the ruins above and the shrine below is a gateway (*kankani*) stupa that formally marked the spatial passage between them (Fig. 7.8). The interior of the stupa is hollowed out, and both the lantern ceiling and the interior walls that support it have paintings well above eye-level.[4] The lantern ceiling, 3.6 meters off the ground, depicts a version of the Vajradhatu *mahāmaṇḍala* with the crowned Akṣobhya Buddha in the center, surrounded by *vajra*-bodhisattvas (*samādhi* deities), offering goddesses, and gate guardians (Figs. 4.96, 7.9–10). The upper interior walls, which suffered greatly from water damage, show the other four crowned Tathāgata Buddhas, each with two bodhisattvas and flanked by dozens of other deities (see Figs. 4.90, 4.92, 4.94, 4.100, 4.103, 7.11, 7A.1–3). There is a deep niche to either side of the passageway, though when I first saw them, both were filled to the brim with *tsha tsha* (small molded images made of clay mixed with pulverized powder from human bones) that villagers had deposited as a kind of memorial to their departed relatives. The interior ceiling paintings intrigued me from the first time I saw them in 1990. They appeared older than the murals in the shrine below, and in fact they looked more like early Central Tibetan painting in comparison with most of the other early paintings I had encountered in Ladakh and Zangskar.

4 See also Linrothe and Kerin, "Deconsecration and Discovery," figs. 9–11d.

Fig. 7.8 (Left): The gateway stupa, or Kadampa chorten, pre-restoration. Photo 1999. (Right): During restoration before the finial is in place. Photo 2016. (Both): Chuchikzhal, Karsha, Zangskar, India.

Fig. 7.9 The painted lantern ceiling with an Akṣobhya mandala, ca. late 12th–early 13th c., inside the Kadampa chorten, Chuchikzhal, Karsha, Zangskar. Photo 2011.

Fig. 7.10 A *vajra*-bodhisattva with "nga" written on his chest to indicate the color; detail from the Akṣobhya mandala on the painted lantern ceiling inside the Kadampa chorten, Chuchikzhal, Karsha, Zangskar. Photo 2018.

Fig. 7.11 A *makara* next to the nimbus of Ratnasambhava, detail from the wall supporting the ceiling inside the Kadampa chorten, Chuchikzhal, Karsha, Zangskar. Photo 2018.

Fig. 7.12 The author conferring with the Karsha Lonpo, Karsha, Zangskar. Photo 1996 by Laura Strand.

The paintings stood out, so I was fascinated to learn the stupa's local name: the Kadampa Chorten. *Kadampa* refers to a Buddhist monastic tradition established in central Tibet that was inspired by the eastern Indian master Atiśa Dipaṇkaraśrījñāna (982–1054). *Chorten* is the Tibetan word for *stūpa*, and the terms are used interchangeably here.

Through the 1990s, I continued to make visits to Karsha during my treks through Ladakh and Zangskar, and gradually got to know the Lonpo's family better. I talked to the Lonpo about the gateway stupa's interior murals, and the problem of access in order to study, measure and photograph them comprehensively (Fig. 7.12). Since it was a consecrated structure, it was deemed inappropriate to climb on it to get close enough to see if there were any inscriptions, or to adequately document it. In the summer of 2000, the Lonpo and I were again talking about this, and he suddenly suggested that I come back next summer and sponsor a DE-consecration. He would arrange for a former abbot of nearby Karsha Monastery to perform the deconsecration, and then I could climb up and photograph it without hurting the religious sentiments of local people. Afterward, it could be reconsecrated and all would be well. He offered to choose an auspicious time for the deconsecration: not only had the Lonpo become a devout monk after his wife died—he was ordained by H. H. the 14th Dalai Lama himself—he was also a trained and respected Amchi, or Tibetan doctor, in the village, and a renowned astrologer (dbon po). Even monastic leaders consulted him in order to choose auspicious days for rituals. We could document the whole process as well as the Buddhist remains.[5]

It was an unparalleled opportunity. At a single stroke, we would learn about early art and about the contemporary rituals that surrounded them.

5 For more on the Karsha Lonpo, see K. Gutschow, "An Economy of Merit," 2–9, 90–91, 348–50; K. Gutschow, "The *smyung gnas* Fast in Zangskar"; and especially K. Gutschow, *Being a Buddhist Nun*, 46–49.

I talked about it to a friend who had spent extensive time in Karsha, Kim Gutschow. At the time, Kim was a graduate student in anthropology at Harvard University, and she had first introduced me to Karsha Lonpo in 1992 after having spent years studying with him and with the nuns who were, with the Lonpo's permission, building a nunnery nearby the shrine. Kim in turn talked about the project with another graduate student interested in Himalayan art, at the time finishing a Master's of Divinity degree at Harvard's Divinity School. She had previously traveled to Ladakh, and was starting in the fall of 2001 in the art history graduate program of the University of Pennsylvania. This was Melissa Kerin, now a professor at Washington and Lee University in Virginia. After Kim talked to her about the project, she got in touch with me. We discussed the unique opportunity, and the three of us collaborated on it that summer, along with the Lonpo's family on 12–15 July 2001. This resulted in an earlier article in *Orientations* by Kerin and me already cited.

✣✣✣

The whole process of "discovery through deconsecration" (as we titled the original *Orientations* article) was exhilarating. Such access allows for documentation such as Figure 7.10, which shows a *vajra*-bodhisattva with a Tibetan letter, a color notation, at his chest. This was part of the underdrawing, a common practice in workshops in which the master-artist draws the outlines and writes the abbreviated name of the intended color for those who later fill in the pigments. Among other unexpected discoveries were a number of fragments of texts and cloth paintings, that, as relics had been respectfully disposed of by placing them into the niches along with thousands of *tsha tsha*. As these were removed we found at the back of each niche a clay sculpture with murals on the side walls. Both the sculptures and murals were in very rough condition, but appear to have been created by local artists a few decades or a century or so after the ceiling paintings were completed. In the left niche (when facing uphill) is a seated Buddha sculpture with murals of monks at his sides **(Figs. 7.13–14)**.[6] The sculpture in the right niche is the four-armed Ṣaḍakṣara Avalokiteśvara **(Figs. 7.15–16)** with colorful but damaged murals of the white Mahāvidyā Ṣaḍakṣarī and the red Manidharin **(Figs. 7.17–18)**.

Although finally getting access to the murals was very satisfying, justifying closer scrutiny, equally enriching and completely new to me was to see

6 Linrothe and Kerin, "Deconsecration and Discovery," figs. 7–8a.

Fig. 7.13 Clay sculpture of Buddha almost covered with *tsha tsha* in one of the niches in the Kadampa chorten, Chuchikzhal, Karsha, Zangskar. Photo 2006.

Fig. 7.14 Clay sculpture of Buddha, ht. 119 cm including lotus base, in one of the niches in the Kadampa chorten with *tsha tsha* removed, revealing painted murals on the walls of the niche, Chuchikzhal, Karsha, Zangskar. Photo 2018.

Fig. 7.15 Clay sculpture of Ṣaḍakṣara Avalokiteśvara almost covered with *tsha tsha* in one of the niches in the Kadampa chorten, Chuchikzhal, Karsha, Zangskar. Photo 2006.

Fig. 7.16 Clay sculpture of Ṣaḍakṣara Avalokiteśvara, ht. 84 cm not counting covered base, in one of the niches of the Kadampa chorten with *tsha tsha* removed, revealing painted murals on the walls of the niche, Chuchikzhal, Karsha, Zangskar. Photo 2018.

Fig. 7.17 Damaged mural next to the Ṣaḍakṣara Avalokiteśvara sculpture depicting Mahāvidyā Ṣaḍakṣarī in one of the niches, now cleared of *tsha tsha* in the Kadampa chorten, Chuchikzhal, Karsha, Zangskar. Photo 2018.

Fig. 7.18 Damaged mural next to the Ṣaḍakṣara Avalokiteśvara sculpture depicting Manidharin in one of the niches, now cleared of *tsha tsha* in the Kadampa chorten, Chuchikzhal, Karsha, Zangskar. Photo 2018.

Fig. 7.19 Altar in Chuchikzhal shrine with specially prepared *torma* (butter offerings) for the deconsecration ritual, Chuchikzhal, Karsha, Zangskar. Photo 2001.

Fig. 7.20 Zurba Tashi and other monks performing deconsecration ritual at the Kadampa Chorten, with Kim Gutschow and Melissa R. Kerin (far left) looking on, Chuchikzhal, Karsha, Zangskar. Photo 2001.

the rituals and the attitudes that surrounded them. On the first day of the ritual, monks from Karsha Monastery came over to make the offering cakes necessary for the deconsecration. These were set up in the second story of the eleven-headed Lokeśvara shrine, on a large altar (Fig. 7.19). The next day, a small company of monks began the rituals in the Lokeśvara shrine, and then processed up to the stupa. A few hours were spent there reciting texts and prayers outside and also inside the stupa (Fig. 7.20). An essential

Fig. 7.21 Zurba Tashi (holding mirror and incense) and other monks performing deconsecration ritual at the Kadampa, Chorten, Chuchikzhal, Karsha, Zangskar. Photo 2001.

Fig. 7.22 Detail of ritual mirror used in consecration and deconsecration rituals, Chuchikzhal, Zangskar. Photo 2001.

part of the *arga* or deconsecration involves a ritual mirror. It was taken by the ex-abbot, Zurba Tashi, who conducted the ritual, and displayed all the way around and inside the stupa (Figs. 7.21–22). Prayers requested the consecrated deities to temporarily reside in the mirror, which was then wrapped up in a white offering-scarf (*katag*) and carefully carried down to the altar in the Lokeśvara shrine. At that point, it was as if a switch had been flipped. Although there was no disrespect shown to the stupa, it was clearly no longer sacred ground. It was now not a problem to climb up on the niches to examine, measure and photograph the murals, as well as to climb onto the upper levels of the dilapidated exterior in order to measure the height of the stupa. All the clay press-molded sculptures (*tsha tsha*) inside the niches were handled as if so many kitchen wares, treated carefully from not reticently, removed from the niches, and placed on plastic tarps laid outside. In the process we "excavated" the two sculptures that had been almost completely covered by the *tsha tsha* in the niches, and discovered some previously unseen but brightly colored murals behind them, as mentioned already (see Figs. 7.14, 7.17–18). Among the *tsha tsha* that were removed, we discovered many fragments of paintings and pages of illuminated texts and were free to photograph them.[7] All these items had been deposited there over centuries. One doesn't throw away such consecrated objects like garbage, but deposits them in shrines such as these stupas.

Unfortunately, an ill-timed medical emergency requiring surgery in New Delhi precipitated a hasty departure before the replacement of the *tsha tsha* and the other relics into the niches and re-consecration, so I was not able to witness it that year. When I returned to Karsha in 2002, everything was back in place and both Karsha Lonpo and (the now late) Zurba Tashi, the former abbot who had conducted the deconsecration, were very keen to hear my conclusions regarding the date and origin of the Kadampa Chorten as well as the methods by which I arrived at them. Close observation during the deconsecration, the continued study of the photographic

7 See Linrothe and Kerin, "Deconsecration and Discovery," figs. 12–15b.

documentation, and consultations with other specialists in the art of the western Himalaya convinced me that the paintings are datable to the late twelfth or early thirteen century. Although my opinions did not confirm their beliefs that this was a site built in the eleventh century by the famous translator Rinchen Zangpo—or, as one often optimistically hears locally, "Just like Alchi!"—they were at least relieved that I did not question the antiquity of the site as among the earliest in Zangskar, which I still believe to be the case. I learned more from them than they from me. Moreover, our investigations had had a positive effect: they informed me that the de- and reconsecration had served to increase local interest in the site. Villagers subsequently told me that they had never actually been up to the stupa before we sponsored the ritual.

Subsequently, I have been able to study my documentation of the images, and to expand the archive of such photographs at opportune moments and with more powerful cameras and lenses. The documentation has allowed for the gradual decipherment of the ceiling *maṇḍala*. Each of the inner and outer offering goddesses, the four gate guardians, and the four *vajra*-bodhisattva, are found in their proper direction as mandated by the main Vajradhatu *mahāmaṇḍala* prescriptions, and in their proper colors.

Even before the deconsecration, I had provided some funds to help structurally reinforce the main shrine at Chuchikzhal, and afterward contributed to the building of a small medical library and treatment room immediately below the main shrine. While construction was only half-finished, I spent the autumn and early winter of 2003–04 in the part of the building that was enclosed, focused on learning to read Tibetan. The Lonpo was then staying in a small room on the top floor of the Chuchikzhal shrine, but after the medical library building was completed, he moved in. He has stayed there ever since, first teaching Tibetan medicine to local students for a few years and then writing several books on Zangskar history, two of which have been published in Tibetan.[8] Over time, he grew increasingly concerned about the condition of the Kadampa Chorten and other sites in the Chuchikzhal complex. Alongside a proprietary interest in this, his inheritance, he felt an inner obligation to arrest as best he could the decay accelerated by cultural and climate change. To this end he has been very active indeed over the last decade and a half, as I am able to document here.

8 Wangchuk, *History of Zangskar Monasteries*. In a draft English translation of the Karsha Lonpo's chapter on the Chuchikzhal Shrine by his grandson, Phuntsok Angchuk, the Lonpo indicates that although the traditional oral understanding of the making and consecration of the sculpture of the 11-headed Chuchikzhal dates to the time of Rinchen Zangpo, he suggests that the sculpture was done by a disciple of the great Lotsava, and that the shrine itself as it exists may date between the mid thirteenth and the early fourteenth century. Personal communication, September 2023.

Virūpa and the Date of the Karsha Kadampa Chorten

Elena Pakhoutova's 2009 Ph.D. dissertation on the Indian formation and transmission of the set of eight great stupas in tenth to thirteenth century Tibet and the western Himalaya has been cited here already multiple times, most often in chapter 3. As part of her research, she closely considered the murals in the Kadampa Chorten above Karsha Chuchikzhal and argued that the paintings in the Kadampa Chorten must date no earlier than the mid-thirteenth-century.[1] As laid out clearly in the dissertation, she based this date on the presence of Mahāsiddha Virūpa in a mural inside the entrance chorten **(Fig. 7A.1)**. He appears on the upper left of the Vairocana-dominated wall, which sadly is in a relatively poor state **(Fig. 7A.2)**. Fortunately, the Virūpa figure is in recognizable condition, and comparison of two photographs taken some twenty years apart demonstrates little significant deterioration. (Figure 7A.1 was taken in 2001, and Figure 7A.3 taken in 2018.) Virūpa appears there in his classic form, pointing with his proper left arm at the sun, to slow its course while he slaked his thirst at a drinking establishment.[2] He appears that way at Tungri, as was illustrated in the previous chapter **(Figs. 6.11–11A)**. The nineteenth century post- or poly-sectarian scholar practioner Jamgön Kongtrul describes him this way:

> On an antelope-skin seat is the revered
> great lord of yogins, Birvapa or Virūpa.
> He is dark brown, short and fat, with a
> large belly. His shortish, curly hair is
> decorated with a garland of flowers.
> He is looking with his eyes gazing fixedly.
> His right hand is raised to the sky in the
> threatening gesture; his left hand holds a
> decorative horn cup filled with nectar. He is
> wearing a triangular hemp skirt and sitting
> with his legs in the posture of royal ease.
> To his left is a yogini from the ḍākinīs' realm,
> appearing as a maiden, holding a vase of
> nectar and offering it to him.[3]

Fig. 7A.1 Virūpa Mahāsiddha on upper left of Vairocana mural inside Kadampa Chorten, Chuchikzhal, Karsha, Zangskar. Photo 2001.

Pakhoutova's reasons for dating it to the mid-thirteenth century or later is based on two interrelated factors and an inference. The first factor is Virūpa's indisputable prominence in the Sakya lineage, from which Pakhoutova seems to (questionably) deduce that ipso facto Virūpa's presence there demonstrates that it is a Sakya monument. The second factor, the relevance of which is dependent on this conclusion, has to do with the timing of the predominance of the Sakyas over west Tibet and the western Himalaya under the Mongols. She points out that "the Sakya religious tradition . . . traces its tantric transmission lineage to Virūpa . . . [and] extended their control to western Himalaya after the reign of western Tibetan [Gugé] king Dragpa De ended

1 Pakhoutova, "Reproducing the Sacred Places," 240.

2 On Virūpa, see "The Tavern Customer," and "Commentary: The Forms of Virūpa," in Linrothe, *Holy Madness*, 28–29, 302–303, and cat. nos. 46, 48–50, and 52–58.

3 Jamgön Kongtrul, *Mahāsiddha Practice*, 65.

Fig. 7A.2 Mural of Vairocana mural ("East wall") inside Kadampa Chorten, Chuchikzhal, Karsha, Zangskar. Photo 2011.

Fig. 7A.3 Virūpa Mahāsiddha on upper left of Vairocana mural inside Kadampa Chorten, Chuchikzhal, Karsha, Zangskar. Photo 2018.

in 1227 [*sic*]."[4] "Therefore," Pakhoutova continues, "the paintings at Karsha stūpa are later than suggested by Linrothe and Kerin and cannot be earlier than around the middle of the thirteenth-century."[5] This is certainly an interesting argument and needs to be considered in detail. As a point of reference, we had dated it to the late twelfth century.[6]

Although in the passage quoted above, 1227 is given as the date for the death of Dragpa De, in fact his dates are 1230–1277 according to the source she cites and indeed as she correctly provides in two other places in her dissertation.[7] That minor typo is meaningless in itself. But if Virūpa is a sign of Sakya patronage at Karsha, and Sakya control was not a factor until after the death in the third quarter of the thirteenth century of Dragpa De, the king of Gugé and Puhrang, then it does not follow that the Kadampa Chorten paintings "cannot be earlier than the middle of the thirteenth-century."[8] If the two prior suppositions

4 Pakhoutova, "Reproducing the Sacred Places," 239–240.

5 Ibid., 240.

6 Linrothe and Kerin, "Deconsecration and Discovery," 63.

7 Vitali, *Kingdoms of Gu.ge Pu.hrang*, 147, 443; Pakhoutova, "Reproducing the Sacred Places," 201, 203.

8 Ibid., 240.

Fig. 7A.4 Phagmo Drupa and Jigten Gonpo in Kagyu Drigung lineage at the Senge Gang shrine at Lamayuru, Ladakh, late thirteenth–early fourteenth c. Photo 2008.

hold, then the paintings cannot be earlier than the very late thirteenth, not its middle. According the same study by Roberto Vitali that Pakhoutova cites, in the mid-thirteenth century, the Drigung lineage, not the Sakya, was empowered in the western Himalaya by the Mongols, in 1240 and confirmed in 1250[9] and only lost control of the region "some time between 1277 and 1280."[10] It was only in 1290 that the Drigung in central Tibetan were defeated by the Sakyas in open warfare and their home monastery devastated.[11] Presumably only then did their fortunes in the western Himalaya quickly collapse. In fact the sources Vitali used are quiet about Drigung activities and those of the Karmapas "after the Sa.skya.pa-s had taken over the lands of sTod [i.e. the farther western Himalaya]."[12] However, if the Karsha Kadampa Chorten had Sakya sponsors, and they did not take control until the very end of the thirteenth-century, then practically we would have to date it to the start of the fourteenth century. That would place it in the same period as Ladakh's Wanla Sumtsek and Lamayuru's Senge Gang shrine. Both are Drigung and employ a localized form-idiom stemming from the central Tibetan refinement of the Magadha mode (see chapter 4 and Fig. 7A.4). Both have murals depicting identifiable Drigung teachers as in Figure 7A.4, and most studies instead place them in the late thirteenth to early fourteenth century.[13] Comparison makes the Karsha Kadampa Chorten paintings, with traces of the subtle modeling, look much earlier than the Ladakhi paintings. The latter represent the (later) western Himalayan localization of the type of central Tibetan versions of eastern Indian (Magadha) painting that the (earlier) Kadampa Chorten murals epitomize.

Textual or inscriptional sources for the Sakya period of control of Ladakh and Zangskar are not granular enough to know of what "control" consisted. More importantly there is evidence, including some that has come to light subsequent to the completion of Pakhoutova's dissertation, to suggest that Virūpa's early appearance in the western Himalaya was not exclusive to the Sakya lineage. Without corroborative evidence that the Kadampa Chorten is Sakya in orientation, and not, as its local name suggest, Kadampa, the date and the extent of the control of the Sakya-Mongol interjection into western Himalayan religious and political life become irrelevant to the date of the Kadampa Chorten.

9 Vitali, *Kingdoms of Gu.ge Pu.hrang*, 389, 418. This empowerment of the Drigung "did not do more than confirm the prevailing religious and political situation" in western Ladakh; ibid., 421.

10 Ibid., 420.

11 Czaja, *Medieval Rule in Tibet*, 1:106–107.

12 Ibid., 424.

13 Luczanits, "Wanla Bkra shis *gsum brtsegs*," 124; Namgyal Institute, *Legacy of a Mountain People*, 1:211.

Fig. 7A.5 Detail of upper proper left thigh of Mañjuśrī Bodhisattva clay sculpture depicting Mahāsiddhas as part of the dhoti decoration; Virūpa is at the upper left; Alchi Sumtsek, Ladakh. Photo 2022.

Fig. 7A.6 Virūpa pointing at the sun, part of a set of eight Mahāsiddhas with Padampa Sangye surrounding Mañjuśrī in right niche on the ground floors of the Wanla Sumtsek, Ladakh, fourteenth century. Photo 2006.

Although Pakhoutova is certainly correct to point to Virūpa's prominence among Sakya practitioners, they were far from the only group of Buddhists to feature him in the western Himalaya, or elsewhere for that matter. For example, he belongs to the selective set of eight "great" Mahāsiddhas who are distributed to the eight charnel grounds surrounding countless mandalas. More specifically, he is found at a site in the western Himalaya datable to the late twelfth or early thirteenth century (though some still maintain an even earlier date) and in a distinctly non-Sakya context: the Alchi Sumtsek. The fact is that Christian Luczanits and I, working together, only recently identified Virūpa on the dhoti of the sculpture of Mañjuśrī at the Sumtsek at Alchi, a decidedly Drigung lineage context (Fig. 7A.5).[14] A set of 84 Mahāsiddhas has long been recognized as having been painted on the bodhisattva's legs. The fact that Virūpa has not been previously identified is probably because he is invisible from the front of the bodhisattva sculpture. He appears at the very extreme upper left edge of the group. In order to see him one must look from the side at the edge of the proper right hip of Mañjuśri. But there he is, pointing at the sun, and embracing his consort. Counter-intuitively, one could say that he is placed at the top left, first among the group, in order to maximize his isolation and thus visibility since he is not surrounded by the dozens of others competing for attention.

There may very well be other reasons to date the Karsha Kadampa Chorten later than late twelfth century that Kerin and I proposed, or to the late twelfth or early thirteenth as I now accept. But dating it on the basis of the presence of Virūpa and Sakya overlordship in my opinion is not viable when we can find him in prominent positions in other groupings of the eight or 84 Mahāsiddhas in the western Himalaya, including at the Wanla Sumtsek (Fig. 7A.6), the Phyang Guru Lhakhang and in the Alchi Shangrong murals. In both of the latter cases, he is in the lower left-hand corner of the group, and thus is closest to the viewer and easiest to see for that reason.

14 See Linrothe, "Note on the *Mahāsiddha*" 2.578–579.

By the mid-2000s some Italian converts to Buddhism had established an NGO called Stupa Onlus which came to Ladakh to rebuild older stupas. Although the group is well-intentioned, its method, at least at first, was to encase old stupas in cement, reshaping them in accord with modern stupa forms, despite the fact that their original designs reflect historically older patterns. For example, around 2008 they turned a dilapidated but still-standing entrance chorten at the old royal palace of Zangla into a pile of brightly painted cement that barely resembled the original. Smaller than the Kadampa Chorten, within just a few years after its renovation by Stupa Onlus the cement was cracking and pieces were already starting to fall off. I worried that the weight of the cement cladding might actually destroy the very interesting, very old murals inside it. (A pre-restoration photograph is included in chapter 5, Figure 5.10, and the murals are discussed and illustrated in chapter 4; see Figures 4.80–82, 4.162.) The Zangla murals have survived, thankfully, but are clad within something of a structural wreck, but a recent one due to the use of disintegrating cement.

Members of the Stupa Onlus team came to the Chuchikzhal complex, drew up some architectural plans and tried to convince the Karsha Lonpo to let them renovate the Kadampa Chorten, offering to pay for its restoration. I pleaded with him to do as he had done with the funds I had given him in the 1990s for the main Chuchikzhal shrine: use local sustainable materials and methods, not cement. As it happened, by this time the Zangla Chorten had started to crack and crumble, and rumors were floated that Karsha Lonpo had approved their plans, implying that he was somehow at fault **(Figs. 7.23–24)**. Before work had started on it, the Lonpo and other honored members of the community were asked to come to a meeting at Zangla to discuss the NGO's offer to repair it at their expense. Not being an architect or mason himself, he had not been asked to weigh in on the plan or the materials. But when he later heard he was being blamed, and I showed him photographs of what it looked like just three years after the "renovation" completion, he decided against that mode of repair for the Kadampa Chorten.

Meanwhile, two ancient closed chorten—not gateway stupas, so without murals—near the Chuchikzhal main shrine were starting to collapse. In the spring and summer of 2013, some Nepali masons were hired to dismantle them after a deconsecration. In early June of that year, I was able to document many of the objects that had been found inside one of the

(anticlockwise from top left):

Fig. 7.23 Zangla Kankani (Gateway) Chorten, a few years after renovation, Zangla, Zangskar. Photo 2012.

Fig. 7.24 Detail of crumbling cement structure of Zangla Kankani Chorten, a few years after renovation, Zangla, Zangskar. Photo 2012.

Fig. 7.25 (Left): Nepali workers during the dismantling of one of the two deteriorating chortens near the Chuchikzhal shrine. (Right): The Karsha Lonpo directing the preservation of ritual deposits found in the chorten. (Both): Chuchikzhal, Karsha, Zangskar, 2013.

chortens. I went on a trek within Zangskar and when I returned to Karsha in July, the other chorten was being dismantled, so I was able to participate in retrieving the *bumpa* (vase with consecration offerings and deposits), extracting *tsha tsha* (Figs. 7.25–26), unfolding painting fragments, and documenting the finds. I photographed a number of objects from the second stupa as they were removed, along with the earlier ones after they had been found. The *tsha tsha* included Kashmiri, Kaṇiṣka-type stupas with small *aṇḍa* and tall superstructures (Fig. 7.27), and a standing two-armed Lokeśvara with sophisticated modeling and posture (Fig. 7.28). Appropriate to the context, a *tsha tsha* featuring a seated, twelve-armed, eleven-headed Avalokiteśvara (Chuchikzhal) was also found in numbers (Fig. 7.29). Most of the paintings were very fragmentary, including small illuminations on torn thick paper. Of the two illustrated, including Amoghasiddhi (Fig. 7.30) and Green Tārā (Fig. 7.31), the Tathāgata painting is the earlier, plausibly thirteenth century, in the central Tibetan idiom derived from Pāla painting like the Kadampa Chorten ceiling paintings.

Fig. 7.26 A vase (*bumpa*) filled with consecration deposits extracted from one of the dismantled chortens, Chuchikzhal, Karsha, Zangskar. Photo 2013.

Fig. 7.28 Molded clay plaque (*tsha tsha*) depicting a standing two-armed Lokeśvara with sophisticated modeling and posture, ht. 8 cm, from one of the dismantled chortens, Chuchikzhal, Karsha, Zangskar. Photo 2013.

Fig. 7.27 Molded clay plaque (*tsha tsha*) depicting a Kashmiri, Kaṇiṣka-type stupa with small *aṇḍa* and tall superstructure, ht. 9 cm, from one of the dismantled chortens, Chuchikzhal, Karsha, Zangskar. Photo 2013.

Fig. 7.29 Molded clay plaque (*tsha tsha*) depicting a seated twelve-armed, eleven-headed Avalokiteśvara (Chuchikzhal), ht. 8 cm, from one of the dismantled chortens, Chuchikzhal, Karsha, Zangskar. Photo 2013.

Fig. 7.30 Text illumination fragment on thick paper showing Amoghasiddhi Tathaāgata, 5 x 4.5 cm, ca. 12th–13th c., from one of the dismantled chortens, Chuchikzhal, Karsha, Zangskar. Photo 2013.

Fig 7.31 Text illumination fragment on thick paper showing Syama (Green) Tārā, ca. 13th c., 4 x 4 cm, from one of the dismantled chortens, Chuchikzhal, Karsha, Zangskar. Photo 2013.

Fig. 7.32 Fragmentary left edge of a painting on cloth depicting Cakrasaṃvara, with bottom still inserted into its painted wooden hanging bar,74 x 11 cm, from one of the dismantled chortens, Chuchikzhal, Karsha, Zangskar. Photo 2013.

Fig. 7.33 Detail of fragmentary ca. 15th c. painting on cloth of Ṣaḍakṣarī Avalokiteśvara, 40 x 37 cm, (same as Figs. 7.34, 7.35) depicting white Ṣaḍakśarī on his right, from one of the dismantled chortens, Chuchikzhal, Karsha, Zangskar. Photo 2013.

Fig. 7.34 Detail of fragmentary ca. 15th c. painting on cloth of Ṣaḍakṣara Avalokiteśvara, 40 x 37 cm (same as Figs. 7.33, 7.35) depicting yellow female Manidharī on his right, from one of the dismantled chortens, Chuchikzhal, Karsha, Zangskar. Photo 2013.

One of the retrieved fragmentary paintings on cloth was a strip of a painting, the left edge of a larger wrathful *yidam*-deity painting (Cakrasaṃvara), the bottom selvedge of which was still inserted into its painted wooden hanging bar (Fig. 7.32). The remains of a second painting with the same theme was also recovered. Another was the very faded and torn central portion of an Amitāyus mandala. An additional one constituted part of a ca. fifteenth century Ṣaḍakṣara Avalokiteśvara painting, with white Ṣaḍakśarī on his right (Fig. 7.33), and a yellow Mandiharī on his left (Fig. 7.34), reversing the usual order. Both are female, when elsewhere Manidharin is most often depicted as male, as he appears in the mural behind the sculpture in the niche of the Kadampa Chorten (see Fig. 7.18).[9] In the upper right corner, the same painting has an intriguing idealized portrait of a figure wearing white sleeves under a monastic-type vest and eye-shades of netting pulled up over his forehead (Fig. 7.35). Also retrieved was a battered Syāma (Green) Tārā of ca. fourteenth or fifteenth century date with a relatively

9 Some paintings do show both of the side figures in the three-deity configuration as female. See nos. 66794 and 65087 on the Himalayan Art Resources website, https://www.himalayanart.org/items/66794 and https://www.himalayanart.org/items/65087, respectively.

Fig. 7.35 Detail of fragmentary ca. 15th c. painting on cloth of Ṣaḍakṣara Avalokiteśvara, 40 x 37 cm (same as Figs. 7.33, 7.34) a lineage figure with net eye-shade, from one of the dismantled chortens, Chuchikzhal, Karsha, Zangskar, Photo 2013.

Fig. 7.37 A nearly intact *circa* late 14th-century painting on cloth of the Buddha Amitabha, 50 x 44 cm, found in one of two dismantled chortens near the Chuchikzhal shrine, Chuchikzhal, Karsha, Zangskar. Photo 2013.

Fig. 7.36 Detail of a fragmentary ca. 14th-century painting on cloth, approx. 42 x 30 cm, of Syama (Green) Tārā depicting a standing Ekajatī, from one of the dismantled chortens, Chuchikzhal, Karsha, Zangskar. Photo 2013.

Fig. 7.38 A nearly intact *circa* 15th-century painting on cloth of an unidentified Kadampa or Gelugpa lama, 59 x 50 cm, found in one of two dismantled chortens near the Chuchikzhal shrine, Chuchikzhal, Karsha, Zangskar. Photo 2013.

intact portion depicting a fine black Ekajatī wearing a snow-leopard-skin bodice and shorts (Fig. 7.36).

From the same chorten came two paintings that were nearly whole, and intriguingly, do not fit easily into identifiable lineages or aesthetic traditions (Figs. 7.37–38). The Amitābha painting, perhaps as early as the fourteenth century, features a strictly arranged, pre-landscape setting and some archaic looking elements. These include the angularly posed standing white Padmapāṇi on the Buddha's left, the accomplished scroll work, the eastern Indian style (rgya gar shar bris[10]) throne, and the luminous stems and flowers against a flat black ground in the empty spaces surrounding the central figure (Figs. 7.39–42). It has a chorten drawn on the back, with cursive inscriptions of prayers (Figs. 7.43–44), which might possibly reveal some historical information though the initial reading by Karsha Lonpo did not uncover any.

10 Heller, "Page from an Artist's Sketchbook," 381.

Fig. 7.39 Detail of Figure 7.37, depicting a standing Padmapāṇi next to *gaja-vyāla* motif on the Buddha's throne. Photo 2013.

Fig. 7.40 Detail of Figure 7.37, depicting Amitābha's arm against scrollwork. Photo 2013.

Fig. 7.41 Detail of Figure 7.37, depicting *makara* on Amitābha Buddha's throneback against the scarlet nimbus. Photo 2013.

Fig. 7.42 Detail of Figure 7.37, depicting lotus throne with elephant and lions, the dark blue background of the background with lotus stems and flowers in an archaic mode. Photo 2013.

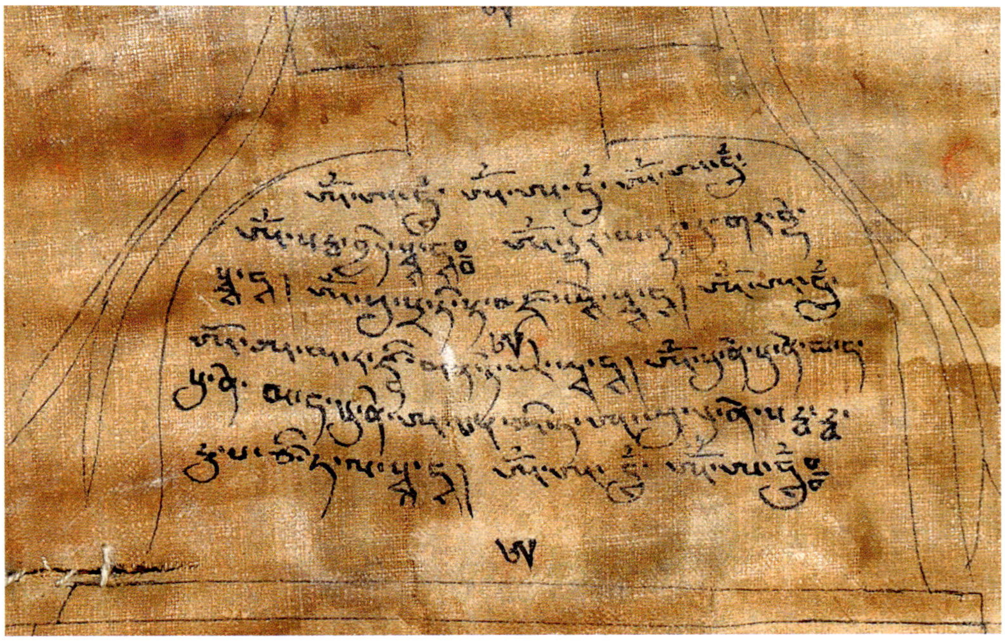

Fig. 7.43 Inscription on the back of the painting on cloth of Amitabha Buddha (Fig. 7.37), Tibetan cursive script within the outline stupa's *aṇḍa*. Photo 2013.

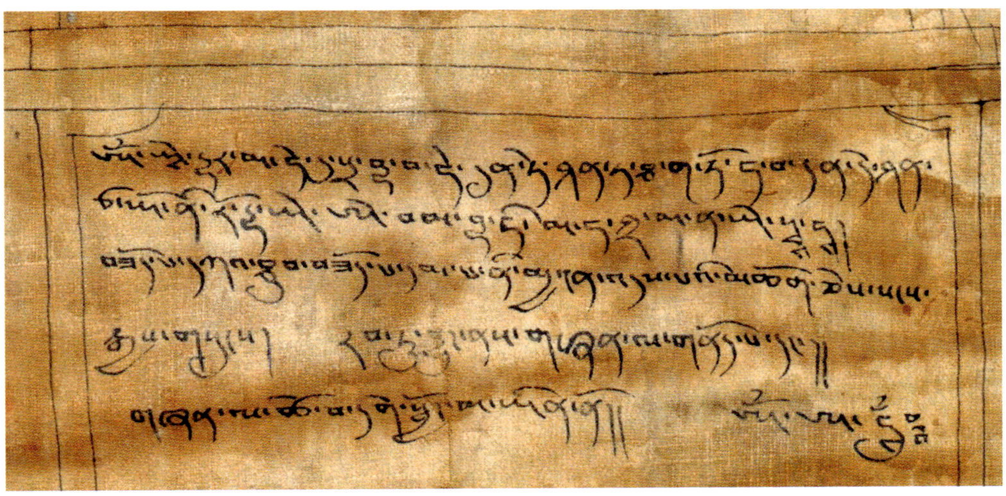

Fig. 7.44 Inscription on the back of the painting on cloth of Amitabha Buddha (Fig. 7.37), Tibetan cursive script within the outline stupa's base. Photo 2013.

Fig. 7.45 Detail of the lower left of Figure 7.38, depicting peaceful and wrathful protectors as well as Padampa Sangye (upper right), with Acala (lower left) and Hayagrīva (lower right). Photo 2013.

Fig. 7.46 Detail of Fig. 7.38, depicting the face of the yellow-hat teacher holding vajra and bell. Photo 2013.

The other painting, of the yellow-hatted monk (see Fig. 7.38), has a number of interesting minor attendant figures, wrathful protectors as well as early inspiring teachers including Padampa Sangye in the lower left (Fig. 7.45, upper right).[11] In the upper portion of the composition, a rich panoply of two dozen lineages figures, unfortunately not identified by inscription, a few wearing distinctly red hats but most of them bare-headed, surround the central figure and his two standing acolytes. It is conceivable that the central monk figure (Fig. 7.46) may be a candidate for representing a Kadampa teacher, a lineage that remained important in Zangskar into the sixteenth century and later as evidenced by the Andus shrine in Langmi village near Karsha that preserves books and statues of late Kadampa teachers.[12] This is the lineage, after all, that the Kadampa Chorten was named after. The Gelugpa, the dominant Tibetan Buddhist lineage to which the Dalai Lamas belong, founded in the fifteenth century, originally called itself the "New Kadampa" lineage.

✣✣✣

To replace the two chorten that had been dismantled before collapsing, the Lonpo and his son, Lama Angchug, engaged a locally-trained *mistri* or mason from Reru in Zangskar named Stanzin Choldan (Fig. 7.47). Using mostly local materials, he constructed a new chorten near the site of the two smaller dismantled ones, between the Chuchikzhal shrine and the nunnery. The only drawback of the traditional method and materials is that the structure has to be given an annual coat of whitewash to protect it. One day in the summer of 2018, I happened to be there when the newly built replacement stupa was in need of whitewashing. Incentivized by some pocket-money from their grandfather, a few of the Lonpo's grandchildren and their friends managed the job in a morning (Figs. 7.48–50). Meanwhile, all the objects removed from the two collapsed chortens—the *tsha tsha*, the text pages, and the painting fragments—were reinstalled in a new repository built nearby. All, that is, except for the two relatively intact paintings (see Figs. 7.37–38) which I urged the Lonpo and Gelong Angchug to keep. I bought some good blue cloth from Delhi and had it brought to Zangskar, and by 2017 the two paintings were remounted and hung in the Chuchikzhal shrine.

At around the same time, the Zangskar Development Authority awarded the Lonpo's family a community grant between 2015 and 2017 to build

11 On other images of this figure in Ladakh and Zangskar, including Karsha, see Linrothe, "Strengthening the Roots."

12 See Linrothe, "Siddhas and Sociality," 187.

Fig. 7.47 The trained craftsman and stupa builder Stanzin Choldan in front of the Karsha Kadampa Chorten, Chuchikzhal, Karsha, Zangskar. Photograph by "Pali" Stanzin Chosgyal, son-in-law of the Karsha Lonpo in 2016.

Fig. 7.48 Some of the Karsha Lonpo's grandchildren and their friends after pouring lime whitewash on the chorten built to replace the two dismantled chortens near the Chuchikzhal shrine, Chuchikzhal, Karsha, Zangskar. Photo 2018.

Fig. 7.49 Pouring lime whitewash on the top of the chorten built to replace the two dismantled chortens near the Chuchikzhal shrine, Chuchikzhal, Karsha, Zangskar. Photo 2018.

(left and right):

Fig. 7.50 In the process of white-washing the newly built replacement chorten, Chuchikzhal, Karsha, Zangskar. Photo 2018.

Fig. 7.51 The Kasha Lonpo hosting the son of Ngari Rinpoche inside the new extension to the Karsha Chuchikzhal Shine, Chuchikzhal, Karsha, Zangskar. Photo 2018.

Fig. 7.52 Young nuns and others attending the school at the Chuchikzhal nunnery awaiting the visit of Ngari Rinpoche's son, presentation scarves at the ready, Chuchikzhal, Karsha, Zangskar. Photo 2018.

a new hall for the *nyungné* (nyung gnas) fasting ritual that takes place annually in the Chuchikzhal shrine as already mentioned. The three-day ritual draws many more lay people than can be accommodated within the shrine itself. The new hall, built of cement, is directly adjacent to the old shrine, and now people can prostrate in both the shrine and in the hall where they can sleep at night. Completed by the summer of 2018, it further serves as a bright new space for other meetings. The son of an honored Tibetan Lama, Ngari Rinpoche (the present incarnation is the current Dalai Lama's brother), visited Karsha that summer, and Karsha Lonopo hosted him for tea in the new prayer hall (Fig. 7.51). Then, he entered the Karsha Chuchikzhal Shrine itself, followed by a visit to the nunnery where he was warmly greeted by all the nuns, including the youngest (Fig. 7.52).

***

Following the repainting and regilding of the face of the eleven-headed Lokeśvara in the main Chuchikzhal shrine by a professional artist in the summer of 2016 (see Fig. 7.4), the Karsha Lonpo was ready to devote his energies to repairing the structure of the Kadampa Chorten. He had found both the right builder—Stanzin Choldan—as well as a donor, a generous and successful Japanese female artist named Yasui Yoko, a longtime friend of Tsewang Yangphel from Hongshet, a village neighboring Karsha. The latter had helped to arrange the connection and was also himself a partial sponsor. The master builder, Stanzin Choldan, having proved his abilities on the previous stupa project was charged with overseeing this one, using local materials exclusively.

Stanzin Choldan (see Fig. 7.47) was originally from Kargyak village in eastern Zanskar. He married a woman from Reru, where he lives with his family. I have met him more than once, and on one occasion had a chance to interview him with Gelong Angchug, the Lonpo's second son, as translator. He started training at sixteen at the Leh Handicrafts Training Institute. He spent three years there, working with a well-known artist from Nimmu, now deceased. He also worked with a statue maker, also now deceased, from Wanla, and learned how to make and repair sculpture. Most formative for his training, he said, was working alongside a stupa-maker in a number of villages. He considers himself an all-around artist, capable in all media although he was come to specialize in stupa-building and repair, and in designs incorporating auspicious symbols of Buddhist culture that are executed in various media. His training was multi- or rather non-sectarian, not specific to a single artistic or Buddhist tradition such as Geluk or Drukpa. His most prestigious commission so far is the 2016 Rohtang Tunnel Changchub Chorten in 2016 at the suggestion of H.H. the 14th Dalai Lama.

On 9 February 2016, a second deconsecration ceremony of the Kadampa Chorten took place, nearly fifteen years after the one we sponsored in 2001. Subsequently, on 8 April 2016 the ritual to appease earth spirits and Nāgās, an earth-cleansing ritual (Tib. *klu 'bum*), in line with classical Indian and Tibetan prescriptions, was carried out before the restoration work began.[13] They included making ritual deposits in the four directions,[14] reciting prayers, inserting offerings into the ground such as barley, sandalwood powder, *tsha tsha*, and other desirable things to appease the earthly spirits (Figs. 7.53–54). Repairs and reconstruction were carried out between April

13 For the ideal prescribed course of such rituals, see Gyaltsen, *Clarifying the Meaning of the Arga and Consecration Rituals*, 73–81. "According to old customs dating from shamanistic, pre-Buddhist times, the local deities had to be placated and measures had to be taken to assure that the project would thrive. The small group [of monks] carried out the necessary geomantic calculations on the cleared land, and in the place indicated by their calculations they buried a vase containing rolls of mantras, incense, and semiprecious stones as offerings. They also performed rituals to request the local deities for their permission and for the peaceful completion of their project." This was for the establishment of the Drikung Kagyu Institute in Dehra Dun. Gruber, *From the Heart of Tibet*, 230.

14 This is probably related to *garbhadhāna*, the "implanting of the seed" in Hindu temple establishment rituals; see Kramrisch, *Hindu Temple*, 1:165.

Figs. 7.53, 7.54 The Karsha Lonpo and other monks from Karsha Monastery carrying out the earth-purification and offering rituals to appease earth spirits, including offerings in the four directions; Chuchikzhal, Karsha, Zangskar. Photographs by "Pali" Stanzin Chosgyal in 2016.

and June of that first year but not completed. The Japanese sponsor arrived in June and inspected the progress.

The objects we had found in 2001 inside the niches (*tsha tsha*, text and painting fragments) had been replaced in the niches with the reconsecration. After the 2016 deconsecration was carried out in order to begin rebuilding, they were once again removed. They were placed inside the Chuchikzhal Shrine while the repairs and structural stabilization were carried out by a team of workers under Stanzin Choldan and overseen by the Lonpo and his family. During the course of the repairs, on 9 August 2016 I was able to confirm that these objects—fragments of paintings and texts—were the very ones we had photographed fifteen years earlier in 2001. There was also an astro-medical chart (Fig. 7.55), a fragment of a painting of a wrathful protector (perhaps Takkirāja) (Fig. 7.56), and a very faded portion of a painting of Drigungpa (Fig. 7.57),[15] objects that I failed to recall or to have documented in 2001.

That summer, the Karsha Lonpo told me that in the course of the rebuilding (Fig. 7.58), they had found some bones among the exposed stones of the upper superstructure (Fig. 7.59). He asked if I would like to examine them. He kept them in a plastic sack outside the medical-library which includes a consecrated shrine-room. He spread them out, outdoors. They were mostly small animal bones, of perhaps sheep, mice, or marmots, even part of a goat horn. The Lonpo reasoned that they had landed atop the chorten when crows or eagles or other predator birds flew up there to eat their carrion. Also at the top of the stupa the workers had also found, wrapped in now-faded yellow silk, some human-cranial parietal fragments—at least, that is what they looked like to me. Looking carefully I noticed that the silk wrapping had a tiny square seal impression on it, depicting the *triratna* (Buddhist three jewels signifying the Buddha, the teachings and the community of practitioners) giving off radiance (Fig. 7.60). Clearly, this was an intentional relic deposit, but Karsha Lonpo had not noticed the seal, and so did not distinguish these bones from the others. I believe that what threw off the Lonpo and the Geshes he had asked about them is that they were found at the top of the stupa. In contemporary practice in Zangskar, relics are part of the consecration deposits, as offerings, and are found below or in the main part of the stupa, not near the top though in older ritual texts and actual excavations they are also placed up there.[16] I concluded that this was an intentional relic deposit, and speculated that it could have been what motivated the stupa's creation in the first place. At first, the Karsha Lonpo was still cautious and kept them wrapped up with the other bones outside his quarters until the next day another very learned Geshe respected by the Lonpo stopped by. We showed the silk and bones to him and after a close look, he also agreed they were different, and from then on, the Karsha Lonpo brought the silk wrapped bone relics inside the shrine room. Whose they are, we can only speculate, but they are not recent.

By late August or early September 2016, all the ritual deposits (painting fragments, most of the *tsha tsha*, etc.) removed from the Karsha Kadampa Chorten were interred nearby in a specially built depository (tsha tsha khang)—not a chorten but still consecrated. By June 2017, Stanzin Choldan

15 Compare this image to a painting Walter Koelz collected at Karsha in July of 1933, now in the University of Michigan Museum of Anthropology, acc. no. 17487; Sinpoli, *Himalayan Journey*, 93–94; Copeland, *Tankas from the Koelz Collection*, fig. 98.

16 A text attributed to Shes rab 'byung gnas (1187–1241) that includes a list of relics inserted into Jigten Gonpo's Tashi Gomang Stupa states that "for the pinnacle, the highest point of the stupa symbolizing the enlightenment, most bone relics (*gdung*) were taken;" Czaja, "Commemorative Stupas at Densathil," 226. In the *Dharmagutaka-Vinaya*, "They did not know how to place the śarīras (i.e., relics). (The Buddha said:) 'They should be placed in a golden *stupa*, silver *stupa*, jewelled *stupa*, or in a *stupa*, (inlaid) with sundry jewels; they should be wrapped in silk (or) cotton cloth, should be wrapped in *patsijaṃlamba* (?) cloth, or *d(h)ud(h)ula (?)* cloth.'" Karashima, "*Stūpas* Described in the Chinese Translations of the *Vinayas*," 452.

(clockwise from top left):

Fig. 7.55 Astro-medical chart painted across two sheets of paper, 28 x 20 cm, found among the objects deposited in the Kadampa Chorten after the deconsecration of 2016, Chuchikzhal, Karsha, Zangskar. Photo 2016.

Fig. 7.56 Fragment, 11 x 9 cm, of a ca. 12th–13th-century damaged painting on cloth deposited in the Kadampa Chorten after the deconsecration of 2016, possibly depicting Takkirāja, Chuchikzhal, Karsha, Zangskar. Photo 2016.

Fig. 7.57 Damaged painting on cloth of a ca. 13th century painting of Drigungpa Rinchen Pel, 36 x 17 cm, found among the objects deposited in the Kadampa Chorten after deconsecration of 2016, Chuchikzhal, Karsha, Zangskar. Photo 2016.

Fig. 7.58 Renovating the exterior of the Kadampa chorten Chuchikzhal, Karsha, Zangskar, India, Chuchikzhal, Karsha, Zangskar, India. Photograph by "Pali" Stanzin Chosgyal in 2016

Fig. 7.59 The upper part of the Kadampa chorten pre-renovation, where animal bones and silk-wrapped relics (probably human cranial fragments) were discovered during the repairs, Chuchikzhal, Karsha, Zangskar. Photo 2015.

(clockwise from top left):

Fig. 7.60 Close up view of a seal impression of the glowing *triratna* ('Three Jewels') design on the yellow silk wrapping bone relics, found in the upper part of the Kadampa chorten during renovation, Chuchikzhal, Karsha, Zangskar. Photo 2016.

Fig. 7.61 The Kadampa chorten after renovations were completed, before reconsecration, Chuchikzhal, Karsha, Zangskar. Photo 2017.

Fig. 7.62 The ritual specialist monks performing the reconsecration of the Kadampa chorten, Chuchikzhal, Karsha, Zangskar, India. Photograph by Gelong Angchug, second eldest son of the Karsha Lonpo in 2017.

Fig. 7.63 The monks, the Lonpo family, the sponsors and other visitor in front of the newly renovated, just-reconsecrated Kadampa chorten, Chuchikzhal, Karsha, Zangskar, India. Photograph by Gelong Angchug in 2017.

Fig. 7.64 The Karsha Lonpo (centre) offering honorific scarves to the sponsors (right) and the monks presiding over the reconsecration of the Kadampa chorten, with the two remounted paintings in Figures 7.37 and 7.38 behind them, Chuchikzhal, Karsha, Zangskar, India. Photograph by Gelong Angchug in 2017.

Fig. 7.65 (Left): The Karsha Lonpo performing an informal 'eye-opening' ceremony for the repainting of the repaired Buddha sculpture in one of the niches inside the Kadampa chorten. (Right): The Lonpo's grandson Pema repainting the Buddha's face. (Both): Chuchikzhal, Karsha, Zangskar in 2019.

Fig. 7.66 The Rigsum Gonbo (3 protectors) Chorten recently built near the Chuchikzhal shrine at Chuchikzhal, Karsha. Photo 2022.

had completed work on the Kadampa Chorten finial (Fig. 7.61), and on 29 and 30 July 2017, the major consecration took place. The Japanese sponsor returned for this important event and notable learned monks were invited to perform it. Among them was the Vajrācārya (rdo rje slob dpon) Geshe Kachen Sherab (dka' chen shes rab), originally from Zangskar, who happened to be visiting from Tashilhunpo in India (Fig. 7.62, right).[17] On the side of the stupa, they hung up the newly remounted paintings that had been found inside the demolished chorten, and so they too were re-consecrated (Figs. 7.63–64). The Lonpo's remaking of the Chuchikzhal complex was almost, but not quite, complete.

In early August 2019, Karsha Lonpo's grandson Pema, who was studying in Dharmasala to be an artist, paid a visit to Karsha and repainted the Buddha sculpture in the niche of the Kadampa Chorten passageway. When he was almost finished, the Lonpo did an informal *rabné* (rab gnas) consecration or "eye-opening" ceremony (Fig. 7.65) using a digest of ritual prayers.[18] (No retouching of the other sculpture, the murals in the niches or the upper mandala paintings has been undertaken to my knowledge.) Subsequently, the Lonpo arranged for the exterior structure to be whitewashed and by May of 2022 had completed building a set of three chortens known as the Rigsum Gonbo (3 protectors) affiliated with the three bodhisattvas Avalokiteśvara, Mañjuśrī and Vajrapāṇi (Fig. 7.66). These were placed next to the new chorten (Figs. 7.48–50) between the Chuchikzhal shrine and the nunnery. Meanwhile, a group of women (including two of the Lonpo's married daughters) living in the Thieur neighborhood of Karsha directly below Chuchikzhal, sponsored the repair and whitewashing of a chorten marking the start of the path up the hill to Chuchikzhal (Fig. 7.67). Finally, the lower area of the Queen's Chorten (Gyalmo Chorten),

17 I am indebted to Yannick Laurent for this identification, as he recognized him in the photograph; personal communication, 30 November 2019.

18 Drepung Loseling Library, *Chos spyod rab gsal skal bzang skye bo'i mgul rgyan zhes bya ba zhugs so*; Shinohara, "Esoteric Buddhist Ritual of Image Installation," 291–92. An abridged version of a *pratiṣṭhā* ritual similar to what the Karsha Lonpo performed from the *Saṃkṣiptapratiṣṭhavidhi* of the *Vajrāvali* is described: "[I]n the case of an abridged consecration of images and other [substrata], immediately after [the meditation on] voidness, [a tantric officiant] should (1) visualise in a moment each *samayasattva* whose eyes, body and other [parts] have been empowered, (2) draw down its *jñānasattva* by means of a ray from the seed- syllable in his hear, (3) cause the *jñānasattva* to enter the *samayasattva* (*tatra*), (4) cause the *tathāgatas* drawn down by means of rays from the seed-syllable in his heart to bathe it with water from jugs while he bathes it himself, worships it, and then (5) [finally] utters its mantra one hundred and eight times. Thus an image and other [substrate] become consecrated." Tanemura, "One Aspect of the Consecration Ceremony of Images in Buddhist Tantrism," 69n5.

Fig. 7.67 Newly renovated and whitewashed chorten at the foot of the path leading up to the Chuchikzhal complex and the associated nunnery, with buildings in the Karsha Monastery in the background at upper right. Photo 2022.

Fig. 7.68 The renovated, newly whitewashed and reconsecrated Kadampa chorten seen from upper Karsha village, with a ruined temple and a set of eight chortens the Lonpo had made *circa* 2003; further down, the Chuchikzhal medical library (with slanted windows) built in 2003–04 together with, right, a nuns' residence, Chuchikzhal, Karsha, Zangskar. Photo 2018.

Fig. 7.69 The renovated, newly whitewashed and reconsecrated Kadampa chorten seen at upper left above Chuchikzhal nunnery; view from lower Karsha village, Zangskar, Photograph by "Pali" Stanzin Chosgyal in 2017.

immediately adjacent to the Chuchikzhal shrine, to which reference is made in chapter 8 (see Fig. 8.25), has been fully enclosed, and is no longer used for storage.[19] As far as I know, these are the last steps in the Lonpo's exhaustive plan to leave the Chuchikzhal complex to future generations in better condition than he himself received it.[20]

One notable difference between the new and the old version of the Karsha Kadampa Chorten (see Fig. 7.8)—now renamed the Duttul (defeating enemies) Chorten—is that the newly rebuilt version is externally much more massive than the old one.[21] The interior, including the important mandala ceiling, the four panels and the two niches are preserved intact, but presumably are now protected and structurally strengthened. At present, the chorten is clearly visible from the foot of the hill below Karsha village and quite prominent even from further away (Figs. 7.68–69). Indeed, it is the new face of Chuchikzhal, and perhaps even Karsha. This is appropriate since it is the oldest surviving part of it, excepting the ruined citadel.

All this has been rather unexpected, however, because when I first visited Karsha in 1990, the Kadampa Chorten had been nearly forgotten.

19 Part of the Queen's Chorten is visible on the right in Figure 7.66; on the extensive late sixteenth-century paintings inside this site chorten, see Linrothe, "Site Unseen."

20 Although the upper paintings were not touched, the repair of the sculptures is in accord with a passage of the *Mūlasarvāstivāda-Vinaya* where it is written that "Figures and clay statues of the Buddha became damaged and broken. Being unsure, the monks dared not redecorate them. The Buddha [said]: 'One should either enlarge [i.e., repair] them or make similar ones as one likes.'" Karashima, "*Stūpa*s Described in the Chinese Translations of the *Vinaya*," 466.

21 Another passage in the *Mūlasarvāstivāda-Vinaya* states that, "Concerning the (re-) construction of stūpa, a small one can be enlarged, while a big one should not be decreased." Karashima, "*Stūpa*s Described in the Chinese Translations of the *Vinaya*," 466.

Fig. 7.70 The Karsha Lonpo with the author in front of the Chuchikzhal shrine Chuchikzhal, Karsha, Zangskar. Photograph by Victoria Andrews in 2018.

In the ensuing three decades, thanks to the Karsha Lonpo (Fig. 7.70), the gateway chorten has been made pertinent to the lives of three generations of contemporary Zangskaris and visitors from afar, like myself. Its survival into the distant future has been made *possible*; however, it is not guaranteed. That will require on the one hand learned, devout, and dedicated people in the mold of the Karsha Lonpo every few generations. On the other hand, it assumes that the devastating impact of climate change that is drastically and rapidly diminishing essential water resources for agriculture and animal husbandry in Zangskar can be mitigated.[22] Desertification and the abandonment not just of agricultural fields, as at present, but of entire villages if not regions of Zangskar, is looming. Thus the future of the preservation of the cultural and physical context of the strengthened Chuchikzhal Kadampa Chorten is facing long odds indeed.

As final corrections were being made for publication,
the Karsha Lonpo, born in 1936, passed away on 2 October, 2023.

22 On the climate crisis in Zangskar, see Mingle, *Fire and Ice*.

CHAPTER 8

Reflections on a Buddhist Painting of Sarasvatī in Zangskar

Hail to the holy Sarasvatī, hail! that goddess, who, having her power manifested as the enlightener of the all, through the gradually evolving faculties commencing with "desire," illuminates the nature of her mansion, the lotus-hearts of the sages,—her, even Sarasvatī, I praise.

—First verse of a Kaśmīri manuscript of Bāṇa's *Harṣcarita*

Several chapters in this volume—3–5, and to an extent 6—are focused on form-idioms, on the visual aspects of painting and sculpture in Zangskar. Others are more attentive to theoretical or thematic issues. This chapter is in the latter vein, and in fact attempts to recover the "meaning"—that is, the social significance and religious implications—of a single theme at a particular moment for an identifiable class of sponsors: Sarasvatī, the goddess associated with learning and arts originating in ancient times in India. Taking as its point of departure and conclusion a painting found in a monastery of Zangskar, the essay traces the nuanced set of associations that developed in South Asia from the early historic period there, and the uses and concentration or narrowing of those associations to a western Himalayan context, itself absorbing the ongoing central Tibetan conventions for this theme.[1]

Introduction

The origin of this sprawling essay is simple and straightforward. It is a ca. late fifteenth- or early sixteenth-century painting in a Buddhist monastery located in Zangskar, the western Himalayan region that is the focus of this volume. The official name of the monastery is the Phugtal Gonpa Ganden Zangpoling (phug thar dgon pa dga ldan bzang po gling), the Phugtal Retreat of the Auspicious Tushita Pure Land.[2] The monastery is built onto a cliff surrounding a deep cave with a water source in the back (Fig. 8.1). In the interior of the cave was constructed a stupa containing the relics of the monk who converted the monastery to the Geluk (dge lugs) order, a student of the Tibetan founder of that order. After the death in central Tibet of the founder (Tsongkhapa, who will be discussed later), his disciple

1 This is a slightly revised and expanded version of a chapter of *Revisiting Himalayan Borderlands, A Bridge Between India and Central Asia*, edited by T. A. Rather, Ajmal Shah, and Mumtaz A. Yatoo, with a preface by Siddiq Wahid. The publication was delayed by the coronavirus pandemic but was released in 2022. The version included here allowed for three times as many illustrations. I wish to thank Shanker Sharma of the Nalanda Archaeological Site Museum for his invaluable assistance to enable me to photograph the sculpture identified as Sarasvatī on Temple 2 at Nalanda (see Fig. 8.22) before the grounds were shut down for Covid protocol on 5 January 2022.

2 Wangchuk, *History of Zangskar Monasteries*, 38. See also map 2, p. x.

Fig 8.1 View of Phugtal Monastery, Zangskar, India. Photo 2018.

Changsem Sherap Zangpo (byang sems shes rab bzang po; 1395–1457) came home to the western Himalaya and apparently died at Phugtal. While in Zangskar, he either sent some local artists for training in west-central Tibet, or brought artists from there, for a disused shrine has darkened murals that are strongly reminiscent of paintings from Gyantse and are unlike local murals (see Fig. 2.6). I have previously written about portraits of Sherap Zangpo found in the inactive shrine room called the Muldung (dngul gdung) shrine, as well as the other murals preserved inside it.[3] Only recently did I begin to consider and wonder about the small painting on cloth still hanging there. Those musings inspired this chapter.

Unveiled, the painting features a smiling light-skinned, two-armed seated female deity holding a musical instrument (Figs. 8.2–3). She is surrounded by scenes of animals, trees, and seated and standing humans with halos. Basic iconography tells us that the central figure is the Brāhmanical Sarasvatī, but what is she doing in a Himalayan Buddhist monastery? Why would someone—presumably the monk who is depicted as the sponsor in the painting—want to make a painting of her, in particular? What did this painting signify or do for him? That is the question that motivated

3 Linrothe, "Preliminary Report on 15th Century Murals in Zangskar"; Linrothe, "Portraiture on the Periphery."

Fig. 8.2 Sarasavatī in Vajrapāṇi's Pure Land, late 15th or early 16th century. Pigments on cloth; approx. 40 x 28 cm. Muldung Shrine, Phugtal Monastery, Zangskar, India. Photo 2018.

Fig. 8.3 Detail of Fig. 8.2. Photo 2018.

the gathering, magpie-like, of strands of meaning with Sarasvatī in, first, South Asian religious (Vedic, popular Hindu, Jaina, Mahāyāna Buddhist, and Tantric) culture. After a detailed description, a pre-iconological examination, of the painting itself, I will draw on literary texts and contexts of greater India. The essay then veers north into Tibet and the Buddhist Himalaya. It is possible to discover Sarasvatī in the portraiture, biographies, and literary compositions of prominent teachers in Tibet, Sherab Zangpo's teacher among them. After presenting this material, I will conclude by weaving together out of these disparate threads a magpie's nest in which an interpretation of this painting's original intended significance might plausibly rest.

Along the way, I hope to layer in the processes of cultural transmission, of cross-cultural fertilization and appropriation. I would expect that the original South Asian writers and thinkers would be surprised to see the uses put to their ideas and conceits, and, perhaps, barely recognize their transmogrified forms and contents. Still, they might draw satisfaction knowing that those who drew on the notions that slipped across cultural borders with Buddhism remained aware that the origins lay to the south of the Himalaya. Indeed, that was one element in their attraction and authenticity, that the texts and images came couched in Sanskrit, "the language of the gods," and from the lands the Buddha walked. For the people of the Himalaya, including Tibetans and Zangskaris, rivers of culture flowed north from India, unlike the literal rivers of the Indus, Ganges, Yamuna, and Brahmaputra. They knew those living rivers originated in the western Himalaya and meander east or west before flowing south to generously, gratefully, water the lands of the Buddhism that sustained so much of their own culture, bridging South and Inner Asia.

The Phugtal Painting

The small painting hangs in front of a larger, newer painting on a wooden pillar with a carved capital facing the door—the only interior source of light besides a bare bulb sometimes weakly charged by a solar panel and fitfully burning (Fig. 8.4). Unlike most of the other cloth paintings in the Muldung shrine, this painting is mounted with two trapezoidal pieces of plain dark-blue linen at the top and the bottom, visible in Figure 8.4. A painted or lacquered hanging bar with a slit into which the bottom edge of the lower cloth once was wedged is now crudely tied to the bottom edges of the blue cloth. The trapezoidal pieces at top and bottom without borders attached to the sides mark this as a relatively archaic mode of mounting. Paintings datable to the seventeenth century or slightly earlier that depict hanging thangkas provide evidence that the more extensive mounting practice currently employed was already in use, having replaced the older style that this painting exhibits.[4] A fine silk dustcover or veil with a mottled tie-dyed pattern is sewn to the top edge of the painting but can easily be lifted to reveal the still-bright painting. The painting itself is approximately 40 x 28 centimeters.

The central figure, a crowned and draped female, dominates the painting. She sits with her knees splayed and raised, her ankles crossed, her feet resting on a pink-patterned carpet or cloth. A tiny smile sweetens her face as she cocks her head toward a stringed musical instrument, the better to hear its resonant sounds. Her palms and fingers are hennaed. She holds the neck of the instrument with her left hand, and appears to be strumming or plucking the strings with a plectrum held in her right hand at the lower gourd-like sounding chamber. The finial of the mandolin-like *vīṇā* is a wrathful head with golden beard, mustache, and eyebrows, the pupils of

4 Recent modes of mounting are illustrated in some of the figures from the later sections of this essay, notably Figures. 8.26 and 8.29.

Fig. 8.4 Interior of Muldung Shrine at Phugtal Monastery, Zangskar, India, with smaller covered Sarasvatī *thangka* painting hanging in front of a larger painting on a central pillar. Photo 2012.

Fig. 8.5 Detail of offering goddess mural, ca. 15th century. On the porch of the Marpo Lhakhang at Tholing, Ngari, Tibet. Photo 2007.

Fig. 8.6 Detail of White Tārā mural, ca. 15th century. Inside the Marpo Lhakhang of Tsaparang, Ngari, Tibet. Photo 2005.

his wide eyes directed at her face. The lady's ornamentation, suggesting both cloth and jeweled metalwork, is layered, patterned, and extensive. She wears two pairs of anklets, armlets, and bracelets, a crown with five medallions, large earrings, chokers, necklaces, and a long golden chain around her shoulders that is caught up by the movement of her right arm. The chain crosses over and under her right elbow like the blue scarf with a green underside (or is it the other way around?). Her crimson skirt (śāṭī) has black curling tendril designs on the lower border and a golden lining.

The lower rim of her headdress surmounts and defines her oval hairline. A precisely arranged fringe of "kiss curls" softens the transition between smooth skin and jewel-encrusted crown. Parallel strands of black curls alternate with slightly splayed individual hair strands that end in red-dyed tips. It is a distinctive hairstyle, very particular and painstaking in application, like the rest of the ornamentation in the painting. To be sure, variants of the kiss-curl treatment appear at other sites in the western Himalaya in the fifteenth century, in west-central Tibet, including in the Gyantse Kumbum,[5] as well as in Ngari, western Tibet (Figs. 8.5–6) and elsewhere in Zangskar (see Figs. 7.33–34).

The main figure sits against a deep-red throneback with a narrow blue inner border, a wider orange outer border, and a matching nimbus. These in turn are set against a dark background, though for contemporary viewers there is a noticeable lack of an illusion of space. The entire background against which she sits, except for the lowest register below her seat, is painted in black against a dark-blue ground with typical fifteenth-century floral whorl patterns derived from Chinese silk lotus- and peony-scroll decor. The same pattern, but in two shades of red, fill her body and head nimbi and their rims and, in pink, the white textile on which the soles of her feet rest. Related motifs appear as the woven patterns of her clothing.

Simple lollipop-like tree-forms grow with trunks angling inward from the cloth painting's outer border and outward from edges of her body nimbus (Fig. 8.7). Round clumps of solid green designate clusters of leaves. Some are limned with leaf outlines, and some are dabbed with red or orange to designate flowers. Here and there, especially at the top, free-falling flowers are strewn against the backdrop. Two ponds with red-bordered cusped outlines appear opposite either elbow. The background is teeming with ducks, white elephants, goats, geese, and other animals. A solitary

5 Linrothe, "Preliminary Report on 15th Century Murals in Zangskar", fig. 14.

Fig. 8.7 Detail of top left of Fig. 8.2. Photo 2018.

Fig. 8.9 Detail of lower middle left of Fig. 8.2. Photo 2018.

Fig. 8.8 Detail of lower middle right of Fig. 8.2. Photo 2018.

Fig. 8.10 Detail of sponsor figure, lower left of Fig. 8.2. Photo 2018.

Fig. 8.11 Detail of lower middle of Fig. 8.2. Photo 2018.

peacock stands on top of one of the tree forms at the central figure's proper right shoulder, below a meditating *yogi* (see Fig. 8.7). The latter's bearded colleague on her other side sits silently surrounded by birds, trees, deer, and the like. At the level of her knees are two seated bodhisattvas, the one on the viewer's left perhaps a goddess, based on the rounded or oval shape of the forehead. Below the one on the viewer's right is another white-colored elephant with a very large trunk and very un-elephantine legs (Fig. 8.8). The elephant wears a crown and harness bearing a *maṇī*-gem or perhaps a dharma-wheel on its back. Beneath the elephant is a pink-bordered pond seen from above, and below that stands a wrathful Vajrapāṇi holding up a *vajra* in his right hand. On the opposite side, two deer—one white, one dark blue—seem to spring into the air above a white elephant balancing on a red round lotus (Fig. 8.9). Below the lotus is a seated, hatless monk wearing a yellow outer cloak, a red monk's robe, and a Tibetan-style golden cutaway vest revealing a nipple (Fig. 8.10). His hands are held at his chest, fingers out, as if making the *dharmacakra mudrā*. His eyes are almond-shaped like hers, his nose long and pointed, his head like an egg at an angle. This is a representation of the painting's sponsor.

The lower register is separated from the rest of the composition by a wave-and-dot border of green that spans the width of the painting (Fig. 8.11).

Below it are nine broad lotus petals, with paired colors starting from the outside: green, cerise, blue, red, and, at the center, another blue. Below these are five elaborate lotus flowers with pointed leaves strewn about. The one in the center floats on a red-bordered pond from which the main stalk of the lotus on which the lady sits emerges (see Fig. 8.2, lower edges).

The central figure's head-nimbus reaches almost to the upper limit of the painting. The painter framed the rectangular space of the composition with a narrow strip of yellow and an outer border of red. To the sides of the nimbus, below the seated figures in the top register, are two asymmetrical groups of standing haloed figures, four on our right and three on the left, all facing toward her, some reaching out to her, one holding a bell. A fourth on the left, completing the symmetrical balance but alone without a halo, is slightly above the others, close to the top of her head nimbus which obscures his body (see Figs. 8.2–3). But his head, shoulders, and arms are visible as he extends a fully opened, long-stemmed blue lotus, as if to insert the fragrant flower into her crown. Near the upper corners, just above the two groups of offering or worshipping figures, are two *apsaras*es emerging out of pink clouds. The one on our left extends a golden vase as if to offer pure water or *amṛit*-nectar (see Fig. 8.7).

Across the very top, interrupted by the slightly off-center head nimbus of the central figure, are six seated figures dressed in monastic robes. All are nimbated, and three of them wear tall pointed yellow hats, likely belonging to the Kadampa lineage, still active in Zangskar at the time, or else to the Geluk who modeled themselves as the "new Kadampa."[6] The two on the outer edges are bare-headed, as is the second from the left. The seventh seated figure—fourth on the left, closest to her head nimbus—is the blue Vajradhāra, an Esoteric Buddhist form of the Buddha (see Figs. 8.2–3).

The setting that surrounds the lady at the center is not so much a visual illusion of coherent landscape as a conceptual construction using landscape elements.[7] Objects are shown either from above or from the side, depending on whether the plan (as with the ponds) or the profile (as with the elephants) yields greater legibility. The constraints of consistent scale—never an overwhelming imperative in Himalayan painting—are not felt deeply by the artist, as long as the viewer can recognize that this is a forest with ponds and streams, and that those are wild animals, *yogi*s, bodhisattvas, and sentient beings of all sorts. An illusion of shared, relational

6 Himalayan Art Resources, no. 595, https://www.himalayanart.org/items/595.

7 Linrothe, "Landscape Elements in Early Tibetan Painting."

being-in-space—below versus above, in front versus in depth—is deemed not worth the trouble. It is the concept, not the *trompe d'oeil*, that succeeds in being conveyed to the viewer, that the goddess resides in an idyllic setting and is attended by divine and other beings. Further, that this is an authentic transmission stemming from Vajradhāra and passing continuously down, teacher to successor, into the artist's and the sponsor's day.

The Brāhmanical Sarasvatī

Sarasvatī (lit. "the flowing one" or "the winding one") needs very little introduction in South Asian contexts. Her Vedic origins, including a holy river named the Sarasvatī along which sages performed sacrifices and sang hymns to divine powers, have faded over time. Like the river itself, they have gone underground but are not completely forgotten. She seems to have merged in the religious subconscious with the goddess Vāc, Sacred Speech.[8] In the Rig Veda, as "deified Holy speech or Utterance . . [Vāc] is so devoid of anthropomorphic qualities as to lack even a minimum of mythology. . . . [H]er personification is hardly more than one of grammatical gender and remains so until the post-Rigvedic period when she has blended with Sarasvatī."[9] The composite Sarasvatī-Vāc survives into the present with a cluster of associations adhering to the name of a personification of aspirational ideals and concepts[10] centered around "the ultimate elevation of the magic power which holy sound is considered to possess."[11] Daughter and consort of Brahmā,[12] with whom she shares the white goose (*haṃsa*) as vehicle,[13] goddess of speech, Sarasvatī "represents the union of power and intelligence from which organized creation arises . . . [She is] the goddess of eloquence, of wisdom, of learning, the patroness of arts and of music . . . She is the mother of poetry."[14] Associations with learning, memory, eloquence, books, and especially art and music remain strong and to an extent cross religious dispensations, including Jain.[15] As for "priests and musicians . . . she is believed to sit on their tongues to guide them."[16] By her form holding and playing the *vīṇā*, she assumes a revered role today in the major musical lineages (*gharana*) whose members cross Hindu and Islamic lines: "Her garlanded image is present in the homes of all musicians, Hindu and Muslim alike."[17] Sarasvatī also enjoys "enduring popularity amongst students who invoke her name, especially at exam time."[18] Down to the present, learned Brāhmanical Hindu religious figures give interpretations of her name (the flowing one, connected to fertility and purification), her white color (she is associated with knowledge, "the antithesis of the

8 There is also apparently some connection to Manasā, a rural folk or tribal goddess propitiated as insurance against snakebites, or to cure them if they occur. Rawson cites the Arthaveda Samhita, where "Sarasvati is spoken of explicitly as the Destroyer of poison, and is identified with a Kirāṭa girl called Ghritāchī who digs up medicines at the top of a mountain with a golden shovel . . . Vogel mentions that the Mahabharata commentators having identified with the river Sarasvatī the Bhogāvatī, meaning 'the Winding One,' which supported a tirtha sacred to [the Nāga] Vāsukī referred to in the epic;" Rawson, "Iconography of the Goddess Manasā," 158). Dimock also points out that Manasā "is at once Sarasvatī and Jāṅgulī, goddesses of healing (Dimock, "Goddess of Snakes," 301), while Haque also suggests a lineage for Manasā from Sarasvatī (Haque, "Manasā Images of Bengal," 136).

9 Brown, "The Creative Role of the Goddess Vāc," 393.

10 Lal, *Female Divinities*, 151–98; Ludvik, *Sarasvatī, Riverine Goddess of Knowledge*; Gombrich, "Sarasvatī Vāc"; Sandness, "Yama and Sarasvatī"; Donaldson, *Tantra and Śākta Art of Orissa*.

11 Brown, "The Creative Role of the Goddess Vāc," 393.

12 Biardeau, "Hindu God with Five Heads."

13 "Sarasvati's white goose, or hamsa, is a visual pun, and reminds us that esoteric meaning underlie puja's images: In Sanskrit, the mantra '*aham sah*' means, 'I am it,' interpreted to mean, 'I am the self (atman).' When 'aham sah' is repeated over and over in meditative repetition (japa), it melds into 'hamsa,' or 'goose.'" Hudson, "Ritual Worship of Devi," 91.

14 Daniélou, *Hindu Polytheism*, 259–60. See also Sinha, "Evolution of Śakti Worship in India," 48.

15 Handa and Agrawal, "A New Jaina Sarasvatī from Rajashthan"; Dehejia, *Devi the Great Goddess*, cat. no. 3; Blurton, *Hindu Art*, 175.

16 Hudson, "Ritual Worship of Devi," 91.

17 Dehejia, *Devi the Great Goddess*, 289.

18 Blurton, *Hindu Art*, 175; H. Smith, "Introduction: Impact of 'God Posters' on Hindus," 22.

darkness of ignorance," so she is pure white), and the manuscript and the *vīṇā* (to show that "intellectual learning, without a heart tempered by higher feelings, sentiments and emotions, is as dry as dust").[19] She has also been reinterpreted by Hindu reformers, such as Swami Dayananda Saraswati, founder of the Arya Samaj, not as an independent goddess "but an aspect of the One God," in the attempt to establish Hinduism's monotheistic philosophy.[20]

Not only students, but also accomplished poets and writers invoke her. The treatise on poetics, the *Kāvyādarśa* by Daṇḍin (7th–8th c.) begins with this prayer to her: "Let Sarasvatī, who is completely white, play in my mind as she always does like a goose in the lotus garden of the four (lotus) faces (of Brahmā)."[21] The epigraph of this chapter does not exhaust Sarasvatī's presence in Bāṇa's *Harṣcarita*: the plot of the entire first chapter of the hagiography of the historical seventh-century ruler Harṣavardhana revolves around Sarasvatī's descent to earth.[22]

In ornate Sanskrit *kāvya* poetry, Sarasvatī the goddess is employed as a figure of speech, standing for the extreme limits of wisdom and eloquence. Tulsīdās (ca. 1543–1623) in the *Rāmacaritamānasa*, uses her this way: "The bliss and prosperity of Rāma's realm neither Serpent King nor Sarasvatī can describe."[23] The ninth-century philosopher of aesthetics Ānandavardhana (ca. 820–890 CE), whose *Dhvanyālokai* inspired the commentary *Locana* by no less than the famed Kaśmīri teacher Abhinavagupta (ca. 950–1016), saw her as "within" great poets, the source and soul of their poetic imagination. It is she who pours forth sweetness as *śabda* (glossed as sound, voice, note, words, language, auditory object).[24]

Besides musicians and poets, visual artists also looked to her for inspiration. Interestingly, architects and sculptors in Karnataka organized themselves in guilds that took Sarasvatī as the patron goddess of their profession, and a number of "early Hoysala artists referred to themselves as *Sarasvatī-gaṇa-dasis* or 'servants of the guild of Sarasvatī.'"[25] Since the late nineteenth century, many of the garlanded pictures of Sarasvatī hanging in schools, homes, and libraries have been popular prints,[26] but as Pal points out those kinds of prints were as familiar as *daal-bhaat*, found "at home, at countless *paan-bidi* (betel and tobacco) shops, car repair garages, in groceries, and, in fact, all over the place."[27] Sarasvatī sitting playing the *vīṇā* in front of a river backdrop became so familiar that by the mid-twentieth

19 Harshananda, *Hindu Gods and Goddesses*, 80–81.

20 Sutherland, "Politics of 'Other Peoples' Myths,'" 155.

21 Gombrich, "Sarasvatī Vāc," 347. See also Donaldson, "Lakulīśa to Rājaguru," 141–42.

22 Cowell and Thomas, *Harsa-carita of Bāṇa*, 5–34.

23 Backer, *Holy Ground*, 65.

24 Ingalls, Masson, and Patwardhan, *The Dhvanyaloka of Anandavardhana with the Locana of Abhinavagupta*, 1990.

25 Collyer, *Hoysala Artists*, 108.

26 Pinney, *Photos of the Gods*, fig. 8.

27 Pal, "Printed Image," 29.

century or so it had served as the model for images for "Tamilttay (Mother Tamil), the Tamil language personified as goddess, mother and maiden."[28] Like many images of Sarasvatī, she too holds a manuscript (*pustaka*) and sits demurely with a musical instrument resting across her lap. To distinguish them, Sarasvatī's *vīṇā* was exchanged with Tamilltay's curved *yal*, a kind of lyre associated with southern India though one that looks very much like the so-called stick-zither commonly held in earlier times by Sarasvatī.[29]

Controversy and the impassioned proprietary claims of devotees constitute another measure of Sarasvatī's continuing relevance into South Asia's late twentieth century. The drawings and paintings of both a clothed and nude Sarasvatī by M. F. Husain (1915–2011) provoked outrage among reactionary Hindutva supporters in the 1990s and early 2000s. That the offense was clearly about the religious identity of the artist and not about the visual qualities of the art, nor any lewdness in its treatment of the theme, is demonstrated by the fact that the works are in a flattened, museumified mode of modernist art that resists the sensuous or the erotic.[30]

The dates offered for the creation and distribution of the *Viṣṇudharmottara Purāṇa*, the vast compendium of religious lore, vary from the early fifth century to the end of the tenth century.[31] Greater accord rests on its relevance for Kaśmīr. It reflected and helped to standardize the iconographic details of the standing four-armed Sarasvatī. In the text, Mārkaṇḍeya tells Vajra:

> Devī Sarasvatī should be made adorned with all kinds of ornaments. Standing and having four hands. In her two right hands, there should be a book and a rosary and in her two left hands, a *vīṇā* [a stringed Indian instrument, often translated as a lute] and a *kamaṇḍalu* (water-vessel). She should stand with feet placed together and her face should be made having a moon-like face. The [four] Vedas should be known as her hands and all the Śāstras or Sciences as the book. O king, the Kamaṇḍalu should be known as [containing] the nectar of all Śāstras and the rosary in her hand is time (Kāla)... [The goddess] should be known as success incarnate. There is no doubt about it.... The eyes of the lotus-eyed one should be known as the moon and the sun. I have narrated to you this very charming and holy form of Sarasvatī, O chief of the kings! The person desiring success should make it and meditate upon it.[32]

28 Ramaswamy, "Body Politic(s)," 46.

29 On the various forms taken by the instrument, see Prajñānānanda, *Historical Development of Indian Music*, 438–61.

30 Guha-Thakurta, "Clothing the Goddess." See also Goswamy, *Conversations*, 51–54.

31 Ludvik, *Sarasvatī, Riverine Goddess of Knowledge*, 118.

32 Shah, *Śrī-Viṣṇudharmottara-Purāṇa*, 169, with minor changes.

The description was no doubt also used as a prescription by artists or their patrons. A detailed examination by Catherine Ludvik of images identified—rightly or mistakenly—as Sarasvatī focuses on those proposed to be earlier than the seventh century.[33] By that time, Sarasvatī's iconography was relatively fixed within recognizable limits, allowing for the identification of many Jaina and Brāhmanical examples from Rajasthan, Bihar, Bengal, Gujarat, and Uttar Pradesh from the period of ca. eighth to thirteenth century.

Probably the most frequent context for Sarasvatī imagery in later art before her appearance in the popular prints mentioned earlier is in eastern Indian stone sculptures of Viṣṇu from the ca. eleventh–thirteenth century where she is one of a pair of his consorts. In a Viṣṇu sculpture in the Patna Museum, a detail of the lower half of which is shown in Figure 8.12, Sarasvatī stands on Viṣṇu's left, while Śrī Lakṣmī, associated with wealth, stands on his right. A lovely depiction of Sarasvatī holding the *vīṇā*, also on the left of a Viṣṇu, is in the National Museum in New Delhi (Fig. 8.13). Gouriswar Bhattacharya suggests that "the two consorts of Vishnu, viz. Shri or Lakshmi and Sarasvati, developed out of Gadadevi and Chakrapurusha respectively in Eastern Indian sculptures."[34] The two, Lakṣmī and Sarasvatī, "are rivals . . . It is said that whenever one of them bestows her boons on a man the other remains away: the wise are not wealthy and the wealthy are not wise."[35] This too becomes a literary conceit as is illustrated in this passage from the *Harṣacarita*: Bāṇa describes Harṣa's necklace dividing his chest from his head as "like the dividing-line which draws the boundary between the respective empires of Śrī and Sarasvatī."[36] Another reference to the tension between Lakṣmī and Sarasvatī in the same source is embedded in the following description of the pink color of Harṣa's forehead formed by a reflection of his crest ornament, "as if it were the lac dye of Lakṣmi's feet which had clung to it, when he sought by prostration to appease her jealousy at the preference shown to Sarasvatī."[37]

Independent sculptures of Sarasvatī were also made in the period of the eleventh to the thirteenth century.[38] One of the most handsome of the many Brāhmanical sculptures of Sarasvatī from eastern India is a twelfth-century stone sculpture in the Malda Archaeological Museum in West Bengal (Fig. 8.14).[39] The four-armed goddess plays a one-stringed *vīṇā* in the shape of a "stick-zither" and holds a (damaged) *pustaka*-manuscript in her raised upper left hand. Her eyes are lowered and heavy lidded, while her head tilts

33 Ludvik, *Sarasvatī, Riverine Goddess of Knowledge*, 225–69.

34 G. Bhattacharya, "How Come Sarasvati Is a Consort of Vishnu in Eastern India?," 117.

35 Zimmer, *Myths and Symbols*, 88. See also H. Smith, "Contemporary Iconic Tradition," 41.

36 Cowell and Thomas, *Harṣa-carita of Bāṇa*, 60.

37 Ibid., 61 (with spelling changes).

38 Donaldson, *Tantra and Śākta Art of Orissa*, 3: figs. 170–172.

39 M. Bhattacharya, *Art in Stone*, pl. 11, fig. 1; M. Bhattacharya, *Art of Bengal*, pl. 27.1; G. Bhattacharya, "How Come Sarasvati Is a Consort of Vishnu in Eastern India?," fig. 9.7; G. Bhattacharya, "Malda Museum of Antiquities," pl. 15, fig. 5.

Fig. 8.12 Detail of lower portion of Viṣṇu with two consorts, ca. 11th–12th century. Stone; dimension of current overall sculpture 120 x 69 cm. From Giriak, Nalanda district, Bihar, India, now in the Patna Museum, Bihar. Patna Museum (acc. no. 1594). Photo 2017.

Fig. 8.13 Detail of the Sarasvatī on Viṣṇu's left, ca. 11th century. Stone; dimension of the overall sculpture 86 x 35 cm. Eastern India, now in the National Museum, New Delhi. National Museum, acc. no. 57.43/1. Photo 2021.

Fig. 8.14 Sarasvatī, ca. 12th century. Stone, 75 x 37.5 cm. Collected from Malda district, Bengal, now in the Malda Archaeological Museum, West Bengal. Malda Archaeological Museum acc. no. RSW-1. Photo 2016.

slightly as if listening intently, with a faint smile on her face. Kiss-curls changing direction at the center of her forehead—bisected by a conch-shaped *ūrnā*—frame her hairline. At her feet are a sponsor couple on the left—the male in front offering a flower garland—and a second, bearded male sponsor on the right. A ram-*vāhana* (instead of the usual *haṃsa*) is displaced rightward from the center of the pedestal by the goddess's pendent right leg and foot.[40] Sarasvatī is richly bejeweled and wears wide, cuff-like bracelets that appear not to constrain the fluent movements of her wrists as she plays the *vīṇā*. The density of the detail and scrollwork on the cutout backslab is beautifully balanced with areas of plain flat ground, as in her concentrically framed nimbus.

Two other sculptures from the tenth and eleventh centuries show the range and the importance of Sarasvatī in eastern and north-central India. In the Gaya Museum, Sarasvatī sits with one knee up, her left elbow balanced against her thigh supporting the neck of a slightly curved stick-zither-type *vīṇā* (Fig. 8.15). Her other hands hold the *akṣamālā* prayer beads, and the vertically-oriented manuscript. Two flying deva proffer garlands, while two female acolytes stand ready with yak-tail

40 G. Bhattacharya, "How Come Sarasvati Is a Consort of Vishnu in Eastern India?," 112.

Fig. 8.15 Sarasavatī, ca. 10th century. Stone, 56.25 x 41.5 cm. Gaya District, Bihar, now in the Gaya Museum. Gaya Museum acc. no. 31. Photo 2016.

Fig. 8.16 Sarasvatī, ca. 11th century. Stone, 60 x 35 cm. Gorakhpur, Uttar Pradesh, now in the State Museum, Lucknow. State Museum Lucknow acc. no. H.23. Photo 2017.

whisks (*cāmara*). A miniature male sponsor figure on viewer's left offers his reverence, seeking knowledge.

A slightly later sculpture, impressive despite the awkwardness of the upper proper left arm in the act of actually pressing a plectrum into the one-string *vīṇā*, draws on the north-central form-idiom associated with Uttar Pradesh (Fig. 8.16). The radiating head-nimbus is also particular to that region. The backdrop is otherwise plain, except for a trilobed niche outline. In this instance, a lowered left hand proffers the manuscript, palm facing outward. She bestows a beatific smile on the sponsor couple on the pedestal below her, the male in front offering a budding flower in his clasped hands. Just to the right of center is an unmistakable rendering of the *haṃsa*, the storied long-necked goose with one wing raised and her beak turned toward it, as if to smooth its feathers. This is an unusual representation since it appears to have originally been six-armed, though only three arms remain. Along with the lowered right hand steadying the *vīṇā*, traces of two other right arms seem to emerge from behind the right shoulder.

The Jaina Sarsvatī

Sarasvatī's importance in Jaina contexts is also worth emphasizing because, while one might associate her with Brāhmanical Hinduism, she is hardly exclusive to any South Asian sectarian division. Still, she is not as prominent in Indian Buddhism as she is in Tibetan Buddhism, or as she is in Jaina practice. "[B]ecause Sarasvatī in the Jain context was visualized as personification of the preachings of Jinas (Jina Vāṇī) with manuscript as one of her attributes, she is given a status equal to the Jinas."[41] Also known as *Śrutadevatā*, "she is the personified form of knowledge in the sacred Jain scriptures preached by Jinas," the foundational *tirthānkaras*.[42]

The Jains in western India in particular seemed to have had a special affinity for Sarasvatī. One of the most impressive representations of her, even shorn as it is now of its densely carved shrine niche (the *prabhatorana*), is now in the National Museum in New Delhi **(Fig. 8.17)**. As Tiwari and Sinha describe it, the "whole composition is endowed with divine grace."[43] It was found in 1917 in Pallu, Rajasthan, by an Italian member of the local Maharaja's court, Dr Luigi Pio Tessitori.[44] Instead of playing the *vīṇā* herself, the two standing retinue figures beside her each hold one, while she holds a full-blown lotus, an elaborately-tied manuscript, a string of prayer beads (*akṣamālā*), and a water-pouring vessel (*kamaṅdalu*). A beautifully detailed sponsor couple, possibly royal, with the queenly figure on the goddess's left, sits reverentially on the pedestal **(Fig. 8.18)**. The male sponsor figure in the Phugtal painting of Sarasvatī **(see Fig. 8.10)** sits on the viewer's left, like the bearded sponsor in the Jaina sculpture, following long-standing precedents.[45] Beneath them, a tiny goose (*haṃsa*), Sarasvatī's vehicle, is just visible.

Jains also had a highly developed painting tradition, and Sarasvatī certainly figures prominently in those *thangka*-like paintings on cloth, or *paṭa*. One such painting is arranged mandala-like with nine square compartments, the central, slightly larger section occupied by Sarasvatī, also in the National Museum, New Delhi **(Fig. 8.19)**. This Sarasvatī is much less naturalistic, more iconic, abstracted, patternized and frontal, yet still compelling. She also holds up a manuscript, but in her proper right hand

41 Tripathi and Jain, "Sarasvatī in Jain Art," 9.

42 Ibid., 9.

43 Tiwari and Sinha, "Concept of Saraswati in Jain Tradition and Art," 692.

44 Handa and Agrawal, "A New Jaina Sarasvatī from Rajashthan," 169n1.

45 Linrothe, "Deeply Rooted Ritual;" Linrothe, "The Human Sphere."

Fig. 8.17 Sarasvatī, ca. 12th century. Stone, 120 x 46 cm. Pallu, Rajasthan, now in the National Museum, New Delhi. National Museum acc. no. 272/6-278. Photo 2019.

Fig. 8.18 Detail of Fig. 8.17 depicting the sponsor couple on the pedestal. Photo 2021.

Fig. 8.19 Jain Sarasvatī Paṭa, detail of center, ca. 15th c. Pigments and gold on cloth; dimensions of cloth painting 54.8 x 44.5 cm. Western India, now in the National Museum, New Delhi. National Museum acc. no, 63.1590. Photo 2021.

Fig. 8.20 Detail of manuscript held by Sarasvatī in Fig. 8.19. Photo 2021.

Fig. 8.21 Detail of miniature *vīṇā* held by Sarasvatī in Fig. 8.19. Photo 2021.

(Fig. 8.20), and holds a schematic *vīṇā* in her upper left hand (Fig. 8.21). In the compartment directly beneath her is the white *haṃsa*, her *vāhana*. The other squares surrounding the central Sarasvatī are filled with musicians and dancers, and one white-clad monk preaching or offering reverence.

Sarasvatī in Early Mahāyāna Buddhism in South Asia

Given her embrace by Brāhmanical and Jaina traditions, it is hardly surprising that Sarasvatī is also visible in Buddhist South Asia. Yet this seems to be easily overlooked, despite her presence in both early Mahāyāna and in later Tantric, or Esoteric Buddhism. Sarasvatī is distinctive in being "the only Hindu goddess adopted into the Mahāyāna pantheon without a change in name or significant alteration of divine persona."[46] The most extensive, well-studied, and earliest expression of her inclusion in Buddhist writings was the *Sūtra of Golden Light*, the *Suvarṇabhāsottama* Sūtra (also known as the *Suvarṇaprabhāsottama Sūtra*). Although the core of the text may go back as early as the first century CE, she is prominent in the earliest Chinese translation of 417 by Dharmakṣema from a lost early Sanskrit version. There Sarasvatī has her own chapter, and she is often mentioned in passing in the other chapters, paired with Śrī (i.e., Lakṣmī), followed by Dṛḍhā Pṛthivī (the earth goddess), who also have their own chapters. According to textual historians, including Emmerick[47] and Ludvik,[48]

46 M. Shaw, *Buddhist Goddesses of India*, 236.

47 Emmerick, *Sūtra of Golden Light*.

48 Ludvik, *Sarasvatī, Riverine Goddess of Knowledge*.

Sarasvatī's chapter was then expanded to include a protective bathing ritual and an invocation as an eight-armed protective goddess, both of which appear in the Chinese translation by 597. The Chinese monk traveler Yijing retranslated the text into Chinese in 703, after his return from India. This influential version "was, in turn, translated into Tibetan, Sogdian, [Tangut] Xia, and Old Uighur."[49] From the earliest extant version, the *Sūtra* draws on post-Vedic associations of Sarasvatī with knowledge, speech, and eloquence, as established in the Brāhmanas, the epic *Mahābhārata* (ca. mid-second c. BCE–0 CE), and Purāṇas such as the *Mārkaṇḍeya* (ca. third c.) and *Viṣṇudharmottara* (ca. fourth–fifth c.).[50]

The early Buddhist treatments did not disrupt but instead reinforced the cluster of associations connected to speech and eloquence that were maintained in the Brāhmanical texts and practices. As with the Brāhmanical examples, only a few random instances can be cited here. The Mahāyāna text *Kāraṇḍavyūha-sūtra* in praise of Lokeśvara Bodhisattva which lists the gods as coming from different parts of his body, has Sarasvatī as emerging from his eye-teeth, and assigns her the task of being "lord over learning."[51] "As her worship is widely prevalent among the Buddhists owing to the belief that like Mañjuśrī and Prajñāpāramitā, she confers wisdom, learning, intelligence, memory, etc. a comparatively large number of Sādhanas is assigned to her in the *Sādhanamālā*."[52] Not all of these forms of her hold the *vīṇā*, are white in color, or are peaceful, like the main form focused on here. Some, such as the one in the later version of the *Sūtra of Golden Light*, are wrathful.

Across sectarian divides in South Asia, then, Sarasvatī maintains a connection with wisdom and articulate speech. Without a context for a sculpture, it can be difficult to declare confidently which is Brāhmanical and which is Mahāyāna Buddhist. Temple 2 at Nalanda is an excellent paradigm of this dilemma, as it is a puzzling anomaly. Its plinth (all that remains of it) is set among Buddhist monasteries and shrines, yet most agree that the more than two hundred stone sculptures placed in architectural niches around the exterior base are variously "pan-Indian" if not Brāhmanical in theme. There is general consensus that the sculptures date to the middle or late seventh century, but less agreement is reached on the nature of their presence there.[53] Among the sculptures is a seated female figure holding the neck of a stringed instrument more like a Central Asian *pipa* than a stick-zither (Fig. 8.22).[54] It appears to be Sarasvatī (as Misra and

49 Ibid., 150.

50 Ibid., 95–141.

51 Lokesh Chandra, *Kāraṇḍa-Vyūha-Sūtra*, xiii–xiv.

52 B. Bhattacharyya, *Indian Buddhist Iconography*, 349. See also Wayman, "Goddess Sarasvatī," 432–33.

53 Deva, "Stone Temple (No. 2) at Nālandā," 84; Asher, *Nalanda*, 59.

54 Misra, *Nālandā*, 2: fig. 33, and 3: fig. 220.

Fig. 8.22 Sarasvatī (?) in a niche at Nalanda Temple 2, ca. late 7th century. Stone, the niche approx. 33 x 38.5 cm. Photo 2022, enabled by Shanker Sharma.

others identify her), although compared with other, later images of her that appear at the site, the identification is not unassailable. By contrast, two metalwork images included by B. N. Misra in the Buddhist section of his three-volume work on Nalanda show the goddess holding a more standard *vīṇā*.[55] Others could consider these all as Brāhmanical, and there certainly have been Brāhmanical stone and metal sculptures excavated at the predominantly Buddhist site of Nalanda. These include Śiva with Parvatī, Gaja-Lakṣmī, Varāha, Balarāma, and Sūrya.[56] It is not always clear why or when such sculptures were acquired by the monastery, or in what capacity they functioned. As Buddhist? As Brāhmanical? Or as both?

Sarasvatī in South Asian Śaiva and Buddhist Tantra

As can be expected in the heterogeneous category of South Asian Tantra, Sarasvatī played varied roles, though her association with speech as sacred sound matched Tantric employment of techniques such as recitation of the sounds and visualization of the written forms of mantra and *bījākṣaras* (seed-syllables). In Trika Tantric Śaivism, one of the five deities at the core of the pantheon is the goddess Parā, who is "an ectype of the goddess Sarasvatī, more precisely of Sarasvatī as embodiment of the Word (Vāgīśvarī) or, which is the same conception, of the alphabet (Mātṛkāsarasvatī, Lipidevī)."[57] In all the forms she takes, the book and *mālā* (a string of prayer beads) are invariable, but not the *vīṇā*. Sometimes the pen replaces the prayer beads. Trika "sees itself as the highest level within Śaiva revelation . . . at the furthest remove from neutral, 'vedic' orthodoxy. It might be somewhat surprising therefore that its highest deity should be an ectype of Sarasvatī, the exoteric, nonsectarian consort of Brahmā."[58] It seems it was the very "nonsectarian neutrality of her image" that "encapsulates the universal essence of the divine Word (*vāk*)."[59] Certainly Sarasvatī held an enduring attraction for compilers of other Hindu Tantric pantheons and, as I will discuss later, in both South Asian and Himalayan Esoteric Buddhism.

55 Ibid., 3: figs. 163–164.

56 Sastri, *Nalanda and Its Epigraphic Material*, 116 and pls. 12b, d; Misra, *Nālandā*, 2: figs. 111, 116, 132, and 3: figs. 171–176, 196.

57 Sanderson, "Visualization of the Deities of the Trika," 43.

58 Ibid., 50.

59 Ibid., 50.

Gudrun Bühnemann notes that Sarasvatī was added to a group of Tantric Mahāvidyā goddesses when at some point that group of ten was expanded to eighteen. She suggests that such a grouping took place in Bengal sometime after the twelfth century and was well-known in Nepal.[60] In those later texts, Sarasvatī is also sometimes named as one of the wives or consorts of Gaṇeśa.[61] In the *Śāradātilaka* by Lakṣmaṇadeśika, nine forms of Sarasvatī are described, along with Śāradā, Vāc or Vāgdevatā, Vāgadhidevatā, and Vāgadhīśā, all of whom Bühnemann considers other forms of Sarasvatī.[62] A manuscript is usually present in her hands but not the *vīṇā*. Still, Vāṇī ("speech") or Haṃsavāgiśvarī has a number of characteristics that reinforce the connection to Sarasvatī, including the moon crescent in her hair, the white "lustre of camphor and jasmine," the *akṣamālā* (prayer beads), manuscript, the goose *vāhana*, and the *vīṇā*.[63]

Among certain South Asian Tantric practitioners and authors (admittedly, a widely varied group), inner yoga and its internal anatomy comes increasingly to the fore. According to some inner yoga texts, the *iḍā* and the *piṅgalā* peripheral channels (*nāḍī*) are identified with the Gaṅgā and the Yamunā Rivers while the central or medial channel, the *suṣumṇā*, is recognized as the Sarasvatī River and goddess.[64] Even here, there is logic to the ascriptions given her association not only with speech but also with her namesake river: "Sarasvatī is the goddess of speech; her home in the body is the tongue. . . . The tongue is connected to the Suṣumṇā *nāḍī*, the central and most important of the 72,000 *nāḍī*s or channels of the body."[65] She is thus engaged in arousing the *kuṇḍalinī*-energy, who slumbers at the base of the *suṣumṇā*. James Mallinson, working on the Tantric group known as the Nāths, explains further:

> Sarasvatī is said to be a synonym of either Kuṇḍalinī or Suṣumṇā. Both identifications make sense because of the different possible referents of Sarasvatī. Kuṇḍalinī and Sarasvatī are both manifestation of Śakti, the feminine principle of the universe; Sarasvatī is also the name of the now mythical river said to meet the Ganges and Yamuna in a triple confluence at Allahabad which is paralleled in the body by the confluence of the Iḍā, Piṅgalā, and Suṣumṇa *nāḍī*s. Both analogues only serve to obscure, however, the location of Sarasvatī in the body . . . In the *Khevarīvidyā*, the tongue is frequently called Vāgīśī, 'Goddess of Speech,' a synonym of Sarasvatī. It is this identification of the Sarasvatī *nāḍī* that makes sense of the compound *sarasvatīcālana*.[66]

60 Bühnemann, *Iconography of Hindu Tantric Deities*, 1:39, 42.

61 Ibid., 1:85. See also Smith 1999; Pal 1981: 142; and Donaldson 2002: 3: fig. 598.

62 Bühnemann, *Iconography of Hindu Tantric Deities*, 2:177, 189, 190, 193.

63 Ibid., 2:191; also Pal 1981: 90.

64 White, *The Alchemical Body*, 227.

65 Mallinson, "The Original *Gorakṣaśataka*," 258.

66 Ibid., 259–60. See also Wayman, "The Goddess Sarasvatī," 431; and Prajñānānanda, *Historical Development of Indian Music*, 40.

The connection among the Nāths and Sarasvatī, as well as between the goddess and Gaṇeśa, may help explain why Gaṇeśa, Sarasvatī, and Jallandranāth are depicted on the first folio of a beautifully rendered ca. 1825 *Nāth Purāṇa* associated with the royal Nāth-devotee Marwar Mahārāja Man Singh (r. 1803–1843) of Jodhpur.[67] The four-armed Sarasvatī carries a stick-zither–type *vīṇā*, a book, a flower and garlands, and a *paraśu* (hatchet) and sits on a white *haṃsa* (goose).

A very ancient strain of what is also called Tantra is much less literary, intellectual, or philosophical than the modes associated with sophisticated thinkers like Abhinavagupta and those of Trika. I refer here to magic of the secretive, coercive sort.[68] Known generally as *abhicāra* in its aggressive darker form and *śānti* (appeasement) in its more defensive or avoidance mode, it is found equally practiced, with very similar rituals, in both Brāhmanical and Buddhist iterations. As Arthur Ewing put it in 1902, sorcery has "its beneficent and terrible aspects. On the one hand, the Mantrin, by proper practices, can obtain almost anything that the heart may wish; on the other hand, he can kill or enable a man to kill his enemy. This is the chief blot upon this Tantra."[69] In Ewing's understanding, Śāradā is another name for Sarasvatī, "who stands first in the list of deities worshipped in connection with various Mantras in the body of the book."[70] Its pacification or appeasement rituals have recently been extensively studied, including a ritual where Sarasvatī is called upon.[71] *Abhicāra* is typically aimed at worldly events, from love to wealth to health. Because it too depends on "spells," it draws on the hoary sacred speech aspect of Sarasvatī. It is she upon whom success depends: "Sarasvatī is speech; verily with speech he [the performer] yokes him [the enemy]."[72] "According to the TS [*Taittirīya-Saṃhitā*] one who practices *abhicāra* 'should offer to Agni and Viṣṇu on eleven potsherds; Sarasvatī should have a portion of the butter, and to Bṛhaspati an oblation [should] be offered).' Agni then is identified with all the gods, Viṣṇu with the sacrifice, Sarasvatī with speech, and Bṛhaspati with *brahman*."[73] To be sure, Sarasvatī is not only invoked in the procedure of directing the yoking and the destruction of enemies, she also *protects* against *abhicāra*.[74]

Sarasvatī is one of eight Brāhmanical goddesses that the practitioner conjures into his or her heart while performing *abhicāra* rituals.[75] But even in those texts proscribing practices with worldly ends, a metaphorical usage for Sarasvatī is found: the name of the goddess becomes a standard

67 Diamond, *Gardens & Cosmos*, cat. no. 39.

68 M. Willis, *Archaeology of Hindu Ritual*, 62, 176.

69 Ewing, "Çārada-tilaka Tantra," 66.

70 Ibid.

71 Geslani, "Ritual Culture of Appeasement," 253–54.

72 Türstig, "The Indian Sorcery Called Abhicāra," 99.

73 Ibid., 98.

74 Ibid., 108.

75 Ullrey, "Grim Grimoires," 601.

praise-reference to learning of all types. Brāhmanical "magic Tantras" using mantras and *mālās* to gain knowledge and learning use Sarasvatī as the basis of comparison for success or as the measure of the effects of rituals.[76] In the *Uddīsatantra* one reads of such a ritual that "causes all perfections: it is the perfection of Sarasvatī."[77] The authors of Digambara Jaina "magic tantra" texts are trenchantly described as "blessed by Sarasvatī" and thus able to speak eloquently and accurately.[78] Similarly, "a great disciple who knew all the scriptures (śāstra)," is compared with Sarasvatī.[79]

Sarasvatī also appears in the texts and contexts of early-stage Esoteric Buddhism. She is incorporated into such early contexts as the *Vairocanābhisaṃbodhi Sūtra*'s main mandala, where she is included in the western quarter along with other Brāhmanical gods and goddesses.[80] Her Buddhicized mantra (*namaḥ samantabuddhānāṃ, sarasvatyai svāhā*) and the *vīṇā mudrā* named after her musical instrument (and which also functions as her *samaya* symbol sometimes representing her in pictorial mandala) are both included elsewhere in the *sūtra*.[81] Since the so-called Garbhadhātu mandala is accepted as at least vaguely based on the *Vairocanābhisaṃbodhi Sūtra* it follows that the version of the mandala transmitted to Japan in the early ninth century corresponds loosely to the text. She is in the section on the gods from the west gate to the northwestern corner.[82] Recently, Kimiaki Tanaka published his remarkable study of the development of mandala in Esoteric Buddhist texts in India, and has identified some texts that indicate "the transition from early esoteric Buddhism to the *Vairocanābhisambhodhisūtra*, although most of them have been lost."[83] One such surviving text is the *Vajrapāṇyabhiṣekhatantra*, and Sarasvatī appears there in the outer zone.[84] Tanaka also reconstructs the Garbha-*maṇḍala* (as he prefers to refer to it) from Indian texts and Tibetan versions based on them, without the modification made during the transmission to Japan via China. Sarasvatī remains as one of eighty-five Hindu deities "who had become protective deities after receiving Śākyamuni's teaching."[85] In an identical manner, Sarasvatī with the *vīṇā* as her attribute is included in various other mandalas, such as the Bhūtaḍāmara mandala[86]—and the Durgati-Pariśodhana mandala,[87] but only as a minor figure.

Once Esoteric Buddhism, or Buddhist Tantra, had been established, one of the important roles played by Sarasvatī is her pairing with Mañjuśrī, who is also known as Vāgīśvara and as Vādirāj, the "King of Speech."[88]

76 Ibid., 163.

77 Ibid., 663.

78 Ibid., 375, 743.

79 Ibid., 371.

80 Giebel, *Vairocanābhisaṃbodhi Sutra*, 33.

81 Ibid., 62, 116, *passim*. See also Giebel, *Two Esoteric Sutras*, 311n6.

82 Snodgrass, *The Matrix and Diamond World Mandalas*, 2:512–13, fig. 255.

83 Tanaka, *Illustrated History of the Maṇḍala*, 61.

84 Ibid., 62.

85 Ibid., 77.

86 Mori, *Vajrāvalī of Abhayākaragupta*, 685, no. 23.15; Lokesh Chandra and Sharma, *Nispanna-Yogāvalī*, 228, also no. 23.15.

87 Lokesh Chandra and Sharma, *Nispanna-Yogāvalī*, 222, no. 66; and Skorupski, *Sarvadurgatipariśodhana Tantra*, 90.

88 Nihom, "Sādhanamālā 256," 214. See also Mukherjee, *Sahaja, in Quest of the Innate*, 16; and Pal, *Hindu Religion and Iconology*, 36.

However, in eastern India of the ca. tenth–thirteenth century, this did not seem to result in images of the two of them together. Overall, the pairing does not appear to be as prominent among late Esoteric Buddhists in eastern India as we will see that it is in Tibet and the Himalayan regions. There are some possible reasons to explain the disparity between texts and archaeology. One is that the images of the independent Sarasvatī recovered from Buddhist sites such as Nalanda have generally lost their original context. For example, were they placed in conjunction to images of Mañjuśrī, in the way that we will see Mañjuśrī and Sarasvatī images are placed together in Himalayan painting? Without the original context of display, her images are reasonably assumed to be Brāhmanical and not Buddhist. Another possibility is that as Buddhist sites like Nalanda gradually fell into desuetude, Sarasvatī imagery was more likely to be retrieved by practicing Hindus in the neighborhood, and so were removed and preserved within Brāhmanical contexts where they are now presumed to have originated.

With this relatively sparse representation of Sarasvatī in demonstrably South Asian Buddhist contexts—both archaeological and textual—it is perhaps ironic that she is rather more prominent in Japanese Buddhism, tantric or otherwise. Among other contexts, she appears in her own right and as one of the *shichifukujin*, or seven gods of good fortune.[89] In addition, she regularly appears as the consort of the chief directional guardian Vaiśravana,[90] who also originated in South Asia in the pre-Mahāyāna period.

The Tibetan and Himalayan Afterlives of Sarasvatī

Sarasvatī entered Tibet and the western Himalayan regions in the context of the wholesale transmission of Indic Buddhism starting at least by the seventh century. During the eighth and ninth centuries of the imperial Pugyal (spu rgyal) dynasty, and through the majority of the Chidar period (phyi dar, "later spread [of Buddhism]" in the late tenth to fourteenth century), the most vibrant developments of Buddhism in northern India were Esoteric or Tantric Buddhism. Accordingly, Mahāyāna and Tantric elements arrived in Himalayan contexts entangled with each other, and with other aspects of South Asian literary culture. Just as Sarasvatī appeared in the early Esoteric Buddhist mandalas mentioned above, she continued to be depicted in later mandalas as the consort of Brahmā in the outer realms reserved for Brāhmanical deities converted to Buddhism.[91] Because in Tibet

89 Ludvik, "La Benzaiten à Huit Bras"; Bakshi, *Hindu Divinities in Japanese Buddhist Pantheon*, 107–27.

90 R. Stein, "Guardian of the Gate," 126, 131.

91 Ricca and Lo Bue, *Great Stupa of Gyantse*, 84 and pl. 58.

there was intense value placed on knowledge of Sanskrit from the eighth-century onward, her more important, independent role as inspiration for writers was also transmitted. Sanskrit language skills were recognized as essential for the major translation efforts of the eighth through the fourteenth century.[92] "Without at least a superficial acquaintance with the intricacies of Sanskrit, the would-be scholar could not hope to comprehend the beginning pages of even Tibetan commentaries on the great Buddhist treatises of India."[93] The title of "Translator" (lo tsā ba), referring to Sanskrit-to-Tibetan translation, carried high status in those centuries.[94] Buton Rinchen Drub (bus ton rin chen grub; 1290–1364), a renowned scholar who collected and helped systematize the expanding canon of Tibetan translations of Buddhist texts, includes a history of Sanskrit grammatical literature in his *History of Buddhism*, and he himself received the *sādhana*s of Sarasvatī from one of his teachers.[95] Already in this period there was considerable interest and familiarity with a range of South Asian Sanskrit literary productions, including *kāvya*-style poetics and that too, not exclusively for Buddhist authors.[96] As we have seen, Sarasvatī appears in many texts, as both river and goddess to be invoked, as a character in a drama, and as metaphor for eloquence.

Starting in the sixteenth century there was a "renewed interest in Sanskrit and the Indic origins of Buddhism among the Tibetan intelligentsia."[97] Increasingly, Sanskrit poetics took its place alongside the study of its grammar. Although Buddhism was certainly localized in its new Himalayan context, given the Indian origins, the leading erudite practitioners of Buddhism in Tibet were aware of, and closely adhered to, most of the rhetorical devices referencing Sarasvatī found in South Asian literature, explicitly Buddhist or otherwise. They were also eager to import the *sādhana*s, visual conventions, and mandalas generated in India. Thus, Sarasvatī's associations with the arts, with eloquent speech, poetic fluency, wisdom, and memory are carried into the Tibetan language discourse generated by these religious leaders. The other most important inheritance from the Indian Buddhist framing of Sarasvatī that carried forward into Tibet and Himalayan regions was the attribution of Sarasvatī as consort to Mañjuśrī.

Sarasvatī figures in the textual and pictorialized biographies of some of the most prominent religious leaders in later Tibetan history. These include the founder of what became the dominant religious school in Tibet, the

92 Davidson, *Tibetan Renaissance*, 117–209.

93 E. Smith, *Among Tibetan Texts*, 191. See also Gold, "Sa-skya Paṇḍita's Buddhist Argument for Linguistic Study," 153, 179.

94 Davidson, *Tibetan Renaissance*, 159.

95 Obermiller, *History of Buddhism in India and Tibet by Bu-Ston*, 167–69; Ruegg, *Life of Bu Ston Rin Po Che*, 86; Dratshadpa, *Handful of Flowers*, 16.

96 Epperson, "Kālidāsa in Tibet," 1–25, 180–84.

97 Lin, "Adapting the Buddha's Biographies," 16.

Geluk, as well as the most well-known reincarnating lineages, including Dalai and Panchen Lamas. Other, even older lineages also underscored their connection with her, including the Black Hat Karmapa and the related Red-Hat Shamar and Tai Situ corollary lineages. An exploratory listing of some of the most prominent examples will illustrate the breadth and depth of her integration into Tibetan Buddhist culture. There we find a consistent deflection on the part of high-standing Tibetan incarnates of the credit for the eloquence and impact of their own writings and teachings onto their evocation of Sarasvatī.

The life of Tsongkhapa Lobzang Drakpa (tsong kha pa blo bzang grags pa; 1357–1419), the teacher of Sherap Zangpo mentioned in the introduction of this chapter, was memorialized both in texts and in paintings, some of which include explanatory captions drawn from biographies. A sponsor in the first half of the eighteenth century created a set of fifteen woodcuts at the monastery of Tashilhunpo depicting the life of Tsongkhapa.[98] Versions of them were widely distributed through the Himalayan Buddhist realm, and the woodblock prints were painted over or were used as the compositional matrix for murals and paintings. In Giuseppe Tucci's treatment of 203 of the inscriptions on the woodcuts and some paintings, three of them mention Sarasvatī.[99] They describe Tsongkhapa as (a) learning rhetoric and—not incidentally—obtaining the realization of Sarasvatī; (b) having a vision of Sarasvatī; and (c) receiving instruction on Sarasvatī from the teacher Bumapa (dbu ma pa) during which he has a vision of Mañjuśrī. A woodblock print that has the latter inscription on it depicts Mañjuśrī and Sarasvatī sitting next to each other above two monks, one wearing a hat and making a teaching gesture, the other hatless but listening, presumably Tsongkhapa receiving the teachings and having the vision.[100]

We learn more details about Tsongkhapa's relationship to Sarasvatī in his biography, including the fact that he "started giving tantric initiations and the teachings related to such practices; especially the permission of Saraswati, a female deity of wisdom, whom some took to be his particular protectress."[101] One of the teachers with whom two of Tsongkhapa's disciples had previously studied came to Tsongkhapa requesting initiation into meditations on Sarasvatī.[102] A Nyingma lama who dreamed of receiving a teaching from Mañjusrī himself, asked Tsongkhapa (who became increasingly identified with Mañjusrī) for instruction. While Tsongkhapa was speaking, the lama saw Maitreya Buddha above

98 Tucci, *Tibetan Painted Scrolls*, 2: figs. 106–120, pls. 88–94.

99 Ibid., 2:418–34, esp. inscription nos. 56, 59, and 82.

100 Ibid., 2: fig. 114.

101 Sherpa Tulku, *Life and Teachings of Tsong-Khapa*, 13.

102 Ibid., 14.

Tsongkhapa's head, Mañjusrī above his right shoulder, and Sarasvatī above his left.[103] Sarasvatī is also said to have appeared to Tsongkhapa in order to warn him of the danger of his dying relatively young, and encouraging him to work hard for sentient beings in the time remaining to him.[104] The danger was averted through prayer, and he lived beyond the originally forecast time.

The Tashilhunpo set of fifteen compositions depicting the life of Tsongkhapa show him in each case at the center of the composition, facing forward. A second set of compositions was also composed, in which the main figures are asymmetrically arranged facing left or right toward an unidentified central image. The alternate asymmetric set was less popular and only variations of two compositions hanging to the right of the central image and two to the left are known.[105] Tucci acquired two paintings of this type from the same set, one facing left, the other right. Typically, he does not reveal where he acquired them, but studied them and suggests that they contain some of the same inscriptions found in the more complete set from Tashilhunpo.[106] In one of the paintings he acquired, Tsongkhapa's heart is pierced by the tip of a sword held by Mañjuśrī, suspended in the space before him, while Sarasvatī is in a similar rainbow-enclosed roundel at the bottom of the painting, before the kneeling Tsongkhapa.

Tsongkhapa and his followers passed along the relationship of Sarasvatī with Mañjuśrī, with wisdom, with beautiful and melodious speech, and with their founder's life and writings. This strong association between Tsongkhapa and Sarasvatī, and even the imagery by which it was conveyed, was transmitted to Qing China. That the episode just described was known in its compositional formality is demonstrated by a mural in the Gugong (Forbidden City), the patron of which was the Qianlong Emperor (r. 1735–1796). An avid supporter of the Geluk lineage, the emperor considered his childhood friend, the 3rd Jangjya Hutukhtu Rölpé Dorjé (lcang skya, rol pa'i rdo rje; 1717–1786) to be his adviser on Tibetan matters and his Tantric guru.[107] Rölpé Dorjé is credited with compiling the so-called Pantheon of 300 deities.[108] In 1772 the emperor began to construct an elaborate shrine complex, the Fanhua Pavilion, in the northern part of the Gugong. One of the main shrines on the upper floor displays three large paintings on cloth hung on the walls behind and to either side of a large sculpture of Tsongkhapa.[109] The murals combine the various episodes in the biographical paintings of Tsongkhapa into three compositions,

103 Ibid., 19.

104 Ibid., 21.

105 Himalayan Art Resources, set no. 1819; www.himalayanart.org/search/set.cfm?setID=1819..

106 Tucci, *Tibetan Painted Scrolls*, plate volume, pls. 95–98. See also Klimburg-Salter, *Discovering Tibet*, cat. nos. 79–80.

107 E. Smith, *Among Tibetan Texts*, 133–46; Chen, "Lcang-skya Rolpavi-rdorje and Emperor Qian Long"; Illich, "Selections from the Life of a Tibetan Buddhist Polymath."

108 Olschak, *Mystic Art of Ancient Tibet*, 113–85; Lokesh Chandra, *Buddhist Iconography*; Luo, *Eulogies*.

109 Wang, *Fanhua Lou*, 1:72–99.

including the ones just discussed. The wall on the left features the seated, hatless Tsongkhapa facing to his right, with his heart area touched by the tip of a long blue blade emerging from the heart of a rainbow-encircled Mañjuśrī floating at his left shoulder (Fig. 8.23). Nearby, also enclosed by a rainbow, is a seated Sarasvatī in a rainbow-striped skirt or pantaloons, in a distinctive pose in between sitting and squatting with her ankles crossed, referred to as "crossed-ankle *utkuṭakāsana*,"[110] playing the *pipa*-like *vīṇā* and appearing just above a praying monk, presumably Tsongkhapa (Fig. 8.24).

One of Tsongkhapa's closest disciples, Gendun Drub (dge 'dun grub pa; 1391–1474), who founded Tashilhunpo (bra shis lhun po) Monastery, was later recognized as the first Dalai Lama, an emanation of Avalokiteśvara. Two years after his death, his reincarnation was recognized, and was retrospectively designated as the 2nd Dalai Lama. This was Gendun Gyatso (dge 'dun rgya mtsho; 1476–1542). In his lifetime he became abbot of three of the most important Geluk monasteries: Tashilhunpo, Drepung ('bras spungs) and Sera (se ra). He was also a poet, and an epic poem he wrote about a pilgrimage he made opens with a verse of homage to Sarasvatī:

> Homage to Sarasvatī, female Bodhisattva of Wisdom.
> Crown jewel of all enlightenment seekers,
> Whose mystical dancing forms, like the full moon,
> Carry rays of light into all directions.
> May the signs of her goodness prevail.[111]

In fact, the 2nd Dalai Lama took Sarasvatī's name in Tibetan, Yangcanma (dbyangs can ma; lit. "she who possesses melodiousness"; "Goddess of Melodious Voice"),[112] dropped the feminine suffix (ma), and added it to his tantric name, "Laughing Vajra," so that his *nom de plume* became "The Melodious Laughing Vajra."[113] It is probably only a coincidence, but in the late sixteenth century Queen's Chorten in Karsha, Sarasvati is painted on the main wall mural (Fig. 8.25), the same wall that depicts the Second Dalai Lama.[114] Next to her is an inscription reading "lha mo yangs can la na mo," or "Praise to the Goddess of Melodious Voice," with a slight misspelling of "dbyangs."

In addition to composing poetry that invokes her, Gendun Gyatso also wrote a *sādhana* with a description of the "The Immutable Sarasvatī" who resides on the shores of a vast ocean.[115] It is an extensive visualization-

110 M. Shaw, *Buddhist Goddesses of India*, 240.
111 Mullin, *Mystical Verses of a Dalai Lama*, 150.
112 M. Shaw, *Buddhist Goddesses of India*, 237.
113 Ibid., 237.
114 Linrothe, "Site Unseen," figs. 12 and 24.
115 Mullin, *Meditations on the Lower Tantras*, 117–23. See also Wayman, "Goddess Sarasvatī," 435.

Fig. 8.23 Detail from a large painting on cloth depicting the life of Tsonkhapa in the Fan Hua Pavilion. After Wang Jiapeng et al. *Fanhua Lou (The Fanhua Pavilion)*, 4 vols. Beijing: The Forbidden City Publishing House, 2009, 1:98, fig. 40-1. Used with permission, courtesy Luo Wenhua.

Fig. 8.24 Sarasvatī, detail of Fig. 8.23. Used with permission, courtesy Luo Wenhua

Fig. 8.25 Sarasvatī, mural in the Queen's Chorten (stupa) at Karsha Chuchikzhal, Zanskar. Photo 2003.

meditation on the goddess, complete with generation, invitation, mantras, offerings, and identification with her, she "who is inseparable from my root Spiritual Master and who is accompanied by hosts of Buddhas and Bodhisattvas."[116]

The description resembles the iconography of her depiction in the Phugtal *thangka* (see Figs. 8.2–3). A white-petaled lotus bearing the syllable ĀḤ transforms itself into a white moon disk, the mind makes offerings of the light, and, thus,

> I emerge as the goddess Sarasvati, white in color. I have one face and two arms. My left hand holds a many-stringed vina—the type used by the celestial musicians. Its main hollow gourd [is] resting by my left side. I pluck its strings with the plectrum-rings that adorn my right fingers. I sit with both legs crossed at the ankles and with both knees raised. I wear a mantle and skirt of various silks, and I am adorned with a precious diadem, a necklace, a longer hanging necklace, and an ornamented belt.[117]

Gendun Gyatso enumerates some of the signs of successful practice of this Sarasvatī *yoga* or union with the deity in terms that will seem familiar from South Asian contexts already discussed: "an improved memory, the ability to recite mantras rapidly and clearly, an understanding into the import of many scriptural texts, and even a wish to write poetry."[118] The *sādhana* practice includes praise

116 Mullin, *Meditations on the Lower Tantras*, 117.

117 Ibid., 118.

118 Ibid., 120.

verses to Sarasvatī, including the following lines, which help underscore the connection to speech, eloquent writing, and mental sharpness:

> I make obeisance at your feet, O Sarasvati;
> Your body, bewitching and entrancing goddess,
> Was engendered from the immaculate speech of Avalokiteshvara.
> . . .
> All the wise are delighted by skillful composition;
> And the defeat of all opponents is the mark of an expert debater
> Lucid expression thrills every sharp mind. So, please
> Bestow on me the wisdoms of expositions, dialectics and composition.[119]

The *sādhana* practice seems to have been particularly suited to a Geluk monastery like the ones where Gendun Gyatso was abbot. The training of Geluk monks is renowned for its emphasis on scriptural memorization, recitation, explanation, and formalized debate. Among the most successful, highly educated monks, these skills produced prized poetic compositions.

The 1st (4th) Panchen Lama Lobzang Chokyi Gyeltsen (blo bzang chos kyi rgyal mtshan; 1570–1662) also had Sarasvatī play a meaningful role according to the accounts of his life. (There are two systems of counting the Panchen Lamas.) When he was fourteen years old "he successfully generated a vision of the White-faced Sarasvatī . . . and from that time he showed the signs of having opened the door to the treasury of intelligence, vast as the sky."[120] In a biography, the Panchen Lama was stated to have been "spiritually supported by the goddess [Sarasvatī] in person."[121] He was one of the teachers of the powerful "Great Fifth": the 5th Dalai Lama Ngawang Lobzang Gyatso (ngag dbang blo bzang rgya mtsho; 1617–1682), whose connections to Sarasvatī are storied, varied, and revealing.

Whether or not the 5th Dalai Lama received reinforcement from the 1st (4th) Panchen Lama for his connection to Sarasvatī, the 5th Dalai Lama seems to have received the actual formal permission-empowerment (rjes snang) from Zurchen Chöying Rangdröl (zur chen chos dbyings rang grol; 1604–1669). This was his "root lama," his "main Nyingma guru and guide in matters of practical magic."[122] In his "outer" autobiography, the 5th Dalai Lama writes that at the end of autumn 1638, while at Drepung monastery:

> I was curious about my ability to learn texts by heart. I requested Lord Zurchen to give me the *jenang* of the white Yangchenma [Sarasvatī]

119 Ibid., 121–22.

120 J. Willis, *Enlightened Beings*, 86–87.

121 J. Willis, *Enlightened Beings*, 209n411.

122 FitzHerbert, "Rituals as War Propaganda," 92.

> as well as instructions on the recitation of the goddess's *mantra*. I entered into a seven-day retreat reciting (*mantra* of the goddess), but my mind was elsewhere throughout the session and so there was no proper concentration at all. Likewise, no experience of any good sign occurred, not even a good dream. However, later one day I could write 15 *shloka* (60 lines) according to the system of Rinpung, or 20 *shloka* according to the system of Nathangpa and Palkhangpa. When my perception was unimpeded I could write the eulogy to Manjushri—when I was in China—in 68 *shloka* . . . . I dictated one *shloka* after the other as fast as lightning . . . (If my skill in writing) is to be taken as the result of the *mantra* of the goddess I recited, it is fine then. So I composed eulogies to Yangchenma and Drolkar (White Tārā).[123]

Six years later, in 1644, the Dalai Lama again referred to the benefits of his visualization of Sarasvatī and the recitation of her *mantra* in the context of a conversation with one of his primary teachers, Lingme Zhabdrung Konchok Chopel (gling smad zhabs drung dkon mchog chos 'phel; 1573–1644), the Thirty-Fifth Ganden Tripa:

> Lingme Zhabdrung had a new embroidered *thangka* of Tsongkhapa made at Sangngag Khar and asked me to compose a prayer of aspiration for it. I immediately composed it . . . and showed it to him. He said: "Before, you found it hard to write a eulogy to the goddess Yangchenma. Lord Gedun Gyatsho [the 2nd Dalai Lama; see above] was favoured by the goddess and so he could do the writing without any impediment. I always wished that you could do as he did. Now my hope has been fulfilled!" He was very pleased.[124]

The Great Fifth composed "an extensive supplication prayer to the Dalai Lama lineage, titled *Yangchen's Lute*," named after Sarasvatī's *vīṇā*.[125] "[T]he opening words of the text in question [were] in honor of the goddess of music, poetry, and learning, also known by her Sanskrit name Sarasvatī." Nancy Lin points out that the verses of praise to Sarasvatī that are attributed to Kālidāsa, the classical Sanskrit author of fifth-century India, were translated into Tibetan and preserved in the Tengyur (the canon of Buddhist commentarial texts). "There she is . . . compared to an ocean that is the source of the wish-granting jewel, fulfilling hopes and coming to the aid of deluded and bewildered beings."[126] The 5th Dalai Lama also wrote a commentary on the *Mirror of Poetics*, the seventh-century treatise on Sanskrit poetics (*Kāvyādarśa*) by Daṇḍin (Tib. Dbyug pa can),

123 Karmay, *Illusive Play*, 137. On contemporary Sarasvatī retreats, see M. Shaw, *Buddhist Goddesses of India*, 242.

124 Karmay, *Illusive Play*, 189.

125 Lin, "Recounting the Fifth Dalai Lama's Rebirth Lineage," 126.

125 Ibid., 140.

first translated into Tibetan in the thirteenth century. The 5th Dalai Lama's commentary was entitled *Song Delighting Sarasvatī*.[127]

Himalayan Buddhists of other persuasions and lineages besides that of the Geluk also paid attention to Sarasvatī. Probably the most celebrated Buddhist hero after the Buddha is the eighth-century Indian Buddhist master Padmsasambhava.[128] On his visits to Tibet he is said to have tamed the resistant local spirits and succeeded in establishing Buddhism there. According to a later legend, his Tibetan consort (he also had an Indian one) was Yeshe Tsogyel (ye ses mtsho rgyal). A seventeenth-century version of her story was written by Taksham Nuden Dorje (stag sham nus ldan rdo rje; fl. 17th c.). It begins by having a form of Padmasambhava think to himself, "The time has come for the goddess Sarasvati to project an emanation so that I can spread the teaching of the Tantra."[129] That emanation was Yeshe Tsogyel. Later, after Yeshe Tsogyel was born, "the goddess Sarasvatī spontaneously appeared to her and bestowed upon her the power of an infallible memory."[130]

The 6th Karmapa Tongwa Donden (mthong ba don ldan; 1416–1453) is depicted with Sarasvatī above him in the set of lineage paintings designed by the 8th Tai Situ, Situ Panchen Chokyi Jungne (si tu paṇ chen chos kyi 'byung gnas; 1700–1774). This portrait composition continues to be followed into the present.[131] The justification for this pictorial pattern is probably to be found in his biography, in which it is stated that the 6th Karmapa had a significant vision of her.[132] In a lineage related to the Karmapas, and contemporary to the 6th Karmapa, the 4th Shamar Chokyi Drakpa (zhwa dmar chos kyi grags pa; 1453–1524) (who became the abbot of Densatil Monastery[133]) also had a vision of Sarasvatī and "[a]s a result of this he was able to learn very quickly."[134] This episode is depicted in portraits of the 4th Shamar surrounded by life events.[135]

The 8th Tai Situ Panchen, just mentioned, designed a set of paintings based on a text known as the *Wish-Fulfilling Vine* by the celebrated Kaśmīri poet Kṣemendra (ca. 990/1010–1070). Ksemendra wrote 107 *avadāna* stories and his son, Somendra, completed his father's work with a numerically auspicious 108th chapter. According to Lin's study of the currency of the Tibetan translation of the text and the paintings it inspired in the seventeenth and eighteenth centuries, Somendra wrote in his preface to the tenth episode that "this compiled *avadāna* [text] fashioned by my father /

127 Lin, "Adapting the Buddha's Biographies," 100; and Lessing and Wayman, *Introduction to the Buddhist Tantric Systems*, 79.

128 Pakhoutova et al., *Second Buddha*.

129 Dowman, *Sky Dancer*, 7.

130 Ibid., 25.

131 Jackson, *Patron and Painter*, fig. 9.18; Pardee et al., *Karmapa*, 24–25.

132 Himalayan Art Resources, nos. 23949 (https://www.himalayanart.org/items/23949) and 61034 (https://www.himalayanart.org/items/61034); Douglas and White, *Karmapa*, 67.

133 Venturi, "Before and After," 107.

134 Douglas and White, *Karmapa*, 145.

135 Himalayan Art Resources, no. 2, https://www.himalayanart.org/items/2.

with the paintbrush of Sarasvatī, through the sequence of various colors, / has great purpose and delights good people."[136] As Lin's sophisticated and insightful analysis reveals, Tai Situ wrote an inscription in 1736 for his design of the extensive set of paintings (in 22, 23, or 25 scrolls) to illustrate the *Wish-Fulfilling Vine*. In it he refers to Somendra's verse, which

> plays with the relationship between image and text: his father's writing process is compared to a paintbrush that applies colors in sequence, gradually composing a complete picture through the accumulation of 107 narrative episodes. The paintbrush, in turn, is placed in the hand of Sarasvatī, the goddess of learning who is regularly invoked by poets for blessings and creative inspiration. . . . While Somendra calls paintings "nectar for the eyes" (*netrāmṛta*), Situ states that paintings "please through sight" *mthong bas dga' mgur bskyed byed pa* [lit. "(things that) produce satisfaction through perception"].[137]

Situ Panchen refers to the whole text of the Kaśmīri authors as "a goddess' song."[138] As we have seen, South Asian intellectuals such as Abhinavagupta similarly attribute the poets' sweet words to Sarasvatī.

Like the 5th Dalai Lama, Tai Situ was as learned an exegete of Sanskrit grammar as he was of its *kāvya* (snyan gnag) poetics. He knew Daṇḍin's *Kāvyādarśa* (which begins with the eulogy to Sarasvatī quoted above) and used Sanskrit commentaries to prepare his own edition of it.[139] The treatise on Sanskrit grammar, the *Sārasvatavyākaraṇa*, which in the Tibetan view was inspired by Sarasvatī herself,[140] was translated and commentaries written by no less than Tāranātha (1585–1634), the famous teacher and Indophile.[141] The 5th Dalai Lama had problems with Tāranātha's translation (and many other aspects of Tāranātha) as well as with another translation. Situ Panchen "compared both of these earlier translations and, ultimately, decided to redo the verses and autocommentary completely in collaboration with the Nepalese scholar Visṇupati."[142]

A contemporary of Tai Situ, the 7th Dalai Lama Lobzang Kelsang Gyatso (blo bzang skal bzang rgya mtsho; 1708–1757), is also associated with Sarasvatī and she is painted in some of his portraits. In fact a set of thirteen blockprint images of the Dalai Lamas and their previous incarnations was carved during the lifetime of the 7th Dalai Lama. His portrait was intended to be hung at the center of the horizontal lineup of cloth-mounted paintings inspired by the compositions disseminated in the woodblock prints.

136 Lin, "Adapting the Buddha's Biographies," 140.

137 Ibid., 140–41.

138 Ibid., 140.

139 E. Smith, *Among Tibetan Texts*, 206–7.

140 Ibid., 199; Ghose, "Study of Sanskrit Grammar in Tibet," 35.

141 Tucci, *Tibetan Painted Scrolls*, 1,72; Linrothe, "Polishing the Past;" Linrothe, "'Utterly False, Utterly Undeniable."

142 E. Smith, *Among Tibetan Texts*, 199.

Therefore he faced forward while the other Dalai Lamas and their predecessors were designed to face inward, toward him, with left- and right-facing compositions in equal number. The woodblocks were sometimes printed on gold silk and lightly painted, as in the complete set in the Tibet House Museum in New Delhi.[143] A second set of seven blockprints was designed and carved that was exclusively devoted to his own inner spiritual attainments and aspirational identities. They too were similarly printed on satiny yellow silk from China and delicately painted with restrained blushes of red color along with white teeth and white eyes with black pupils.[144] In the central or main painting of both sets, what is termed in Tibetan the *tso bo*, Sarasvatī is found next to Mañjuśrī in the upper right corner. While neither silk set in the Tibet House (New Delhi) collection has inscriptions, an early twentieth-century painting presented to King George V of Britain on behalf of the 13th Dalai Lama and now in the Victoria and Albert Museum, London, does have inscriptions written in gold on several of the depicted biographical events surrounding the main figure. The painting identifies the scene in the upper right corner as a vision that the 7th Dalai Lama had of White Mañjuśrī and Sarasvatī as he withdrew to meditate.[145]

It may be that the 7th Dalai Lama transmitted the permission-empowerment and practice of the Sarasvatī visualization to his student, the 3rd (6th) Panchen Lama Losang Penden Yeshe (blo bzang dpal dan ye shes; 1738–1780). In a painted portrait of the 3rd Panchen Lama photographed at Kyi Monastery in Spiti (Himachal Pradesh) **(Figs. 8.26–27)**, Sarasvatī appears buoyed in the sky by a cluster of multihued pastel clouds, playing her *vīṇā* and creating an "ocean of sounds" for the Panchen Lama seated on a throne on the flat roof of a monastic building (or a courtyard between buildings?). He seems delighted by the vision and sounds, which the seated student in front of him apparently cannot see or hear. The large central figure in the composition leans forward over an altar table on which rest a mandala offering and ritual implements. A similarly equipped table rests below a large painted sculpture (or is this too a vision?) of Cakrasaṃvara and his consort Vajravārāhī. At the center of the lower portion is the wealth deity Black Jambhala.[146] Based on the cloud formations, the relatively dark sky, and the treatment of the landscape and lake, this painting was probably brought to Kyi Monastery from Tashilhunpo, the seat of the Panchen Lamas, where many Geluk monks from Ladakh, Zangskar, and Spiti used to go for training before the political events of 1950 (the "peaceful liberation" of Tibet by the People's Republic of China) prevented them.

143 Himalayan Art Resources, no. 686, https://www.himalayanart.org/items/686.

144 Himalayan Art Resources, no. 687, https://www.himalayanart.org/items/687.

145 Kapstein 2005: 71–73.

146 Himalayan Art Resources, no. 1053, https://www.himalayanart.org/items/1053.

Fig. 8.26 Overall of mounted painting depicting the 3rd (6th) Panchen Lama, part of a set of five biographical paintings, ca. 19th century, central Tibet. Pigments on cloth with silk mounting; painting 72 x 45 cm. Kyi Gompa, Spiti, Himachal Pradesh, India. Photo 2005.

Fig 8.27 Detail of Fig. 8.26 depicting the Panchen Lama having a vision of Sarasvatī. Photo 2005.

Originally, the painting was also probably part of a set of at least five paintings depicting the life of the 3rd (6th) Panchen Lama. Four paintings of the same size, mounting, style, and date are in a private collection identified as the Chaofu Collection.[147] They include the same composition as the one in Kyi Gompa, but the Chaofu painting and a nearly identical one in the Mead Art Museum at Amherst College[148] have inscriptions. In these other paintings, but not the one in Spiti, a golden thread that appears to emanate from Sarasvatī links her to the heart of the seated lama. An inscription placed in the sky between the two in the Mead painting identifies this as "the vision of Sarasvatī" (dbyangs can ma'i gzigs snang).[149] The inscription beneath the Cakrasaṃvara is translated as "Vision at the occasion of listening to the empowerment in front of the victorious Kelsang Gyatso," which Marylin Rhie rightly understands as referring to the 3rd (6th) Panchen Lama's teacher, the 7th Dalai Lama Lobzang Kelsang Gyatso.[150] She argues cautiously that the main episode depicts "the young third Panchen Lama receiving the empowerment (initiation) of the *Chakrasamvara* Tantra by the 7th Dalai Lama."[151] The scene at the upper right is inscribed to signify visions and blessings attained while meditating at the Dechen Rabgye (bde chen rab rgyes), which Rhie interprets as indicating the hall at Tashilhunpo Monastery in which he was meditating. That the buildings shown were all meant to represent Tashilhunpo, by then the seat of the Panchen Lamas, is indubitable since an inscription between the building at center left and Sarasvatī is labeled as such (bkra shis lhun po).

Five paintings, of identical size and mounted with the same types of cloth, are preserved at Kyi Gompa. The hitherto unrecognized fifth painting in the life of the 3rd (6th) Panchen Lama (Fig. 8.28) seems to be a combination of (1) the Khedrub Geleg Pal Zangpo composition;[152] and (2) that of the 2nd Panchen Lama Lobzang Yeshe,[153] both from the earlier, original Panchen Lama set.[154] Comparing the Khedrub composition with the "missing" painting of the 3rd Panchen Lama (see Fig. 8.28), both of the main figures are hatless, facing toward their right and seeing a vision in the sky. The composition of the second comparison is similar in those ways, but the vision that the 2nd Panchen Lama is seeing is dominated by Vajrabhairava above Mañjuśrī, whereas in the 3rd Panchen Lama set it is Vajrabhairava above Śākyamuni, Vajrapāṇi, Green Tārā, and Garuḍa; Vajrabhairava is larger than all the others.

147 Himalayan Art Resources, no. 848, https://www.himalayanart.org/items/848.

148 Rhie, *Picturing Enlightenment*, cat. no. 1.

149 Ibid., 49.

150 Ibid., 46.

151 Ibid., 46–49.

152 Himalayan Art Resources, no. 529, https://www.himalayanart.org/items/529.

153 Himalayan Art Resources, set no. 980, https://www.himalayanart.org/search/set.cfm?setID=980.

154 Himalayan Art Resources, no. 689, https://www.himalayanart.org/items/689.

Fig. 8.28 "Missing" painting of the five-painting set depicting the 3rd (6th) Panchen Lama biography, ca. 19th century, central Tibet. Pigments on cloth with silk mounting; painting 72 x 45 cm. Kyi Gompa, Spiti, Himachal Pradesh, India. Photo 2005.

Another distinction to be made between the Kyi Gompa set of five paintings depicting the life of the 3rd (6th) Panchen Lama and the two partial sets recognized to date and just discussed has to do with the wrathful protectors and wealth deities at the bottom of the paintings. In the Chaofu partial set, only the central painting with the 3rd (6th) Panchen Lama facing forward has wrathful protectors below his throne. At center is Magzor Gyalmo (dmag zor rgyal mo), sometimes considered the wrathful form of Sarasvatī just as Paldan Lhamo (dpal ldan lha mo) is considered the wrathful form of Śrī Devī Lakśmī. On her right is the blue four-headed, four-armed standing Mahākala carrying skullcup, *kartri*-chopper, sword, and *triśūla*-tipped staff. On her left is the armored Begtse Chen holding a sword in his left hand and in his right a fresh heart held up to his mouth with an archer's bow in the crook of his elbow. The central image of the complete set in Kyi Gompa has these three as well, but sharing the center with Magzor Gyalmo, between her and Begtse Chen, is Black Jambhala.[155] Black Jamabhala appears in each of the other four paintings in the Kyi Gompa set as well, at the bottom center. As he is a powerful wealth deity, I hesitate to speculate on the significance of adding Black Jambhala into each composition of the set.

The 3rd (6th) Panchen Lama may also have helped consolidate or reinforce the Qianlong Emperor's interest in Tsongkhapa and his knowledge of the latter's affiliation to Sarasvatī. However, the Fanhua Pavilion, with its large mural of Tsongkhapa's vision of Sarasvatī (see Figs. 8.23–24) was completed a few years before the Panchen Lama was induced to visit the Emperor in Qing China. After declining the emperor's repeated invitations—in part because of his fear of smallpox—the Panchen Lama finally acceded to the imperial request by agreeing to attend the celebrations of the emperor's seventieth birthday. After months of travel, the Panchen Lama had arrived by August 20, 1780, and the lama and emperor saw each other over the next six weeks in Chengde and in Beijing. By December, however, the Panchen Lama tragically had succumbed to smallpox.[156]

The *Rinjung Gyatso* (rin 'byung brgya rtsa) compiled by Tāranātha (1575–1634) and amplified by the 4th (7th) Panchen Lama Lobzang Tenpai Nyima (blo bzang bstan pa'i nyi ma; 1782–1853) includes an extensive meditative visualization of the White Sarasvatī (dbyangs can ma dkar mo) and an identification with her as "the goddess of sound."[157] Some of the descriptive phrases in the *sādhana* recall the painting from Phugtal Monastery as well

155 Himalayan Art Resources, no. 1053, https://www.himalayanart.org/items/1053.

156 Cammann, "Panchen Lama's Visit to China in 1780."

157 Willson and Brauen, *Deities of Tibetan Buddhism*, 239–40 and no. 8.

as the painting in the Fanhua Pavilion (see Figs. 8.2–3, 8.23–24), including the fact that "the fringe of her hair [is] adorned with various jewels," her "fluttering lower garments [are] variegated like a rainbow," and she wears "earrings, choker bracelets, anklets, rings, girdle, pendant necklace, long necklace, and strings of little bells (on the feet)."[158] Here she is also recognized as the consort of Mañjughoṣa.[159] That the associations with wisdom are here as well is indicated by the explicit request in the ritual to the four-armed White Sarasvatī, "Please increase my intelligence," while the ritual that focused on the Red Sarasvatī similarly promises that its performance is "very quick for developing intelligence."[160]

Another great literary figure cemented his visionary links to Sarasvatī in his poetry: the Nyingmapa Amodowa, Zhabkar Tsokdruk Rangdrol (zhabs dkar tshogs drug rang grol; 1781–1851). At the same time, he reinforces her connection with Mañjuśrī:

> Another day, in a vision, I saw the faces of Manjushri, of Knowledge, and Sarasvati, Mistress of Speech. Smiling and laughing, they emanated rays of light that filled the sky like clouds, in the midst of which were flowers, banners, points of light, symbolic letters, forms of deities, medicines, and all sorts of beautiful objects . . . falling in a gentle rain, they dissolved into my body, which became as if insubstantial, ethereal. I had an inconceivable realization of bliss-emptiness.[161]

The next day he sang "Laughter of Manjushri and Sarasvati." The repeated chorus of the second half of the song was "Sarasvati, as well, will laugh in delight—ko re!"[162]

Sarasvatī remained an important part of the pantheon of Buddhist deities in Tibet into the late nineteenth century. Alex Wayman drew on the work of the great consolidator of disparate traditions, Jamgön Kongtrul Lodrö Thayé (1813–1900). Kongtrul's fourteen-volume *Compendium of All Sadhanas* (*Druptap Kuntü*) places Sarasvatī as the third deity in the first volume among the "Three White Deities," and lists seven different forms of her within her own category, second only to Mañjuśrī in the "Deities of Wisdom" section in the second volume. He includes her again in the seventh volume under "Deities of Enrichment."[163]

It is not possible to cite all of the contexts in which Sarasvatī appears in Tibetan thought and art, although offering at least a few final examples

158 Ibid., 240.

159 Ibid., 289.

160 Ibid., 290–91.

161 Ricard, *Life of Shabkar*, 171.

162 Ibid.

163 Jamgön Kongtrul, *Autobiography of Jamgön Kongtrul*, 532–43.

that extend into the present is warranted. One is part of the diaspora of late Buddhist culture back into India as part of the reconstitution of Tibetan monasteries in India after the Chinese absorption of Tibet in 1950 and the persecution of Buddhists and their institutions between 1958 and 1974. At a Nyingmapa monastery in the Mysore district of Karnataka, a four-armed Mañjuśrī is depicted in a wall mural "in union with his white two-armed partner Sarasvatī," who holds the neck of the *vīṇā* in her left hand, while the instrument's body is behind Mañjuśrī's back.[164]

Sarasvatī is also incorporated in a set of early twentieth-century silk weavings made in Hangzhou, eastern China, depicting the Panchen Lamas and the predecessors that they appropriated as belonging to their pre-incarnation lineage. This is a well-known woven set that is based on the eighteenth-century painted and woodblock printed sets that originally were centered on the 3rd (6th) Panchen Lama Lobzang Palden Yeshé. Patricia Berger, who has reviewed the scholarship on the complex history of the production in various media, argues that Qing court records "affirm that the 6th Panchen Lama himself presented the Qianlong emperor with a full set of twelve painted portraits of his lineage in 1770, a decade before his trip to Chengde" in 1780.[165] The 6th (9th) Panchen Lama Tubten Chokyi Nyima (thub bstan chos kyi nyi ma; 1883–1937), who collaborated with the Republican Nationalist government—the successors of the Manchu Qing dynasty after it fell in 1911—was gifted by them with a woven portrait of himself in 1932 in the general style of the older painted, woodblock-carved, and printed set.[166] In 1934, while the Panchen Lama was actually in Hangzhou, the Chinese governor of Zhejiang (in which Hangzhou is located) commissioned one of the local silk factories equipped with sophisticated Jacquard looms to create the punch-card programs for an updated set of images of the Panchen Lamas and their predecessors. They portrayed all of them, including the 6th (9th), and as Berger puts it, "bales of his portraits [that is, the Panchen Lama and his predecessors] . . . seem to have flowed freely over the borders."[167]

Karsha Monastery in Zangksar owns the woven set of fifteen images including the 6th (9th) Panchen Lama. They are mounted together and displayed during special occasions, for example the annual Karsha masked dance ritual, which usually occurs in July, when I photographed them in the main upper Dukhang in both 2018 and 2019 (Fig. 8.29). The previously mentioned Kyi Gompa in northern Spiti also has a full set of these weavings.

164 Herrmann-Pfandt, *Copper-Coloured Palace*, 2:471, fig. 4-11.

165 Berger, "Reincarnation in an Age of Mechanical Reproduction," 734.

166 Ibid., 740 and fig. 8.

167 Ibid., 744.

Fig. 8.29 Left side of the set of 1934 Hangzhou woven portraits of the Panchen Lamas and their predecessors at the upper Dukhang (assembly hall) at Karsha Monastery. Note: 5th (8th) Panchen Lama's portrait is on the far left. Karsha, Zangskar, India. Photo 2019.

They are beautifully mounted in Chinese silk brocade. In August 2005 they were in pristine condition as they had been stored inside a locked trunk in the Zimshung (gzims gzhung). Among the Panchen Lamas in both sets in the western Himalaya is the 5th (8th) Panchen Lama Lobzang Tenpai Wangchug (blo bzang bstan pa'i dbang phyug; 1854/55–1882) (Fig. 8.30). The design for this addition to the earlier sets was perhaps made at the same time as the weaving in the mid-1930s. At any rate, very few examples are known except as part of these woven sets.[168] At the level of the Panchen Lama's hat are the paired Mañjuśrī and Sarasvatī, on the viewer's left and right, respectively.

Finally, mention might be made of Sarasvatī's continuing prominence throughout the Tibetan horizon into the present. North of the Tibetan Autonomous Region, in Qinghai Province of China, the ethnically Tibetan painter in the Golog region, known as Golog Sherab, who studied with the renowned Amdo Jampa, included three paintings of Sarasvatī in his trilingual book *Tangkas in Golog: The Tangka Album by Xi Re Bu.*[169] The one included here (Fig. 8.31) was captioned in Tibetan, Chinese, and English, "Beautiful and gentle Sarasvati." The other two were captioned "Sarasvati in the heavenly lake," and "Sarasvati making the sound[s] of [Buddhist] preaching," respectively. In a probable reference to Sarasvatī as a deity personifying artistic skill-in-means, a cropped version of Figure 8.31 featured on the cover of the Golog painter's book. Note the pair of long-necked geese, reminiscent of the *haṃsa*, Sarasvatī's *vāhana*. A detail of them in his book is captioned, "Two geese listening to the music."[170] Additionally, as with the Phugtal painting, the musical instruments she holds has a head—in this case, that of a dragon-like beast—as the finial at the tip of the neck.

168 Himalayan Art Objects, no. 58981, https://www.himalayanart.org/items/58981.

169 Golog Sherab, *Tangkas in Golog*, 28–31.

170 Ibid., 29.

Fig. 8.30 Woven portrait of the 5th (8th) Panchen Lama Lobzang Tenpai Wangchug. Tapestry of silk woven in 1934 in Hangzhou, Zhengzhou, China; 69 x 41 cm. Kyi Gompa, Spiti, Himachal Pradesh, India. Photo 2005.

Fig. 8.31 "Beautiful and gentle Sarasvati." Painting on cloth by Golog Sherab. After Hungkar, *Tankas in Golog,* 28.

Sarasvatī as Metaphor within the Tibetan Buddhist Horizon

Ultimately inherited from classical, dramaturgical, and Buddhist literature of India, Sarasvatī's significance within the regions practicing Buddhism in its developed Himalayan modality was associated most strongly with eloquence in the expression of wisdom, particularly Buddhist wisdom. The 5th Dalai Lama used Sarasvatī as a synecdoche and cynosure of eloquence; he is quoted as praising a travelogue of Tsarchen Losal Gyatso (tsar chen blo gsal rgya mtsho; 1502–1566) in these terms: "Styled in finely alternating verse and prose[,] were Sarasvatī to have appeared in his throat and spoken, what more could she have said than that?"[171] Tsarchen himself "spent time in retreat meditating on Sarasvatī, the goddess of the fine arts. During the retreat a rain of white flowers fell, he heard the sweet sound of Sarasvatī's lute, and finally saw her face and received her prophetic words. This caused an incredible gift of eloquence to blossom, and whatever he wrote naturally came forth as poetry."[172] Such references echo those found in the *kāvya* Sanskrit texts that scholars such as the Great Fifth studied. The *Harṣacarita* also suggests that Sarasvatī "inhabited his mouth."[173] Similar phrasing is found in the *Saundaryalaharī* ("Flood of Beauty"): "Unweariedly muttering (jāpa) in repetition tales of your lord's many achievements, / your tongue, O mother, lovely as the China rose (japā), is supreme; / as Sarasvatī sits at its tip, her beauteous crystal-clear / form changes until it looks like a ruby."[174] Likewise, the first recitation of the *Skandapurāṇa* in front of Harṣavardhana was so eloquent it evoked, in the words of Bāṇa, "the tinkling of the anklets of Sarasvatī, as she presents herself in his mouth, while it seems as if, by the sparkling of his teeth, he whitewashes the ink-stained syllables and worships the book with showers of white flowers."[175] As late as the ca. eleventh century, the *Rāmacaritaṁ* of Sandhyākaranandi use the same trope of someone having the goddess Sarasvatī "located in his mouth."[176] References to Sarasvatī, especially those by the later Tibetan teacher-scholars, were themselves self-referential displays of wisdom, of knowledge of Sanskrit and Buddhism, of her blessings. The references that have been assembled above from (auto) biographies of Tibetan savants where the vision of Sarasvatī precedes the bestowal of "[p]erfection in the skills of exposition, dialectics, and composition"[177] make clear that she was synonymous with memory and with eloquence of both speech and writing, a metaphor to live and thrive by.

171 Stearns, *Song of the Road*, 4.

172 Stearns, *Song of the Road*, 6.

173 Cowell and Thomas, *Harṣa-carita of Bāṇa*, 61.

174 Brown, *Saundaryalaharī*, 72, verse 64.

175 Bakker, *Holy Ground*, 607.

176 Majumdar, Bask and Banerji, *Rāmacaritaṁ of Sandhyākaranandin*, canto 1, verse 17A-B.

177 Mullin, *Meditations on the Lower Tantras*, 122.

Those values are enshrined at the heart of Himalayan Buddhist culture, by any measure one of the most highly literate in the world. For whatever reasons, Tibetan and Himalayan cultures have little in the way of an impressive tradition of high-fired ceramics or intricately woven tapestries (thus excluding appliqués), content to import both from China. For a region with astounding natural terrain, its visual artists were surprisingly uninterested in pictorial landscape, and its instrumental music cannot hold its own in rhythmic complexity or melodic power in comparison with Indian classical music. But it more than makes up for these deficits or disinterest, if those are what they are, by the refinement and dimensions of its literary production.

> The volumes of Tibetan literature that today crowd libraries around the world speak to centuries of such scholarship and the efforts of scribes, scholars, editors, and artisans who spent their lives working with ink, paper, wood and chisel. The making of books was such a prominent aspect of Tibetan cultural life that it could even come to define a person.[178]

A multitude of different scripts—not sufficiently captured by simple categories such as printed and cursive—were and are regularly employed and deciphered. There were elaborate rules for punctuation,[179] and for the transcription of Sanskrit-derived mantras. Although only a few such genres have been drawn on in the course of this study, there are highly developed varieties of history, biography, autobiography ("inner," "outer," and "secret"), hagiography, poetry and song, guidebooks, commentaries, textbooks, grammars, epistolary collections, assemblies of memorable verses encapsulating practical advice, compilations of inscriptions, manuals for meditation and for pronunciation, and studies of religious, literary, philological, astronomical, medical, and other sciences.[180]

It was contemplative practice along with literary skills that drew "[s]tudents from Ngari [and from Zangskar] in the far west to Kham and Amdo in the east,"[181] in order to sit at the feet of scholars such as Zhalu Lotsawa Chökyong Zangpo (zhwa lu lo tsa ba chos skyong bzang po; 1441–1527) in west-central Tibet. They studied grammatical works and admired his expertise in Indian and Tibetan grammatical systems, his "firm command not only of different languages but also of poetics, synonomics, as well as a deep knowledge of scriptures."[182]

178 Schaeffer, *Culture of the Book in Tibet*, 3.

179 Schaeffer, "Letter to the Editors," 270.

180 Nearly thirty genres are treated with separate essays in Cabezón and Jackson, eds. *Tibetan Literature: Studies in Genre*.

181 Schaeffer, *Culture of the Book in Tibet*, 49.

182 Ibid., 51.

Within the same monastic contexts, there developed an emphasis comparable to that of learned *written* articulateness, that of *spoken* eloquence, particularly expressed in the format of debate.[183] Monastic debate "evolved into a prestigious form of learning and language socialization at the major monasteries of the Geluk sect, a sect that emerged as a hegemonic force over much of central Tibetan beginning in the mid-seventeenth century."[184] At early stages of monastic education, debate helps to "distinguish monks from their lay peers and set off the subcategory of the elite monk who does well in philosophy and ends up pursuing a Geshe degree [analogous to a PhD] from the kind of monk who does not do well on the debating courtyard and ends up shuttled into monastic labor and service."[185] Monks train one-on-one in the courtyards of the monasteries on a daily basis, switching roles between the standing challenger and the seated defendant (Figs. 8.32–33). At the Geluk monastery of Phugtal in Zangskar, to which the Sarasvatī painting that provoked this study belongs, I have myself seen young monks being trained in debate by monks with advanced degrees (Geshés) from relocated Tibetan monasteries in south India. At a much more advanced level, there are public debates with a great deal at stake, including status-conferring degrees. Even intrinsically esteemed, recognized, reincarnating lamas are expected to excel in such vocal contests. Doing badly in debates, including exhibiting signs of hesitation, incoherence, or poor memorization skills, provoke taunts by the challenger or challengers.

As long as Sarasvatī remained "on the tip of one's tongue," bolstering one's memory of scripture to use in debate or teaching, and providing inspiration at the tip of one's pen, monks in particular could thrive in the Tibetan monastic system. Those are the very associations that we have seen being described in texts and being explained in those images that appear to illustrate descriptions of visions of Sarasvatī. The 5th (8th) Panchen Lama (see Fig. 8.30) image then is paradigmatic of the promise in her presence. Mañjuśrī and Sarasvatī perch just above the lama, right and left. The Panchen Lama holds the wheel of the Buddha dharma in his left hand, along with the stem of a lotus that blossoms at his left cheek, and bears the text of the *Perfection of Wisdom* (*Prājnāparamitā*) *Sūtra*, echoing the lotus and book held by Mañjuśrī. With his right hand, the Panchen Lama makes the *vitarka mudra*, the gesture of exposition, or teaching *mudra*.
It is as if Mañjuśrī and Sarasvatī are whispering the message he should preach into his ears and mind. Together, a melodious and wise ocean

183 Dreyfus, *Sound of Two Hands Clapping*; Lempert, *Discipline and Debate*.

184 Lempert, *Discipline and Debate*, 51.

185 Ibid., 36.

Fig. 8.32 Monks in a courtyard of Rongwo Tosam Namgyel Ling training in debate, in the Rebkong's Tongren County, Qinghai, PRC. Photo 2007.

Fig. 8.33 Monks in the courtyard of Sakya Monastery training in debate, Tsang area of the Tibetan Autonomous Region, PRC. Photo 2007.

of sound emerges from his mouth, reshaping the understanding of his listeners and deepening their faith.

This, then, is the cultural context in which the painter of Phugtal's Sarasvatī could assume was ingrained in the sponsor of the painting. Getting at those assumptions are what I consider the essential task of the historian, to expose the "period eye." The case is made easier in this instance by the fact that this is not a work for "the public," in the sense of a generic population, but rather for a member of particular social class known to be highly literate. As Clifford Geertz expressed it, placing a work of art "within other modes of social activity," revealing how it is incorporated "into the texture of a particular pattern of life . . . [and] giving to art objects a cultural significance, is always a local matter."[186] It is not so much universal values in play as a universal capacity to fathom the values that others may devise. In this case, the social and religious values dear to the sponsor of the painting seem to me to have clearly included eloquence in spoken and written registers and related memorization of noble texts. As a prompt and aid to visualization of the culturally validated source of such skills, the painting could provide functional and psychological assistance to its sponsor. The act of sponsorship was itself an offering to the deity. In the Buddhist worldview, the world in which we live is governed by *karma*. The acts of offering were therefore transactional, at least to a certain extent. No good deed is left unrecompensed, and the arena in which Sarasvatī could pay back that reverence was well defined. All this the painter could take into account in designing the composition and executing lines, shapes, and colors. The painting, if it was not in a sense the manifestation of the sponsor's internal visualization of Sarasvatī, might instead have been of some assistance in his conjuring and identification with her. As the sixteenth-century 2nd Dalai Lama Gendun Gyatso described in the *sadhana* quoted above, the Tantric practitioner "becomes" Sarasvatī in the process known as *ahaṃkāra*.

In this light, we can resist or dismiss a few things in our interpretation of the painting. Referring to works of art in a Christian religious context, Geertz makes an important point valid for the Himalayan Buddhist ones as well, *mutatis mutandis*. "[T]he relation between religious ideas and pictorial images . . . was not simply expositive; they were not Sunday school illustrations."[187] In other words, such a painting was not intended for illustrating some narrative that needed reinforcing, much less for

186 Geertz, "Art as a Cultural System," 1475.

187 Ibid., 1483.

beautification of the cloister's walls. Sarasvatī's character could not be known from the painting itself, only through other, extra-visual associations. Nor was the painting designed for abstract contemplation of "tonal progressions, color relations, or prosodic shapes."[188] Such a work was purposeful, not bootless, and "traffics . . . in the moral substance of [its] culture."[189] Even if we accept that it signified an attempt to fill a need other than an aesthetic one, we can reject the seemingly obvious connection between *vīṇā*-playing and music, or the fulfillment of the desire for virtuosic musical skill. In the Tibetan monastery where the painting hangs, there were no musical solos or improvisatory leads. Our sponsor was not praying to become the sixteenth-century equivalent of Vilayat Khan or Nusrat Fateh Ali Khan. Instead, ambition lay in the direction of becoming a credible teacher to the community of monks and villages in Zangskar, making his nearby or local family proud, composing tracts worthy of copying or even woodcut duplication, and fashioning a reputation that might spread regionally by coming to the ears of the kings and wealthy patrons in Padum or Zangla, or farther afield in the kingdoms of Ladakh, Spiti, or Gugé.

While the goal conveyed by such a painting was not to acquire skill in music per se, it still was all about sound, about *śabda*. In Sanskrit and in its Tibetan translation, *śabda* is both sound and word.[190] It can denote sound, term, auditory object, voice, term, word, speech, or note. If the Phugtal painting may be summed up in a single such word, it would be *śabda* or, the Tibetan སྒྲ (*sgra*).

An Iconological Rereading of the Phugtal Sarasvatī Painting

Melodious sound emanates from the *vīṇā* (see Figs. 8.2–3, 8.7–11). Its first listener is Sarasvatī, her almond-shaped eyes almost closed in delight, her head tilted in concentration, her smile in response. All the beings in her synesthetic world are attracted by the sight of this beautiful goddess, and especially by the sounds she is producing. The beaks of the attentive ducks, geese, and peacock are clasped in silence. The two siddhas or *yogis* are similarly rapt, sitting up straight, eyes open, listening. The bodhisattva on the left near Sarasvatī's right knee sways dance-like toward her, hand to ear. The one on the right has his hands in positions identical to hers, and might actually be playing another *vīṇā* in harmony. The fish in the blue waters of the ponds surface for an opportunity to hear the sound. Their gills gasping, they ignore the long-necked birds nearby who, though natural fishers, are

188 Ibid., 1474.

189 Ibid., 1488.

190 De Körös, *Sanskrit-Tibetan-English Vocabulary*, 331.

similarly transfixed by the celestial sounds. The standing bodhisattvas and the two cloud-borne heavenly beings are all concentrating on Sarasvatī and responding to the pervading sound with appropriate welcoming or admiring gestures. The six monks at the top are actually paired, facing each other as if to share their enchantment with the sounds and communicate their wonder at its perfection.

The "extra" register at the bottom is particularly intriguing. It seems like a peculiar indulgence, an additional panel that adds little to the narrative but has an abstract order and logic, and an underlying, nearly invisible pattern of repetition and rotation. In that sense, it is musical, like a Bach fugue or variation, like a classical Indian *rāga*, an improvisation on a set sequence of notes.[191] It alerts us to attend to the non-narrative, purely visual elements reinforcing the central message. The sensuous color, rhythm, and flickering movement in and out, dark and bright, are the aesthetic subconscious means and goals of this religious art, rather than fidelity to three-dimensional proportionality and the mimicking of colored and textured surfaces in particularized conditions of lighting. The envelopment of recognizable facets of divine perfection within staged environments of appropriately belabored ornament (*alaṁkāra*) is closely analogous to *kāvya*, the vaunted methods of which are punning ornamentation, elaboration, and implicature. Here the goal, the message, is the prompt for aesthetic-religious response.[192] The largest area of plain, unadorned color is the moon-like brightness of the goddess's face and skin, established and emphasized in Puranic if not Vedic sources.[193]

The painter's visual heritage has been mobilized in order to respond to the sponsor's desire for a painting of Sarasvatī. The sponsor's need was related to the religious and social dimensions of his life. Reading behind the explicit theme of the monk able to envision her, the artist shows her in the realm of Ālaka (lcang lo can), Vajrapāṇi's abode endowed with beautiful sounds and peace.[194] There, she is being intently listened to, just as the monk wishes his fluent discourse to be heard in the world by sentient beings, protected by Vajrapāṇi, overseen by Vajradhāra, commended by and channeling his distinguished Tibetan and South Asian predecessors and colleagues.

191 As might be expected, there is a '*rāga Sarasvatī*.'

192 Bhikshu Sangharakshita contends that "even from the orthodox Buddhist point of view, the content of art is not incompatible with the content of spirituality, and that the religious life does not exclude artistic interests," including visual, auditory, and literary. Sangharakshita, "*Meaning of Buddhism*," 40.

193 Lal, *Female Divinities* 197. See also Willson and Brauen, *Deities of Tibetan Buddhism*, 240.

194 The environment over which she presides is the visual equivalent of the poetic description of the setting for the goddess Hirmā (Hidimbā) in the Kulu Valley (two mountain passes south of Zangskar) in its "inaccessible regions of forests, and on mountain-breasts with blossoming trees . . . on sylvan streams with beautiful banks, and mountain currents, in picturesque woods with blossoming trees and creepers, in Himālayan bowers, and various caves, on crystal pools smiling with lotusses [sic] . . . woods sacred to the gods and on hill-sides in the regions of Guhyakas and ascetics, on the banks of [Lake] Mānasasarawara, abounding with fruits and flowers of every season;" Pratāpa Chandra Rāy, translator, *The Mahabharata of Krishna Dwaipayana Vyasa*, canto CLVII; quoted in P. H. Pott, "The Goddess Hirmā in Kulū Valley," 559.

Bibliography

Abhayadatta. *Buddha's Lions: The Lives of the Eighty-Four Siddhas, Caturaśīti-siddha-pravṛtti*. Translated by James B. Robinson. Berkeley, CA: Dharma, 1979.

Ahmad, Iqbal. *Kushans in Kashmir*. Srinagar: Gulshan Books, 2011.

Ahmad, Zahiruddin. "New Light on the Tibet-Ladakh-Mughal War of 1679–84." *East and West* 18, nos. 3–4 (1968): 340–61.

Ahmed, Monisha, and Clare Harris. Introduction to *Ladakh: Culture at the Crossroads*, edited by Monisha Ahmed and Clare Harris, 10–20. Mumbai: Marg, 2005.

Aldenderfer, Mark. "On Text, Materiality, and the Tibetan Buddhist Religious Architecture at Piyang." In *Religion, Archaeology, and the Material World*, edited by Lars Fogelin, 339–58. Occasional Paper 36. Carbondale: Southern Illinois University Carbondale, Center for Archaeological Investigations, 2008.

Aldenderfer, Mark. "Piyang: A Tibetan Buddhist Temple and Monastic Complex of the 10th–11th Centuries AD in Far Western Tibet." *Archaeology, Ethnology & Anthropology of Eurasia* 4, no. 8 (2001): 138–46.

Aldenderfer, Mark, and Holley Moyes. "Excavations at Dindun, a Pre-Buddhist Village Site in Far Western Tibet." In *Xizang Kaogu yu Yishu: Guoji Xueshu Taolunhui wenji* (Tibetan Archaeology and Art: Proceedings from the International Research Conference), edited by Huo Wei and Li Yongxian, 47–69. Chengdu: Sichuan Renmin Chubanshe, 2004.

Aldenderfer, Mark, and Holley Moyes. "In the Valley of the Eagle: Zhang-zhung, Kyunglung, and the Pre-Buddhist Sites of Far Western Tibet." *Expedition* 47, no. 2 (2005): 28–34.

Alder, Garry. *Beyond Bokhara: The Life of William Moorcroft, Asian Explorer and Pioneer Veterinary Surgeon, 1767–1825*. 2nd ed. with new introduction and postscript. Delhi: Low Price Publications, 2012.

Alexander, André. *The Temples of Lhasa: Tibetan Buddhist Architecture from the 7th to the 21st Centuries*. Chicago: Serindia, 2005.

Alexander, André, and Sam van Schaik. "The Stone Maitreya of Leh: The Rediscovery and Recovery of an Early Tibetan Monument." *Journal of the Royal Asiatic Society* 21, no. 4 (2011): 421–39.

Alley, Kelly D. *On the Banks of the Gangā: When Wastewater Meets a Sacred River*. Ann Arbor: University of Michigan Press, 2002.

Allinger, Eva. "An Early West Tibetan Manuscript from Hanle Monastery, Ladakh." In Allinger et al., *Interaction in the Himalayas and Central Asia*, 147–71.

Allinger, Eva. "*Thang ka*s Dedicated to the Vajradhātumaṇḍala: Questions of Stylistic Connections." In *Art in Tibet: Issues in Traditional Tibetan Art from the Seventh to the Twentieth Century*. PIATS 2003: Tibetan Studies: Proceedings of the Tenth Seminar of the International Association for Tibetan Studies, Oxford, 2003, edited by Erberto F. Lo Bue, 53–61. Leiden: Brill, 2011.

Allinger, Eva, Frantz Grenet, Christian Jahoda, Maria-Katharina Lang, Anne Vergati, eds. *Interaction in the Himalayas and Central Asia: Processes of Transfer, Translation and Transformation in Art, Archaeology, Religion and Polity*. Vienna: Austrian Academy of Sciences, 2017

Almond, Philip C. *The British Discovery of Buddhism*. Cambridge: Cambridge University Press, 1988.

Anand, Dibyesh. "Archive and the Poetics of 'Exotica Tibet.'" In Klieger, *Tibetan Borderlands*, 49–66.

Antiquities of Northern Pakistan: Reports and Studies. Vol. 1, *Rock Inscriptions in the Indus Valley*. Edited by Karl Jettmar in collaboration with Ditte König and Volker Thewalt. Mainz: Philipp von Zabern, 1989.

Antiquities of Northern Pakistan: Reports and Studies. Vol. 2. Edited by Karl Jettmar in collaboration with Ditte König and Martin Bemmann. Mainz: Philipp von Zabern, 1993.

Antiquities of Northern Pakistan: Reports and Studies. Vol. 3. Edited by Gérard Fussman and Karl Jettmar in collaboration with Ditte König. Mainz: Philipp von Zabern, 1994.

Asboe, Walter. "Pottery in Ladakh, Western Tibet." *Man* 46 (1946): 9–10.

Asboe, Walter. "Sacrifices in Western Tibet." *Man* 36 (1936): 75–76.

Asher, Frederick M. *The Art of Eastern India, 300–800*. Minneapolis: University of Minnesota, 1980.

Asher, Frederick M. *Nalanda: Situating the Great Monastery*. Mumbai: Marg, 2015.

Astley, Ian. "An Example of Vajrasattva in the Sino-Japanese Tantric Buddhist Tradition." *Studies in Central and East Asian Religions* 1 (1988): 67–87.

Atil, Esin, W. T. Chase, and Paul Jett. *Islamic Metalwork in the Freer Gallery of Art*. Washington, D.C.: Freer Gallery of Art, Smithsonian Institution, 1985.

Azarpay, Guitty, with A. M. Belenitskii, B. I. Marshak, and Mark J. Drescen. *Sogdian Painting: The Pictorial Epic in Oriental Art*. Berkeley: University of California Press, 1981.

Bachhofer, Ludwig. *Early Indian Sculpture*. 1939; reprint, New Delhi: Munshiram Manoharlal, 1973.

Bagley, Robert. "Styles, Period, and the Life Cycle of the Goblin." *Gombrich among the Egyptians and Other Essays in the History of Art*, 22–47. Seattle: Marquand Books, 2015.

Bailey, H. W. "An Itinerary in Khotanese Saka." *Acta Orientalia* 14, no. 4 (1936): 258–67.

Bajpai, K. D. "Role of Indian Rivers and Tīrthas in National Integration." In *Pilgrimage Studies: Text and Context, Srī Phalāhārī Bābā Commemoration Volume*, edited by D. P. Dubey and Lallanji Gopa, 22–25. Allahabad: Society of Pilgrimage Studies, 1990.

Bakker, Hans Teye. *Holy Ground, Where Art and Text Meet: Studies in the Cultural History of India*. Leiden: Brill, 2019.

Bakshi, D. N. *Hindu Divinities in Japanese Buddhist Pantheon: A Comparative Study*. Calcutta: Benten, 1979.

Bamzai, P. N. K. *Culture and Political History of Kashmir*. 3 vols. New Delhi: M.D. Publications, 1994.

Bandini-König, Ditte, Martin Bemmann, and Harald Hauptmann. "Rock Art in the Upper Indus Valley." In *The Indus: Cradle and Crossroads of Civilizations, Pakistan-German Archaeological Research*, edited by Harald Hauptmann, 29–70. Islamabad: Embassy of the Federal Republic of Germany, 1997.

Baxandall, Michael. *Patterns of Intention: On the Historical Explanation of Pictures*. New Haven, CT: Yale University Press, 1985.

Bazin, Nathalie. "Fragrant Ritual Offerings in the Art of Tibetan Buddhism." Special issue, *Journal of the Royal Asiatic Society* 23, no. 1 (2013): 31–38.

Beal, Samuel. *Si-Yu-Ki: Buddhist Records of the Western World Translated from the Chinese of Hiuen Tsiang (A.D. 629)*. 1884; reprint, Delhi: Motilal Banarsidass, 1981. 1884 edition available online from Wisdom Library: https://www.wisdomlib.org/south-asia/book/buddhist-records-of-the-western-world-xuanzang.

Beck, Michael. *Tibet–Guge: The Cultural Relics of Ancient Western Tibet*. Kathmandu: Vajra Books, 2018.

Beckwith, Christopher I. *The Tibetan Empire in Central Asia: A History of the Struggle for Great Power among Tibetans, Turks, Arabs, and Chinese during the Early Middle Ages*. Princeton: Princeton University Press, 1987.

Beek, Martijn van. "Contested Classifications of People in Ladakh: An Analysis of the Census of Jammu & Kashmir 1873–1941." In *Tibetan Studies: Proceedings of the 7th Seminar of the International Association for Tibetan Studies, Graz 1995, Vol. 1*, edited by Helmut Krasser et al., 35–49. Vienna: Österreichische Akademie der Wissenschaften, 1997.

Benavides, Gustavo. "Giuseppe Tucci, or Buddhology in the Age of Fascism." In *Curators of the Buddha: The Study of Buddhism Under Colonialism*, edited by Donald S. Lopez Jr., 161–96. Chicago: University of Chicago Press, 1995.

Bénisti, Mireille. *Contribution à l'Étude du Stūpa Bouddhique Indien: Les Stūpa Mineurs de Bodhi-Gayā et de Ratnagiri*. 2 vols. Paris: École Française d'Extrême-Orient, 1981.

Bentor, Yael. "The Content of Stūpas and Images and the Indo-Tibetan Concept of Relics." *Tibet Journal* 28 nos. 1&2 (2003): 21–48.

Berger, Patricia. "Reincarnation in an Age of Mechanical Reproduction: The Career of the Narthang Panchen Lama Portraits." In *Images of Tibet in the 19th and 20th Centuries*, edited by Monica Esposito, 727–45. Paris: École Française de'Extrême-Orient, 2008.

Bernbaum, Edwin. *The Way to Shambhala*. Garden City: Anchor Books, 1980.

Bernier, François. *Travels in the Mogul Empire, A.D. 1656–1668*. Translated by Archibald Constable (1891). 2nd ed., edited by Vincent A. Smith. London: Humphrey Milford, Oxford University Press, 1916.

Beszterda, Rafal. *The Moravian Brethren and Himalayan Cultures: Evangelisation, Society, Industry*. New Delhi: Munshiram Manoharlal, 2013.

Bhattacharya, Gouriswar. "Buddha Śākyamuni and *Pañca-Tathāgatas*: Dilemma in Bihar-Bengal." In *South Asian Archaeology 1985*, 350–71.

Bhattacharya, Gouriswar. "How Come Sarasvati Is a Consort of Vishnu in Eastern India?" In *Art, Icon and Architecture in South Asia: Essays in Honour of Dr. Devangana Desai*, edited by Anila Verghese and Anna L. Dallapiccola, 105–20. New Delhi: Aryan, 2015.

Bhattacharya, Gouriswar. "Malda Museum of Antiquities." *Baha* 7 (2014): 51–55.

Bhattacharya, Malaysankar. *Art in Stone: A Catalogue of Sculptures in Malda Museum*. Malda: Malda Museum, 1982.

Bhattacharya, Malaysankar. *Art of Bengal: The Sculptures of the Mahānandā-Karatoyā Valley*. Vol. 1. Kolkata: Indian Institute of Oriental Studies & Research, 2002.

Bhattacharya-Haesner, Chhaya. "Indo-Tibetan Influences in Banners from Dunhuang." In *Prajñādhara: Essays on Asian Art, History, Epigraphy and Culture in Honour of Gouriswar Bhattacharya*. 2 vols. Edited by Gerd J.R. Mevissen and Arundhati Banerji, 2.479–490. New Delhi: Kaveri Books: 2009.

Bhattacharyya, Benoytosh. *The Indian Buddhist Iconography: Mainly Based on the Sādhanamālā and Cognate Tāntric Texts of Rituals*. 2nd ed., rev. and enl. 1958; reprint, Calcutta: Firma K. L. Mukhopadhyay.

Bhattacharyya, D. C. *Pratimālakṣaṇa of the Viṣṇudharmottara*. New Delhi: Harman, 1991.

Bialek, Joanna. "'Tibetan'—All Inclusive? Rethinking the 'Tibetanity' of the 'Tibetan Empire.'" In *The Social and the Religious in the Making of Tibetan Societies: New Perspectives on Imperial Tibet*, edited by Guntram Hazod, Mathias Fermer, and Christian Jahoda. Vienna: Österreichische Akademie der Wissenschaften, 2022.

Bialostocki, Jan. Review of *The Shape of Time* by Georg Kubler. *Art Bulletin* 47, no. 1 (1965): 135–39.

Biardeau, Madeleine. "The Hindu God with Five Heads (*Pañcamukha*)." In *Asian Mythologies*, edited by Yves Bennefoy and Wendy Doniger, 50–52. Translated by David White. Chicago: University of Chicago Press, 1993.

Biasutti, Renato, and Giotto Dainelli. *I Tipi Umani*. Spedizione Italiana de Filippi Nell'Himàlaia, Caracorùm e Turchestàn Cinese (1913–1914), Serie II: Resultati Geologici e Geografici 9. Bologna: Nicola Zanichelli, 1925.

Bishop, Peter. *Dreams of Power: Tibetan Buddhism and the Western Imagination*. New Delhi: Adarsh Enterprises, 2001.

Bishop, Peter. *The Myth of Shangri-La: Tibet, Travel Writing, and the Western Creation of Sacred Landscape*. London: Athlone, 1989.

Bjerken, Zeff. "On Mandalas, Monarchs, and Mortuary Magic: Siting the *Sarvadurgatipariśodhana Tantra* in Tibet." *Journal of the American Academy of Religion* 73, no. 3 (2005): 813–41.

Blurton, T. Richard. *Hindu Art*. 1992; Cambridge, MA: Harvard University Press, 1993.

Bosch, F.D.K. "Pratiṣṭhā Symbols: Additional Remarks to Professor Vogel's Monograph on 'The Goose in Indian Literature and Art.'" In *Pratidānam: Indian, Iranian and Indo-European Studies Presented to Franciscus Bernardus Jacobus Kuiper on His Sixtieth Birthday*. Edited by J. C. Heesterman, G. H. Schokker, and V. I. Subramoniam, 533–38. The Hague: Mouton, 1968.

Bose, Partha Pratim. "A Note on Some Interesting Icons from Nalanda." *Indian Museum Bulletin* 20 (1985): 85–86, figs. 1–6.

Brancaccio, Pia. *The Buddhist Caves at Aurangabad: Transformations in Art and Religion*. Leiden: Brill, 2011.

Brauen, Martin. *Dreamworld Tibet: Western Illusions.* 1st English ed. Bangkok: Orchid Press, 2004.

Bray, John, ed. *Ladakhi Histories: Local and Regional Perspectives*. 2005; reprint, Dharamsala: Library of Tibetan Works and Archives, 2011.

Bray, John. "Early Protestant Missionary Engagement with the Himalayan Region and Tibet." In Bray, *Ladakhi Histories*, 249–70.

Bray, John. "The Lapchak Mission from Ladakh to Lhasa in British Indian Foreign Policy," *Tibet Journal* 15, no. 4 (1990): 75–96.

Brown, W. Norman. "The Creative Role of the Goddess Vāc in the Rig Veda." In *Pratidānam: Indian, Iranian and Indo-European Studies Presented to Franciscus Bernardus Jacobus Kuiper on His Sixtieth Birthday*. Edited by J. C. Heesterman, G. H. Schokker, and V. I. Subramoniam, 393–97. The Hague: Mouton, 1968.

Brown, W. Norman, trans. *The Saundaryalaharī or Flood of Beauty Traditionally Ascribed to* Śaṅkarācārya. Cambridge, MA: Harvard University Press, 1958.

Bruneau, Laurianne. "Influence of the Indian Cultural Area in Ladakh in the 1st Millennium AD: The Rock Inscription Evidence." *Purātattva* 41 (2011): 179–90, 9 pls.: pp. 31–33.

Buffetrille, Katia. "The Increasing Visibility of the Tibetan 'Borderlands.'" In Gros, *Frontier Tibet*, 85–113.

Bühnemann, Gudrun. *The Iconography of Hindu Tantric Deities*. Vol. 1, *The Pantheon of the Mantramahodadhi*; vol. 2, *The Pantheons of the Prapañcasāra and the* Śāradātilaka. Two volumes bound in one. 2000; rev. ed., New Delhi: Aditya Prakashan, 2016.

Cabezón, José Ignacio, and Roger R. Jackson, eds. *Tibetan Literature; Studies in Genre*. Ithaca: Snow Lion, 1996.

Cammann, Schuyler. "The Panchen Lama's Visit to China in 1780: An Episode in Anglo-Tibetan Relations." *Far Eastern Quarterly* 9, no. 1 (1949): 3–19.

Casson, Lionel. *The 'Periplus Maris Erythraei': Text with Introduction, Translation, and Commentary*. Princeton: Princeton University Press, 1989.

Chen, Qingying. "Lcang-skya Rolpavi-rdorje and Emperor Qian Long." In *Theses on Tibetology in China*, compiled by Hu Tan, 67–90. Beijing: China Tibetology, 1991. [NB: "Rolpavi" is correct according to the Chinese system of transcribing Tibetan into English, the "v" standing for the " ' " used in the English Wylie transcriptions.]

Ching, Dora C.Y., ed. *Visualizing Dunhuang: The Lo Archive Photographs of the Mogao and Yulin Caves*. 9 vols. Princeton: P.Y. and Kinmay W. Tang Center for East Asian Art in association with Princeton University Press, 2021.

Chopel, Gendun. *Grains of Gold: Tales of a Cosmopolitan Traveler*. Translated by Thupten Jinpa and Donald S. Lopez Jr. Chicago: University of Chicago Press, 2014.

Chou, Yi-liang. "Tantrism in China." *Harvard Journal of Asiatic Studies* 8, no. 3/4 (1945): 241–332.

Clark, Graham E. "Who Were the Dards? A Review of the Ethnographic Literature of the North-Western Himalaya." *Kailash* 5, no. 4 (1977): 323–56.

Clarke, John. "Hindu Trading Pilgrims." In *Pilgrimage in Tibet*, edited by Alex McKay, 52–70. Richmond: Curzon, 1998.

Collyer, Kelleson. *The Hoysala Artists: Their Identity and Styles*. Mysore: Directorate of Archaeology and Museum, 1990.

Copeland, Carolyn. *Tankas from the Koelz Collection: Museum of Anthropology, The University of Michigan*. Ann Arbor: University of Michigan Center for South and Southeast Asian Studies, 1980.

Cowell, E. B., and F. W. Thomas, trans. *The Harṣa-carita of Bāṇa.* London: Royal Asiatic Society, 1897.

Cribb, Joe. "Coins and the Chronology of Gandhara." In Luczanits, *Gandhara, the Buddhist Heritage of Pakistan*, 64–69.

Cribb, Joe. "The Origin of the Buddha Image: The Numismatic Evidence." In *South Asian Archaeology 1981*, 231–44.

Crook, John H. "The History of Zangskar." In Crook and Osmaston, eds., *Himalayan Buddhist Villages: Environment, Resources, Society and Religious Life in Zangskar, Ladakh*, 435–74.

Crook, John H., and Henry Osmaston, eds. *Himalayan Buddhist Villages: Environment, Resources, Society and Religious Life in Zangskar, Ladakh*. Bristol: University of Bristol, 1994.

Crook, John H., and Tsering Shakya. "Monastic Communities in Zangskar: Location, Function and Organisation." In Crook and Osmaston, eds., *Himalayan Buddhist Villages: Environment, Resources, Society and Religious Life in Zangskar, Ladakh*, 559–600.

Crowden, James. "Butter Trading Down the Zangskar Gorge: The Winter Journey." In Crook and Osmaston, eds., *Himalayan Buddhist Villages: Environment, Resources, Society and Religious Life in Zangskar, Ladakh*, 285–92.

Crowden, James. *The Frozen River: Seeking Silence in the Himalaya*. London: William Collins, 2020.

Cunningham, Alexander. "Correspondence of the Commissioners Deputed to the Tibetan Frontier." *Journal of the Asiatic Society of Bengal* 17, pt. 1 (1848): 89–132.

Cunningham, Alexander. *Ladák, Physical, Statistical, and Historical; with Notices of the Surrounding Countries*. London: Wm. H. Allen, 1854.

Czaja, Olaf. "The Commemorative Stupas at Densathil: A Preliminary Study." In Lo Bue and Luczanits, *Tibetan Art and Architecture in Context*, 197–280.

Czaja, Olaf. *Medieval Rule in Tibet: The Rlangs Clan and the Political and Religious History of the Ruling House of Phag mo grup pa, with a Study of the Monastic Art of Gdan sa mthil.* 2 vols. Vienna: Verlag der Österreichischen Akademie der Wissenschaften, 2013.

Czaja, Olaf, and Adriana Proser, eds. *Golden Visions of Densatil: A Tibetan Buddhist Monastery*. New York: Asia Society Museum, 2014.

Czuma, Stanislaw. "Ivory Sculpture." In *Art and Architecture of Ancient Kashmir*, edited by Pratapaditya Pal, 57–76. Bombay: Marg, 1989.

Dalton, Jacob P. *The Gathering of Intentions: A History of a Tibetan Tantra*. New York: Columbia University Press, 2016.

Dalton, Jacob P. *The Taming of the Demons: Violence and Liberation in Tibetan Buddhism*. New Haven, CT: Yale University Press, 2011.

Dani, Ahmad Hasan. "Carvings on a Thalpan Rock." In *Ethnologie und Geschichte: Festschrift für Karl Jettmar*, edited by Peter Snoy, 89–95. Wiesbaden: Franz Steiner, 1983.

Dani, Ahmad Hasan. *Human Records on Karakorum Highway*. Lahore: Seng-e-meel, 1995.

Daniélou, Alain. *Hindu Polytheism*. New York: Pantheon Books, 1964.

Dar, Saifur Rahman. "Rock-Cut Standing Figure at Kargah, near Gilgit: Some Thoughts on Its Identification, Origin and Date." *Journal of Central Asia* 8, no. 2 (1985): 191–211.

Dargyay, Eva K. "Buddhism in Adaptation: Ancestor Gods and Their Tantric Counterparts in the Religious Life of Zanskar." *History of Religions* 28, no. 2 (1988): 123–34.

Darrah, Henry Zouch. *Sport in the Highlands of Kashmir*. London: Rowland Ward, 1898.

Dasser, Karl Ludwig. "Appendix: Some Observations on the Technology of the Wall Paintings of the Sumtsek." In *Alchi: Ladakh's Hidden Buddhist Sanctuary, The Sumtsek*, edited by Roger Goepper, 273–76, 279. Boston: Shambhala, 1996.

Davidson, Ronald M. "Himalayan Buddhist Valleys as Tantric Ecologies." In *Buddhist Himalaya: Studies in Religion, History and Culture, Proceedings of the Golden Jubilee Conference of the Namgyal Institute of Tibetology, Gangtok, 2008*. 3 vols., edited by Alex McKay and Anna Balikci-Denjongpa. Vol. 1, *Tibet and the Himalaya*, 135–50. Gangtok: Namgyal Institute of Tibetology, 2011.

Davidson, Ronald M. *Tibetan Renaissance: Tantric Buddhism in the Rebirth of Tibetan Culture*. New York: Columbia University, 2005.

De Filippi, Filippo. *Karakoram and Western Himalaya 1909: An Account of the Expedition of H.R.H. Prince Luigi Amedeo of Savoy, Duke of the Abruzzi*. New York: E. P. Dutton, 1912. The Italian edition was titled *La Spedizione nel Karakoram e nell'Imalaia Occidentale 1909. S.A.R. il Principe Luigi Amedeo di Savoia, Duca degli Abruzzi*.

De Kőrös, Alexander Csoma. "Geographical Notice of Tibet." *The Journal of the Asiatic Society of Bengal* 1, no. 4 (1832): 121–27.

De Kőrös, Alexander Csoma. *Sanskrit–Tibetan–English Vocabulary: Being an Edition and Translation of the Mahāvyutpatti*. Edited by J. Terjék. Budapest: Akadémiai Kiadó, 1984. Originally published in *Memoirs of the Asiatic Society of Bengal*, edited by E. Denison Ross, 1910.

De Marco, Giuseppe. "The Stūpa as a Funerary Monument: New Iconographical Evidence." *East and West* 37, no. 1/4 (1987): 191–246.

De Rossi Filibeck, Elena. "Poetical Prefaces of Manuscripts from Western Tibet." In *Discoveries in Western Tibet and the Western Himalayas: Essays on History, Literature, Archaeology and Art*, edited by Amy Heller and Giacomella Orofino, 151–72. Leiden: Brill, 2007.

Deambi, B. K. Kaul. *Corpus of* Śāradā *Inscriptions of Kashmir*. Delhi: Agam Kala Prakashan, 1982.

Deeg, Max. "Has Huichao Been Back to India? On a Chinese Inscription on the Back of a Pāla Bronze and the Chronology of Indian Esoteric Buddhism." In *From Turfan to Ajanta: Festschrift for Dieter Schlingloff on the Occasion of His Eightieth Birthday*, edited by Eli Franco and Monika Zin, 197–213. Kathmandu: Lumbini International Research Institute, 2010.

Dehejia, Vidya, ed. *Devi the Great Goddess: Female Divinity in South Asian Art*. Washington, DC: Smithsonian Institution, 1999.

Dehejia, Vidya. *Indian Art*. London: Phaidon Press, 1997.

Denwood, Philip. "Early Connections between Ladakh/Baltistan and Amdo/Kham." In Bray, *Ladakhi Histories*, 31–39.

Denwood, Philip. "Rock Inscriptions." In David L. Snellgrove and Tadeusz Skorupski, *The Cultural Heritage of Ladakh*. Vol. 2, *Zangskar and the Cave Temples of Ladakh*, 155–64. New Delhi: Vikas, 1980.

Denwood, Philip. "The Tibetanisation of Ladakh: The Linguistic Evidence." In *Recent Research on Ladakh 4 & 5: Proceedings of the Fourth and Fifth International Colloquia on Ladakh*, edited by Henry Osmaston and Philip Denwood, 281–287. Delhi: Motilal Banarsidass, 1985.

Denwood, Philip. "The Tibetans in the Western Himalayas and Karakoram, Seventh–Eleventh Centuries: Rock Art and Inscriptions." *Journal of Inner Asian Art and Archaeology* 2 (2007): 49–58.

Denwood, Philip. "The Tibetans in the West, Part I." *Journal of Inner Asian Art and Archaeology* 3 (2008): 7–21.

Denwood, Philip. "The Tibetans in the West, Part II." *Journal of Inner Asian Art and Archaeology* 4 (2009): 149–60.

Denwood, Philip T., and Neal F. Howard. "Inscriptions at Balukhar and Char Zampa and Archaeological Observations on the Fort of Balukhar and Its Environs." In *Indo-Tibetan Studies: Papers in Honour and Appreciation of Professor David L. Snellgrove's Contribution to Indo-Tibetan Studies*, edited by Tadeusz Skorupski, 81–88. Tring: Institute of Buddhist Studies, 1990.

Desideri, Ippolito. *Mission to Tibet: The Extraordinary Eighteenth-Century Account of Father Ippolito Desideri, S. J.* Translated by Michael J. Sweet. Edited by Leonard Zwilling. Somerville, MA: Wisdom, 2010.

Devers, Quentin. "Archaeological Ladakh: Recent Discoveries Redefining the History of a Key Region between the Pamirs and the Himalayas." *Central Asiatic Journal* 61, no. 1 (2018): 103–32.

Devers, Quentin. "An Architectural Survey of the Temples of Ladakh, Ruined and Intact, until the Mid-15th Century." Forthcoming.

Devers, Quentin. "Buddhism before the First Diffusion? The Case of Tangol, Dras, Phikhar and Sani-Tarungtse in Purig and Zanskar (Ladakh)." In *Ladakh through the Ages: A Volume on Art History and Archaeology*, edited by Quentin Devers, Gerald Kozicz, and Heinrich Pöll. *Études* mongoles et sibériennes, centrasiatiques et tibétaines 51. Paris: Oriens, 2020. https://doi.org/10.4000/emscat.4131

Devers, Quentin. "Charting Ancient Routes in Ladakh: An Archaeological Documentation." In Allinger et al., *Interaction in the Himalayas and Central Asia,* 321–29.

Devers, Quentin. "Fortifications of Ladakh: A Brief Chrono-Typology." In *Visible Heritage: Essays on the Art and Architecture of Greater Ladakh*, edited by Rob Linrothe and Heinrich Pöll, 41–64. New Delhi: Studio Orientale, 2016.

Devers, Quentin. *Historical Sites of Changthang, Leh, Ladakh*. New Delhi: Indian National Trust for Art and Cultural Heritage, 2019.

Devers, Quentin. *Historical Sites of Purig, Kargil District, Jammu & Kashmir*. New Delhi: Indian National Trust for Art and Cultural Heritage, 2017.

Devers, Quentin. *Historical Sites of Zanskar: Kargil District, Ladakh*. New Delhi: Indian National Trust for Art and Cultural Heritage, 2022.

Devers, Quentin, Laurianne Bruneau and Martin Vernier. "An Archaeological Account of Ten Ancient Painted Chortens in Ladakh and Zanskar." In *Art and Architecture in Ladakh: Cross-Cultural Transmissions in the Himalayas and Karakoram*, edited by Erberto Lo Bue and John Bray, 100–140. Leiden: Brill, 2014.

Devy, G. N. *A Nomad Called Thief: Reflections on Adivasi Silence*. New Delhi: Orient Longman, 2006.

Di Mattia, Marialaura. "The Divine Palaces of the Buddha: Architectural Frames in Western Himalayan Art." In *Discoveries in Western Tibet and the Western Himalayas: Essays on History, Literature, Archaeology and Art. Proceedings of the Tenth IATS, Oxford 2003*, edited by Amy Heller and Giacomella Orofino, 55–81. Leiden: Brill, 2007.

Diamond, Debra. *Gardens & Cosmos: The Royal Paintings of Jodhpur*. Washington, DC: Smithsonian Institution, 2008.

Diemberger, Hildegard. "Beyul Khenbalung, the Hidden Valley of the Artemisia: On Himalayan Communities and Their Sacred Landscape." In *Maṇḍala and Landscape*, edited by A. W. Macdonald, 287–334. New Delhi: D. K Printworld, 1997.

Dimock, Edward C., Jr. "The Goddess of Snakes in Medieval Bengali Literature." *History of Religions* 1, no. 2 (1962): 307–21.

Dobbins, James C. *Behold the Buddha: Religious Meanings of Japanese Buddhist Icons*. Honolulu: University of Hawai'i Press, 2020.

Dodin, Thierry, and Heinz Räther. *Imagining Tibet: Perceptions, Projections, & Fantasies*. Boston: Wisdom, 2001.

Dodin, Thierry. "Transregional Buddhist Organizations in Indian Himalayas." In *Perspectives on History and Change in Karakorum, Hindukush, and Himalaya*, edited by Irmtraud Stellrecht and Matthias Winiger, 189–213. Cologne: Rüdiger Köppe, 1997.

Dollfus, Pascale. "The Seven Rongtsan Brothers in Ladakh: Myth, Territory and Possession." *Études mongoles et sibériennes, centrasiatiques et tibétaines* 36–37 (2006).

Donaldson, Thomas E. "Lakulīśa to Rājaguru: Metamorphosis of the 'Teacher' in the Iconographic Program of the Orissan Temple." In *Studies in Hindu and Buddhist Art*, edited by P. K. Mishra, 129–53. New Delhi: Abhinav, 1999.

Donaldson, Thomas E. *Tantra and* Śākta *Art of Orissa*. 3 vols. New Delhi: D. K. Printworld, 2002.

Dorjee, Pema. *Stūpa and Its Technology: A Tibeto-Buddhist Perspective*. New Delhi: Indira Gandhi National Centre for the Arts; Delhi: Motilal Banarsidass, 1996.

Douglas, Nik, and Meryl White. *Karmapa: The Black Hat Lama of Tibet*. London: Luzac, 1976.

Dowman, Keith. *Sky Dancer: The Secret Life and Songs of the Lady Yeshe Tsogyel*. 1984; reprint, London: Arkana, 1989.

Dowman, Keith. *Masters of Mahāmudrā: Songs and Histories of the Eighty-Four Buddhist Siddhas*. Albany: State University of New York Press, 1985.

Dratshadpa Rinchen Namgyal. *A Handful of Flowers: A Brief Biography of Buton Rinchen Drub*. Translated by Hans Van den Bogaert. Dharamsala: Library of Tibetan Works and Archive, 1996.

Drepung Loseling Library Society. *Chos spyod rab gsal skal bzang skye bo'i mgul rgyan zhes bya ba zhugs so (A Collection of Devotional and Dedicational Prayers Recited in Religious Services in All Gelug Monasteries Including the Three Main Sects of Drepung, Sera and Ganden)*. Mondgod, Karnataka, Drepung Loseling Library Society, 2001. Title translation follows Gerke, *Long Lives and Untimely Deaths*, 350.

Drew, Frederick. *The Northern Barrier of India: A Popular Account of the Jummoo and Kashmir Territories*. London: Edward Stanford, 1877.

Dreyfus, Georges. *The Sound of Two Hands Clapping*. Berkeley: University of California, 2003.

Duka, Theodore. *Life and Works of Alexander Csoma De Körös: A Biography Compiled Chiefly from Hitherto Unpublished Data.* London: Trübner & Co., 1885. Reprint edition, London: Routledge, 2000.

Duncan, Jane E. *A Summer Ride through Western Tibet*. London: Smith, Elder, 1906.

Durand, Algernon. *The Making of a Frontier: Five Years' Experience and Adventures in Gilgit, Hunza, Nagar, Chitral, and the Eastern Hindu-Kush*. London: John Murray, 1900.

Ebert, Jorinde. "Niches, Columns, and Figures in Some Petroglyphic Stūpa Depictions of the Karakorum Highway." *Artibus Asiae* 54, nos. 3–4 (1994): 268–95.

Eck, Diana L. "India's *Tīrthas*: 'Crossings' in Sacred Geography." *History of Religions* 20, no. 4 (1981): 323–44.

Efurd, David S. "Early Buddhist Caves of Western India ca. Second Century BCE through the Third Century CE: Core Elements, Functions and Buddhist Practices." PhD diss., Ohio State University, 2008.

Egerton, Philip Henry. *Journal of a Tour through Spiti, to the Frontier of Chinese Tibet*. London: Cundall, Downes, 1864.

Emmer, Gerhard. "dGa' ldan Tshe dbang dPal bzang po and the Tibet-Ladakh-Mughal War of 1679–84." In *The Mongolia-Tibet Interface: Opening New Research Terrains in Inner Asia*, edited by Uradyn E. Bulag and Hildegard G.M. Diemberger, 81–107. Proceedings of the Tenth Seminar of the International Association for Tibetan Studies, Oxford, 2003. Leiden: Brill, 2007.

Emmerick, R. E. *The Sūtra of Golden Light, Being a Translation of the Suvarṇabhāsottamasūtra*. Oxford: Pali Text Society, 1992.

Epperson, Erin Hillary. "Kālidāsa in Tibet: Messenger Poetry in Translation." PhD diss., University of Chicago, 2017.

Ewing, Arthur H. "The Çārada-tilaka Tantra." *Journal of the American Oriental Society* 23 (1902): 65–76.

Faccenna, Domenico, and Anna Filigenzi. *Repertory of Terms for Cataloguing Gandharan Sculptures Based on Materials from the IsIAO Italian Archaeological Mission in Swat, Pakistan*. Translated by Pia Brancaccio et al. Rome: Istituto Italiano per l'Africa e l'Oriente, 2007.

Fewkes, Jacqueline H., and Abdul Nasir Khan. "Social Networks and Transnational Trade in Early 20th Century Ladakh." In Bray, *Ladakhi Histories*, 321–34.

Filigenzi, Anna. *Art and Landscape: Buddhist Rock Sculptures of Late Antique Swat/Uḍḍiyāna*. Vienna: Österreichische Akademie der Wissenschaften, 2015.

Filigenzi, Anna. *Il Bodhisattva Maitreya nell'arte rupestre dello Swat: Appunti sull'iconografia e sul culto del Buddha venture*. Rome: Istituto Italiano per l'Africa e l'Oriente, 1999.

Finnin, Rory. "How the West Gets Ukraine Wrong—and Helps Putin as a Result." *Politico*, February 12, 2022. Available online, https://www.politico.com/news/magazine/2022/02/12/west-gets-ukraine-wrong-helps-putin-little-russia-00007977

Fisher, Robert E. "The Enigma of Harwan." *Art International* 25, no. 9 (1982): 33–45.

FitzHerbert, Solomon G. "Rituals as War Propaganda in the Establishment of the Tibetan Ganden Phodrang State in the Mid-17th Century." *Cahiers d'Extrême-Asie* 27 (2018): 49–119.

Flood, Finbarr B. *Objects of Translation: Material Culture and Medieval "Hindu-Muslim" Encounter*. Princeton: Princeton University Press, 2009.

Flood, Finbarr B. "A Turk in the Dukhang? Comparative Perspectives on Elite Dress in Medieval Ladakh and the Caucasus." In Allinger et al., *Interaction in the Himalayas and Central Asia*, 227–53.

Fonia, R. S. "Ladakh Corridor to Central Asia: An Investigative Report of Prehistoric Cultures." *Journal of Central Asian Studies* 4 (1993): 34–41.

Foucher, Alfred. *The Beginnings of Buddhist Art and Other Essays in Indian and Central-Asian Archaeology*. Revised by the author and translated by L. A. Thomas and F. W. Thomas. Paris: Paul Geuthner, 1917.

Francfort, Henri-Paul, Daniel Klodzinski, and Georges Mascle. "Archaic Petroglyphs of Ladakh and Zanskar." In *Rock Art in the Old World: Papers presented in Symposium A of the Aura Congress, Darwin (Australia) 1988*, ed. Michel Lorblanchet, 147–92. New Delhi: Indira Gandhi National Centre for the Arts, 1992.

Francke, A. H. *Antiquities of Indian Tibet*. 2 vols. 1914; 1926; reprint, New Delhi: Low Price, 1999.

Francke, A. H. *Antiquities of Indian Tibet*. Vol. 1, *Personal Narrative*, edited by J. Ph. Vogel. Calcutta: Archaeological Survey of India, Superintendent Government Printing. 1914; reprint, New Delhi: Asian Educational Services, 1992.

Francke, A. H. *Antiquities of Indian Tibet*. Vol. 2, *The Chronicles of Ladakh and Minor Chronicles*, edited by F. W. Thomas. Calcutta: Archaeological Survey of India, Superintendent Government Printing. 1926; reprint, New Delhi: Asian Educational Services, 1992.

Francke, A. H. "Archaeological Notes on Balu-mkhar in Western Tibet." *Indian Antiquary* 34 (1905): 203–11.

Francke, A. H. "Archaeology in Western Tibet." *Indian Antiquary* 35 (1906): 237–41, 325–33; 36 (1907): 85–98, 148.

Francke, A. H. "The Dards at Khalatse in Western Tibet." *Memoirs of the Asiatic Society of Bengal* 1 (1906): 413–19.

Francke, A. H. "Historische Dokumente von Khalatse in West-Tibet (Ladakh)." *Zeitschrift der Deutschen Morgenländischen Gesellschaft* 36 (1907): 583–614.

Francke, A. H. *A History of Western Tibet: One of the Unknown Empires*. London: Partridge, 1907; reprint, Delhi: Pilgrims Books, 1999.

Francke, A. H. "Kleine archäologische Erträge einer Missionsreise nach Zangskar in Westtibet." *Zeitschriften der Deutschen Morgenländischen Gesellschaft* 61 (1906): 645–61.

Francke, A. H. "The Ladakhi Pre-Buddhist Marriage Ritual." *Indian Antiquary* 30 (1901): 131–49.

Francke, A. H. "A Language Map of West Tibet with Notes." *Journal of the Asiatic Society of Bengal* 73, pt. 1, no. 4 (1907): 362–67.

Francke, A. H. "Notes on Rock-Carvings from Lower Ladakh." *Indian Antiquary* 31 (1902): 398–401.

Francke, A. H. "Remarks on a Photograph, near Ating, taken by the Hon. Eric Upton, During a Tour in Zangskar in 1907." *Indian Antiquary* 37 (1908): 332–33.

Francke, A. H. "Some More Rock Carvings from Lower Ladakh." *Indian Antiquary* 32 (1903): 361–63.

Francke, A. H. "A Tibetan Inscription of the Darkōt Pass." In Sir Aurel Stein, *Innermost Asia: Detailed Report of Explorations in Central Asia, Kan-su and Eastern Iran*, 2:1050–51. 4 vols. Oxford: Clarendon Press, 1928.

Frye, Richard N. "The Merchant World of the Sogdians." *The Heritage of Central Asia: From Antiquity to the Turkish Expansion*, 183–98. Princeton: Markus Wiener, 1996.

Fussman, Gérard. "Chilas, Hatun et les Bronzes Bouddhiques du Cashemire." In *Antiquities of Northern Pakistan*, 2 (1993):1–60.

Fussman, Gérard. "Une Peinture sur Pierre: Le Triptypque au Stūpa de Shatial." In *Antiquities of Northern Pakistan*, 3 (1994): 1–56.

Gagné, Karine. *Caring for Glaciers: Land, Animals, and Humanity in the Himalayas*. Seattle: University of Washington, 2018.

Garland Encyclopedia of World Music Volume 5: South Asia: The Indian Subcontinent. Edited by Alison Arnold. New York: Routledge, 1999. https://www.routledge.com/The-Garland-Encyclopedia-of-World-Music-South-Asia-The-Indian-Subcontinent/Arnold/p/book/9780824049461.

Garrone, Renzo. *The Cashmere Journey and the Nomad Shepherds of Ladakh: A Report about Pashmina*. Avegno Genova: Associazione RAM, 2015.

Geertz, Clifford. "Art as a Cultural System." *Modern Language Notes* 91 (1976): 1473–99.

Genoud, Charles. *Buddhist Wall-Painting of Ladakh*. Photographs by Takao Inoue. Geneva: Editions Olizane, 1981.

Gerke, Barbara. *Long Lives and Untimely Deaths: Life-span Concepts and Longevity Practices among Tibetans in the Darjeeling Hills, India*. Leiden: Brill, 2012.

Geslani, Marko Allen. "The Ritual Culture of Appeasement: Śānti Rites in Post-Vedic Sources." PhD diss., Yale University, 2011.

Ghose, Bhajagovinda. "Study of Sanskrit Grammar in Tibet." *Bulletin of Tibetology* 7, no. 2 (1970): 21–41.

Ghosh, Amitav. *The Nutmeg's Curse: Parables for a Planet in Crisis.* Chicago: University of Chicago, 2021.

Ghosh, Pika, ed. *Fashioning the Divine: South Asian Sculpture at the Ackland Art Museum*. Chapel Hill: Ackland Art Museum, University of North Carolina at Chapel Hill, 2006.

Giebel, Rolf W. The *Chin-kang-ting ching yü-ch'ieh shi-pa-hui chih-kuei*: An Annotated Translation." *Naritasan Bukkyō Kenkyūjo kiyō* 18–19 (1995–96): 107–201.

Giebel, Rolf W. *Two Esoteric Sutras: The Adamantine Pinnacle Sutra, The Susiddhikara Sutra*. Translated from the Chinese (*Taishō* vol. 18, nos. 865, 893). Berkeley, CA: Numata Center for Buddhist Translation and Research, 2001.

Giebel, Rolf W. *The Vairocanābhisaṃbodhi Sutra*. Translated from the Chinese (*Taishō* vol. 18, no. 848). Berkeley, CA: Numata Center for Buddhist Translation and Research, 2005.

Giès, Jacques, and Monique Cohen, eds. *Sérinde, Terre de Bouddha: Dix Siècles d'Art sur la Route de la Soie*. Paris: Réunion des Musées Nationaux, 1995.

Godwin-Austen, H. H., with photography by Alexander Brodie Melville. "Description of a Mystic Play, as Performed in Ladak, Zaskar, &c." *Journal of the Asiatic Society of Bengal* 34, pt. 1, no. 2 (1864): 71–79.

Godwin-Austen, H. H. "On the System Employed in Outlining Figures of Deities and Other Religious Drawings, as Practised in Ladakh, Zaskar etc." *Journal of the Asiatic Society of Bengal* 33, no. 294 (1865): 151–54.

Goepper, Roger. *Alchi: Buddhas, Göttinnen, Mandalas: Wandmalerei in einem Himalaya-Kloster*. Cologne: DuMont, 1982.

Goepper, Roger, and Jaroslav Poncar, with contributions by Robert Linrothe and Karl Dasser et al. *Alchi: Ladakh's Hidden Buddhist Sanctuary, the Sumtsek*. Boston: Shambhala; London: Serindia, 1996.

Goepper, Roger. "Dressing the Temple: Textile Representations in the Frescoes at Alchi." In Jill Tilden, *Asian Art: The Second Hali Annual*, 100–117, 191. London: Worldwide Hali Publications, 1995.

Goepper, Roger. "The Four Kinds of Rites at the Altar: Paragraph Six of the Hizō-ki." In *Das Andere China: Festscrhift für Wolfgang Bauer zum 65. Geburtstag*, edited by Helwig Schmidt-Glintzer, 183–208. Wiesbaden: Harrassowitz, 1995.

Goepper, Roger. "More Evidence for Dating the Sumtsek in Alchi and Its Relations with Kashmir." In *Dating Tibetan Art: Essays on the Possibilities and Impossibilities of Chronology from the Lempert Symposium, Cologne*, edited by Ingrid Kreide-Damani, 15–24. Wiesbaden: Dr. Ludwig Reichert Verlag, 2003.

Goepper, Roger, and Christian Luczanits, with photography by Jaroslav Poncar and contributions by Holder Neuwirth, Carmen Auer, Rob Linrothe and Nils Martin. *Alchi: Ladakh's Hidden Buddhist Sanctuary.* 2 vols. Bangkok: Serindia, 2023.

Goetz, Hermann. "The Beginnings of Medieval Art in Kashmir." *Studies in the History and Art of Kashmir and the Indian Himalaya*, 37–67. Wiesbaden: Otto Harrassowitz, 1969. Originally published in *Journal of the University of Bombay* 21, pt. 23 (1952): 63ff.

Gold, Jonathan C. "Sa-skya Paṇḍita's Buddhist Argument for Linguistic Study." *Journal of Indian Philosophy* 33 (2005): 151–85.

Gombrich, Sanjukta Gupta. "Sarasvatī Vāc, the Sacral Word and the Supreme Cosmic Goddess." In *Studies in Hindu and Buddhist Art*, edited by P. K. Mishra, 337–50. New Delhi: Abhinav, 1999.

Gonda, Jan. "The Meaning of the Word Alaṃkāra." In *Selected Studies*. Vol. 2, *Sanskrit Word Studies*, 257–74. Leiden: Brill, 1975.

Gore, St. George. "Mr. Freshfield's Paper on the Glaciers of Kangchenjunga." *Geographical Journal* 20, no. 2 (1902): 235–37.

Goswamy, Brijinder Nath. *Conversations: Indian's Leading Art Historian Engages with 101 Themes & More*. Gurugram: Penguin Random House India, 2022.

Goswamy, Brijinder Nath. "Introductory Speech: The Stūpa: Some Uninformed Questions about Terminological Equivalents." In *The Stūpa: Its Religious, Historical and Architectural Significance*, edited by Anna Libera Dallapiccola with Stephanie Zingel-Avé Lallemant, 1–11. Wiesbaden: Franz Steiner, 1980.

Granoff, Phyllis. "A Portable Buddhist Shrine from Central Asia." *Archives of Asian Art* 22 (1968/1969): 80–95.

Grenet, Frantz, and Zhang Guangda. "The Last Refuge of the Sogdian Religion: Dunhuang in the Ninth and Tenth Centuries." *Bulletin of the Asia Institute* 10 (1998): 175–86.

Gros, Stéphane. "Frontier (of) Experience: Introduction and Prolegomenon." In *Frontier Tibet: Patterns of Change in the Sino-Tibetan Borderlands*, edited by Stéphane Gros, 41–83. Asian Borderlands 6. Amsterdam: Amsterdam University Press, 2019.

Gruber, Elmar R. *From the Heart of Tibet: The Biography of Drikung Chetsang Rinpoche, the Holder of the Drikung Kagyu Lineage*. Boston: Shambhala, 2010.

Guha-Thakurta, Tapati. "Clothing the Goddess: The Modern Context of Representations of Devi." In *Devi the Great Goddess: Female Divinity in South Asian Art*, edited by Vidya Dehejia, 157–70. Washington, DC: Smithsonian Institution, 1999.

Gupta, S. P. *Kushāṇa Sculptures from Sanghol (1st–2nd Century A.D.): A Recent Discovery*. New Delhi: National Museum, 1985.

Gutschow, Kim. *Being a Buddhist Nun: The Struggle for Enlightenment in the Himalayas*. Cambridge, Mass.: Harvard University Press, 2004.

Gutschow, Kim. "An Economy of Merit: Women and Buddhist Monasticism in Zangskar, Northwest India." PhD diss., Harvard University, 1998.

Gutschow, Kim. "The *smyung gnas* Fast in Zangskar: How Liminality Depends on Structure." In *Ladakh: Culture, History, and Development between Himalaya and Karakoram: Recent Research on Ladakh 8*, edited by Martijn van Beek, Kristoffer Brix Bertelsen, and Poul Pedersen, 153–73. New Delhi: Sterling, 1999.

Gutschow, Kim, and Niels Gutschow. "A Landscape Dissolved: Households, Fields, and Irrigation in Rinam, Northwest India." In *Sacred Landscape of the Himalaya: Proceedings of an International Conference at Heidelberg, 25–27 May 1998*, edited by Niels Gutschow, Axel Michaels, Charles Ramble, Ernst Steinkellner, 111–36. Vienna: Austrian Academy of Sciences Press, 2003.

Gutschow, Niels. *Architecture of the Newars: A History of Building Typologies and Details in Nepal*. Vol. 1, *The Kathmandu Valley and Urban Context: The Early Periods (200–1350)*. Chicago: Serindia, 2011.

Gyalpo, Tshering, and Christiane Kalantari, in cooperation with Christian Jahoda. "The Buddhist Monuments of Khartse Valley, Western Tibet." *AAS Working Papers in Social Anthropology* 9 (January 2009): 1–28. http://hw.oeaw.ac.at/wpsa9flyer. 9. 10.1553/wpsa9s1.

Gyaltsen, Jetsün Dragpa. *Clarifying the Meaning of the Arga and Consecration Rituals*. Translated and introduced by Yael Bentor. Kathmandu: Vajra Books, 2015.

Ham, Peter van. *Guge—Ages of Gold: The West-Tibetan Masterpieces*. Munich: Hirmer, 2016.

Ham, Peter van. *Indian Tibet / Tibetan India: The Cultural Legacy of the Western Himalayas*, edited by Gita Rajan. First English, rev. ed. New Delhi: Niyogi, 2015.

Ham, Peter van. *Indiens Tibet—Tibets Indien: Das Kulturelle Vermächtnis des Westhimalaya*. Munich: Hirmer, 2009.

Ham, Peter van, and Aglaja Stirn. *The Forgotten Gods of Tibet: Early Buddhist Art in the Western Himalayas*. Paris: Mengès, 1997.

Handa, Devendra, and Govind Agrawal. "A New Jaina Sarasvatī from Rajashthan." *East and West* 23, no. 1 (1973): 169–70.

Haque, Enamul. "The Manasā Images of Bengal." *Bangladesh Lalit Kalaā: Journal of the Dacca Museum* 1, no. 2 (1975): 135–44.

Hardy, R. Spence. *A Manual of Buddhism in Its Modern Development*. Translated from Singhalese manuscripts. London: Partridge and Oakey, 1853.

Harshananda, Swami. *Hindu Gods and Goddesses*. 1981; reprint, Madras: Sri Ramakrishna Math, 1987.

Hauptmann, Harald. "Pre-Islamic Heritage in the Northern Areas of Pakistan." In *Karakoram: Hidden Treasures in the Northern Areas of Pakistan*, edited by Stefano Bianca, 21–39, 317–19. Turin: Aga Khan Trust for Culture, 2005.

Hauptmann, Harald. "Rock Art in the Upper Indus Region." In Luczanits, *Gandhara, the Buddhist Heritage of Pakistan*, 352–57.

Heber, Adolph Reeve, and Kathleen Mary Heber. *Himalayan Tibet & Ladakh: A Description of Its Cheery Folk, Their Ways & Religion, of the Rigours of the Climate & Beauties of the Country, Its Fauna & Flora*. 1926 [under title *In Himalayan Tibet*]; reprint, Delhi: Ess Ess, 1976.

Hedin, Sven. *My Life as an Explorer*. Translated by Alfhild Huebsch. Garden City, NY: Garden City, 1925.

Heller, Amy. "Buddhist Images and Rock Inscriptions from Eastern Tibet, VIIIth to Xth Century, Part IV." In *Proceedings of the 7th Seminar of the International Association for Tibetan Studies, Graz 1995*, Vol. 1, *Tibetan Studies*, edited by Helmut Krasser et al., 385–98. Vienna: Österreichische Akademie der Wissenschaften, 1997.

Heller, Amy. "Early Ninth Century Images of Vairochana from Eastern Tibet." *Orientations* 26, no. 6 (June 1994): 74–79.

Heller, Amy. "Indian Style, Kashmiri Style: Aesthetics of Choice in Eleventh Century Tibet." *Orientations* 32, no. 10 (December 2001): 18–23.

Heller, Amy. "A Page from an Artist's Sketchbook." In *Gateways to Tibetan Studies: A Collection of Essays in Honour of David P. Jackson on the Occasion of His 70th Birthday*, edited by Volker Caumanns, Jörg Heimbel, Kazuo Kano, and Alexander Schiller, 1:381–98. 2 vols. Hamburg: Department of Indian and Tibetan Studies, Universität Hamburg, 2021.

Heller, Amy. "*P.T. 7A, P.T. 108, P.T. 240* and *Beijing Bstan'Gyur 3489*: Ancient Tibetan Rituals Dedicated to Vairocana." In *The Pandita and the Siddha: Tibetan Studies in Honour of E. Gene Smith*, edited by Ramon N. Prats, 85–91. Dharamsala: Amnye Machen Institute, 2007.

Heller, Amy. "Preliminary Remarks on the Donor Inscriptions and Iconography of an 11th-Century *mChod rten* at Tholing." In Lo Bue and Luczanits, *Tibetan Art and Architecture in Context*, 43–74.

Heller, Amy. *Tibetan Art: Tracing the Development of Spiritual Ideals and Art in Tibet: 600–2000 A.D.* Milan: Jaca, 1999.

Heller, Amy, and Giacomella Orofino, eds. *Discoveries in Western Tibet and the Western Himalayas: Essays on History, Literature, Archaeology and Art*. Leiden: Brill, 2007.

Henss, Michael. *The Cultural Monuments of Tibet: The Central Regions*. Vol. 1, *The Central Tibetan Province of Ü*. Vol. 2: *The Southern Tibetan Province of Tsang*. Munich: Prestel, 2014.

Herrmann-Pfandt, Adelheid. *The Copper-Coloured Palace: Iconography of the rÑiṅ ma School of Tibetan Buddhism*. 3 vols. Delhi: Agam Kala Prakashan, 2018.

Heyde, Christian. "The Early History of the Moravian Mission in the Western Himalayas: The Life and Work of Wilhelm and Marie Heyde." In Bray, *Ladakhi Histories*, 271–80.

Hinüber, Oskar von. "Brāhmī Inscriptions on the History and Culture of the Upper Indus Valley." In *Antiquities of Northern Pakistan*, 1:41–71.

Hinüber, Oskar von. "Buddhism in Gilgit between India and Central Asia." In *The Countries of South Asia: Boundaries, Extensions, and Interrelations*, edited by Peter Gaeffke and David A. Utz, 40–48. Philadelphia: University of Pennsylvania, 1988.

Hooker, Joseph Dalton. *A Sketch of the Flora of British India*. London: Eyre and Spottiswoode, 1904.

Hooker, Joseph Dalton, and Thomas Thomson. *Flora Indica: Being a Systematic Account of the Plants of British India Together with Observations on the Structure and Affinities of Their Natural Orders and Genera*. Vol. 1, *Ranunculaceae to Fumariaceae, with an Introductory Essay*. (No further volumes issued.) London: W. Pamplin, 1855.

Howard, Angela, Wu Hung, Li Song, and Yang Hong. *Chinese Sculpture*. New Haven, CT: Yale University Press, 2006.

Howard, Kath. "Archaeological Notes on Chorten (*mChod-rten*) Types in Ladakh and Zanskar from the 11th–15th Centuries." In *Recent Research on Ladakh 4 & 5: Proceedings of the Fourth and Fifth International Colloquia on Ladakh*, edited by Henry Osmaston and Philip Denwood, 61–78. Delhi: Motilal Banarsidass, 1985.

Howard, Meghan. "Translator's Introduction." In H. H. the Drikung Kyabgon Chetsang, *A History of the Tibetan Empire: Drawn from the Dunhuang Manuscripts*, translated by Meghan Howard with Tsultrim Nakchu, xxv–xxxiv. Dehra Dun: Songtsen Library: Center for Tibetan and Himalayan Studies, 2011.

Howard, Neil. "Ancient Painted Pottery from Ladakh." In *Ladakh: Culture, History, and Development Between Himalaya and Karakoram; Recent Research on Ladakh 8*, edited by Martijn van Beek, Kristoffer Briz Bertelsen, and Poul Pedersen, 222–36. Denmark: Aarhus University Press, 1999.

Howard, Neil. "The Development of the Boundary between the State of Jammu & Kashmir and British India, and Its Representation on Maps of the Lingti Plain." In Bray, *Ladakhi Histories*, 217–34.

Howard, Neil. "The Development of the Fortresses of Ladakh c. 950 to 1650 A.D." *East and West* 39, nos. 1–4 (1989): 217–88.

Howard, Neil. "The Fortified Places of Zanskar." In *Recent Research on Ladakh 4 & 5: Proceedings of the Fourth and Fifth International Colloquia on Ladakh*, edited by Henry Osmaston and Philip Denwood, 79–99. Delhi: Motilal Banarsidass, 1995.

Howard, Neil. "Sultan Zain-ul Abidin's Raid into Ladakh." In Bray, *Ladakhi Histories*, 125–45.

Howard, Neil, and Kath Howard. "Historic Ruins in the Gya Valley, Eastern Ladakh, and a Consideration of Their Relationship to the History of Ladakh and Maryul." In *Art and Architecture in Ladakh: Cross-Cultural Transmissions in the Himalayas and Karakoram*, edited by Erberto Lo Bue and John Bray, 68–99. Leiden: Brill, 2014.

Huber, Toni. "Some 11th-Century Indian Buddhist Clay Tablets (*tsha-tsha*) from Central Tibet." In *Tibetan Studies: Proceedings of the 5th Seminar of the International Association for Tibetan Studies, Narita 1989*. Vol. 2, edited by S. Ihara and Z. Yamaguchi, 493–96. Narita: Naritasan Shinshoji, 1992.

Hudson, Dennis. "The Ritual Worship of Devi." In *Devi the Great Goddess: Female Divinity in South Asian Art*, edited by Vidya Dehejia, 72–97. Washington D.C.: Arthur M. Sackler Gallery, Smithsonian Institution, 1999.

Hungkar, Dorje. *Tangkas in Golog: The Tangka Album by Xi Re Bu*. English translation by Chogyi and Kelley Lynch. Beijing: Zhongguo da bai ke quan chu ban she, 2001.

Hunter, Harriet. "Faquan's Transmission of the *Susiddhi* Category of the Esoteric Buddhist Teachings." *Journal of the International College for Advanced Buddhist Studies* 8 (2004): 43–93.

Huntington, John C. "Cave Six at Aurangabad: A Tantrayāna Monument?" In *Kalādarśana: American Studies in the Art of India*, edited by Joanna G. Williams, 47–55. New Delhi: Oxford and IBH in collaboration with the American Institute of Indian Studies, 1981.

Huntington, John C. "Gu-ge Bris: A Stylistic Amalgam." In *Aspects of Indian Art: Papers Presented in a Symposium at the Los Angeles County Museum of Art October, 1970*, edited by Pratapaditya Pal, 105–117. Leiden: Brill, 1972.

Huntington, Susan L. "Compassion in a Mountain Abode: A Pala Period Image of Avalokiteshvara." *Orientations* 48, no. 5 (2017): 78–87.

Huntington, Susan L. *The "Pāla-Sena" Schools of Sculpture*. Studies in South Asian Culture 10. Leiden: E. J. Brill, 1984.

Huo, Wei. "Newly Discovered Early Buddhist Grottos in Western Tibet." In *Discoveries in Western Tibet and the Western Himalayas: Essays on History, Literature, Archaeology and Art*, edited by Amy Heller and Giacomella Orofino, 23–39. Leiden: Brill, 2007.

Huo, Wei. "Xizang xibu Shiku bihua zhong ji zhong yishu fengge de fenxi" (Analysis of the Principal Artistic Styles of Cave Murals in Western Tibet). In *Xizang Kaogu yu Yishu: Guoji Xueshu Taolunhui Wenji* (Tibetan Archaeology and Art: Proceedings from the International Research Conference), 245–72. Chengdu: Sichuan Renmin Chubanshe, 2004.

Huo, Wei, and Yongxian Li. *Nishi Chibetto Sekkutsu Iseki: Piyan to Tonga no Sekkutsu hekiga*. Tokyo: Shueisha, 1997.

Huo, Wei, and Yongxian Li. *Xizang Xibu Fojiao Yishu*. Chengdu: Sichuan Renmin Chubanshe, 2001.

Huxley, Leonard. *Life and Letters of Sir Joseph Dalton Hooker, Based on Materials Collected and Arranged by Lady Hooker*. London: J. Murray, 1918.

Illich, Marina. "Selections from the Life of a Tibetan Buddhist Polymath: Chankya Rolpai Dorje (Lcang skya rol pa'i rdo rje), 1717–1786." PhD diss., Columbia University, 2006.

Ingalls, Daniel H. H., Jeffrey Moussaieff Masson, and M. V. Patwardhan. *The* Dhvanyaloka *of Anandavardhana with the* Locana *of Abhinavagupta*. Cambridge, MA: Harvard University Press, 1990.

Ingold, Tim. "Temporality of the Landscape." *World Archaeology* 25, no. 2 (1993): 152–74.

Iyanaga, Nobumi. "Récits de la Soumission de Mahesvara par Trailokyavijaya: D'apres les Sources Chinoises et Japonaises." *Tantric and Taoist Studies III In Honor of R. A. Stein*, edited by Michel Strickmann. Brussels: Institut Belge des Hautes Études Chinoises, 1985.

Jackson, David P. *The Nepalese Legacy in Tibetan Painting*. New York: Rubin Museum of Art, 2010.

Jackson, David P. *Painting Traditions of the Drigung Kagyu School*. New York: Rubin Museum of Art, 2015.

Jackson, David P. *Patron and Painter: Situ Panchen and the Revival of the Encampment Style*. New York: Rubin Museum of Art, 2009.

Jackson, David P., and Janice A. Jackson. *Tibetan Thangka Painting: Methods and Materials*. Boulder, CO: Shambhala, 1984.

Jahoda, Christian. "The Social and the Religious in Early Post-Imperial Tibet: The Case of 10th–11th Century Western Tibet and Its Antecedents." In *The Social and the Religious in the Making of Tibetan Societies: New Perspectives on Imperial Tibet*, edited by Guntram Hazod, Mathias Fermer, and Christian Jahoda, 149–88. Vienna: Österreichische Akademie der Wissenschaften, 2022.

Jahoda, Christian. "Socio-economic Organisations of Village Communities and Monasteries in Spiti, H.P., India: The Case of a Religious Administrative Unit (Chos gzhis)." In *Discoveries in Western Tibet and the Western Himalayas: Essays on History, Literature, Archaeology and Art*, edited by Amy Heller and Giacomella Orofino, 215–40. Leiden: Brill, 2007.

Jamgön Kongtrul Lodrö Thayé. *The Autobiography of Jamgön Kongtrul: A Gem of Many Colors*. Translated by Richard Barron. Ithaca, NY: Snow Lion, 2003.

Jamgön Kongtrul Lodrö Thayé. *Mahāsiddha Practice, From Mitrayogin and Other Masters: The Treasury of Precious Instructions: Essential Teachings of the Eight Practice Lineages of Tibet, Volume 16*. Translated by the Padamakara Translation Group. Boulder: Tsadra Foundation, 2021.

Jäschke, H. A. *A Tibetan-English Dictionary: With Special Reference to the Prevailing Dialects.* 1881; reprint, London: Routledge and Kegan Paul, 1968.

Jettmar, Karl. "Exploration in Baltistan." In *South Asian Archaeology 1987*, 2:801–13.

Jettmar, Karl. "The Main Buddhist Period as Represented in the Petroglyphs at Chilas and Thalpan." In *South Asian Archaeology 1985*, 407–11.

Jettmar, Karl. "Non-Buddhist Traditions in the Petroglyphs of the Indus Valley." In *South Asian Archaeology 1983*, 2:751–77.

Jettmar, Karl. "The Paṭolas, Their Governors and Their Successors." In *Antiquities of Northern Pakistan*, 2:77–122.

Jettmar, Karl, Klaus Sagaster, and Loden Sherab Dagyab. "Ein Tibetisches Heiligtum in Punyal." In *Antiquities of Northern Pakistan*, 2:123–39.

Jettmar, Karl, and Volker Thewalt. *Between Gandhāra and the Silk Roads: Rock-carvings along the Karakorum Highway, Discoveries by German-Pakistani Expeditions 1979–1984*. Mainz am Rhein: Philipp von Zabern, 1987.

Jinpa, Geshe Gelek, Charles Ramble, and Carroll Dunham. *Sacred Landscape and Pilgrimage in Tibet: In Search of the Lost Kingdom of Bön*. Photographs by Thomas L. Kelly. New York: Abbeville Press, 2005.

Jinpa, Nawang (Estelle Atlan). "Why Did Tibet and Ladakh Clash in the 17th Century? Rethinking the Background to the 'Mongol War' in Ngari (1679–1684)." *Tibet Journal* 40, no. 2 (2015): 113–50.

Jinpa, Nawang (Estelle Atlan), and Jigme Shide, "In Praise of the Incarnation Line of 'Kyabgon Staktsang Rinpoche': Documents Issued by the Dalai Lamas to the Kings of Ladakh," unpublished ms. for the planned publication of papers from the 17th International Association of Ladakh Studies Conference Kargil, *Visible Heritage 2: essays on the Art and Architecture of Greater Ladakh*, edited by Christian Luczanits and Heinrich Pöll.

Joldan, Sonam. *Ladakh's Traditional Ties with Buddhist Tibet*. Delhi: Kalpaz, 2012.

Jolden, Tsering, and Rinchen Tundup. "Cultural Relationship between the People of Ladakh and Tibet." *Tibet Journal* 43, no. 2 (2018): 65–71.

Kak, Ram Chandra. *Ancient Monuments of Kashmir*. London: India Society, 1933.

Kalantari, Christiane. "The Art of Khorchag and Khartse in the Fabric of Western Himalayan Buddhist Art (10th–14th Centuries): Questions of Style II." In Allinger et al., *Interaction in the Himalayas and Central Asia*, 191–225.

Kalantari, Christiane, and Eva Allinger. "The Spiritual Quest of the Buddha in the Dungkar Cave Temple—Indian Sources and Western Tibetan Image-making. Part 1: The Narrative Cycle from Tuṣita Heaven up to the Enlightenment." *Études mongoles et sibériennes, centrasiatiques et tibétaines* 51 (2020). https://journals.openedition.org/emscat/4308.

Kapstein, Matthew T. "The Seventh Dalai Lama Kalsang Gyatso." In *The Dalai Lamas: A Visual History*, edited by Martin Brauen [English ed. editors Patrick A. McCormick and Shane Suvikapakornkul], 102–15. 1st English ed. Chicago: Serindia, 2005.

Kapstein, Matthew T. *The Tibetan Assimilation of Buddhism: Conversion, Contestation, and Memory*. 2000; reprint, New York: Oxford University Press, 2002.

Kapstein, Matthew T. "Weaving the World: The Ritual Art of the 'Paṭa' in Pala Buddhism and Its Legacy in Tibet." *History of Religions* 34, no. 3 (1995): 241–62.

Karashima, Seishi. "*Stūpa*s Described in the Chinese Translations of the *Vinayas*." *ARIRIAB* 21 (2018): 439–69.

Karmay, Samten G. "A Decree of lHa Bla ma Ye shes 'od." in *Cultural Flows across the Western Himalaya*, edited by Patrick McAllister, Cristina Scherrer-Schaub, and Helmut Krasser, 477–85. Vienna: Österreichische Akademie der Wissenshaften, 2015.

Karmay, Samten G. *The Illusive Play: The Autobiography of the Fifth Dalai Lama*. Chicago: Serindia, 2014.

Karmay, Samten G. "The Ordinance of lHa Bla-ma Ye-shes-'od." In *Tibetan Studies in Honour of Hugh Richardson*, edited by Michael Aris and Aung San Suu Kyi, 150–62. New Delhi: Vikas, 1980.

Karmay, Samten G. "A Recently Discovered rNam thar of Lha bla ma Ye shes 'od." In *Tibet after Empire: Culture, Society, and Religion between 850–1000: Proceedings of the Seminar Held in Lumbini, Nepal, March 2011*, edited by Christoph Cüppers, Robert Mayer, and Michael Walter, 229–38. Lumbini: Lumbini International Research Institute, 2013.

Kerin, Melissa R. *Art and Devotion at a Buddhist Temple in the Indian Himalaya.* Bloomington: Indiana University Press, 2015.

Kerin, Melissa R. "From Emulation to Interpretation: Trends in the Late-Medieval Ngari Painting Tradition of the Guge Kingdom and Beyond." In Linrothe, *Collecting Paradise*, 150–95.

Kerin, Melissa R. "Re-tracing Lines of Devotion: Religious Identities and Political Ideologies in Fifteenth–Sixteenth-Century Western Himalayan Wall Painting." PhD diss., University of Pennsylvania, 2008.

Kerin, Melissa R., and Rob Linrothe. "Recollecting Kashmir: Cleveland's Eleven-headed, Thousand-armed Avalokiteshvara." *Orientations* 46, no. 1 (2015): 68–76.

Khamtrul, Garje Rinpoche. "A History and Geography of Shambhala." *Tibet Journal* 3, no. 3 (1981): 3–11.

Khān, Ḥashmatullāh Lakhna'vī. *History of Tibet and Great Tibet*. Translated by Zain-ul-Aabedin Aabedi. New Delhi: Atlantic, 2014.

Khān, Ḥashmatullāh Lakhna'vī. *Tarikh e-Jammu: Tarikh e-Kishtwar, Tibbat e-Asli (Lhasa), Tibbat e-buzurg (Ladakh), Tibbat e-Khurd (Baltistan), Purig (Kargil wa Zanskar), Gilgit (Dardistan)*. 1939; reprint, Mirpūr: Verīnāg, 1991.

Khan, M. Nasim. *Buddhist Paintings in Gandhara*. Peshawar: M. Nasim Khan, 2000.

Khan, M. Nasim. "Chaghdo Rock Paintings, Baltistan, Northern Areas." *Journal of Asian Civilizations* 21, no. 1 (1998): 100–104.

Khan, M. Nasim. "Rock-Carvings at Kinro Kor: A Prehistoric Site of the Northern Areas of Pakistan." *Lahore Museum Bulletin* 13, no. 2 (2000): 2–7.

Khan, Nazir, Abdul Nisar, Luca M. Olivieri, and Matteo Vitali. "The Recent Discovery of Cave Paintings in Swat: A Preliminary Note." *East and West* 45, nos. 1–4 (1995): 333–53.

Khoo, Michael. "Preliminary Remarks Concerning Solar Observation, Solar Calendars, and Festivals in Ladakh and the Western Himalaya." In *Recent Research on Ladakh 7: Proceedings of the 7th Colloquium of the International Association for Ladakh Studies Held in Bonn/Sankt Augustin, 12–15 June 1995*, edited by Thierry Dodin and Heinz Räther, 235–69. Bonn: Universität Bonn, 1997.

Khosla, Romi. *Buddhist Monasteries in the Western Himalaya*. Kathmandu: Ratna Pustak Bhadar, 1979.

Klieger, P. Christiaan, ed. *Tibetan Borderlands: PIATS 2003: Tibetan Studies: Proceedings of the Tenth Seminar of the International Association for Tibetan Studies, Oxford, 2003.* Leiden: Brill, 2006.

Klimburg-Salter, Deborah E., ed. *Discovering Tibet: The Tucci Expeditions and Tibetan Paintings*. Milan: Skira, 2015.

Klimburg-Salter, Deborah E. "Dung dkar/Phyi dbang, West Tibet, and the Influences of Tangut Buddhist Art." *East and West* 51, nos. 3–4 (2001): 323–48.

Klimburg-Salter, Deborah E. "The Gilgit Manuscript Covers and the 'Cult of the Book.'" In *South Asian Archaeology 1987*, 2:815–30.

Klimburg-Salter, Deborah E. "Imagining the World of Ye Shes 'od: 10th-Century Painting in Tabo." In *The Cultural History of Western Tibet: Recent Research from the China Tibetology Research Center and the University of Vienna*, edited by Deborah Klimburg-Salter, Liang Junyan, Helmut Tauscher, and Zhou Yuan, 231–86. Beijing: China Tibetology Research Center; Vienna: Arbeitskreis für Tibetische und Buddhistische Studien, Universität Wien, 2008.

Klimburg-Salter, Deborah E. "Is There an Inner Asian International Style 12th to 14th Centuries? Definition of the Problem and Present State of Research." In *The Inner Asian International Style 12th–14th Centuries: Papers Presented at a Panel of the 7th Seminar of the International Association for Tibetan Studies*, edited by Deborah E. Klimburg-Salter and Eva Allinger, 1–13. Vienna: Österreichische Akademie der Wissenschaften, 1998.

Klimburg-Salter, Deborah E. "Note on the Origin of the Tibetan Book Cover Decoration." *Tibet Journal* 16, no. 1 (1991): 115–27.

Klimburg-Salter, Deborah E. "Notes on Two Gilgit Manuscript Cover-Paintings." In *The Art of Ajanta: New Perspectives*, edited by Ratan Parimoo, 521–36. New Delhi: Books & Books, 1991.

Klimburg-Salter, Deborah E., ed. *The Silk Route and the Diamond Path: Esoteric Buddhist Art on the Trans-Himalayan Trade Routes*. Los Angeles: UCLA Art Council, 1982.

Klimburg-Salter, Deborah E. "Some Thoughts on Style in Tibetan Art." *Tibet Journal* 24, no. 4 (2000): 83–90.

Klimburg-Salter, Deborah E. "Style in Western Tibetan Painting: The Archaeological Evidence." *East and West* 46, nos. 3-4 (1996): 319–336.

Klimburg-Salter, Deborah E. *Tabo, a Lamp for the Kingdom: Early Indo-Tibetan Buddhist Art in the Western Himalaya*. Milan: Skira, 1997.

Klimburg-Salter, Deborah E. *Tabo Monastery: Art and History, With an Interview of Geshe Sonam Wangdu by Peter Stefan and a Tibetan Summary.* Vienna: (publisher not indicated), 2005.

Klimburg-Salter, Deborah E. "The Tibetan Himalayan Style: The Art of the Western Domains, 8th–11th Centuries." In *Cultural Flows across the Western Himalaya*, edited by Patrick McAllister, Cristina Scherrer-Schaub, and Helmut Krasser, 427–75. Vienna: Österreichische Akademie der Wissenschaften, 2015.

Klimburg-Salter, Deborah E., ed. "The Tucci Archives Preliminary Study, 1: Notes on the Chronology of Ta pho *'Du Khaṅ*." *East and West* 35, nos. 1–3 (1985): 11–41.

Klimburg-Salter, Deborah E. "Tucci Himalayan Archives Report, 2: The 1991 Expedition to Himachal Pradesh." *East and West* 44, no. 1 (1994): 13–82.

Knight, E. F. *Where Three Empires Meet: A Narrative of Recent Travel in Kashmir, Western Tibet, Gilgit, and the Adjoining Countries*. New ed., London: Longmans, Green, 1896.

Koelz, Walter. "The Roof of the World: From the Diary of a Traveler in Tibet." *Michigan Alumnus, Quarterly Review* 41, no. 11 (1935): 283–92.

Kollmar-Paulenz, Karénina. "Utopian Thought in Tibetan Buddhism: A Survey of the Śambhala Concept and Its Sources." *Studies in Central & East Asian Religions* 5/6 (1992–93): 78–96.

Konow, Sten. *Kharoshṭhī Inscriptions, with the Exception of Those of Aśoka*. Corpus Inscriptionum Indicarum 2, pt. 1. 1929; reprint, Varanasi: Indological Book House, 1969.

Kossak, Steven. *Painted Images of Enlightenment: Early Tibetan Thankas, 1050–1450*. Mumbai: Marg, 2010.

Kossak, Steven. "Pala Painting Style and Its Tibetan Variant." In Kossak, *Painted Images of Enlightenment*, 38–63.

Kozicz, Gerald. "Collapsed, Fragmented, and Reassembled: The Temple Complex of Swaim." *Orientations* 53, no. 3 (2022): 94–100.

Kozicz, Gerald. "One *Stūpa* and Three *Lha thos*: The Monuments of Tashigang." *Revue d'Etudes Tibétaines* 41 (2017): 226–48.

Kramrisch, Stella. "Emblems of the Universal Being." In *Exploring India's Sacred Art: Selected Writings of Stella Kramrisch*, edited by Barbara Stoler Miller, 130–40. Philadelphia: University of Pennsylvania Press, 1983.

Kramrisch, Stella. *The Hindu Temple.* Photographs by Raymond Burnier. 2 vols. 1946; reprint, Delhi: Motilal Banarsidass, 1976.

Kramrisch, Stella. "Pala and Sena Sculpture." *Rupam* 40 (1929): 107–126.

Krishna Deva. "The Stone Temple at Nālandā." *Journal of the Uttar Pradesh Historical Society* 23 (1950): 198–212.

Krishna Deva. "Stone Temple (No. 2) at Nālandā." *Journal of the Indian Society of Oriental Art*, n.s. 11 (1980): 80–84.

Krist, Gabriela, ed. *Nako: Research and Conservation in the Western Himalayas*. Vienna: Böhlau, 2016.

Krist, Gabriella, and Tatjana Bayerová, eds. *Heritage Conservation and Research in India: 60 Years of Indo-Austrian Collaboration*. Vienna: Böhlau, 2010.

Kubler, George. "The Shape of Time: Reconsidered." *Perspecta* 19 (1982): 112–21.

Kubler, George. *The Shape of Time: Remarks on the History of Things*. 1962; reprint, New Haven, CT: Yale University Press, 2008.

Kuijp, Leonard W. J. van der. "The Bird-faced Monk and the Beginnings of the New Tantric Tradition, Part One." In *Tibetan Genealogies: Studies in Memorium of Guge Tsering Gyalpo (1961–2015)*, edited by Guntram Hazod and Shen Weirong, 403–50. Beijing: China Tibetology, 2018.

Kuijp, Leonard W. J. van der. "The Bird-faced Monk and the Beginnings of the New Tantric Tradition, Part Two. Journal of Tibetology 19 (2018): 86–127.

Kuijp, Leonard W. J. van der. "Notes Apropos of the Transmission of the Sarvadurgatipariśodhana-tantra in Tibet." *Studein zur Indologie und Iranistik* 16 (1992): 109–25.

Kuijp, Leonard W. J. van der. "On the Lives of Śākyaśrībhadra (?–?1225)." *Journal of the American Oriental Society* 114, no. 4 (1994): 599–616.

Kuijp, Leonard W. J. van der. "Tibetan Belles-Lettres: The Influence of Daṇḍin and Kṣemendra." In *Tibetan Literature; Studies in Genre*, edited by José Ignacio Cabezón and Roger R. Jackson, 393–410. Ithaca: Snow Lion, 1996.

Kurita, Isao. *Gandāra bijutsu* [Gandhāran Art], Vol. 1, *Butsuden* [The Buddha's Life Story]. Tokyo: Nigensha, 2003.

Kvaerne, Per. "The Beggar from Amdo." *Tibet Journal* 12, no. 3 (1987): 68–69.

Kvaerne, Per. "Tibet Images among Researchers on Tibet." In *Imagining Tibet: Perceptions, Projections, and Fantasies*, edited by Thierry Dodin and Heinz Räther, 47–63. Boston: Wisdom, 2001.

La Vaissière, Étienne de. *Sogdian Traders: A History*. Leiden: Brill, 2005.

Lakoff, George, and Mark Johnson. *Metaphors We Live By*. Chicago: University of Chicago Press, 1980.

Lal, Shyam Kishore. *Female Divinities in Hindu Mythology and Ritual*. Pune: University of Poona, 1980.

Lalou, Marcelle. "Les Textes Bouddhiques au temps du roi Khri-Sroṅ-lde-bcan." *Journal Asiatique* 241 (1953): 313–53.

Lamotte, Étienne. *History of Indian Buddhism: From the Origins to the* Śaka *Era*. Translated from the French by Sara Webb-Boin under the supervision of Jean Dantinne. 1958; reprint, Louvain-la-Neuve: Université Catholique de Louvain, Institut Orientaliste, 1988.

Lawson, Graeme. "An Anglo-Saxon Harp and Lyre of the Ninth Century." In *Music and Tradition: Essays on Asian and Other Musics Presented to Laurence Picken*, edited by D. R. Widdess and R. F. Wolpert, 229–44. Cambridge: Cambridge University Press, 1981.

Le Calloc'h, Bernard. "Francisco De Azevedo's Travels in Guge and Ladakh." *Tibet Journal* 16, no. 2 (1991): 55–66.

Leidy, Denise Patry. "Kashmir and China: A Note about Styles and Dates." *Orientations* 28, no. 2 (1997): 66–70.

Lempert, Michael. *Discipline and Debate: The Language of Violence in a Tibetan Buddhist Monastery.* Berkeley: University of California Press, 2012.

Lessing, F. D., and A. Wayman. *Introduction to the Buddhist Tantric Systems Translated from mKhas grub rJe's Rgyud sde spiḥi rnam par gzag pa rgyas par brjod*. 1968; reprint, Delhi: Motilal Banarsidass, 1983.

Lin, Nancy Grace. "Adapting the Buddha's Biographies: A Culture History of the *Wish-Fulfilling Vine* in Tibet, Seventeenth to Eighteenth Centuries." PhD diss., University of California, Berkeley, 2011.

Lin, Nancy Grace. "Recounting the Fifth Dalai Lama's Rebirth Lineage." *Revue d'Études Tibétaines* 38 (2017): 119–56.

Linrothe, Rob. "Art Historical Evidence for a Cult of the Trloknāth Lokeśvara in Zangskar." *Journal of Tibetology* 21, no. 2 (2019): 177–204.

Linrothe, Rob. "Dating the Mangyu Style." In *Heavenly Himalayas: The Murals of Mangyu and Other Discoveries in Ladakh*, edited by Peter van Ham, 159–61. Munich: Prestel, 2011.

Linrothe, Rob. "Deeply Rooted Ritual: The Plurality of Sponsor Couples in Eastern Indian Sculpture, ca. Eighth to Thirteenth Century, and an Explanatory Hypothesis." *Journal of Bengal Art* 24 (2019): 123–50.

Linrothe, Rob, ed. *Holy Madness: Portraits of Tantric Siddhas.* New York: Rubin Museum of Art and Serindia Publications, 2006.

Linrothe, Rob. "The Human Sphere: Comparative Analysis of Sponsor Images in the Jaina Caves of Ellora." *Journal of Bengal Art (Dedicated to Claudine Bautze-Picron)* 26 (2021): 215–232.

Linrothe, Rob. "Kashmiri 'Loving-Kindness' in Ladakh: A Tall Order?" *Himalayan Art in 108 Objects*, edited by Karl Debreczeny and Elena Pakhoutova, object no. 17, 92–95. New York: Rubin Museum of Art, 2023.

Linrothe, Rob. "Landscape Elements in Early Tibetan Painting." In *Looking at Asian Art*, edited by Katherine R. Tsiang and Martin Powers, 159–77. Chicago: Center for the Art of East Asia, University of Chicago, Art Media Resources, 2012.

Linrothe, Rob. "Mirror Image: Deity and Donor as Vajrasattva." *History of Religions* 54, no. 1 (2014): 5–33.

Linrothe, Rob. "The Murals of Mangyu: A Distillation of Mature Esoteric Buddhist Icongraphy." *Orientations* 25, no. 11 (1994): 92–102.

Linrothe, Rob. "Note on the *Mahāsiddha*," Goepper and Luczanits, *Alchi: Ladakh's Hidden Buddhist Sanctuary*, 2.578–79.

Linrothe, Rob. "Origins of the Kashmiri Style in the Western Himalayas: Sculpture of the 7th–11th Centuries." In Meinert, *Transfer of Buddhism across Central Asian Networks (7th to 13th Centuries)*, 147–88.

Linrothe, Rob. "Polishing the Past: The Style of a Seventeenth-Century Tibetan Mural." *Artibus Asiae* 71, no. 2 (2011): 247–81.

Linrothe, Rob. "Portraiture on the Periphery: Recognizing Changsem Sherab Zangpo."*Archives of Asian Art* 63, no. 1 (2013): 59–86.

Linrothe, Rob. "Preliminary Report on 15th Century Murals in Zangskar." *Orientations* 43, no. 5 (2012): 36–43.

Linrothe, Rob. *Reenchantment: Masterworks of Sculpture in Village Temples of Bihar and Orissa*. New Delhi: Studio Orientalia, 2021.

Linrothe, Rob. *Ruthless Compassion: Wrathful Deities in Early Indo-Tibetan Esoteric Buddhist Art*. London: Serindia, 1999.

Linrothe, Rob. *Seeing into Stone: Pre-Buddhist Petroglyphs and Zangskar's Early Inhabitants*. New Delhi and Berlin: Studio Orientalia, 2016.

Linrothe, Rob. "Siddhas and Sociality: A Seventeenth-Century Lay Illustrated Buddhist Manuscript in Kumik Village, Zangskar (A Preliminary Report)." In *Visible Heritage: Essays on the Art and Architecture of Greater Ladakh*, edited by Rob Linrothe and Heinrich Pöll, 169–202. New Delhi: Studio Orientale, 2016.

Linrothe, Rob. "Site Unseen: Approaching a Royal Buddhist Monument of Zangskar (Western Himalayas)." *Tibet Journal* 40, no. 2 (2015): 29–88.

Linrothe, Rob. "Skirting the Bodhisattva: Fabricating Visionary Art." Études *Mongoles & Sibériennes, Centrasiatiques & Tibétaines* 42 (2011). https://journals.openedition.org/emscat/1803.

Linrothe, Rob. "Strengthening the Roots: An Indian Yogi in Early Drigung Paintings of Ladakh and Zangskar." *Orientations* 38, no. 4 (2007): 65–71.

Linrothe, Rob. "'Structure and Subject Matter' at Dunhuang," review of Michelle C. Wang's *Maṇḍalas in the Making: Visual Culture of Esoteric Buddhism at Dunhuang* (2018). *Archives of Asian Art* 72, no. 1 (2022): 255–72.

Linrothe, Rob. "A Summer in the Field." *Orientations* 30, no. 5 (1999): 57–67.

Linrothe, Rob. "Thirty Years On: Revisiting the Chuchikzhal Complex in Karsha." *Orientations* 51, no. 6 (2020): 30–44.

Linrothe, Rob. "'Utterly False, Utterly Undeniable': The Akaniṣṭha Lhakhang Murals of Takden Phuntsokling Monastery." *Archives of Asian Art* 67, no. 2 (2017): 143–87.

Linrothe, Rob. "A Winter in the Field." *Orientations* 38, no. 4 (2007): 40–53.

Linrothe, Rob, ed., with contributions by Melissa R. Kerin and Christian Luczanits. *Collecting Paradise: Buddhist Art of Kashmir and Its Legacies*. New York: Rubin Museum of Art; Evanston, IL: Block Museum of Art, 2014.

Linrothe, Rob, and Melissa R. Kerin. "Discovery through Deconsecration: The Art of the Karsha Kadampa Chorten Revealed." *Orientations* 32, no. 10 (2001): 52–63.

Lo Bue, Erberto. Review article of *Tibetan Painted Scrolls* by Giuseppe Tucci. *Tibet Journal* 27, nos. 3–4 (2002): 183–91.

Lo Bue, Eberto. "Sculptural Styles According to Pema Karpo." In *Tibetan Art: Towards a Definition of Style*, edited by Jane Casey Singer and Philip Denwood, 242–53. London: Laurence King, 1997.

Lo Bue, Erberto, and John Bray, eds. *Art and Architecture in Ladakh: Cross-Cultural Transmissions in the Himalayas and Karakoram*. Leiden: Brill, 2014.

Lo Bue, Erberto, and Christian Luczanits, eds. *Tibetan Art and Architecture in Context. PIATS 2006: Tibetan Studies: Proceedings of the Eleventh Seminar of the International Association for Tibetan Studies, Königwinter 2006*. Halle: International Insitute for Tibetan and Buddhist Studies, 2010.

Lojda, Linda, Deborah Klimburg-Salter, and Monica Strinu. "The Tibetan Himalayan Style: Considering the Central Asian Connection." In Meinert, *Transfer of Buddhism across Central Asian Networks (7th to 13th Centuries)*, 121–46.

Lokesh Chandra, ed. *Buddhist Iconography (Begun by the Late Prof. Raghu Vira)*. Compact ed. New Delhi: International Academy of Indian Culture, Aditya Prakashan, 1991.

Lokesh Chandra. Introduction to Giuseppe Tucci, *Stupa: Art, Architectonics and Symbolism, English Version of Indo-Tibetica I*, v–xxxvi. Translated by Uma Marina Vesci. New Delhi: Aditya Prakashan, 1988. Italian edition 1932.

Lokesh Chandra. *Kāraṇḍa-Vyūha-Sūtra, or The Supernal Virtues of Avalokiteśvara*. New Delhi: International Academy of Indian Culture and Aditya Prakashan, 1999.

Lokesh Chandra. *A Ninth Century Scroll of the Vajradhātu Maṇḍala*. New Delhi: International Academy of Indian Culture and Aditya Prakashan, 1997.

Lokesh Chandra. "Preface: Synoptic View of the Book." In Tucci, *Temples of Western Tibet*, xii–xliv.

Lokesh Chandra, and Nirmala Sharma. *Buddhist Paintings of Tun-huang in the National Museum, New Delhi*. New Delhi: Niyogi Books, 2012.

Lokesh Chandra and Nirmala Sharma. *Nispanna-Yogāvalī: Sanskrit and Tibetan Texts with English Translation*. 1986; reprint, New Delhi: International Academy of Indian Culture and Aditya Prakashan, 2015.

Lopez, Donald S., Jr. *Hyecho's Journey: The World of Buddhism*. Chicago and London: University of Chicago Press, 2017.

Luczanits, Christian. "Beneficial To See: Early Drigung Painting." In *Painting Traditions of the Drigung Kagyu School*, edited by David P. Jackson, 214–59. New York: Rubin Museum of Art, 2015.

Luczanits, Christian. *Buddhist Sculpture in Clay: Early Western Himalayan Art, Late 10th to Early 13th Centuries*. Chicago: Serindia, 2004.

Luczanits, Christian. "The Early Buddhist Heritage of Ladakh Reconsidered." In Bray, *Ladakhi Histories*, 65–96.

Luczanits, Christian. "From Kashmir to Western Tibet: The Many Faces of a Regional Style." In Linrothe, *Collecting Paradise*, 108–49.

Luczanits, Christian, comp. *Gandhara, the Buddhist Heritage of Pakistan: Legends, Monasteries, and Paradise*. Berlin: Kunst-und Ausstellungshalle der Bundesrepublik Deutschland, 2008.

Luczanits, Christian. "Methodological Comments Regarding Recent Research on Tibetan Art." *Wiener Zeitschrift* für die Kunde *Südasiens* 45 (2001): 125–45.

Luczanits, Christian. "The Nako Monuments in Context." In *Nako: Research and Conservation in the Western Himalayas*, edited by Gabriela Krist, 19–45. Vienna: Böhlau, 2016.

Luczanits, Christian. "On an Unusual Painting Style in Ladakh." In *The Inner Asian International Style 12th–14th Centuries*, edited by Deborah E. Klimburg-Salter and Eva Allinger, 151–69. Vienna: Österreichische Akademie der Wissenschaften, 1998.

Luczanits, Christian. "On the Earliest Mandalas in a Buddhist Context." In *Mahayana Buddhism: History and Culture,* edited by M. Darrol Bryant and Susan Bryant, 111–36. New Delhi: Tibet House, 2008.

Luczanits, Christian. "On the Iconography of Tibetan Scroll Paintings (*Thang ka*) Dedicated to the Five Tathāgatas." In *Art in Tibet: PIATS 2003: Tibetan Studies: Proceedings of the Tenth Seminar of the International Association for Tibetan Studies, Oxford, 2003*, edited by Erberto F. Lo Bue, 37–51. Leiden: Brill, 2011.

Luczanits, Christian. "Styles in Western Himalayan Art." In *Han-Zang Fojiao Meishu Yanjiu* (Research in Han-Tibetan Buddhist Fine Arts), edited by Xie Jisheng, Xiong Wenbing, Luo Wenhua, and Jing Anning, 133–50. Shanghai: Shanghai Guji Chubanshe, 2009.

Luczanits, Christian. "The Wanla Bkra shis *gsum brtsegs*." In *Buddhist Art and Tibetan Patronage: Ninth to Fourteenth Centuries: PIATS 2000: Tibetan Studies, Proceedings of the Ninth Seminar of the International Association for Tibetan Studies, Leiden 2000*, edited by Deborah Klimburg-Salter and Eva Allinger, 115–25. Leiden: Brill, 2002.

Luczanits, Christian, and Holger Neuwirth. "The Development of the Alchi Temple Complex: An Interdisciplinary Approach. In *Heritage Conservation and Research in India: 60 Years of Indo-Austrian Collaboration*, edited by Gabriella Krist and Tatjana Bayerová, 79–84. Vienna: Böhlau, 2010.

Ludvik, Catherine. "La Benzaiten à Huit Bras: Durgā déesse guerrière sous l'apparence de Sarasvatī." *Cahiers d'Extrême-Orient* 11 (1999–2000): 292–338.

Ludvik, Catherine. *Sarasvatī, Riverine Goddess of Knowledge: From the Manuscript-carrying* Vīṇā*-player to the Weapon-wielding Defender of the Dharma*. Leiden: Brill, 2007.

Luo, Wenhua. *Eulogies to the Sacred Images of the Buddhas and Bodhisattvas*. Beijing: Zhongguo Zangxue Chubanshe, 2008.

Mallinson, James. "The Original *Gorakṣaśataka*." In *Yoga in Practice*, edited by David Gordon White, 257–72. Princeton: Princeton University Press, 2012.

Marshak, Boris. *Legends, Tales, and Fables in the Art of Sogdiana*. New York: Bibliotheca Persica Press, 2002.

Martin, Dan. "Zhangzhung Dictionary—Introduction." *Revue d'Etudes Tibétaines* 18 (2012): 5–32.

Martin, Nils. "A Solemn Praise to an 11th Century West-Tibetan Councillor at Kharul, Purik." *Zentralasiatische Studien* 46 (2017): 189–232.

Maurer, Petra. "Isn't Life Miserable? The Youth of the Yogin Ngawang Tshering." *Tibet Journal* 40, no. 2 (2015): 89–112.

Maxwell, T. S. "Lākhamaṇḍal and Trilokināth: The Transformed Functions of Hindu Architecture in Two Cross-Cultural Zones of the Western Himalaya." *Art International* 24, nos. 1–2 (1980): 9–74.

McCorkel, Christine. "Sense and Sensibility: An Epistemological Approach to the Philosophy of Art History." *Journal of Aesthetics and Art Criticism* 34, no. 1 (1975): 35–50.

Meinert, Carmen, ed. *Transfer of Buddhism across Central Asian Networks (7th to 13th Centuries)*. Dynamics in the History of Religion 8. Leiden: Brill, 2016.

Meister, Michael W. "Mountain Temples and Temple-Mountains: Masrur." *Journal of the Society of Architectural Historians* 65, no. 1 (2006): 26–49.

Melikian-Chirvani, Assadullah Souren. *Islamic Metalwork from the Iranian World 8th–18th Centuries: Victoria and Albert Museum Catalogue*. London: H.M.S.O., 1982.

Melville, Stephen. "The Temptation of New Perspectives." *October* 52 (1990): 3–15.

Michaud, Éric. *The Barbarian Invasions: A Genealogy of the History of Art*. Translated by Nicholas Huckle. Cambridge, MA: MIT Press, 2019.

Mingle, Jonathan. *Fire and Ice: Soot, Solidarity, and Survival on the Roof of the World*. New York: St. Martin's Press, 2015.

Mīrzā, Ḥaidar, Dughlát. *The Tarikh-I-Rashidi of Mirza Muhammad Haidar, Dughlát: A History of the Moghuls of Central Asia*. Translated by E. Denison Ross and edited by N. Elias. London: Sampson Low, Marston, 1895.

Misra, Bhāskaranātha N. *Nālandā*. 3 vols. Delhi: B.R. Publishing, 1998.

Mitra, Debala. "A Brief Survey of the Representations of *Aṣṭa-Mahā Bodhisattva-Maṇḍala* in India and Bangladesh." *Journal of Bengal Art* 2 (1997): 59–77.

Mitra, Debala. *Ratnagiri (1958–1961)*. 2 vols. New Delhi: Archaeological Survey of India, 1981, 1983.

Mohammed, Jigar. "Mughal Sources on Medieval Ladakh." In Bray, *Ladakhi Histories*, 147–60.

Moorcroft, William. "A Journey to Lake Mánasaróvara in U'n- dés, a Province of Little Tibet." *Asiatick Researches* 12 (1818): 380–536.

Morelli, Giovanni. *Italian Painters: Critical Studies of Their Works*. Translated by Constance Jocelyn Foulkes. London: John Murray, 1892.

Morgan, Peter. "Samanid Pottery: Types and Techniques." In *Cobalt and Lustre: The First Centuries of Islamic Pottery*, edited by Ernst J. Grube, 55–113. London: Nour Foundation, in association with Azimuth Editions and Oxford University Press, 1994.

Mori, Masahide. *Vajrāvalī of Abhayākaragupta*. Tring, UK: Institute of Buddhist Studies, 2009.

Mukherjee, Prithwindra. *Sahaja, in Quest of the Innate: An Esoteric Fusion of Bengal Poetry through the Charyā and the Baul Songs*. New Delhi: Aditya Prakashan, 2018.

Mukherji, Parul Dave. *The* Citrasūtra *of the* Visṇudharmottara Purāṇa. New Delhi: Indira Gandhi National Centre for the Arts; Delhi: Motilal Banarsidass, 2001.

Mullin, Glenn H., comp. and ed. *Meditations on the Lower Tantras: From the Collected Works of the Previous Dalai Lamas*. 1983; reprint, Dharamsala: Library of Tibetan Works & Archives, 1997.

Mullin, Glenn H. *Mystical Verses of a Dalai Lama*. New Delhi: New Age, 2003. Originally published in 1994 as *Mystical Verses of a Mad Dalai Lama*.

Murray, Charles Adolphus, the 7th Earl of Dunmore. *The Pamirs; being a Narrative of a Year's Expedition on Horseback and on Foot through Kashmir, Western Tibet, Chinese Tartary, and Russian Central Asia*. 2 vols. London: John Murray, 1893.

Nagaraja Rao, M. S. "The Stupa at Sanghol." In Gupta, *Kushāṇa Sculptures from Sanghol*, 21–24.

Namdak Tsukphu. *mChod rten gyi dpe ris blo gsar mgul rgyan bzhugs (Bon Stupa: Illustrations and Explanations)*. Solan: Tibeto Zhang-Zhung Research Centre, 1998.

Namgial, Eshey. "Ladakhi: An Offsoot of Classical Tibetan Language." *Tibet Journal* 43, no. 1 (2018): 35–47.

Namgyal, Phuntsok. *Tuolin Si (Ntho-ling Monastery)*. Beijing: Zhongguo Dabaike, 2001.

Namgyal Institute for Research on Ladakhi Art and Culture. *Legacy of a Mountain People: Inventory of Cultural Resources of Ladakh. 4 Volumes* New Delhi: NIRLAC, 2008.

Neelis, Jason. *Early Buddhist Transmission and Trade Networks: Mobility and Exchange within and beyond the Northwestern Borderlands of South Asia*. Leiden: Brill, 2011.

Neumann, Helmut F. "The Cave of the Offering Goddesses: Early Painting in Western Tibet." *Oriental Art* 44, no. 4 (1998–99): 52–60.

Neumann, Helmut F. "Wall Paintings of Western Tibet: A Stylistic Analysis." *Orientations* 30, no. 8 (1999): 74–83.

Neumann, Helmut F., and Heidi A. Neumann. "Defining the Sacred Space: Painted Ceilings in Dung dkar and Tsaparang in Western Tibet." In *The Temple in South Asia*, edited by Adam Hardy, 139–48. "Volume 2 of the proceedings of the 18th Conference of the European Association of South Asian Archaeologists, London, 2005." London: British Association for South Asian Studies, 2007.

Neuwirth, Holger. "The Temple of Lalung." In *The Ancient Monastic Complex of Dangkhar: Buddhist Architecture in the Western Himalayas*, edited by Holger Neuwirth, 275–89. Graz: Graz University of Technology, 2013.

Neuwirth, Holger, and Carmen Auer, eds. *The Ancient Monastic Complexes of Tholing, Nyarma and Tabo*. Buddhist Architecture in the Western Himalayas 3. Graz: Graz University of Technology, 2021.

Neve, Ernest F. *Beyond the Pir Panjal: Life among the Mountains and Valleys of Kashmir*. London: T. Fisher Unwin, 1912.

Newman, John. "Itineraries to Sambhala." In *Tibetan Literature: Studies in Genre*, edited by José Ignacio Cabezón and Roger R. Jackson, 481–99. Ithaca, NY: Snow Lion, 1995.

Nihom, Max. "Sādhanamālā 256: A Pāśupata-Bauddha Tantristic Sādhana." *Wiener Zeitschrift für die Kunde Südasiens* 38 (1994): 213–29.

Norberg-Hodge, Helena. *Ancient Futures: Learning from Ladakh*. London: Rider, 1992.

O'Brien, Seamus. *In the Footsteps of Joseph Dalton Hooker: A Sikkim Adventure*. Kew: Kew, Royal Botanic Gardens, 2018.

O'Donnell, C. Oliver. "Revisiting David Summers' *Real Spaces*: A Neo-pragmatist Interpretation." *World Art* 8, no. 1 (2018): 21–38.

Obermiller, E., trans. *The History of Buddhism in India and Tibet by Bu-Ston*. 1932; 1st Indian ed., New Delhi: Paljor, 1999.

Ogilby, John. *Asia, the First Part: Being an Accurate Description of Persia, and the Several Provinces thereof: The Vast Empire of the Great Mogol, and other Parts of India, and Their Several Kingdoms and Regions. . . .* London: Printed by the author, 1673.

Olschak, Blanche C., in collaboration with Geshé Thupten Wangyal. *Mystic Art of Ancient Tibet*. 1973; reprint, Boston: Shambhala, 1987.

Orofino, Giacomella. "A Note on Some Petroglyphs of the Ladakh Area." *East and West* 40, no. 1–4 (1990): 173–200.

Pächt, Otto. *The Practice of Art History: Reflections on Method*. Translated from the German by David Britt. 1st English ed. London: Harvey Miller, 1999.

Pakhoutova, Elena A. "Reproducing the Sacred Places: The Eight Great Events of the Buddha's Life and Their Commemorative Stūpas in the Medieval Art of Tibet (10th–13th century)." PhD diss., University of Virginia, 2009.

Pakhoutova, Elena, Lewis Doney, Daniel A. Hirshberg, and Benjamin Bogin. *The Second Buddha: Master of Time*. Munich: Delmonico/Prestel, 2018.

Pal, Pratapaditya. "The *Aiḍūka* of the *Viṣṇudharmottarapurāṇa* and Certain Aspects of Stūpa Symbolism." *Journal of the Indian Society of Oriental Art* 4 (1972): 49–62.

Pal, Pratapaditya, ed. *The Arts of Kashmir*. New York: Asia Society, 2007.

Pal, Pratapaditya. "A Brāhmanical Triad from Kashmir and Some Related Icons." *Archives of Asian Art* 27 (1973–74): 33–45.

Pal, Pratapaditya, ed. *Himalayas: An Aesthetic Adventure*. Chicago: Art Institute of Chicago, 2003.

Pal, Pratapaditya. *Hindu Religion and Iconology According to the Tantrasāra*. Los Angeles: Vichitra Press, 1981.

Pal, Pratapaditya. "Kashmir and the Tibetan Connection." *Marg* 40, no. 2 (1987): 57–75.

Pal, Pratapaditya. "The Printed Image: An Iconographic Excursus." In Gerald James Larson, Pratapaditya Pal, and H. Daniel Smith, *Changing Myths and Images: Twentieth-Century Popular Art in India*, 29–38. Bloomington: Indiana University Art Museum, 1997.

Paldan, Thubstan. *The Guide to the Buddhist Monasteries and Royal Castles of Ladakh*. Delhi: Jayed Press, 1997.

Paljor, Tsewang. "Ladakh: An Example of Living Museum." In *Museums and Changing Cultural Landscape: Proceedings of the International Seminar*, edited by Manvi Seth, 183–87. Gurgaon: Shubhi, 2016.

Pallis, Marco. *Peaks and Lamas*. 1939; rev. ed., Washington, DC: Shoemaker & Hoard, 1949.

Papa-Kalantari, Christiane. "The Art of the Court: Some Remarks on the Historical Stratigraphy of Eastern Iranian Elements in Early Buddhist Painting of Alchi, Ladakh." In *Proceedings of the Tenth Seminar of the IATS, 2003, vol. 7, Text, Image and Song in Transdisciplinary Dialogue*, edited by Deborah Klimburg-Salter, Kurt Tropper, and Christian Jahoda, 167–228. Leiden: Brill, 2007.

Papa-Kalantari, Christiane. "The Ceiling Paintings of the Alchi *gsum brtsegs*: Problems of Style." In *Buddhist Art and Tibetan Patronage: Ninth to Fourteenth Centuries: PIATS 2000: Tibetan Studies, Proceedings of the Ninth Seminar of the International Association for Tibetan Studies, Leiden 2000*, edited by Deborah Klimburg-Salter and Eva Allinger, 85–113. Leiden: Brill, 2002.

Papa-Kalantari, Christiane. "From Textile Dress to Vault of Heaven: Some Observations on the Function and Symbolism of Ceiling Decorations in the Western Himalayan Buddhist Temples of Nako, Himachal Pradesh, India." In *The Temple in South Asia*, edited by Adam Hardy, 149–78. "Volume 2 of the proceedings of the 18th Conference of the European Association of South Asian Archaeologists, London, 2005." London: British Association for South Asian Studies, 2007.

Pardee, Thomas, Susan Skolnick, Eric Swanson, and Willa Baker. *Karmapa, the Sacred Prophecy*. Wappingers Falls, NY: Kagyu Thubten Chöling Publications Committee, 1999.

Parimoo, Ratan. "A Critique of Ananda Coomaraswamy's Presuppositions for a Philosophy of Indian Art." *Studies in Indian Sculpture: Regional Genres and Interpretations*, 1:1–31. 2 vols. New Delhi: Books & Books, 2000.

Peissel, Michel. *Tibet: The Secret Continent*. London: Cassell Illustrated, 2002.

Peissel, Michel. *Zanskar: The Hidden Kingdom*. New York: E.P. Dutton, 1979.

Petech, Luciano. *A Study on the Chronicles of Ladakh*. 1939; reprint, New Delhi: Low Price, 1999.

Petech, Luciano. *The Kingdom of Ladakh: C. 950–1842 A.D.* Rome: Istituto Italiano per il Medio ed Estremo Oriente, 1977.

Phun-tshogs-rnam-rgyal and Zhang Jianlin. *Tuo lin Si (mtho gling dgon pa; ntho-ling* [sic] *monastery*). Beijing: Zhongguo Dabai Kequan Shu Chubanshe, 2001.

Phun-tshogs-rnam-rgyal. *Zhongguo Xizang: Xizang Ali Dongga Bihua Ku* (China's Tibet: Donggar Murals Cave in Ngari Prefecture, Tibet; 中国西藏阿里東 壁画). Beijing: Zhongguo da bai ke quan shu chu ban she, 2008.

Pinney, Christopher. *Photos of the Gods: The Printed Image and Political Struggle in India*. London: Reaktion, 2004.

Pöll, Heinrich. "Trees-of-Life, Aquatic Creatures, and Other Enigmatic Motifs on Ladakh Wood Art: What They Tell Us about Art History." In *Visible Heritage: Essays on the Art and Architecture of Greater Ladakh, 16th Conference of the International Association for Ladakh Studies Heidelberg 17–20 April 2013*, edited by Rob Linrothe and Heinrich Pöll, 203–34. New Delhi: Studio Orientalia, 2016.

Pott, P. H. "The Goddess Hirmā in Kulū Valley." In *Pratidānam: Indian, Iranian and Indo-European Studies Presented to Franciscus Bernardus Jacobus Kuiper on His Sixtieth Birthday*. Edited by J. C. Heesterman, G. H. Schokker, and V. I. Subramoniam, 556–62. The Hague: Mouton, 1968.

Powers, John, and David Templeman. *Historical Dictionary of Tibet*. Lanham, MD: Scarecrow Press, 2012.

Prajñānānanda, Swāmī. *Historical Development of Indian Music: A Critical Study*. 1960; reprint, Calcutta: K. L. Mukhopadhyay, 1973.

Preziosi, Donald, ed. *The Art of Art History: A Critical Anthology*. New ed., Oxford: Oxford University Press, 2009.

Pritzker, David Thomas. "Allegories of Kingship: A Preliminary Study of a Western Central Asian Gold Ewer in the Royal Court of Tibet." In Allinger et al., *Interaction in the Himalayas and Central Asia*, 105–25.

Pritzker, Thomas J. "A Preliminary Report on Early Cave Paintings of Western Tibet." In *Art of Tibet: Selected Articles from* Orientations *1981–1997*, [1996] 206–27. Hong Kong: Orientations Magazine, 1998.

Pritzker, Thomas J. "The Wall Paintings of Nyag Lhakhang Kharpo." *Orientations* 39, no. 2 (2008): 102–12.

Procida, Mary A. "A Tale Begun in Other Days: British Travelers in Tibet in the Late Nineteenth Century." *Journal of Social History* 30, no. 1 (1996): 185–208.

Radhu, Abdul Wahid. *Tibetan Caravans: Journeys from Leh to Lhasa*. New Delhi: Speaking Tiger Publishing, 2017.

Ramaswamy, Samathi. "Body Politic(s): Maps and Mother Goddesses in Modern India." In *Picturing the Nation: Iconographies of Modern India*, edited by Richard H. Davis, 32–50. New Delhi: Orient Longman, 2007.

Ramble, Charles. "Whither, Indeed, the Tsampa Eaters." *Himal* 6, no. 5 (1993): 21–25.

Ramsay, H. (British Joint-Commissioner, Ladak). *Western Tibet: A Practical Dictionary of the Language and Customs of the Districts included in the Ladák Wazarat*. Lahore: W. Ball, 1890.

Rather, T. A., M A. Shah, and M. A. Yatoo. *Revisiting Himalayan Borderlands, A Bridge Between India and Central Asia*. Srinagar: Jay Kay Books, 2022.

Rawson, P. S. "The Iconography of the Goddess Manasā." *Oriental Art* n.s. 1, no. 4 (1955): 151–58.

Rāy, Pratāpa Chandra, trans. *The Mahabharata of Krishna Dwaipayana Vyasa*. Calcutta: Bhārata Press, 1893.

Rayner, Hugh Ashley, ed. *Photographic Journeys in the Himalayas: Comprising the Complete Texts of Four Series of Letters to the* British Journal of Photography, *Published between July 1st 1863 and April 1st 1870*. 2nd rev. and enl. ed. Bath: Pagoda Tree Press, 2004.

Reimer, Paula J., William E. N. Austin, Edouard Bard, Alex Bayliss, Paul G. Blackwell, Christopher Bronk Ramsey, Martin Butzin, et al. "The IntCal20 Northern Hemisphere Radiocarbon Age Calibration Curve (0–55 Cal kBP)." *Radiocarbon* 62, no. 4 (August 2020): 725–57. doi: 10.1017/RDC.2020.41.

Rhie, Marylin M. "Interrelationships between the Buddhist Art of China and the Art of India and Central Asia from 618–755 A.D." *Supplemento n. 54 agli Annali 48, fasc. 1, 1–44, with 67 figures in 32 plates*. Naples: Istituto Universitario Orientale, 1988.

Rhie, Marylin M., ed. *Picturing Enlightenment: Tibetan Tangkas in the Mead Art Museum at Amherst College*. Amherst, MA: Mead Art Museum, 2013.

Rhie, Marylin M. "The Statue of Songzen Gampo in the Potala, Lhasa." *Orientalia Iosephi Tucci Memoriae Dicata; Serie Orientale Roma* 56, no. 3 (1988): 1201–19.

Rhie, Marylin M. "A T'ang Period Stele Inscription and Cave XXI at T'ien-Lung Shan." *Archives of Asian Art* 28 (1974–75): 6–33.

Rhie, Marylin M. "Tibetan Painting: Styles, Sources and Schools." In Marylin M. Rhie and Robert A.F. Thurman, *Worlds of Transformation: Tibetan Art of Wisdom and Compassion*, 45–74. New York: Tibet House, 1999.

Riaboff, Isabelle. "Gzhon nu mdung lag, Mountain God of Zanskar: A Regional Scale Divinity and Its Cult's Territorial Ordering." In *Reflections of the Mountain: Essays on the History and Social Meaning of the Mountain Cult in Tibet and the Himalaya*, edited by Anne-Marie Blondeau and Ernst Steinkellner, 23–37. Vienna: Österreichische Akademie der Wissenschaften, 1996.

Riaboff, Isabelle. "Notes sur les rituals agraires au Zanskar: Terre, Terroirs, Territoires." In *Tibetan Studies: Proceedings of the 7th Seminar of the International Association for Tibetan Studies, Graz 1995, Vol. 2*, edited by Helmut Krasser, 803–16. Vienna: Österreichische Akademie der Wissenschaften, 1997.

Ricard, Matthieu, trans. *The Life of Shabkar: The Autobiography of a Tibetan Yogin*. 1994; reprint, Ithaca, NY: Snow Lion, 2001.

Ricca, Franco, and Erberto Lo Bue. *The Great Stupa of Gyantse: A Complete Tibetan Pantheon of the Fifteenth Century*. London: Serindia, 1993.

Richardson, Hugh E. "The Cult of Vairocana in Early Tibet." In *Indo-Tibetan Studies: Papers in Honour and Appreciation of Professor David L. Snellgrove's Contribution to Indo-Tibetan Studies*, edited by Tadeusz Skorupski, 271–74. Buddhica Britannica Series Continua 2. Tring, UK: Institute of Buddhist Studies, 1990.

Richardson, Sarah. "When Walls Could Talk: The Powers of Tibetan Paintings in a Buddhist Library." *Archives of Asian Art* 71, no. 2 (2021): 243–68.

Riegel, Caroline. *Semeuses de Joie (Sowers of Joy)*. Paris: Hemeria, 2021.

Rizvi, Janet. "Trade and Migrant Labour: Inflow of Resources at the Grassroots." In Bray, *Ladakhi Histories*, 309–19.

Roth, Gustav. "Symbolism of the Buddhist Stūpa." In *The Stūpa: Its Religious, Historical, and Architectural Significance*, edited by Anna Libera Dallapiccola with Stephanie Zingel-Avé Lallemant, 183–209. Wiesbaden: Franz Steiner, 1980.

Rozwadowski, Andrzej. *Symbols through Time: Interpreting the Rock Art of Central Asia*. Poznań: Institute of Eastern Studies, Adam Mickiewicz University, 2004.

Ruegg, David Seyfort. *The Life of Bu Ston Rin Po Che*. Rome: Istituto Italiano per il Medio ed Estremo Oriente, 1966.

Ryavec, Karl E. *A Historical Atlas of Tibet*. Chicago: University of Chicago Press, 2015.

Salomon, Richard, Quentin Devers, and Tashi Ldawa. "Kharoṣṭhī and Brāhmī Inscriptions from Ladakh." *Bulletin of the Asia Institute* 30 (2020–2021): 93–111.

Sanderson, Alexis. "The Visualization of the Deities of the Trika." In *L'Image Divine, Culte et Méditation dans l'Hindousime*, edited by André Padoux, 31–88. Paris: Éditions du CNRS, 1990.

Sandness, Adéla. "Yama and Sarasvatī: On Perceptions of Death and the Continuity of Life in Early Vedic Literature." *Annals of the Bhandarkar Oriental Research Insitute* 88 (2007): 81–97.

Sangharakshita, Bhikshu. "The Meaning of Buddhism and the Value of Art." *The Religion of Art*, 19–57. Glasgow: Windhorse Publications, 1988. First published in 1956 by the Maha Bodhi Society under the title *Buddhism and Art*.

Sardar-Afkhami, Abdol-Hamid. "The Buddha's Secret Gardens: End Times and Hidden-lands in Tibetan Imagination." PhD diss., Harvard University, 2001.

Sastri, Asoke Chatterjee. *The Citralaksana, an Old Text of Indian Art*. Bibliotheca Indica 315. Calcutta: Asiatic Society, 1987.

Sastri, Hiranandi. *Nalanda and Its Epigraphic Material*. 1942; reprint, Delhi: Satguru, 1986.

Schaeffer, Kurtis. *The Culture of the Book in Tibet*. New York: Columbia University Press, 2009.

Schaeffer, Kurtis. "A Letter to the Editors of the Buddhist Canon in Fourteenth-Century Tibet: The *Yig mkhan rnams la gdams pa* of Bu ston Rin chden grub." *Journal of the American Oriental Society* 124, no. 2 (2004): 265–81.

Schafer, Edward H. *The Golden Peaches of Samarkand: A Study of T'ang Exotics*. Berkeley: University of California Press, 1963.

Scherrer-Schaub, Christina. "A Perusal of Early Tibetan Inscriptions in Light of the Buddhist World of the 7th to 9th Centuries A.D." In *Epigraphic Evidence in the Pre-Modern Buddhist World: Proceedings of the Eponymous Conference Held in Vienna, 14–125 Oct. 2011*, edited by Kurt Tropper, 117–65. Vienna: Arbeitskreis für Tibetische und Buddhistische Studien Universität Wien, 2014.

Schopen, Gregory. "Burial *'Ad Sanctos'* and the Physical Presence of the Buddha in Early Indian Buddhism: A Study in the Archaeology of Religions." *Religion* 17, no. 3 (1987): 193–225.

Schopen, Gregory. "An Old Inscription from Amarāvatī and the Cult of the Local Monastic Dead in Indian Buddhist Monasteries." *Journal of the International Association of Buddhist Studies* 14, no. 2 (1991): 289–329.

Schopen, Gregory. "*Stūpa* and *Tīrtha*: Tibetan Mortuary Practices and an Unrecognized Form of Burial Ad Sanctos at Buddhist Sites in India." *Figments and Fragments of Mahāyāna Buddhism in India: More Collected Papers*, 350–69. Honolulu: University of Hawai'i Press, 2005.

Schopen, Gregory. "What's in a Name: The Religious Function of the Early Donative Inscriptions." *Buddhist Monks and Business Matters: Still More Papers on Monastic Buddhism in India*, 382–94. Honolulu: University of Hawai'i Press, 2004. Originally published in *Unseen Presence: The Buddha and Sanchi*, edited by V. Dehejia (Bombay: Marg, 1996), 58–73.

Schuh, Dieter, and Ajaz Hussain Munshi. *Travel into the History of Purig: Preliminary Report about a Journey to Purig in 2013*. Beiträge zur Zentralasienforschung 29. Andiast: International Institute for Tibetan and Buddhist Studies (IITBS), 2014.

Schwieger, Peter. "Kathog Rigzin Tsewang Norbu's (Kah-thog-rig-'dzin Tshe-dbang-nor-bu) Diplomatic Mission to Ladakh in the 18th Century." In *Recent Research on Ladakh 6: Proceedings of the Sixth International Colloquium on Ladakh, Leh 1993*, edited by Henry Osmaston and Nawang Tsering, 219–30. Delhi: Motilal Banarsidass, 1997.

Schwieger, Peter. "Stag-tshang Ras-pa's Exceptional Life as a Pilgrim." *Kailash* 18, no. 1–2 (1996): 81–107.

Shah, Ahmad. *Four Years in Tibet*. Benares: E. J. Lazarus, 1906.

Shah, Priyabala, trans. *Śrī-Viṣṇudharmottara-Purāṇa: Third Khaṇḍa (A Text on Ancient Indian Arts)*. Delhi: Parimal, 2002.

Shakya, Tsering. "Whither the Tsampa Eaters?" *Himal* 6, no. 5 (1993): 8–11.

Shali, S. L. *Kashmir: History and Archaeology through the Ages*. New Delhi: Indus, 1993.

Shastri, Ajay Mitra. *India, As Seen in the* Kuṭṭanī-Mata *of Dāmodaragupta*. Delhi: Motilal Banarsidass, 1975.

Shaw, Julia. "Stūpas, Monasteries, and Relics in the Landscape: Typological, Spatial, and Temporal Patterns in the Sanchi Area." In *Buddhist Stupas in South Asia: Recent Archaeological, Art-Historical, and Historical Perspectives*, edited by Jason Hawkes and Akira Shimada, 114–45. New Delhi: Oxford University Press, 2009.

Shaw, Miranda. *Buddhist Goddesses of India*. Princeton: Princeton University Press, 2006.

Sheikh, Abdul Ghani. "Economic Conditions in Ladakh during the Dogra Period." In *Ladakh: Culture, History, and Development between Himalaya and Karakoram: Recent Research on Ladakh 8*, edited by Martijn van Beek, Kristoffer Brix Bertelsen, and Poul Pedersen, 339–49. New Delhi: Sterling, 1999.

Sheikh, Abdul Ghani. *Reflections on Ladakh, Tibet and Central Asia*. India: Inamullah Khawaja, 2014.

Sherpa Tulku et al., trans. *The Life and Teachings of Tsong-Khapa*. Edited by Robert A. F. Thurman. 1982; reprint, Dharamsala: Library of Tibetan Works and Archives, 1993.

Sherring, Charles A. *Western Tibet and the British Borderland: The Sacred Country of Hindus and Buddhists, With an Account of the Government, Religion, and Customs of Its Peoples*. London: Edward Arnold, 1906.

Shinohara, Koichi. "The Esoteric Buddhist Ritual of Image Installation." In *Buddhist and Jaina Studies: Proceedings of the Conference in Lumbini, February 2013*, edited by Jayandra Soni, Michael Pahlke, and Christoph Cüppers, 265–98. Lumbini, 2014.

Shneiderman, Sara. "Barbarians at the Border and Civilising Projects: Analysing Ethnic and National Identities in the Tibetan Context." In Klieger, *Tibetan Borderlands*, 9–34.

Sichuan Daxue. *Piyang, Dongga yi zhi kao gu bao gao*. Chengdu: Sichuan ren min chu ban she, 2008.

Sichuan Daxue Zhongguo Zhangxue Yanjiu Suo (Sichuan University China-Tibet Research Institute). "Xizang Ali Xiangquan he Liuyu Kazi hegu Fojiao Weicun de Kaogu Diaocha yu Yanjiu" [Archaeological Survey and Study of Buddhist Remains across the Khatse River Valley in the Xiangquan River Basin within Ngari Prefecture, Tibet]. *Kaogu Xuebao* (Acta Archaeologica Sinica), no. 4 (2009): 547–77.

Silver, Larry. "Introduction: Canons in World Perspective—Definitions, Deformations, and Discourses." In *Canons and Values: Ancient to Modern*, edited by Larry Silver and Kevin Terraciano, 1–21. Los Angeles: Getty Research Institute, 2019.

Simpson, William. *The Autobiography of William Simpson, R.I. (Crimean Simpson)*. Edited by George Eyre-Todd. London: T. Fisher Unwin, 1903.

Simpson, William. "A Sculptured Tope on an Old Stone at Dras, Ladak." *Journal of the Royal Asiatic Society of Great Britain and Ireland*, n.s. 14 (1882): 28–38.

Sims-Williams, Nicholas. "The Sogdian Merchants in China and India." In *Cina e Iran: Da Alessandro Magno alla dinastia Tang*, edited by Alfredo Cadonna and Lionello Lanciotti, 45–67. Orientalia Venetiana 5. Florence: L. S. Olschki, 1996.

Singh, Madanjeet. *Himalayan Art: Wall-painting and Sculpture in Ladakh, Lahaul and Spiti, the Siwalik Ranges, Nepal, Sikkim, and Bhutan*. 1968; reprint, New York: Macmillan, 1971.

Singh, Tejpal, and Sanjib Kumar Singh. *Ecstasy of Classical Art, Indian Bronze: National Museum Collection*. New Delhi: National Museum, New Delhi, 2016.

Sinha, B. P. "Evolution of Śakti Worship in India." In *The Śakti Cult and Tārā*, edited by D. C. Sircar, 45–55. Calcutta: University of Calcutta, 1967.

Sinopoli, Carla M. *The Himalayan Journey of Walter N. Koelz: The University of Michigan Himalayan Expedition, 1932-1934*. Ann Arbor: Museum of Anthropology, University of Michigan, 2013.

Siudmak, John. "The Development of the Classical Buddha Image from Kashmir, and Some Observations on Kashmirian Influence on the Sculpture of West Tibet." *Oriental Art* 46, no. 2 (2000): 36–46.

Siudmak, John. "Religious Architecture (500–1200)." In Pal, *Arts of Kashmir*, 44–59.

Skorupski, Tadeusz. *The Sarvadurgatipariśodhana Tantra: Elimination of All Evil Destinies.* Delhi: Motilal Banarsidass, 1983.

Skorupski, Tadeusz. "Tibetan Homa Rites: The Durgatipariśodhana and Its Maṇḍalas." In *Agni, the Vedic Ritual of the Fire Altar*, edited by Frits Staal, 403–17. Berkeley: Asian Humanities Press, 1983.

Smith, E. Gene. *Among Tibetan Texts: History & Literature of the Himalayan Plateau*, edited by Kurtis R. Schaeffer. Boston: Wisdom, 2001.

Smith, H. Daniel. "A Contemporary Iconic Tradition: Lakṣmī, Gaṇeśa, Sarasvatī—An Emerging, 'New' Hindu Trimūrti." In *Studies in Hindu and Buddhist Art*, edited by P. K. Mishra, 11–48. New Delhi: Abhinav, 1999.

Smith, H. Daniel. "Introduction: Impact of 'God Posters' on Hindus and Their Devotional Traditions." In Gerald James Larson, Pratapaditya Pal, and H. Daniel Smith, *Changing Myths and Images: Twentieth-Century Popular Art in India*, 17–23. Bloomington: Indiana University Art Museum, 1997.

Snellgrove, David L. "Buddhism in North India and the Western Himalayas, Seventh to Thirteenth Centuries." In *The Silk Route and the Diamond Path: Esoteric Buddhist Art on the Trans-Himalayan Trade Routes*, edited by Deborah E. Klimburg-Salter, 65–80. Los Angeles: UCLA Art Council, 1982.

Snellgrove, David L. "Indo-Tibetan Liturgy and Its Relationship to Iconography." In *Mahayanist Art after A.D. 900: Proceedings of a Colloquy held 28 June–1 July 1971 at the Percival David Foundation of Chinese Art, London*, edited by William Watson, 36–45. Colloquies on Art and Archaeology in Asia 2. London: University of London, 1972.

Snellgrove, David L. Introduction to *Sarva-Tathāgata-Tattva-Saṅgraha: Facsimile Reproduction of a Tenth Century Sanskrit Manuscript from Nepal*, edited by Lokesh Chandra and David L. Snellgrove, 5–67. New Delhi: Mrs. Sharada Rani, 1981.

Snellgrove, David L. *The Nine Ways of Bon: Excerpts from gZi-brjid.* London: Oxford University Press, 1967.

Snellgrove, David L., and Tadeusz Skorupski. *The Cultural Heritage of Ladakh*. Vol. 1, *Central Ladakh*. Boulder, CO: Prajña Press, 1977.

Snellgrove, David L., and Tadeusz Skorupski. *The Cultural Heritage of Ladakh*. Vol. 2, *Zangskar and the Cave Temples of Ladakh*. New Delhi: Vikas, 1980.

Snodgrass, Adrian. *The Matrix and Diamond World Mandalas in Shingon Buddhism*. 2 vols. New Delhi: Aditya Prakashan,1988.

Sørensen, Per K. Review of Ernst Steinkellner, *Sudhana's Miraculous Journey: The Inscriptional Text of the Tibetan* Gandavyūhasūtra *Edited with Introductory Remarks* (Rome: Istituto Italiano per l'Africa e l'Oriente, 1995), in *Studies in Central & East Asian Religions* 10 (1997): 69–73.

South Asian Archaeology 1981: Proceedings of the Sixth International Conference of the Association of South Asian Archaeologists in Western Europe held in Cambridge University, 5–10 July 1981, edited by Bridget Allchin. Cambridge: Cambridge University Press, 1984.

South Asian Archaeology 1983: Papers from the Seventh International Conference of the Association of South Asian Archaeologists in Western Europe, in the Musées Royaux d'art et d'histoire, Brussels, Vol. 2, edited by Janine Schotsmans and Maurizio Taddei. Naples: Istituto Universitario Orientale, 1985.

South Asian Archaeology 1985: Papers from the Eighth International Conference of South Asian Archaeologists in Western Europe, held at Moesgaard Museum, Denmark, 1–5 July 1985, edited by Karen Frifelt and Per Sørensen. London: Curzon Press, 1989.

South Asian Archaeology 1987: Proceedings of the Ninth International Conference of the Association of South Asian Archaeologists in Western Europe, held in the Fondazione Giorgio Cini, Island of San Giorgio Maggiore, Venice, edited by Maurizio Taddei and Pierfrancesco Callieri. Rome: Istituto Italiano per il Medio ed Estremo Oriente, 1990.

South Asian Archaeology, 1993: Proceedings of the Twelfth International Conference of the European Association of South Asian Archaeologists held in Helsinki University, 5–9 July 1993, edited by Asko Parpola and Petteri Koskikallio. Helsinki: Suomalainen Tiedeakatemia, 1994.

Spengen, Wim van. "Chone and Thewu: Territoriality, Local Power, and Political Control on the Southern Gansu-Tibetan Frontier, 1880–1940." In Klieger, *Tibetan Borderlands*, 209–30.

Sperling, Elliot. "A Captivity in Ninth Century Tibet." *Tibet Journal* 4, no. 4 (1979): 17–67.

Srinivasan, Doris Meth, and Lore Sander. "Viśvarūpa Vyūya Avatāra: Reappraisals on an Inscribed Bronze from the Northwest Dated to the Early 5th Century A.D." *East and West* 47, no. 1 (1997): 105–70.

Stacul, Giorgio. "Neolithic Inner Asian Traditions in Northern Indo-Pakistani Valleys." In *South Asian Archaeology 1993*, 2:707–14.

Stearns, Cyrus. *The Buddha from Dolpo: A Study of the Life and Thought of the Tibetan Master Dolpopa Sherab Gyaltsen*. Albany: State University of New York, 1999.

Stearns, Cyrus. *Song of the Road: The Poetic Travel Journal of Tsarchen Losal Gyatso*. Boston: Wisdom, 2012.

Stein, M. A. [Sir Aurel]. "Archaeological Notes from the Hindukush Region." *Journal of the Royal Asiatic Society*, no. 2 (1944): 5–24.

Stein, M. A. [Sir Aurel]. *Innermost Asia: Detailed Report of Explorations in Central Asia, Kan-su and Eastern Iran*. 4 vols. Oxford: Clarendon Press, 1928.

Stein, M. A. [Sir Aurel]. *Kalhana's Rajatarangini: A Chronicle of the Kings of Kashmir*. 3 vols. 1900; reprint, Srinagar, Kashmir: Gulshan, 2007.

Stein, M. A. [Sir Aurel]. *Report of Archaeological Survey Work in the North-West Frontier Province and Baluchistan*. Peshawar: Government Press, North-west Frontier Provinces, 1905.

Stein, Rolf A. "The Guardian of the Gate: An Example of Buddhist Mythology, from India to Japan." Translated by Gerald Honigsblum in *Asian Mythologies*, compiled by Yves Bennefoy, edited by Wendy Doniger, 122–36. Chicago: University of Chicago Press, 1993.

Stewart, Mary L. *Nālandā Mahāvihāra: A Study of an Indian Pāla Period Buddhist Site and British Historical Archaeology, 1861–1938*. BAR International Series 529. Oxford: B.A.R., 1989.

Stoddard, Heather 1998. "The 'Indian Style' *rGyal lugs* on an Early Tibetan Book Cover." In *The Inner Asian International Style 12th–14th Centuries: Papers Presented at a Panel of the 7th Seminar of the International Association for Tibetan Studies, Graz 1995*, edited by Deborah E. Klimburg-Salter and Eva Allinger, 121–32. Vienna: Osterreichische Akademie der Wissenschaften.

Stoddard, Heather. *Early Sino-Tibetan Art*. 1975; 2nd ed. Bangkok: Orchid Press, 2008.

Strachey, Henry. "Narrative of a Journey to Cho Lagan (Rákas Tal), Cho Mapan (Mánasaróvar), and the Valley of Pruang [*sic*] in Gnari, Húndés, in September and October 1846." *Journal of the Asiatic Society of Bengal* 17, pt. 2 (1848): 98–120, 127–82, 327–51.

Strachey, Henry. "Note on the Construction of the Map of the British Himalayan Frontier in Kumaon and Garhwál." *Journal of the Asiatic Society of Bengal* 17, pt. 2 (1848): 532–38.

Strachey, Richard. "Narrative of a Journey to the Lakes Rakas-Tal and Manasarowar, in Western Tibet, Under-Taken in September, 1848." *Geographical Journal* 15, no. 2 (1900): 150–70; no. 3 (1900): 243–64; no. 4 (1900): 394–415.

Strickmann, Michel. "The Longest Taoist Scripture." *History of Religions* 17, no. 3 (1978): 331–54.

Strong, John S. *Relics of the Buddha*. Princeton: Princeton University Press, 2004.

Sutherland, Gail. "The Politics of 'Other Peoples' Myths.'" In *Notes from a* Maṇḍala*: Essays in the History of Indian Religions in Honor of Wendy Doniger*, edited by Laurie L. Patton and David L. Haberman, 150–63. Newark: University of Delaware Press. 2010.

Taddei, Maurizio. "Inscribed Clay Tablets and Miniature Stūpas from Ġaznī." *East and West* 20, no. 1/2 (1970): 70–86.

Takeuchi, Tsuguhito. "Old Tibetan Rock Inscriptions near Alchi." Unpublished manuscript, 2009. (I am indebted to Quentin Devers for providing a photocopy.)

Takeuchi, Tsuguhito. "Old Tibetan Rock Inscriptions near Alchi." *Journal of Research Institute* 49 (2013): 29–69, special issue, *Historical Development of the Tibetan Languages*.

Takeuchi, Tsuguhito. "The Tibetan Military System and Its Activities from Khotan to Lop-Nor." In *The Silk Road: Trade, Travel, War and Faith*, edited by Susan Whitfield with Ursula Sims-Williams, 50–56. Chicago: Serindia and The British Library, 2004.

Tanabe, Katsumi. *Silk Road Coins: The Hirayama Collection*. Kamakura: Institute of Silk Road Studies, 1993.

Tanaka, Kimiaki. *An Illustrated History of the Maṇḍala: From Its Genesis to the Kālacakratantra.* Somerville, MA: Wisdom, 2018.

Tanemura, Ryugen. "One Aspect of the Consecration Ceremony of Images in Buddhist Tantrism: 'The Ten Rites' Prescribed in the *Kriyāsaṃgrahapañjikā* and Their Background." *Journal of the Japanese Association for South Asian Studies* 13 (2001): 52–75.

Tartakov, Gary Michael, and Vidya Dehejia. "Sharing, Intrusion, and Influence: The Mahiṣāsuramardinī Imagery of the Calukyas and the Pallavas." *Artibus Asiae* 45, no. 4 (1984): 287–345.

Tharchin, Lopon Konchok, and Geshes Konchok Namgail. *Recollections of Tibet*. Edited by Francesca Merritt. New Delhi: Sona Printers, [2000s].

Tharoor, Shashi. *Inglorious Empire: What the British Did to India*. Melbourne: Scribe Publications, 2018.

Thewalt, Volker. "Rockcarvings and Inscriptions along the Indus: The Buddhist Tradition." In *South Asian Archaeology 1983*, 2:779–800.

Thomson, Thomas. *Western Himalaya and Tibet: A Narrative of a Journey through the Mountains of Northern India during the Years 1847–8*. London: Reeve and Co., 1852.

Tiwari, Maruti Nandan Pd., and Shanti Swaroop Sinha. "Concept of Saraswati in Jain Tradition and Art." *Indian Journal of Archaeology* 3, no. 2 (2018): 677–700.

Tobdan, and C. Dorje. *Moravian Missionaries in Western Trans-Himalaya: Lahul, Ladakh and Kinnaur*. New Delhi: Kaveri Books, 2008.

Todaro, Dale Allen. "An Annotated Translation of the *Tattvasaṃgraha* (Part 1) with an Explanation of the Role of the *Tattvasaṃgraha* Lineage in the Teachings of Kūkai." PhD diss., Columbia University, 1985.

Tong, Tao. *The Silk Roads of the Northern Tibetan Plateau during the Early Midde Ages (from the Han to Tang Dynasty): As Reconstructed from Archaeological and Written Sources.* BAR International Series 2521. Oxford: Archaeopress, 2013.

Torrens, Henry D'Oyley. *Travels in Ladâk, Tartary, and Kashmir.* London: Saunders, Otley, 1862.

Tribe, Anthony. "Mañjuśrī as Ādibuddha: The Identity of an Eight-armed Form of Mañjuśri Found in Early Western Himalayan Buddhist Art in the Light of Three *Nāmasaṃgīti*-Related Texts." In Śaivism *and Tantric Traditions: Essays in Honour of Alexis G.J.S. Sanderson*, edited by Dominic Goodall, Shaman Hatley, Harunaga Isaacson, and Srilata Raman, 539–68. Leiden: Brill, 2020.

Tribe, Anthony. *Tantric Buddhist Practice in India: Vilāsavajra's Commentary on the* Mañjuśrī-nāmasaṃgīti: *A Critical Edition and Annotated Translation of Chapters 1–5 with Introductions.* London: Routledge, 2016.

Trinle Tharchin. *Qiangu Juehui: Zhongguo Xizang Ali Gudai Bihua Xuanji (Masterpieces throughout the Ages: Select Compilation of Ancient Murals of Ngari in China's Tibet.* In Chinese, Tibetan, and English. Lhasa: Xizang Renmin Chubanshe, 2001.

Tripathi, S.V., and Pawan Jain. "Sarasvatī in Jain Art." *National Museum Bulletin* 10 (2018): 5–13.

Tropper, Kurt. *The Founding Inscription in the gSer khaṅ of Lalung (Spiti, Himachal Pradesh): Edition and Annotated Translation.* Dharamsala: Library of Tibetan Works and Archives, 2008.

Tsering, Nawang. *Buddhism in Ladakh: A Study of the Life and Works of the Eighteenth Century Ladakhi Saint Scholar.* New Delhi: Sterling, 1979.

Tsomu, Yudru. "Traders as Cultural Brokers on the Sino-Tibetan Borderland during the Republican Period." *Journal of Tibetology* 14 (2016): 177–210.

Tsuchiya, Haruko. "Preliminary Report on Field Research along the Ancient Routes in the Northern Areas of Pakistan and Related Historical and Art Historical Information (September, 1991) [I]." *Sophia International Review* 15 (1993): 27–39.

Tsuchiya, Haruko. "Preliminary Report on Field Research along the Ancient Routes in the Northern Areas of Pakistan and Related Historical and Art Historical Information (September, 1991) [II]." *Journal of the Japanese Association for South Asian Studies* 5 (1993): 1–38.

Tsuchiya, Haruko. "Tracing Ancient Routes in Northern Pakistan: Field Research (1991–1996) (Preliminary Report)." In *Coins, Art, and Chronology: Essays on the Pre-Islamic History of the Indo-Iranian Borderlands*, edited by Michael Alram and Deborah E. Klimburg-Salter, 353–90. Vienna: Österreichische Akademie der Wissenschaften, 1999.

Tucci, Giuseppe. Indo-Tibetica: 3., *I templi del Tibet occidentale e il loro simbolismo artistico. Parte 1, Spiti e Kunavar.* Rome: Reale Accademia d'Italia, 1935.

Tucci, Giuseppe. "On Swāt: The Dards and Connected Problems." *East and West* 27, no. 1/4 (1977): 9–103.

Tucci, Giuseppe. *Rin-chen-bzan-po and the Renaissance of Buddhism in Tibet around the Millenium, English Version of Indo-Tibetica II*, edited by Lokesh Chandra. Translated into English by Nancy Kipp Smith. New Delhi: Aditya Prakashan, 1988. Originally published in Italian in 1932.

Tucci, Giuseppe. "Stupa and Votive Stupa (mchod-rten and tsha-tsha)." *Stupa: Art, Architectonics and Symbolism, English Version of Indo-Tibetica I*, edited by Lokesh Chandra, 11–70. Translated into English by Uma Marina Vesci. New Delhi: Aditya Prakashan, 1988. Italian ed. 1932.

Tucci, Giuseppe. *The Temples of Western Tibet and Their Artistic Symbolism: The Monasteries of Spiti and Kunavar, English Version of Indo-Tibetica III.1*, edited by Lokesh Chandra. Translated into English by Uma Marina Vesci et al. New Delhi: Aditya Prakashan, 1988. Originally published in Italian in 1935.

Tucci, Giuseppe. "Tibetan Book-Covers." In *Art and Thought: Issued in Honour of Dr. Ananda K. Coomaraswamy on the Occasion of His 70th Birthday*, edited by K. Bharatha Iyer, 63–68. London: Luzac, 1947.

Tucci, Giuseppe. *Tibetan Painted Scrolls.* 3 vols. Rome: Libreria dello Stato, 1949.

Tucci, Giuseppe. *Transhimalaya.* Translated from the French by James Hogarth. Delhi: Vikas, 1973.

Tucci, Giuseppe, and E. Ghersi. *Secrets of Tibet: Being the Chronicle of the Tucci Scientific Expedition to Western Tibet (1933).* Translated from the Italian edition by Mary A. Johnstone. London: Blackie & Son, 1935.

Tucci, Giuseppe, and E. Ghersi. *Shrines of a Thousand Buddhas: Exploring for Tibet's Hidden Art.* 1936; new ed., Varanasi: Pilgrims Publishing, 2008.

Turin, Mark. "Rethinking Tibeto-Burman: Linguistic Identities and Classifications in the Himalayan Periphery." In Klieger, *Tibetan Borderlands*, 35–48.

Türstig, Hans-Georg. "The Indian Sorcery Called *Abhicāra*." *Wiener Zeitschrift für die Kunde Südasiens* 29 (1985): 69–117.

Twist, Rebecca L. "Patronage, Devotion and Politics: A Buddhological Study of the Paṭola Śāhi Dynasty's Visual Record." PhD diss., Ohio State University, 2008.

Tyndale Biscoe, E. E. *Kashmir in Sunlight & Shade.* Philadelphia: J.B. Lippincott, 1922.

Ujfalvy, Karl Eugen [Károly Jenő] von. *Aus dem Westlichen Himalaja: Erlebnisse und Forschungen.* Leipzig: F. A. Brockhaus, 1884.

Ullrey, Aaron Michael. "Grim Grimoires: Pragmatic Ritual in the Magic Tantras." PhD diss., University of California, Santa Barbara, 2016.

Uray, Geza. "Tibet's Connections with Nestorianism and Manicheism in the 8th–10th Centuries." In *Proceedings of the Csoma de Kőrös Symposium: Held at Velm-Vienna, Austria, 13–19 September 1981*, 3:399–429. Vienna: Arbeitskreis für Tibetische und Buddhistische Studien Universität Wien, 1983.

Vasudeva, Somadeva. "The Transport of the Haṃsas: A Śakta Rāsalīlā as Rajayoga in Eighteenth-Century Benares." In *Yoga in Practice*, edited by David Gordon White, 242–54. Princeton: Princeton University Press, 2012.

Venturi, Adolfo. *Storia dell'arte italiana*, 11 vols. Milan: Hoepli, 1901–1940.

Venturi, Federica. "Before and After: A Perspective on the Fifteenth Century in Tibet." In *Fifteenth Century Tibet: Cultural Blossoming and Political Unrest, Proceedings of a Conference Held in Lumbini, Nepal, March 2015*, edited by Volker Caumanns and Marta Sernesi, 97–114. Lumbini: Lumbini International Research Institute, 2017.

Verma, T. P. "Chandra Śrī Deva Vikramāditya of the Sacred Rock of Hunza." In *Studies in Indian History and Culture*, edited by T. P. Verma and O. P. Tandon, 109–31. Varanasi: Bharat Kala Bhavan, 1968.

Vernier, Martin. *Exploration et Documentation des Pétroglyphes du Ladakh 1996–2006*. Sierre, Switzerland: Foundation Carlo Leone et Mariena Montandon, 2007.

Vernier, Martin. "Zamthang, epicenter of Zangskar's rock art heritage." *Revue d'Etudes Tibétaines* 35 (2016): 53–105.

Vigne, G. T. *Travels in Kashmir, Ladak, Iskardo, the Countries Adjoining the Mountain-Course of the Indus and the Himalaya, North of the Panjab*. London: Henry Colburn, 1842.

Vinding, Michael, and Per K. Sørensen. "Miscellanea Himalaica: Thakali *rhab*, *mi dpon* bKra shis bzang po and Bam steng Tulku." In *Gateways to Tibetan Studies: A Collection of Essays in Honour of David P. Jackson on the Occasion of His 70th Birthday*, edited by Volker Caumanns, Jörg Heimbel, Kazuo Kano, and Alexander Schiller, 1:979–1017. 2 vols. Hamburg: Department of Indian and Tibetan Studies, Universität Hamburg, 2021.

Vitali, Roberto. *Early Temples of Central Tibet*. London: Serindia, 1990.

Vitali, Roberto. *The Kingdoms of Gu.ge Pu.hrang according to mNga'.ris rgyal.rabs by Gu.ge mkhan.chen Ngag.dbang grags. pa*. Dharamsala: Tho.ling gtsug.lag.khang lo.gcig.stong, 1996.

Vitali, Roberto. *Records of Tho-ling: A Literary and Visual Reconstruction of the "Mother" Monastery in Gu-ge*. Dharamshala: High Asia, 1999.

Vogel, Jean Philippe. *The Goose in Indian Literature and Art*. Leiden: E. J. Brill, 1962.

Vohra, Rohit. "Ethnographic Notes on the Buddhist Dards of Ladakh: The Brog-Pā." *Zeitschrift für Ethnologie* 107, no. 1 (1982): 69–94.

Vohra, Rohit. "Ethno-Historicity of the Dards in Ladakh-Baltistan: Observations and Analysis." In *Tibetan Studies: Proceedings of the 4th Seminar of the International Association for Tibetan Studies. Schloss Hohenkammer—Munich 1985*, edited by Helga Uebach and Jampa L. Panglung, 529–46. Munich: Kommission für Zentralasiatische Studien Bayerische Akademie der Wissenschaften, 1988.

Vohra, Rohit. "Sogdian Inscriptions from Tangtse in Ladakh." In *Tibetan Studies: Proceedings of the 6th Seminar of the International Association for Tibetan Studies, Fagernes, 1992*, edited by Per Kvaerne, 920–29. Oslo: Institute for Comparative Research, 1994.

von Schroeder, Ulrich. *Buddhist Sculptures in Tibet*. 2 vols. Hong Kong: Visual Dharma, 2001.

Wandl, Erna. "The Representation of Costumes and Textiles." In *Tabo: A Lamp for the Kingdom: Early Indo-Tibetan Buddhist Art in the Western Himalaya*, edited by Deborah E. Klimburg-Salter, 178–87. Milan: Skira, 1997; New York: Thames and Hudson, 1998.

Wandl, Erna. "Textile Depictions from the 10th/11th Century in the Tabo Main Temple." In *Tabo Studies II: Manuscripts, Texts, Inscriptions, and the Arts*, edited by Cristina Anna Scherrer-Schaub and Ernst Steinkellner, 277–98. Rome: Istituto Italiano per l'Africa e l'Oriente, 1999.

Wang, Jiapeng et al. *Fanhua Lou*. 4 vols. Beijing: Zi jin cheng chu ban she, 2009.

Wang, Michelle C. *Maṇḍalas in the Making: The Visual Culture of Esoteric Buddhism at Dunhaung*. Leiden: Brill, 2018.

Wangchuk, Sonam the Karsha Lonpo (dkar sha'i blon po bsod nams dbang chyug). *History of Zangskar Monasteries* (zangs dkar chos 'byung gsal ba'i me long bzhugs so). Delhi: Himalayan Buddhist Cultural Association, 2013.

Warikoo, Kulbushan. "Karakoram Himalayas and Central Asia: The Buddhist Connection." In *The Other Kashmir: Society, Culture and Politics in the Karakoram Himalayas*, edited by Kulbushan Warikoo, 13–35. New Delhi: Institute for Defence Studies and Analyses; Pentagon Press, 2014.

Warikoo, Kulbushan. "The Making of a Frontier: The Relationship between Kashmir and Its Frontier Territories." In *The Other Kashmir: Society, Culture and Politics in the Karakoram Himalayas*, edited by Kulbushan Warikoo, 98–124. New Delhi: Institute for Defence Studies and Analyses; Pentagon Press, 2014.

Warikoo, Kulbushan. "Political Linkages between Ladakh and Eastern Turkestan under the Dogras during the 19th Century." In Bray, *Ladakhi Histories*, 235–48.

Watson, Oliver. *Ceramics from Islamic Lands.* London: Thames and Hudson, in association with the al-Sabah Collection, Dar al-Athar al-Islamiyyah, Kuwait National Museum, 2004.

Watt, Jeff. "An Introduction to Bon Art." In *Bon, the Magic Word: The Indigenous Religion of Tibet*, edited by Samten G. Karmay and Jeff Watt, 19–53. New York: Rubin Museum of Art, 2007.

Wayman, Alex. "The Goddess Sarasvatī—From India to Tibet." *Buddhist Insight: Essays*, edited by George Elder, 431–39. Delhi: Motilal Banarsidass, 1984. Originally published in *Kailash: A Journal of Himalayan Studies* 3 (1977): 45–51.

Weinberger, Steven Neal. "The Significance of Yoga Tantra and the *Compendium of Principles* (*Tattvasaṃgraha Tantra*) within Tantric Buddhism in India and Tibet." PhD diss., University of Virginia, 2003.

White, David Gordon. *The Alchemical Body: Siddha Traditions in Medieval India*. Chicago: University of Chicago Press, 1996.

Whitfield, Roderick. *The Art of Central Asia: The Stein Collection in the British Museum*. 3 vols. Tokyo: Kodansha International in cooperation with the Trustees of the British Museum, 1982–85.

Wilkinson, Charles K. "The Glazed Pottery of Nishapur and Samarkand." *The Metropolitan Museum of Art Bulletin* n.s. 20, no. 3 (1961): 102–15.

Willemen, Charles. "The Buddhist Pratimālakṣaṇa: 'Defining the Image.'" *Pacific World* 3rd ser., 9 (2007): 151–68.

Willemen, Charles. "Tripiṭaka Shan-wu-wei's Name: A Chinese Translation from Prākrit." *T'oung Pao*, 67, no. 3/5 (1981): 362–65.

Willis, Janice D. *Enlightened Beings: Life Stories from the Ganden Oral Tradition*. Boston: Wisdom, 1995.

Willis, Michael. *The Archaeology of Hindu Ritual: Temples and the Establishment of the Gods*. Cambridge: Cambridge University Press, 2009.

Willis, Michael. "Relics of the Buddha: Body, Essence, Text." In *The Heritage of Nalanda*, edited by C. Mani, 136–42. New Delhi: Aryan Books International, Asoka Mission, 2008.

Willson, Martin, and Martin Brauen. *Deities of Tibetan Buddhism: The Zürich Paintings of the Icons Worthwhile to See (Bris sku mthoṅ ba don ldan)*. Boston: Wisdom, 2000.

Wilson, Horace Hayman. *Travels in the Himalayan Provinces of Hindustan and the Panjab; in Ladakh and Kashmir; in Peshawar, Kabul, Kunduz, and Bokhara; by Mr. William Moorcroft and Mr. George Trebeck from 1819 to 1825*. 2 vols. London: John Murray, 1841.

Wölfflin, Heinrich. *Principles of Art History: The Problem of the Development of Style in Early Modern Art*. Translated by Jonathan Blower. Los Angeles: Getty Research Institute, 2015.

Wood, Frances. "The Spread of Trade and Religions: Tocharians and Sogdians." *The Silk Road: Two Thousand Years in the Heart of Asia*, 61–74. Berkeley: University of California Press, 2002.

Xizang Zizhiqu Wenwu Ju (Cultural Artifacts Bureau of the Tibetan Autonomous Region) and Sichuan Lianhe Daxue Kaogu Ye (Sichuan United University Archaeological Department). "Xizang Ali Dongga, Piyang Shiku Kaogu Diaocha Jianbao" (Brief report on the archaeological investigations at Dungga [Dunkar] and Piyang [Chyiwang] Caves in Ali [Ngari] Province of Tibet). *Wenwu*, no. 9 (1997): 6–22, inside back cover and back cover.

Xuanzang. *The Great Tang Dynasty Record of the Western Regions (Taishō volume 51, number 2087)*. Translated by Li Rongxi. Moraga, CA: Bukkyo Dendo Kyokai America, 1996.

Yaldiz, Marianne, et al. *Magische Götterwelten: Werke aus dem Museum für Indische Kunst Berlin*. Berlin: Staatliche Museen zu Berlin, Preussischer Kulturbesitz, 2000.

Yang, Han-Sung, Jan Yün-hua, Iida Shotaro, and Laurence W. Preston. *The Hye-Ch'o Diary: Memoir of the Pilgrimage to the Five Regions of India*. Berkeley, CA: Asian Humanities Press; Seoul: Po Chin Chai, 1984.

Yijing. *Buddhist Monastic Traditions of Southern Asia: A Record of the Inner Law Sent Home from the South Seas (Taishō vol. 54, no. 2125)*. Translated by Li Ronxi. Berkeley, CA: Numata Center for Buddhist Translation and Research, 2000.

Yijing (I-tsing). *A Record of the Buddhist Religion as Practised in India and the Malay Archipelago (A.D. 671–695)*. Translated by J. Takakusu. Oxford: Clarendon Press, 1896.

Yoritomi, Motohiro. "An Iconographic Study of the Eight Bodhisattvas in Tibet." In *Indo-Tibetan Studies: Papers in Honour and Appreciation of Professor David L. Snellgrove's Contribution to Indo-Tibetan Studies*, edited by Tadeusz Skorupski. Tring, UK: Institute of Buddhist Studies, 1990.

Zartman, I. William. "Identity, Movement, and Response" and "Borderland Policy: Keeping Up with Change." In *Understanding Life in the Borderlands: Boundaries in Depth and in Motion*, edited by I. William Zartman, 1–18 and 245–50. Athens: University of Georgia Press, 2010.

Zeisler, Bettina. "East of the Moon and West of the Sun? Approaches to a Land with Many Names, North of Ancient India and South of Khotan." Special issue, *Tibet Journal* 34, no. 3; and 35, no. 1 (Autumn 2009–Summer 2010): 371–463.

Zeisler, Bettina. "On the Position of Ladakhi and Balti in the Tibetan Language Family." In Bray, *Ladakhi Histories*, 41–64.

Zeisler, Bettina. Review of *Historical Dictionary of Tibet* by John Powers and David Templeman (Lanham, MD: Scarecrow Press, 2012), in *Revue d'Etudes Tibétaines* 30 (2014): 225–46.

Zhang, Changhong, and Wei Huo. *Bod kyi mdzes rtsal kun btus; rtsom sgrig tshogs pas bsgrigs* (Zangzu meishu ji cheng, Huihua yishu, Bihua, Ali juan; Mural Painting Art from Ngari). Chengdu: Sichuan Minzu Chubanshe, 2017.

Zimmer, Heinrich. *Myths and Symbols in Indian Art and Civilization*, edited by Joseph Campbell. Bollingen Series 6. 1946; reprint, Princeton: Princeton University Press, 1972.

Zimmer, Heinrich. *Philosophies of India*, edited by Joseph Campbell. Bollingen Series 26. New York: Pantheon Books, 1951.

Zurick, David. *The Himalaya: Encounters with the Roof of the World.* Chicago: Center for American Places at Columbia College Chicago, 2011.

Zurick, David, and Julsun Pacheco, with Basanta Shrestha and Birendra Bajracharya. *Illustrated Atlas of the Himalaya*. Lexington: University Press of Kentucky, 2006.

Zwalf, W., ed. *Buddhism: Art and Faith*. New York: Macmillan, 1985.

Websites

Dictionary of Art Historians. Edited by Lee Sorensen. www.dictionaryofarthistorians.org/venturia.htm.

HAR, Himalayan Art Resources. http://www.himalayanart.org.

Huntington Archive of Buddhist and Asian Art. https://huntingtonarchive.org/.

Index and Glossary

Abbreviations

ASI = Archaeological Survey of India

DVMm = Dharmadhātu Vāgīśvara Mañjuśrī mandala

FD = Female Deity

FF = Forward-facing

FS = Female Sponsor

IF = Inward-facing

k-v = *krodha-vighnāntaka* (wrathful obstacle-destroyer)

LZSKLB = Ladakh, Zangskar, Spiti, Kinnaur, Lahaul, Baltistan, etc.

MkK = Malakartse Khar

MS = Male Sponsor

STTS = *Sarvatathāgata Tattva Saṃgraha*

TPS = *Tibetan Painted Scrolls*

WD = Wrathful Deity